THE BOOK OF FLY PATTERNS

Also by Eric Leiser

THE METZ BOOK OF HACKLE

FLY TYING MATERIALS

STONEFLIES FOR THE ANGLER
(with Robert H. Boyle)

THE CADDIS AND THE ANGLER
(with Larry Solomon)

THE COMPLETE BOOK OF FLY TYING

The Book of
FLY PATTERNS

BY ERIC LEISER

PHOTOGRAPHS BY MATTHEW VINCIGUERRA

DRAWINGS BY ERNEST LUSSIER

SKYHORSE PUBLISHING

Skyhorse Publishing books may be purchased in bulk at special discounts for sales promotion, corporate gifts, fund-raising, or educational purposes. Special editions can also be created to specifications. For details, contact the Special Sales Department, Skyhorse Publishing, 307 West 36th Street, 11th Floor, New York, NY 10018 or info@skyhorsepublishing.com.

Skyhorse® and Skyhorse Publishing® are registered trademarks of Skyhorse Publishing, Inc.®, a Delaware corporation.

Visit our website at www.skyhorsepublishing.com.

10 9 8 7 6 5 4 3 2 1

Library of Congress Cataloging-in-Publication Data is available on file.

ISBN: 978-1-61608-389-2

Printed in China

Contents

Acknowledgments

IT'S QUITE obvious that an undertaking such as this is not accomplished without the help of many others. When those of you who have contributed to these pages come across a familiar sequence, a recipe for a particular fly pattern, a reference to a material, or perhaps a photograph or illustration of a fly you've tied or submitted, I hope you say to yourself, "I've had something to do with that!" I, for one, am grateful that you did. I couldn't have done it without you.

Where to begin?

The supporting cast of most productions is usually listed alphabetically. Why not? So then, here's to:

John Bailey, for the flies, the letters, and the special attention to detail; Dave Baker, Reg Baird, and Barry and Cathy Beck for flies and pattern recipes; John Betts, who picks me up when I'm down; Gary Borger and Dick Bovyn, for valued correspondence; Dick Brady, hunter, angler, and friend, for some special landlocked salmon flies; Alan Bramley of Partridge for a lesson in the fine art of hook making and the many free samples; Jay and Kathy Buchner for their superb flies; the Danville Chenille Company for samples and an education in chenilles and threads; the Dettes, Walt, Winnie, and Mary, whose fifty-plus years of fly tying have made this a better book, for checking the accuracy of many of the listed patterns in the dry and wet flies sections and for tying the flies for some of the plates, but most of all for their special friendship; Herb Dickerson, for always offering to help and for many of the flies for photos and illustrations; Jerry Doak, Rodney Flagg, David Footer, and Dick Frost for flies, pattern recipes, and valuable information; Keith Fulsher and Charles Krom, for the hair wing salmon flies for the plate and for playing devil's advocate for the salmon section; Jack Gartside, for sharing some original thoughts and patterns; Ted Gerken, for the flies and the standing invitation to fish Alaska; David Goulet and Everett Hale, for flies, pattern recipes, and some new ideas; Ed Haas, the only free spirit I know who's willing to pay the price, for his friendship and the exquisite flies tied for Plate X; Rudi Heger, for remembering and for the new materials; John Harder, friend through many seasons, and the Orvis Company, for invaluable assistance, for the loan of the store; Jim Hopkins, for the invitation and the flies and the methods; Bill Hunter, for more than he knows; Chris Jacklin, for getting the mail out; Randy Kaufmann, for the flies but especially the encouragement; Lefty Kreh, the best act in town, for being a buddy and checking out the saltwater category; Mike Lawson and Craig Mathews for flies, recipes, and needed information; Mike Mercer and the Fly Shop for flies, recipes, samples of new materials, and above-and-beyond correspondence; Jack Mickievicz, always ready to help a friend regardless of time or weather, for an in-depth study on materials which is freely shared; Harry Murray and Jay Neve for flies, pattern recipes, and histories and origins; Fred Oswalt, for research, new approaches, research, special ideas for photography and research; Tom Pellis and Larry Larese of the Fishing Post for flies and pattern recipes; Andre Puyans for flies, pattern recipes, and a few things I should have known, but didn't; Eddie Reif, Bob Rifchin, Polly Rosborough, Bill Ryer, and Robert Schneider for flies, pattern recipes, and extra attention to detail; Tom Rosenbauer, for special delivery service; Ed Shenk, for sharing as he always does; Tom Schmuecker, for his kindness and many samples of various materials; Joe Sterling, Dick Stewart, Taylor Streit, and Don Traver, for flies, pattern recipes, and selected information in their respective fields; Al Troth, for his tricks of the trade, his innovative patterns, and some exceptionally tied flies; Phillip Turner and Si Upson for some unusual patterns and much information regarding them; the Universal Vise Corp., for information and encouragement; VMC for all the hook samples and informative correspondence; Robert Veverka for some exceptional flies and interesting patterns; Ken Walters, for flies, pattern recipes, and loyalty; Lee and Joan Wulff, for taking time out on a very busy day to explain flies, patterns, and histories; Rod Yerger, for some innovative and beautifully tied terrestrial patterns; and Peter Zito, for flies, suggestions, but more than anything for being a fishing partner and friend.

A special thanks also to those not mentioned but who, through casual conversation at various clinics, outings, and fishing club presentations, have also contributed; and to the many mail-order houses and fly shops who sent their catalogs upon request and other information as I needed it.

And finally, an extra special thanks:

To Bobbie Bristol, my editor, for taking the chance.

To Verlyn Klinkenborg, for the many helpful comments, but mostly for the encouragement.

To Ernest Lussier, for a lesson in values and for the superb artwork.

To Matty Vinciguerra, so easy to be with, and his camera.

And to Angus, for just about everything.

Preface

THIS IS not a book about how to learn the art of tying flies. At least not as such. Although it does contain certain techniques and procedures related to various patterns, it is presumed that the reader has already acquired a basic knowledge of fly tying from other books, classes, or instructors specializing in this field. The instructional details, tips, and advice regarding certain constructions are simply to assist the tyer in understanding the specific pattern and leading him or her to a simpler or more direct route to its achievement. For those who have as yet to tie their first fly or are in the very beginning stages, may I suggest you obtain a copy of *The Complete Book of Fly Tying,* which I wrote with the express purpose of leading you very carefully, step by step, through the various styles of fly tying, whether for fresh-water or saltwater fishing. There are also a number of books listed in the bibliography written by exceptionally gifted fly tyers that cover this area very well.

This *is* a book about flies and the pieces of feathers, furs, and other materials that go into their makeup. It is a book of specific recipes, if you will, that give names to the flies we use. We call them fly patterns. One would think that a particular assemblage and arrangement of materials, their color, and the manner of construction, such as, for example, the Adams, would be clearly established and would not be confused with any other pattern. Oh, how I wish that were true! It would have made this task so much easier. Unfortunately, there are innumerable interpretations among fly tyers of the exact shadings that are used in an Adams. And here, perhaps, lies one of the reasons for the writing of yet another book relating to fly patterns.

A number of seasons ago I had the opportunity of operating my own fly shop. In addition to the usual array of fly rods, reels, lines, tools, hooks, and materials, I decided to try to stock the most complete line of flies to be found anywhere. I ordered the various dries, wets, nymphs, and streamers from some dozen fly tyers throughout the country and learned two things: (1) American fly tyers still tied the best flies and (2) the patterns were as individualized in their makeup (from tyer to tyer) as the quality was good.

Our customers liked the flies and they sold well, but I could not, under these circumstances, guarantee consistency in the makeup of individual fly patterns without personally tying and mailing to each of our fly tyers samples of many of our listed flies. Since there were numerous pattern books on the market and each commercial tyer had his favorite or his own interpretation of the pattern listed, I decided, at that time, to produce my own little pamphlet which would indicate what *I* wanted for the ingredients in the flies that were tied for our company.

Still, I was not altogether sure that my own knowledge of the various patterns was complete or accurate enough. Therefore, I sent photocopies of my interpretations to a number of colleagues in specific fields whose opinions I valued highly. Salmon fly patterns were sent to Poul Jorgensen, saltwater flies to Lefty Kreh. Larry Solomon and Matthew Vinciguerra checked many of the dries, wets, and nymphs. And there were many others. Of course, even the most expert of us differs as to what exact shade of color the body should be or whether the wing should be longer or shorter. Nevertheless, I felt that the result would at least give us a kind of standard, the most consistent representation to be found anywhere.

I printed the pamphlet, which was titled *A Professional Fly Tyer's Guide to Pattern Recipes,* and sold it through our catalog, in order to offset the cost of supplying copies free of charge to our fly tyers. It became quite popular and was reprinted a number of times. Even after we closed our shop in 1982, I still received requests for it, but it is now out of print. It was this pamphlet that provided me with a basic concept for this book.

Though there were plenty of fly pattern books on the market, I decided to broaden the scope of my original intent so as to put together a book containing the most often used, the most effective, and therefore the most popular fly patterns currently being fished with and answering the questions that both amateurs and professionals have concerning the tying of a particular fly or its recipe.

I began by writing letters requesting all the fly-fishing catalogs I could find listed in the advertising sections of magazines. I worked through the catalogs, lifting out fly patterns and separating them into categories of dries, wets, streamers, nymphs, and others.

I next contacted the owners of various fly shops whom I had come to know over the years. They supplied me with other patterns, not listed in catalogs, that had been used effectively by local anglers. I phoned and wrote to colleagues and friends for more patterns and bought, begged, and borrowed flies everywhere I could, stipulating that they send only the effective or popular flies. In the mail came handwritten notes, computer printouts, and in quite a number of cases, the flies themselves.

Next I checked the pattern descriptions and filled them in along with suggested hooks and threads. The more flies and the more contemporary patterns I examined, the more disparities I found among the authors of pattern books. Which pattern was correct? Trying to trace origins was of little avail since many patterns, even classic ones, had evolved and been improved upon to suit the modern angler and to accommodate particular fishing situations, acquiring different overtones depending on where they were fished or who interpreted what they should be. I decided to stay with the pattern whose construction and materials best served its purpose. In dry flies and other surface patterns I leaned toward those using materials that best supported the fly on the water and in subsurface imitations those which breathed and pulsed and gave an impression of life, providing, of course, that the overall color scheme was correct.

Making the recipes understood was another matter. As the flies paraded by, I realized there was something unique about each and every one of them. Certain categories were more disciplined than others and held to somewhat general proportions. Others, especially streamers, nymphs, terrestrials, and saltwater flies, were more wayward, and defied any attempt at strict classification.

I devised a method which used certain flies as models for others with similar techniques or difficulty factors. Some patterns, however, no matter how carefully I tried to describe them in the text, required still further clarification of detail and, as such, needed illustrations to explain them.

Some of the flies shown in the plates and illustrations were tied by others. Most of them I tied myself. When you tie flies, even those you've tied many times before, you begin to see again all the little movements and wrinkles that go into a particular pattern. Just the act of tying all those flies added more detail to the descriptions and sometimes more illustrations to clarify them further.

When at last everything seemed to be coming together, another thought occurred to me. What about the materials that are used to make the flies? Will they be fully understood? And what about the many varied terms used in fly tying? But certainly everyone will know what a dubbing loop or wing pad is, won't they? I hesitated, and then, as usually happens, I remembered the advice given by Angus Cameron, my first editor at Knopf: "Don't take anything for granted. If they already know it, it doesn't matter that much. But if they don't, it makes a world of difference." And so, page by page, I went through the manuscript and compiled a glossary of the terms used in fly tying and a list of the materials used by tyers; you will find them at the end of the book. I also added the names of the dealers who carry some of the scarcer materials and indicated the materials that can be substituted for items that are no longer available. I then made up a list of the catalog houses, along with their specialties, and finally, I compiled a bibliography of the most useful books and a list of bookdealers for rare and out-of-print titles.

I stared at the pile of paper before me. It contained the recipes of the most commonly used flies for all types of fishing. Trout, salmon, steelhead, bass, tarpon, bonefish; dry flies, caddis, terrestrials, and all manner of subsurface imitations were represented. Though I'd fished for many species of fish in both fresh and salt water and I'd tied most of the patterns, there were still areas in which I was not as knowledgeable as I would like to have been. I grew doubtful and a bit depressed. A year and a half had gone by and the mountain of paper stared back at me asking, accusingly: "Am I correct? Am I complete? Do you really know what you're doing? Will the fly tyer who reads me get his money's worth?" Frantically, I copied sections of the manuscript and, as I did with the original pamphlet, mailed them to those I considered truly expert. Lefty Kreh again received the saltwater data. The salmon flies went to Keith Fulsher and Charles Krom. Ed Haas, who tied the steelhead flies for Plate XI, was reluctant to criticize but nevertheless gave me much-needed inside information in this area. Bill Hunter read through the pages concerning streamer patterns. The dry flies, other surface patterns, and the wet flies sections were mailed to Walt and Winnie Dette. In addition, I went back to the library and re-read Wulff, Combs, Brooks, Flick, Jorgensen, Hellekson, Rosborough, and other authors. As the responses to my queries arrived, I added more text and made necessary changes.

Finally, I retyped the manuscript and delivered it, greatly overweight and long overdue. I was sure the extra volume of words and illustrations would see me shown to the door. My editor, God bless her, understood.

Looking back, I've asked myself: What was I trying to accomplish? Why did I go to all this trouble and who's going to benefit from it? In a way, I suppose, I did it for myself and for those with the same problems I had when we looked up a fly pattern and asked, "What does he mean by that? How is this part formed? Where do I get the materials?" If I've answered these and other pertinent questions I'll have done my homework. If I haven't, you'll know it and, in turn, so will I.

How to Use This Book

THE PURPOSE of any reference work is to impart information to the reader quickly, easily, and with a complete understanding of the details or problems involved. We are concerned here with the makeup of any one of a number of fly patterns and the solving of fly-tying problems related to specific patterns.

For obvious reasons, this book is broken down into categories, sections, and subsections. For example, surface patterns are not all alphabetized into one overall grouping but are divided into the standard dry flies, the hair wings, the adult caddis imitations, the parachutes, and so on. This has been done to keep together certain methods and procedures that are peculiar to each group and to make cross-references easier.

The index will tell you where to find a particular fly pattern. In cases where a fly, such as a Light Cahill, may be represented as a dry, a wet, a nymph, or an emerger, the index will distinguish between them and indicate on which page the specific recipe can be found. Once you have located the fly pattern desired, you will find the ingredients required and the suggested hooks and threads to be used. In all cases, the materials that make up a specific pattern will be listed in the order in which they are to be attached to the hook.

After the components listed for each fly, I have added in many cases some "remarks," which may simply be a historical note about the originator or the pattern. More often, however, I will describe a procedure or technique peculiar to some part of the fly or some special tricks of the trade. For example, for the body of the Quill Gordon dry fly a stripped peacock quill is called for. Under the "remarks" for that pattern, you will find a listing of substitutes that are equal to or better than the peacock quill and also certain methods you can use to prepare this type of material. Since there are other flies which use the same type of quill for the body, I have labeled the Quill Gordon as the "model" fly for all of them. When, for instance, you come across the Ginger Quill dry fly, which uses the same kind of body, you will find after the words "Body: Stripped peacock quill" the notation "(see model, Quill Gordon)." Throughout this book you will find other fly patterns which have been designated as models and they will serve as the answer to problems for all other patterns having a similar construction, whether it be in the body, wing, tail, or any other part of the fly. Most of these cross-references to a model fly will occur within a specific section of a particular category. Now and then, however, the same technique may apply to two or more categories. For example, the Blue Dun wet fly is the model which shows how a wet fly hackle is folded, prepared, and then wound as a hackle collar. In the category of salmon flies, the pattern Cosseboom also uses a similar wet fly collar and therefore you will be referred to the Blue Dun because the procedure is exactly the same regardless of the type of fly.

Certain patterns that require unique construction methods or are especially difficult will be illustrated with particular focus on those aspects of their construction.

When you come across a material that is unfamiliar, the index will refer you to any special discussion of it in the text or you can move directly to the list of fly-tying materials at the back of the book, where you should find it alphabetically under the bird or mammal that the particular feather or fur is derived from. If the material is synthetic, you will find it under its trade name. I have tried to follow my peculiar fly tyer's logic here; therefore, turkey wing quills are discussed under TURKEY; polar bear is found under POLAR BEAR; but imitation polar bear is found under POLAR BEAR, IMITATION, and ringneck pheasant and golden pheasant are listed under RINGNECK PHEASANT and GOLDEN PHEASANT, respectively, because that is the way that fly tyers (not ornithologists) refer to them. If the material is difficult to find, I have listed the names of some of the dealers who carry it, and if it is very rare or restricted by law, I have listed substitutes.

The names and addresses of a number of mail-order houses have been listed in a section of their own, with specific reference to the materials or services they offer. Where I mention a dealer in the "remarks" section of a pattern, this is the only source for the material known to me; refer to the dealer list for the address. Occasionally I have mentioned the exclusive source for a particular fly (it is often the originator), and for those who would like to order that fly as a model, I have included the address in the "remarks."

When you come across a term which is unfamiliar or ambiguous, the glossary should shed some light. The glossary does not list specific materials, so if you are interested in duck quills, for instance, you should look in the materials section. If, however, you are unsure what is meant by the word "quill," which has many meanings, go directly to the glossary.

In addition to the plates and photographic and line-drawing sequences of certain techniques, you will find a number of ink drawings of flies strategically placed next to some of the patterns throughout the book. The purpose of these drawings is to give the fly tyer a silhouette of the completed fly showing its correct proportions and outline. (They are not intended to show the detail of specific materials.) To make a comparison, you must remove a completed fly from your vise and hold it up to the light to see if its silhouette matches that in the book. Each silhouette drawing also represents other patterns having a similar outline. Flies that appear in the plates are not repeated as silhouette drawings.

Note: Even though drawings and photographs have been supplied to assist you in understanding the printed recipe more fully, the recipe itself should be carefully read and checked for every detail.

Part I

RECIPES FOR SURFACE PATTERNS

Standard or Classic Dry Flies

THE FOLLOWING patterns are those of the standard or conventional type of dry fly. Some of them have been with us for more than half a century and are still being fished by anglers everywhere. The classic design and basic construction of these patterns are what anglers envision when we refer to the dry fly.

Although we are more familiar with this type of fly than with any other, some of us have problems here and there with a particular recipe. The "remarks" section for that recipe should make things a little easier, whether by suggesting techniques or listing substitute materials. If you have never tried some of the suggestions mentioned in the "remarks" section, you owe it to yourself to investigate them. They are procedures that have been fine-tuned after hundreds of hours

at the tying vise, not only by myself but by a number of professional and amateur fly tyers. If the pattern you are interested in presents a problem, be sure also to check any referral to a model fly which may show construction procedures for wing, body, tail, or some other part of the fly.

The hooks listed for most of the standard dry flies are the Mustad model 94840 and the Partridge L3A. This does not mean that you cannot use another hook of equivalent design, such as a TIEMCO (TMC) or a VMC or, for that matter, that of any other manufacturer. In many cases some of these other hooks may be preferable for the design of your pattern. Nor does it mean that you cannot use a variation such as a barbless or one made of extra-fine wire if this is your bent when fishing the dry fly. There are many new hooks

on the market and others are constantly being introduced. I've used the Mustad and Partridge as the suggested hooks only because they've been with us a long time and have proven themselves for most situations over the years.

For nearly all of the standard dry flies the Flymaster brand of thread is recommended. This is a 6/0 thread which lies fairly flat. It comes pre-waxed and in a variety of colors. Some tyers prefer to tie with silk thread, which is fine. A 6/0 silk thread has no stretch whatsoever and, though slightly weaker than nylon, firmly secures the materials to the hook shank. Silk threads should first be waxed so they will lie flatter on the shank and adhere more readily. Silk threads of any quality are usually available only in black and white and these colors do not always fit into the overall color scheme of the fly patterns to be tied. If you do use silk thread, stick with the white for all patterns unless black is specifically called for. The waxing of white silk thread will soften it into a somewhat more neutral shade.

Threads that should not be used for standard dry flies are the Monocords and those of heavier gauge than a size 5/0. Monocord, though it lies flat and is used on some of the other types of patterns, has just a bit too much stretch in it to make for a securely tied fly. Heavy threads simply take up too much room on the shank and prevent the materials from behaving properly, especially in the setting of the wings.

Hook sizes listed for each recipe are those on which the pattern is commonly tied. For example, the Quill Gordon, which imitates the early mayfly *Epeoris pleuralis,* is usually sold in sizes 12 and 14 because these sizes most closely simulate the natural. If you feel that a size 18 Quill Gordon is a killer on Upper Muddy Creek, by all means tie it in that size. For the most part, and within the restrictions of your materials, you can tie any of the patterns in this book on any size or style of hook you desire.

The ingredients for each pattern recipe are listed *in the order in which they are attached to the hook.*

The primary function of a surface fly is to float, and to that end those materials which best support the fly on the water should be used without changing the pattern itself. The pattern derives its name from the ingredients used in its recipe, and unless we give a par-

ticular fly another name, it is not wise to change the ingredients. There are, however, certain basic rules we can follow without violating tradition.

If the body is made of a water-absorbent material, it will not float very long, and will perform poorly where a long drift is required to reach the lie of a fish. On standard dry flies, it is still best to use natural furs where a dubbed body is called for. Yes, we do have a number of synthetic furs and blends which are supposed to be lighter than water. Actually, the synthetics, for the most part, absorb water like a sponge and should be avoided on a dry fly except in special cases. There is ample room in the fly tyer's repertoire for the use of synthetics, primarily in the wet fly and nymph categories.

Certain dry flies, especially the more traditional patterns, call for floss or floss-and-tinsel bodies. If we change from floss to a less absorbent fur body, we must also change the name of the pattern. If you are going to tie a fly according to its pattern (and generally you should, since we have too much confusion already), you will have to stay with the materials called for. However, if you wish to experiment with some of the standard patterns by substituting fur for the body, by all means do so. If you are a commercial tyer and wish to sell a fly with this change in it, you will have to announce the variation. For example, the Pink Lady pattern calls for a pink floss body. If you substitute pink fur, you should call this fly pattern Pink Lady, Fur Body.

Another example is the use of woodchuck

guard hair fibers in forming the wing and tail of the Irresistible. Woodchuck is easier to tie with, is more durable, and makes for a more pronounced wing. If you use woodchuck, though, you should call your fly the Woodchuck Irresistible to differentiate it from the original pattern, in which the wing and tail are formed with deer body hair fibers.

You should always try to use the best materials for the job. Sometimes this is not possible, as in the tying of the wings of such standard dry flies as the Quill Gordon and the Light Cahill. Many tyers, because of the scarcity and costliness of natural woodchuck flank, will use mallard flank that has been dyed to imitate the natural wood duck color. This is a perfectly acceptable solution and no notation regarding the pattern is required. (Mallard flank, however, is not quite as stiff as natural wood duck and will not stand quite as proudly erect as a dry fly wing.)

The proportions of the standard dry fly are generalized below. The dimensions of

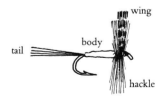

General Proportions for a Standard Dry Fly
WING HEIGHT: Hook-shank length
TAIL LENGTH: Hook-shank length
BODY LENGTH: Three-quarters shank length
HEIGHT OF HACKLE: Three-quarters height of wing

wing height, tail length, and hackle height are as they apply to a standard-sized hook such as the Mustad 94840. For long- or short-shanked hooks these proportions should be adjusted. For the most part, keep the tail and hackle fibers just long and high enough so that the bottom bend of the hook barely rests on the surface of the water. The wing, of course, should protrude slightly above the hackle tips.

ADAMS
(Plate I)

HOOK: Mustad 94840, Partridge L3A
   (10–20)
THREAD: Gray or black (Flymaster 6/0)
WING: Grizzly hackle tips
TAIL: Brown and grizzly hackle mixed
BODY: Gray muskrat dubbing fur
HACKLE: Brown and grizzly mixed

REMARKS: It is fitting that the single most popular dry fly in North America is the very first fly listed. The wing of the Adams can be difficult to set. Trying to divide the wing with a crisscross winding of thread leaves too many fibers exposed, while stripping away most of the fibers before the tips are tied in makes for a flimsy wing. The following technique, shown to me by Walt Dette, has simplified this procedure: After lashing and propping the hackle tips to a vertical position on the hook shank, you should bring the thread *in back of the wings,* take one turn of thread around the hook shank *in back of the wings,* and then proceed with a *reverse-figure-eight* winding of thread around and between the hackle tips. The thread will be coming toward you and you will be encircling the base of the hackle tips in such a manner that the thread will close around all the fibers on each wing.

Tying the Adams Hackle Tip Wing

a. Hackle tip wings have been lashed to hook shank.

b. Thread is brought around outside base of far-side hackle tip then through and between hackle tips.

c. Thread is wound one turn (counterclockwise) around hook shank in back of wing.

d. Thread is brought around outside base of near-side hackle tip then through and between hackle tips to back of wings. Thread is now again moving in a clockwise manner.

e. One complete turn of thread is taken around shank in back of wings.

f. Hackle tip wings properly secured.

The standard recipe calls for rooster hackle tips, but many tyers prefer to use hackle tips from grizzly hen necks. Hen hackle, because of its webbiness, has more density and presents a better silhouette when being fished, whereas rooster hackle tips almost disappear inside the hackle collar. Hen hackle is much less expensive than the lowest-grade rooster neck, and the tips are easier to tie in and divide. A normal figure eight of thread will do the job without leaving a number of prickly, wispy, wayward fibers which have to be trimmed. Oversized hen hackle feathers can be shaped into cut wings, again lending more prominence to the Adams pattern.

The wing for the Adams may also be made from teal flank fibers. The flank feathers from a drake teal are very darkly barred and, as a wing, strongly pronounced. In this case the name of the fly should be Adams, Teal Wing.

The Adams calls for a tail of two colors of hackle, brown and grizzly mixed, which have to be aligned at the tips. The easiest way to achieve proper alignment is to pluck the section of fibers from a brown hackle feather and lay them on the table. Then pluck the section of grizzly fibers and, holding them with tweezers, place them on top of the section of brown hackle fibers so the tips are even. Place your index finger on top of the combined sections of hackle fibers and remove the tweezers. Then pick up the combined (and aligned) sections of fibers with the tweezers and transfer them to your thumb and index finger for placement on the hook shank.

In setting the tail, it is much easier if you tie in the tail so that the unit appears to be too short and take one turn of thread around the hook shank to hold the fibers loosely in place. Then all you have to do is pull the entire section rearward until the tail is as long as it should be.

The hackle for the Adams is then prepared and wound for the dry fly collar. It should be noted, however, that because you will be using hackles from two different rooster necks, chances are that the fibers on one may be slightly longer than those on the other. Always wind the hackle having the longer fibers first, then wind the second hackle, the one with the shorter fibers.

The Adams was developed by Leonard Halladay of Mayfield, Michigan. It was first used in 1922 by Charles F. Adams of Lorain, Ohio, and because of the unusual success Adams had with the fly on Michigan's Boardman River, the fly was named in his honor. The original Adams pattern was tied as a spent wing. Today, the general practice is to tie it upright and divided. When it is to be tied as a spent wing, it will be so noted.

ADAMS QUILL
(Plate II)

HOOK: Mustad 94840, Partridge L3A
   (12–16)
THREAD: Black (Flymaster 6/0)
WING: Grizzly hackle tips tied semi-spent
   (see model, Adams)
TAIL: Wood duck flank fibers
BODY: Stripped peacock quill dyed a light
   rusty brown (see model, Quill Gordon)
HACKLE: Brown and grizzly mixed

REMARKS: This fly, developed by Everett Caryl of Spokane, Washington, is one of a number of improvisations on the Adams. The tail of wood duck fibers requires that you select only the stiffest of fibers. If these are

Tying In the Adams Tail

a. Section of brown hackle fibers placed on table.

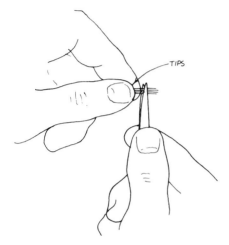

b. Section of grizzly hackle fibers placed between tweezers.

c. Section of grizzly hackle fibers being aligned with brown hackle fibers.

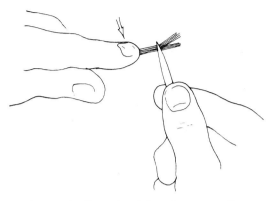

d. Grizzly fibers placed directly on top of brown fibers and held in place with fingertip.

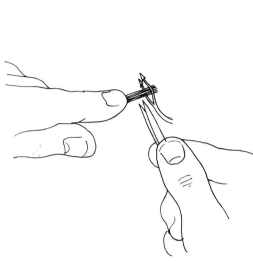

f. Tweezers scooping and grasping aligned section of both grizzly and brown fibers as a unit.

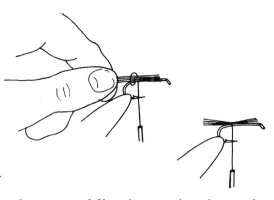

h. Section of fibers being tied in short with one turn of thread.

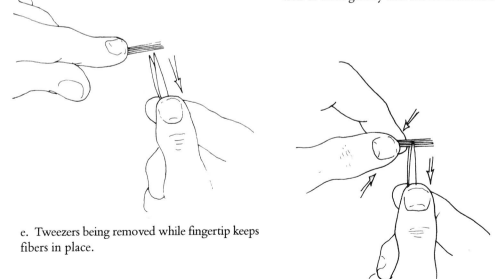

e. Tweezers being removed while fingertip keeps fibers in place.

g. Section of tail fibers being transferred to left thumb and forefinger.

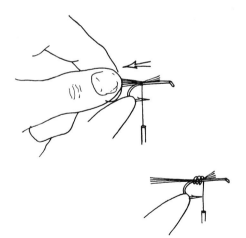

i. Section of fibers being pulled rearward until proper length is attained.

not available, use brown and grizzly hackle mixed as in the standard Adams.

ADAMS SPENT WING

The same as Adams except that the grizzly hackle tip wings are tied in a horizontal position to represent a spent or dying mayfly.

AMERICAN MARCH BROWN
(see March Brown)

BADGER VARIANT
(Plate II)

HOOK: Mustad 94840, Partridge L3A (12–16)
THREAD: Brown (Flymaster 6/0)
WING: Dark cream hackle tips (see model, Adams)
TAIL: Dark cream hackle tips
BODY: Stripped peacock quill (see model, Quill Gordon)
HACKLE: Badger (tied oversized)

REMARKS: Variant type flies do not usually have a wing as this pattern does.

BASIC WHITE FLY

HOOK: Mustad 94840, Partridge L3A (12–14)
THREAD: White (Flymaster 6/0)
WING: None
TAIL: White hackle fibers
BODY: White mink dubbing fur
HACKLE: White and blue dun mixed

BEAVERKILL

HOOK: Mustad 94840, Partridge L3A (10–16)
THREAD: Black (Flymaster 6/0)
WING: Mallard (or equivalent) wing quill sections (see model, Black Gnat)
TAIL: Brown hackle fibers
PALMER RIB: Brown hackle palmered through body
BODY: White floss
HACKLE: Brown

REMARKS: Use a slightly shorter-fibered hackle for the palmer rib than for the front hackle. On a size 14 hook use a size 16 hackle to palmer through the body. Tie the rib in at the butt end as you would for a hackle collar. Keep the floss body fairly thin, so that it will be easier to palmer the hackle.

BEAVERKILL RED FOX

HOOK: Mustad 94840, Partridge L3A (10–16)
THREAD: Black (Flymaster 6/0)
WING: None
TAIL: Dark ginger hackle fibers
RIB: Fine flat gold tinsel
BODY: Muskrat dubbing fur
HACKLE: Golden ginger followed by medium blue dun to eye

REMARKS: It is always a good idea to tie the rib of tinsel in near the center of the hook shank and wind it rearward toward the bend, securing it at that point with a turn or two of thread. This will program the tinsel to wind

properly around the shank when the first turn is made after the body has been formed.

The hackle collar on this fly is not a mixed hackle as in the Adams. The simplest way to form this two-tone collar is to first tie the ginger hackle to the shank, then the blue dun hackle slightly forward of the ginger. Bend the blue dun hackle forward and beyond the eye of the hook and take one turn of thread around it to keep it out of the way while you make your turns of the ginger hackle. After the ginger hackle collar has been secured, wind the blue dun hackle in front of it to the eye to complete the collar.

Bivisibles

The term "bivisible" means that the fly is visible not only to the trout but also to the angler. A bivisible dry fly may be made in any color, including purple, as long as the front hackle is white or cream. In other words, the front hackle must be light enough to be visible. Bivisibles generally do not have wings. The most popular bivisible is the Brown Bivisible.

BROWN BIVISIBLE
(Plate I)

HOOK: Mustad 94840, Partridge L3A (10–16)
THREAD: Black (Flymaster 6/0)
HACKLE: White

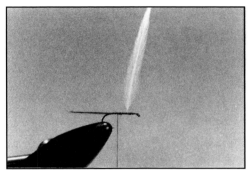

Hackle Sequence for Bivisible
a. White front hackle tied to shank.

b. Brown hackle being wound forward to a point in front of white hackle.

c. White hackle has been wound to eye to complete fly.

TAIL: Brown hackle fibers
BODY: Brown hackle wound in connecting spirals two-thirds of the hook-shank length

REMARKS: The trick to this pattern is to first tie in the front white hackle and force it slightly forward with a turn or two of thread so that it is out of the way. Then proceed by tying in the tail, and then winding two or three (or whatever it takes) brown hackles around the shank in closely connecting spirals to the point where the white hackle was previously tied in. It's not a bad idea to wind the last of the brown hackles one or two turns beyond the front white hackle. This will result in a gradual blend from brown to all-white after the white hackle has been wound forward to the eye. For better visibility take at least five or six turns of the white hackle around the shank to form the front collar.

Other commonly listed bivisibles are:

BLACK BIVISIBLE
With black tail and black hackle body

BADGER BIVISIBLE
With badger hackle tail and badger hackle body

GINGER BIVISIBLE
With ginger tail and ginger hackle body

GRIZZLY BIVISIBLE
With grizzly tail and grizzly hackle body

BLUE DUN BIVISIBLE
With blue dun tail and blue dun hackle body

Again, all bivisibles have a white or cream front hackle collar.

BLACK GNAT
(Plate I)

HOOK: Mustad 94840, Partridge L3A (12–18)
THREAD: Black (Flymaster 6/0)
WING: Mallard (or equivalent) wing quill sections
TAIL: Black hackle fibers
BODY: Dyed black dubbing fur
HACKLE: Black

REMARKS: While many earlier pattern descriptions of this fly call for the use of black chenille for the body, this material is much too water-absorbent to be used on a dry fly. Anglers in the know prefer the fur body. The wing of the Black Gnat consists of two wing quill segments, a left and a right, from a mallard or similar water duck. A wing made from this material is generally not very durable and has a tendency to split while it is being fastened to the shank unless certain precautions are taken. The wing quill sections should be taken from that part of the duck quill flight feather which is neither too soft (the lower section of the quill) nor too brittle (the upper portion of the shaft). The most usable portion on most feathers is generally the middle third of the the feather.

There is a line of demarcation running down the entire length of this feather dividing the outer softer portion from the inner hard and glossier section. When a left and a right section are cut from their respective quills, the thread should never come down on the glossy hardness of the inner section of quill. This will cause splitting of the fibers. If the quill sections to be used are not long enough for the particular size of fly to allow the thread to crimp down on the softer outer section of quill, find another feather which will accommodate the hook size used. On very large flies you may have to resort to goose quills.

Once the left and right quill segments have been paired and evenly aligned (a pair of tweezers makes this job much easier), they are lashed to the top of the hook shank with two firm windings of thread. Do not use more than two turns of thread since this may cause splitting of the fibers, or, when you pass the thread between the wing quill segments to force the wing apart into a natural position, the bulking of thread may splay the segments into an unnatural alignment.

Once the wing quills have been fastened to the shank, take a turn or two of thread in front of them so that they stand erect. Then bring the thread in back of the wings and take one turn of thread around the hook shank only. Now bring your thread through the wing division from rear to front and then take one turn of thread around the hook shank only in front of the wings. Now bring the thread through the wing division to the back of the wings and again take one turn of thread around the shank in back of the wings. You are now ready to proceed with the rest of the fly.

A Matched Pair of Duck Wing Quills

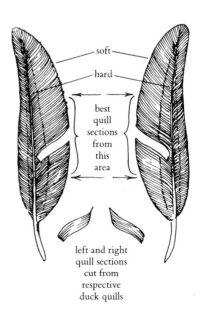

soft

hard

best quill sections from this area

left and right quill sections cut from respective duck quills

Preparing Wing Quills for Black Gnat

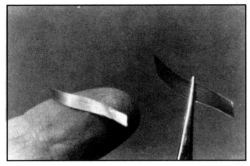

a. Left quill section placed on fingertip. Right quill section held in tweezers.

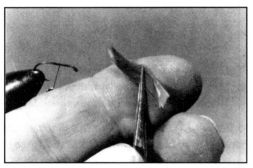

b. Right quill section placed on top and in alignment with left quill section.

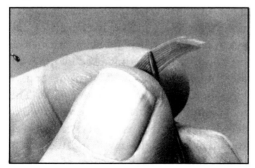

c. Paired quill sections grasped between left thumb and forefinger.

d. Quill sections fastened to hook shank.

e. Completed Black Gnat.

The question always arises whether the tips of the duck quill sections should point forward over the eye or rearward toward the bend. You will see this type of fly tied both ways. I like to point them forward over the eye of the hook for purely aesthetic reasons. Others prefer the wing sections to point and slant rearward because they believe the fly behaves better when being cast. Unless you are tying for resale and your customer has a certain preference, the tip position of the wings is up to you.

Incidentally, when you trim the butts which face toward the bend, use the stagger-cut method so that you will have a slight taper upon which to build the body of your fly when you come to that operation.

BLACK HACKLE
(sometimes listed as Black Hackle, Peacock)

HOOK: Mustad 94840, Partridge L3A (10–16)
THREAD: Black (Flymaster 6/0)
WING: None
TAIL: Dyed bright red hackle fibers
BODY: Peacock herl
HACKLE: Black

REMARKS: Sometimes a tag of fine flat gold tinsel is added on this pattern.

BLACK QUILL

HOOK: Mustad 94840, Partridge L3A (12–16)
THREAD: Black (Flymaster 6/0)
WING: Mallard (or equivalent) wing quill sections (dark) (see model, Black Gnat)
TAIL: Black hackle fibers
BODY: Stripped peacock quill (or equivalent) (see model, Quill Gordon)
HACKLE: Black

BLACK QUILL (Variation)
(Plate II)

HOOK: Mustad 94840, 94863, Partridge L3A (12–14)
THREAD: Black (Flymaster 6/0)
WING: Wood duck flank fibers (see model, Dark Hendrickson)
TAIL: Darkest natural dun, almost black
BODY: Peacock eye herl dyed black then stripped with wax (see model, Quill Gordon)
HACKLE: Darkest natural dun

REMARKS: This variation of the Black Quill was designed by Jack Mickievicz, who uses it to imitate an unidentified natural he has found in some of the wilder and more remote streams still harboring native brook trout.

BLUE DUN
(Plate I)

HOOK: Mustad 94840, Partridge L3A (12–18)
THREAD: Gray (Flymaster 6/0)
WING: Mallard (or equivalent) wing quill sections (see model, Black Gnat)
TAIL: Medium blue dun hackle fibers
BODY: Muskrat dubbing fur
HACKLE: Medium blue dun

BLUE FOX

HOOK: Mustad 94840, Partridge L3A (10–16)
THREAD: Black (Flymaster 6/0)

WING: None
TAIL: Dark ginger hackle fibers
RIB: Fine flat gold tinsel
BODY: Muskrat dubbing fur
HACKLE: Dark ginger followed by blue dun to eye (see model, Beaverkill Red Fox)

BLUE QUILL

HOOK: Mustad 94840, Partridge L3A (12–18)
THREAD: Gray (Flymaster 6/0)
WING: Mallard (or equivalent) wing quill sections (see model, Black Gnat)
TAIL: Medium blue dun hackle fibers
BODY: Stripped peacock quill (or equivalent) (see model, Quill Gordon)
HACKLE: Medium blue dun

BLUE WINGED OLIVE

HOOK: Mustad 94840, Partridge L3A (12–18)
THREAD: Olive (Flymaster 6/0)
WING: Pale dun hackle tips (see model, Adams)
TAIL: Dark dun hackle fibers
BODY: Medium olive dubbing fur
HACKLE: Dark dun

REMARKS: The body color of this very popular pattern is often tied lighter or darker because the natural insect changes color from the time it first emerges (dark olive) till it actually lifts off the water (light olive). Some anglers will fish a dark-bodied emerger or dry fly at the head of the pool where it is emerging and a lighter-shaded fly at the tail of the pool. There are a few variations of this pattern but the above is the one most commonly used.

BLUE WINGED OLIVE (Flick)
(Plate I)

HOOK: Mustad 94840 (16–18)
THREAD: Olive (Flymaster 6/0)
WING: None
TAIL: Natural dark dun hackle fibers
BODY: A blend of shredded olive wool yarn with a hint of muskrat dubbing mixed in (olive cast must show through)
HACKLE: Natural dark dun, slightly oversized

REMARKS: This pattern by Art Flick is another version quite often tied when the Blue Winged Olive is called for.

BORCHER SPECIAL
(Plate II)

HOOK: Mustad 94840, Partridge L3A (8–20)
THREAD: Black (Flymaster 6/0)
WING: Blue dun hackle tips (see model, Adams)
TAIL: Mahogany ringneck pheasant tail fibers (banded)
BODY: Mottled turkey fibers
HACKLE: Brown and grizzly mixed

REMARKS: The body of this pattern uses individual turkey wing quill fibers, two or three of which are tied in near the bend and wound forward as you would a section of floss.

The pattern was originated by Anne Schwiegert, who for many years ran a fly shop in Roscommon, Michigan. The original hackle was brown, and when Ernie Borcher added grizzly to the hackle collar, the pattern became known as the Borcher Special.

BROWN DRAKE
(see page 36)

BROWN HACKLE

HOOK: Mustad 94840, Partridge L3A (12–18)
THREAD: Brown or black (Flymaster 6/0)
WING: None
TAIL: Dyed red hackle fibers
RIB: Fine flat gold tinsel
BODY: Medium brown dubbing fur
HACKLE: Brown

BROWN HACKLE, PEACOCK
(Plate II)

HOOK: Mustad 94840, Partridge L3A (12–18)
THREAD: Black (Flymaster 6/0)
WING: None
TAIL: Dyed red hackle fibers
RIB: Fine gold wire
BODY: Peacock herl
HACKLE: Brown

BROWN HACKLE, YELLOW

HOOK: Mustad 94840, Partridge L3A (12–18)
THREAD: Brown (Flymaster 6/0)
WING: None
TAIL: Brown hackle fibers
RIB: Fine flat gold tinsel
BODY: Dyed yellow dubbing fur
HACKLE: Brown

BROWN MAYFLY
(Plate II)

HOOK: Mustad 94840, Partridge L3A (12–16)
THREAD: Tan (Flymaster 6/0)
WING: Wood duck flank fibers (see model, Dark Hendrickson)
TAIL: Mahogany ringneck pheasant tail fibers (enough to support fly)
RIB: Stripped peacock herl (see model, Quill Gordon)
BODY: Natural tan raffia
HACKLE: Brown

REMARKS: This pattern, listed by the Orvis Company, uses the stripped peacock quill as an open-spiraled rib with the tan raffia showing between the spirals. The mahogany pheasant tail fibers are tied in as a unit or clump to form the tail.

BURR'S BRIGHT
(Plate II)

HOOK: Mustad 94840, Partridge L3A (12–16)
THREAD: Black (Flymaster 6/0)
WING: None
TAIL: White hackle fibers
BODY: Fluorescent green wool
HACKLE: Grizzly

REMARKS: This fly was originated by Walter Burr of Dennis, Massachusetts, for fishing during the hours of maximum ultra-violet light, from dawn to sunrise, from sundown to darkness.

CAHILL, DARK
(see Dark Cahill)

CAHILL, LIGHT
(see Light Cahill)

CAHILL QUILL

HOOK: Mustad 94840, Partridge L3A (12–18)
THREAD: Cream (Flymaster 6/0)
WING: Wood duck flank fibers (see model, Dark Hendrickson)
TAIL: Dark cream hackle fibers
BODY: Stripped peacock quill (or equivalent) (see model, Quill Gordon)
HACKLE: Dark Cream

CALIFORNIA MOSQUITO
(Plate II)

HOOK: Mustad 94840, Partridge L3A (10–18)
THREAD: Black (Flymaster 6/0)
TAIL: Grizzly hackle fibers
RIB: White silk thread
BODY: Black floss
WING: Two grizzly hackle tips aligned back to back and tied slanting rearward at a 45-degree angle over the body to the center of the tail
HACKLE: Grizzly

REMARKS: This pattern employs a semi-downwing effect with the grizzly tips extending rearward slightly above the body. In this case, the construction procedure is easier if the tail is tied in first, followed by rib, body, wing, and finally the hackle.

COACHMAN
(see under Royal Coachman, which lists all in this series)

COCK Y BONDHU

HOOK: Mustad 94840, Partridge L3A (10–16)
THREAD: Black (Flymaster 6/0)
WING: None
TAIL: Cock Y Bondhu hackle fibers
BODY: Peacock herl
HACKLE: Cock Y Bondhu

COFFIN FLY
(see page 37)

COMPARA DUNS
(see page 37)

CONOVER
(Plate I)

HOOK: Mustad 94840 (10–18)
THREAD: Claret (Flymaster 6/0)
WING: None
TAIL: Golden badger hackle fibers
BODY: Muskrat, red wool, and a hint of white lamb's wool blended together
HACKLE: Golden badger (without a black edge)

REMARKS: Originated by Walt Dette and named after J. Scott Conover, who frequented the Beaverkill and Willowemoc rivers in New York in the late 1930s and early 1940s. It is still tied by the Dette family and used very successfully on these and other streams. It doubles as both a mayfly and a caddis fly imitation.

COWDUNG

HOOK: Mustad 94840, Partridge L3A (12–16)
THREAD: Black (Flymaster 6/0)
WING: Dark gray duck wing quill sections (see model, Black Gnat)
TAIL: Brown hackle
TAG: Fine flat gold tinsel
BODY: Dark olive dubbing fur
HACKLE: Brown

REMARKS: This pattern is generally known and tied as a wet fly though it is listed and used, now and then, as a floater. The wet fly version employs dark olive floss for the body but the dry fly version floats better with a dubbed fur body of the same color.

CREAM VARIANT
(Plate I)

HOOK: Mustad 94836, 94837, Partridge L3A (14–16)
THREAD: Cream (Flymaster 6/0)
WING: None
TAIL: Dark cream hackle fibers
BODY: The center stem quill from a dark cream rooster neck or saddle hackle feather
HACKLE: Dark cream tied oversize, usually two or three sizes larger than the hook size used (e.g., a size 16 hook would require a size 10 hackle)

REMARKS: This pattern is one of the flies highlighted by Art Flick in his *Streamside Guide* and is used to represent the large colored mayfly *Potomanthus distinctus,* which appears on many eastern streams in June.

The body of this pattern is not difficult to form but occasionally fly tyers have problems keeping the bumps, lumps, and humps out of the lower abdomen when making the first turn of quill around the shank. This bubble effect can be avoided by tying the fine end of the quill to the center of the hook shank and first winding rearward before progressing forward toward the eye. Try this method the next time you tie this pattern

Tying In Stripped Quill for Cream Variant

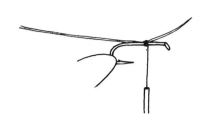

a. Quill tied to hook shank.

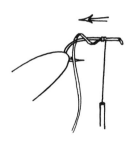

b. Quill wound rearward and around shank to bend.

c. Quill being wound forward to form body.

and see if you don't obtain a more even and natural taper. It is a good idea, after the fly is completed, to brush a coat of head lacquer or varnish over the quill body.

CROSS SPECIAL

HOOK: Mustad 94840, Partridge L3A (12–18)
THREAD: Gray (Flymaster 6/0)
WING: Lemon wood duck flank fibers (see model, Dark Hendrickson)
TAIL: Light blue dun hackle fibers
BODY: Pale gray fox fur dubbing (or equivalent)
HACKLE: Light blue dun

DARK CAHILL
(Plate I)

HOOK: Mustad 94840, Partridge L3A (12–18)
THREAD: Tan, gray, or black (Flymaster 6/0)
WING: Lemon wood duck flank fibers (see model, Dark Hendrickson)
TAIL: Dark ginger hackle fibers
BODY: Muskrat dubbing fur
HACKLE: Dark ginger

DARK HENDRICKSON

HOOK: Mustad 94840, Partridge L3A (12–18)
WING: Lemon wood duck flank fibers
TAIL: Medium bronze dun hackle fibers
BODY: Muskrat dubbing fur
HACKLE: Medium bronze dun

REMARKS: The wing of the Dark Hendrickson is representative of a multitude of dry fly patterns. It may, in fact, be the most popular and most commonly used type of wing in the dry fly category. Its construction, if one uses the natural wood duck flank as opposed to the dyed mallard substitute, is not overly difficult. Still, there are those who have trouble getting a compact and distinct appearance after its formation. The wispy fibers, instead of springing upward from the hook shank in a concentrated yet slightly flaring V shape, seem to follow their own bent, going this way and that. The solution, as with the Adams, is to pass the thread around and between the divided wing sections in such a manner as to lock the fibers tightly at the wing base (where they are lashed to the shank) and yet allow the upper tips to fan outward just a bit and thus present a silhouette resembling the wing of the natural.

After you have lashed the appropriate clump of wood duck fibers to the hook shank and propped them erect, bring your thread between the clump of fibers from front to rear, dividing them equally. Now bring the thread around the hook shank and then through the clump of fibers from rear to front. This operation simply divides the clump of fibers into two separate clumps. Now bring your thread to the rear of the wings and take one complete turn of thread around the hook shank in back of them.

Encircle the clump of fibers on the far side of the shank with one turn of thread. The thread will be coming toward you in a reverse figure eight. After you have completely encircled the clump of fibers at their base, bring the thread through the division of the left and right wing (and again toward yourself) and continue with the thread to encircle the clump of fibers nearest you with one turn of thread. After you have made one turn of thread around the fibers at the base of those nearest you, continue with the thread through the division to the rear of the wings. Take one turn of thread around the hook shank in back of the wings. If this procedure is followed, your wings should stand perfectly erect and neatly divided.

Stagger-cut the butt ends of the excess wood duck fibers before bringing your thread toward the bend to tie in the tail in order that the body you will shortly be constructing has an inclining foundation upon which to build a natural taper.

The hackle color of this pattern (and that of the Light Hendrickson) will vary from shop to shop and from tyer to tyer. The medium bronze dun color I have listed is the most commonly used and most anglers agree that it is the color they see on the natural insects. Even then, that color may vary from stream to stream; moreover, anglers see colors differently from one another.

Winging Method for Wood Duck
Type Wing (Dark Hendrickson)

a. Wood duck fibers, with tips forward, are lashed to shank.

b. Clump of wood duck has been propped erect and a number of turns of thread are taken in front of the base of fibers to support wing clump in a vertical position.

c. Wood duck fibers have been separated into two equal sections. Wing section on near side is being held out of the way as thread is brought from front to rear between the two sections.

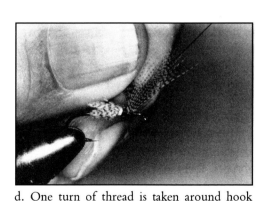

d. One turn of thread is taken around hook shank in back of the wings. Fibers on far side are now held out of the way as thread is brought from rear to front between the two sections of wood duck fibers. After the wing clump has been roughly divided with this figure-eight winding of thread, the thread is brought to a position in back of the wings and one extra turn of thread is taken around the hook shank in back of the wings.

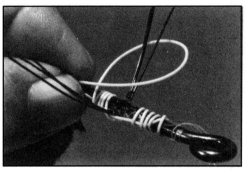

e. (This step illustrates a reverse-figure-eight procedure. However, I've learned that when using a small hook and conventional tying thread many tyers cannot easily distinguish the movements during the process. Therefore, I've substituted an extra-large hook and replaced the black thread with a white fly line so you can see exactly what takes place in this important step. Metal prongs which have been glued to the 20/0 hook represent the wood duck wings.) The thread (line) is brought around the outside of the wing, then through and between the wings toward the tyer. (This reverse loop of thread should be snug against the base of the fibers.) The thread is then brought around the hook shank behind the wings in a counterclockwise direction for one or two turns.

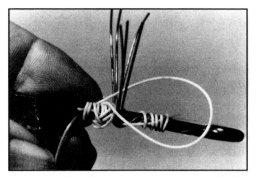

f. Thread (line) is now brought around the outside of the near wing, then through and between divided wings and down the far side of the hook shank. (Again, thread should be snugged against base of wing section.) One or two turns of thread are then taken around hook shank in back of wings.

g. After wing has been secured, excess butts are trimmed and tail body and hackle are tied in to complete fly as in this completed Dark Hendrickson.

For hair-winged flies additional turns of thread are used around the base of each wing to compact wayward fibers such as calf tail or deer hair. This particular and continuing process is shown with the model fly Ausable Wulff (page 35).

DEEP HOLLOW SPECIAL

HOOK: Mustad 94840 (12–16)
THREAD: Black (Flymaster 6/0)
WING: None
TAIL: Dark cream hackle fibers
BODY: Dubbing fur dyed a shade of light-colored mustard
HACKLE: Dyed light but bright yellow

REMARKS: Originated by Don Traver of Don's Tackle in Poughkeepsie, New York, this fly is used on some of the smaller local streams when conventional imitations do not seem to produce.

DEER FLY

HOOK: Mustad 94840 (10–14)
THREAD: Black (Flymaster 6/0)
WING: White duck wing quill (see model, Black Gnat)
TAIL: Black hackle fibers
BODY: Dyed green dubbing fur
HACKLE: White

DELAWARE ADAMS
(Plate I)

HOOK: Mustad 94840 (10–16)
THREAD: Black (Flymaster 6/0)
WING: Grizzly hackle tips (see model, Adams)
TAIL: Grizzly hackle fibers
BODY: Olive floss palmered with grizzly hackle one size smaller than hackle collar
HACKLE: Brown and grizzly mixed

REMARKS: Originated by Walt Dette, this pattern is becoming more popular on the rivers of New York State with each passing season.

DORATO HARE'S EAR
(Plate II)

HOOK: Mustad 94840 (10–14)
THREAD: Brown (Flymaster 6/0)
WING: Lemon wood duck flank feather as single clump
TAIL: Grizzly hackle fibers (half the length of hook shank)
BODY: Hare's ear dubbing fur (the body should have a scraggly appearance even though tapered)
HACKLE: Light to dark ginger and grizzly mixed and trimmed top and bottom

REMARKS: When setting the wing, take a number of turns of thread around the base of the wood duck fibers after they have been propped erect to a vertical position, and force them rearward with pressure from the thread as you make the turns. Holding the clump rearward as the turns are being made also helps. They will fight their way forward again but not quite as far as they would if this extra precaution had not been taken.

The trimming of the hackle, especially on the bottom, allows the fly to ride flush on the water, presenting a fuller silhouette.

DUN VARIANT
(Plate I)

HOOK: Mustad 94836, 94837, Partridge L3A (12–16)

THREAD: Olive (Flymaster 6/0)

WING: None

TAIL: Dark dun hackle fibers

BODY: The center stem quill from a brown rooster neck or saddle feather (see model, Red Quill)

HACKLE: Dark dun (two to three sizes oversize) (see model, Cream Variant)

REMARKS: This pattern was introduced by Art Flick.

EASY HEX
(Plate II)

HOOK: Mustad 37187 (Stinger), Mustad 94840 (2–6)

THREAD: Yellow (Flymaster 6/0)

WING: None

TAIL: Two stripped ginger hackle stems (tied at a 75-degree angle)

BODY: Light brown and yellow fur coarsely mixed

HACKLE: Two ginger and one grizzly mixed (heavy)

REMARKS: Originated by Jay Neve of Bellevue, Michigan. Neve trims the hackle even with the hook point for dun imitations and further trims the hackle almost down to the shank for the spinner fall. It has proven very effective and durable during the "Hex" hatch on Michigan's South Branch of the Au Sable River.

EVENING WHITE FLY
(Plate II)

HOOK: Mustad 94840 (14)

THREAD: Cream (Flymaster 6/0)

WING: Light, sandy ringneck hen pheasant body feather formed into cut wing

EGG SAC: Bright yellow buttercup dubbing fur ball

TAIL: Golden ginger hackle fibers

BODY: Light yellow dubbing fur

HACKLE: Cream ginger

REMARKS: Jack Mickievicz designed this pattern to imitate *Ephoron lucon,* the white mayfly that hatches in the silty sections of certain streams. (The Yellow Breeches in Pennsylvania has a white fly hatch.) In this pattern Mickievicz is imitating the female, which has a bright yellow egg sac and an overall dun color when it lays its eggs. The pattern is highly effective during a hatch.

If hen pheasant neck feathers are unavailable, the light, sandy mottled feathers from a hen chicken may be used.

FEMALE ADAMS

HOOK: Mustad 94840, Partridge L3A (12–18)

THREAD: Gray (Flymaster 6/0)

WING: Grizzly hackle tips (see model, Adams)

EGG SAC: Dyed yellow dubbing fur ball

TAIL: Brown and grizzly hackle fibers mixed

BODY: Muskrat dubbing fur

HACKLE: Brown and grizzly mixed

FEMALE BEAVERKILL
(Plate I)

HOOK: Mustad 94840, Partridge L3A (12–16)

THREAD: Gray (Flymaster 6/0)

WING: Mallard quill sections (or equivalent) (see model, Black Gnat)

EGG SAC: One turn of extra-fine yellow chenille

TAIL: Dark ginger hackle fibers

BODY: Muskrat dubbing fur

HACKLE: Dark ginger

GINGER QUILL
(Plate I)

HOOK: Mustad 94840, Partridge L3A (12–18)

THREAD: Yellow (Flymaster 6/0)

WING: Mallard wing quill sections (see model, Black Gnat)

TAIL: Golden ginger hackle fibers

BODY: Stripped peacock quill (see model, Quill Gordon)

HACKLE: Golden ginger

GOLD-RIBBED HARE'S EAR
(Plate II)

HOOK: Mustad 94840 (12–18)

THREAD: Brown (Flymaster 6/0)

WING: Mallard wing quill sections (see model, Black Gnat)
TAIL: Brown hackle fibers
RIB (optional): Fine gold wire
BODY: Hare's mask and ear fur blended together
HACKLE: Brown

REMARKS: This pattern is rarely listed as a dry fly and that is unfortunate, since it is exceptionally productive.

GORDON

HOOK: Mustad 94840, Partridge L3A (12–16)
THREAD: Cream (Flymaster 6/0)
WING: Lemon wood duck flank fibers (see model, Dark Hendrickson)
TAIL: Badger hackle fibers
RIB: Fine gold wire
BODY: Gold floss
HACKLE: Cream badger

GORDON QUILL
(see Quill Gordon)

GRAY FOX
(Plate I)

HOOK: Mustad 94840, Partridge L3A (12–14)
THREAD: Primrose (yellow) (Flymaster 6/0)
WING: Mallard flank fibers (see model, Dark Hendrickson)
TAIL: Golden ginger hackle fibers

BODY: Fawn/beige fox dubbing fur or equivalent
HACKLE: Light-cast grizzly and golden ginger mixed

REMARKS: This pattern, originated by Preston Jennings, may perhaps owe most of its popularity to Art Flick. The elusive color of light fawn-colored fur from the red fox may be obtained by blending most cream and tan furs, such as fox, hare's mask, or Australian opossum.

GRAY FOX VARIANT
(Plate I)

HOOK: Mustad 94836, 94837, Partridge L3A (12–16)
THREAD: Primrose (Flymaster 6/0)
WING: None
TAIL: Golden ginger hackle fibers
BODY: Center stem quill from dark cream rooster neck or saddle hackle feather (see model, Cream Variant)
HACKLE: Golden ginger, dark ginger, and grizzly mixed (two to three sizes oversize) (see model, Cream Variant)

REMARKS: Art Flick, who is responsible for this popular version of a very important fly, has often said, "If I had one fly to fish, the Gray Fox Variant would be my choice."
When tying in the triple hackle collar, be sure that the longest-fibered hackle is the first to be wound forward so that when all of them have been wound the tips are fairly evenly aligned. The collar itself should be as

compact as possible without throwing it into disarray.

GRAY HACKLE, PEACOCK

HOOK: Mustad 94840, Partridge L3A (12–16)
THREAD: Black (Flymaster 6/0)
WING: None
TAIL: Dyed red hackle fibers
RIB: Fine gold wire
BODY: Peacock herl
HACKLE: Grizzly

GRAY HACKLE, YELLOW

HOOK: Mustad 94840, Partridge L3A (12–16)
THREAD: Black (Flymaster 6/0)
WING: None
TAIL: Red hackle fibers
RIB: Fine flat gold tinsel
BODY: Dyed yellow dubbing fur
HACKLE: Grizzly

GREEN DRAKE (Grimm)
(Plate II)

HOOK: Mustad 94833 (8–10)
THREAD: White (Flymaster 6/0)
TAIL AND BODY: One long-fibered white hackle feather, the tip of which has been V-notched so that it resembles a forked tail while the fibers of the rest of the hackle are pulled forward to form the body

Preparing Extended Forked Tail and Body for Green Drake (Grimm)

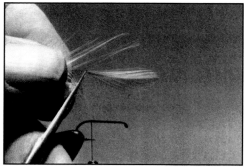

a. Tip being cut from hackle feather.

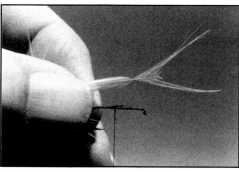

b. Hackle fibers pulled rearward and held in position prior to tying to shank.

c. Hackle being tied to shank to form both tail and body.

d. Completed Green Drake.

WING: White hackle tips (see model, Adams)

HACKLE: White badger trimmed square on bottom

REMARKS: The style of using a hackle feather to form both tail and body was introduced by Harry Darbee in a pattern called the Two-Feather Fly. Emil Grimm used this type of construction but then added a conventional hackle tip wing and a bottom-trimmed hackle collar for his design of the Green Drake.

The hackle feather forming both tail and body is tied to the hook shank only at that point before the wing area where the wing is to be tied. A white hackle feather having extra-long fibers is first measured for proper length so that a quarter of an inch of the body extends past the hook bend and two fibers from each side angle outward as a forked tail beyond the body. Those fibers below the forked tail are pulled forward against the grain of the feather and secured with thread behind the wing area.

After the tail and body sections have been completed, the hackle tip wings and then the hackle are tied in to complete the fly.

HENDRICKSON, DARK
(see Dark Hendrickson)

HENDRICKSON, LIGHT
(see Light Hendrickson)

HENRYVILLE SPECIAL
(see page 67)

HENWING BOMBER

HOOK: Mustad 94840 (6–12)

THREAD: Gray (Flymaster 6/0)

WING: Hen grizzly hackle tips (tied three-quarters spent) (see model, Adams)

TAIL: Gray mink tail guard hair fibers

PALMER RIB: Grizzly hackle palmered through body

BODY: Dyed yellow mink fur and gray/brown muskrat fur blended together to form a coarse dubbing fur

HACKLE: Grizzly and brown mixed

REMARKS: This Michigan pattern serves as an all-purpose fly for adult stoneflies and caddis. It also serves well during the famed "Hex" hatch on various rivers. Designed by Jay Neve and Don Fox.

IRON BLUE DUN

HOOK: Mustad 94840, Partridge L3A (12–18)

THREAD: Black (Flymaster 6/0)

WING: Mallard (or equivalent) wing quill sections (see model, Black Gnat)

TAIL: Cock Y Bondhu hackle fibers

TAG: Red wool

BODY: Muskrat dubbing fur

HACKLE: Furnace or brown

KATTERMAN
(Plate I)

HOOK: Mustad 94840, Partridge L3A (12–16)

THREAD: Cream

WING: None

HACKLE: White

TAIL: Brown hackle fibers

PALMER BODY: Dark brown hackle in connecting spirals

BODY: Peacock herl

REMARKS: This pattern, originated by Walt Dette, is constructed more easily if you first tie in the white hackle which is to become the front collar and then proceed with tail, rib, palmer, and body. (See Brown Bivisible for construction.)

KETTLE CREEK HENDRICKSON
(Plate II)

HOOK: Mustad 94840 (12–14)

THREAD: Cream

WING: Blue dun cut wings

TAIL: Dark dun hackle fibers

BODY: Hare's mask dubbing fur dyed light claret

HACKLE: Dark iron dun (almost black)

REMARKS: This pattern is used by Jack Mickievicz when fishing Kettle Creek in Pennsylvania.

KING OF WATERS

HOOK: Mustad 94840, Partridge L3A (10–16)

THREAD: Black (Flymaster 6/0)

WING: Mallard flank fibers (see model, Dark Hendrickson)

TAIL: Grizzly hackle fibers

PALMER RIB: Brown hackle palmered through body

BODY: Red floss

HACKLE: Brown

LACEWING
(Plate II)

HOOK: Mustad 94840 (14)

THREAD: Yellow (Flymaster 6/0)

WING: None

TAIL: Cream hackle fibers, short (half shank length)

BODY: Dubbing made of green nylon tow

HACKLE: Cream, short (gap width in length)

REMARKS: This slightly unusual pattern is featured in the North Country Angler catalog.

LEADWING COACHMAN

HOOK: Mustad 94840, Partridge L3A (12–18)

THREAD: Black (Flymaster 6/0)

WING: Dark-shade mallard wing quill sections (see model, Black Gnat)

TAIL: Brown hackle fibers

BODY: Peacock herl

HACKLE: Brown

LIGHT CAHILL
(Plate I)

HOOK: Mustad 94840, Partridge L3A
  (10–20)
THREAD: Cream, pale yellow (Flymaster
  6/0)
WING: Lemon wood duck flank fibers (see
  model, Dark Hendrickson)
TAIL: Dark cream hackle fibers
BODY: Creamy yellow dubbing fur
HACKLE: Dark cream

REMARKS: Hackle and body shades vary
with tyer's preference from cream to straw,
from dark cream to golden ginger and various shades in between. This second most
popular dry fly, originated by Dan Cahill,
imitates a variety of light-colored insects.

LIGHT HENDRICKSON
(Plate I)

HOOK: Mustad 94840, Partridge L3A
  (12–14)
THREAD: Gray (Flymaster 6/0)
WING: Lemon wood duck flank fibers (see
  model, Dark Hendrickson)
TAIL: Medium bronze dun hackle fibers
BODY: Urine-stained fox belly fur
HACKLE: Medium bronze dun

REMARKS: The hackle color is generally
listed as blue dun and occasionally rusty dun.
The medium bronze dun used here is very
close to what the natural insect, *Ephemerella
subvaria*, looks like to most anglers. The above
recipe is the one most likely to be used today

though it differs slightly from the original,
which was created by Roy Steenrod and
named after A. E. Hendrickson.

The body fur of urine-stained fox was introduced by Art Flick and it may have been the
color Preston Jennings refers to when he calls
for fawn-colored fox belly in his *Book of
Trout Flies*. Needless to say, it is one of
our most important early flies of the season
throughout the East and the northern tier
states of Michigan, Minnesota, and Wisconsin.

LITTLE MARRYAT

HOOK: Mustad 94840, Partridge L3A
  (10–18)
THREAD: Cream (Flymaster 6/0)
WING: Mallard wing quill sections (see
  model, Black Gnat)
TAIL: Brown hackle fibers
BODY: Light gray dubbing fur
HACKLE: Brown

LITTLE SULFUR DUN
(see under Sulfur Duns)

LUNN'S PARTICULAR

HOOK: Mustad 94840, Partridge L3A
  (12–18)
THREAD: Black (Flymaster 6/0)
WING: Light blue dun hackle tips (tied
  spent) (see model, Adams)
TAIL: Brown hackle fibers (sparse)
BODY: Stripped center stem quill from

brown rooster neck or saddle hackle feather
  (see model, Red Quill)
HACKLE: Brown (sparse)

MALE BEAVERKILL
(see Beaverkill)

MARCH BROWN
(Plate I)

HOOK: Mustad 94840, Partridge L3A
  (12–14)
THREAD: Orange (Flymaster 6/0)
WING: Mallard flank with bronze tinge or
  well-marked wood duck flank fibers (see
  model, Dark Hendrickson)
TAIL: Dark ginger hackle fibers
BODY: Sandy beige dubbing fur
HACKLE: Dark ginger and grizzly mixed

REMARKS: This pattern, also known as
the American March Brown, is the result of
research done by Preston Jennings and Art
Flick. In both of the original patterns the
dark ginger (red game) hackle is wound in
first and the grizzly hackle last as a fronting
collar. Most tyers today simply mix the two
hackles to represent the legs.

The body of the original Jennings recipe
lists red fox belly mixed with sandy poll
from a hare's ear but does not list the ratio of
ingredients. The Flick variation simply lists
light fawn-colored fox fur from the red fox,
which may be incorrectly interpreted by some
tyers. For that matter, so may sandy beige,
which I've used to describe this pattern, but
then, without a sample, it is a difficult shade

to describe. I just wonder how much thought the trout has given to all this.

The original Jennings pattern calls for a wing fashioned from the pearl-barred gray mallard flank feather but this does not really suggest the subtle brownish bronze tints in the natural. Mixing a few bronze dun fibers with the pearl gray or simply using wood duck flank comes a little closer.

McGINTY

HOOK: Mustad 94833, Partridge L3A (10–16)
THREAD: Black (Flymaster 6/0)
WING: Blue with white-tipped secondary feather from mallard duck known as "Mc-Ginty" feather (tied upright and divided in manner of model fly, Black Gnat)
TAIL: Dyed red hackle fibers
BODY: Alternate bands of black and yellow chenille
HACKLE: Brown

REMARKS: This old stand-by, which is sometimes used as a bee imitation, requires a light wire hook to float the absorbent chenille. Chenille size depends on hook size. For sizes 10 to 16, extra fine is recommended.

MELOCHE
(Plate II)

HOOK: Mustad 94840, Partridge L3A (10–20)
THREAD: Tan (Flymaster 6/0)
WING: Light-cast grizzly hackle tips (see model, Adams)
TAIL: Cream ginger hackle fibers
BODY: Tan dubbing fur (as in tan fox)
HACKLE: Cream ginger

REMARKS: This pattern was originated when one Gilbert Meloche came rushing into Dan Bailey's Fly Shop on August 8, 1938, carrying a pale, cream-colored mayfly in his hat. Dan Bailey tied an imitation and Meloche ran out of the store with it and back to the stream. Some two hours later he returned with a 4-pound 8-ounce trout, which became the first fish on the famous Bailey wall of lunkers. Bailey named the fly after Meloche.

MOSQUITO
(Plate I)

HOOK: Partridge L3A (12–20)
THREAD: Gray (Flymaster 6/0)
WING: Grizzly hackle tips (see model, Adams)
TAIL: Grizzly hackle fibers
BODY: Stripped center stem quill from grizzly rooster neck or saddle feather (see model, Cream Variant)
HACKLE: Grizzly

REMARKS: The body of this pattern may also be made from black and white moose

mane fibers tied in and wound simultaneously to form alternate bands of black and white segmentation, or stripped peacock quill may be used.

NEAR ENOUGH

HOOK: Partridge L3A (12–16)
THREAD: Gray (Flymaster 6/0)
WING: Lemon wood duck flank fibers (see model, Dark Hendrickson)
TAIL: Two stripped grizzly hackle stems tied in as a forked tail, extra long (twice shank length)
BODY: Two stripped center stem quills from grizzly rooster wound simultaneously to form body (see model, Cream Variant)
HACKLE: Golden ginger and grizzly mixed

OLIVE DUN, DARK

HOOK: Mustad 94840, Partridge L3A (10–20)
THREAD: Olive (Flymaster 6/0)
WING: Dark-shade mallard wing quill sections (see model, Black Gnat)
TAIL: Dark olive hackle fibers
BODY: Medium to dark olive dun dubbing fur
HACKLE: Dark olive

OLIVE DUN, LIGHT

HOOK: Mustad 94840, Partridge L3A (10–20)
THREAD: Olive (Flymaster 6/0)
WING: Light-shade mallard wing quill sections (see model, Black Gnat)
TAIL: Light olive hackle fibers
BODY: Pale olive dubbing fur
HACKLE: Light olive

OLIVE QUILL, DARK

HOOK: Mustad 94840, Partridge L3A (10–20)
THREAD: Olive (Flymaster 6/0)
WING: Dark-shade mallard wing quill sections (see model, Black Gnat)
TAIL: Medium to dark olive hackle fibers
BODY: Stripped peacock quill (or equivalent) (see model, Quill Gordon)
HACKLE: Dark Olive

OLIVE QUILL, LIGHT

HOOK: Mustad 94840, Partridge L3A (10–20)
THREAD: Olive (Flymaster 6/0)
WING: Light-shade mallard wing quill sections (see model, Black Gnat)
TAIL: Light olive hackle fibers
BODY: Stripped peacock quill (or equivalent) (see model, Quill Gordon)
HACKLE: Light olive

PALE EVENING DUN

HOOK: Mustad 94840, Partridge L3A (14–20)
THREAD: Cream or primrose (Flymaster 6/0)
WING: Light dun hackle tips (see model, Adams)
TAIL: Light blue dun hackle fibers
BODY: Pale yellow dubbing fur
HACKLE: Light blue dun

REMARKS: This is but one version of the fly that imitates the mayfly *Ephemerella dorothea*. Other versions are Pale Watery Dun, Sulfur Dun, and Little Sulfur Dun. See also Little Sulfur Dun (under Sulfur Duns) for other pattern recipes.

PALE WATERY DUN

HOOK: Mustad 94840, Partridge L3A (16–18)
THREAD: Gray (Flymaster 6/0)
WING: Mallard wing quill sections (see model, Black Gnat)
TAIL: Pale dun hackle fibers
BODY: Light-shade muskrat or mink dubbing fur
HACKLE: Pale dun

PINK LADY

HOOK: Partridge L3A (12–16)
THREAD: Cream (Flymaster 6/0)
WING: Mallard wing quill sections (see model, Black Gnat)

TAIL: Golden pheasant tippet fibers (enough to support fly)
RIB: Fine flat gold tinsel
BODY: Pink floss
HACKLE: Golden ginger

QUEEN OF WATERS

HOOK: Partridge L3A (12–16)
THREAD: Cream (Flymaster 6/0)
WING: Mallard flank fibers (see model, Dark Hendrickson)
TAIL: Golden ginger hackle fibers
PALMER RIB: Golden ginger hackle palmered through body
BODY: Orange floss
HACKLE: Golden ginger

QUILL GORDON
(still known as the Gordon Quill in parts of the Catskill region of New York)
(Plate I)

HOOK: Mustad 94840, Partridge L3A (12–14)
THREAD: Gray (Flymaster 6/0)
WING: Lemon wood duck flank fibers (see model, Dark Hendrickson)
TAIL: Medium to dark dun hackle fibers
BODY: Stripped peacock quill
HACKLE: Medium to dark dun

REMARKS: The body of this pattern, as in many others, calls for a stripped peacock quill, which, at best, is a fairly fragile material. In fact, expletives have been hurled at this material by professional fly tyers because, in the case of an especially weak peacock eye quill, the fiber tends to break as it is being wound around the shank. There are, however, a few solutions to this problem. Certain substitutes can be used if you can find them. One is the stripped quill of a condor flight feather, which is much tougher than peacock quill and in some cases has more definition of segmentation. You cannot buy condor because the birds are protected. If, however, you have a friend in the aviary department of your local zoo, ask him to save these feathers for you when the bird molts. Another substitute is the outer pointer flight feather from the brown or wild turkey. This feather is barred black and white. The quills you want from this feather are those which have a predominance of the black barring. These will be dark enough, whereas those from the white area will be too light. (Lighter fibers can be darkened in a tan dye bath.) While condor and peacock quills must be stripped of their flues, turkey quill fibers may be used as is since they do not have an overabundance of these fine barbules.

If you cannot find a suitable substitute and you are forced to use the stripped peacock quill, you can strengthen the quill by counterwrapping it with fine gold wire after the body has been formed. If you are not happy with the aesthetics of the gold wire, you can use a method employed by the Dettes. After the quill body has been formed, a strand of 6/0 white silk thread is lashed to the hook shank behind the wings, from where it is wound to the bend in an open spiral and then, in crisscross fashion, back to the starting point, where it is secured with the tying thread. The crisscross windings of white silk thread and the quill body of the fly are then covered with spar varnish and allowed to dry. The interaction between the silk and the varnish causes the windings of silk thread to become almost invisible to the naked eye, and the body has been made much more durable.

Preparation

When preparing bodies for such flies as the Quill Gordon, Ginger Quill, and the like, many of us would dip the peacock eye quill in Clorox to remove the fine barbules. This method is no longer recommended because it severely weakens the quill. (The Clorox method is still recommended for the bodies of such flies as the Red Quill and the Dun Variant, since in these instances we are dealing with a much stronger and fuller hackle stem quill.)

The stripping of flues from the peacock eye quill by hand—that is, running the fiber through the fingernails of forefinger and thumb—weakens the quill less than any other method. If you strip your quills in this manner, try stripping two or three of them simultaneously. It seems to work better and, of course, the results are doubled or tripled. If

An Easy Way to Strip a Peacock Quill

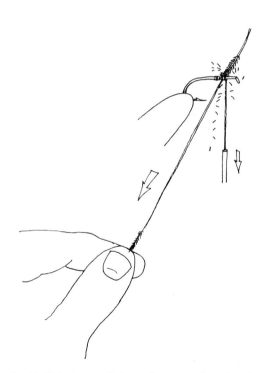

a. One turn of thread wound around peacock eye quill.

b. Quill being pulled out between thread and hook shank and stripping off tiny barbules.

you have a particularly stubborn quill and the barbules refuse to be removed, here is another method that seldom fails. Place a hook in your vise and attach tying thread to the center of the hook shank. Now place the peacock quill fiber against the shank and take just one turn of thread over it. Pull the peacock quill from between the thread and the shank. Repeat this procedure until all the flues have been removed. It usually takes only three to five such maneuvers to rid the quill of unwanted fuzz.

If you wish to have peacock quills in quantity, melt some paraffin wax in an old pot. When the wax is fluid, dip an entire peacock eye into the liquid. Remove it after a second or two and place it on newspaper to dry. When it has dried to a caked and unrecognizable glob, it is ready. Simply remove one of the quills and peel the wax from the quill by running it between the nails of your thumb and forefinger.

RED ANT
(Plate II)

HOOK: Mustad 94840, Partridge L3A (10–20)
THREAD: Black (Flymaster 6/0)
WING: Mallard wing quills (or equivalent) (see model, Black Gnat)
TAIL: Brown hackle fibers
BUTT: Peacock herl
BODY: Red floss
HACKLE: Brown

REMARKS: This pattern, which predates the Royal Coachman, may have been created to imitate a red or flying red ant. Its construction, however, is in the manner of other flies in this category and totally unlike the dressings given for ants in the section pertaining to terrestrials. Therefore, it is listed here. This antique pattern, which was originally tied without a tail and with a wing made from starling wing quill feathers, is still listed in the Dan Bailey catalog.

RED FOX

HOOK: Mustad 94840, Partridge L3A (10–16)
THREAD: Orange (Flymaster 6/0)
WING: Lemon wood duck flank fibers (see model, Dark Hendrickson)
TAIL: Dark ginger hackle fibers
BODY: Urine-stained fox fur dubbing
HACKLE: Dark ginger

RED IBIS

HOOK: Partridge L3A (12–16)
THREAD: Red (Flymaster 6/0)
WING: Dyed red duck wing quill sections (see model, Black Gnat)
TAIL: Red hackle fibers
RIB: Fine flat gold tinsel
BODY: Red floss
HACKLE: Dyed red

REMARKS: This brightly dressed old pattern listed in Joe's Tackle catalog is often used as an attractor fly for native brook trout in the brooks and ponds of the Northeast.

RED QUILL (Flick)

HOOK: Mustad 94840, Partridge L3A (12–14)
THREAD: Gray (Flymaster 6/0)
WING: Lemon wood duck flank fibers (see model, Dark Hendrickson)
TAIL: Medium bronze dun hackle fibers
BODY: Center stem quill from brown rooster neck or saddle hackle having reddish cast (see model, Cream Variant)
HACKLE: Medium bronze dun

REMARKS: The quill stem forming the body of this pattern should have a dark reddish-brown cast. Preparation of the quill by most tyers involves stripping the hackle fibers from the stem by hand. This procedure, however, removes, along with the fibers, some of the pigmentation that produces the desired color. A quill for the Red Quill and other flies using this body can be prepared by immersing it in a solution of Clorox and, when the feather fibers have been dissolved, removing the quill and washing it thoroughly in clear water or immersing it in a solution of baking soda and water to halt the chemical action. If a number of quill bodies are desired, it is suggested that the entire back end of an appropriately shaded brown neck be immersed in the Clorox solution, leaving, in effect, a half neck of red quills, which can be plucked from the skin as needed.

When soaking this or any other quill in Clorox, you must stay and observe the process so that the quills can be removed immediately after the feather fibers have dissolved.

Leaving them beyond the proper time may result in the disintegration of the entire quill stem.

Quills which are too light may be darkened in a dye bath or shaded the proper color with a marking pen.

A Half Neck of Red Quill Material After Having Been Soaked in Clorox Solution

RED TAIL MOSQUITO
(Plate II)

HOOK: Mustad 94840, Partridge L3A (12–18)
THREAD: Black (Flymaster 6/0)
TAIL: Dyed red hackle fibers
RIB: Black silk thread
BODY: White floss
WING: Two grizzly hackle tips (back to back) (tied slanting back at a 45-degree angle to center of tail)
HACKLE: Grizzly

RENEGADE
(Plate II)

HOOK: Mustad 94840 (10–18)
THREAD: Black (Flymaster 6/0)
REAR HACKLE: Brown
BODY: Peacock herl
FRONT HACKLE: White

REMARKS: This pattern, similar to the old Fore and Aft, is a favorite among western fly fishermen. The rear hackle collar should be slightly smaller than the front hackle collar.

RIO GRANDE KING
(Plate II)

HOOK: Mustad 94840 (10–16)
THREAD: Black (Flymaster 6/0)
WING: White duck wing quill sections (see model, Black Gnat)
TAIL: Golden pheasant tippet fibers
BODY: Black chenille (fine to extra fine depending on hook size)
HACKLE: Brown

REMARKS: When I tie this pattern, I use black dubbing fur for the body since chenille is too water-absorbent.

ROYAL COACHMAN
(Plate I)

HOOK: Mustad 94840, Partridge L3A (10–18)
THREAD: Black (Flymaster 6/0)
WING: White duck wing quill sections (see model, Black Gnat)
TAIL: Golden pheasant tippet fibers
BODY: Peacock herl divided by band of red floss
HACKLE: Brown to dark brown

REMARKS: If you ask a non–fly-fishing angler to give you the name of a fly, more than likely he will mention the Royal Coachman. Though this pattern has lost some of its popularity over the last two decades, it is still known quite well, both in and out of fishing circles. The Royal Coachman, according to Harold Hinsdale Smedley in his book *Fly Patterns and Their Origins,* was created by John Haily of New York in 1878 and given its name by L. C. Orvis to distinguish it from the original Coachman, which did not have the band of red floss dividing the peacock herl.

The Coachman pattern has quite a number of offspring, some of which are:

COACHMAN

HOOK: Partridge L3A (10–16)
THREAD: Black (Flymaster 6/0)
WING: White duck wing quill sections (see model, Black Gnat)
TAIL: Golden pheasant tippet fibers
BODY: Peacock herl
HACKLE: Brown to dark brown

CALIFORNIA COACHMAN
The same as the Royal Coachman except that it has a band of yellow floss at the center.

FAN WING
ROYAL COACHMAN
(Plate I)

The recipe for this particular pattern is the same as that for the Royal Coachman except that the wing is made from the white breast feathers of a duck. The breast of the male wood duck is excellent. Fan wings are not tied to the hook in the usual manner. The easiest way to secure a fan wing to the hook so that it does not twist or cant is to allow the stems of the breast feathers to straddle the hook shank, one on each side. When the stems are pointing downward, bring the thread around the shank and behind the stems for three or four turns. Let's illustrate this procedure.

1. Strip excess fibers from two white duck breast feathers. Align breast feathers so tips are even and flare away from each other.

2. Grasp aligned breast feathers between right thumb and forefinger and bring them down onto the hook shank so that the stems straddle downward past the hook shank.

3. With your left hand, take one or two turns of thread around the shank and the stems. Thumb and forefinger of the right hand should keep the tips firmly in position while this winding of thread is taking place. The thread should be going around the stems at a point immediately below the feather fibers.

4. You can now let go of the duck breast feathers. Take two or three more turns of thread diagonally around the stems and the hook shank for added security.

5. Bring the butt ends (stems) forward along the underside of the hook shank and pointing beyond the eye of the hook. Take three or four turns of thread around the butts and the hook shank directly in front of the fan wings.

6. Take four or five turns of thread around the base of the wings. You will not be going around the hook shank but simply winding around the base on a horizontal plane. Cut away the excess butts.

7. Bring your thread to the bend and proceed with the construction of the rest of the fly.

Winging Sequence for Fan Wing Royal Coachman

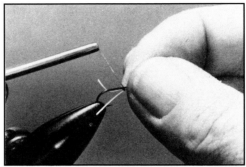

a. Note that stems straddle hook shank downward toward bend. Wing tips are held between right thumb and forefinger while thread is wound around stems and shank.

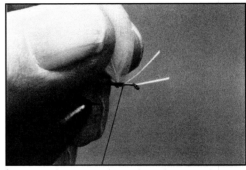

b. Stems have now been forced forward under shank and are bound down with thread in front of wing.

c. Thread is wound around base of both feathers.

d. Completed Fan Wing Royal Coachman.

HAIR WING ROYAL COACHMAN
(see Royal Coachman, Hair Wing, page 49)

ROYAL WULFF
(see page 49)

ROYAL RENEGADE
(Plate II)

HOOK: Mustad 94840, Partridge L3A (10–16)
THREAD: Black (Flymaster 6/0)
WING: None
TIP: Fine flat gold tinsel
TAIL: Golden pheasant tippet fibers
REAR HACKLE: Brown (should only slightly exceed the hook gap to ensure proper float)
BODY: Peacock herl divided by band of red floss
FRONT HACKLE: White or cream (normal for hook size used)

REMARKS: This new pattern designed by Everett M. Hale evolved from the Royal Coachman and the Renegade. Except for the tail, it is tied in the same manner as the Renegade.

SIERRA BRIGHT DOT
(Plate II)

HOOK: Mustad 94840
THREAD: Black (Flymaster 6/0)
WING: None
TAIL: Golden pheasant tippet fibers

REAR HACKLE: Grizzly (tied undersize)
BODY: Red floss (very thin)
FRONT HACKLE: Grizzly (tied oversize)

REMARKS: This pattern, submitted by Joe Sterling, uses a construction the same as that for the Renegade except that the difference in hackle size between the rear hackle and the front one is accented. The rear hackle is tied about two sizes smaller than related hook size while the front hackle is two sizes larger.

SNOW FLY

HOOK: Mustad 94840, Partridge L3A (16–18)
THREAD: Gray (Flymaster 6/0)
WING: Mallard wing quill sections (see model, Black Gnat)
TAIL: Mallard flank fibers, sparse
BODY: Stripped peacock quill (see model, Quill Gordon)
HACKLE: Grizzly

REMARKS: This pattern, submitted by Taylor Streit of Taos, New Mexico, features a tail of mallard flank. This is a rather soft fiber for the tail on a dry fly, but since the fly is tied only on smaller-sized hooks there should be no problem. On hooks larger than size 16, I would prefer a tail of grizzly hackle fibers.

SNOW FLY CLUSTER
(Plate II)

HOOK: Mustad 94840, Partridge L3A (14–18)
THREAD: Gray

WING: None
TAIL: None
BODY: Muskrat dubbing fur
HACKLE: Grizzly palmered through body

REMARKS: This pattern, also from Taylor Streit, is used on the Rio Grande in late November to represent a cluster of midges. The fly is very effective when these small flies are grouped together for "mating."

SOFA PILLOW
(see page 89)

Spiders

Generally speaking, spiders are patterns with long tails and oversize hackles; hence the name. They are never tied with a wing but occasionally you will find one which has a fur or peacock herl body under the hackle. Spiders may be tied in almost any color combination. The following are the ones most often cataloged by fly shops.

BADGER SPIDER
(Plate II)

HOOK: Mustad 94838, 9479 (14–16)
THREAD: Black (Flymaster 6/0)
TAIL: Badger hackle fibers, long (1½ shank lengths)
BODY (optional): Flat gold tinsel
HACKLE: Badger (tied three to four sizes

oversize; for example, a size 16 hook would use a size 10 or 8 hackle)

REMARKS: The Mustad 9479 hook has a very short shank and is listed as a spider or variant hook. It is, however, much easier to work with the Mustad 94838 2X short and still not lose the overall spider effect.

BLACK SPIDER

HOOK: Mustad 94838, 9479 (14–16)
THREAD: Black (Flymaster 6/0)
TAIL: Black hackle fibers, long (1½ shank lengths)
HACKLE: Black, oversize

BLUE DUN SPIDER

HOOK: Mustad 94838, 9479 (14–16)
THREAD: Gray (Flymaster 6/0)
TAIL: Blue dun hackle fibers, long (1½ shank lengths)
HACKLE: Blue dun, oversize

GINGER SPIDER

HOOK: Mustad 94838, 9479 (14–16)
THREAD: Cream (Flymaster 6/0)
TAIL: Ginger hackle fibers, long (1½ shank lengths)
HACKLE: Ginger, oversize

Closely related to the spiders are the skaters, which have no tail. It is rare to find a listing for skaters today simply because it is difficult to find enough extra-large hackle to tie one properly. A true skater should display stiff fibers radiating from the hook shank which exceed the diameter of a silver dollar—also difficult to find. Skaters, like spiders, can be tied in any color. Generally, two hackles with concave sides facing each other are tied to the shank and, after having been wound as a collar, are pushed together by thumb and forefinger to achieve compactness and density. When fished, skaters are skittered across the surface of the water. They are primarily used when trout are disinterested in feeding and the skittering, or skating, action arouses their interest. Once a rise is observed many anglers will switch to more conventional fare. (see Troth Super Skater, page 52.)

SPIRIT OF PITTSFORD MILLS
(Plate II)

HOOK: Mustad 94840, Partridge L3A (12–16)
THREAD: Gray (Flymaster 6/0)
WING: Light-shade grizzly hackle tips (see model, Adams)
TAIL: Golden ginger hackle fibers
PALMER RIB: Clipped ginger hackle
BODY: Grayish-brown duck down dubbed to thread like fur
HACKLE: Golden ginger

REMARKS: The rib of the ginger hackle may be trimmed prior to tying to the hook shank or after it has been wound as a rib.

The effect to be achieved is one of stubby hackle fibers protruding from the body no more than one-half the width of the hook gap.

Sulfur Duns

There is a wide range of opinion as to how this fly should be tied and which type is the most effective. Sulfur Duns, for the most part, imitate the mayflies *Ephemerella dorothea* and *Epeorus vitria*. The most commonly listed recipe is, perhaps, that of the Little Sulfur Dun.

LITTLE SULFUR DUN
(Plate I)

HOOK: Mustad 94840 (16–18)
THREAD: Yellow, primrose (Flymaster 6/0)
WING: Pale dun hackle tips (see model, Adams)
TAIL: Dark cream hackle fibers
BODY: Yellow cream fur blended with a small amount of orange fur (a yellow with an orange overtone)
HACKLE: Dark cream

Ed Shenk, in the September 1984 issue of *Fly Fisherman* magazine, went to the trouble of researching no fewer than ten other dressings of sulfur duns, all by anglers who themselves do their homework on the stream. Shenk's listing follows. All patterns can be tied on Mustad 94840 or Partridge L3A. Size 16 prevails. Thread is cream.

LETORT SULFUR DUN

WING: None
TAIL: Cream hackle fibers
BODY: Cream thorax and abdomen
HACKLE: Cream or buff over thorax

REMARKS: In this pattern the tapered fur body is carried through to the eye of the hook and the hackle wound through the fur for the collar at the thorax or fore end of the body.

SULFUR DUN (Charles Fox)
(Plate II)

WING: Cream hackle tips (tied upright and slightly spread) (see model, Adams)
TAIL: Palest blue dun hackle fibers
BODY: Cream fox fur or dyed pale yellow dubbing fur
HACKLE: Palest blue dun

SULFUR DUN (Ed Shenk)
(Plate II)

WING: None
TAIL: Stiff cream hackle fibers
BODY: Cream for abdomen, orange for thorax
HACKLE: Buff, light ginger, cream (one of each)

REMARKS: Hackles wound through thorax area should be spread so that the orange color shows through. No more than three turns of each hackle.

SULFUR DUN THORAX
(Vince Marinaro)
(Plate II)

WING: Pale blue dun body feathers (shaped with wing cutter)
TAIL: Pale blue dun (tied at an up angle to the body)
BODY: Cream for abdomen and thorax
HACKLE: Pale blue dun (tied thorax style; see page 104)

CUT WING SULFUR DUN

WING: Pale blue dun body feather (shaped with wing cutter)
TAIL: Brown bucktail (split into V shape)
BODY: Cream or pale yellow for thorax and abdomen
HACKLE: Cream or buff (tied thorax style; see page 104)

HARVEY SULFUR (George Harvey)
(Plate II)

WING: Cream hackle tips
TAIL: Cream hackle fibers
BODY: Cream fur
HACKLE: Two cream and one dyed orange mixed

FASTWATER SULFUR (Ed Shenk)

WING: None
TAIL: Tan deer hair fibers
BODY: Tan deer hair (or dyed pale yellow) (spun and clipped short) (for construction, see model, Irresistible, page 45)
HACKLE: Buff (tied full, using three hackles)

FOX SPINNER (Charles Fox)

WING: None
TAIL: Pale blue dun hackle fibers
BODY: Fluorescent orange floss
HACKLE: Pale blue dun

SPENT WING SULFUR DUN

WING: Cream hackle (tied short, as hackle collar)
TAIL: Cream hackle fibers (tied split, in V shape)
BODY: Blended tan fur with a dash of orange
HACKLE: Used as wing

REMARKS: Shenk explains that the wing is formed by crisscrossing the thread over the hackle fibers to form a wing coming from the sides of the thorax. I've found it simpler if the hackle, after having been wound as a collar, is trimmed top and bottom, leaving only those fibers coming out of the sides of the thorax to represent the spinner wing.

POLY WING SULFUR SPINNER (Barry Beck)

TAIL: Tan bucktail (tied split, in V shape)
WING: Poly yarn (tied spent) (pale blue dun)
BODY: Bright orange fur (or cinnamon) for abdomen, thorax, and head
HACKLE: None

And yet another Sulfur Dun pattern comes from Jack Mickievicz, who has his own special formula.

SULFUR DUN (Mickievicz)
(Plate II)

WING: Light dun body feathers (shaped with wing cutter)
TAIL: Light dun hackle fibers
BODY: Abdomen, white and yellow rabbit mixed; thorax, orange rabbit
HACKLE: Light dun

For those tyers who are dressing flies commercially, the first pattern listed in this series, the Little Sulfur Dun, is the one you will most likely be required to tie. For those of you who wish to see which performs best on the stream, you have a variety to choose from.

TUPS INDISPENSABLE

HOOK: Mustad 94840 (12–16)
THREAD: Cream (Flymaster 6/0)
WING: None
TAIL: Honey dun hackle fibers (straw shade with hint of dun)
BODY: Creamy pink dubbing fur
HACKLE: Honey dun

REMARKS: Honey dun hackle is sometimes scarce. A mix of cream ginger and medium light dun hackles can be substituted for both tail and hackle collar.

Variants

Most patterns which go under the name "variant" have oversize hackle collars, usually two to three times larger than standard. In this they are similar to the spiders, which also have oversize hackle collars. Variants do have bodies and in many cases wings, whereas spiders rarely do.

You would expect that the word "variant" would imply a variation or difference in color scheme, but except for the flies that use mixed hackle shades, such as the Gray Fox Variant, it does not.

VARIANT BROWN

HOOK: Mustad 94840, Partridge L3A (12–16)
THREAD: Gray (Flymaster 6/0)
WING: Lemon wood duck flank fibers (see model, Dark Hendrickson)
TAIL: Dark brown hackle fibers
BODY: Gray center stem quill from dark dun rooster neck or saddle hackle feather (see model, Cream Variant)
HACKLE: Dark brown

VARIANT TAN

HOOK: Mustad 94840, Partridge L3A (12–16)
THREAD: Cream (Flymaster 6/0)
WING: Lemon wood duck flank fibers (see model, Dark Hendrickson)
TAIL: Light brown hackle fibers (dark ginger)
BODY: Center stem quill from dark cream rooster neck or saddle hackle feather (see model, Cream Variant)
HACKLE: Light brown (dark ginger)

WHITCRAFT

HOOK: Mustad 94840, Partridge L3A (10–18)
THREAD: Gray (Flymaster 6/0)
WING: Grizzly hackle tips (see model, Adams)
TAIL: Brown hackle fibers
BODY: Stripped peacock quill (see model, Quill Gordon)
HACKLE: Brown and grizzly mixed

REMARKS: This pattern is identical to the Adams Quill except that it has all-brown hackle for the tail. The Whitcraft was originally listed in the *Noll Guide to Trout Flies* and is still carried under this name in some catalogs.

THE BOOK OF FLY PATTERNS   33

WHITE MILLER

HOOK: Mustad 94840 (10–18)
THREAD: White (Flymaster 6/0)
WING: White duck wing quill sections (see model, Black Gnat)
TAIL: White hackle fibers
BODY: White dubbing fur
HACKLE: White

YELLOW ADAMS

HOOK: Mustad 94840, Partridge L3A (10–18)
THREAD: Gray (Flymaster 6/0)
WING: Grizzly hackle tips (see model, Adams)
TAIL: Brown and grizzly hackle fibers mixed
BODY: Yellow dubbing fur
HACKLE: Brown and grizzly mixed

Hair-Winged and Deer-Bodied Flies

WHEN HAIR-WINGED flies first came into vogue, many of the patterns were made from bucktail or deer body hair fibers. Today the average fly tyer will use calf tail or calf skin fibers since these are much finer, do not flare when tied to the shank, and are easier to align. If a choice can be made between calf tail and calf skin, I would choose the latter, for the simple reason that the fibers are straighter and even out quickly when tamped in a hair stacker.

In patterns that call for the use of deer body hair for the construction of wings and tails, the fibers from moose and elk may be substituted. Unlike the body hair from either the white-tailed or the mule deer, moose hair and elk hair are not as hollow and thus do not flare. Hair that flares readily, such as that of the white-tailed deer, mule deer, caribou,

and antelope, is, of course, desirable for spinning bodies. A familiarity with the various animal fibers is an advantage when working with this type of fly.

ADAMS IRRESISTIBLE
(Plate III)

HOOK: Mustad 94840 (10–16)
THREAD: Gray (Flymaster 6/0)
WING: Grizzly hackle tips (see model, Adams, page 5)
TAIL: Brown and grizzly hackle fibers mixed
BODY: Natural gray deer hair (spun and trimmed to shape) (see model, Irresistible)
HACKLE: Brown and grizzly mixed

REMARKS: Sometimes the hackle fibers which make up the tail on the larger deer-

bodied flies will not support it. With this pattern, tail fibers made from woodchuck guard hairs, which are very close in color, make an excellent substitute.

ADAMS WULFF
(Plate III)

HOOK: Mustad 94840 (10–16)
THREAD: Black (Flymaster 6/0)
WING: Woodchuck guard hair fibers (see model, Ausable Wulff)
TAIL: Woodchuck guard hair fibers
BODY: Muskrat dubbing fur
HACKLE: Brown and grizzly mixed

REMARKS: Submitted by Peter Burton, this pattern, except for the body, is identical to the Woodchuck Wulff listed in the category of salmon dry flies.

AUSABLE WULFF
(Plate III)

HOOK: Mustad 94840 (8–18)
THREAD: Red or fluorescent fire orange
(Flymaster 6/0)
WING: White calf tail or calf skin fibers
TAIL: Guard hair fibers from tail of
woodchuck
BODY: Buff tan dubbing fur with rusty
orange highlight
HACKLE: Brown and grizzly mixed

REMARKS: The calf tail wing is divided
with thread in the manner of a wood duck
wing such as used on the Dark Hendrickson
standard dry fly. However, the fibers of calf
tail have a tendency to splay about; to control this behavior it is recommended that an
extra turn, or two, be taken around the base
of the fibers of both left and right portions of
the wing. This maneuver will compact the
fibers and present a tighter yet *natural* flare
at the tips.

This pattern, which was originated by
Francis Betters for use on the fast-moving
and riffling waters of the Ausable River of
New York, has found acceptance all over the
country and abroad. The color of the body
was formerly derived from the fur of bleached
Australian opossum, but now almost any fur
of that shade is used. The addition of a bit of
gray fox fur that has been immersed in a hot
orange dye bath enhances the overall effect.

BLACK GOOFUS BUG
(see Black Humpy)

Compacting a Calf Tail Type Wing

Calf tail type wings are secured to the shank in
the same manner as a wood duck flank (see
model, Dark Hendrickson). However, because
these hairs tend to be crinkly and more difficult
to control than other fibers, an additional turn
or two of thread is taken around the base before
completing a reverse-figure-eight turn of thread.

The photos that follow are a continuation of
the series used for the Dark Hendrickson, showing the process on the extra-large hook which
has had metal prongs glued to it to represent
wings and a white fly line substituting for the
thread.

a. After the clump of calf tail has been divided
with a figure-eight turn of thread, the thread is
wound around the shank in back of the wings.
It is then brought around the outside of the
wings and *encircles the base of the fibers two or
three times* before being brought through the
division and around the hook shank in back of
the wings.

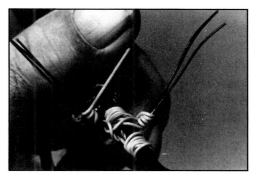

b. Thread (line) is brought around the outside
of the near wing and *encircles the base of the fibers
two or three times* before being brought through
the division and down and around the hook
shank in back of the wings.

Note: Turns of thread around the wing clumps
are at the base and snug. If too much pressure is
applied the thread will slip and flip off the
fibers. It takes but a little practice to determine
the proper amount of thread pressure.

BLACK WULFF

HOOK: Mustad 94840 (8–14)
THREAD: Black (Flymaster 6/0)
WING: Black calf tail fibers (see model,
Ausable Wulff)
TAIL: Black calf tail fibers
BODY: Pink floss (substitute: pink dub-
bing fur)
HACKLE: Black

REMARKS: This pattern and the White,
Royal, Gray, Brown, Grizzly, and Blonde
Wulffs represent a style of flies developed by
Lee Wulff in 1930.

Strangely, were it not for Dan Bailey the Wulff category of dry flies might have had a nondescript name that did not commemorate the originator. Bailey suggested that Wulff name the flies after himself and did, in fact, design and contribute the Grizzly Wulff to the series. The first in this group of hair-winged dry flies were the White, Royal, and Gray Wulffs.

You will find that there are a variety of other fly patterns called Wulffs, such as the Ausable Wulff and the Adams Wulff, which use the design originated by Lee, and do honor to the originator of these fast water flies.

Other patterns, such as the Irresistible and the Rat-Faced McDougal, probably owe their existence to the Wulff patterns. Lee Wulff is the first to have used this particular style of dry fly and to this day still ties it by hand, as he does all his patterns, including the minuscule 22s.

The first flies were tied with a wing and tail of bucktail, but today calf tail is the most commonly used hair fiber for these patterns.

BLONDE GOOFUS BUG
(see Blonde Humpy)

BLONDE WULFF

HOOK: Mustad 94840 (6-16)
THREAD: Tan (Flymaster 6/0)
WING: Bleached ginger deer hair or natural light tan deer or elk hair fibers (see model, Irresistible)

TAIL: Light tan deer hair fibers (see model, Irresistible)
BODY: Buff tan dubbing fur
HACKLE: Golden ginger

BROWN DRAKE
(Plate III)

HOOK: Mustad 94840 (10)
THREAD: Tan (Flymaster 6/0)
WING: Light brown elk hair fibers (see model, Irresistible)
TAIL: Dark moose hair fibers
RIB: Yellow floss
BODY: Yellow tan dubbing fur
HACKLE: Grizzly dyed yellow tan

REMARKS: This is a western tie, carried primarily in Idaho, Montana, and Colorado. The pattern description was submitted by Mike Lawson.

BROWN WULFF

HOOK: Mustad 94840 (6-16)
THREAD: Black (Flymaster 6/0)
WING: Brown calf tail (see model, Ausable Wulff)
TAIL: Brown calf tail fibers
BODY: Yellow dubbing fur
HACKLE: Badger

COACHMAN TRUDE
(Plate III)

HOOK: Mustad 94840, Partridge L3A (6-16)

THREAD: Black (Flymaster 6/0)
TIP: Flat gold tinsel
TAIL: Brown hackle fibers
BODY: Peacock herl
WING: White calf tail downwing style to center of tail
HACKLE: Brown

REMARKS: The wing of this pattern is characteristic of all Trude flies in that it is a downwing type, much in the manner of an adult caddis imitation. The Trude series of flies are named after or may have evolved from the patterns of A. S. Trude, a rancher in Idaho during the early 1900s. Joseph D. Bates, Jr., in his book *Atlantic Salmon Flies and Fishing,* says that as far as we know, Trude was the father of the hair fly, or bucktail fly, in this country. Harold Hinsdale Smedley, in his *Fly Patterns and Their Origins,* relates that Carter H. Harrison, the onetime mayor of Chicago, created the first hair wing, using red worsted from a rug for the body and a bunch of hair from a red spaniel dog, and presented it in jest to Trude. Trude thought this was something worth looking into and he (perhaps with Carter Harrison) made further innovations which proved successful on the Snake River. Whatever the origin, the name Trude today connotes, in general, a dry fly with a downwing made of bucktail or calf tail.

The above pattern is also occasionally tied with a tail made of golden pheasant tippet fibers. It is listed in the Dan Bailey catalog.

COFFIN FLY
(Plate III)

HOOK: Mustad 94831 (10–12)
THREAD: Black
WING: Barred teal flank fibers (tied spent)
(see model, Dark Hendrickson, page 15)
TAIL: Two peccary fibers (tied forked)
BODY: Spun and trimmed white deer hair
(see model, Irresistible)
HACKLE: Badger

REMARKS: This pattern was originated by Walt Dette in 1930. It was the first pattern so named. Coffin flies are generally tied to represent the spinner of the green drake *(Ephemera guttulata)*

Compara Duns

The name Compara Dun was coined by Al Caucci and Bob Nastasi in their book *Hatches.* It represents a type or style of dry fly which features deer hair fibers, especially those from the face, or mask, of the white-tailed deer, spread fanlike across the shank of the hook for 180 degrees. This particular type of construction, one of many which eliminate the use of a hackle to support the fly on the water, was first introduced over thirty years ago by Francis Betters in a pattern called the Haystack.

Incidentally, the idea of a hackleless fly is not new. Ray Bergman and Herb Howard had their own versions of such a design in the early 1930s. Ted Niemeyer, in 1967, created a realistic imitation without the use of a hackle collar. The most popular innovations were, of course, the no-hackle flies designed by Swisher and Richards in their now standard *Selective Trout,* published in 1971.

The Compara Duns (and the Haystack) have one extra attribute going for them and that is their durability. They are almost indestructible. The trick to tying these patterns lies primarily in the setting of the wings.

Setting the Compara Dun Wings

Deer hair fibers for the variously shaded Compara Dun wings may be found on the face, ears, legs, and body of the white-tailed deer. The hair from the mask, ears, and legs is a little finer than the body hair and will not flare quite as much, which makes it ideal for this type of construction. Any color shading not found in the natural hair can, of course, be produced by dyeing.

A base of thread should be wound on the hook shank to cover the fore portion of a Mustad 94840 or other designated hook. The thread is left at a position one-third behind the eye of the hook. A small clump of fibers (approximately the diameter of a round toothpick) is cut from the hide and evenly aligned. The use of a hair stacker quickly facilitates the alignment of the hair fibers.

1. The clump of hair fibers is held on top of the hook shank with the tips of the fibers pointing forward beyond the eye of the hook.

2. Four or five turns of thread are taken around the clump of fibers as the left thumb pushes down on the fibers (between turns of thread) so that some of the fibers are actually being bound along the sides of the hook shank. You are, in effect, tying the clump of fibers to the top and both sides of the hook shank.

3. Lift the fibers to a vertical position and take a good number of turns of thread (ten to twelve) directly in front of the fibers. Keep pushing the fibers rearward with the pad of your right thumb after every two or three windings of thread. They should automatically fan upward and outward to form an arc- or fan-shaped wing describing 180 degrees. If it does not achieve that exact effect, a little tugging and pulling in the right places will set the fibers in proper order. Any fibers which have misbehaved or protrude below the horizontal plane can simply be snipped away.

4. Bring the thread to a position directly behind the wings. Trim and stagger-cut the excess deer hair butts so that there is a natural incline for the building of a tapered body.

Compara Dun Tails

The tails of the Compara Dun flies are usually made up of stiff hackle fibers tied outrigger style. A small ball of fur is wound around the shank of the hook at the bend and three

Tying Steps for Compara Dun Type Fly

c. Properly secured wing.

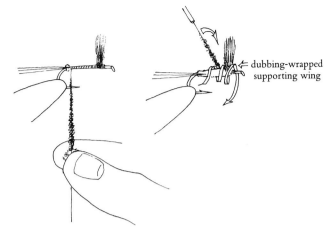

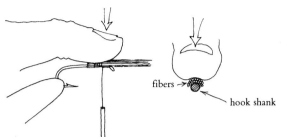

a. After deer hair has been snugly but not too tightly lashed to the shank, thumb is used to push fibers downward so that they spread partly down the sides of the shank.

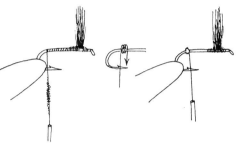

d. Thread is brought to position just before bend and a small ball of fur is dubbed onto the shank.

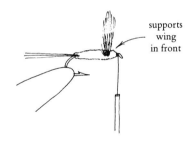

f. Thread is dubbed with fur and wound forward to form body.

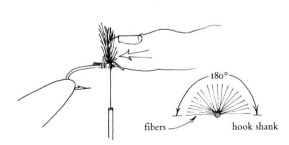

b. Thread is brought down tightly in back of wing clump and then in front of it while thumb is used to push against clump so that fibers stand erect yet spread in a 180-degree fan.

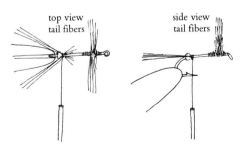

e. A few deer hair fibers are tied against the ball of fur near the bend so that they flare outward.

g. Dubbed thread is also used in front of wing and against base of wing to help support it in its vertical position.

h. Completed Compara Dun fly.

or four hackle fibers are crimped against each side of the fur ball so that they flare and angle outward at approximately a 45-degree angle.

Compara Dun Bodies

The dubbed fur bodies of these flies are formed in the conventional manner—that is, by spinning fur onto the thread and winding it forward. They differ from the standard patterns in that the dubbed thread is brought forward past the position of the wing all the way to the eye of the hook, thus forming a full thorax in addition to an abdomen. When winding the dubbed thread forward, be sure to place an extra turn or two in front of and against the wings. You will not only be building the thorax area but also using the fur to assist in keeping the wings erect.

The following are some of the most commonly cataloged Compara Dun patterns. In some cases, the popular name, such as Hendrickson, is used, and in other cases, the name of the natural insect imitated, such as *Ephemerella subvaria,* is listed.

The standard hook listed for these patterns will often be the Mustad 94840 even though a 2XL is often recommended.

Many tyers prefer the standard shank because it has more strength and the overall proportions in relation to the natural can be adjusted in tail length and wing height.

COMPARA DUN
BLUE WINGED OLIVE
(Ephemerella attenuata)

HOOK: Mustad 94840 (16–18)
THREAD: Yellow (Flymaster 6/0)
WING: Medium dark deer hair fibers
TAIL: Golden ginger hackle fibers
BODY: Yellow/olive dubbing fur

COMPARA DUN
DUN VARIANT
(Isonychria bicolor)

HOOK: Mustad 94831, 94840 (10–12)
THREAD: Black (Flymaster 6/0)
WING: Dark gray deer hair
TAIL: Dark ginger hackle fibers
BODY: Reddish-brown dubbing fur

COMPARA DUN GRAY FOX
(Stenonema fuscum)

HOOK: Mustad 94840 (12–14)
THREAD: Yellow (Flymaster 6/0)
WING: M edium light gray deer hair
TAIL: Medium dun hackle fibers
BODY: Yellowish cream dubbing fur

COMPARA DUN
GREEN DRAKE
(Ephemera guttulata)

HOOK: Mustad 94831, 94840 (10–12)
THREAD: Yellow (Flymaster 6/0)
WING: Light brown/gray deer hair
TAIL: Dark brown mink tail fibers
BODY: Creamy white dubbing fur

COMPARA DUN
HENDRICKSON
(Ephemerella subvaria)

HOOK: Mustad 94840 (12–14)
THREAD: Yellow (Flymaster 6/0)
WING: Medium gray deer hair
TAIL: Medium gray hackle fibers
BODY: Yellow gray dubbing fur

REMARKS: Body colors on the Hendrickson may be varied to simulate Dark Hendrickson, Light Hendrickson, or ribbed with thread for the Red Quill.

COMPARA DUN
LIGHT CAHILL
(Stenonema canadensis)

HOOK: Mustad 94840 (12–18)
THREAD: Cream or primrose (Flymaster 6/0)
WING: Light grayish cream deer hair
TAIL: Cream hackle fibers
BODY: Cream dubbing fur

COMPARA DUN
LITTLE SULFUR DUN
(Ephemerella dorothea)

HOOK: Mustad 94840 (16)
THREAD: Yellow (Flymaster 6/0)
WING: Pale gray deer hair
TAIL: Pale gray hackle fibers
BODY: Pale yellow dubbing fur

COMPARA DUN
MARCH BROWN
(Stenonema vicarium)

HOOK: Mustad 94840 (10–12)
THREAD: Yellow (Flymaster 6/0)
WING: Brown deer hair fibers
TAIL: Brown hackle fibers
BODY: Yellow/tan dubbing fur

COMPARA DUN
QUILL GORDON
(Epeoris pleuralis)

HOOK: Mustad 94840 (12–14)
THREAD: Olive
WING: Medium gray deer hair
TAIL: Dark gray hackle fibers
BODY: Light gray with hint of yellow dubbing fur

GOOFUS BUG
(Plate III)

HOOK: Mustad 94840 (10–16)
THREAD: Gray (Flymaster 6/0)
TAIL: Natural gray/brown deer hair fibers
BODY: Half of tail pulled forward to form hood or hump
WING: Formed with tips of pulled-forward deer hair
HACKLE: Grizzly and brown mixed

REMARKS: This pattern is identical to the Humpy except that it does not have an underbody. For construction, see Humpy series.

GRAY WULFF
(Plate III)

HOOK: Mustad 94840 (8–14)
THREAD: Black (Flymaster 6/0)
WING: Natural brown calf tail fibers (see model, Ausable Wulff)
TAIL: Natural brown calf tail fibers
BODY: Muskrat dubbing fur
HACKLE: Medium blue dun

GREEN DRAKE (WESTERN)
(Plate III)

HOOK: Mustad 94840 (10–12)
THREAD: Olive (Flymaster 6/0)
WING: Dark gray elk hair (see model, Irresistible)
TAIL: Dark moose hair fibers
RIB: Yellow floss
BODY: Dark olive dubbing fur
HACKLE: Grizzly dyed bright yellow and tinted with olive

GREEN DRAKE WULFF

HOOK: Mustad 94840 (8–14)
THREAD: Brown (Flymaster 6/0)
WING: Moose body hair (see model, Ausable Wulff)
TAIL: Moose body hair fibers
RIB: Light olive floss
BODY: Medium olive dubbing fur
HACKLE: One dyed yellow hackle and one grizzly mixed

GRIZZLY WULFF
(Plate III)

HOOK: Mustad 94840, Partridge L3A (8–14)
THREAD: Gray (Flymaster 6/0)
WING: Dark brown calf tail (see model, Ausable Wulff)
TAIL: Dark brown calf tail fibers
BODY: Yellow floss (substitute: yellow dubbing fur)
HACKLE: Brown and grizzly mixed

H & L VARIANT
(also known as House and Lot)
(Plate III)

HOOK: Mustad 94840, Partridge L3A (10–16)
THREAD: Black (Flymaster 6/0)
WING: White calf tail (see model, Ausable Wulff)
TAIL: White calf tail fibers

BODY: Rear half, stripped peacock herl; fore half, peacock herl
HACKLE: Furnace

HAYSTACK
(Plate III)

HOOK: Mustad 94840 (10–16)
THREAD: Red (Flymaster 6/0)
TAIL: Deer hair fibers bleached to a tan/ cream, short and stubby (barely past bend)
WING: Bleached cream/tan deer hair, tied just forward of the center of the hook shank and fanned 180 degrees so that the lower fibers support the fly on the surface of the water
BODY: Cream dubbing fur heavily applied both behind and in front of wing (body fur helps support wing in vertical position)

REMARKS: The same construction methods used for the Compara Dun wings are applied here (see Compara Duns). This pattern was introduced by Francis Betters. It is also tied in a dark version using natural gray/brown deer hair for the wing and tail and muskrat dubbing for the body. This is the pattern which inspired the famous Compara Duns featured by Caucci and Nastasi in *Hatches*.

HOUSE AND LOT
(see H & L Variant)

HUMPY
(Plate III)

HOOK: Mustad 94840, 7957B (10–16)

THREAD: Red (Flymaster 6/0)
TAIL: Natural brown/gray deer hair or moose body fibers
UNDERBODY: Red floss
BODY: Natural deer hair (pulled forward to form hump)
WING: Formed from pulled-forward deer hair fibers
HACKLE: Brown and grizzly mixed

REMARKS: This particular western pattern, including its many variations, is, according to Terry Hellekson in *Popular Fly Patterns*, a takeoff on a pattern called Horner's Deer Hair, created by Jack Horner. The tying procedures for both are identical. Most angler/ tyers would rather fish the fly than tie it. The construction, if anything, is far from the norm. However, it can be assembled with little difficulty if certain procedures are followed.

1. Tie in the tail. (Moose body fibers are a bit stiffer than deer hair and easier to control.) The butt ends of the tail should be fastened to the shank from the center of the hook to the bend.

2. Cut a clump of deer hair the diameter of which is about that of a wooden matchstick. (This is for a size 12 fly. Fewer fibers would be required for smaller sizes.) Align the tips in a hair stacker. Your thread should be at the center of the hook shank. Measure the deer hair clump so the tips extend past the tips of the tail a distance of one-half the length of the hook shank. Trim the butt ends so that when they are tied in they are at the exact center of the hook shank (exactly even with the tail butts tied in previously).

Lash the deer hair clump to the shank by winding over both deer hair and shank commencing from the center of the hook shank to the bend. (Remember to take a couple of turns of thread around the bare shank after you have begun binding down the deer hair so that the fibers are not accidentally pulled off from the top of the hook shank. Leave your thread idling at a position near the bend.)

3. Tie in a section of single-strand red floss. Bring your thread forward to a position just in front of the lashed-down deer hair. Bring your floss forward over the bound-down deer hair to the thread and secure it. Clip the excess.

4. Grasp the tips of the deer hair clump (they will have flared, so you will have to gather them together) and pull them forward to the thread, forming a hump over the floss. Hold the tips tautly out over the eye of the hook and with your left hand bring the thread over the deer hair fibers, securing them just beyond the floss underbody. Take another couple of turns of thread in the same area to make sure they do not slip rearward.

5. Lift the tips of the deer hair fibers to a vertical position and take a few turns of thread around the hook shank in front of them to keep them erect.

Divide the vertical hair fibers with a figure-eight crisscrossing of thread and also reverse figure eights of thread encircling the base of each (see model, Ausable Wulff) thus forming a divided wing.

Proceed with the hackling of the fly as you would for any other pattern.

Tying Steps for Humpy

a. Tail has been tied in.

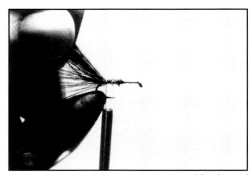

b. Section which is to form humped body and wing has been measured and tied in.

c. Red floss being tied in for underbody.

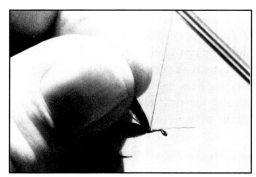

e. Tips of deer hair held erect while turns of tying thread are wound in front of base of wing.

f. Fibers have been divided with figure-eight and reverse-figure-eight turns of thread to form wing.

g. Hackle being tied in.

Other flies in this series include the following:

BLACK HUMPY
The same as Humpy except has black floss underbody.

BLONDE HUMPY

HOOK: Mustad 94840 (10–16)
THREAD: Cream (Flymaster 6/0)
TAIL: White calf tail fibers
UNDERBODY: Yellow floss
BODY: White deer hair (pulled forward to form hump)
WING: White calf tail
HACKLE: Cream ginger

EASTERN HUMPY
(Plate III)

HOOK: Mustad 94840 (10–16)
THREAD: Red (Flymaster 6/0)
TAIL: Woodchuck guard hair fibers
UNDERBODY: Red floss
BODY: Woodchuck guard hairs (pulled forward to form hump)
WING: Woodchuck guard hairs
HACKLE: Brown and grizzly mixed

POLY HUMPY

HOOK: Mustad 94840 (12–16)
THREAD: Yellow (Flymaster 6/0)
TAIL: Light cream bucktail fibers

UNDERBODY: Yellow floss
BODY: Yellow poly yarn (pulled forward to form hump)
WING: Yellow poly yarn
HACKLE: Cream

ROYAL HUMPY
The same as Humpy except has white calf tail for tail and wings.

YELLOW HUMPY
The same as Humpy except has yellow floss underbody.

Humpy flies may be made with a variety of materials. Deer, elk, and moose are the most commonly used.

IRRESISTIBLE

HOOK: Mustad 94840 (10–16)
THREAD: Gray (Flymaster 6/0)
TAIL: Natural gray deer hair fibers
BODY: Spun and trimmed deer hair
WING: Natural brown gray deer hair
HACKLE: Medium blue dun

REMARKS: The popular Irresistible is a good model for other patterns with similar wings, tails, and bodies because it uses deer hair for every part except the hackle.

This pattern is one of the exceptions to the rule of always tying in the wing first on a dry fly. Obviously, if you tried to trim the spun deer hair body with the wings already in place you might accidentally clip the wing fibers.

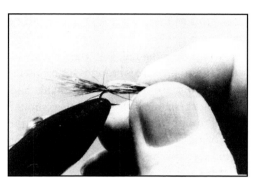

d. Deer hair pulled forward to form hump or shell.

h. Completed Humpy.

Tail

Deer hair is both good news and bad news, depending on what you want to do with it. The good news is that it will flare readily when you want to spin it for a clipped deer hair body. The bad news is that it will also flare when you don't want it to, such as in the construction of a tail or a wing.

When tying in deer hair fibers for a tail, two or three snug—but not tight—turns of thread should be taken around the fibers and the hook shank at the rearmost portion of the shank. All you want to do is encircle the fibers with thread as closely as possible without having the thread bite into them. Once these gentle turns have compacted the fibers, the thread is brought slightly forward and tight turns are made which secure the fibers to the shank. Be sure also to take one or two turns of thread around the bare hook shank and then back around the fibers once more so they do not slip over the side of the shank.

The excess butts should be trimmed as close to the bend without losing security. A certain amount of bare hook shank is necessary for the proper spinning of deer body hair, which follows.

Clipped Deer Hair Body

For a size 12 fly you will need approximately three matchstick-sized clumps of deer hair for spinning the entire body. Remove as much of the fuzz from the deer hair as you can before spinning. I find that a hair comb works well for removing just about all the fuzz. The easiest method I know of, and it is almost foolproof, for spinning deer hair is the one Walt Dette showed me a number of seasons ago.

Place the section of deer hair to be spun against the hook shank so that the butt ends point diagonally downward and forward toward the eye.

Bring your thread around the hair fibers and the hook shank for two complete turns. The turns of thread should be neither tight nor loose. They should just snug up to both hair and shank without making the fibers flare. When both turns of thread have been made, apply pressure and pull the thread toward you as you let go of the tip ends which have been held between your left thumb and forefinger. Continue going around the hook shank and fibers with your thread for a third turn and then a fourth in the same area. The hair will flare and radiate around the shank. Take one more turn of thread through the same area. By the fourth or fifth turn of thread around the shank and fibers, the hair will stop spinning and radiating. Pull the fibers rearward and place a turn of thread in front of the flared fibers. Repeat this procedure two more times with the other clumps of deer hair until half the hook is covered with spun and flared hair.

Remove the semi-completed fly from the vise and trim the body to a miniature ice-cream-cone shape, the narrowest end of which is at the bend. Then trim the bottom of the deer hair body fairly flush to the shank so that there is enough hook-gap clearance to strike the fish.

Replace the trimmed fly in the vise and proceed with the wings.

Deer Hair Wings

The wings, like the tail, will flare if uncontrolled thread pressure is brought against them. After lashing the fibers to the shank and propping them vertically erect, they should first be roughly divided with figure-eight turns of thread. The thread is then brought around the hook shank in back of the wings and a reverse figure eight of thread is performed through the division of fibers (the same way as in the Ausable Wulff and Adams). The thread is again brought in back of the wings and the thread is brought around the base of the wing section furthest from you, in a clockwise circle two or three times. These turns around the base are, again, snug but not tight. The thread is then brought through the division of fibers and the near wing is encircled in a counterclockwise manner for two or three turns. After the base of the fibers on the near wing has been compacted, the thread is brought through the division of fibers from front to rear and two turns of thread are taken around the hook shank in back of the wings. The excess butts are now trimmed away. You need only to tie in the hackle for the collar and complete the fly.

IRRESISTIBLE, WHITE

HOOK: Mustad 94840 (10–16)
THREAD: White (Flymaster 6/0)

Building Tail, Body, and Wing of Irresistible

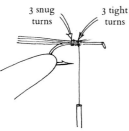

3 snug turns   3 tight turns

a. Tail tied in using three snug, then three tight turns of thread.

b. Excess butts being trimmed.

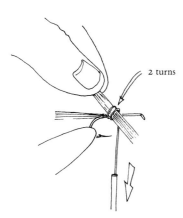

2 turns

c. A clump of deer hair placed diagonally against shank and two turns of thread taken around clump and shank.

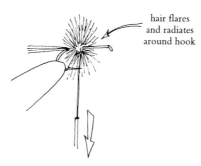

hair flares and radiates around hook

d. Thread is pulled down (and then around shank and hair once more), causing deer hair to flare.

e. Thread is brought around shank in front of flared deer hair.

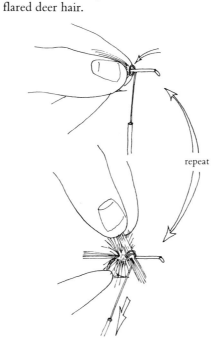

repeat

f. Another clump of deer hair is added prior to flaring.

g. Fly has been removed from vise and is being trimmed to shape.

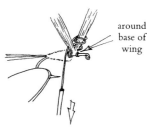

around base of wing

h. Deer hair has been tied in for wing, and far wing is being wound with reverse-figure-eight turns of thread which are snug but not tight.

i. Thread has been brought through wing division and once around hook shank in back of wings.

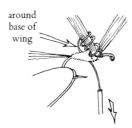

around base of wing

j. Near wing is encircled with thread, after which fly is hackled for completion.

TAIL: White deer hair fibers (or white calf tail fibers)

BODY: Clipped white deer hair (see model, Irresistible)

WING: White calf tail fibers

HACKLE: Badger

REMARKS: The wing is sometimes made from badger hackle tips.

IRRESISTIBLE, WOODCHUCK

HOOK: Mustad 94840 (10–16)

THREAD: Gray (Flymaster 6/0)

TAIL: Woodchuck guard hair fibers

BODY: Spun and trimmed natural gray deer hair (see model, Irresistible)

WING: Woodchuck guard hair fibers (see model, Ausable Wulff)

HACKLE: Brown and grizzly mixed

REMARKS: The use of woodchuck guard hair fibers for the tail and wing makes for easier tying and a more realistic imitation. Combined with the rusty dun effect of the grizzly and brown hackle mix, this pattern is an extremely buggy-looking and effective fly.

KENNEBEGO

HOOK: Mustad 94840, Partridge L3A (8–14)

THREAD: Gray (Flymaster 6/0)

WING: Brown deer hair (see model, Irresistible)

TAIL: Brown deer hair (see model, Irresistible)

BODY: Medium gray wool (substitute: muskrat dubbing fur)

HACKLE: Medium blue dun

REMARKS: Submitted by Dick Frost.

KEN'S NO-HACKLE HEX
(Plate III)

HOOK: Mustad 94840 (6–10)

THREAD: Yellow

TAIL AND BODY: Deer hair lashed to shank from behind eye to bend with the fibers continuing past the bend a full shank length; tips of fibers will form tail; color of deer hair is a bleached tan

WINGS AND LEGS: Deer hair flared upward and slightly rearward to resemble wing, then all excess trimmed except for twenty to twenty-five hair fibers on each side to represent legs

REMARKS: The purpose of the design as originated by Ken Mers was to create a fly that would be relatively durable, since fishing the "Hex" hatch in Michigan (mayfly *Hexegenia limbata*) is done during the early hours of night when changing flies is difficult.

A clump of deer hair fibers which will form both body and tail is lashed to the hook shank, with the butt ends tied down just before the wing position. The thread is wound around both fibers and hook shank to the bend and then continues past the bend, going around the deer fibers only for a distance equal to half the hook-shank length.

Thread is then reversed and brought back to its starting point in crisscross fashion over previous thread windings to its starting point.

A drop of head lacquer is placed at the rearmost winding of thread just where the tail fibers begin to form.

Most deer hair fibers in the center of the tail section are cut away, leaving a few fibers on each side to form a forked, or split, tail.

The wing is constructed by flaring deer hair on top of the hook shank just forward of where the body ends (about one-third of the distance back from the eye). The fibers are not allowed to spin or rotate around the shank. This is done by holding the clump of fibers in place and bringing the thread tautly around fibers and shank so that they flare but do not rotate. After they have been flared, the thread is brought in front of the hair and wound two times around the hook shank.

The tips extending upward and rearward are left as such while the butt ends protruding forward and off to the side are trimmed so that only 20 to 25 fibers remain protruding from the side of the shank pointing outward and slightly forward. It helps in the formation of the wing if the butt-end fibers are first roughly divided into position as you would a standard wing. Remember, however, to divide them in a spent fashion and then trim them to shape.

KOLZER YELLOW
(Plate III)

HOOK: Mustad 94840 (8–14)

THREAD: Black (Flymaster 6/0)

Tying Steps for Ken's No-Hackle Hex

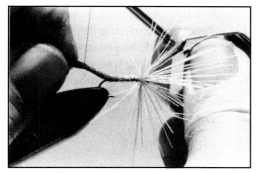

a. Hair fibers have been tied to shank before hook eye and thread is being wound in an open spiral around both shank and hair and then around hair fibers only.

b. Thread has been reversed and wound in an open spiral back to starting point, forming a diamond-shaped wrap.

c. A clump of deer hair is being tied in to simulate wing.

d. Butt ends of deer hair being divided with thread and forced to a more horizontal position.

e. Divided butt ends being trimmed to size.

f. Completed Ken's No-Hackle Hex, showing center fibers cut from tail to give impression of natural insect.

WING: Tan elk hair fibers with black tips (see model, Ausable Wulff)
TAIL: Tan elk hair fibers with black tips
PALMER RIB: Brown hackle palmered through body
BODY: Fluorescent yellow wool or fur
HACKLE: Brown

REMARKS: This pattern as featured in the Dan Bailey catalog is also tied with fluorescent red or fluorescent orange bodies.

MICHIGAN CADDIS
(Plate III)

HOOK: Mustad 94840 (6–10)
THREAD: Black (Flymaster 6/0)
TAIL: Natural brown/gray deer hair fibers
BODY: Deer hair (spun and trimmed to shape) (see model, Irresistible)
HACKLE: Grizzly (trimmed top and bottom)
WING: Grizzly hackle tips (tied spent) (a full-feathered hackle should be used)

REMARKS: This pattern was submitted by Jay Neve, who observes: "For many years, and to some extent even now, Michigan's fly fishermen called the giant Michigan mayfly the 'Michigan Caddis.' Where this originated no one is sure, but most imitations of the 'Great Hex' were named accordingly for many years." According to Neve, this design by Art Winnie is still one of the most popular dressings in Michigan when fishing the "hex" hatch.

MR. RAPIDAN
(Plate III)

HOOK: Mustad 94838, Partridge L3A (12–18)
THREAD: Tan (Flymaster 6/0)
WING: Dyed yellow calf tail (see model, Ausable Wulff)
TAIL: Stiff dark moose body fibers
BODY: A blend of super-fine polypropylene consisting of 50% #34 (Quill Gordon Fly-Rite) and 50% #30 (March Brown Fly-Rite)
HACKLE: One medium brown and one grizzly mixed (tied sparse)

REMARKS: This pattern was submitted by Harry Murray, who says that it is a fly he will not go astream without. It is a favorite among anglers on Big Hunting Creek in Maryland.

O'CONNER TRUDE
(see Rio Grande King Trude)

POLAR HEX
(Plate III)

HOOK: Mustad 37187 (Stinger) (2–6)
THREAD: Yellow
WING: Polar bear hair (tied spent and sparse) (see model, Ausable Wulff) (substitute: white calf tail)
TAIL: Two stripped ginger hackle quills (tied at a 45-degree angle)
BODY: Light brown and yellow poly dubbing mixed (or same shades of dubbing fur blended together)
HACKLE: Ginger (clipped top and bottom)

REMARKS: Originated by Jay Neve, this fly is very effective during the "hex" spinner fall. The fly should be presented to the trout directly in the feeding lane, since the fish will rarely move from its position when these spent mayflies are drifting down to it.

POWDER PUFF

HOOK: Mustad 94840 (10–16)
THREAD: Gray (Flymaster 6/0)
WING: White calf tail (see model, Ausable Wulff)
TAIL: White calf tail fibers
BODY: Medium gray wool (substitute: muskrat dubbing fur)
HACKLE: Medium blue dun

RAT-FACED McDOUGAL

HOOK: Mustad 94840 (10–16)
THREAD: Gray (Flymaster 6/0) (or tan or black)
TAIL: Dark ginger hackle fibers
BODY: Caribou hair (spun and trimmed) (see model, Irresistible)
WING: Grizzly hackle tips (see model, Adams, page 5)
HACKLE: Dark ginger

REMARKS: Gray thread is used for tail and spinning the body. Tan or black thread is used to tie in hackle and wings.

RED GOOFUS BUG
(see Humpy)

Riffle Flies

Riffle flies are nothing more than versions of Wulff type flies. The name "riffle" was coined by Dick Surette, and, as the name implies, they are used in fast or broken water. The white wing and tail assure the angler of higher visibility, especially at dusk. They are carried as standard fare in the North Country Angler's catalog.

BROWN RIFFLE

HOOK: Mustad 9671, 94831 (6–16)
THREAD: Brown (Flymaster 6/0)
WING: White calf tail tied oversize (see model, Ausable Wulff)
TAIL: White calf tail fibers
BODY: Medium tan/brown dubbing fur
HACKLE: Brown

REMARKS: The wing fibers are half again as long as standard, adding to their visibility.

GRIZZLY RIFFLE

HOOK: Mustad 9671, 94831 (6–16)
THREAD: Black (Flymaster 6/0)
WING: White calf tail fibers (tied oversize) (see model, Ausable Wulff)
TAIL: White calf tail fibers
BODY: Gray muskrat dubbing fur
HACKLE: Grizzly

REMARKS: The Mustad 9671 should be used for the smaller hooks and the 94831 for the larger.

RIO GRANDE KING TRUDE
(also known as O'Conner Trude)

HOOK: Mustad 94840, Partridge L3A (6–16)
THREAD: Black (Flymaster 6/0)
TIP: Fine flat gold tinsel
TAIL: Golden pheasant tippet fibers
BODY: Black chenille (to proportionate size)
WING: White calf tail (to center of tail) (see model, Coachman Trude)
HACKLE: Brown

REMARKS: This pattern is listed as the O'Conner Trude in the Dan Bailey catalog.

ROYAL COACHMAN, HAIRWING

HOOK: Mustad 94840 (10–18)
THREAD: Black (Flymaster 6/0)
WING: White calf tail (See model Ausable Wulff)
TAIL: Golden pheasant tippet fibers
BODY: Peacock herl divided by band of red floss
HACKLE: Brown

ROYAL COACHMAN TRUDE

HOOK: Mustad 94840, Partridge L3A (6–16)

THREAD: Black (Flymaster 6/0)
TAIL: Golden pheasant tippet fibers
BODY: Peacock herl divided by band of red floss
WING: White calf tail (to center of tail) (see model, Coachman Trude)
HACKLE: Medium to dark brown

REMARKS: This pattern is also tied with a tail of dyed red hackle fibers.

ROYAL GOOFUS BUG
(see Royal Humpy)

ROYAL TRUDE
(see Royal Coachman Trude)

ROYAL WULFF
(Plate III)

HOOK: Mustad 94840, Partridge L3A (8–16)
THREAD: Black (Flymaster 6/0)
WING: White calf tail (see model, Ausable Wulff)
TAIL: Brown bucktail or calf tail fibers
BODY: Peacock herl divided by band of red floss
HACKLE: Dark brown

REMARKS: Occasionally, you will see this pattern tied with a tail of white calf tail fibers. However, after checking with Lee Wulff, I've been assured that the tail should be of brown calf tail or deer tail fibers.

SODA BUTTE SPECIAL
(Plate III)

HOOK: Mustad 94831 (8–12)
THREAD: Gray (Flymaster 6/0)
TAIL: A small bunch (10 to 14 fibers) of woodchuck guard hairs (gap width in length)
PALMER RIB: Brown hackle spiraled through body (use related hook size as if for hackle collar)
BODY: Blue dun hackle wound full to eye and trimmed to bullet shape (as if it were deer hair) or deer hair dyed blue dun gray and spun and trimmed to shape

REMARKS: After the tail is tied in, the palmer rib is fastened to the shank at the bend and left idling. Then the hackle for the body is wound tightly in connecting spirals to the eye. The hook is removed from the vise and the hackle trimmed to shape as you would deer hair. The fly is placed back in the vise and the palmer rib is wound through the body in a normal open spiral to the eye.

The fly was submitted by Peter Burton, who first discovered the fly in the "Junk Box" at Dan Bailey's Fly Shop quite a number of seasons ago. It is now a favorite where he fishes on the Middlebury River in Vermont.

Sparkle Duns

This is a relatively new introduction by Craig Mathews of Blue Ribbon Flies. These patterns feature a soft, short (hook-gap width in length) tail consisting of a sparkle yarn material. The wings and body are similar to those of the Compara Dun series of flies. Mathews relates that these patterns have become their best-selling dry flies.

CALLIBAETIS SPARKLE DUN

HOOK: Mustad 94840 (12–16)
THREAD: Tan (Flymaster 6/0)
WING: Tan deer body fibers (tied spread, 180 degrees) (see model, Compara Dun)
TAIL: Olive sparkle yarn
BODY: Tan dubbing fur (covering entire shank)

REMARKS: The wing on these patterns sits closer to the center of the hook shank, while the dubbing fur, which helps support the wing in its upright yet spread position, is wound around the shank in back and in front of the wing from the bend to the eye. The body taper increases as it reaches the wing area and diminishes as it reaches the eye.

HENDRICKSON SPARKLE DUN
(Plate III)

HOOK: Mustad 94840 (12–14)
THREAD: Gray (Flymaster 6/0)
WING: Tan/gray deer body fibers (tied spread, 180 degrees) (see model, Compara Dun)
TAIL: Gray/brown sparkle yarn
BODY: Reddish-brown dubbing fur (covering entire shank)

PALE MORNING DUN SPARKLE DUN

HOOK: Mustad 94840 (16–18)
THREAD: Orange (Flymaster 6/0)
WING: Light dun deer body fibers (tied spread, 180 degrees) (see model, Compara Dun)
TAIL: Dark gray sparkle yarn
BODY: Yellowish-orange dubbing fur (covering entire shank)

REMARKS: Mathews states that this pattern, if tied in a lighter shade, serves well as an imitation for the pale evening dun in the East.

SLATE AND OLIVE SPARKLE DUN

HOOK: Mustad 94840 (12–14)
THREAD: Olive (Flymaster 6/0)

Tying Steps for Troth Hair Spider

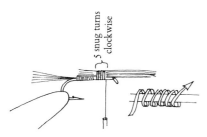

a. Elk mane tail tied in and clump of elk mane tied in for hair collar. Note five turns of thread taken around hair which is to form collar. Turns are snug but not tight. (Do not flare hair at this time.)

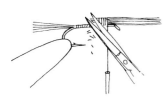

b. Excess butts of mane hair being trimmed.

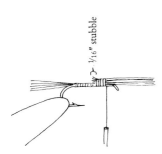

c. Butts trimmed back so only short stubble remains.

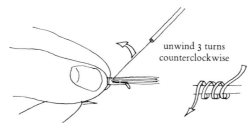

d. Three turns of thread being unwound from mane and shank.

e. Thread is now pulled tight to make it flare and radiate around hook shank.

f. Thread has been wound around shank and through hair fibers once more.

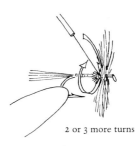

g. Two or three more turns of thread are taken around shank and through hair fibers and then brought directly in front of the hackle collar.

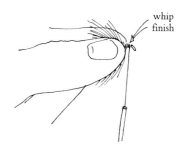

h. Hair fibers are held out of the way while whip-finish knot is applied.

i. Completed Troth Hair Spider.

WING: Medium to dark dun deer body fibers (tied spread, 180 degrees) (see model, Compara Dun)

TAIL: Dark olive sparkle yarn

BODY: Dark olive dubbing fur (covering entire shank)

SPRUCE FLY

HOOK: Mustad 94840, Partridge L3A (10–16)

THREAD: Black (Flymaster 6/0)

WING: Badger hackle tips (see model, Adams, page 5)

TAIL: Moose body hair fibers

BODY: Rear half, red floss; fore half, peacock herl

HACKLE: Badger

REMARKS: This pattern is more famous as a streamer fly, though a few houses do carry it in this dry fly form.

TROTH HAIR SPIDER
(Plate III)

HOOK: Mustad 94840 (12)

THREAD: Yellow (Monocord size A)

TAIL: Natural tan with black-tipped elk mane fibers

BODY: Yellow Monocord

HACKLE: Flared cow elk flank hair (tan with fine black tips) (radiated symmetrically around shank)

REMARKS: This pattern, designed by Al Troth of Dillon, Montana, presented a few problems for me until I received his letter regarding its construction. Here's how Troth ties it.

1. Tie in the tail fibers and use the yellow Monocord to form the body. The body should end just past the midway point of the hook shank.

2. Cut a clump of elk mane fibers (about matchstick size, perhaps a bit more) and align the tips in a hair stacker.

3. Place the fibers, tips pointing forward beyond the eye of the hook, on the hook shank just forward of the body and take five turns of thread around the fibers and the shank. The turns of thread should not be tight enough to cause the hair to flare yet they should be snug enough to hold the fibers in place.

4. Trim all the butt ends evenly, leaving a stubble no more than one-sixteenth of an inch long.

5. Unwind the thread three turns, while holding on to the short stubs with left thumb and forefinger. Loosen the thread slightly and then cinch tightly, flaring the fibers around the shank. As you pull the thread toward you, continue around the area with two or three more turns of thread. After the fibers have stopped radiating, bring the thread in front of the fibers as you pull them rear-ward with your left thumb and forefinger and out of the way. Whip-finish your thread.

It takes but one or two attempts at this pattern to get the idea and a few more to get it right. Between you and me, though, I still can't make it look as good as the model fly sent me by Troth. (See preceding page for illustrations.)

TROTH SUPER SKATER

HOOK: Mustad 94840 (6–10)

THREAD: Yellow (Monocord size A)

REAR HACKLE: Flared deer or elk hair

BODY: Yellow Monocord

FORE HACKLE: Flared deer hair (or elk) (oversize)

REMARKS: Tied as you would a Troth Spider except it has two hair fiber collars and no tail.

THE USUAL
(Plate III)

HOOK: Mustad 94840 (14–18)

THREAD: Gray (Flymaster 6/0)

TAIL: Guard hairs from between the rear foot pads of a snowshoe rabbit (tied short and stubby, barely past bend)

WING: Same as tail, tied just forward of the center of the hook shank and fanned 180 degrees so that lower fibers support the fly on the water

BODY: Gray dun underfur of snowshoe rabbit applied heavily both behind and in front of the wing to help support it vertically

REMARKS: Except for the proportions, this pattern is tied in the manner of the Compara Dun series. It was originated by Francis Betters and popularized by Bill Phillips, who has, at times, fished this pattern for an entire season on various rivers. Phillips loves it when other anglers, watching him take fish after fish, ask, "What are you using?" His answer, "The Usual," is fairly annoying at times. The Usual is perhaps one of the most unusual of flies with its coarse makeup of snowshoe rabbit foot guard hairs, a material many tyers will have trouble obtaining. But who can argue with success?

The pattern is first fished dry, then as drag begins after the free float, it is fished under like a wet fly or caddis pupa.

WELCH

HOOK: Mustad 94840, Partridge L3A (8–14)
THREAD: Black or tan (Flymaster 6/0)
WING: Red fox squirrel tail fibers (see model, Ausable Wulff)
TAIL: Red fox squirrel tail fibers
BODY: Bright yellow wool (substitute: bright yellow dubbing fur)
HACKLE: Dark ginger

REMARKS: This pattern was submitted by Dick Frost.

WHITE WULFF
(Plate III)

HOOK: Mustad 94840, Partridge L3A

THREAD: Black (Flymaster 6/0)
WING: White calf tail (see model, Ausable Wulff)
TAIL: White calf tail fibers
BODY: Cream wool (substitute: cream dubbing fur)
HACKLE: Light badger

REMARKS: Many times used for the spinner fall of the green drake on New York's Ausable River.

WOODCHUCK IRRESISTIBLE
(see Irresistible, Woodchuck)

YELLOW GOOFUS BUG
(see Humpy, Yellow)

Midges

MIDGE-TYPE flies are normally tied on hooks in sizes of 20 and smaller. There is no need to use an extra-fine-wire hook as is called for in some of the larger classic dry flies. There is so little weight to these tiny hooks that they almost float by themselves. Some anglers even go to a heavier-gauged hook when fishing this category of flies to ensure against the wire straightening out. The hook most commonly used for midges is the Mustad model 94859. This is a standard-wire dry fly hook which features a straight ringed eye for greater gap clearance. An up-eye hook, such as the Mustad model 94842, also allows gap clearance but has a tendency to hinge on the leader and throw the fly out of posture. (Most anglers use clinch knots on these small flies since there is too little room for a turle behind the hook eye.)

When tying midges, the trick is to go slowly and carefully and think small. If, when you begin to tie these flies, you really concentrate on the proportions during the construction of the first few flies, you'll be amazed at how easily and correctly they can be tied. Midges usually do not have wings and require fewer materials and fewer turns of hackle to form the collar. This endears them to many commercial tyers, for they can be turned out quickly and at greater profit.

When forming the bodies of midges that call for dubbing fur, it is a good idea to use much less than you think you'll need. A finely spun thread of dubbing fur about half an inch long is usually enough to give the impression of an abdomen. Nor should the body be too long. I find that if I wind the dubbed thread halfway along the shank, I have adequate space to tie in the butt or butts of the hackle feathers as well as an uncrowded head area to which I can easily attach my leader when fishing.

Some fly tyers like to use a specially manufactured midge thread for these small flies, but I've found it to be a nuisance because it attracts static electricity and loops and twines all over the place. The Flymaster brand of tying thread is sufficient for all midges.

ADAMS MIDGE
(Plate V)

HOOK: Mustad 94859 (20–24)
THREAD: Gray (Flymaster 6/0)
TAIL: Brown and grizzly hackle fibers mixed
BODY: Muskrat dubbing fur
HACKLE: Brown and grizzly mixed (about three turns of each)

REMARKS: This is, perhaps, the only midge pattern that uses two hackles for the collar and may require three turns of each brown and grizzly hackle to achieve its speckled effect. For most midge flies, especially those in sizes 22 and 24, a total of three turns of hackle to form the collar is usually sufficient.

BLACK MIDGE

HOOK: Mustad 94859 (20–22)
THREAD: Black (Flymaster 6/0)
TAIL: Black hackle fibers
BODY: Black dubbing fur
HACKLE: Black

BLACK AND WHITE SPINNER
(see Tricorythodes Male Spinner, page 60)

BLUE DUN MIDGE

HOOK: Mustad 94859 (20–22)
THREAD: Gray (Flymaster 6/0)
TAIL: Medium blue dun hackle fibers
BODY: Muskrat dubbing fur
HACKLE: Medium blue dun

BLUE WINGED OLIVE MIDGE

HOOK: Mustad 94859 (20–22)
THREAD: Dark olive (Flymaster 6/0)
TAIL: Dark dun hackle fibers
BODY: Medium olive dubbing fur
HACKLE: Dark dun

BROWN MIDGE

HOOK: Mustad 94859 (20–22)
THREAD: Brown or tan (Flymaster 6/0)
TAIL: Brown hackle fibers
BODY: Medium brown dubbing fur
HACKLE: Brown

CAENIS DUN
(see Tricorythodes Dun)

CREAM MIDGE

HOOK: Mustad 94859 (20–22)
THREAD: Cream (Flymaster 6/0)
TAIL: Cream hackle fibers
BODY: Cream dubbing fur
HACKLE: Cream

MOSQUITO MIDGE

HOOK: Mustad 94859 (20–22)
THREAD: Gray (Flymaster 6/0)
TAIL: Grizzly hackle fibers
BODY: Black and white moose mane fibers (wound simultaneously)
HACKLE: Grizzly

REMARKS: Stripped peacock herl may be used for the body. However, moose mane is advised since the diameter of the fibers is narrower than the width of the flat peacock herl and gives a more pronounced segmentation. A touch of head lacquer to the body will help protect it.

OLIVE MIDGE

HOOK: Mustad 94859 (20–22)
THREAD: Olive (Flymaster 6/0)
TAIL: Dyed medium olive hackle fibers
BODY: Medium olive dubbing fur
HACKLE: Medium olive

TRICORYTHODES BADGER DUN

HOOK: Mustad 94859 (22–24)
THREAD: Black (Flymaster 6/0)
TAIL: None
WING: None
HACKLE: Badger

REMARKS: This pattern, used by Matthew Vinciguerra in seasons past, has almost become a forgotten pattern, because of the limited quantity of badger hackle in the very small sizes required. If you can locate white or silver badger in a size 22 or less, you simply wind this hackle around the center of the hook shank and fish it.

TRICORYTHODES DUN
(Plate V)

HOOK: Mustad 94859 (22–24)
THREAD: Black (Flymaster 6/0)
TAIL: Dark dun hackle fibers (tied forked) (see model, Brown Drake Spinner, page 56)
WING: Upright clump of gray poly yarn
BODY: Black dubbing fur

REMARKS: The upright clump of poly yarn is tied in extra long so that the dubbed thread can be easily worked around it when forming the body. After the fly is completed the upright clump is cut down to appropriate size and combed.

Spinners

NOT VERY long ago, spinner, or spent, flies were tied with the wings constructed of hackle tips, calf tail, or other feather or hair fibers. Today, most fly tyers have switched to the use of poly yarn and other synthetics because the density of these fibers is very fine, they are usually lighter than water, and the amount of filament in a given wing can be controlled.

Spinners, in general, are fairly easy to tie, but because of slightly different tying procedures, they have been grouped in a category by themselves for easier referral. Because they are intended to ride in the surface film, the choice of hooks and body materials is not critical. If, in fact, some of these flies begin to submerge ever so slightly, it may just be an added advantage, since this behavior is not unlike the natural.

The first recipe listed, the Brown Drake Spinner, will become our model for all spinners having a wing made of poly yarn.

BLACK AND WHITE SPINNER
(see Tricorythodes Male Spinner)

BROWN DRAKE SPINNER
(Plate V)

HOOK: Mustad 94840 (10–12)
THREAD: Tan (Flymaster 6/0)
TAIL: Brown hackle fibers (tied forked)
BODY: Yellowish-brown fur
WING: Light gray poly yarn

REMARKS: The easiest method for tying most spinners, especially those of size 18 and smaller, is as follows:

1. Spin a small amount of dubbing onto your thread and wind it around the shank at the bend, forming a small ball of fur. Tie five or six hackle fibers against each side of the fur ball so they flare at a 45-degree angle as the pressure of thread against the fur pushes them outward. Normally only one or two hackle fibers on each side are required for the forked tail. However, quite often they do not snug up in the proper horizontal plane from the bend. Some tilt upward, others downward. By tying in extra hackle fibers you can, after the fly has been completed, snip the excess fibers, particularly those that do not conform to a precise forked tail.

2. The body of the fly is normally formed as the next step in the construction of spinner

Tying Steps for Brown Drake Spinner

a. Tail fibers tied in against each side of fur ball.

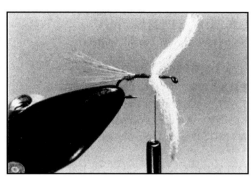

b. A long length of poly yarn tied in for wing.

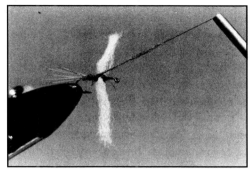

c. Dubbing fur being wound around shank and between wing for body and thorax.

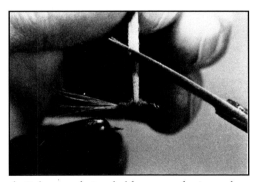

d. Poly yarn being held erect and trimmed to proper wing size.

e. Fibers not representing a forked tail being cut away.

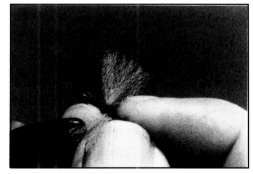

f. Completed Brown Drake Spinner. Poly yarn fibers have been combed.

patterns. However, on flies smaller than size 16, it is best to tie in the wing of poly yarn and then go back and form the body.

3. Tie the poly yarn wing in extra long. This way you will have something to hold on to when you want to move the wing backward or forward and out of the way as the body is being formed. Incidentally, the poly yarn wing should be sparse and should be combed out after the wing is formed.

4. Spin the dubbing fur onto your thread and build the abdomen area in a natural taper to the wings. Bring the dubbed thread between the wings in crisscross fashion and taper down to the eye. This maneuver will not only build a heavier and more natural thorax area, but will also set your wings more securely in their spent position. (On some of the tiny 20 and 22 spinners you will not have that much room for an abdomen and your turns of dubbed thread will very quickly get into the thorax area.)

When you have completed the fly and whip-finished the head you must still trim the oversized wings to proper size. Simply lift both ends of the poly yarn to a vertical position and cut both simultaneously to the proper length.

CAENIS SPINNER
(see Tricorythodes Spinner)

GREEN DRAKE SPINNER
(see model, Brown Drake Spinner)

HOOK: Mustad 94831 (10–12)
THREAD: Primrose (Flymaster 6/0)
TAIL: Cream hackle fibers (tied forked)
BODY: Cream dubbing fur
WING: Pale dun poly yarn

GREEN SPINNER
(see model, Brown Drake Spinner)

HOOK: Mustad 94840 (12–18)
THREAD: Olive (Flymaster 6/0)
TAIL: Cream hackle fibers (tied forked)
BODY: Medium olive dubbing fur
WING: Light tan poly yarn (tied spent)

HEXEGENIA SPINNER
(Plate V)

HOOK: Mustad 94831 (6–8)
THREAD: Brown (Flymaster 6/0)
TAIL: Deer hair fibers from extended body
BODY: Natural gray/brown deer hair diamond-wrapped (crisscrossed with thread) to shank
WING: Grizzly hackle tips (tied spent)
HACKLE: Grizzly and brown mixed

REMARKS: Body and tail are formed from one clump of deer hair fibers. Tie the fibers first to the shank just behind the wing area. Then wind the thread rearward in an open spiral over both the fibers and the hook shank. The thread continues on past the bend but only around the deer hair to within one-eighth inch of the tips. Then reverse the thread and wind back in crisscross fashion over the tail fibers and subsequently over both fibers and shank to its starting point. Trim away tips of the deer fibers beyond the thread until only three tips remain, one point-

Tying Steps for Hexegenia Spinner

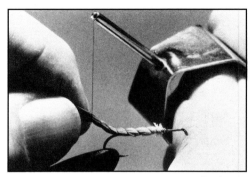

a. Deer hair has been tied to shank and is being wrapped in an open spiral with thread first around shank and hair, then around hair only.

e. Hackle is being trimmed on top and bottom, leaving only the side fibers.

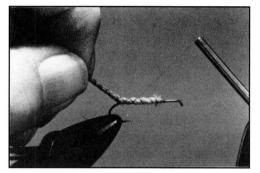

b. Thread has been reversed and is being wound forward in a crisscross manner to starting point.

c. Grizzly hackle tips have been tied spent in front of body.

d. Brown and grizzly hackles have been attached and are being wound for the collar.

f. Most of tail fibers are being cut away to leave three or four to resemble spread tails of natural insect.

g. Completed Hexegenia Spinner.

ing to the left, one to the right, and one straight back from the center. An application of head lacquer to the thread windings on the tail section helps preserve the shape of the extended body. The overall length of both body and tail unit past the bend equals the length of the hook shank.

The wing, which is tied in next, is set in place and tied down spent fashion using reverse-figure-eight turns of thread (described in the tying of the Adams wing, page 5).

After you have wound the hackle as a dry fly collar, trim it on top and bottom. The hackle fibers left protruding from the sides of the shank help support the fly in the surface film.

PALE OLIVE SPINNER

HOOK: Mustad 94840 (16–20)
THREAD: Olive (Flymaster 6/0)
TAIL: Pale dun hackle fibers (tied forked) (see model, Brown Drake Spinner)
WING: Pale dun poly yarn fibers (see model, Brown Drake Spinner)
BODY: Light olive dubbing fur

PALE SULFUR SPINNER

HOOK: Mustad 94840 (14–18)
THREAD: Primrose (Flymaster 6/0)
TAIL: Pale dun hackle fibers (tied forked) (see model, Brown Drake Spinner)
BODY: Yellowish creamy dubbing fur

WING: Pale dun poly yarn (see model, Brown Drake Spinner)

RUSTY BROWN SPINNER

HOOK: Mustad 94840 (12–22)
THREAD: Brown (Flymaster 6/0)
TAIL: Bronze dun hackle fibers (tied forked) (see model, Brown Drake Spinner)
BODY: Rusty-brown dubbing fur (reddish brown)
WING: Light gray poly yarn (see model, Brown Drake Spinner)

REMARKS: Just a reminder that the poly yarn wing on this and all other spinners should not be dense. Wings should be sparse, combed, and slightly spread to simulate the ephemeral veining of the natural fly.

SHERRY SPINNER

HOOK: Mustad 94840 (12–18)
THREAD: Cream (Flymaster 6/0)
WING: Pale dun hackle tips (tied spent) (see model, Adams, page 5)
TAIL: Honey dun or dark cream hackle fibers
RIB: Fine gold wire
BODY: Amber seal dubbing fur or equivalent
HACKLE: Cream ginger

REMARKS: This rather old pattern, which is still carried by some fly shops, is tied in the

manner of the classic dry rather than the newer spinner style.

TRICORYTHODES FEMALE SPINNER
(Plate V)

HOOK: Mustad 94859 (22–24)
THREAD: Black (Flymaster 6/0)
TAIL: Dark dun hackle fibers (tied forked) (see model, Brown Drake Spinner)
WING: White poly yarn (tied spent) (see model, Brown Drake Spinner)
BODY: Rear portion, white; thorax, black

REMARKS: On this pattern the fur ball used to flare the forked hackle tail is made of white dubbing fur which in turn forms the rear abdomen.

TRICORYTHODES MALE SPINNER
(also called Black and White Spinner)
(Plate V)

HOOK: Mustad 94859 (22–24)
THREAD: Black (Flymaster 6/0)
TAIL: Dark dun hackle fibers (tied forked) (see model, Brown Drake Spinner)
WING: White poly yarn (tied spent) (see model, Brown Drake Spinner)
BODY: Black dubbing fur

There are many other versions of the Tricorythodes Spinner, using different shadings of color and other materials. Today, however, the poly wing type is the one most commonly used.

Caddis Flies
(Downwing Patterns)

THERE ARE almost as many caddis type patterns in the various catalogs as there are mayfly imitations of the standard variety. More and more anglers are realizing that the caddis is the mainstay, whereas the mayfly has its day in the sun only every now and then.

Although caddis patterns are among the easiest of all flies to tie, care must be taken in the setting of the wing so that it is not easily pulled out. Wing fibers such as mink tail guard hairs and woodchuck are smooth and slippery. It is best always to taper the body almost to the eye (reverse taper) and fill in the area between the end of the fur body and the eye with a base of thread. A touch of head lacquer at the point where the wing is to be fastened will give added security.

On all patterns where hackle is to be wound over a previously tied-in wing, it is advisable to use a hackle size a half size smaller than normal. For example, a size 12 caddis fly should employ a size 13 hackle. The reason for this is that the tying in of the wing has increased the diameter of the base around the hook shank and standard-size hackle for the related hook would be too large.

Materials for caddis patterns should be of such texture and quality that they float well and can be twitched or popped. Deer hair, woodchuck, elk, and moose fibers are particularly effective for this. Hooks used for the adult caddis are more or less the same as those used for standard dry flies.

Caddis Fly Proportions
Drawings that follow are for general purposes only and relate to a standard-size hook.

BODY: Reverse taper to eye
WING: As long as hook shank plus one-third
HACKLE: Radiated tips as high as three-quarters of hook shank
PALMER RIB: One size smaller than related hook size
TAIL (if any): Usually one-third shank length past bend

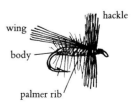

AU SABLE KING
(Plate IV)

HOOK: Mustad 94833, 94840 (10–16; use 94840 for sizes 14 and 16 and 94833 for sizes 10 and 12)
THREAD: Black (Flymaster 6/0)
TAIL: Dark ginger hackle fibers
BODY: Peacock herl
WING: Grizzly hackle tips (tied tent style)
HACKLE: Dark ginger

REMARKS: This pattern was submitted by Frank Cupp, a superlative custom fly tyer, who writes: "This is one of my favorite flies. ...It was introduced by Anne Schwiegert (Roscommon, Michigan) many years ago. I have used it since 1970 and wouldn't be caught on the river without it."

The construction is standard except for the wings, which are tied in after the tail and the body have been formed. The grizzly hackle tip wings are tied in tent style—that is, one side edge of each hackle tip wing is even with the bottom of the body while the other, or upper, edge is over the body. The two upper edges meet above the body somewhat like the top of a tent. The wing extends to the middle of the tail. The hackle collar is tied and wound after the wings have been secured.

BLACK CADDIS

HOOK: Mustad 94840, Partridge L3A (14–18)
THREAD: Black (Flymaster 6/0)
BODY: Black dubbing fur
WING: Black mink tail guard hair fibers
HACKLE: Black

REMARKS: We'll use this pattern as our model fly for many similar patterns to follow.

1. The dubbing fur is wound around the shank in a reverse taper—that is, it is heavier near the bend and narrower as it approaches the eye of the hook. When the body has been completed, wind the thread over what is left of a bare shank to the eye, forming a base upon which to tie the wing.

2. Cut small a bunch of fibers, depending on the size of the pattern to be tied, from a black mink tail and align them in a stacker. (For a size 12 fly a bunch of fibers about half the size of a wooden matchstick is sufficient.)

Tie the fibers to the shank at a point about one-third back from the hook eye. The tips extend beyond the bend for approximately one-third the hook-shank length. Take three turns of thread around both fibers and shank to keep them in place and with your scissors angle-cut the excess butts protruding beyond the eye. An angling type of cut is necessary because you don't want the hackle stem to slip off a ledge when winding the hackle for the collar.

Once the butt ends have been trimmed, wind the thread forward to the eye and back to its starting point. This should keep the mink fibers well in place. A drop of head cement under the fibers before placing the wings on the shank is always a great help.

3. Select two hackle feathers which measure slightly less than would normally be used for the related hook size and tie them in by the butts. For example, if you are tying a size 14 Black Caddis, use a size 15 hackle. Wind the hackle collar but use one or two more turns of hackle than you would normally use. The extra hackle turns are for those situations when you may wish to twitch or skitter the caddis on the surface of the water. The use of two hackles as opposed to one, regardless of hook size, also helps the hackle fibers support one another.

BUCKTAIL CADDIS

HOOK: Mustad 94840, Partridge L3A (10–16)
THREAD: Brown (Flymaster 6/0)
TAIL: Natural brown/gray deer hair fibers (tied short)
PALMER RIB: Brown hackle palmered through body
WING: Natural brown/gray deer hair
HACKLE: Brown

REMARKS: This particular pattern from Frank Johnson of Missoula, Montana, features a palmer rib of brown hackle winding through the body which not only keeps the fly riding high but also keeps the deer hair wing angled upward, almost as if the fly is ready to take off from the surface. It is a good pattern to skitter and twitch, much in the manner of the Henryville Caddis.

Tying Steps for Black Caddis

a. A reverse-tapered body has just been formed and a bit of head cement is being applied to the top of the fore third of body to help prevent wing fibers from pulling out.

b. Wing has been tied in and excess is being cut away at an angle to assure smooth taper for winding hackle.

c. Wing has been secured. Note thread wraps covering fore third of hair and shank.

d. Hackles have been tied in, ready for winding for a collar.

e. Completed Black Caddis.

The wing of this pattern does not require a loose turn of thread to compact the fibers. A slight upward flare is natural and will keep the wing above the palmer rib hackle. The Bucktail Caddis is also tied with bodies in yellow and orange.

CADDIS TAIL FLY

HOOK: Mustad 94840 (12–18)
THREAD: Brown (Flymaster 6/0)
TAIL: A short section of mottled brown turkey quill (V-notched and lacquered)
PALMER RIB: Grizzly hackle palmered through body
BODY: Gray/brown hare's ear fur
HACKLE: Brown

REMARKS: This unusual pattern, originated by Warren Johns, does away with the wing, using only the suggestion of one with the V-notched turkey tail.

CHIMARRA CADDIS (No. 2)

HOOK: Mustad 94840, Partridge L3A (16–18)
THREAD: Black (Flymaster 6/0)
BODY: Black dubbing fur
WING: White-tailed doe deer face hair
HACKLE: Black

REMARKS: A favorite pattern of its originator, Dr. William Priest. The hair fibers

from the mask of a deer are not as hollow as those from the body, and thus do not require as careful a setting to prevent flaring as with other deer hair wing patterns.

CHUCK CADDIS
(Plate IV)

HOOK: Mustad 94840, Partridge L3A (12–18)
THREAD: Orange, gray, or brown
BODY: Dirty orange dubbing fur
WING: Guard hairs from back of woodchuck (see model, Black Caddis)
HACKLE: Brown and grizzly mixed

REMARKS: This all-purpose pattern is also tied in body colors of gray, olive, black, tan, and yellow. The wing and hackle colors remain the same. Woodchuck guard hair fibers are perhaps one of the easiest materials to work with and have the additional advantages of being banded (black with white tip) in color, durable (three to four times stronger than deer hair), and floatable. They perform well in fast or broken water and require very little fly dope to keep them high and dry.

The Chuck Caddis is one of the more popular of the newer patterns because it takes fish during the entire season and in all parts of the country.

COLORADO KING

HOOK: Mustad 94840, Partridge L3A (10–18)
THREAD: Black (Flymaster 6/0)

TAIL: Two peccary fibers (tied long and forked)
PALMER RIB: Grizzly hackle palmered through body
BODY: Dyed yellow rabbit dubbing fur
WING: Elk hair fibers slightly longer than shank

REMARKS: This pattern by George Bodmer is also tied using muskrat for the body and dark elk hair for the wing.

DARK CADDIS (Rosborough)
(Plate IV)

HOOK: Mustad 94840 (6–8)
THREAD: Black (Flymaster 6/0)
BODY: Dirty orange dubbing fur
WING: Very dark brown deer hair
HACKLE: Very dark brown

REMARKS: This pattern was originated by E. H. "Polly" Rosborough. When tying a wing of deer hair fibers, loose turns of thread should be taken over the rearmost section of fibers receiving the thread windings lashing the hair to the shank; otherwise, the hair will flare upward and outward in unwanted directions. (see model, Irresistible, page 45.) Once the gentle curls of thread have been made, it is possible to crimp down with adequate pressure below that point and tie the hair securely to the shank.

Remember also to take one or two turns of thread around the bare shank and then back over the fibers to prevent them from flipping over the side.

As in the Black Caddis, an angle cut should be made when trimming the excess butts in front of the eye so that the hackle, when wound, does not slide off an abrupt ledge.

Tying Deer Hair Wing Caddis Fly

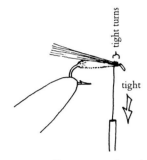

a. Hair wing fibers are tied to shank with tight turns of thread behind eye.

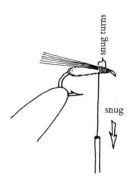

b. Snug (but not tight) turns of thread taken rearward of first turns so that hair does not flare.

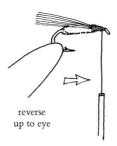

c. Thread is wound back to position before eye, where it is whip-finished.

d. Completed deer hair wing caddis fly.

DELTA WING CADDIS, GRAY
(Plate IV)

HOOK: Mustad 94840 (10–22)
THREAD: Gray (Flymaster 6/0)
BODY: Gray dubbing fur (muskrat)
WING: Blue dun hen hackle tips (tied delta style)
HACKLE: Bronze dun

REMARKS: As the name implies, the hackle tip wings are tied "delta wing" style—that is, at approximately a 45-degree angle from the hook shank at a point one-third back from the eye of the hook. The best hackle tips for this type of fly are those from a hen neck, as opposed to those from a rooster or from saddle patches.

The wings are attached one at a time, with turns of thread setting the proper angle.

DELTA WING CADDIS, OLIVE

HOOK: Mustad 94840 (12–22)
THREAD: Olive (Flymaster 6/0)
BODY: Olive with a gray-cast dubbing fur
WING: Blue dun hen hackle tips (tied delta style)
HACKLE: Dark ginger

REMARKS: The delta wing construction of this type of pattern was originated by Larry Solomon.

DESCHUTES CADDIS

HOOK: Mustad 94840 (8–12)
THREAD: Brown (Flymaster 6/0)
TAIL: Natural brown/gray deer hair (tied short, one-third normal)
BODY: Yellow dubbing fur
WING: Light brown deer hair (see model, Dark Caddis)
HACKLE: Dark ginger

ELK HAIR CADDIS
(Plate IV)

HOOK: Mustad 94840, Partridge L3A (10–20)
THREAD: Tan or brown (Flymaster 6/0)

PALMER RIB: Furnace or brown hackle palmered through body

BODY: Hare's ear and mask dubbing fur

WING: Tan-colored elk hair fibers (tilting slightly upward)

HEAD: Trimmed butts of elk hair wing

REMARKS: After the elk hair wing has been lashed to the hook shank, the butt ends are trimmed so that a small portion of them still protrude to form a squared-off head. Lacquer should be applied under the wings prior to tying them to the shank and also to the windings after the fly has been completed.

Al Troth is the originator of this remarkable fly which has become the equal of the Henryville Special as an all-purpose caddis imitation. Troth has contributed greatly to the angler's fly box with his innovations. Some of his designs include Terrible Troth, Troth Salmon Fly, Golden Stone (Troth version), Gulper Special, Hairy Brown Leech, Baby Bullhead, Troth Scud, and his own version of many others (Troth Matuka Sculpin).

The Elk Hair Caddis is today carried in most catalogs in every conceivable color combination. Troth, in his catalog, offers them in gold, black, and green, which may be all you need to cover the hatches. This pattern is a very high floater and one that can easily be twitched, skittered, and popped.

FLAT WING CADDIS, BLACK

HOOK: Mustad 94840 (14–20)

THREAD: Black (Flymaster 6/0)

PALMER RIB: Black hackle palmered through body (trimmed top and bottom)

WING: Mottled turkey wing quill section (or equivalent) (end V-notched)

HACKLE: Black (trimmed on bottom)

REMARKS: The trimmed rib and hackle allow this fly to ride close to the water surface.

FLAT WING CADDIS, GRAY

HOOK: Mustad 94840 (14–20)

THREAD: Gray (Flymaster 6/0)

PALMER RIB: Brown hackle palmered through body (trimmed top and bottom)

BODY: Muskrat dubbing fur

WING: Mottled turkey wing quill section (or equivalent) (end V-notched)

HACKLE: Brown (trimmed on bottom)

FLAT WING CADDIS, OLIVE

HOOK: Mustad 94840 (14–20)

THREAD: Olive (Flymaster 6/0)

PALMER RIB: Grizzly hackle palmered through body (trimmed top and bottom)

BODY: Medium olive dubbing fur

WING: Mottled turkey wing quill section (or equivalent) (end V-notched)

HACKLE: Brown (trimmed on bottom)

FLAT WING CADDIS, TAN

HOOK: Mustad 94840 (14–20)

THREAD: Tan or light brown (Flymaster 6/0)

PALMER RIB: Brown hackle palmered through body (trimmed top and bottom)

BODY: Beige/tan dubbing fur (tan hare's mask fur is fine)

WING: Mottled turkey wing quill section (or equivalent) (end V-notched)

HACKLE: Brown (trimmed on bottom)

FLUTTERING CADDIS
(see Wright Skittering Caddis)

GODDARD CADDIS
(Plate IV)

HOOK: Mustad 94840 (10–16)

THREAD: Brown (Flymaster 6/0)

BODY: Natural gray deer hair (spun and trimmed to body and wing shape of adult caddis; for technique, see model, Irresistible, page 45)

ANTENNAE: Stripped hackle stems from brown hackle feather

HACKLE: Brown

REMARKS: Designed by John Goddard and Andre Puyans, this pattern is an excellent choice for fast and turbulent waters.

GRAY SEDGE

HOOK: Mustad 94840 (8–10)

THREAD: Black (Flymaster 6/0)

TAIL: Dyed red hackle fibers
RIB: Fine oval gold tinsel
BODY: Muskrat dubbing fur
WING: Mallard flank fibers (tied flat over shank)
HACKLE: Dark ginger

GUS'S GRANNOM
(Plate IV)

HOOK: Mustad 94840 (12–16)
THREAD: Brown (Flymaster 6/0)
BODY: Lacquered quill stem from dark brown rooster (see model, Red Quill, page 26)
WING: Mallard wing quill section (cupped and lacquered)
HACKLE: Brown or pale rusty dun

REMARKS: Originated by Gus Nevros. The mallard quill is trimmed round at the end and bent or cupped slightly as it is fastened to the shank. It extends past the bend for one-quarter of the hook-shank length.

HARE'S EAR CADDIS

HOOK: Mustad 94840 (10–18)
THREAD: Gray (Flymaster 6/0)
TAIL: Grizzly hackle fibers (tied short, one-third normal length)
BODY: Hare's ear dubbing fur blend
HACKLE: Brown and grizzly mixed

REMARKS: This pattern is also called the Vermont Caddis.

HARE'S EAR FLUTTERING CADDIS
(Plate IV)

HOOK: Mustad 94840 (10–18)
THREAD: Tan or gray (Flymaster 6/0)
TAIL: A pinch of hare's mask fibers (half shank length)
BODY: Hare's ear and mask dubbing fur
WING: A pinch of hare's mask fibers
HACKLE: Dun grizzly or dun variant (or one grizzly and one dun hackle mixed)

REMARKS: This pattern from Jack Mickievicz looks like an organized fuzz ball and is highly effective. Mickievicz uses it to represent an ovipositing or fluttering caddis. It should be twitched and popped during the float.

HEMINGWAY CADDIS
(Plate IV)

HOOK: Mustad 94840 (12–20)
THREAD: Olive (Flymaster 6/0)
PALMER RIB: Medium blue dun hackle palmered through body
BODY: Medium olive fur
UNDERWING: Wood duck flank fibers
WING: Mallard wing quill section (tied to cup over body; end of quill trimmed round)
HACKLE: Medium blue dun (wound over base of peacock herl)

REMARKS: This pattern features a construction similar to that of the Henryville Special except that the wing is made of one section and cupped slightly over the body. Before the hackle is wound for the collar, a peacock eye herl is tied in behind the hook eye and wound two turns around the shank.

HENRYVILLE SPECIAL
(Plate I)

HOOK: Mustad 94840 (12–18)
THREAD: Gray (Flymaster 6/0)
PALMER RIB: Grizzly hackle palmered through body (hackle size slightly less than that of hackle collar)
BODY: Olive floss
UNDERWING: Wood duck flank fibers
WING: Mallard quill sections (tied to flare outward from body)
HACKLE: Brown

REMARKS: The palmer rib of grizzly hackle should be trimmed on top before the underwing of wood duck flank is tied in.

The simplest method of attaching the wing to this pattern is to pick up the quill section which is to form the far side of the wing and hold it in place with the pad of the index finger of your left hand. Then pick up the quill section for the near side of the wing in a pair of tweezers and hold it against the shank, aligning the tips and sides against the far wing. Once aligned, cover both quill sections by pressing your thumb pad against your index finger pad and remove the tweezers. (This method is much more efficient than trying to manipulate and align the two quill

Special Winging Techniques for Henryville Special

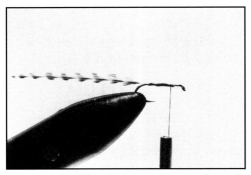

a. Grizzly hackle which later forms palmer rib is first tied in.

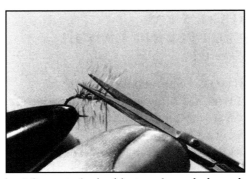

b. After grizzly hackle is palmered through floss body it is trimmed on top.

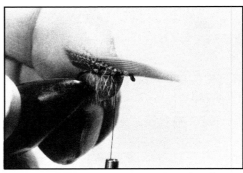

c. Duck quill section forming far side of wing is held in place with tip of forefinger.

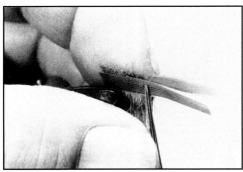

d. Tweezers are used to hold near-side duck quill section in place before thumb closes over it and the thread binds both sections to the shank.

e. Both quill sections have been tied to shank flaring away from each other.

f. Brown hackle has been wound for the fronting collar and fly is completed.

sections with your fingers and thumbs only.) Bring your thread between your finger and thumb pads and down on both wing quills. They should set up perfectly. The lower sides of the quill sections should be parallel to the hook shank and body.

The brown front hackle collar requires but three or four turns of hackle.

This grand old fly was first introduced by Hiram Brobst while fishing the Henryville section of Broadhead Creek in Pennsylvania. The original body color was red floss. This pattern is now universally accepted as *the* caddis pattern.

In addition to the olive body, it is also tied in floss body colors of fluorescent green and burnt orange.

HERMAPHRODITE, BLACK

HOOK: Mustad 94840 (14–20)
THREAD: Black (Flymaster 6/0)
BODY: Black dubbing fur
WING: Two very fine slips of mallard wing quill (a left and a right) laid one on top of the other to appear as a single wing
HACKLE: Black

REMARKS: The series of patterns called Hermaphrodites were originated by Al Brewster and are carried exclusively by the Classic and Custom Fly Shop.

HERMAPHRODITE, DIRTY ORANGE

The same as above except has dirty orange fur body and brown hackle.

HERMAPHRODITE, HARE'S EAR

The same as above except has hare's ear and mask fur blend for the body and a brown hackle collar.

HERMAPHRODITE, OLIVE
(Plate IV)

The same as above except has olive fur body and olive hackle.

KENNY'S CADDIS

HOOK: Mustad 94840 (12–18)
THREAD: Gray (Flymaster 6/0)
PALMER RIB: Pale dun hackle palmered through body (clipped short)
BODY: Tan dubbing fur
WING: Mallard wing quill section (tied flat and slightly cupped, rounded at end)
ANTENNAE: Two fine hackle stems protruding beyond eye
HACKLE: Cock Y Bondhu

REMARKS: Originated by Ken Schram of Wyncote, Pennsylvania.

KING'S RIVER CADDIS

HOOK: Mustad 94840 (12–18)
THREAD: Dark brown (Flymaster 6/0)

BODY: Tan brown dubbing fur
WING: Mottled turkey wing quill (or equivalent) (end V-notched)
HACKLE: Brown

LIGHT GINGER CADDIS
(Rosborough)

HOOK: Mustad 94840 (2–8)
THREAD: Orange (Monocord 3/0)
PALMER RIB: Golden ginger hackle palmered through body
BODY: Tan/orange dubbing fur
WING: Buff ginger deer hair (see model, Dark Caddis)

LITTLE BLACK CADDIS

HOOK: Mustad 94840 (16–18)
THREAD: Black (Flymaster 6/0)
BODY: Black horsehair or zebra mane (substitute: moose mane)
WING: Hair fibers from white-tailed deer mask
HACKLE: Black

REMARKS: This pattern from William Priest features a segmented body in miniature windings for imitating the small *Chimarra* adult caddis.

McKENZIE GREEN CADDIS

HOOK: Mustad 94840 (12–14)
THREAD: Gray (Flymaster 6/0)
BODY: Greenish pale blue dubbing fur

WING: Dyed medium blue dun deer hair (see model, Dark Caddis)

HACKLE: Brown and grizzly mixed

NAT'S CADDIS

HOOK: Mustad 94840 (12–16)
THREAD: Cream (Flymaster 6/0)
BODY: Cream dubbing fur
WING: Mottled turkey wing quill (or equivalent) (end V-notched)
HACKLE: Golden ginger

REMARKS: Originated by Nat Long.

OCTOBER CADDIS
(Plate IV)

HOOK: Mustad 9672 (8)
THREAD: Black (Monocord 3/0)
TAIL: Black moose body hair fibers (gap width in length)
PALMER RIB: Brown hackle palmered through body
BODY: Burnt orange dubbing fur
WING: Black moose body hair (to center of tail)
HACKLE: Cream ginger (wound full)

ORANGE CADDIS

HOOK: Mustad 94840 (6–8)
THREAD: Orange (Monocord 3/0)
BODY: Pale orange dubbing fur
WING: Natural gray deer hair (see model, Dark Caddis)
HACKLE: Dyed orange and grizzly mixed

REMARKS: Submitted by Dave McNeese of Salem, Oregon.

OREGON ORANGE CADDIS

HOOK: Mustad 9672 (8–12)
THREAD: Black (Flymaster 6/0)

PALMER RIB: Orange saddle hackle palmered through body (trimmed short and stubby)
BODY: Dirty orange dubbing fur
WING: Natural mule deer body hair (see model, Dark Caddis)
HACKLE: Grizzly

REMARKS: This pattern, like some others, features a long-shanked hook to better imitate some of the larger natural adult caddis.

OZARK CADDIS

HOOK: Mustad 94840 (10–14)
THREAD: Brown (Flymaster 6/0)
BODY: Orange poly yarn
WING: Red fox squirrel tail fibers
HACKLE: Furnace or reddish brown

REMARKS: Originated by Robert Schneider, this is a favorite among anglers fishing the White River in Arkansas.

PEACOCK CADDIS
(Plate IV)

HOOK: Mustad 94840, Partridge L3A (8–14)
THREAD: Black (Flymaster 6/0)
BODY: Peacock herl
WING: Tan elk hair fibers (see model, Dark Caddis)
HACKLE: Brown and grizzly mixed

PHEASANT CADDIS
(Plate IV)

HOOK: Mustad 94840 (8–14)
THREAD: Black (Flymaster 6/0)
PALMER RIB: Dark ginger hackle (clipped to gap size) palmered through body
BODY: Tan dubbing fur
WING: Mottled brown feather from hen or cock ringneck pheasant (lacquered, end V-notched)
HACKLE: Brown or dark ginger

REMARKS: Originated by Jack Gartside.

PM CADDIS

HOOK: Mustad 94840 (10–18)
THREAD: Olive (Flymaster 6/0)
BODY: Olive dubbing fur
WING: Natural fine brown deer hair (see model, Dark Caddis)
HACKLE: Brown and grizzly mixed

REMARKS: This is also tied with a muskrat body for a darker version.

SACO CADDIS
(Plate IV)

HOOK: Mustad 94833 (14)
THREAD: Tan (Flymaster 6/0)
EGG SAC: Bright green dubbing fur
PALMER RIB: Brown hackle palmered through body
BODY: Dark green dubbing fur
WING: Natural dark brown deer hair (see model, Dark Caddis)

SID NEFF
HAIR WING, BROWN

HOOK: Mustad 94840, Partridge L3A (12–18)
THREAD: Brown (Flymaster 6/0)
BODY: Light brown dubbing fur
WING: Tan/gray deer hair
HEAD: Deer hair butts (trimmed square)

REMARKS: The squared-off, blunted head on this pattern, and others in this series, is made by trimming the butts of the wing squarely behind the eye. No attempt is made to shape the head further. Similar to the head of the Elk Hair Caddis. The wing should flare upward. Designed by Sid Neff.

SID NEFF HAIR WING, GRAY

HOOK: Mustad 94840, Partridge L3A (12–18)
THREAD: Gray (Flymaster 6/0)
BODY: Muskrat dubbing fur
WING: Deer hair dyed dark gray
HEAD: Deer hair butts (trimmed square)

SID NEFF
HAIR WING, OLIVE

HOOK: Mustad 94840, Partridge L3A (12–18)
THREAD: Olive (Flymaster 6/0)
BODY: Olive dubbing fur
WING: Tan/brown deer hair
HEAD: Deer hair butts (trimmed square)

SOLOMON'S
HAIR WING, GRAY
(Plate IV)

HOOK: Mustad 94840 (12–20)
THREAD: Gray (Flymaster 6/0)
BODY: Olive dubbing fur with a hint of muskrat gray
WING: Tan/gray deer hair (see model, Dark Caddis)
HACKLE: Dark ginger

REMARKS: This pattern and the three others to follow were originated by Larry Solomon.

SOLOMON'S
HAIR WING, OLIVE

HOOK: Mustad 94840 (14–20)

THREAD: Olive (Flymaster 6/0)
BODY: Medium olive dubbing fur
WING: Natural brown deer hair (see model, Dark Caddis)
HACKLE: Bronze dun

SOLOMON'S HAIR WING,
PALE YELLOW

HOOK: Mustad 94840 (14–20)
THREAD: Beige or light brown (Flymaster 6/0)
BODY: Pale yellow dubbing fur
WING: Tan deer hair (see model, Dark Caddis)
HACKLE: Golden ginger and dark ginger mixed

SOLOMON'S
HAIR WING, TAN

HOOK: Mustad 94840 (12–20)
THREAD: Beige or light brown (Flymaster 6/0)
BODY: Tan ginger dubbing fur
WING: Tan brown deer hair (see model, Dark Caddis)
HACKLE: Dark cream

SPENT PARTRIDGE CADDIS
(Plate IV)

HOOK: Mustad 94840 (14–20)
THREAD: Olive (Flymaster 6/0)
BODY: Dark olive dubbing fur
WING: Two mottled partridge feathers (tied flat one over the other)

HACKLE: Brown and grizzly over a base of peacock herl (trimmed top and bottom)

REMARKS: This pattern submitted by Mike Lawson employs a couple of turns of peacock eye herl at the head area before the hackle is wound as a collar. When the fly is completed, the hackle fibers on top and bottom are trimmed flush to the shank, leaving only the side fibers protruding from the thorax area.

STALKER CADDIS, EVENING

HOOK: Mustad 94840 (10)
THREAD: Black (Flymaster 6/0)
BODY: Muskrat dubbing fur
WING: Dark brown deer hair from scent gland area (gap width past bend)
HACKLE: Brown and grizzly mixed, hackle collar one size larger than related hook size (trimmed almost flat on bottom)

REMARKS: This pattern is fished prior to nightfall during evening dusk hours. The stalker series also includes one pattern that is tied all-black.

STALKER CADDIS, NIGHT
(Plate IV)

HOOK: Mustad 94840 (10)
THREAD: Cream (Flymaster 6/0)
BODY: Cream fox dubbing fur
WING: Cream elk hair fibers (gap width past bend)
HACKLE: Cream, one size larger than hook size (wrapped full and trimmed almost flat on bottom)

REMARKS: Developed by Peter Burton and a number of angling friends for fishing the west branch of the Penobscot River in Maine during the night hours.

TROTH ELK HAIR CADDIS
(see Elk Hair Caddis)

TRY IT

HOOK: Mustad 94831 (14–16)
THREAD: Red (Flymaster 6/0)
BODY: Muskrat dubbing fur
WING: Deer body hair, fairly full (half a shank length past bend) (fibers allowed to flare upward slightly)
HEAD: Clipped ends of deer hair wing

REMARKS: Developed by Bill Phillips, this is often popped like a bass bug to create interest. Body colors may be varied according to the natural insect being imitated. This pattern is similar to the Sid Neff Hair Wing.

VERMONT CADDIS
(see Hare's Ear Caddis)

VINCENT SEDGE

HOOK: Mustad 94840 (10–12)
THREAD: Olive (Flymaster 6/0)
BODY: Dark olive dubbing fur
WING: Mottled turkey wing quill section (or equivalent) (end V-notched) (tied slightly tented)
HACKLE: Brown or cree

REMARKS: A far western favorite.

WHARRY CADDIS

HOOK: Mustad 94840 (10–16)
THREAD: Black (Flymaster 6/0)
TAIL: Light tan elk hair fibers (gap width past bend)
BODY: Dark brown (Monocord 3/0)
WING: Light tan elk hair (to end of tail fibers)
HACKLE: Badger

WILD TURKEY

HOOK: Mustad 94840 (10–16)
THREAD: Black (Flymaster 6/0)
TAIL: Brown hackle fibers
PALMER RIB: Brown hackle palmered through body
BODY: Black tying thread
WING: Mottled turkey wing quill sections (or equivalent) (cupped against each other tenting rearward; opposite of Henryville Special wing)
HACKLE: Brown

REMARKS: A local favorite in the Hudson Valley in New York.

WISCONSIN FANCY
(Plate IV)

HOOK: Mustad 94840 (12–18)
THREAD: Black (Flymaster 6/0)

TAIL: Brown hackle fibers

PALMER RIB: One brown and one grizzly hackle palmered through body

BODY: Cream dubbing fur or ginger red fox dubbing

REMARKS: This pattern, listed in the Little Dixie Flies catalog, features a mixed hackle palmer rib, and is similar to the bivisibles except that it has no fronting collar.

WRIGHT SKITTERING CADDIS, BLACK

HOOK: Mustad 94840 (12–16)

THREAD: Black (Flymaster 6/0)

BODY: Black dubbing fur

WING: Black mink tail guard hairs (see model, Black Caddis)

HACKLE: Dark rusty dun

REMARKS: Originated by Leonard Wright

and first featured in his book *Fishing the Dry Fly as a Living Insect.* The original fly in this series featured a wing made of long, stiff spade hackles. This material, however, is so scarce that a switch was made to mink tail guard hairs.

WRIGHT SKITTERING CADDIS, CINNAMON

HOOK: Mustad 94840 (12–16)

THREAD: Orange (Flymaster 6/0)

BODY: Dyed cinnamon dubbing fur

WING: Dark brown mink tail guard hairs (see model, Black Caddis)

HACKLE: Rusty dun

WRIGHT SKITTERING CADDIS, GRAY

HOOK: Mustad 94840 (12–16)

THREAD: Gray (Flymaster 6/0)

BODY: Muskrat dubbing fur

WING: Blue dun mink tail guard hairs (see model, Black Caddis)

HACKLE: Rusty dun

WRIGHT SKITTERING CADDIS, OLIVE

HOOK: Mustad 94840 (12–16)

THREAD: Olive (Flymaster 6/0)

BODY: Medium olive dubbing fur

WING: Dark brown mink tail guard hairs (see model, Black Caddis)

HACKLE: Rusty dun

Terrestrials

THERE IS very little that can be called standard in this category, nor is there a set rule for even general proportions. Imitations of these land insects, which may vary widely in size and color, have been interpreted very differently by fly tyers.

AL'S HAIR CRICKET

HOOK: Mustad 9671 (10–14)
THREAD: Black (Monocord 3/0)
RIB: Black thread
BODY: Black elk hair fibers (reversed)
WING: A black goose wing quill section, rounded at its end and tied flat over the body extending to the bend. This is partially covered with elk hair fibers flared rearward while spinning the head. A single black goose quill fiber is also tied on each side as an outrigger (as long as the wing)
HEAD: Black elk hair, spun and trimmed to cricket or hopper shape
REMARKS: This pattern, developed by Al Troth, is tied in the following manner:

1. Thread is wound onto the hook shank to the bend, with an excess strand of about five inches left hanging out of the way.

2. A clump of black elk hair fibers with butt ends facing toward eye is lashed to the hook shank from a point one-quarter of the shank length before the eye to the bend. (Thickness of clump on a size 10 hook is about equal to that of a wooden matchstick.) Extra turns of thread are taken around the fibers and shank at the bend area. Thread is then brought forward to a point directly in front of the butts.

3. The elk hair extending rearward beyond the bend is now reversed and pulled forward. The fibers should entirely surround the hook shank. They are pulled taut as the thread is brought around them in front of the butts. Four or five turns of thread should secure them.

4. The excess thread left idling in the rear is now wound forward in an open spiral over the elk hair. The thread spirals should be tight enough to create a segmentation effect on the body. The thread forming the segmentation is now tied down with the tying thread. All excesses are trimmed away.

5. The black goose quill section is tied in for the wing.

6. Black elk hair is spun around the hook shank before the eye of the hook. (see Irresistible, page 45, for spinning method.) Some

Tying Steps for Al's Hair Cricket

a. Thread wound onto shank with a five-inch excess left dangling rearward.

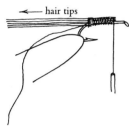

← hair tips

b. Black elk hair fibers, with tips rearward, are lashed to shank from a point one-quarter shank length behind the eye to the bend.

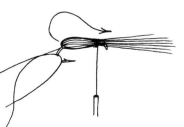

c. Fibers are pulled forward beyond hook eye and bound to shank one-quarter shank length before eye.

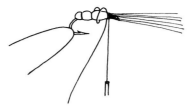

d. Excess thread is now wound around elk hair body in an open spiral forming segmentation.

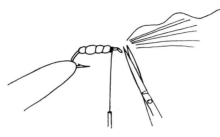

e. Excess butts are trimmed.

f. Black goose quill section is tied in for wing.

g. Black elk hair is spun around shank behind eye. A few butt fibers are allowed to trail rearward over wing.

h. A single black goose fiber is tied to each side of head.

i. Black spun elk hair is trimmed to cricket-shaped head.

j. Completed Al's Hair Cricket.

of the flared fibers are allowed to stray over the top part of the wing.

7. A single black goose quill fiber is tied onto each side of the head. It should splay outward from the sides of the body to the end of the wing like an outrigger.

8. Fly is removed from vise, and head is trimmed to shape.

Beetles

There are a number of patterns known simply as Beetle, even though they are dressed a bit differently from each other. Two of the more commonly tied versions follow.

BEETLE

HOOK: Mustad 94840 (16–18)
THREAD: Gray (Flymaster 6/0)
SHELL: Natural gray deer hair (pulled forward over body)
BODY: Peacock herl
LEGS: Three fibers cut loose from the shell at the bend
HEAD: Clipped ends of deer hair

REMARKS: The following photo sequence will illustrate this procedure.

1. Tie a small clump of deer hair to the hook shank at the bend.

2. Tie a strand of peacock herl in at the bend and wind it around the shank to form the body. Leave the thread hanging just before the eye of the hook.

3. Pull the deer hair forward over the body and tie it down with the thread. The deer hair should cover the top and half the sides of the body.

4. Whip-finish the thread and cut the excess deer hair even with the eye of the hook so that a small stubby section remains. This forms the squared-off head.

5. With the point of the scissors, cut three fibers of deer hair loose from the shell where they emerge at the bend. Push them forward so they extend at right angles to the front of the body and resemble the legs.

BEETLE
(Plate IV)

HOOK: Mustad 94840 (16–18)
THREAD: Gray (Flymaster 6/0)
SHELL: Natural gray deer hair (pulled forward over shank and hackle-palmered legs)
LEGS: Brown hackle palmered along shank (trimmed top and bottom)
HEAD: Clipped ends of deer hair

REMARKS: The remaining hackle fibers form the legs, so there is no need to cut loose part of the deer hair shell.

Some fly tyers prefer to lacquer the fibers of the deer hair shell on these patterns, both for durability and for the glossy effect of the natural.

BLACK BEETLE

HOOK: Mustad 94840 (14–20)
THREAD: Black (Flymaster 6/0)
SHELL: Natural dark gray goose quill section (pulled over body)

Tying Steps for a Beetle

a. Deer hair, with tips rearward, has been lashed to shank from a point one-third behind eye to bend. Extra turns are taken at bend area.

d. Excess deer hair is trimmed, leaving only a short stub to represent the head.

LEGS: Brown hackle palmered through body (trimmed on bottom)

BODY: Peacock herl

REMARKS: This pattern is a combination of the two previous ones except for the goose quill shell. It does not have a clipped head.

BLACK CROWE BEETLE

HOOK: Mustad 94840 (14–20)

THREAD: Black (Flymaster 6/0)

SHELL: Black deer hair (pulled forward over shank)

LEGS: Black deer hair fibers (three on each side)

HEAD: Clipped ends of excess deer hair

REMARKS: This pattern is similar to the first Beetle except that after the clump of fibers has been tied in for the shell, three individual strands of deer hair are lashed to the center of the hook shank and crisscrossed with thread to separate them. These are then trimmed to a length to simulate a beetle's legs. Once the legs have been secured, the deer hair clump is pulled forward, tied down, and the excess trimmed to a squared-off head.

BLACK ANT

HOOK: Mustad 94840 (14–20)

THREAD: Black (Flymaster 6/0)

ABDOMEN: Dyed black dubbing fur ball (on rear half of shank)

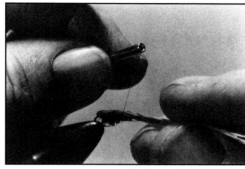

b. Peacock herl has been tied in and wound forward to form underpart of body.

c. Deer hair is pulled forward beyond eye and turns of thread are taken around hair and shank to secure it.

e. Three strands of deer hair are cut loose from each side of shank at bend area to represent legs.

f. Completed Beetle.

HACKLE (LEGS): Black (at waist between abdomen and thorax)

THORAX: Dyed black dubbing fur ball
(on fore half of shank)

BLACK FLYING ANT
(see Flying Ant, Black)

CALCATERRA ANT

HOOK: Mustad 94840 (12–22)

THREAD: Black (Flymaster 6/0)

BODY, LEGS, AND THORAX: A
clump of deer hair is tied in at the bend
and folded forward to the center of the
shank and the tying thread secures the
fibers, thus forming the rear hump. At
this time three fibers are pricked loose on
each side near the bend to form the legs.
(See Beetle, peacock body.) Thread is then
brought forward to the eye and remainder of hair fibers is pulled forward and
secured, thus forming forward hump. Entire body is lacquered.

REMARKS: Originated by Paul Calcaterra.

CINNAMON ANT

HOOK: Mustad 94840 (18–20)

THREAD: Brown (Flymaster 6/0)

ABDOMEN: Cinnamon fur-blend ball (on
rear half of shank)

HACKLE (LEGS): Dark ginger (at waist
between abdomen and thorax)

THORAX: Cinnamon fur-blend ball (on
fore half of shank)

DAN'S DEER HOPPER

HOOK: Mustad 94831, 9672 (6–12)

THREAD: Yellow for body, then brown
(Monocord 3/0)

TAIL: Dyed red hackle fibers (gap width
in length)

BODY: Spun and clipped dyed yellow deer
hair (see model, Irresistible, page 45)

WING: Mottled turkey wing quill section
(or equivalent)

HACKLE: Brown and grizzly mixed

REMARKS: The trick of setting the wings
so that they snug naturally to the body is in
the trimming of the deer hair to a hopper
body shape. That part of the deer hair body
where the wings are to be tied should be
trimmed almost flush to the hook shank.

The wings should be tied directly onto the
forward side portion of the body, not onto
the hook shank in front of it; otherwise, the
ledge of clipped deer body hair will cause
the wings to flare outward. (If it is a single
flat turkey wing quill section to be tied on
top of the body, as in some other patterns,
then the top of the deer hair is trimmed
almost flush to the hook shank.)

Turkey wing quill sections should be lacquered and allowed to dry before they are
used as wings. It's a good idea to lacquer a
complete pair of wing quills just for hoppers

and cut the sections from them as they are
needed. Plio Bond and vinyl cement are excellent lacquers for this process.

The clipped deer hair body of the fly should
extend no more than two-thirds of the shank
length from the bend to the eye, leaving
adequate space for hackle and/or head.

DAVE'S HOPPER

HOOK: Mustad 9672 (4–12)

THREAD: Gray (Monocord 3/0)

TAIL: Dyed red deer hair fibers (gap width
in length)

PALMER RIB: Brown hackle palmered
through body

BODY: Yellow yarn with a small loop of
yarn hovering above bend

UNDERWING: Yellow calf tail fibers (to
bend)

WING: Two lacquered turkey wing quill sections (tied tented over body, the upward-
curved tips mirroring hook bend)

HEAD: Natural brown/gray deer hair, spun
and trimmed to shape

REMARKS: The spinning of the deer hair
for the head employs the technique used for
the dry fly Irresistible (page 45). Sometimes,
however, as in this case, butt ends of previously
tied-in materials cover the shank where the
spinning of hair is to occur. Deer hair spins
readily only on a bare shank. For this pattern,
and others like it, you may have to spot and
flare the hair in place until all areas are covered and until you get to the bare shank
section of the hook. If a void or sparse area
occurs, simply place a small clump of deer

fibers over it and bring the thread tightly around hair and hook shank, causing the fibers to flare in place and fill in the void.

Some of the flared ends of deer hair are allowed to extend rearward over the body and partially cover the wing. This creates an illusion of movement when the hopper is being fished.

This pattern was originated by Dave Whitlock.

DEER HOPPER
(see Dan's Deer Hopper)

DOODLEBUG, RED AND WHITE

HOOK: Mustad 9671 (8–12)
THREAD: Black (Flymaster 6/0)
BODY: Medium red chenille (size 1)
SHELL or COVER: White deer hair lashed down at both bend and before eye. Deer hair butts are trimmed off squarely at both ends. These trimmed and slightly flared butts do not extend beyond the eye or the bend.

REMARKS: This pattern is tied in a variety of colors, varying and alternating in both body and shell.

ELK HAIR FLYING ANT
(Plate IV)

HOOK: Mustad 94859 (12–18)
THREAD: Black or orange (Flymaster 6/0)

ABDOMEN: Elongated black or cinnamon fur ball (on rear half of shank)
WING: Natural tan elk hair fibers (tied in at center of shank, tilting slightly upward and extending just beyond bend)
HACKLE: Two or three turns of black hackle (tied over wing butts between abdomen and thorax)
THORAX: Black or cinnamon dubbed fur ball

REMARKS: This Jack Gartside pattern, though taken readily as a terrestrial, is also effective when neither black nor cinnamon ants are prevalent. The slightly angled elk hair wing also creates the illusion of an adult caddis fly struggling to become airborne.

FLYING ANT, BLACK

HOOK: Mustad 94840 (14–18)
THREAD: Black (Flymaster 6/0)
ABDOMEN: Elongated black fur ball (on rear half of shank)

WING: Black hackle tips (tied delta style; see Delta Wing Caddis, page 65) (slightly past bend)
HACKLE: Black (at waist)
THORAX: Oval black fur ball (on fore half of shank)

FLYING ANT, RED

HOOK: Mustad 94840 (14–18)
THREAD: Orange (Flymaster 6/0)
ABDOMEN: Elongated reddish-brown fur ball (on rear half of shank)
WING: Medium blue dun hackle tips (tied delta style) (slightly past bend)
HACKLE: Blue dun (at division of rear and front fur segments)
THORAX: Oval reddish-brown fur ball (on fore half of shank)

GARTSIDE PHEASANT HOPPER
(Plate IV)

HOOK: Mustad 94831 (6–12)
THREAD: Yellow or to match body color (Monocord 3/0)
TAIL: Dark moose body hair fibers (gap width in length)
PALMER RIB: Furnace saddle hackle, trimmed on top and cut at a tapered angle on bottom so that the fibers are half a gap width at the hook point area to almost a full gap width before the head
BODY: Yellow poly yarn (or other appropriate colors, such as tan, gray, or olive)
UNDERWING: A dozen very fine natural brown deer hair fibers (may be dyed other shades for desired imitation) (to center of tail)
WING: A mottled ringneck pheasant back feather (dipped in spar varnish and dried; tip V-notched and extending to center of

tail; feather cupped slightly over under-wing and body)

COLLAR: A dozen natural brown deer hair fibers (tied in along the sides of the body to extend rearward half a shank length)

HEAD: Deer hair spun and trimmed fairly square in shape (color may be natural gray or dyed tan, olive, or other desired shades)

REMARKS: Originated by Jack Gartside, a former English teacher and currently a taxi driver, who spends more time away from home than his budget would seem to allow. Many of his designs are from the feathers he finds along the banks of the streams he fishes. A favorite haunt is Yellowstone Park, where he remains encamped from runoff until the bears chase him out in the fall. He has been known to extract a certain amount of dubbing fur from a dun-colored cat named Tobermory, a traveling companion who shares Gartside's wanderlust, in spite of being cropped of his overcoat now and again. When his budget gets tight, Gartside will sell his flies. Since he is an exceptionally gifted fly tyer, there is always a waiting list of those seeking his flies.

GREEN HOPPER

The same as Joe's Hopper except for green chenille body.

GREEN LEAF HOPPER
(Plate IV)

HOOK: Mustad 94840 (16–22)

THREAD: Pale yellow or cream (Flymaster 6/0)

PALMER RIB: Dyed insect green hackle palmered through body (trimmed flush top and bottom)

BODY: A thin layer of white floss

WING: Dyed insect green mallard breast or flank feather (lacquered and cut to ovoid shape and tied flat over body)

HENRY'S FORK HOPPER
(Plate IV)

HOOK: Mustad 94831, 9672 (8–12)

THREAD: Yellow (waxed Monocord 3/0)

BODY: Cream-colored elk rump fibers (reversed and segmented with excess thread; see model, Al's Hair Cricket)

UNDERWING: Yellow deer hair (tied flat over body to bend)

WING: A single mottled hen pheasant feather (rounded at tip; lacquered and tied flat on top, cupping slightly downward on each side; extending gap width past bend)

LEGS: Knotted ringneck pheasant tail fibers (see model, Jay/Dave's Hopper)

HEAD: Elk hair (pulled back to form bullet head: same technique used in Thunder Creek series of streamer and bucktail flies, page 236; the tannish tips of elk hair allowed to flare back for three-quarters of the hook shank on top and sides)

REMARKS: Listed in the Henry's Fork Anglers catalog.

INCHWORM
(Plate IV)

HOOK: Mustad 94831 (14)

THREAD: Green (Monocord size A), then black for head (Flymaster 6/0)

BODY: Dyed bright green deer hair (tied down, then reversed and pulled forward)

RIB: Green thread left over from original tie-in (wound in open spiral for segmentation)

HEAD: Peacock herl

REMARKS: This employs the same method as described for the body of Al's Hair Cricket.

JAPANESE BEETLE

HOOK: Mustad 94840 (14)

THREAD: Black (Flymaster 6/0)

SHELL: Black poly yarn (pulled over)

LEGS: Dark brown hackle (clipped top and bottom and short on the sides; wound through after body has been formed)

BODY: Fairly thick olive/brown dubbing, over which is wound peacock herl

JASSID
(Plate IV)

HOOK: Mustad 94840, 94859 (20–22)

THREAD: Black (Flymaster 6/0)

BODY: Black hackle (wound in connecting spirals over shank and trimmed top and bottom)

WING: One small jungle cock nail feather (slightly past bend)

REMARKS: Any other dark feather which has been lacquered and cut to ovoid shape may be used in place of the scarce jungle cock nail. White lacquer can be used to paint the top of the back for angler visibility. This pattern was originated by Vince Marinaro and introduced in his *A Modern Dry Fly Code.*

JAY/DAVE'S HOPPER
(Plate IV)

HOOK: Mustad 94831, 9671, 9672 (8–12)
THREAD: Brown (Monocord 3/0)
TAIL: Dyed red calf tail fibers (or deer hair)
PALMER RIB: Brown hackle palmered through body (trimmed short)
BODY: Yellow yarn with loop of yarn past bend half as long as tail
UNDERWING: Yellow calf tail or deer hair fibers (to center of tail)
WING: Section of mottled turkey wing quill (or equivalent), rounded at tip to center of tail (section should be wide enough so that it can be cupped slightly over sides); lacquered before tying in
LEGS: Section of golden or ringneck pheasant tail fibers knotted for legs
HEAD: Spun, flared, and trimmed deer hair (see model, Dave's Hopper)

REMARKS: This pattern is a Dave's Hopper with legs. Jay Buchner, who designed it, added knotted legs to a standard Dave's (Whitlock) Hopper.

Making Legs for Jay/Dave's Hopper

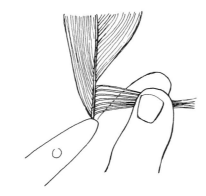

a. Section of pheasant fibers separated from feather.

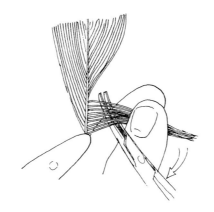

b. Pair of forceps (or tweezers) being placed under and against section of fibers.

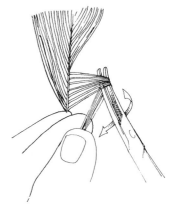

c. Section of fibers being pulled round forceps.

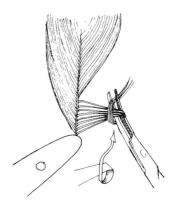

d. Tip of feather fibers being grasped by tip of forceps.

(continued)

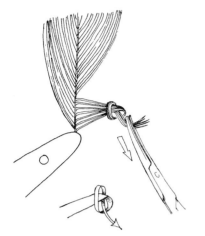

e. Tip of feather fibers being pulled through loop as in an overhand knot.

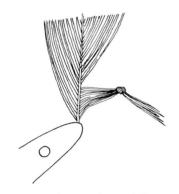

f. Completed knotted leg of fibers. Head cement should be added to the knot area.

JOE'S HOPPER

HOOK: Mustad 38941, 9672 (6–14)
THREAD: Brown (Flymaster 6/0)
TAIL: Dyed red hackle fibers (gap width in length)
PALMER RIB: Brown hackle palmered through body (trimmed short)
BODY: Yellow chenille (or yarn)
WING: Mottled turkey wing quill sections (or equivalent) (tied tented; see model, Dave's Hopper)
HACKLE: Brown and grizzly mixed

REMARKS: This pattern is also called Michigan Hopper, although the actual Michigan Hopper sometimes uses a body made of yellow wool. Another version omits the clipped palmer rib. (See Michigan Hopper.)

JOHN'S ELK HAIR HOPPER
(Plate IV)

HOOK: Mustad 38941, 9672 (6–12)
THREAD: Brown (Monocord 3/0)
TAIL: Dyed red hackle fibers (gap width in length)
PALMER RIB: Brown hackle palmered through body (trimmed short)
BODY: Yellow poly yarn; a stub of yarn allowed to extend past bend for half the length of tail
WING: Elk hair, tied in to flare slightly upward and outward to resemble hopper wing just beginning to open for takeoff (length to center of tail)
HACKLE: Brown and grizzly mixed

REMARKS: This pattern was designed by John Bailey because of the scarcity of mottled turkey wing quills. It has become one of the best sellers in Dan Bailey's Fly Shop.

LADYBUG

HOOK: Mustad 94840, Partridge L3A (14)
THREAD: Black (Flymaster 6/0)
SHELL: Orange deer hair (pulled forward and lacquered with vinyl cement; when dry, four black dots are painted on shell which trout do not see)
BODY: Black hackle palmered over shank (clipped top and bottom)
HEAD: Clipped ends of deer hair

LETORT CRICKET
(Plate IV)

HOOK: Mustad 9671 (12–16)
THREAD: Black (Flymaster 6/0)
BODY: Black dubbing fur
WING: Black crow or dyed black goose quill section (rounded at tip and curving

slightly downward on sides; extending to bend)

HEAD: Spun and clipped black deer hair, with some flared ends allowed to extend rearward over top and sides of wing (see model, Irresistible, page 45, and Dave's Hopper)

LETORT HOPPER

HOOK: Mustad 94831, 9671 (8–16)
THREAD: Gray (Monocord 3/0 to size 10, Flymaster 6/0 to size 16)
BODY: Yellow dubbing fur
WING: One mottled turkey wing quill section (or equivalent) (V-notched at tip and tied flat over body with slight curve downward at sides)
HEAD: Natural gray deer hair, spun and clipped to hopper shape, with some of the flaring fibers allowed to cover wing and sides of body (see Irresistible, page 45, and Dave's Hopper)

REMARKS: Credit for both the Letort Hopper and the Letort Cricket go to Ed Shenk.

MAGGOT FLY

HOOK: Mustad 9671 (10–12)
THREAD: White (Flymaster 6/0)
BODY: White deer hair, spun and trimmed to a very thin cigar shape (like a maggot) (see model, Irresistible, page 45)

REMARKS: Ted Gerken, who runs the Iliaska Lodge (Fly Fishing Only) in Illiamna, Alaska, relates that at certain times in the season when the water is low and stranded decomposing salmon litter the shores, maggots develop in the carcasses. When rain brings the water level up once more, the maggots are washed into the stream and the fish gorge on them. At such times, this pattern is the deadliest of all.

McMURRAY ANT
(Plate IV)

HOOK: Mustad 94840 (12–22)
THREAD: Black (Flymaster 6/0)
BODY: Black-lacquered balsa wood in two parts connected by monofilament
HACKLE: Black (at waist)

REMARKS: This particular pattern was created by Ed Sutryn, who manufactures the components and sells them, along with instructions, to his distributors.

While these flies can be made by following the above pattern recipe, most tyers feel that cutting and shaping the balsa wood pieces and then connecting them with monofilament and glue is simply too much bother. By using the ready-made parts, which are relatively inexpensive, this pattern can be made in a minute or so.

The McMurray Ants are also made in cinnamon with brown hackle and red-headed with grizzly hackle.

Sutryn also manufactures parts for emergers, ladybugs, stoneflies, caddis flies, and midges. For source see Beaverkill Angler.

MICHIGAN HOPPER
(Plate IV)

HOOK: Mustad 94831 (6–14)
THREAD: Yellow (Flymaster 6/0)
TAIL: Dyed red hackle fibers (gap width in length)
BODY: Yellow chenille (substitute: fur)
WING: Mottled turkey
HACKLE: Brown

REMARKS: Originated by Art Winnie, a professional fly tyer in the 1950s, who was responsible for many innovations in the fly-tying field. He may be best known for the Michigan Hopper, which may have been the first fly that used a turkey feather wing.

MUDDLER HOPPER
(Plate IV)

HOOK: Mustad 94831, 9672 (6–10)
THREAD: Yellow (Monocord 3/0)
TAIL: Narrow section of red duck or goose quill (gap width in length)
PALMER RIB: Brown saddle hackle palmered through body (not trimmed) (fibers gap width in length)
BODY: Yellow wool, the end of which protrudes over bend as a loop (same as in Dave's Hopper)
WING: Flared natural brown deer hair surrounding body (as long as tail)
HEAD: Dyed yellow deer hair, spun and clipped to hopper shape (see model, Irresistible, page 45, and Dave's Hopper)

ORANGE HOPPER

The same as Joe's Hopper except for orange chenille body.

RED FLYING ANT
(see Flying Ant, Red)

ROD'S BLACK ANT
(Plate IV)

HOOK: Mustad 94840 (12–22)
THREAD: Black (Flymaster 6/0)
ABDOMEN: Pre-shaped balsa cylinder strung on a piece of monofilament and painted black
THORAX, HEAD, AND LEGS: Black deer hair

REMARKS: This very realistic pattern by Rod Yerger is similar to the McMurray Ant in that the abdomen is made of balsa wood. Yerger, like Ed Sutryn, furnishes components and instructions for this and similar patterns. The series of Yerger terrestrials inlcudes Rod's Cinnamon Ant, Rod's Cricket, Rod's Hopper, and Rod's Meadow Hopper. It's advisable to buy the parts from Yerger, who has the machinery set up to produce them at a reasonable price. Instructions and components for these patterns may be obtained by writing to Rod Yerger, Box 294, Lawrence, Pennsylvania 15055.

SUTRYN McMURRAY ANT
(see McMurray Ant)

WOODCHUCK HOPPER
(Plate IV)

HOOK: Mustad 9672 (8–12)
THREAD: Light brown or yellow (Flymaster 6/0)
TAIL: Dyed red hackle fibers (gap width in length)
PALMER RIB: Brown hackle palmered through body (trimmed)
BODY: Natural gray/brown deer hair dyed yellow, spun and trimmed to hopper shape (see model, Irresistible, page 45)
WING: Guard hairs from back of woodchuck (tied slightly spread to imitate grasshopper prior to taking off)
HACKLE: Brown and grizzly mixed

REMARKS: Be sure to trim top of clipped deer hair fairly flush to the shank or the wing fibers will flare upward too severely. The reason for using woodchuck as a flared wing is that it has the proper color breakup (black with white tips), resembling many hoppers. It is also a very high floater.

Adult Stoneflies

THIS TYPE of pattern is not used very much in the East, except possibly at night. Probably its most important application is during the hatch of *Pteronarcys californica,* popularly called the salmon fly hatch on the rivers of the West, especially in Montana, Idaho, and Wyoming.

Many stonefly patterns are similar to some of our hopper flies and, in a pinch, can be interchanged if one is astream without one or the other.

BI-FLY YELLOW
(Plate V)

HOOK: Mustad 79580 (6–12)
THREAD: Black (Flymaster 6/0 or Monocord 3/0 on large sizes)
TAIL: Brown elk hair fibers (gap width in length)

BODY: Yellow floss coated with acetone or lacquered
HACKLE: Light-shade grizzly
WING: Elk hair fibers (tied downwing style over hackle collar to end of tail), topped with four or five strands of white bucktail
HEAD: Black with top half lacquered red

REMARKS: This pattern from Dan Bailey's Fly Shop is also tied with an orange body.

ELK HAIR SALMON FLY

HOOK: Mustad 79580 (4–6)
THREAD: Black (Monocord 3/0)
TAIL: Natural elk hair fibers (gap width in length)
PALMER RIB: Brown hackle palmered through body (clipped short)
BODY: Burnt orange poly yarn or floss
WING: Natural elk hair fibers (to center of tail)
HACKLE: Brown

FLUTTERING GOLDEN STONEFLY
(Plate V)

HOOK: Mustad 3906 (6–8)
THREAD: Yellow (waxed Monocord 3/0)
BODY: Yellow poly yarn twisted into extended body (see model, Fluttering Salmon Fly)

WING: Light elk hair fibers (as long as body), full and slightly flared

ANTENNAE: Eight-pound-test monofilament dyed gold (substitute: gold hackle stem quills)

HACKLE: Dark ginger saddle hackle, full (fifteen turns)

REMARKS: The design of this and the following pattern evolved from a fly tied by Nevin Stephenson, who conceived the idea of crossing the MacIntosh, a salmon dry fly (page 118), and the Sofa Pillow.

FLUTTERING SALMON FLY

HOOK: Mustad 3906 (4–6)

THREAD: Orange (waxed Monocord 3/0)

BODY: Salmon-colored poly yarn twisted into rope and tied as extended body running the length of shank past bend

WING: Dark gray elk hair fibers (as long as the body)

ANTENNAE: Monofilament dyed brown (substitute: stripped hackle stem quills dyed brown)

HACKLE: Brown saddle hackle, full (fifteen to twenty turns)

REMARKS: Tying methods and procedures for both this pattern and the Fluttering Golden Stonefly are identical.

The body of this fly is formed by tying in a single strand of poly yarn near the bend, attaching a pair of hackle pliers, and twisting in one direction. (You'll need at least a two- to three-inch strand for this.) After twisting,

the yarn is folded in two, forming a twisted rope of sorts. The fold should be made so that the poly rope is the same length as the hook shank. The doubled half of the yarn is now secured to the shank in the same area where the single strand of poly was first tied in. Excesses are trimmed away.

The elk hair fibers, which are gathered into a fair-sized clump (almost two wooden matchsticks in diameter), are lashed to the shank where the poly yarn was tied in. The tips of the fibers extend rearward as far as the extended body. The elk hair should be allowed to flare upward and outward just a bit to simulate a fluttering fly. The antennae are now tied in to extend a hook-gap width beyond the eye of the hook.

The fifteen turns of brown saddle hackle cover the portion of elk hair fibers that is lashed to the shank. Hackle size is standard for related hook size—that is, for a size 8 fly, use size 8 hackle.

GOLDEN STONE

HOOK: Mustad 9672 (4–10)

THREAD: Black (Monocord 3/0)

TAIL: Light-shade elk hair fibers (gap width in length)

PALMER RIB: Golden ginger hackle palmered through body

BODY: Yellow poly yarn

WING: Light-shade elk hair fibers, fairly full (to end of tail)

HACKLE: Golden ginger, heavily hackled

Tying Steps for Fluttering Salmon Fly

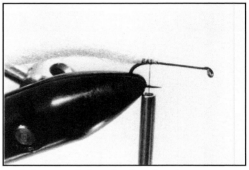

a. Poly yarn tied to shank at bend.

d. A large clump of elk hair fibers being tied to shank over poly yarn.

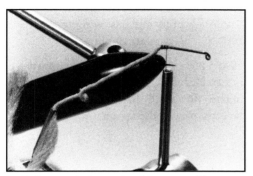

b. Poly yarn being twisted into ropelike structure with hackle pliers.

c. Poly yarn rope has been doubled over and secured to hook shank.

e. Wing is complete and hackle has been tied to be wound as hackle collar, and two pieces of brown monofilament have been tied in to represent the antennae.

f. Hackle collar has been wound and fly is complete.

HENRY'S FORK SALMON FLY
(Plate V)

HOOK: Mustad 9672 (4–10)
THREAD: Orange (waxed Monocord 3/0)
TAIL: Dark (almost black) moose body fibers (gap width in length)
PALMER RIB: Medium to light blue dun hackle fibers palmered over body (trimmed short)
BODY: Light orange poly yarn
WING: Natural tan elk hair fibers, full (to end of tail)
HEAD: Dark (almost black) moose body hair, tied with tips extending beyond eye and then pulled rearward to form bullet-shaped head (reverse Humpy technique). Flared ends of moose fibers form a half skirt around elk hair with fringe or tips extending to a point two-thirds back on the hook shank.

REMARKS: This pattern was tied and submitted by Rob Van Kirk of Henry's Fork Anglers. For further information on forming a bullet-head type of wing, see also Thunder Creek series (page 236).

JUGHEAD
(Plate V)

HOOK: Mustad 9672 (4–6)
THREAD: Orange (Monocord 3/0)
TAIL: Tan elk hair fibers (gap width in length)
PALMER RIB: Brown saddle hackle palm-

ered through body (trimmed to half the size of gap width)

BODY: Orange poly yarn

WING: Tan elk hair fibers, over which red fox squirrel tail fibers, fairly full (both to end of tail)

HEAD: Spun and trimmed antelope hair (see model, Irresistible, page 45, and Dave's Hopper)

REMARKS: This is another imitation of the giant stonefly *Pteronarcys californica*.

K'S BUTT SALMON FLY
(Plate V)

HOOK: Mustad 36620 (2–6)

THREAD: Orange (Flymaster 6/0)

BODY: Butt end of peacock quill stem (this quill is one piece and serves as abdomen, thorax, and head)

RIB OR SEGMENTATION: Size D black thread

TAIL (optional): Two strands of dark gray rubber hackle

LEGS: Six strands of dark gray rubber hackle

WING: Two mallard flank feathers dipped in Plio Bond cement

ANTENNAE: Two strands of dark gray rubber hackle

REMARKS: This pattern, originated by Robert Boyle, was field-tested by Charles Brooks and other anglers in the rivers of Montana and Idaho and reported to be perhaps the most effective adult stonefly imitation they had ever used.

The idea of using a hollow quill for float-ing a fly is not new, yet in this case the size and shape of the quill and the other parts of the pattern come extremely close to imitat-ing the natural. The strands of rubber used for the legs, tail, and antennae create the movement which is so attractive to trout and other fish.

The K's Butt Salmon Fly is not difficult to tie. It is, in fact, more a matter of assembly of parts.

The quill, which forms the abdomen, thorax, and head, is slotted underneath and wedged into the top of the hook shank. It is then painted orange with a Pantone marker and covered with lacquer to seal any open-ings and prevent the entry of water. Two strands of rubber are tied in to form the tail and black size D thread is wound in an open spiral to form the segmentation. Six rubber legs are then affixed at equal distances (three on each side) on the lower sides of the thorax area and two more strands of rubber hackle are tied in to protrude beyond the hook eye to represent the antennae.

For the wing, two fairly large mallard flank feathers are required, because after they have been dipped in Plio Bond head cement they shrink to a somewhat oblong shape. When they are dry, they are affixed to the top of the body, one on top of the other, and extend to the center of the tail.

LITTLE BLACK STONEFLY

HOOK: Mustad 94840 (10–18)

THREAD: Black (Flymaster 6/0)

WING: Dark gray to black hen hackle tips (tied three-quarters spent) (see model, Adams, page 5)

TAIL: Black mink tail guard hair fibers

PALMER RIB: Black hackle palmered through body and past wing to eye

BODY: Black mink dubbing fur

REMARKS: This pattern is constructed in standard dry fly fashion. It is used to imitate the small black stoneflies during the early part of the season.

MacSALMON (Troth)
(Plate V)

HOOK: Mustad 79580 (2–8)

THREAD: Brown (Monocord 3/0)

BODY: Macramé yarn, extending half a shank length past bend

WING: Light cream elk hair fibers extending past the end of the body by half a shank length, tied fairly full and slightly flared

COLLAR: A slightly flared skirt of dyed dark brown deer hair extending just past the center of the hook shank and com-pletely surrounding the body and wing

HEAD: Dyed dark brown deer hair, spun and trimmed to a rounded bullet-head shape (see model, Irresistible, page 45)

REMARKS: This design by Al Troth fea-tures macramé yarn for the body. The yarn is cut to proper size and the point of the hook pushed through one end and out the bottom at a point where the yarn leaves the shank almost at the bend. The end of yarn near the eye is secured with thread while the rear-ward end, extending past the hook shank for half its length, is fused closed with a cigarette lighter flame.

The flared skirt of dark brown deer hair is formed with the first clump of deer hair to be spun for the head. The deer hair tips which surround the shank after the hair has been spun are tied down snugly (but not tightly) with turns of thread wound rearward, thus forming a collar or skirt extending just past the center of the body. The thread is then brought forward again and the rest of the deer hair is spun for the head and later trimmed to shape.

POLAR COMMANDER

HOOK: Mustad 9672 (2–10)
THREAD: Yellow (Monocord 3/0)
TAIL: Two dyed ginger goose biots (tied forked)
BODY: Yellow deer hair, tied lengthwise surrounding hook shank and secured by crisscross windings of thread (diamond-wrapped)
WING: Polar bear hair (or calf tail) (to end of tail)
HACKLE: Brown and grizzly mixed

REMARKS: This pattern by Jay Neve and Don Fox is used primarily as a night fly to imitate the nocturnal *Pteronarcys dorsata,* one of our largest eastern stoneflies.

PTERONARCYS CALIFORNICA ADULT

HOOK: Mustad 9575 (4–8)
THREAD: Orange (Monocord 3/0)

TAIL: Two brown goose biots (tied slightly forked)
PALMER RIB: Dark blue dun hackle palmered through body
BODY: A blend of black, brown, and orange dubbing fur to achieve a dark dirty orange
WING: Dark-shade elk hair fibers set low over body (to end of tail) (matchstick-sized clump)
HACKLE: Dark blue dun, heavily hackled

REG'S LITTLE STONEFLY
(Plate V)

HOOK: Mustad 94833, Partridge L3A (14–16)
THREAD: Tan (Flymaster 6/0)
BODY: Dark-shade hackle stem feather stripped and lacquered (see model, Red Quill, page 26)
WING: Two cream badger hackle tips (tied slightly delta-wing style, extending just past bend)
HACKLE: Dark dun

REMARKS: This pattern is also tied in a lighter shade using pale dun hackle for the collar. It was originated by Reg Baird for the hatches in Nova Scotia.

SOFA PILLOW
(Plate V)

HOOK: Mustad 94831 (6–8)
THREAD: Tan (Flymaster 6/0)
TAIL: Yellow duck wing quill section (or equivalent) (gap width in length)

BODY: Yellow floss
WING: Gray squirrel tail (to end of tail)
HACKLE: Grizzly, wound full

SOFA PILLOW
(Variation)

HOOK: Mustad 94831 (6–8)
THREAD: Tan (Flymaster 6/0)
TAIL: Dyed orange deer or elk hair (gap width in length)
PALMER RIB: Dark ginger hackle palmered through body
BODY: Orange poly yarn
WING: Woodchuck guard hairs or elk hairs
HACKLE: Dark ginger and grizzly mixed, wound full

REMARKS: Another version of this pattern, called the Improved Sofa Pillow, features an elk hair body palmered with brown hackle. The use of floss on the standard Sofa Pillow does not help its buoyancy. That pattern would do well with a body made of spun and trimmed yellow deer hair.

STIMULATOR
(Plate V)

HOOK: Mustad 94831, 79580 (4–16)
THREAD: Fluorescent fire orange (Flymaster 6/0)
TAIL: Natural elk or deer hair fibers (slightly longer than gap width)
PALMER RIB: Brown or furnace hackle palmered through body
BODY: Dubbed Hairtron in yellow, orange,

or olive to suit (substitute: seal fur in same colors)

WING: Elk or deer hair (to center of tail, angling slightly upward)

HEAD: Amber goat with grizzly hackle wound through as hackle collar (substitute: amber seal fur)

REMARKS: This pattern is not only a superb stonefly imitation but doubles as a hopper as well. In the smaller sizes it is used to imitate caddis flies.

SWANN'S STONEFLY
(Plate V)

HOOK: Mustad 94831 (4–12)

THREAD: Black (Flymaster 6/0)

TAIL: Mottled turkey wing quill section (three or four fibers gap width in length)

PALMER RIB: Blue dun hackle palmered through body

BODY: Yellow or orange poly yarn

UNDERWING: Brown elk hair fibers, sparse (to bend)

WING: Two sections (a left and a right) of mottled turkey wing quill (tied flat on top of shank with tips flaring away from each other)

HACKLE: Brown, fairly full and collaring forward one-third of shank

REMARKS: Submitted by Robert Schneider of Berkeley, Missouri. This pattern also doubles as a hopper.

TROTH SALMON FLY

HOOK: Mustad 79580 (4–6)

THREAD: Orange (flat waxed nylon size A)

TAIL: Black moose hair fibers (gap width in length)

RIB: Doubled thread

UNDERBODY: Orange poly in cigar shape with taper forward

BODY: Elk rump fibers dyed orange (Humpy technique)

WING: Brown elk hair fibers (to end of tail), over which a small bunch of dyed fluorescent orange calf tail (fibers as long as elk fibers)

HEAD AND COLLAR: Elk rump hair dyed black; tied as bullet head in reverse Humpy fashion with tips forming skirt around body of fly a third of the distance before the bend (see Henry's Fork Salmon Fly)

Parachute Flies

THE IDEA of tying a dry fly with the hackle collar wound above the hook shank on a horizontal plane has been with us for some time, and it may have been the first attempt in modern times to bring the body of the fly closer to the water and thus present a better silhouette. In the following patterns, you'll see how the dry fly has gone through an evolutionary process—especially in the concepts of thorax, cut wings, and no-hackles—to make it appear more natural to the trout and still keep it floating correctly.

ADAMS PARACHUTE
(Plate V)

HOOK: Mustad 94840 (10–16)
THREAD: Gray (Flymaster 6/0)
WING: A single upright clump of white calf tail fibers
HACKLE: Brown and grizzly mixed
TAIL: Brown and grizzly mixed
BODY: Muskrat dubbing fur
REMARKS: The greatest difficulty with parachute flies lies in the winding of the hackle on a horizontal plane around the base of the wing material. The method I've come to like better than any other involves the winding of two hackles simultaneously.

The clump of calf tail fibers which forms the upright wing should be full enough to withstand the pressure of the winding of hackles around its base. If it is too thin, the fibers will bend and the hackle will slip off as it is being wound. If it is too full, it will create an imbalance and cause the fly to sink too quickly when it is being fished. The correct ratio of fibers in this clump to hook size used will become apparent after you have tied a few flies.

After tying in the clump of calf tail, which is propped vertically erect with thread and the butts stagger-cut toward the bend, prepare two hackle feathers, in this case one brown and one grizzly, as you normally would for a standard dry fly. The size of the hackle on a parachute fly should be slightly larger than what you would normally select for a related hook size. In other words, if you are tying a size 14 parachute fly you can use a size 13, or even 12, hackle.

Place both hackles on the far side of the calf tail clump with the butts pointing toward the bend and the feathers past the hook eye. I find that it is easier to hold them in position with my right thumb and forefinger while I bind the butts down with the bobbin in my left hand. When the hackles have been secured, bring your thread rearward toward the bend.

Tie in the tail of the fly.

Tying the Adams Parachute

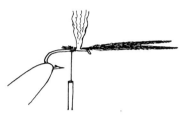

a. Calf tail wing and two hackles have been tied in.

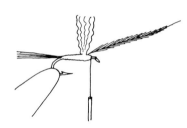

b. Tail and body have been constructed. Note that body is formed to a point in front of wing.

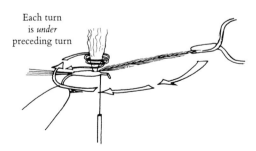

c. Hackles are being wound in a clockwise manner around base of calf tail wing. Note each turn of the hackles is under the preceding turn. Three turns are made.

Each turn is *under* preceding turn

Thread goes over hackle held in pliers and under wound hackle

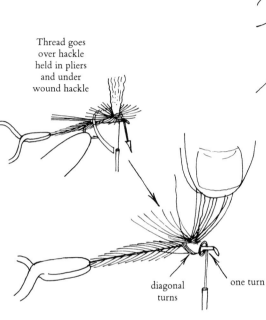

diagonal turns   one turn

d. When securing hackle, note that thread passes *under* the hackle collar but *over* the excess hackle tips in a diagonal movement around body and shank. One final turn of thread is taken around hook shank only in front of body. Collar fibers must be lifted for this last turn.

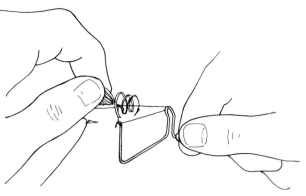

e. While bobbin is cradled in left hand (hidden from view) front fibers of hackle collar are lifted out of the way and a whip-finish knot is applied with a Matarelli whip finisher.

f. Excess thread is cut away, as is excess hackle tip.

Build your body of muskrat dubbing fur and taper it past the upright wing of calf tail. This will form a level platform for the horizontal hackle to be wound next. Leave the thread dangling in front of the clump of calf tail fibers.

Grasp the tips of both hackles between the jaws of your pliers and bring them toward you. Keep the hackles facing flat on a horizontal plane. Bring them all the way around the base of the calf tail clump for two more turns. You will have to switch your hackle pliers from right hand to left hand for each turn you make around the clump so the hackles do not twist. Each turn of hackle is wound under the preceding one.

When you complete the third turn of hackle around the calf tail clump, hold the pliers tautly so that the hackle feathers are pointing rearward beyond the tail of the fly.

Bring your thread diagonally over the hackle feathers directly in back of the wing and back to its starting position. Take two more turns of thread through the same area.

Remove the hackle pliers from the hackle feathers.

Lift the hackle fibers radiating from the front side of the calf tail wing and take one turn of thread around the shank in front of the wing (between the wing clump and the eye of the hook).

The whip-finish knot on a parachute fly is a bit more difficult because the horizontal hackle fibers, pointing beyond the eye of the hook, are in the way. I've devised my own method to accomplish this and with a little practice it becomes fairly easy.

For this operation I use a Matarelli type whip finisher. Spool about three inches of thread from your bobbin. Cradle the bobbin in the palm of your left hand and let your little (pinky) finger hold it there. This will free your thumb, forefinger, and middle finger.

Affix the Matarelli whip finisher to the thread.

With your thumb and first two fingers of your left hand lift the forward-pointing hackles of the hackle collar up and out of the way and with your right hand apply the whip-finish knot.

If you have spooled too much thread from your bobbin, you will not be able to reach the hackle fibers with your thumb and first two fingers. If you have spooled too little thread, you will not have enough room to work the whip finish. Hands come in different sizes. You will be the best judge as to exactly how much thread to spool off.

When the whip-finish knot has been completed, the thread is cut away. Now remove the fly from the vise and cut away the excess hackle tip from underneath the hackle collar.

BLACK GNAT PARACHUTE

HOOK: Mustad 94840 (12–16)
THREAD: Black (Flymaster 6/0)
WING: A single clump of upright calf tail fibers (white)
HACKLE: Black
TAIL: Black hackle fibers
BODY: Black dubbing fur

BLACKTOP
(see Carrottop)

BLUE DUN PARACHUTE

HOOK: Mustad 94840 (12–16)
THREAD: Gray (Flymaster 6/0)
WING: A single upright clump of calf tail fibers (white)
HACKLE: Medium blue dun
TAIL: Medium blue dun hackle fibers
BODY: Muskrat dubbing fur

BROWN DRAKE PARADRAKE
(Plate V)

HOOK: Mustad 94840, 7957B (10–12)
THREAD: Black (Monocord 3/0)
TAIL: Three peccary fibers
WING: Single upright clump of tan elk hair
BODY: Natural tan/brown elk hair fibers as extended body
HACKLE: Grizzly dyed yellow

REMARKS: I received this pattern from Mike Lawson of Henry's Fork Anglers. The design is impressive but required a number of practice sessions on my part to get it right. Once learned, however, it is a fun fly to tie and results in a durable and high-floating imitation. The procedures are as follows.

1. Place a size 10 hook in your vise and cover the shank with thread. Leave the thread hanging near the bend.

2. Select four or five black-tipped peccary fibers and tie them in so that the tips extend a shank length and a half past the bend. (The extra fiber or two are added just in case one or two are accidentally cut during the trimming of excess elk hair.) Cut the excess butts.

3. Bring the thread to a point just forward of the center of the hook shank.

4. Cut a section of fibers from a piece of elk hide. These should be at least one and a half inches long. The exact size of the clump is fairly important. The one I found most suitable contained 71 fibers. Comb out all the fuzz and the shorter hairs and align the tips in a hair stacker.

5. Place the clump of elk hair on top of the hook shank with the tips facing the bend and the butts protruding beyond the eye. (This is the reverse of the normal procedure when tying in a hair wing.) Measure the tip section so that when it is propped up the height will be equal to the hook length.

6. Tie the clump of elk hair to the shank with tight turns of thread. (A drop of head cement on the shank before tying the fibers down helps.) Lift the butt ends of the elk hair out of the way and spiral the thread forward around the shank to a point directly behind the eye.

7. Bring the thread around the butt sections and the hook shank directly behind the eye. Make sure the turns of thread are tight so that the hair cannot slide forward when it is later reversed.

8. Bring the thread in back of the tips of the elk hair. Lift the tips of the elk hair and prop them up with thread. You are forming an upright wing out of a single clump of fibers. You will need extra turns of thread against the base of the wing to help it maintain its vertical posture. Leave the thread hanging directly in back of the wing.

9. Grasp the butt ends protruding beyond the eye and divide them into two equal sec-

tions with your thumbs and forefingers. Bring half the butt-end fibers rearward along the near side of the shank, hold them tautly, and bring thread around them and the hook shank directly in back of the wings. Bring the rest of the butt ends along the far side of the shank and tie them down with the thread directly behind the wings.

10. Wind the thread in an open spiral around the elk hair and the hook shank to the bend and continue in an open spiral around the elk hair only (the peccary fibers by this time will have become lost among the many elk hair fibers) to a point equal to three-quarters of the hook-shank length. At this point take three or four wraps of thread in the same place, then reverse the thread and, going in an open spiral (crisscrossing the thread), wind the thread back to its starting point. Bring the thread directly in front of the wing.

11. Prepare two dyed yellow grizzly hackles and tie them in with the thread on the near side of the wing.

12. Wind the hackles around the base of the wing as described in the Adams Parachute and tie off.

13. Remove the fly from the vise and trim away all the elk hairs beyond the last spiral wrap. Be careful not to cut any of the black-tipped peccary fibers. Leave three divided (forked) peccary fibers for the tail. Place a drop of Super Glue at the point where the peccary fibers emerge from the elk hair to keep the thread windings from unraveling. Lacquer the entire body with Plio Bond or vinyl cement.

Tying Steps for Brown Drake Paradrake

a. Four to five peccary fibers are tied in to extend a shank-and-a-half length beyond bend.

e. Tips of elk hair which will form upright wing clump are now encircled with thread and forced into a vertical position. When wing clump has been secured, thread is brought to a position directly in back of wing.

b. A clump of elk hair fibers is tied in with tips rearward.

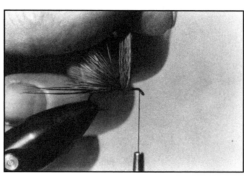

c. Excess butts of elk fibers are lifted vertically while thread is being brought to a position directly before eye.

d. Butt fibers are pulled forward while turns of thread are taken around them and shank directly before hook eye.

f. Half of the elk hair butts are pulled rearward and alongside the shank and are secured at a position just rear of the wing.

g. The other half of the elk hair butts are pulled rearward along the shank on the far side and also secured in the same area.

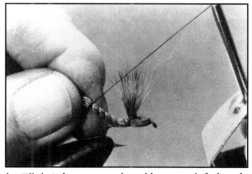

h. Elk hair butts are gathered between left thumb and forefinger and held rearward while thread is wound in an open spiral first around fibers and shank and then around hair fibers only for a full shank length past bend.

i. Thread has been reversed and wound back to starting point in a crisscross manner for a diamond-shaped effect. Two dyed yellow grizzly hackles are now tied in for the parachute collar.

j. Parachute collar has been wound around elk hair wing post.

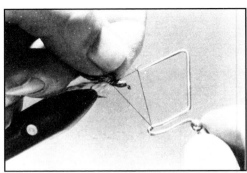

k. Hackle collar is held out of the way while a whip-finish knot is applied with a Matarelli whip finisher.

l. Excess elk hair butts are now being trimmed. Be careful not to cut hidden peccary fibers.

m. Three peccary fibers are left to resemble tail. Drop of Super Glue is being placed on completed Paradrake.

CARROTTOP

HOOK: Mustad 94842 (14–16)
THREAD: Gray or olive (Flymaster 6/0)
WING: A single upright clump of dyed deep orange deer or elk hair fibers
HACKLE: Grizzly
TAIL: Three dark moose body fibers (tied forked)
BODY: Poly fur dubbing in gray or olive or other desired color

REMARKS: Originated by Jack Gartside, who states that this pattern produced well on the Madison, Gallatin, and Beaverkill rivers and was a resounding success on the Avon in England. The parachute hackles on two flies I received from him were sparsely wound.

There is another version of the Carrottop, called the Blacktop, which features a dyed black upright clump of deer or elk hair fibers for the wing and a tan/brown body.

CLUMPER MIDGE
(Plate V)

HOOK: Mustad 94840 (14)
THREAD: Black (Flymaster 6/0)
WING: Black poly yarn tied as an upright clump and spread at the top (like an ice-cream cone); clump tied to center of hook shank
HACKLE: Black
TAIL: Two stiff black moose body fibers (tied forked)
BODY: Black poly yarn

REMARKS: This pattern, originated by Si Upson, represents a midge colony. Upson states: "At certain times on the San Juan River in New Mexico these insects form in colonies or clumps numbering from twenty to fifty midges. During these occurrences the trout take the one-quarter- to one-half-inch clumps with great abandon and *this pattern is a must.*" This phenomenon as reported in Gary Borger's book *Naturals,* occurs when the female Chironomidae (midges) are surrounded by the male of the species, forming clusters or colonies. Of course, this also take place on other streams.

The fly should be tied so that when viewed from above it appears to resemble a black disk.

ELK WING PARACHUTE CADDIS (Rosenbauer)
(Plate V)

HOOK: Mustad 94840 (12–16)
THREAD: Tan (Flymaster 6/0)
RIB: Fine copper wire
BODY: Tan dubbing fur
WING: Tan elk hair fibers (tied slightly spread)
HACKLE: Brown

REMARKS: This pattern, designed by Tom Rosenbauer, can also be tied with a gray body with a blue dun hackle, or it can be tied to imitate the body and leg colors of a number of species of caddis flies. It is used primarily in quiet or slow-moving waters.

After forming the body, tie in a small clump of elk hair fibers for the wing. The butt ends are *not* trimmed at this time. Instead, they are propped to a vertical position to form the post around which the hackle is wound parachute style. When the hackle collar has been secured, trim the post just above the topmost hackle so all that remains is a short stub.

GULPER SPECIAL

HOOK: Mustad 94840 (12–20)
THREAD: Olive (Flymaster 6/0)
WING: White poly yarn (enough to support hackle)
HACKLE: Grizzly
TAIL: Grizzly hackle fibers
BODY: Medium olive dubbing fur

REMARKS: This pattern by Al Troth is also tied in body colors of gray or tan. When winding hackle parachute style around a clump of poly yarn, you may have to hold the yarn upright and taut as you make your first turn of hackle around the base so that the clump does not flip over.

LIGHT CAHILL PARACHUTE

HOOK: Mustad 94840 (10–16)
THREAD: Cream or yellow (Flymaster 6/0)
WING: Upright clump of calf tail fibers (white)
HACKLE: Dark cream
TAIL: Dark cream hackle fibers
BODY: Cream with hint of yellow dubbing fur

Tying a Loop Wing Paradun

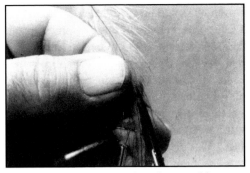

a. Hackle being trimmed to form stubby stem for wing.

b. Trimmed stem forced into loop and being tied to shank.

c. Two dyed light olive grizzly hackles tied to shank on far side of wing.

d. Tail has been tied in and body is being wound forward.

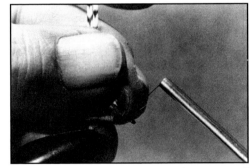

e. Light olive dubbing fur has been wound past looped wing, forming a full thorax. Thread is left in front of wing.

f. Parachute hackle collar has been formed and is being secured with diagonal turns of thread. (For detailed procedure, see Adams Parachute.)

g. Completed Loop Wing Paradun.

LOOP WING
PARADUN, OLIVE
(Plate V)

HOOK: Mustad 94840 (14–16)
THREAD: Olive (Flymaster 6/0)
WING: Trimmed blue dun hackle stem tied
to shank as loop
HACKLE: Grizzly dyed light olive
TAIL: Light blue dun hackle fibers
BODY: Stripped hackle stem quill dyed
light olive (see model, Red Quill, page
26)
THORAX: Light olive dubbing fur

REMARKS: The loop wing is formed by
simply tying one end to the hook shank,
bending the stubby hackle stem into a loop,
and tying in the other end. Sometimes with
this type of pattern two loops are used for
the wing. The idea of using this type of
material for the wing originated with Andre
Puyans.

OLIVE DUN PARACHUTE

HOOK: Mustad 94840 (14–16)
THREAD: Yellow (Flymaster 6/0)
WING: A single clump of upright yellow
poly yarn

HACKLE: Light olive
TAIL: Light olive hackle fibers
BODY: Light olive dubbing fur

REMARKS: Designed by Al Troth.

PALE EVENING
DUN PARACHUTE

HOOK: Mustad 94840 (12–16)
THREAD: Black (Flymaster 6/0)
WING: A single upright clump of white
calf tail
HACKLE: Pale dun
TAIL: Pale dun hackle fibers
BODY: Pale yellow dubbing fur

RIO GRANDE
KING PARACHUTE
(Plate V)

HOOK: Mustad 94840 (12–16)
THREAD: Black (Flymaster 6/0)
WING: A single upright clump of white
calf tail
HACKLE: Brown
TAIL: Golden pheasant tippet fibers
BODY: Black dubbing fur

ROYAL COACHMAN
PARACHUTE

HOOK: Mustad 94840 (12–16)
THREAD: Black (Flymaster 6/0)
WING: A single upright clump of white
calf tail
HACKLE: Dark brown
TAIL: Golden pheasant tippet fibers
BODY: Peacock herl divided by band of
red floss

WESTERN DRAKE
PARADRAKE

HOOK: Mustad 94840 (10–12)
THREAD: Yellow (Monocord 3/0)
BODY: Dyed olive elk hair fibers as ex-
tended body
TAIL: Three peccary fibers
RIB: Yellow Monocord diamond-wrapped
to tail and back
WING: A single upright clump of dyed
dark dun elk hair fibers
HACKLE: Grizzly dyed light olive

REMARKS: Tied in the same manner as
Brown Drake Paradrake. (see page 93)

No-Hackle Flies

A NO-HACKLE or hackleless fly is one that does not have a hackle collar. The term "no-hackle" is generally attributed to Doug Swisher and Carl Richards, who introduced this particular type of pattern to anglers and fly tyers in their now standard *Selective Trout.* Eliminating the hackle on many of the standard dry flies brings the fly flush with the surface of the water and creates a silhouette more closely resembling the natural insect. This is accomplished by constructing the wing and tail in such a manner that the fly still floats.

No-hackle flies can be tied to imitate any number of mayfly patterns, but I have restricted the listing to include only those patterns commonly found in current fly-fishing catalogs. For those who wish to take this type of construction a bit further, I recommend another book by Swisher and Richards, entitled *Tying the Swisher/Richards Flies.*

GRAY/OLIVE NO-HACKLE

HOOK: Mustad 94840 (16–22)
THREAD: Olive (Flymaster 6/0)
TAIL: Medium dun hackle fibers (tied forked) (see model, Brown Drake Spinner, page 57)
BODY: Medium olive dubbing fur
WING: Dark gray duck shoulder (see model, Fan Wing Royal Coachman, page 28)

REMARKS: The dubbed fur body is brought past the wing to the eye of the hook.

GRAY/YELLOW NO-HACKLE
(Plate V)

HOOK: Mustad 94840 (16–20)
THREAD: Gray (Flymaster 6/0)
TAIL: Medium blue dun hackle fibers (tied forked) (see model, Brown Drake Spinner, page 57)
BODY: Pale yellow dubbing fur
WING: Light-shade duck wing quill section

REMARKS: The body should be formed from the bend in a gradually increasing taper to a point one-third before the eye of the hook. The wing is then attached against the front slope of the dubbed fur body so that when thread pressure is brought against the wing it flares outward and slightly upward.

When setting the wing quills, bring them down along the sides of the body so that the

Winging a No-Hackle Pattern

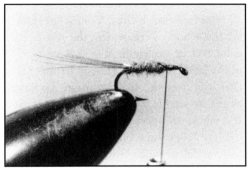

a. Split outrigger type of tail and body have been formed. Note thread is just forward of ledge of dubbed body.

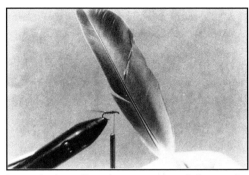

b. A duck quill with a pronounced flare to its leading edge.

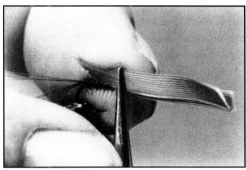

c. A duck quill section on the near side being matched to one on the far side with tweezers. Note that the lower edge of the quills is fairly even with the bottom of the dubbed body.

d. Thread has been brought around quill and body. Because they are tied in just forward of the dubbed body ledge and because of the inherent curve and flare of the feather, the wings swoop outward and slightly upward, while the bottom edge still lends support on the water when the fly is fished.

e. Dubbing fur being added for thorax area of fly.

f. Completed no-hackle fly.

lowest fiber is even with the bottom of the fly. This helps support and float the fly on the water when it is being fished.

When selecting wing quill sections for no-hackle flies, choose those that have a pronounced flare or curve at the tips. This will help achieve the effect desired. Duck wing quills which are relatively straight-edged will not make a proper wing. The no-hackle wing is often referred to as a "sidewinder."

After the wing has been set in place, more dubbing fur is added to the shank between the wing and the eye to achieve a natural full-bodied taper.

SLATE/TAN NO-HACKLE

HOOK: Mustad 94840 (14–20)
THREAD: Brown (Flymaster 6/0)
TAIL: Light brown hackle fibers (tied forked) (see model, Brown Drake Spinner, page 57)
BODY: Tan dubbing fur
WING: Dark gray duck wing quill sections (see model, Gray/Yellow No-Hackle)

SLATE/OLIVE NO-HACKLE
(Plate V)

HOOK: Mustad 94840 (16–20)
THREAD: Olive (Flymaster 6/0)
TAIL: Blue dun hackle fibers (tied forked) (see model, Brown Drake Spinner, page 57)
WING: Dark gray duck wing quill sections (see model, Gray/Yellow No-Hackle)
REMARKS: Perhaps the the most proficient tyer of no-hackle flies is Rene Harrop of St. Anthony, Idaho. Harrop has the touch that produces the most exquisite formation of the no-hackle wing. It almost seems as if the wings are indeed growing right out of the body. For those of you who want a perfect model to work from, they can be had from Harrop himself or the Henry's Fork Anglers.

Thorax Dry Flies

VINCE MARINARO, in *A Modern Dry Fly Code,* may have been the first to expound the use of what has come to be known as the "thorax tie." Most of the fly tyers I've talked to, however, feel that the method he used was too difficult.

Thorax flies today, in their simplest form, employ the basic maneuver of cutting away with a pair of scissors those hackles that prevent the fly from settling down. With these hackles removed, the thorax and body can lie flush with the surface of the water and create the proper silhouette of the natural insect. Why not?

ADAMS THORAX
(Plate V)

HOOK: Mustad 94840, Partridge L3A (10–18)

THREAD: Gray (Flymaster 6/0)
WING: Grizzly hackle tips (see model, Adams, page 5)
TAIL: Brown and grizzly mixed
BODY: Muskrat dubbing fur
HACKLE: Brown and grizzly mixed

REMARKS: The wing on a thorax-style dry fly is positioned slightly forward of the center of the hook shank, so that it is much farther rearward toward the bend than on a standard dry fly. This wing position closer to the hook's center gives the fly a better balance and more closely simulates the sloped-back wings of a natural mayfly.

The tail fibers may or may not be tied in a forked fashion, though this outrigger style helps the fly maintain proper position when being fished. With the Adams, on which two colors of hackle fibers are normally used, it is suggested that only grizzly be employed if the tails are to be tied forked.

The body of thorax flies continues past the wing section and is tapered to its fullest at the thorax area and diminishes as it approaches the eye of the hook.

When the fly has been completed, remove it from the vise and trim most of the hackle from the underside. If you place the fly on the tying table, you will see how it will settle on the surface of the stream when it is being fished.

BLUE WINGED OLIVE THORAX

HOOK: Mustad 94840, Partridge L3A (14–20)
THREAD: Olive (Flymaster 6/0)
WING: Dark blue dun "turkey flat"

Thorax-Style Tying Method

a. Wings are tied to shank just slightly forward of center.

b. Tail and part of body are constructed, then hackles are tied in.

c. Body is now completed, being brought forward to a position just before the eye of the hook.

d. Hackle collar has been wound. Thread is then whip-finished and removed from vise.

e. Hackle is trimmed flush with body on bottom.

f. Front view of a completed Adams Thorax.

TAIL: Medium blue dun hackle fibers (tied forked) (see model, Brown Drake Spinner, page 57)

BODY: Medium olive dubbing fur

HACKLE: Medium blue dun

REMARKS: This pattern is in the style tied and sold by the Orvis Company of Manchester, Vermont. They require their fly tyers to use turkey body feathers. These feathers are triangular or wedge-shaped and squared off at the top. White turkey body feathers are most commonly used since they can be easily dyed to any desirable shade.

For a wing, turkey body feathers, or "flats" as they are called, are placed back to back so that they flare away from each other and are secured to the hook shank in the manner of a hackle tip wing. They can be allowed to retain their fan wing shape or they can be crushed together to form a compact fibered wing somewhat in the manner of a wood duck wing.

John Harder of the Orvis Company feels that this type of wing is much more durable and presents a better silhouette, and the material is readily available. He has a point.

BROWN DRAKE THORAX
(Plate V)

HOOK: Mustad 94840 (8–12)

THREAD: Light brown (Flymaster 6/0)

WING: Medium blue dun turkey flat

TAIL: Brown hackle fibers (tied forked) (see model, Brown Drake Spinner, page 57)

BODY: Yellowish brown dubbing fur

HACKLE: Brown

DARK HENDRICKSON THORAX

HOOK: Mustad 94840, Partridge L3A (12–18)

THREAD: Gray (Flymaster 6/0)

WING: Wood duck flank fibers (see model, Dark Hendrickson, page 15)

TAIL: Medium bronze dun hackle fibers

BODY: Muskrat dubbing fur

HACKLE: Medium bronze dun

GRAY FOX THORAX

HOOK: Mustad 94840, Partridge L3A (12–14)

THREAD: Pale yellow (Flymaster 6/0)

WING: Well-marked mallard breast, tufted

TAIL: Golden ginger hackle fibers (tied forked) (see model, Brown Drake Spinner, page 57)

BODY: Fawn-colored red fox fur

HACKLE: Golden ginger and grizzly mixed

REMARKS: A tufted wing is one in which two fully shaped feathers, such as mallard breast or pheasant breast, have been aligned properly between thumb and forefinger and then crushed so that the fibers bunch together. They are tied in as an upright divided clump like wood duck flank.

GREEN DRAKE THORAX

HOOK: Mustad 94840, Partridge L3A (8–12)

THREAD: Tan (Flymaster 6/0)

WING: Pale brownish olive turkey flat (see model, Blue Winged Olive Thorax)

TAIL: Brown hackle fibers (tied forked) (see model, Brown Drake Spinner, page 57)

BODY: Cream dubbing fur

HACKLE: Light bronze dun and grizzly mixed

HENDRICKSON THORAX

HOOK: Mustad 94840, Partridge L3A (12–16)

THREAD: Gray (Flymaster 6/0)

WING: Medium dun turkey flat (see model, Blue Winged Olive Thorax)

TAIL: Medium dun hackle fibers (tied forked) (see model, Brown Drake Spinner, page 57)

BODY: Urine-burned fox belly fur or pale pink dyed dubbing fur

HACKLE: Medium bronze dun

IRON BLUE DUN THORAX

HOOK: Mustad 94840, Partridge L3A (16–20)

THREAD: Brown (Flymaster 6/0)

WING: Dark dun turkey flat (see model, Blue Winged Olive Thorax)

TAIL: Dark dun hackle fibers (tied forked)

(see model, Brown Drake Spinner, page 57)

BODY: Dyed mahogany dubbing fur

HACKLE: Dark dun

LIGHT CAHILL THORAX

HOOK: Mustad 94840, Partridge L3A (10–20)

THREAD: Yellow or cream (Flymaster 6/0)

WING: Wood duck flank (or lemon wood duck breast, tufted) (see model, Dark Hendrickson, page 15)

TAIL: Dark cream hackle fibers

BODY: Creamy yellow dubbing fur

HACKLE: Dark cream

LIGHT HENDRICKSON THORAX

HOOK: Mustad 94840, Partridge L3A (12–16)

THREAD: Gray (Flymaster 6/0)

WING: Wood duck flank (or lemon wood duck breast, tufted) (see model, Dark Hendrickson, page 15)

TAIL: Medium bronze dun hackle fibers

BODY: Urine-stained fox belly fur (or pale pink dyed dubbing fur)

HACKLE: Medium bronze dun

MARCH BROWN THORAX

HOOK: Mustad 94840, Partridge L3A (12–14)

THREAD: Orange

WING: Well-marked dark lemon wood duck breast, tufted

TAIL: Dark ginger hackle fibers (tied forked) (see model, Brown Drake Spinner, page 57)

BODY: Sandy beige dubbing fur (see model, March Brown, page 22)

HACKLE: Brown and light-cast grizzly mixed

PALE MORNING DUN THORAX

HOOK: Mustad 94840, Partridge L3A (14–20)

THREAD: Pale yellow (Flymaster 6/0)

WING: Light blue dun turkey flats (see model, Blue Winged Olive Thorax)

TAIL: Light blue dun hackle fibers (tied forked) (see model, Brown Drake Spinner, page 57)

BODY: Pale yellow dubbing fur

HACKLE: Light blue dun

QUILL GORDON THORAX
(Fur Body)
(Plate V)

HOOK: Mustad 94840, Partridge L3A (12–14)

THREAD: Gray (Flymaster 6/0)

WING: Dark dun turkey flats (see model, Blue Winged Olive Thorax)

TAIL: Dark dun hackle fibers (tied forked) (see model, Brown Drake Spinner, page 57)

BODY: Tan dubbing fur

HACKLE: Dark dun

REMARKS: This pattern and the Red Quill following are, in their standard or classic forms, always tied with bodies made of a quill material. In fact, they derive their name from the use of these quill materials. The nature of the thorax style of dressing a fly makes it impractical to use quill in that this material cannot be carried forward past the wing area without disrupting its flow or smoothness. When flies such as these are tied with materials other than those associated with them, the name of the pattern should be changed or a notation made, such as Quill Gordon Thorax, Fur Body, or Red Quill Thorax, Fur Body.

It is also possible to have your cake and eat it too by constructing these flies with an abdomen of quill and a thorax made of fur, but in this style, in which the wing is set back almost to the center of the hook shank, the abdomen will appear unnaturally short.

RED QUILL THORAX
(Fur Body)
(Orvis)

HOOK: Mustad 94840, Partridge L3A (12–14)

THREAD: Gray (Flymaster 6/0)

WING: Dark dun turkey flats (see model, Blue Winged Olive Thorax)

TAIL: Bronze dun hackle fibers (tied forked) (see model, Brown Drake Spinner, page 57)

BODY: Reddish-brown (mahogany) dubbing fur
HACKLE: Medium bronze dun

TRICORYTHODES THORAX

HOOK: Mustad 94859 (20–24)

THREAD: Black (Flymaster 6/0)
TAIL: Black hackle fibers (tied forked) (see model, Brown Drake Spinner, page 57)
WING: White turkey flats (see model, Blue Winged Olive Thorax)
BODY: Black dubbing fur
HACKLE: Black

REMARKS: On this small pattern, it is advisable first to tie in the tail, then the wing hackle and body. This procedure assures a bit more working space when tying in these parts. The turkey flat wing, in this case, requires only a very small tip of the turkey flat comprising but a very few fibers.

Cut Wings and Other Concepts

IN THE last few categories of dry flies that have been covered you may have noticed a trend toward the creation of more realism in the imitation of some of our natural mayflies. The parachutes and the thorax patterns have, more or less, taken the standard pattern and constructed it in a different manner with newer procedures. The Compara Duns and the no-hackles, while not necessarily retaining the names of the standards, have tried to duplicate the same insects with still another approach.

In recent years there has been another attempt at realism, primarily concerned with the wing, and, in some cases, the wing and the extension of the body. The cut wing, as it is called, which has been cut from a neck or body feather, usually from a hen chicken, is shaped to resemble the upright wing of a natural mayfly.

The newer cut wings and extended bodies also incorporate some earlier innovations such as the parachute hackle collar and the thorax tie. There have been and always will be new designs and approaches in fly tying, since it is, after all, a creative art. But for every new concept that proves itself and is accepted by the majority of anglers, there are dozens that fail to see the light of day, or if they do, they are as ephemeral as the mayfly after its day in the sun. Consider this: The best-selling flies continue to be the standard or classic types of dry flies, even though, as most of us know, they do not present the proper silhouette as seen through the fish's eye. But they work, and because of that they sell. This is not to imply that some of the newer concepts do not perform well—indeed, some outperform many of the classics. However, many of them have never been given a sporting chance by the angler who, when he has found a successful fly or lure, is reluctant to change. Yes, he may purchase one or two or even a dozen of the newer models, tie one to his leader, and then, if nothing happens after a few casts, change back to his favorite Adams because he knows that the classic pattern has taken fish before and . . . why take the chance?

Following is a representative sampling of some of the more recent innovations on the market today.

IWAMASA DUN (March Brown)

HOOK: Mustad 94840, Partridge L3A (12–16)
THREAD: Tan (Flymaster 6/0)
LEGS: Medium dun hackle fibers
TAIL: Medium dun hackle fibers (tied

forked) (see model, Brown Drake Spinner, page 57)

BODY: Tan dubbing fur or poly

WING: Hungarian partridge (cut or burned to shape)

REMARKS: This pattern by Ken Iwamasa features a cut wing which imitates the natural more realistically and lies rearward along the back of the body, again somewhat like the natural.

There is no hackle collar. Hackle fibers are simply tied to the shank to extend outward from the thorax on a horizontal plane and thus support the fly on the water. The forked tail also adds to this support.

IWAMASA DUN
(Hendrickson)

HOOK: Mustad 94840, Partridge L3A (12–16)

THREAD: Tan (Flymaster 6/0)

LEGS: Light-shade elk hair

TAIL: Medium dun hackle fibers (tied forked) (see model, Brown Drake Spinner, page 57)

RIB: Black thread

BODY: Reddish-brown poly dubbing with reddish-brown elk hair pulled over (Humpy style)

WING: Dark dun hen body feather (cut or burned to shape)

REMARKS: The Iwamasa style of cut wings is featured in Fred Arbona's Streamlife Innovations catalog.

MARCH BROWN
(McCarthy)

HOOK: Mustad 94840, Partridge L3A (12–14)

THREAD: Orange (Flymaster 6/0)

TAIL: Three golden pheasant tail fibers

BODY: Sandy beige dubbing fur as extended body

WING: Mottled tan/brown hen feather (cut to shape of natural insect)

HACKLE: Brown and grizzly mixed

REMARKS: This particular pattern, designed by Dave McCarthy, is perhaps one of the better examples of a cut wing dry fly featuring an extended body. It creates an overall impression of realism while still maintaining a common-sense approach in the use of materials and producing a useful and effective pattern.

Shaping wings and forming an elongated body to resemble a natural mayfly is not a new idea. William E. Blades, author of *Fishing Flies and Fly Tying,* was creating realistic imitations of this type prior to 1950. But the credit for making them popular belongs to Poul Jorgensen, a student of Blades, who greatly improved upon this method by using natural materials with better floating properties.

In the past, various tools and gadgets were manufactured to assist the tyer in the construction of extended bodies. The most ingenious device I have ever used was invented by Ed Thomas, a Connecticut fly tyer. It consists of a wooden scaffold with two holes, approximately four to five inches apart, drilled into the top bar. A string is passed through the holes and a two-ounce lead sinker attached to the end farther from the vise and a pair of Thompson non-skid pliers to the other end. (Thompson non-skid pliers have two rubber surfaces.) The pliers are clamped to the quill, deer hair, thread, or whatever material is used as the core of the extended body, while the weight of the sinker keeps the core material rigid enough so that fur, ribbing, or whatever is called for can be wound. You don't, however, have to go to all the trouble of building a scaffold. I've simplified Thomas's idea using only a rubber band and pliers. In the following photo sequence, you will notice that I have looped the rubber band through a pair of teardrop pliers and attached the other end to another vise, one with a heavy metal base. Any arrangement that gives tension to the material used for the extended body will do.

Though some tyers feel that tying this type of fly is too much trouble, it is actually much less difficult than it appears. Certainly the result, both in appearance and in effectiveness astream, is much more gratifying than more conventional dry flies.

Procedure

1. Place a size 10 hook in your vise and spiral your thread onto the shank from behind the eye to the center.

2. Strip a rooster or saddle hackle feather of its fibers. (Any color will do.) Tie it in at the center of the hook shank with the narrow end pointing beyond the bend. It's a

good idea to apply a drop of head lacquer to the shank and tie the hackle stem down with enough turns of thread so that it does not slip under the tension of the pliers.

3. Attach the hackle pliers to the tip of the hackle stem.

4. Tie in three golden pheasant fibers so that the tips extend past the bend a distance of two shank lengths. (Or use any equivalent fiber having a similar barring, such as the fibers from a ringneck pheasant.)

5. Spiral the thread first around the hook shank, quill stem, and pheasant fibers, then rearward around the quill and pheasant fibers only for half the length of the pheasant fibers.

6. Spin a small amount of dubbing fur onto your thread and wind it around the quill and pheasant fibers, working back to the hook in a natural taper. Continue with the taper around quill, pheasant fibers, and hook shank so that the transition onto the hook shank is smooth and even. Trim all excesses forward.

7. Select two mottled tannish-brown feathers from the back of a hen saddle skin and with a pair of scissors trim each feather close to the center stem. Since one will form the left side of the wing and the other the right, you will have to trim these feathers on alternate sides. Incidentally, while there are no wing cutters on the market which exactly match this shape, those of the Iwamasa brand do come close. Or you can forge your own as Dave McCarthy does.

8. Place the pre-shaped wings on top of the hook shank directly in front of the body with the narrow edge facing forward and the feathers flaring slightly away from each other. If it resembles the wing posture of a newly emerged mayfly dun just beginning to spread its wings, you will have placed them perfectly. If the wings twist or cant when you tie them in, apply a reverse turn of thread to bring them back to proper position. Trim all excesses.

9. In this pattern the turns of hackle forming the collar are in front of the wing. Wind the collar of grizzly and brown and whip-finish.

10. Remove the fly from the vise and trim the excess hackle stem where it emerges from the body. Place a drop of Super Glue at the junction where the body ends and the pheasant tail fibers emerge. The tail fibers should form three distinct tails and if they are positioned properly the glue will help keep them in place.

Tying the March Brown (McCarthy)

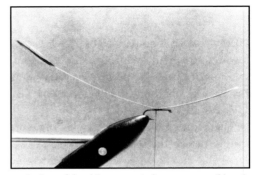

a. Stripped hackle stem tied to center of hook shank.

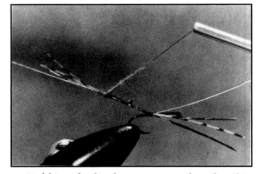

e. Dubbing fur has been spun on thread and is being wound down and around tail fibers and stem to build the extended body.

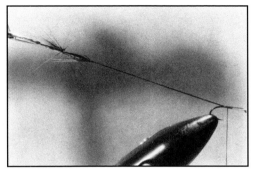

b. Impromptu device of hackle pliers and rubber band to provide tension to stripped quill.

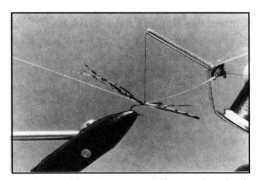

c. Three golden pheasant tail fibers tied to shank at center, the tips extending two shank lengths past bend.

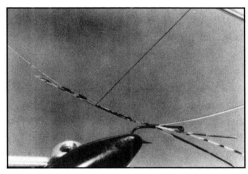

d. Thread has been wound halfway up and around tail fibers and quill.

f. Body has been completed and wings are being attached.

g. Quill stem support being cut away.

h. A drop of Super Glue being applied to juncture of tail and body of completed fly.

Almost two decades ago I was shown a Royal Coachman fly that had been tied by Ralph Graves. It contained all the proper ingredients and they were secured to the shank in the right places. The one major difference was that the fly had been tied inverted—that is, tied upside down on the shank.

Since then I've seen other inverted flies, some published in articles and books, yet I have never noticed a single listing in any of the catalogs. A number of seasons ago, when the no-hackles, the Compara Duns, and the thorax-tied flies became prevalent, I decided to try my own hand at presenting a proper silhouette in fly form to those trout that refused the standard or conventional offering. I made a few slight modifications on the inverted type of pattern and found they were quite successful. If, for example, the standard Adams tie was refused, I switched to a modified inverted Adams of the same size and took the fish. Most of these situations occurred on still or glide water in which the trout had ample time to inspect the offering. I've come to refer to these flies as my silhouette patterns and they can be made using any of the standard recipes listed for most dry flies imitating a mayfly. The following example, using the Adams, should give you the idea.

ADAMS SILHOUETTE

HOOK: Mustad 94842 (10–16)
THREAD: Black or gray (Flymaster 6/0)
TAIL: Woodchuck guard hair fibers
WING: Grizzly hackle tips or cut wing grizzly body feathers

BODY: Muskrat dubbing fur
HACKLE: Brown and grizzly mixed

REMARKS: In creating a pattern to closely imitate the silhouette of a natural, anything that does not contribute to the resemblance should be removed or moved out of the way. Hence the inverted position of the hook. The following steps explain how I dress this type of fly.

1. Place a Mustad 94842 size 12 hook in your vise and spiral the thread onto the shank, terminating near the bend.

2. From a piece of woodchuck skin, cut half a dozen fibers and align the tips. (The reason woodchuck fibers replace the hackle normally used on this pattern is that they can be obtained in a longer length without losing some of the resiliency. You can also use fewer of them.) Tie the woodchuck fibers on top of the hook shank near the bend. The fibers should be half again as long as those normally used for a dry fly, in this case, about a hook shank and a half long. The thread should be wound part of the way down into the bend, forcing the woodchuck fibers downward. Clip the excess butts.

3. Spin a very small amount of dubbing fur onto the thread and wind part of the body from the point where the last windings of thread secure the tail in the bend to a point on the shank just before the bend. If this is not done now, it will be almost impossible to do after the hook has been inverted. Bring your thread to the wing position on the shank.

4. Remove the hook from the vise and reinsert it in an upside-down position. From

Tying Steps for Adams Silhouette

a. Woodchuck guard hair fibers tied to shank and then forced down into bend with wraps of thread.

e. The brown and grizzly hackles have been tied to shank.

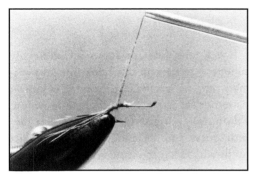

b. The portion of the body for the hook-bend area being formed with dubbed thread.

c. Hook has been inverted and more dubbing applied.

d. Hen grizzly tips have been tied in for the wing.

f. Dubbed body has now been formed to eye of hook.

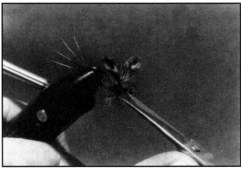

g. Bottom hackles are being trimmed flush to body.

h. Completed Adams Silhouette fly. Note how close body sits to surface while tails extend slightly upward and flared as in natural insect.

this point on you may be sorry you ever heard of this method if you attempt to tie any of these silhouette flies. Since the hook is now above the shank, an area you will be working in, it will grab you now and again until you become accustomed to its position. (In the unlikely event that these patterns ever become popular—as they are with me—and if you are a commercial fly tyer, you may condemn me for ever having brought them to light. They take much longer to tie, you may be wearing Band-Aids or calluses on your left index finger, and you will have to charge your dealer half again as much for your time. The only reason I tie them is for the fishing. Nevertheless, we shall go on.)

5. Select a pair of grizzly hen hackle tips or cut a similar pair with your wing former and tie the wings to the hook shank about one-third in back of the eye. (Or as far back to that point as you can get. On smaller sizes this is difficult since the hook point is much closer to your working fingers.) The wings should be affixed to the shank in a normal upright divided manner.

6. Prepare the two hackles that are to be the collar and tie them in behind the wings. Once they are secured, take an extra turn or two of thread around the hackle stems, forcing the hackle feathers upward and temporarily out of the way as you form the body.

7. Spin the rest of your muskrat dubbing onto the thread and build a tapered body, past the wings and to the eye of the hook.

8. Wind the hackles for your collar. Since you will be winding them through a dubbed body, you'll find they behave much better. When the collar has been formed, whip-finish, cut the thread away, and remove the fly from the vise.

9. Trim all the hackle from the underpart of the body in the same manner you would on a thorax tie. The trimming should be such that when the fly is placed on your tying table (or cast on the water) its posture is just as you want it.

If you have taken the trouble to tie one of these silhouette patterns, you may wish to examine it more closely and count some of its advantages. The tail, which at first you forced down into the bend, is now angling upward somewhat like that of a natural. The hook point, barb, and lower bend no longer form an unnatural protrusion. The fly will ride with its abdomen and thorax on the surface supported partly by the legs, or hackle, coming off the sides, also a bit more natural. The hook that was used, normally an up-eye, which gives more gap clearance when striking a fish, is now a down-eye of sorts, or imitative of the head of a mayfly.

Should you decide to pursue this line of activity, there are only two suggestions I might make for the conversion of some of the standards to silhouettes. First, you should select an equivalent fiber for the tail of the fly that will not only imitate the markings of the natural but will be of appropriate strength and length for the purpose. Second, the construction of a cut wing or the use of hen body material will give you a more prominent silhouette.

I was a bit hesitant about including my silhouette pattern in this book since my primary purpose was to make the tying of known patterns a bit easier for the fly tyer. However, I do have a purpose for this digression into progressive and realistic fly tying and it has to do with what the trout sees and reacts to, and not what we, as anglers, think the trout sees or what its reaction should be. Theories about this have preoccupied fishermen from the time the first artificial fly was dressed on a hook shank and, inevitably, will continue as long as we try to outwit a fish with fur, feather, and tinsel.

If you will take a look at Plate VI, you will see a number of flies from the classics down through the parachutes, thoraxes, no-hackles, and finally the silhouettes just described. The photographs were taken by Dr. Fred Oswalt of Battle Creek, Michigan, using a Hasselblad ELM with a bellows-mounted 120mm Planar. A slant tank was constructed based on the principles described by Ronalds and Hewitt. The lighting was provided by five electronic flash units from above in order to illuminate for the tyer what the fish sees through *its* window, regardless of actual lighting conditions in the stream.

Salmon Dry Flies

ALTHOUGH MOST salmon dry flies are pattern duplicates of standard and classic dry flies and tied in basically the same manner using the same procedures, the amount of material used is greater than that of the conventional-sized (12 to 18) flies. Whereas many trout patterns require only a normal amount of turns for the hackle collar (and in some cases less for a sparse presentation), salmon flies are generally tied over-hackled in order to present as large a puff ball as possible. Hooks used for salmon are, of course, larger than standard trout fare and thus require a few extra turns of hackle just to support them. Yet salmon flies are hackled beyond the necessary flotation point.

Most salmon dry fly patterns incorporate the use of a japanned black upturned eye hook, usually a Mustad 90240 or a Wilson Dry Fly. Of the two, the Wilson has a long shank, which makes it a bit heavier and also forces the fly tyer to adjust his proportions. Which hook to use is a matter of individual preference. I find the Mustad more suitable to my own tastes. This type of hook, whether the Mustad 90240 or the Wilson Dry Fly, is more a matter of tradition than a practical choice. There is no reason you cannot use a larger-sized trout hook, such as the Mustad 94840 or the Partridge L3A, if you so choose. The black up-eye hook does have a grander appearance and it is the one most fly shops will insist upon if you tie for them on a commercial basis.

Though just about any pattern can be dressed as a salmon dry fly, the following are the ones most commonly cataloged and used. This has nothing to do with effectiveness, as those of you who have fished for salmon know.

AUSABLE WULFF
(Plate X)

HOOK: Mustad 90240, Wilson Dry Fly (4–10)

THREAD: Fluorescent fire orange (Flymaster 6/0)

WING: White calf tail (or calf skin) fibers (see model, Ausable Wulff, page 35)

TAIL: Woodchuck tail guard hair fibers

BODY: Buff ginger to dirty orange dubbing fur

HACKLE: Grizzly and brown mixed

REMARKS: Hackle for this pattern, and others in this category, may be a problem, especially in sizes 4 and 6. Most genetically raised rooster necks do not have stiff hackle for hook sizes larger than 10 or 12 since they are primarily raised for the smaller-sized quality hackle. You will have to resort to Indian or Philippine necks or use saddle hackle feathers for these patterns. Saddle hackle is usually quite stiff and in many cases will form the appropriate size hackle collar. However, now and again you will come across saddle hackle feathers that have a tendency to lean or twist. If such is the case, be sure to combine the wayward feather with one or two that have proven to be good winding hackles.

The length of the hackle and the size of the hook to be collared will determine how many hackle feathers you will need. On a size 4 hook I have had to use as many as five or six hackles in order to obtain a full and bushy collar. Then again, in some instances, I've been fortunate enough to locate some very long web-free saddle hackles that required the use of only two hackle feathers for the same size 4 hook.

If you're going to be tying salmon dry flies, it's a good idea to keep your eyes open for some of the larger rooster necks, even the barnyard domestic variety. Usually these necks are less expensive than those with the smaller trout-sized hackles. You will need them primarily in brown, ginger, cream, white, grizzly, and badger. The white necks can, of course, be dyed into duns and other colors, as can some of the lighter variant type necks.

The wings of the Ausable Wulff and similar hair wing patterns are made of calf tail or calf body fibers. Because of the large size of these flies, you will need fibers that are fairly long without being overly scraggly. The fibers from a calf skin are excellent but not always quite long enough.

BADGER BIVISIBLE

HOOK: Mustad 90240 (4–10)
THREAD: Black (Flymaster 6/0)
TAIL: Cream badger hackle fibers
BODY: Closely palmered badger hackle
HACKLE: White

REMARKS: For construction procedures, see Bivisibles (page 8). This pattern calls for the use of badger hackle fibers for the tail. You may not want to use a hackle in which the black portion of the hackle shows beyond the bend, because the black area on all badger (or furnace) hackles is soft and webby. If this black part is tied in at the bend, the tail will be too weak to support the fly properly. Use only the stiffer outer fibers, which will give you a cream tail rather than a two-toned badger effect. The salmon won't mind.

BOMBER
(Plate X)

HOOK: Mustad 79580 (2–4)
THREAD: Gray (flat waxed nylon size A or Monocord size A)
TAIL: Woodchuck guard hair fibers
PALMER RIB: Brown saddle hackle palmered through body
WING: Woodchuck guard hairs slanting forward at a 45-degree angle
BODY: Natural gray deer hair spun and trimmed to cigar shape (see model, Irresistible, page 45)

REMARKS: This pattern looks more like a deer hair bass bug than one of the most popular salmon dry flies used in Canada. Because it takes a bit of time to tie one, I like to tie in two brown saddle hackles for palmering the body. If one should accidentally be clipped while the body is being trimmed, or if one of them breaks because of a weak stem, I still have another with which to try again. The extra hackle is simply cut away if it is not needed after the palmer has been completed.

Bomber wings and tails are also made from deer hair fibers. In many cases, the wing is not divided as in the above pattern but consists of a single clump facing forward. The divided style allows the fly to set up a better balance on the surface of the water, and the woodchuck fibers are much easier to control during the tying process in addition to having a more desirable color marking.

When the spun deer hair body is being trimmed to cigar shape, the bottom part of the fly should receive a little extra pruning, especially under the hook-point area, to allow for a greater gap clearance and surer setting of the hook when striking the fish. In fact, the more knowledgeable angler will insist that the cigar-shaped body extend no farther rearward than the hook point.

Some other Bomber patterns follow.

BLACK AND YELLOW BOMBER

HOOK: Mustad 79580 (2–4)
THREAD: Black (flat waxed nylon size A or Monocord size A)
TAIL: White calf tail
PALMER RIB: Badger saddle hackle
BODY: Rear half, black clipped deer hair; fore half, yellow clipped deer hair
WING: White calf tail (divided clump)

REMARKS: This pattern is a favorite of Angus Cameron, who I don't think has missed a season fishing for salmon in the last forty years or so. "For some reason," he says, "this pattern gets results when other Bomber types fail."

BROWN BOMBER, WHITE TAIL

HOOK: Mustad 79580 (2–4)
THREAD: Gray (flat waxed nylon size A or Monocord size A)
TAIL: White bucktail (or calf tail)
PALMER RIB: Brown saddle hackle
BODY: Natural gray deer hair spun and trimmed to shape
WING: White bucktail (or calf tail)

REMARKS: This pattern is the number one seller for this type of fly on the Miramichi River in New Brunswick. The single clumps of bucktail or calf tail at each end of the hook are sometimes referred to as "tails," as opposed to being a wing and a tail.

WHITE BOMBER, ORANGE HACKLE

Has white tail and wing, clipped white deer body hair, and is palmered with dyed orange saddle hackle. Use white thread.

BROWN BIVISIBLE

HOOK: Mustad 90240, Wilson Dry Fly (4–10)
THREAD: Black (Flymaster 6/0)
TAIL: Brown hackle fibers
BODY: Closely palmered brown hackle
HACKLE: White

REMARKS: For construction methods, see Brown Bivisible (page 8).

BUCK BUG
(Plate X)

HOOK: Mustad 38941 (6–12)
THREAD: Gray (Monocord 3/0 or Flymaster 6/0)
TAIL: A stub of fluorescent orange floss (barely past bend)
PALMER RIB: Brown hackle palmered through body and clipped fairly close to body (a stubby effect)
BODY: Natural gray deer hair spun and trimmed to a slender cigar shape

REMARKS: This pattern is similar to the Bomber except that it does not have wings of a woodchuck or deer hair or tails. It is also tied on smaller hooks.

The Buck Bug, at this time, may be the one most popular salmon dry fly being fished, at least in the northern and eastern Canadian provinces. It is available in a variety of color combinations. The number one producer, according to Jerry Doak, is the Green Buck Bug, also known in New Brunswick as the Green Machine because it takes so many salmon. Though the Buck Bug is considered a dry fly, it is often fished wet. Some angler/tyers will employ a heavy hook, or a double, just to get it under a bit more.

BROWN BUCK BUG
The same as the Buck Bug except that it is tied with a green butt (as opposed to a short tail) or an orange butt, red butt, or green and red butt.

BLACK BUCK BUG

HOOK: Mustad 38941 (6–12)
THREAD: Gray (Monocord 3/0 or Flymaster 6/0)
BUTT: Fluorescent green floss
PALMER RIB: Brown hackle palmered and clipped short
BODY: Dyed black deer hair spun and trimmed

REMARKS: There is also a Black Buck Bug with a dual-colored butt of red and green.

GREEN BUCK BUG

HOOK: Mustad 38941 (6–12)

THREAD: Green (Monocord 3/0 or Fly-master 6/0)

BUTT: Fluorescent green floss

PALMER RIB: Brown hackle palmered and clipped short

BODY: Dyed green spun and trimmed deer hair

REMARKS: The Green Buck Bug is also tied with a dual-colored green and red butt.

WHITE BUCK BUG

HOOK: Mustad 38941 (6–12)

THREAD: White (Monocord 3/0 or Fly-master 6/0)

BUTT: Orange floss

PALMER RIB: Orange hackle palmered and clipped short

BODY: White deer hair spun and trimmed

REMARKS: This pattern is sometimes palmered with dyed red hackle.

RED BUCK BUG

HOOK: Mustad 38941 (6–12)

THREAD: Red (Monocord 3/0 or Fly-master 6/0)

BUTT: Fluorescent red floss

PALMER RIB: Brown hackle palmered and clipped short

BODY: Dyed red deer hair spun and trimmed

FIREFLY

HOOK: Wilson Dry Fly (4–10)

THREAD: Black (Flymaster 6/0)

WING: White calf tail (or calf skin) fibers (see model, Ausable Wulff, page 35)

TAIL: White calf tail fibers

BODY: Fluorescent red/orange wool

HACKLE: Ginger

REMARKS: This pattern is a favorite in the Labrador region.

GRAY WULFF

HOOK: Mustad 90240, Wilson Dry Fly (4–10)

THREAD: Black (Flymaster 6/0)

WING: Natural brown calf tail (see model, Ausable Wulff, page 35)

TAIL: Natural brown calf tail fibers

BODY: Muskrat dubbing fur

HACKLE: Medium blue dun

IRRESISTIBLE

HOOK: Mustad 90240, Wilson Dry Fly (4–10)

THREAD: Gray for spinning body, black for wings and hackle (Flymaster 6/0 or Monocord 3/0)

TAIL: Natural gray deer hair fibers

BODY: Natural gray deer hair spun and trimmed to shape (see model, Irresistible, page 45)

WING: Natural brown/gray deer hair fibers (see model, Irresistible, page 45)

HACKLE: Medium blue dun

REMARKS: This pattern is also tied using woodchuck guard hair fibers for the wing and tail because of the better marking and the ease of tying.

MacINTOSH
(Plate X)

HOOK: Mustad 90240, Wilson Dry Fly (2–8)

THREAD: Black (Flymaster 6/0)

WING (AND TAIL): Red fox squirrel tail fibers (from center of shank to shank length past bend)

HACKLE: Brown saddle hackle heavily wound from center of shank to eye

REMARKS: According to Phillip Turner of Turner's Fly Shop in Aspen, Nova Scotia, the above is the correct dressing for the original MacIntosh fly. He was kind enough to send me two flies tied by Dan MacIntosh, Jr., the son of the late originator. MacIntosh patterns (which are based on the original) are now tied with varying body colors made of floss or wool. (The original version used only the black tying thread for the body.) The wing is sometimes made of gray squirrel tail and the hackle may be blue dun gray. The pattern itself is intended to represent both adult caddis and stoneflies. Here are some of the color variations:

Hackle	Wing	Body Color
Yellow	Gray	Green
Orange	Gray	Green
White	Gray	Maroon
White	Brown	Red
Brown	Brown	Red
White	Brown	Red

RAT-FACED McDOUGAL

HOOK: Mustad 90240, Wilson Dry Fly (4–10)

THREAD: Gray for body, then black for wing and hackle (Flymaster 6/0; Monocord 3/0 for body only)

TAIL: Dark ginger hackle fibers

BODY: Natural gray deer hair spun and trimmed (see model, Irresistible, page 45)

WING: Grizzly hackle tips (see model, Adams, page 5)

HACKLE: Dark ginger

REMARKS: If quality hackle cannot be found to tail this pattern properly and support it, use the guard hair fibers from under the leg of a woodchuck, which come close to the dark ginger color. Other fibers you may use as a substitute are those from the scent gland of white-tailed deer. They are of a fiery brown shade and very stiff.

ROYAL WULFF

HOOK: Mustad 90240, Wilson Dry Fly (4–10)

THREAD: Black (Flymaster 6/0)

WING: White calf tail (or calf skin) fibers (see model, Ausable Wulff, page 35)

TAIL: Brown bucktail or calf tail fibers (see model, Royal Wulff, page 49)

BODY: Peacock herl divided by band of red floss

HACKLE: Dark brown

SKITTERBUG

HOOK: Mustad 94840 (4–10)

THREAD: Gray (Monocord 3/0)

BODY/HACKLE: Natural gray/brown deer hair flared as a skater collar

REMARKS: This pattern is actually a skater fly originated by Dick Stewart. The style of tying is similar to that of the Troth Hair Spider (see page 51) except that it uses two sections of deer hair, one section with the butts facing rearward and the other with the butts forward. When both clumps of deer hair have been flared properly around the shank, they are pushed together to the center of the hook shank and both butt ends are trimmed.

SOLDIER PALMER

HOOK: Mustad 90240 (2–8)

THREAD: Black (Flymaster 6/0)

TAIL: Brown hackle fibers

PALMER RIB: Brown hackle palmered through body

RIB: Fine flat silver tinsel

BODY: Dyed red dubbing fur

HACKLE: A few extra turns of brown hackle for a collar

WHISKERS

HOOK: Mustad 90240 (4–10)

THREAD: Black (Flymaster 6/0)

WING: Natural brown/gray deer hair, fanned 180 degrees above hook shank as in the style of Compara Dun or Haystack patterns (see pages 37 and 41)

TAIL: Gray squirrel tail, long and full

PALMER RIB: Brown hackle palmered through body

BODY: Dyed red dubbing fur

WHITE IRRESISTIBLE

HOOK: Mustad 90240 (4–10)

THREAD: White (Monocord 3/0) for

body, then black (Flymaster 6/0) for wing and hackle

TAIL: White calf tail (or white calf skin) fibers

BODY: White deer hair spun and trimmed to shape (see model, Irresistible, page 45)

WING: White calf tail (or calf skin) fibers (see model, Ausable Wulff, page 35)

HACKLE: Badger

WHITE WULFF

HOOK: Mustad 90240, Wilson Dry Fly (4–10)

THREAD: Black (Flymaster 6/0)

WING: White calf tail (or calf skin) fibers (see model, Ausable Wulff, page 35)

TAIL: White calf tail (or calf skin) fibers

BODY: Cream wool or dubbing fur

HACKLE: White badger

WOODCHUCK WULFF
(Plate X)

HOOK: Mustad 90240 (4–10)

THREAD: Black (Flymaster 6/0)

WING: Woodchuck guard hair fibers (see model, Ausable Wulff, page 35)

TAIL: Woodchuck guard hair fibers

BODY: A blend of fawn tan and rusty orange dubbing fur

HACKLE: Grizzly and brown mixed

Part II

PATTERNS REPRESENTING SUBSURFACE INSECT LIFE

Wet Flies

THERE WAS a time when wet flies comprised the greatest percentage of all fly patterns. Long before dries, nymphs, and the current trend toward realism, the wet fly was king. Just a glance through the color plates of Bergman's *Trout,* which first appeared on the market in the early 1930s, shows how well this type of pattern was once represented.

Today, though still listed in fair number in most catalogs, the old standard wet fly seems to be diminishing in popularity. And that's too bad. For these easy-to-tie patterns still take their share of trout, and have, in fact, saved the day astream more often than not for one or another of our more sophisticated anglers. As one native Catskill fly tyer puts it, "If they're not taking anything else, you can always pick up a few on a wet fly."

More than any other category, wet flies seem to have a consistency of formula in their construction. Though you will find the variable and the offbeat, generally speaking, if you can tie a selected three or four patterns, you can tie most of them. Because of this consistency, few models and few details are required to explain problems that may arise.

The hooks used for most wet flies are the Mustad models 3906 and 3906B. Again, this does not mean they are better, but simply that they have been listed by others so often in the past. You may wish to try equivalent hooks from Partridge or VMC. I've listed some of these in addition to the Mustad under certain patterns. For those of you who like a heavier hook on which to dress your pattern, the Partridge G3A will accommodate you.

Materials for wet flies are as the pattern calls for them. If, however, you find that some other material serves the purpose more efficiently, by all means use it. Wet flies are intended to be fished beneath the surface of the water and anything that will enhance that priority, as long as it does not detract from the pattern in other ways, should be used. Again, if the pattern is changed, the change should be noted in the pattern name.

General Proportions for a Wet Fly
TAIL: Three-quarters wing length (or hook-shank length)
WING: Length of hook shank to bend
HACKLE: Rearward to hook point

ALDER

HOOK: Mustad 3906 (10–16)
THREAD: Black (Flymaster 6/0)
TAG: Fine flat gold tinsel
BODY: Peacock herl
HACKLE: Black hen hackle (see model, Blue Dun)
WING: Speckled turkey wing quill sections (or equivalent) (see model, Blue Dun)

ALEXANDRA

HOOK: Mustad 3906B (10–16)
THREAD: Black (Flymaster 6/0)
TAIL: A small section, or slip, of dyed red duck quill (curving upward)
BODY: Medium or fine flat silver tinsel
HACKLE: Black hen hackle (see model, Blue Dun)
WING: Peacock sword fibers straddled by a strip of dyed red duck quill on each side

REMARKS: The tail is composed of a very thin section of duck quill fibers (depending on hook size, anywhere from three to five fibers). The peacock sword wing requires about half a dozen fibers to be full enough to accommodate the thin strip of red duck quill which straddles it on each side.

BADGER

HOOK: Mustad 3906 (12–16)
THREAD: Black (Flymaster 6/0)

TAIL: Light blue dun hackle fibers
BODY: Fine flat silver tinsel
HACKLE: Badger as folded hackle collar (see model, Blue Dun)
WING: None

BLACK GNAT
(Plate VII)

HOOK: Mustad 3906 (8–16)
THREAD: Black (Flymaster 6/0)
TAIL: None
BODY: Fine black chenille (related to hook size)
HACKLE: Black (see model, Blue Dun)
WING: Slate mallard wing quill sections (see model, Blue Dun)

BLACK PRINCE

HOOK: Mustad 3906 (10–16)
THREAD: Black (Flymaster 6/0)
TAIL: Dyed red hackle fibers
RIB: Fine flat gold tinsel
BODY: Black floss
HACKLE: Black (see model, Blue Dun)
WING: Dyed black mallard wing quill section (see model, Blue Dun)

BLACK QUILL

HOOK: Mustad 3906 (10–16)
THREAD: Black (Flymaster 6/0)
TAIL: Black hackle fibers
BODY: Stripped peacock quill (see model, Quill Gordon, pages 24–6)
HACKLE: Black (see model, Blue Dun)

WING: Mallard wing quill sections (see model, Blue Dun)

BLUE DUN
(Plate VII)

HOOK: Mustad 3906 (10–16)
THREAD: Black (Flymaster 6/0)
TAIL: Medium blue dun hackle fibers
BODY: Muskrat dubbing fur
HACKLE: Medium blue dun
WING: Mallard wing quill sections

REMARKS: This pattern will be our model for the construction of the wing and hackle for many of the flies in this category.

The Hackle

Wet fly hackle collars are formed by tying them in at the tip after they have been folded and then winding them around the shank for two or three turns.

The folding of a hackle is not difficult, but it does require a little practice before the fingers feel comfortable with the newly acquired technique.

1. Select a long rooster hackle feather and grasp the butt end of it between the third and fourth fingers of your left hand.

2. Grasp the tip of the hackle feather between the thumb and forefinger of your right hand. The shiny side of the feather should be facing you.

3. Extend your left thumb and forefinger so they hover over the hackle feather near the tip. Press the pad of your left thumb against the pad of your left forefinger.

4. Pull the hackle feather, held by the tip

between your right thumb and forefinger, through the closed thumb and forefinger of your left hand. You will be moving the feather in an upward direction. Keep a slight pressure against the feather as it passes between the pads of left thumb and forefinger.

When you release the feather, the fibers should have taken a permanent downward set or fold in the area that has passed between the pads of your thumb and forefinger. If it has not, then you did not apply enough pressure. If this is the case, try it one more time, only this time wet the pads of your left thumb and forefinger before pulling the feather through them. (Pretend you're licking a postage stamp.) The wetting of the finger pads creates just a little extra tension and friction, which usually turns the trick. Incidentally, if you apply too much pressure you may strip the hackle fibers from the stem. After a few trial runs, you will be able to judge the proper amount of pressure between thumb and forefinger.

Once you have folded one area of the feather you simply move your left thumb and forefinger farther along the hackle and fold that area.

In the case of hen hackle or other small feathers such as partridge or guinea fowl, the feather may not be long enough to accommodate all the fingers and thumbs involved. In such cases, attach a pair of hackle pliers to the tip of the feather and proceed as before.

Now and again you will find a feather that simply refuses to be folded. This usually occurs with birds other than chickens. Don't be concerned. Tie in the hackle by the tip as you would a folded hackle and stroke the fibers rearward as the turns are being made around the shank.

5. A folded hackle is tied in at the tip at the point where the folded hackles begin. Once the tip section has been securely fastened to the shank with thread, the excess tip is cut away.

6. The hackle is wound around the shank, one turn in front (toward the eye) of the other for two or three turns (enough to simulate a proper hackle collar), and then it is also secured with thread and the excess butt trimmed away. There are no turns of thread around the hackle collar itself, for the fibers should be free to move and pulse in the water when fished. When making the turns around the shank, stroke the fibers rearward to position them properly as each turn is made.

The folded hackle is a basic technique in forming not only wet fly collars but also many of the hackle collars on streamers, nymphs, and salmon flies. It is absolutely essential that this technique be mastered so that it becomes second nature and part of every fly tyer's repertoire. You will, in fact, quite often be referred back to this model pattern when perusing certain patterns in the categories of streamers, nymphs, and salmon flies.

Note: You will, now and then, see reference made to a wet fly collar that is *pulled down*. This simply means that the collar is formed in the standard manner using a folded hackle and that the fibers on top of the shank are stroked or pushed downward and secured in that position with a turn or two of thread. The purpose of this maneuver is to keep the fibers on top of the shank from protruding

Folding a Hackle

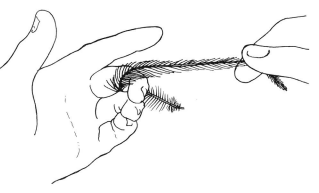

a. Hackle being held between third and fourth fingers of left hand and by its tip between right thumb and forefinger. (Shiny side should face tyer.)

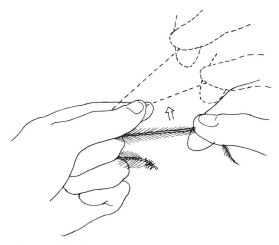

b. Left thumb and forefinger are extended above hackle, which will be pulled upward and to the left between closed thumb and finger pads.

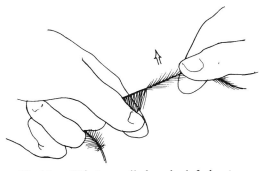

e. Hackle, still being pulled to the left, has just passed between thumb and finger pads. If proper pressure has been applied, the result should be a folded hackle.

h. Excess hackle tip is trimmed away.

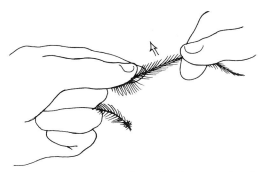

c. Hackle beginning to be pulled between closed thumb and finger pads. Some of the fibers are beginning to fold downward.

f. A properly folded hackle. If entire feather is to be folded, it must be done one section at a time.

i. Hackle is now being wound around hook shank. About three turns are required, depending on hackle density. Each turn is in front (to the right in drawing) of the previous one.

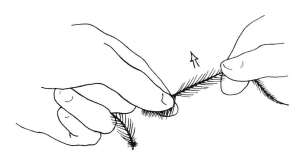

d. Hackle halfway through closed thumb and finger pads. Hackle is now being pulled to the left rather than upward.

g. Hackle is tied to shank between end of body and hook eye. Four to five turns of thread should be taken over tip end to make certain it does not pull out when being wound as a collar.

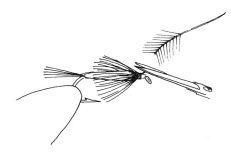

j. Hackle has been tied down with thread and excess butt snipped away. Be sure that when tying over excess butt the thread does not cover any portion of the previously folded and wound hackle collar.

through the wing. It seems to be more an aesthetic than a practical procedure. Frankly, I would just as soon see a fly tyer cut the top fibers as opposed to binding them downward, because it defeats the purpose of the folded hackle—that is, free-moving fibers radiating only from a hackle stem. Nevertheless, this is the manner in which some designers want their patterns tied.

Wet Fly Quill Wings

The secret to properly setting wing quills made from the flight feathers of birds, such as mallard and turkey, is a pair of tweezers. A similar handling of these quills is described in the dry fly section under Black Gnat (pages 9–11). Preparation for the quill wings on a wet fly differs only slightly.

1. Cut a section of quill from a left and a right mallard (or similar duck) flight feather. On a size 12 fly the width of the sections is approximately one-sixteenth of an inch. As a wing the concave sides of both sections of quill will face each other and they should form a slight tenting effect coming off the top sides of the body. The flared curve of the quills should be upward from the bend and, in effect, mirror the curve of the bend.

2. Pick up the section of quill that will form the far side of the wing and hold it in place with the pad of the index finger of your left hand. The lower edge of the quill should be resting just to the side of the top of the body and barely down alongside of it.

3. Using the tweezers, pick up the quill section for the near side and place it against

The Dette Method for Setting a Wet Fly Wing

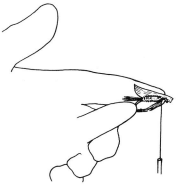

a. Wing quill section that is to form far side of wing is held in place with fingertip.

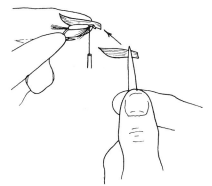

b. Quill section that is to form near side of wing is picked up with a tweezers and placed against far wing section for easy and perfect alignment.

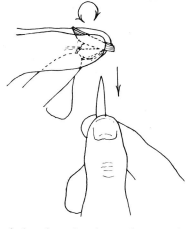

c. Left thumb is placed over finger pad to keep both quills in place while tweezers are removed.

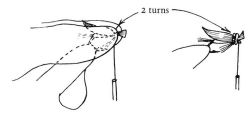

d. Thread is brought through finger and thumb pads and over and around quills and hook shank for two turns to secure wings sections firmly to shank.

e. Excess butts are trimmed and head is whip-finished with thread to complete fly.

the first so that the top, sides, and tip of both feathers are perfectly aligned.

4. Place your thumb pad against both quills and finger pad and remove the tweezers.

5. Bring two turns of thread around the wing quills, securing them to the shank. Snip the excess and finish the fly.

Sometimes you will come across a pattern with a bulky body which forces the wing quill sections outward instead of allowing them to hug and tent neatly. The Black Gnat with its chenille body is such an example. In such cases, trim the forward part of the body very close to the shank and then proceed with the setting of the wings.

BLUE PROFESSOR

HOOK: Mustad 3906, Partridge L2A (10–16)
THREAD: Black (Flymaster 6/0)
TAIL; Dyed red hackle fibers
RIB: Fine flat gold tinsel
BODY: Medium blue floss
HACKLE: Brown partridge (or equivalent), collar pulled down (see model, Blue Dun)
WING: Mallard flank fibers (see model, Dark Cahill)

BLUE QUILL

HOOK: Mustad 94840, Partridge L2A (12–16)
THREAD: Black (Flymaster 6/0)
TAIL: Medium blue dun hackle fibers
RIB (optional): Fine gold wire counter-wound
BODY: Stripped peacock herl (see model, Quill Gordon, pages 24–6)

HACKLE: Medium blue dun (see model, Blue Dun)
WING: Mallard wing quill sections (or equivalent) (see model, Blue Dun)

BLUE WINGED OLIVE

HOOK: Mustad 3906 (14–18)
THREAD: Olive (Flymaster 6/0)
TAIL: Dark dun hackle fibers
BODY: Medium olive with a hint of gray dubbing fur
HACKLE: Dark blue dun (see model, Blue Dun)
WING: Mallard wing quill sections (or equivalent) (see model, Blue Dun)

BROWN BOMBER

HOOK: Mustad 38941 (4–12)
THREAD: Black (Flymaster 6/0)
TAIL: Dyed red hackle fibers
BODY: Black chenille (related to hook size)
HACKLE: Three brown hackle collars dry fly style. One at a point one-third of the hook shank forward of the bend, one at the center of the shank, and one before the head of the fly. This is really like a Woolly Worm (which see) except the hackle is not palmered but spotted at precise places on the shank.

REMARKS: This pattern is featured in the Dan Bailey catalog.

BROWN HACKLE

HOOK: Mustad 3906, Partridge L2A (10–16)
THREAD: Black (Flymaster 6/0)
TAIL: Red floss or wool (tied short, barely past bend)
BODY: Peacock herl
HACKLE: Brown (see model, Blue Dun)
WING: None

BUTCHER

HOOK: Mustad 3906, Partridge L2A (10–16)
THREAD: Black (Flymaster 6/0)
TAIL: Red hackle fibers
RIB: Fine oval silver tinsel
BODY: Medium or fine flat silver tinsel
HACKLE: Black (see model, Blue Dun)
WING: Dark Canada goose wing quill sections (see model, Blue Dun)

CALIFORNIA COACHMAN

HOOK: Mustad 3906 (10–16)
THREAD: Black (Flymaster 6/0)
TAIL: Golden pheasant tippet fibers
BODY: Peacock herl divided by band of yellow floss

HACKLE: Dyed yellow hen hackle (see model, Blue Dun)

WING: White duck wing quill sections (see model, Blue Dun)

CAPTAIN

HOOK: Mustad 3906, Partridge L2A (10–16)
THREAD: Black (Flymaster 6/0)
TAIL: Yellow and red hackle fibers mixed
BODY: Black floss
HACKLE: Brown (see model, Blue Dun)
WING: Mallard wing quill section (or equivalent) (see model, Blue Dun)

CARDINAL

HOOK: Mustad 3906 (12–16)
THREAD: Black (Flymaster 6/0)
TAIL: Dyed fluorescent red hackle fibers
RIB: Fine flat gold tinsel
BODY: Fluorescent red floss
HACKLE: Fluorescent red (see model, Blue Dun)
WING: Dyed fluorescent red duck quill sections (see model, Blue Dun)

CAREY SPECIAL

HOOK: Mustad 3906B (4–12)
THREAD: Black (Flymaster 6/0)
TAIL: Ringneck pheasant breast fibers, tan shade
RIB: Fine flat silver tinsel
BODY: Brown chenille (related to hook size)
HACKLE: Ringneck pheasant flank or

rump feather tied as a folded hackle (see model, Blue Dun); fibers extend as far back as bend

REMARKS: This pattern is sometimes listed as a steelhead fly and is used as a general-purpose pattern mostly in the northwestern states and British Columbia.

CATSKILL

HOOK: Mustad 3906 (10–16)
THREAD: Cream (Flymaster 6/0)
TAIL: Wood duck flank fibers
PALMER RIB: Brown hackle palmered through body, with two extra turns near head for a collar
BODY: Brown floss
WING: Wood duck flank fibers (see model, Dark Cahill)

REMARKS: On a wet fly, the palmer rib hackle is tied in by the tip as a folded hackle (see model, Blue Dun) and then palmered forward in an open spiral. This method keeps the fibers slanting rearward so that the fly submerges more easily yet still pulses and moves to simulate life as in a natural insect.

CLARET GNAT

HOOK: Mustad 3906 (10–14)
THREAD: Black (Flymaster 6/0)
TAIL: None
BODY: Claret chenille
HACKLE: Hen dyed claret (see model, Blue Dun)
WING: Mallard wing quill sections (or equivalent) (see model, Blue Dun)

CLARET QUILL

HOOK: Mustad 3906 (10–16)
THREAD: Black (Flymaster 6/0)
TAIL: Claret hackle fibers
RIB: Stripped peacock quill closely spiraled yet permitting body color to show through
BODY: Claret floss
HACKLE: Claret hen hackle (see model, Blue Dun)
WING: Mallard wing quill sections (or equivalent) (see model, Blue Dun)

COACHMAN
(Plate VII)

HOOK: Mustad 3906, Partridge L2A (10–16)
THREAD: Black (Flymaster 6/0)
TAIL: None
TAG: Fine flat gold tinsel
BODY: Peacock herl
HACKLE: Brown (see model, Blue Dun)
WING: White duck wing quill sections (see model, Blue Dun)

COLONEL FULLER

HOOK: Mustad 3906B (12–16)
THREAD: Black (Flymaster 6/0)
TAIL: Black hackle fibers
RIB: Fine oval gold tinsel
BODY: Flat gold tinsel
HACKLE: Light yellow hackle fibers, beard style
WING: Married sections of yellow, then red, then yellow duck wing quill sections

REMARKS: Thin strips (three fibers each on size 12, two fibers each on smaller sizes) of duck quill section are hinged together (married) to form a unit comprising a duck quill section of alternating yellow, red, and yellow bands. This unit is then treated as a wing using the procedure outlined under the Blue Dun model pattern. You will, of course, have to make two units, one for the left and one for the right side of the wing.

If goose quills are used, only two strips of quill section are needed since their fibers are a bit heavier.

CONNEMARA BLACK

HOOK: Mustad 3906B, Partridge L2A (10–16)
THREAD: Black (Flymaster 6/0)
TAIL: Golden pheasant crest feather (upward curve)
RIB: Fine oval silver tinsel
BODY: Black seal fur (or equivalent)
HACKLE: Black fronted by blue
WING: Bronze mallard flank (see model, Dark Cahill)

REMARKS: The hackle is tied in as a folded hackle (see model, Blue Dun). First two turns of black, clip excess, then two turns of blue.

COWDUNG
(Plate VII)

HOOK: Mustad 3906 (12–16)
THREAD: Black (Flymaster 6/0)
TAG: Flat gold tinsel
BODY: Dark olive floss
HACKLE: Brown (see model, Blue Dun)
WING: Cinnamon turkey wing quill (or equivalent) (see model, Blue Dun)

REMARKS: If cinnamon turkey wing quills cannot be obtained in their natural shading, white duck quills may be dyed or mottled turkey wing quills may be substituted.

DARK CAHILL
(Plate VII)

HOOK: Mustad 3906 (10–16)
THREAD: Black (Flymaster 6/0)
TAIL: Wood duck flank fibers
BODY: Muskrat dubbing fur
HACKLE: Dark ginger (see model, Blue Dun)
WING: Wood duck flank fibers

REMARKS: The wing of this pattern is made from the lemon brown-barred flank feathers of the male wood duck. A section of fibers is snipped from the flank feather (about a half-inch section for a size 12 fly) and the tips are aligned. They are then tied to the hook shank just before the eye of the hook as one unit and allowed to extend slightly past the bend. If natural wood duck is unavailable, mallard flank may be dyed to imitate the proper shade.

DARK HENDRICKSON
(Plate VII)

HOOK: Mustad 3906 (10–16)
THREAD: Black (Flymaster 6/0)
TAIL: Wood duck flank fibers
BODY: Muskrat dubbing fur
HACKLE: Medium bronze dun (see model, Blue Dun)
WING: Wood duck flank fibers (see model, Dark Cahill)

DELAWARE FLYMPH

HOOK: Mustad 3906 (12–16)
THREAD: Orange (Flymaster 6/0)
TAIL: None
RIB: Heavy brown carpet thread
BODY: Tan hare's mask fur (obtained by blending all the colors of the mask) mixed with the reddish-yellow cream of red fox squirrel belly. (Body hairs should be picked out with a dubbing needle after fly is completed to make for a scraggly appearance.)
HACKLE: Dark ginger dry fly hackle tied as a wet fly collar (see model, Blue Dun)

REMARKS: This pattern is intended to be fished in fast or riffle water, hence the stiffer hackle collar. It is also tied with a dropper arrangement using the same pattern as the tail and the dropper fly. According to Dave

Baker, who developed it, this pattern works exceptionally well during the Hendrickson hatch on the Delaware.

DUSTY MILLER

HOOK: Mustad 3906, Partridge L2A (10–16)
THREAD: Black (Flymaster 6/0)
TAIL: Brown hackle fibers
TIP: Fine flat gold tinsel
BODY: Muskrat dubbing fur
HACKLE: Grizzly (see model, Blue Dun)
WING: Mallard wing quill sections (see model, Blue Dun)

FEMALE BEAVERKILL
(Plate VII)

HOOK: Mustad 3906 (10–16)
THREAD: Gray (Flymaster 6/0)
EGG SAC: Fine yellow chenille
TAIL: Mallard flank fibers
BODY: Muskrat dubbing fur
HACKLE: Brown (see model, Blue Dun)
WING: Mallard wing quill sections (see model, Blue Dun)

GINGER QUILL
(Plate VII)

HOOK: Mustad 3906 (10–16)
THREAD: Gray (Flymaster 6/0)
TAIL: Golden ginger hackle fibers
BODY: Stripped peacock quill (see model, Quill Gordon, pages 24–6)
HACKLE: Golden ginger (see model, Blue Dun)

WING: Mallard wing quill sections (see model, Blue Dun)

GOLD-RIBBED HARE'S EAR
(Plate VII)

HOOK: Mustad 3906B, 3906 (8–16)
THREAD: Black (Flymaster 6/0)
TAIL: Brown hackle fibers
RIB: Fine oval gold tinsel
BODY: Coarse and soft fur from hare's ears and mask blended together
WING: Mallard wing quill sections (or equivalent) (see model, Blue Dun)
HACKLE: Plucked-out guard hairs from thorax area

REMARKS: The hair fibers are easily plucked out with a dubbing needle or dubbing teaser to form the legs under the thorax area.

GORDON

HOOK: Mustad 3906 (10–16)
THREAD: Cream (Flymaster 6/0)
TAIL: Wood duck flank fibers
RIB: Fine oval gold tinsel
BODY: Gold floss
HACKLE: Badger (see model, Blue Dun)
WING: Wood duck flank fibers (see model, Dark Cahill)

GOVERNOR

HOOK: Mustad 3906 (10–16)
THREAD: Black
TAIL: None

TIP: Red floss
BODY: Peacock herl
HACKLE: Brown (see model, Blue Dun)
WING: Mottled turkey wing quill sections (or equivalent) (see model, Blue Dun)

GRANNOM

HOOK: Mustad 3906B (10–14)
THREAD: Black
EGG SAC: Green chenille
TAIL: Dyed olive hackle fibers
BODY: Dark brown wool or fur
HACKLE: Brown (see model, Blue Dun)
WING: Mottled turkey wing quill sections (or equivalent) (see model, Blue Dun)

GRAY HACKLE, PEACOCK

HOOK: Mustad 3906 (10–14)
THREAD: Black (Flymaster 6/0)
TAIL: Red hackle fibers
BODY: Peacock herl
HACKLE: Grizzly (see model, Blue Dun)
WING: None

GREENWELL'S GLORY

HOOK: Mustad 3906, Partridge L2A (10–16)
THREAD: Black (Flymaster 6/0)
TAIL: Golden ginger hackle fibers
RIB: Fine oval gold tinsel
BODY: Medium olive floss
HACKLE: Golden ginger (see model, Blue Dun)
WING: Mallard wing quill sections (or equivalent) (see model, Blue Dun)

GRIZZLY KING

HOOK: Mustad 3906B (10–14)
THREAD: Black (Flymaster 6/0)
TAIL: Dyed red duck or goose quill section (see model, Alexandra)
RIB: Fine flat gold tinsel
BODY: Bright green floss
HACKLE: Grizzly (see model, Blue Dun)
WING: Mallard flank fibers (see model, Dark Cahill)

GROUSE AND CLARET

HOOK: Mustad 3906, Partridge L2A (10–16)
THREAD: Black (Flymaster 6/0)
TAIL: Golden pheasant tippet fibers
BODY: Claret wool
HACKLE: Claret (see model, Blue Dun)
WING: Grouse hackle (see model, Dark Cahill)

HARDY'S FAVORITE

HOOK: Mustad 3906, Partridge L2A (10–16)
THREAD: Black (Flymaster 6/0)
TAIL: Bronze mallard fibers
RIB: Silver wire
BODY: Brown wool
HACKLE: Brown partridge (see model, Blue Dun)
WING: Brown partridge (see model, Blue Dun)

REMARKS: Sometimes it is difficult to find partridge hackles small enough to form the correct-sized hackle collar. In such cases, simply tie in the partridge fibers beard style.

IRON BLUE DUN

HOOK: Mustad 3906 (10–16)
THREAD: Black (Flymaster 6/0)
TAIL: Cock Y Bondhu hackle fibers
TAG: Red floss
BODY: Muskrat dubbing fur
HACKLE: Cock Y Bondhu hen (see model, Blue Dun)
WING: Dark mallard wing quill sections (or equivalent) (see model, Blue Dun)

KING OF WATERS

HOOK: Mustad 3906 (10–16)
THREAD: Black
TIP: Fine flat silver tinsel
TAIL: Mallard flank fibers
PALMER RIB: Brown hackle palmered through body as a folded hackle (see model, Blue Dun)
BODY: Red floss
WING: Mallard flank fibers (see model, Dark Cahill)

LEADWING COACHMAN
(Plate VII)

HOOK: Mustad 3906 (6–16)
THREAD: Black (Flymaster 6/0)
TIP (optional): Fine flat gold tinsel
TAIL: None
BODY: Peacock herl
HACKLE: Brown (see model, Blue Dun)
WING: Mallard wing quill sections (or equivalent) (see model, Blue Dun)

REMARKS: This pattern, along with the Gold-Ribbed Hare's Ear, is perhaps one of the most effective of all wet fly patterns. It does not represent a spent submerged mayfly so much as an egg-laying caddis returning to the surface.

LIGHT CAHILL
(Plate VII)

HOOK: Mustad 3906 (10–16)
THREAD: Yellow (Flymaster 6/0)
TAIL: Wood duck flank fibers
BODY: Creamy yellow dubbing fur
HACKLE: Dark cream (see model, Blue Dun)
WING: Wood duck flank fibers (see model, Dark Cahill)

LIGHT HENDRICKSON
(Plate VII)

HOOK: Mustad 3906 (12–16)
THREAD: Gray (Flymaster 6/0)
TAIL: Wood duck flank fibers
BODY: Fawn-colored fox fur dubbing

HACKLE: Medium bronze dun (see model, Blue Dun)

WING: Wood duck flank fibers (see model, Dark Cahill)

LITTLE MARRYAT

HOOK: Mustad 3906, Partridge L2A (12–16)
THREAD: White (Flymaster 6/0)
TAIL: Cream ginger hackle fibers
BODY: Creamy yellow dubbing fur
HACKLE: Cream ginger (see model, Blue Dun)
WING: Light-shade mallard wing quill section (or equivalent) (see model, Blue Dun)

MALLARD AND CLARET

HOOK: Mustad 3906, Partridge L2A (10–16)
THREAD: Black (Flymaster 6/0)
TAIL: Golden pheasant tippet fibers
RIB: Gold wire
BODY: Claret wool
HACKLE: Brown (see model, Blue Dun)
WING: Bronze mallard fibers (see model, Dark Cahill)

MALLARD QUILL

HOOK: Mustad 3906 (10–16)
THREAD: Black (Flymaster 6/0)
TAIL: Bronze mallard flank fibers
BODY: Stripped peacock quill (see model, Quill Gordon, pages 24–6)
HACKLE: Dark brown (see model, Blue Dun)

WING: Bronze mallard flank fibers (see model, Dark Cahill)

MARCH BROWN
(Plate VII)

HOOK: Mustad 3906B (10–14)
THREAD: Brown (Flymaster 6/0)
TAIL: Wood duck flank fibers
RIB: Yellow cotton thread
BODY: Hare's mask dubbing fur
HACKLE: Grouse or wood duck flank, as beard
WING: Speckled turkey wing quill sections (or equivalent) (see model, Blue Dun)

MARCH BROWN SPIDER

HOOK: Mustad 3906 (10–16)
THREAD: Orange (Flymaster 6/0)
RIB: Fine oval gold tinsel
BODY: Hare's mask dubbing fur
HACKLE: Brown partridge (to bend) (see model, Blue Dun)

McGINTY

HOOK: Mustad 3906B, Partridge L2A (10–14)

THREAD: Black (Flymaster 6/0)
TAIL: Barred teal fibers over red hackle fibers
BODY: Alternate bands of black and yellow chenille
HACKLE: Brown (see model, Blue Dun)
WING: McGinty feather from drake mallard (a blue secondary feather with a white tip) (see model, Blue Dun)

REMARKS: The black and yellow chenille body is formed by winding both colors simultaneously. Use fine or extra-fine chenille, depending on hook size.

MONTREAL

HOOK: Mustad 3906 (10–16)
THREAD: Black (Flymaster 6/0)
TAIL: Dyed claret hackle fibers
RIB: Fine flat gold tinsel
BODY: Claret floss
HACKLE: Dyed claret (see model, Blue Dun)
WING: Speckled hen or turkey wing quill sections (see model, Blue Dun)

MORMON GIRL

HOOK: Mustad 3906 (10–16)
THREAD: Gray (Flymaster 6/0)

TAG: Red floss
PALMER RIB: Grizzly as a folded hackle palmered through body (see model, Blue Dun)
BODY: Yellow floss
WING: Mallard flank fibers (see model, Dark Cahill)

ORANGE FISH HAWK

HOOK: Mustad 3906 (10–16)
THREAD: Black (Flymaster 6/0)
TAIL: None
TAG: Flat gold tinsel
RIB: Fine flat gold tinsel
BODY: Orange floss
HACKLE: Light cream badger
WING: None

PALE EVENING DUN
(Plate VII)

HOOK: Mustad 3906 (14–18)
THREAD: Pale yellow (Flymaster 6/0)
TAIL: Light dun hackle fibers
BODY: Pale yellow dubbing fur
HACKLE: Pale dun (see model, Blue Dun)
WING: Light gray mallard wing quill sections (or equivalent) (see model, Blue Dun)

PARMACHENE BELLE

HOOK: Mustad 3906, Partridge L2A (10–16)
THREAD: Black (Flymaster 6/0)
TAIL: Red and white hackle fibers mixed
RIB: Fine flat gold tinsel
BODY: Yellow floss

HACKLE: Red and white mixed (see model, Blue Dun)
WING: Married sections of white, then red, then white duck quills (see model, Colonel Fuller)

REMARKS: The hackle should be wound as a double-folded hackle—that is, one feather inside the other. Two turns of the double-folded hackle are enough to form the collar.

PARSON

HOOK: Mustad 3906, Partridge L2A (10–16)
THREAD: Black (Flymaster 6/0)
TIP: Orange floss
TAIL: Golden pheasant crest feather (upward curve)
RIB: Fine flat silver tinsel
PALMER RIB: Black hackle palmered through body with two extra turns near collar area (see model, Blue Dun)
BODY: Gray wool
WING: Light brown mottled turkey wing quill sections (or equivalent) (see model, Blue Dun)

PARTRIDGE AND GREEN

HOOK: Mustad 3906 (10–16)
THREAD: Black (Flymaster 6/0)
BODY: Green floss
HACKLE: Gray partridge (see model, Blue Dun) (to bend)

REMARKS: This and the three following easy-to-tie patterns are part of a group known as soft-hackled flies which are of English origin. This very effective type of pattern was reintroduced to anglers here by Sylvester Nemes in his *The Soft-Hackled Fly*.

PARTRIDGE AND HARE'S EAR

HOOK: Mustad 3906 (10–16)
THREAD: Black (Flymaster 6/0)
BODY: Orange, green, or yellow floss
THORAX: Hare's ear dubbing fur
HACKLE: Brown partridge (see model, Blue Dun)

REMARKS: The thorax should be picked out with a dubbing needle and the coarse guard hairs made to resemble legs.

PARTRIDGE AND ORANGE

HOOK: Mustad 3906 (10–16)
THREAD: Black (Flymaster 6/0)
BODY: Orange floss
HACKLE: Brown partridge (see model, Blue Dun)

PARTRIDGE AND YELLOW

HOOK: Mustad 3906 (10–16)
THREAD: Black (Flymaster 6/0)
BODY: Yellow floss
HACKLE: Brown partridge (see model, Blue Dun)

PETER ROSS (or PETE ROSS)

HOOK: Mustad 3906B (10–14)
THREAD: Black (Flymaster 6/0)
TAIL: Golden pheasant tippet fibers
BODY AND RIB: Rear half, flat silver tinsel; fore half, red floss ribbed with fine oval silver tinsel
HACKLE: Black hackle fibers as beard
WING: Mallard flank fibers (see model, Dark Cahill)

REMARKS: The wing of this pattern is sometimes made of teal flank and the fore half of the body of dyed red seal fur.

PHEASANT TAIL

HOOK: Mustad 3906, Partridge L2A (10–16)
THREAD: Brown (Flymaster 6/0)
TAIL: Three fibers from the center tail of a male ringneck pheasant
RIB: Fine copper wire
BODY: Fibers from the center tail of a male ringneck pheasant
HACKLE: Brown partridge (see model, Blue Dun)

REMARKS: The body may be formed by clamping both copper wire and pheasant fibers between the jaws of a hackle pliers and twisting them into a rope before winding along the shank to form the body.

PICKET PIN

HOOK: Mustad 9672 (8–12)
THREAD: Black (Flymaster 6/0)

TAIL: Brown hackle fibers
PALMER RIB: Brown hackle palmered through body as folded hackle (see model, Blue Dun)
BODY: Peacock herl wound full (use herl with long flues)
WING: Gray squirrel tail (to end of tail)
HEAD: Peacock herl wound full to form head

REMARKS: This pattern is nearly always listed in the wet fly section of books and catalogs. Its structure, however, indicates that it can easily be fished as a streamer fly, or if made with a more supportive material for the body, could also be used as an adult stonefly, an adult caddis fly, or even a hopper imitation.

PINK LADY

HOOK: Mustad 3906 (10–16)
THREAD: Gray (Flymaster 6/0)
TAIL: Golden pheasant tippet fibers
RIB: Fine flat gold tinsel
BODY: Pink floss
HACKLE: Golden ginger (see model, Blue Dun)
WING: Mallard wing quill sections (or equivalent) (see model, Blue Dun)

PROFESSOR

HOOK: Mustad 3906 (10–16)
THREAD: Black (Flymaster 6/0)
TAIL: Dyed red hackle fibers
RIB: Fine flat gold tinsel
BODY: Yellow floss

HACKLE: Brown partridge (see model, Blue Dun)
WING: Mallard flank fibers (see model, Dark Cahill)

QUEEN OF WATERS

HOOK: Mustad 3906 (10–16)
THREAD: Cream (Flymaster 6/0)
TAIL: Mallard flank fibers
RIB: Fine flat gold tinsel
PALMER RIB: Golden ginger palmered through body as a folded hackle (see model, Blue Dun) with two extra turns for collar area
BODY: Orange floss
WING: Mallard flank fibers (see model, Dark Cahill)

QUILL GORDON
(Plate VII)

HOOK: Mustad 3906 (10–14)
THREAD: Black (Flymaster 6/0)
TAIL: Wood duck flank fibers
BODY: Stripped peacock herl (see model, Quill Gordon, pages 24–6)
HACKLE: Medium to dark blue dun (see model, Blue Dun)
WING: Wood duck flank fibers (see model, Dark Cahill)

REMARKS: Sometimes the black tying thread will show through a light-shaded or similar stripped quill. In this case, use a yellow thread until the body has been formed.

RIO GRANDE KING

HOOK: Mustad 3906 (10–16)
THREAD: Black (Flymaster 6/0)
TIP: Fine flat gold tinsel
BODY: Black chenille (related to hook size)
HACKLE: Brown (see model, Blue Dun)
WING: White duck wing quill sections (see model, Blue Dun)

RIO GRANDE KING HAIR WING TRUDE

HOOK: Mustad 3906B (8–12)
THREAD: Black (Flymaster 6/0)
TAIL: Golden pheasant tippet fibers
BODY: Black chenille (related to hook size)
HACKLE: Brown (pulled down) (see model, Blue Dun)
WING: White calf tail fibers

ROYAL COACHMAN
(Plate VII)

HOOK: Mustad 3906B (10–16)
THREAD: Black (Flymaster 6/0)
TAIL: Golden pheasant tippet fibers
BODY: Peacock herl divided by band of red floss
HACKLE: Dark brown (see model, Blue Dun)
WING: White duck wing quill sections (see model, Blue Dun)

RUBE WOOD

HOOK: Mustad 3906 (10–16)
THREAD: Cream (Flymaster 6/0)
TAIL: Teal flank fibers
BODY: White dubbing fur
HACKLE: Brown (see model, Blue Dun)
WING: Mallard flank fibers (see model, Dark Cahill)

SALLY

HOOK: Mustad 3906 (12–16)
THREAD: Black (Flymaster 6/0)
TAIL: Three peacock sword fibers
BODY: Peacock herl
HACKLE: Brown (see model, Blue Dun)
WING: One section of teal fibers (tied flat over top)

SCARLET IBIS

HOOK: Mustad 3906, Partridge L2A (10–16)
THREAD: Black (Flymaster 6/0)
TAIL: A slip of dyed red duck quill (see model, Alexandra)
RIB: Fine oval gold tinsel
BODY: Bright red floss
HACKLE: Bright red (see model, Blue Dun)
WING: Bright red duck wing quill sections (see model, Blue Dun)

REMARKS: When this pattern first came on the market many law changes ago, the red feathers from the ibis were used. It is strange that this all-red pattern—which does not imi-tate any of our natural aquatic insects—has persisted to find its way into some of our catalogs today.

SILVER PRINCE

HOOK: Mustad 3906 (10–16)
THREAD: Black (Flymaster 6/0)
TAIL: Three strands of peacock herl (cut short, gap width in length)
RIB: Fine oval silver tinsel
UNDERBODY: White floss to shape body
BODY: Flat silver tinsel in connecting spirals
HACKLE: Black (see model, Blue Dun)
WING: Bronze mallard fibers (see model, Dark Cahill)

SPITFIRE

HOOK: Mustad 3906B (8–14)
THREAD: Black (Flymaster 6/0)
TAIL: A slip of red duck quill (see model, Alexandra)
PALMER RIB: Brown hackle palmered through body as folded hackle (see model, Blue Dun)
BODY: Black chenille (related to hook size)
HACKLE: Guinea hen as collar (see model, Blue Dun)
WING: None

REMARKS: Originated by Don Gapen.

STARLING AND HERL

HOOK: Mustad 3906, Partridge L2A (10–16)
THREAD: Black (Flymaster 6/0)
BODY: Peacock herl
HACKLE: Covert feather from starling wing (see model, Blue Dun)

REMARKS: For the hackle collar, there are also some body feathers on the starling which work very nicely.

SULFUR DUN

HOOK: Mustad 3906 (12–18)
THREAD: Yellow (Flymaster 6/0)
TAIL: Dark cream hackle fibers
BODY: Pale yellow dubbing fur
HACKLE: Dark cream (see model, Blue Dun)
WING: Pale gray mallard wing quill sections (or equivalent) (see model, Blue Dun)

TEAL AND BLUE

HOOK: Mustad 3906, Partridge L2A (10–16)
THREAD: Black (Flymaster 6/0)
TAIL: Golden pheasant tippet fibers
RIB: Gold wire
BODY: Blue floss
HACKLE: Black (see model, Blue Dun)
WING: Teal flank fibers (see model, Dark Cahill)

TEAL AND RED

HOOK: Mustad 3906, Partridge L2A (10–16)
THREAD: Black
TAIL: Golden pheasant tippet fibers
RIB: Gold wire
BODY: Red floss
HACKLE: Olive (see model, Blue Dun)
WING: Teal flank fibers (see model, Dark Cahill)

TROUT FIN

HOOK: Mustad 3906 (10–16)
THREAD: Black (Flymaster 6/0)
TAIL: Red duck quill strip (see model, Alexandra)
BODY: Flat silver tinsel
HACKLE: Badger (see model, Blue Dun)
WING: Duck quill, married sections of red, black, and white (white forms the top portion of the wing) (see model, Colonel Fuller)

REMARKS: This pattern is also tied as a streamer fly. Like the Parmachene Belle and other brightly colored flies, it is used primarily for brook trout.

TROUT FIN
(Variation)

HOOK: Mustad 3906 (10–16)
THREAD: Black (Flymaster 6/0)

TAIL: None
PALMER RIB: Dark ginger hackle palmered through body as a folded hackle (see model, Blue Dun)
BODY: Orange wool
HACKLE: Red and black mixed (see model, Blue Dun); use a double-folded hackle
WING: White duck wing quill sections (see model, Blue Dun)

TUPS INDISPENSABLE

HOOK: Mustad 3906, Partridge L2A (10–16)
THREAD: Black (Flymaster 6/0)
TAIL: Blue dun hen hackle fibers, sparse
BODY: Yellow floss
THORAX: Pale pink dubbing fur
HACKLE: Blue dun hen (see model, Blue Dun)

WESTERN BEE

HOOK: Mustad 3906 (10–14)
THREAD: Black (Flymaster 6/0)
TAIL: None
TAG: Flat gold tinsel

BODY: Alternate bands of yellow and black chenille (see model, McGinty)
HACKLE: Golden ginger (see model, Blue Dun)
WING: Mallard wing quill sections (or equivalent) (see model, Blue Dun)

WHIRLING BLUE DUN

HOOK: Mustad 3906 (10–16)
THREAD: Black (Flymaster 6/0)
TAIL: Blue dun hackle fibers
RIB: Fine flat gold tinsel
BODY: Muskrat dubbing fur
HACKLE: Medium blue dun (see model, Blue Dun)
WING: Slate gray mallard wing quill sections (or equivalent) (see model, Blue Dun)

WHITE MILLER

HOOK: Mustad 3906, Partridge L2A (10–16)
THREAD: White (Flymaster 6/0)
TAIL: None
RIB: Fine flat silver tinsel
BODY: White floss
HACKLE: White hen hackle (see model, Blue Dun)
WING: White duck wing quill sections (see model, Blue Dun)

WHITE MOTH

HOOK: Mustad 3906 (10–18)
THREAD: White (Flymaster 6/0)

TAIL: None
TAG: Orange floss
BODY: White chenille
HACKLE: White hen hackle (see model, Blue Dun)
WING: White duck wing quill sections (see model, Blue Dun)

WICKHAM'S FANCY

HOOK: Mustad 3906, Partridge L2A (10–16)
THREAD: Black (Flymaster 6/0)
TAIL: Golden ginger hackle fibers
RIB: Gold wire
PALMER RIB: Golden ginger palmered through body as a folded hackle (see model, Blue Dun)
BODY: Flat gold tinsel
WING: Mallard wing quill sections (or equivalent) (see model, Blue Dun)

WOOLLY WORM, BLACK

HOOK: Mustad 38941 (6–12)
THREAD: Black
TAIL: Red hackle fibers (gap width in length)
PALMER RIB: Grizzly hackle palmered through body
RIB: Flat silver tinsel (related to hook size)
BODY: Black chenille (related to hook size)

REMARKS: The palmer hackle of Woolly Worms is generally wound so that it stands erect as in a dry fly collar. I find that if you tie it in by the tip (do not fold the hackle)

and wind it through the chenille by forcing the shiny side of the hackle against the hook shank, all the fibers pop erect as the turns are being made.

WOOLLY WORM, BROWN

HOOK: Mustad 38941 (6–12)
THREAD: Black (Flymaster 6/0)
TAIL: Red hackle fibers
PALMER RIB: Grizzly hackle palmered through body
BODY: Medium brown chenille (related to hook size)

WOOLLY WORM, OLIVE

HOOK: Mustad 38941 (6–12)
THREAD: Black (Flymaster 6/0)
TAIL: Red hackle fibers
PALMER RIB: Grizzly hackle palmered through body
BODY: Olive chenille (related to hook size)

WOOLLY WORM, YELLOW

HOOK: Mustad 38941 (6–12)
THREAD: Black (Flymaster 6/0)
TAIL: Red hackle fibers
PALMER RIB: Grizzly hackle palmered through body
BODY: Yellow chenille (related to hook size)

REMARKS: Woolly Worms can, of course,

be made of various body colors and hackle combinations. They can also be tied with an underbody of lead wire so they can be fished deep if desired.

YELLOW MAY

HOOK: Mustad 3906 (12–16)
THREAD: White (Flymaster 6/0)
TAIL: Dyed yellow mallard flank fibers
RIB: Fine flat gold tinsel
BODY: Yellow floss
HACKLE: Brown

WING: Dyed yellow mallard flank fibers (see model, Dark Cahill)

YELLOW SALLY

HOOK: Mustad 3906 (10–16)
THREAD: Yellow (Flymaster 6/0)
TAIL: Dyed yellow duck quill strip (see model, Alexandra)
RIB: Fine flat gold tinsel
BODY: Yellow floss
HACKLE: Dyed yellow (see model, Blue Dun)

WING: Dyed yellow duck wing quill sections (see model, Blue Dun)

ZULU

HOOK: Mustad 3906B (10–16)
THREAD: Black (Flymaster 6/0)
TAIL: Red wool (tied short, barely past bend)
PALMER RIB: Black hackle palmered through body as a folded hackle (see model, Blue Dun)
BODY: Peacock herl
WING: None

Larvae, Pupae, and Shrimp

THIS CATEGORY of flies is sometimes included in wet fly listings and at other times under the labeling of nymphs. Though they are similar to both, these patterns are tied just differently enough to warrant their own section in this book.

Larvae, pupae, and shrimp are not generally tied weighted, though they will adapt themselves to lead wire quite readily. Pupae are actually fished off the bottom and used, at times, to simulate the emerging stage in the surface film. The materials used on most shrimp and larvae are such that the fly sinks rapidly enough to be fished on or just off the bottom. If you want the additional weight, by all means add it.

BLACK MIDGE PUPA

HOOK: Mustad 3906B, 94831 (12–14)
THREAD: Pale clear gray nylon or gray thread (Flymaster 6/0)
HEAD: Black ostrich herl
GILLS: Grizzly hackle (size 16 dry fly quality)
RIB: Gray thread (slightly darker than tying thread)
BODY: Two-ply gray Orlon yarn

REMARKS: This pattern by Polly Rosborough is tied in reverse progression on the hook shank. That is, the head of the fly is at the hook bend and the body terminates at the eye. In his book *Tying and Fishing the Fuzzy Nymphs,* Rosborough states that the fly is actually fished as an adult in the surface film. The hackle, therefore, should be tied as a dry fly collar.

The Orlon body is wound so that the narrowest taper is near the eye of the hook.

CADDIS CREEPER

HOOK: Mustad 9671 (10–14)
THREAD: Black (Flymaster 6/0)
TAIL: Two peacock sword fibers (one-quarter inch past bend)
BODY: Rear third, peacock herl; middle third, yellow floss ribbed with gold wire; fore third, peacock herl
WING: Three to four peacock sword fibers to bend

CREAM PEEKING CADDIS
(Plate VII)

HOOK: Mustad 9671 (10–14)
THREAD: Black (Flymaster 6/0)

RIB: Silver wire
BODY: Gray dubbing fur
THORAX: A thin band of cream latex (one-sixteenth inch)
LEGS: Brown partridge hackle, beard style (to hook point)
HEAD: Black ostrich herl

REMARKS: This pattern imitates a cased larva with just a portion of the cream larva showing outside of its case near the head.

CRO CADDIS
(Plate VII)

HOOK: Mustad 7957BX (8–10)
THREAD: Black (Flymaster 6/0)
TAIL: Cream hackle fibers, sparse
WING CASE OR SHELL: Fine black chenille pulled over body
PALMER RIB: Cream hackle palmered through body
BODY: Cream wool

REMARKS: Originated by Ted Fay.

DARK GRAY LARVA

HOOK: Mustad 38941 (12–16)
THREAD: Brown (Flymaster 6/0)
RIB: Fine gold wire
BODY: Hare's ear and mask dubbing fur
LEGS: Brown partridge (or equivalent), beard style
HEAD: Dark brown dubbing fur

EMERGENT PUPA, BROWN

HOOK: Mustad 94840 (12–16)
THREAD: Brown (Flymaster 6/0)
UNDERBODY: An equal blend of brown dubbing fur and brown sparkle yarn
OVERBODY: Brown sparkle yarn pulled loosely over body
TRAILER: A few strands of sparkle yarn allowed to hang behind the bend like a tail to represent a loosening sheath
WING: A few strands of natural brown deer hair reaching almost to the bend
HEAD: Brown marabou or brown fur

REMARKS: The name "emergent pupa," is used by Gary LaFontaine in his book *Caddisflies* to describe a series of pupal imitations. LaFontaine employs as his basic material a nylon yarn, manufactured by Du Pont, known as Antron. Antron is transparent and traps air bubbles and thus gives a good imitation of the gases released by the natural insect as it propels itself to the surface. However, as with so many manufactured synthetic materials, if you don't buy a lifetime supply while it is available, later on you may not be able to obtain it at all. When fashions change, so do the by-products.

In addition to Antron, there are other brands of sparkle yarn on the market. Just look for anything that has a glitter and is translucent and coarse enough to trap air bubbles. It may not be exactly what is described in LaFontaine's book, but you will be able to tie the various caddis pupa patterns with it.

The tying steps for this pattern and others in this series are fairly basic. The under-body is wound on the shank in conventional manner. The overbody is tied in and pulled forward like a shell completely surrounding the hook shank. The trailer is formed by freeing some of the excess fibers near the head so that they extend rearward from the bend and then cutting them to about the length of a wet fly tail. Incidentally, the shell type overbody is not pulled taut but left in a puffy, loose fashion so that it can breathe and also trap a quantity of air bubbles.

Another version of this series of patterns, called the Deep Pupa, does not have a wing or a trailer. The Deep Pupa is also tied with a bit of fine lead wire around the hook shank.

EMERGENT PUPA, GRAY

HOOK: Mustad 94840 (14–16)
THREAD: Gray (Flymaster 6/0)
UNDERBODY: An equal blend of muskrat dubbing fur and brown sparkle yarn
OVERBODY: Gray sparkle yarn pulled loosely over body
TRAILER: A few strands of sparkle yarn allowed to hang behind the bend like a tail to represent a loosening sheath
WING: A few strands of natural dark gray deer hair reaching almost to the bend
HEAD: Dark gray marabou or dark gray fur

REMARKS: When marabou is used, the head is formed by twisting four or five strands into a rope with the hackle pliers and winding them around the shank behind the eye.

EMERGENT PUPA, GINGER
(Plate VII)

HOOK: Mustad 94840 (8–10)
THREAD: Brown (Flymaster 6/0)
UNDERBODY: An equal blend of ginger dubbing fur and amber sparkle yarn
OVERBODY: Amber sparkle yarn pulled loosely over body
TRAILER: A few strands of sparkle yarn allowed to hang behind the bend like a tail to represent a loosening sheath
WING: A few strands of natural tan/brown deer hair reaching almost to the bend
HEAD: Cream marabou or cream fur

REMARKS: LaFontaine provides a more than adequate list of pupa imitations in his book. The foregoing patterns are among those generally cataloged.

FRESH WATER SHRIMP
(Rosborough)

HOOK: Mustad 3906 (6–12)
THREAD: Gray or olive (Flymaster 6/0)
TAIL: Pale gray/olive hackle tip tied down into bend
HACKLE: Pale gray saddle hackle palmered through body, after which all fibers are trimmed except those below the body
BODY: Gray/olive fuzzy yarn
HEAD: Tying thread to complete taper

GILL RIBBED LARVA
(Plate VII)

HOOK: Mustad 37160 or Yorkshire Sedge (14–20)
THREAD: Black (Flymaster 6/0)
RIB: Peacock herl counter-wound with fine gold wire
BODY: Bright green floss
HEAD: Peacock herl

REMARKS: On all larva patterns calling for Mustad hook number 37160, use a hook two sizes smaller than pattern size. For example, when tying a number 14 caddis larva, use a size 18 hook. The Gill Ribbed Larva was originated by Larry Solomon.

GRANNOM PUPA

HOOK: Mustad 3906B (12–16)
THREAD: Brown (Flymaster 6/0)
RIB: Fine gold wire
BODY: Reddish-brown Australian opossum dubbing fur
WING SLATS: Mallard wing quill sections with tips slanting downward
LEGS: Brown partridge (or equivalent), beard style
HEAD: Dark brown dubbing fur

REMARKS: The wing slats should be tied on the forward side of the body and not on the hook shank in front of it. This will prevent the quill sections from flaring outward. Wing slats should be half the length of the hook shank.

GREAT BROWN SEDGE

HOOK: Mustad 3906B (8–12)
THREAD: Brown (Flymaster 6/0)
RIB: Fine gold wire
BODY: Dark brown dubbing fur
WING SLATS: Mallard wing quill sections (see model, Grannom Pupa)
LEGS: Brown partridge (or equivalent), beard style
HEAD: Brown/black dubbing fur (almost black)

GREEN ROCK WORM
(Rosborough)

HOOK: Mustad 3906B (8–12)
THREAD: Black (Flymaster 6/0)
BODY: Green mohair or similar yarn (or seal fur or equivalent)
LEGS: Half a dozen guinea hen fibers dyed green, beard style
HEAD: Black ostrich herl

HONEYBUG

HOOK: Mustad 3906, 3906B (10–14)
THREAD: Black or brown (Flymaster 6/0)
BODY: Cotton chenille in cream, tan, olive, brown, or gray, depending on species being imitated

REMARKS: This larval imitation is perhaps the simplest of all flies to tie, since it only involves the wrapping of the shank with soft cotton chenille. Introduced by Jack Mickievicz and very popular in Pennsylvania waters.

JORGENSEN FUR CADDIS PUPA, GRAY
(Plate VII)

HOOK: Mustad 3906B (8–14)
THREAD: Gray (Flymaster 6/0)
BODY: Gray seal fur (or equivalent)
WING SLATS: Mallard wing quill sections (see model, Grannom Pupa)
HEAD: Natural gray/brown rabbit with guard hairs roped and spun as a wet fly collar (see model, Jorgensen Fur Caddis Pupa, Olive)

JORGENSEN FUR CADDIS PUPA, OLIVE

HOOK: Mustad 3906B (8–14)
THREAD: Olive (Flymaster 6/0)
BODY: Olive seal fur (or equivalent)
WING SLATS: Mallard wing quill sections (see model, Grannom Pupa)
HEAD: Natural gray/brown rabbit fur with guard hairs left in, twisted into dubbing rope and wound wet fly style as a collar and pulled downward so that most of the hair fibers form a tuft of beard (legs) under the forward part of the thorax

JORGENSEN FUR CADDIS PUPA, TAN

HOOK: Mustad 3906B (8–14)
THREAD: Light brown (Flymaster 6/0)
BODY: Tan seal fur (or equivalent)
WING SLATS: Mallard wing quill sections (see model, Grannom Pupa)

HEAD: Natural gray/brown rabbit fur with guard hairs roped and spun and wound as wet fly collar (see Jorgensen Fur Caddis Pupa, Olive)

LATEX LARVA, CREAM
(Plate VII)

HOOK: Mustad 37160 or Yorkshire Sedge (10–16) (for hook sizing, see Gill Ribbed Larva)
THREAD: Cream (Flymaster 6/0)
UNDERBODY: Cream floss
BODY: Cream latex
HEAD: Peacock herl

REMARKS: This pattern may also be tied using Swannundaze nymph material or V-rib material.

LATEX LARVA, OLIVE

HOOK: Mustad 37160 or Yorkshire Sedge (10–16) (for hook sizing, see Gill Ribbed Larva)
THREAD: Olive (Flymaster 6/0)
UNDERBODY: Dark green or olive floss lacquered with clear cement
BODY: Cream latex wound over cement-wet body
HEAD: Peacock herl

REMARKS: The style of using latex strips to form larval imitations was originated by Raleigh Boaze, Jr.

LIGHT CADDIS PUPA
(Rosborough)

HOOK: Mustad 3906B (6–8)
THREAD: Black (Flymaster 6/0)
RIB: Medium yellow sewing thread
BODY: Creamy yellow Dazzle-Aire (or similar yarn which is fuzzy and has sparkle or glitter)
LEGS: Light ginger hackle wound as wet fly collar with fibers extending to bend, then trimmed top and bottom (see model, Blue Dun, page 124); only the fibers along the sides of the body allowed to remain
HEAD: Tan ostrich herl

LITTLE SAND SEDGE

HOOK: Mustad 3906B (14–18)
THREAD: Brown (Flymaster 6/0)
BODY: Pale yellow dubbing fur
WING SLATS: Mallard wing quill sections (see model, Grannom Pupa)
LEGS: Brown partridge (or equivalent), beard style
HEAD: Medium brown fur

MOSQUITO LARVA

HOOK: Mustad 9671 (14–20)
THREAD: Black (Flymaster 6/0)
TAIL: Grizzly hackle fibers
BODY: Stripped peacock quill (see model, Quill Gordon, pages 24–6)
THORAX: Peacock herl

OLIVE SCUD
(Plate VII)

HOOK: Mustad 3906B (10–16)
THREAD: Olive (Flymaster 6/0)
TAIL: Pale olive dubbing fur
RIB: Fine gold wire
WING CASE OR SHELL: Mallard wing quill section hooded over entire body
LEGS: Picked-out body fur

REMARKS: Tail may easily be formed by using a stringy type of fur such as rabbit or muskrat or, even easier, using a section of olive angora yarn.

OLIVE SEDGE

HOOK: Mustad 3906 (14–18)
THREAD: Brown (Flymaster 6/0)
BODY: Pale olive dubbing fur
WING SLATS: Mallard wing quill sections (see model, Grannom Pupa)
LEGS: Brown partridge (or equivalent), beard style
HEAD: Dark brown dubbing fur

PALE OLIVE LARVA

HOOK: Mustad 38941 or Yorkshire Sedge (12–16)
THREAD: Brown (Flymaster 6/0)
RIB: Fine gold wire
BODY: Pale olive dubbing fur
LEGS: Brown partridge (or equivalent), beard style
HEAD: Dark brown dubbing fur

SMALL BLACK PUPA

HOOK: Mustad 3906B (16–20)
THREAD: Brown (Flymaster 6/0)
BODY: Black/brown (almost black) dubbing fur
LEGS: Black hen hackle, beard style
HEAD: Black/brown dubbing fur

SMALL DARK PUPA

HOOK: Mustad 3906B (16–22)
THREAD: Brown (Flymaster 6/0)
BODY: Hare's ear dubbing fur
LEGS: Brown partridge (or equivalent), beard style
HEAD: Hare's ear dubbing fur

SMALL GREEN PUPA

HOOK: Mustad 3906B (16–20)
THREAD: Olive (Flymaster 6/0)
BODY: Bright olive green dubbing fur
LEGS: Brown partridge (or equivalent), beard style
HEAD: Bright olive green dubbing fur

SOLOMON'S CADDIS PUPA, GRAY
(Plate VII)

HOOK: Mustad 3906B (8–14)
THREAD: Gray (Flymaster 6/0)
RIB: Brown Monocord
BODY: Gray dubbing fur (or synthetic equivalent)
WING SLATS: Mallard wing quill sections (see model, Grannom Pupa)
LEGS: Gray partridge (or equivalent), beard style (to point of hook)
ANTENNAE: Gray partridge (or equivalent) (to bend)
HEAD: Peacock herl

REMARKS: The antennae of this pattern do not extend beyond the eye but slant backwards over the top of the hook to the bend. Both antennae and legs are very sparse.
The Solomon's Caddis Pupa series was originated by Larry Solomon of New York.

SOLOMON'S CADDIS PUPA, OLIVE

HOOK: Mustad 3906B (8–14)
THREAD: Olive (Flymaster 6/0)
RIB: Brown Monocord
BODY: Olive dubbing fur (or Unseal or equivalent)
WING SLATS: Mallard wing quill sections (see model, Grannom Pupa)
LEGS: Brown partridge (or equivalent), sparse (to point of hook)
ANTENNAE: Brown partridge (or equivalent) (to bend) (see Solomon's Caddis Pupa, Gray)
HEAD: Peacock herl

SOLOMON'S CADDIS PUPA, TAN

HOOK: Mustad 3906B (8–14)
THREAD: Brown (Flymaster 6/0)

RIB: Brown Monocord

BODY: Tan dubbing fur (or Unseal or equivalent)

WING SLATS: Mallard wing quill sections (see model, Grannom Pupa)

LEGS: Brown partridge (or equivalent) (see Solomon's Caddis Pupa, Gray)

HEAD: Peacock herl

SOW BUG
(Plate VII)

HOOK: Mustad 3906B (10–16)

THREAD: Gray (Flymaster 6/0)

TAIL: Two mallard wing quill fibers (tied forked)

RIB: Fine silver wire

WING CASE OR SHELL: Polyethylene strip over entire top of body

BODY: Muskrat dubbing fur

LEGS: Dubbing fur picked out with dubbing needle

SPECKLED SEDGE
(Plate VII)

HOOK: Mustad 3906B (12–16)

THREAD: Brown (Flymaster 6/0)

RIB: Reddish-brown Australian opossum dubbing fur thinly but firmly spun onto tying thread

BODY: Light brown mink dubbing fur or equivalent

WING SLATS: Mallard wing quill sections (see model, Grannom Pupa)

LEGS: Brown partridge (or equivalent), beard style

HEAD: Dark brown dubbing fur

WHITE LARVA

HOOK: Mustad 38941 or Yorkshire Sedge (10–16)

THREAD: Brown (Flymaster 6/0)

RIB: Fine gold wire

BODY: Dirty white dubbing fur

LEGS: Brown partridge (or equivalent), beard style

HEAD: Dark brown dubbing fur

YELLOW LARVA

HOOK: Mustad 38941 or Yorkshire Sedge (12–16)

THREAD: Brown (Flymaster 6/0)

RIB: Fine gold wire

BODY: Pale yellow dubbing fur

LEGS: Brown partridge (or equivalent), beard style

HEAD: Dark brown dubbing fur

Emergers (Floating Nymphs)

EMERGERS, OR floating nymphs as they are often called, represent that stage in the life of aquatic insects when they are in the act of transformation. The body colors have begun to change slightly and the wings are just about ready to pop out of their shell. Their somewhat helpless condition during this period makes them easy prey for trout and other fish.

This category falls somewhere between the wet flies and the dry flies. Though it is not considered a subsurface imitation, neither does it have all the characteristics of a dry fly.

The trick in selecting hooks and materials for this type of fly is to think of a balance between not being heavy enough to sink and yet not being so light as to float high on the surface.

I've included the emergers in this section with the nymphs and wet flies simply because they are dressed in a similar fashion. Actually, I suppose they belong to the surface pattern group since they do float, though just barely.

When tied on a standard-size hook, such as the Mustad 94840, emerger imitations take on proportions similar to those of a standard dry fly, except that they do not have an upright wing or a stiff supportive hackle collar. In general, the following applies to most types of emergers.

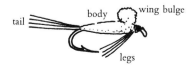

General Proportions for Emergers
TAIL: Length of a standard shank
BODY: Length of shank, tapered

LEGS: Not quite to hook point, usually tied beard style
WING BULGE: Over body where wing case normally appears in a nymph

BLUE WINGED OLIVE FLOATING NYMPH

HOOK: Mustad 94840 (20–22)
THREAD: Olive (Flymaster 6/0)
TAIL: Medium dark blue dun hackle fibers
BODY: Light olive dubbing fur or Spectrum synthetic fur #5
WING BULGE: Medium gray dubbing fur or Spectrum synthetic fur No. 28
LEGS: Medium blue dun hackle fibers, beard style

REMARKS: The wing bulge and legs for this type of fly are formed in the following manner.

1. Spin dubbing fur onto the tying thread.

2. Raise the tying thread to a vertical position above the hook shank and push the fur on the thread down onto the shank so that it forms a ball.

3. Wind the thread around the shank and then around the base of the dubbing ball and once more around the shank. Bring the thread to a position just in front of the dubbing ball.

4. Tie in the hackle for the legs under the hook shank directly in front of (but under) the wing bulge.

5. Spin a small amount of dubbing onto the thread and wind to the eye so that the clipped excess butts of the hackle legs are neatly covered up and there is a natural taper to the eye.

CREAM EMERGER

HOOK: Mustad 94840 (14–18)
THREAD: Cream (Flymaster 6/0)
TAIL: Cream hackle fibers
BODY: Cream dubbing fur
WING BULGE: Amber dubbing fur (see model, Blue Winged Olive Floating Nymph)
LEGS: Cream hackle fibers, beard style

GRAY EMERGER

HOOK: Mustad 94840 (14–20)
THREAD: Gray (Flymaster 6/0)
TAIL: Medium blue dun hackle fibers

Forming the Wing Bulge on an Emerger

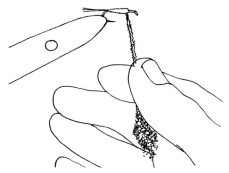

a. Tail and body have been formed and now dubbing fur is spun onto thread.

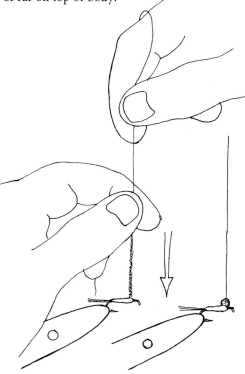

b. Dubbed thread is lifted to vertical position and dubbing is slid down thread and left as ball of fur on top of body.

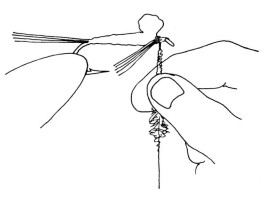

c. Thread is crossed around fur ball and hook shank and also around base of fur ball to secure it in place.

d. Leg fibers are now added and then more dubbing is spun on thread to complete forward end of body.

e. Completed emerger.

BODY: Muskrat dubbing fur

WING BULGE: Muskrat dubbing fur (see model, Blue Winged Olive Floating Nymph)

LEGS: Medium dun hackle fibers, beard style

GREEN DRAKE EMERGER
(Plate VIII)

HOOK: Mustad 94842 (10–14)

THREAD: Olive (Flymaster 6/0)

TAIL: Three wood duck flank fibers (tied spread)

ABDOMEN: A single goose wing quill fiber dyed bright yellow

THORAX: Bright olive seal fur

LEGS: Four turns of grizzly dyed yellow followed by two turns of black hen hackle, both as wet fly collar (see model, Blue Dun, page 124)

REMARKS: This pattern, fished by Rene Harrop and described by him in the Mid-Season issue of *Fly Fisherman* magazine in 1982, is constructed in the manner of a soft-hackled fly. It is dressed with floatant to keep it in the surface film.

MAHOGANY DUN FLOATING NYMPH

HOOK: Mustad 94840 (16–18)

THREAD: Brown (Flymaster 6/0)

TAIL: Dark dun hackle fibers

BODY: Rusty dun dubbing fur or Spectrum synthetic fur No. 35

WING BULGE: Dark gray dubbing fur or Spectrum synthetic fur No. 1 (see model, Blue Winged Olive Floating Nymph)

LEGS: Dark dun hackle fibers, beard style

MOSQUITO EMERGER
(Plate VIII)

HOOK: Mustad 94840 (14–20)

THREAD: Black (Flymaster 6/0)

TAIL: Grizzly hackle fibers

ABDOMEN: Stripped peacock herl (see model, Quill Gordon, pages 24–6)

THORAX: Peacock herl

WING: Grizzly hackle tips tied short and flat on top of body (half the distance from eye to bend)

OLIVE EMERGER

HOOK: Mustad 94840 (14–20)

THREAD: Olive (Flymaster 6/0)

TAIL: Dark dun hackle fibers

BODY: Medium olive with a hint of gray dubbing fur

WING BULGE: Dark dun dubbing fur (see model, Blue Winged Olive Floating Nymph)

LEGS: Dark dun hackle fibers, beard style

PALE MORNING DUN FLOATING NYMPH

HOOK: Mustad 94840 (16–18)

THREAD: Pale yellow (Flymaster 6/0)

TAIL: Light dun hackle fibers

BODY: Olive yellow dubbing fur or Spectrum synthetic fur No. 20

WING BULGE: Light gray dubbing fur or Spectrum synthetic fur No. 47 (see model, Blue Winged Olive Floating Nymph)

LEGS: Light dun hackle fibers, beard style

PARTRIDGE AND ORANGE EMERGER
(Plate VIII)

HOOK: Mustad 3906 (12–18)

THREAD: Brown (Flymaster 6/0)

TAIL: A few (sparse) wood duck flank fibers

BODY: Dirty orange to rust dubbing fur

HACKLE: Brown partridge tied as a dry fly collar

REMARKS: This particular version of a soft-hackle pattern by Jack Mickievicz is designed to imitate the emerging forms of mayflies, such as the blue winged olive. The fuzzier fur body and the hackle tied as a dry fly collar add more movement and pulsation to the fly. The body of this pattern should be coated with fly dope to keep it in the surface film.

PHILO CADDIS EMERGER
(Plate VIII)

HOOK: Mustad 3906 or 3399A (10–14)

THREAD: Gray (Flymaster 6/0)

BODY: A blend of rabbit underfur and gray fox squirrel body fur with guard hairs left in (either may be used in their natural gray colors or dyed into other imitative shades such as olive or tan)

LEGS: Partridge hackle (brown or gray), beard style

WING: A pheasant rump aftershaft feather wound as a wet fly hackle then clipped on top; the simulated undeveloped wing extended rearward to the point of the hook covering the beard of partridge hackle (see "aftershaft" in the glossary)

ANTENNAE: A single wood duck fiber on each side slanting rearward along the top sides of the body to the bend

REMARKS: This effective design by Jack Gartside may more appropriately belong in the section on caddis pupae and larvae. However, because of its name, and its slightly different structure, it is listed here with other emergers.

PHILO MAYFLY EMERGER
(Plate VIII)

HOOK: Mustad 9671 (10–16)

THREAD: To blend with body color (Flymaster 6/0)

TAIL: Three wood duck or partridge hackle fibers

BODY: A blend of rabbit underfur and gray fox squirrel body fur with guard hairs left in (color to be imitative of natural insect being simulated)

WING: Gray pheasant aftershaft feather wound as a wet fly hackle and clipped on bottom. Enough turns should be taken to assure a fluffy clump of fibers imitating a

partially open wing extending rearward to center of shank.

LEGS: Partridge fibers, beard style

REMARKS: I've had occasion to observe Gartside fishing these emergers on the Willowemoc River in New York. Of half a dozen anglers on this particular stretch, he was the only one consistently into fish, and I believe it was due, in part, to the use of the soft, fluffy, and highly pulsating aftershaft feather which represents the unfolding wing.

RUSTY BROWN EMERGER

HOOK: Mustad 94840 (14–18)

THREAD: Brown (Flymaster 6/0)

TAIL: Medium blue dun hackle fibers

BODY: Rusty brown dubbing fur

WING BULGE: Muskrat dubbing fur (see model, Blue Winged Olive Floating Nymph)

LEGS: Medium blue dun hackle fibers, beard style

TIMBERLINE EMERGER
(Plate VIII)

HOOK: Mustad 3906 (10–16)

THREAD: Gray (Flymaster 6/0)

TAIL: Three black moose body hair fibers (tied spread)

BODY: A blend of 30% muskrat and 70% gray seal fur (or seal fur substitute)

LEGS: Two turns of brown hackle as wet fly collar (see model, Blue Dun, page 124)

WING: Two grizzly hackle tips tied flat over body and extending rearward to center of body

REMARKS: This original pattern by Randall Kaufmann appears somewhat like a wet fly with undeveloped wings. It is used by Kaufmann primarily for fishing lakes in high elevations.

Turkey Flat Emergers

This is a new design introduced by Barry Beck. The primary feature is a crushed turkey body feather (turkey "flat") tied to the shank behind the eye to create a semi-formed wing in the process of coming out of its case. This semi-formed wing is fairly full-bodied and reaches rearward about half the length of the shank. It also has a slight upward angle. Turkey Flat Emergers are dressed in important variations for related mayfly species.

What makes this emerger preferable to others, according to Barry Beck, is that it presents an exceptionally good silhouette of a partially opened wing case and the material, though inexpensive, is very durable and easily available in a full color range. More importantly, the turkey material holds silicone fly dope very well and keeps the fly suspended in the surface film exactly where it belongs.

Turkey Flat Emergers are designated by the abbreviation T.F.E. The following are representative of the most popular patterns in this series.

T.F.E. BLUE WINGED OLIVE

HOOK: Mustad 94840 (16–20)
THREAD: Olive (Flymaster 6/0)
TAIL: Two blue dun hackle fibers on each side (tied forked)
BODY: Light olive Spectrum or Fly-Rite poly dubbing
LEGS: Light blue dun hen hackle fibers, sparse, as short beard (about half the gap width)
WING: Dark blue dun turkey flat fibers extending rearward slightly past center of shank.

REMARKS: The wing is formed by snipping a section of turkey flat fibers and compacting them as you would a clump of wood duck fibers and tying them to the shank as a short wing. This method applies for all Turkey Flat Emergers.

T.F.E. HENDRICKSON

HOOK: Mustad 94840 (14)
THREAD: Gray (Flymaster 6/0)
TAIL: Blue dun hackle fibers, two on each side (tied forked)

BODY: Reddish-brown Spectrum or Fly-Rite poly dubbing
LEGS: Blue dun hen fibers, sparse, as short beard (about half the gap width)
WING: Medium blue dun turkey flat fibers extending rearward slightly past center of shank

T.F.E. LIGHT CAHILL

HOOK: Mustad 94840 (14)
THREAD: Cream or primrose (Flymaster 6/0)
TAIL: Cream hackle fibers, two on each side (tied forked)
BODY: Cream Spectrum or Fly-Rite poly dubbing
LEGS: Cream hen hackle fibers, sparse, as short beard
WING: Cream turkey flat fibers extending rearward slightly past center of shank

T.F.E. LITTLE RED QUILL

HOOK: Mustad 94840 (14)
THREAD: Gray (Flymaster 6/0)
TAIL: Blue dun hackle fibers, two on each side (tied forked)
BODY: Mahogany brown Spectrum or Fly-Rite poly dubbing fur
LEGS: Blue dun hen hackle fibers, sparse, as short beard (about half the gap width)
WING: Dark blue dun turkey flat fibers extending rearward slightly past center of shank

T.F.E. MARCH BROWN

HOOK: Mustad 94840 (12)
THREAD: Orange (Flymaster 6/0)
TAIL: Dark ginger hackle fibers, two on each side (tied forked)
RIB: Brown cotton thread
BODY: Buff/tan Spectrum or Fly-Rite poly dubbing fur
LEGS: Ginger hen hackle fibers, sparse, as short beard (about half the gap width)
WING: Medium tan turkey flat extending rearward slightly past center of shank

T.F.E. QUILL GORDON

HOOK: Mustad 94840 (14)
THREAD: Gray (Flymaster 6/0)
TAIL: Blue dun hackle fibers, two on each side (tied forked)
BODY: Cream/olive Spectrum or Fly-Rite poly dubbing fur
LEGS: Blue dun hen hackle fibers, sparse, as short beard (about half the gap width)
WING: Dark blue dun turkey flat fibers extending rearward slightly past center of shank

T.F.E. SULFUR

HOOK: Mustad 94840 (18)
THREAD: Primrose (pale yellow) (Flymaster 6/0)
TAIL: Cream hackle fibers, two on each side (tied forked)
BODY: Pale yellow Spectrum or Fly-Rite poly dubbing fur

Steps for Tying Turkey Flat Emergers (by Beck)

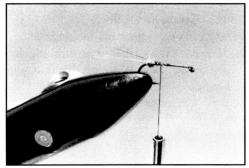

a. Forked tails have been tied in.

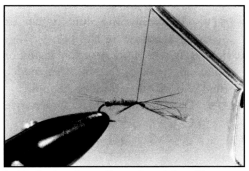

b. Body has been formed and leg fibers are being tied in.

c. A section of fibers being cut from a turkey flat feather.

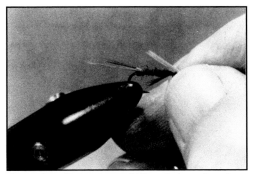

d. Turkey flat section of fibers being placed on hook shank over body prior to being tied in.

e. Completed Turkey Flat Emerger.

LEGS: Cream hen hackle fibers, sparse, as short beard (about half the gap width)

WING: Pale gray turkey flat fibers extending rearward slightly past center of shank

WESTERN DRAKE
FLOATING NYMPH

HOOK: Mustad 94840 (16–18)

THREAD: Brown (Flymaster 6/0)

TAIL: Dark dun hackle fibers

BODY: Brownish-olive dubbing fur or Spectrum synthetic fur No. 34

WING BULGE: Dark gray dubbing fur or Spectrum synthetic fur No. 1 (see model, Blue Winged Olive Floating Nymph)

LEGS: Dark dun hackle fibers, beard style

YELLOW EMERGER

HOOK: Mustad 94840 (14–20)

THREAD: Yellow (Flymaster 6/0)

TAIL: Cream hackle fibers

BODY: Yellowish-cream dubbing fur

WING BULGE: Pale dun dubbing fur (see model, Blue Winged Olive Floating Nymph)

LEGS: Cream hackle fibers

Nymphs (General)

AFTER THE dry fly, the nymph is the most commonly fished imitation. Of all types of flies attached to a leader, they are perhaps the deadliest. Nymphs are intended to be fished on or very near the bottom of the stream. To accomplish this, they require materials that absorb water quickly and sink rapidly. At the same time, the materials must be such that they give the impression of life. This does not necessarily mean that they have to look like the natural insect, but rather that they should move, pulse, and vibrate in the manner of a crawling or swimming insect in the nymphal or larval stage. This element of *life* is more important in this category of flies than in any other. If a choice has to be made between water absorbency in a material and lifelike impression, the latter has first priority. In some of the pattern listings that follow,

you will find a simple description for either the abdomen or the thorax, giving only general material requirements such as amber fur or brown dubbing fur. The description may not specify what kind of fur or synthetic is required. If given the option, try to use a fur, whether natural or synthetic, that has a scraggly or fuzzy appearance, such as hare's mask, seal fur, seal fur substitute, or fuzzy yarn. The results will become apparent on the stream.

Most of the nymphs in the following pages will be described without the listing of an underbody of lead wire. Yet most of these patterns may, and in certain situations should, be weighted. The lead wire underbody should be constructed in such a manner that it does not clash with the overall appearance of the pattern. It can, in fact, enhance it if properly

configured. An example would be the weighting of the hook with strips of lead wire lashed to the sides of the shank so that there is a simulation of a flat-bodied or oval-flat-bodied appearance in the completed fly, thus imitating the shape of many of our nymphs.

The proper diameter of lead wire for relative hook sizes should also be considered. You don't want to wind a 3 amp (.036 diameter) wire on a size 12 hook, or a very fine wire on a size 2 stonefly nymph which is to be fished in deep water. Common sense will dictate the proper amount of wire. Just keep in mind the shape of the natural insect to be imitated, the materials to be wound over the lead wire underbody, and the depth and current speed of the water to be fished.

Proportions

It is difficult to suggest even a generalized scale for the proportions of a nymph since the naturals imitated differ so much. Hooks used for nymph patterns range from a 2X long to a 4X long, and as you will see in the section on stonefly nymphs, a 6XL long is not uncommon.

Some tyers try for accents involving tails, gills, legs, and feelers to bring more life to their creations, while others strive for exact duplication. Thus, for this section, I have omitted a diagrammatic scale drawing of the proportions of a nymph.

ALBINO NYMPH
(see White Nymph)

ALL-PURPOSE NYMPHS
(see Orvis All-Purpose Nymphs)

AMBER MARABOU NYMPH
(see Marabou Nymph)

Andre Puyans Nymph Series

(also known as A.P. Nymphs)

The following series was designed by Andre Puyans. The patterns are intended to imitate mayfly nymphs, which are important to the angler. Puyans has made the job relatively simple by designing a basic structure for all of them, adjusting only the size, shape, and color in relation to the natural.

A.P. HARE'S EAR/BEAVER NYMPH

HOOK: Mustad 3906B (10–14)
THREAD: Tan (Flymaster 6/0)
TAIL: Bronze mallard flank fibers
WING CASE: Bronze mallard flank
LEGS: Bronze mallard flank fibers
RIB: Gold wire over abdomen
ABDOMEN: A dubbing blend of equal parts hare's ear and beaver fur
THORAX: Same as abdomen
HEAD: Tan Flymaster thread, varnished.

A.P. MUSKRAT NYMPH (No. 1)

HOOK: Mustad 3906B (10–14)
THREAD: Gray (Flymaster 6/0)
TAIL: Blue dun hackle fibers
WING CASE: Bronze mallard flank (medium shade)
LEGS: Bronze mallard flank fibers (medium shade)
RIB: Gold wire (.006) over abdomen only
ABDOMEN: Dark-shade muskrat dubbing fur
THORAX: Same as abdomen
HEAD: Gray Flymaster thread, varnished, or same dubbing used on abdomen

A.P. CLARET AND BEAVER NYMPH

HOOK: Mustad 3906B (10–14)
THREAD: Black (Flymaster 6/0)
TAIL: Dark moose hair fibers
WING CASE: Dark moose hair
LEGS: Dark moose hair fibers
RIB: Gold or copper wire (.006) over abdomen only
ABDOMEN: A dubbing blend of 40% medium-shade beaver, 20% claret seal fur (or substitute), 20% fiery brown seal fur (or substitute), and 20% hare's ear fur
THORAX: Same as abdomen
HEAD: Black Flymaster thread, varnished, or same dubbing used on abdomen

A.P. OLIVE NYMPH

HOOK: Mustad 3906B (10–14)
THREAD: Olive (Flymaster 6/0)
TAIL: Finely marked mallard flank fibers dyed olive
WING CASE: Finely marked mallard flank dyed olive
LEGS: Finely marked mallard flank fibers dyed olive
RIB: Gold wire (.006) over abdomen only
ABDOMEN: Beaver dubbing fur dyed medium olive
THORAX: Same as abdomen
HEAD: Olive Flymaster thread, varnished, or same dubbing used on abdomen

REMARKS: Certain olive nymphs have a very dark wing case. In such instances, the wing case may be darkened with a black marking pen.

A.P. BEAVER NYMPH

HOOK: Mustad 3906B (10–14)
THREAD: Black (Flymaster 6/0)
TAIL: Dark moose hair fibers
WING CASE: Dark moose hair
LEGS: Dark moose hair fibers
RIB: Copper wire (.006) over abdomen only
ABDOMEN: Dark-shade beaver dubbing fur
THORAX: Same as abdomen
HEAD: Same as abdomen

A.P. MUSKRAT NYMPH (No. 2)

HOOK: Mustad 3906B (10–14)
THREAD: Gray (Flymaster 6/0)
TAIL: Dark moose hair fibers
WING CASE: Dark moose hair
LEGS: Dark moose hair fibers
RIB: Gold wire (.006) over abdomen only
ABDOMEN: Dark-shade muskrat dubbing fur
THORAX: Same as abdomen
HEAD: Gray Flymaster thread, varnished, or same dubbing used on abdomen

A.P. HENDRICKSON NYMPH

HOOK: Mustad 3906B (10–14)
THREAD: Tan (Flymaster 6/0)
TAIL: Bronze mallard flank fibers or dark elk hair fibers
WING CASE: Bronze mallard flank or dark elk hair
LEGS: Bronze mallard flank fibers or dark elk hair fibers
RIB: Copper wire (.006) over abdomen only
ABDOMEN: Beaver dubbing fur dyed reddish brown
THORAX: Same as abdomen
HEAD: Tan Flymaster thread, varnished, or same dubbing used on abdomen

A.P. BLACK BEAVER NYMPH

HOOK: Mustad 3906B (10–14)
THREAD: Black (Flymaster 6/0)
TAIL: Dark moose hair fibers
WING CASE: Dark moose hair fibers
LEGS: Dark moose hair fibers
RIB: Copper wire (.006) over abdomen only
ABDOMEN: Dyed black beaver dubbing fur
THORAX: Same as abdomen
HEAD: Black Flymaster thread, varnished, or same dubbing used on abdomen

A.P. PEACOCK AND PHEASANT

HOOK: Mustad 3906B (10–14)
THREAD: Black (Flymaster 6/0)
TAIL: Fibers from center tail of male ringneck pheasant
WING CASE: Center tail section of ringneck pheasant with dark barring used for pulled-over case
LEGS: Fibers from center tail of ringneck pheasant
RIB: Copper wire (.006) over abdomen only
ABDOMEN: Bronze peacock herl
THORAX: Same as abdomen
HEAD: Black Flymaster thread, varnished

The following instructions apply to all the patterns in the A.P. Nymph series.

1. These nymphs are tied weighted. Wrap .015 lead wire around shank at the thorax area only. Secure ends of wire with thread and taper off naturally.

2. Tie in material for tail, wing case, and legs directly behind lead wire. Measure material for wing case only. Bring thread to a position over the hook point.

3. Trim excess material from tail. In the case of flank fibers, usually about half. With moose body fibers, until only three to five remain. Tail is as long as hook gap is wide.

4. Bring a turn of thread under the tail fibers and around the shank to lift them slightly upward.

5. Tie in the ribbing material. Spin dubbing material onto thread and wind it in a counterclockwise manner to the wing case area.

6. Spiral the rib forward in a clockwise manner to the wing case and snip the excess.

7. Lift the remaining material which will form the wing case out of the way and spin

Tying Steps for the A.P. Nymph Series

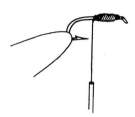

a. Lead wire has been wound and secured to hook shank.

b. Material for tail, wings, and legs has been tied in.

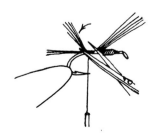

c. Excess tail material being cut away.

d. Tail fibers are lifted so turn of thread can be taken under them.

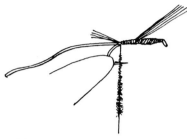

e. Ribbing material has been tied in and thread is spun with dubbing fur.

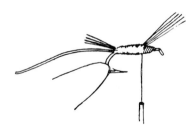

f. Dubbed thread has been wound forward to form abdomen.

g. Ribbing has been spiraled forward over body to form segmentation and excess ribbing is cut away. Then more dubbing is spun onto thread.

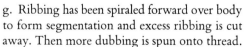

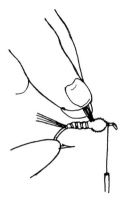

h. Dubbing is wound over shank to form thorax area. Wing case fibers are lifted slightly rearward and some of dubbed thread is wound against base of fibers so that a hump or bulge is formed when they are next folded over.

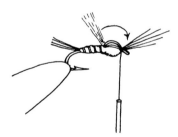

i. Wing case fibers are folded forward and over top of thorax.

j. Three excess fibers from wing case are forced rearward and secured with thread to form legs extending from sides of thorax.

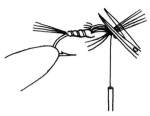

k. Remainder of excess wing case fibers are now trimmed off.

l. More dubbing is spun onto the thread and wound around the shank before the eye to form the head.

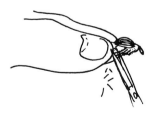

m. Leg fibers are now trimmed to proper size.

n. Completed A.P. Nymph.

fur onto thread and form the thorax. Thorax is fuller than abdomen.

8. Leave thread a short distance before the eye. Bring wing case material forward and tie it down.

9. The legs are formed by separating three fibers from each side of the thorax and securing them in an outstretched position with the tying thread. All excess material is now trimmed away.

10. Head is formed using either the tying thread or the dubbing material. Trim the leg fibers so that they extend just past the rear of the thorax. Apply head lacquer to the head if tying thread has been used.

Puyans believes that fur from aquatic animals has a better breathing and pulsing action when fished than fur from land animals such as rabbit and raccoon. The fur from a hare's ear or mask is, of course, an exception since the texture here is scraggly and thus beneficial in creating a lifelike action.

ANYTIME, ANYWHERE

HOOK: Mustad 9672 (4-12)
THREAD: Black (Flymaster 6/0 or Monocord 3/0)
TAIL: Wood duck flank fibers, very heavy and as long as the hook shank
PALMER RIB: Grizzly hackle trimmed

fairly close to the body to produce a stubby effect
BODY: Black chenille

REMARKS: This pattern, which was submitted by Gary Merriman of the Fish Hawk in Atlanta, Georgia, is generally tied weighted. Like the Woolly Worm, the Woolly Bugger, and the Leech, all of which it resembles, the pattern is very effective for a wide range of fish, including salmon, steelhead, bonefish, bream, bass, and, of course, trout. Merriman calls it a nymph though it does not have the characteristic appearance of a nymph. Nevertheless, it is fished as such and seems to live up to its name, and so it is here listed.

ATHERTON MEDIUM

HOOK: Mustad 3906B (10-16)
THREAD: Black (Flymaster 6/0)
TAIL: Three fibers from the center tail of a male ringneck pheasant (tied short, not quite gap width in length)
RIB: Fine oval gold tinsel
ABDOMEN: Hare's mask dubbing fur, picked out to make it coarser after the ribbing has been wound
WING CASE: Goose wing quill section dyed medium bright blue
THORAX: Mixed hare's mask and ear fur wound fuller than abdomen
LEGS: Brown partridge hackle (or equivalent)

REMARKS: This pattern, from among a number of nymphs originated by John Atherton and listed in his book *The Fly and the Fish,* is still a favorite among anglers. Atherton, an artist, believed in impressionism in the flies he tied. To him, it was more important to give the impression of life than to create an exact image of the natural he was imitating. An excellent expression of this theory is the use of hare's ear fur and the extra trouble he went to in picking out the fur fibers with a dubbing needle so that the fly would pulse and breathe.

Today, the partridge fiber legs and the wing case structure are, for the most part, tied in the conventional style described in our model fly, the Hendrickson Nymph. The partridge legs, however, may also be tied beard style or divided beard style.

BAETIS NYMPH

HOOK: Mustad 3906B (14–20)
THREAD: Olive (Flymaster 6/0)
TAIL: Gray partridge fibers (or equivalent)
RIB: Dark gray thread
BODY: Dark gray/brown wool or fur
WING CASE: Gray goose quill section
LEGS: Gray partridge fibers (or equivalent) (for wing case and legs, see model, Hendrickson Nymph)

BEAVER NYMPH

HOOK: Mustad 9671 (10–16)
THREAD: Gray (Flymaster 6/0)

TAIL: Wood duck flank fibers (gap width in length)
RIB: Fine gold wire
BODY: Beaver dubbing fur (medium shade)
LEGS: Brown partridge (or equivalent), beard style

BIRD'S NEST
(Plate VIII)

HOOK: Mustad 9672 (8–12)
THREAD: Tan or brown (Flymaster 6/0)
TAIL: Mallard or teal flank fibers dyed bronze, sparse
RIB: Medium copper wire
BODY: Heather tan dubbing material (No. 16 Buggy Nymph Material)
WING: Four separate sparse sections of mallard or teal flank fibers, dyed bronze, spaced over top half and sides of hook shank (four or five fibers in each section), extending to bend
THORAX OR HEAD: Same material that is used for the body but fuller. The material is actually wound in the thorax area, and the remainder of the hook shank to the eye, about an eighth of an inch, is covered only with thread windings and lacquered.

REMARKS: Originated by Cal Bird.

BITCH CREEK NYMPH

HOOK: Mustad 79580 (4–8)
THREAD: Black (Flymaster 6/0 or Monocord 3/0)

UNDERBODY: A strip of lead wire on each side of the shank
TAIL: Two strands of white rubber hackle (gap width past bend)
ANTENNAE: Two strands of white rubber hackle (same length as tail)
ABDOMEN: Orange chenille on bottom, black chenille on top
LEGS: Brown hackle palmered through thorax
THORAX: Black chenille

REMARKS: There are several ways to achieve the two-tone effect for the abdomen, one of which involves the weaving of the orange and black chenille around the hook shank. This is the most time-consuming but, in my opinion, obtains the best result. I use the following steps when constructing a two-tone body, whether it is of chenille, floss, monofilament, or other suitable material. It was shown to me many years ago by Ralph Graves. See pp. 160–1.

After the underbody of lead wire strips and the rubber hackle strands for the tail have been tied in, a black and an orange piece of extra-fine chenille (size 00) are tied in at the bend. The thread is then whip-finished and cut and the vise is turned so that it points directly at the tyer.

Grasp the orange chenille in one hand and the black in the other and bring them toward you and in front of the hook. Make an overhand knot and slip the black chenille over the top of the shank and the orange underneath it. Bring the unclosed knot to the rear of the shank and pull the chenille tight, making sure that the black stays on top and the orange on the bottom. Chenille is not a very strong material, so you will have to be careful as you tighten it. Again bring the chenille forward and go into another overhand knot. Once more slip it over the hook shank with the black on top and the orange on the bottom.

Keep making overhand knots until you have progressed to a point on the shank slightly forward of center.

Wind the tying thread back onto the shank and tie down a short section of the leftover chenille. Clip the excess chenille.

Tie in the brown hackle that will later be palmered through the thorax.

Tie in the next-largest size of black chenille (size 0 or 1).

Tie in the rubber strands to form the antennae.

Wind the black chenille forward, forming the thorax.

Wind the brown hackle through the thorax, forming the legs.

A two-tone body may also be formed by tying in the black chenille along the top of the shank near the bend and the orange chenille under the shank in the same area. The thread is then brought forward to the thorax area and the black chenille pulled along the top and the orange along the bottom. Both are secured with thread at the thorax area. This method, however, leaves something to be desired, since trout and other fish can easily render the fly useless. When this method is used, the brown hackle is usually palmered through both abdomen and thorax.

There is, of course, the lazy tyer's method, which requires only that the abdomen be wrapped with orange chenille and the top half painted black with a marking pen.

BLACK CREEPER

HOOK: Mustad 9671 (10–14)
THREAD: Black (Flymaster 6/0)
TAIL: Black hackle fibers
RIB: Fine flat gold tinsel
ABDOMEN: Black floss
THORAX: Black dubbing fur
LEGS or FEELERS: Black hen hackle tied to sides of thorax, extending outward at 90-degree angle

BLACK DRAKE NYMPH
(Rosborough)

HOOK: Mustad 38941 (10)
THREAD: Gray (Flymaster 6/0)
TAIL: Four to six guinea hen body fibers
BODY: A dubbing blend of 80% light-shade muskrat or beaver fur and 20% jackrabbit back (hare's mask dubbing fur may be substituted for jackrabbit) with guard hairs removed; thorax fuller than abdomen.
LEGS: Guinea hen fibers, divided beard style (three fibers on each side)
HEAD: Gray tying thread. Head is slightly longer than normal and pressed flat. Two coats of head lacquer are called for.

BLACK FORKED TAIL
(see Prince Nymph)

BLACK MARABOU NYMPH
(see Marabou Nymph)

BLACK MARTINEZ
(see Martinez Black Nymph)

BLONDE BURLAP (Rosborough)

HOOK: Mustad 3906B (2–10)
THREAD: Tan or beige (Flymaster 6/0 or Monocord 3/0)
TAIL: A thick clump of honey dun hackle tied to the bend so it points downward like the tail of a shrimp
UNDERBODY: Two-ply tan yarn (any kind) to cover shank, tapered at both ends and heavily cemented with head lacquer
BODY: Three bleached strands of jute from a burlap bag or gunny sack which have been twisted into a rope with hackle pliers and wound forward over the underbody (twisting of the fibers causes the segmentation in the body form)
LEGS: Five or six turns of soft honey dun hackle in front of the body wound as a wet fly collar (see model, Blue Dun, page 124)

REMARKS: The honey dun color referred to here is that of a straw- or honey-colored feather having a light dun center.

BLUE QUILL NYMPH

HOOK: Mustad 3906B (12–18)
THREAD: Black (Flymaster 6/0)

Weaving Body and Tying Steps for Bitch Creek Nymph

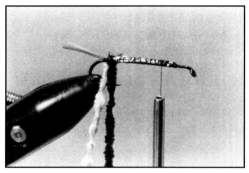

a. Rubber hackle tails have been tied in at bend; body has been weighted with strips of lead wire on each side of shank; orange and black chenille have been tied in at bend.

b. Lead wire and shank have also been covered with poly yarn to add bulk and give more definition to woven body to come.

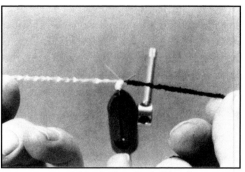

c. Orange and black chenille held in horizontal position prior to being brought forward for overhand knotting. When knot is being tightened to shank, always hold chenille (or any other suitable material) in this horizontal position before tightening to shank.

g. When the two-tone body has been woven for about two-thirds of the hook shank to the eye, a few turns of thread are used to secure the weavings and the orange chenille is cut away.

h. A black saddle hackle feather is now tied in directly in front of the woven body and the excess tip cut away.

i. Two strands of rubber hackle are first tied in to represent the antennae and then the remaining strand of black chenille is wound forward to the eye to form the thorax. Excess chenille is trimmed away.

d. Overhand loop of two colors of chenille being brought tight against shank.

e. To illustrate the knot and the process more clearly, Matt Vinciguerra, my photographer, used strands of black and white electric wire as an extra insert for this procedure.

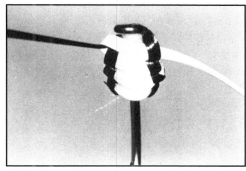

f. Another insert showing very clearly the completed weaving process.

j. Side view after hackle has been wound through thorax and fly completed.

k. Bottom view of completed fly.

TAIL: Three fibers from center tail of male ringneck pheasant
ABDOMEN: Amber dubbing fur
WING CASE: Dyed black goose wing quill section (folded over)
THORAX: Amber dubbing fur, full
LEGS: Guinea hen hackle, divided beard style

BLUE WINGED DUN NYMPH
(Troth)

This pattern is identical to the Dark Hendrickson Nymph (Troth) except that it is tied in sizes 16–18.

BLUE WINGED OLIVE NYMPH

HOOK: Mustad 3906B (14–18)
THREAD: Olive (Flymaster 6/0)
TAIL: Lemon wood duck flank fibers
RIB: Brown cotton thread or single strand of brown floss
BODY: Gray/brown/olive dubbing fur
WING CASE: Dark gray goose wing quill section
LEGS: Brown partridge (or equivalent) (for legs and wing case, see model, Hendrickson Nymph)

REMARKS: The body color of the nymph of the blue winged olive is much darker than the dun and has overtones of gray and brown in with the olive.

BRASSIE
(Plate VIII)

HOOK: Mustad 9671 (8–20)
THREAD: Black (Flymaster 6/0)
BODY: Copper wire
HEAD: Light-shade muskrat dubbing fur

REMARKS: This pattern is very popular in the southwestern states. It was originated by Gene Lynch and improvised upon by many others. Si Upson ties versions in yellow and orange to imitate some of the differently shaded midge larvae on the San Juan River in New Mexico. Some Brassies are tied with a dubbed fur head and some without. The wire for the body, which can be purchased in a variety of colors in an electronics/video parts house, is available in a range of diameters. Wire gauge should be adjusted to relative hook size.

The Brassie is similar to the Breadcrust, but its wire construction enables it to get down deeper.

BREADCRUST
(Plate VIII)

HOOK: Mustad 3906B (8–16)
THREAD: Orange or brown (Flymaster 6/0)
RIB: The center quill stem from a brown rooster hackle (see model, Red Quill, page 26)
BODY: Burnt orange seal fur (or equivalent)
HACKLE: Grizzly as a folded wet fly collar (see model, Blue Dun, page 124)

REMARKS: Orange wool is sometimes used to build an underbody before applying the expensive seal fur. This pattern is sometimes listed in the wet fly category of books and catalogs. It is also used as a caddis larva imitation. It is, in short, one of those all-purpose patterns that are very effective most of the time on most streams.

BROWN DRAKE NYMPH (Troth)

HOOK: Mustad 9672 (8–10)
THREAD: Yellow (Flymaster 6/0)
TAIL: Gray/brown marabou (tied short)
ABDOMEN: Dyed gold rabbit dubbing fur painted black along the sides with a marking pen
WING: Gray/brown marabou tied in between abdomen and thorax to extend rearward over abdomen to base of tail
WING CASE: Gray goose wing quill section (folded over)
THORAX: Dyed gold rabbit dubbing fur
HACKLE (LEGS): Brown partridge along sides of thorax and beneath thorax
HEAD: Dyed gold rabbit dubbing fur

REMARKS: The legs may be formed in the manner of the Montana Nymph.

BROWN FORKED TAIL
(Plate VIII)

HOOK: Mustad 9671 (10–14)
THREAD: Black (Flymaster 6/0)
TAIL: Two brown goose biots (tied forked) (gap width in length)

RIB: Fine flat gold tinsel

BODY: Peacock herl

HACKLE: Dark brown as wet fly collar (see model, Blue Dun, page 124)

WING: Two white goose biots tied in the form of a V so that tips flare slightly upward and extend to bend of hook

REMARKS: This pattern, originated by Doug Prince, is another version of the Prince Nymph, or Black Forked Tail (see Prince Nymph).

BROWN MARABOU NYMPH
(see Marabou Nymph)

BROWN SPRITE

HOOK: Mustad 3906B (12–16)

THREAD: Black (Flymaster 6/0)

TAIL: Dark ginger hackle fibers

BODY: Light cream poly yarn coated with head lacquer

HACKLE: Dark ginger as a wet fly collar (see model, Blue Dun, page 124)

BULL MOOSE

HOOK: Mustad 3906B (12–16)

THREAD: Black (Flymaster 6/0)

TAIL: None

RIB: Fine oval gold tinsel

BODY: Blue dun muskrat dubbing fur

HACKLE (LEGS): Brown partridge wound as a wet fly collar (see model, Blue Dun, page 124) with tips extending to bend of hook

REMARKS: This pattern, listed by Joe's Tackle, resembles a soft-hackled wet fly more than it does a nymph, though it is fished as the latter.

CAENIS NYMPH
(see Tricorythodes Nymph)

CAREY SPECIAL
(Plate VIII)

HOOK: Mustad 9672 (8–14)

THREAD: Black (Flymaster 6/0)

TAIL: Male ringneck pheasant rump fibers (1½ gap widths in length)

BODY: Peacock herl counter-wound with gold wire

HACKLE: Male ringneck pheasant rump feathers wound spey fashion as a folded hackle (see model, Blue Dun, page 124)

REMARKS: The body may be formed by twisting the gold wire and the peacock herl together using a pair of hackle pliers. Clamp both the wire and the peacock herl between the jaws of the pliers and spin, then wind forward for the body. The body may also be formed in a more conventional manner by winding the gold wire through the peacock herl after a peacock body has been formed.

The tips of the spey hackle collar extend rearward to the center of the tail fibers.

CASUAL DRESS

HOOK: Mustad 9672 (6–12)

THREAD: Black (Flymaster 6/0 or Mono-cord 3/0)

TAIL: Muskrat guard hairs with some underfur left in

BODY: Muskrat fur with guard hairs twisted into a dubbing rope

COLLAR: Muskrat fur with guard hairs twisted into a rope and wound as a wet fly collar

HEAD: Black ostrich herl

REMARKS: This superlative pattern by Polly Rosborough shows what can be accomplished by the proper use of both fur and fibers. The result here is an effective pattern that breathes and pulses with life when being fished.

Both body and collar dubbing rope are formed by trapping fur and hair fibers between two strands of thread and twisting them in one direction so they are permanently locked in. A bit of head cement on the thread before the hair and fur fibers are inserted helps them to adhere in place until the twisting motion is begun.

The collar is wound in the manner of a wet fly collar—that is, winding one turn of hackle in front of the other and stroking the fibers rearward as each turn is made. This is the same method used in the wet fly Blue Dun, except that there is no hackle to be folded.

As the turns of fur rope for either body or collar are made around the hook shank, the hackle pliers should be rotated clockwise, one turn for each turn around the shank, to prevent unraveling of the twisted fur rope.

Tying Steps for Casual Dress

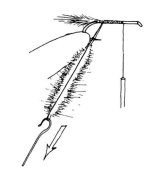

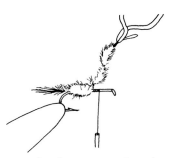

a. Bushy tail of fur and guard hairs has been tied in at bend.

b. Thread has been doubled over on itself, forming a loop, and tied down. Both sides of thread loop have been brushed with head cement.

c. A prepared elongated piece of muskrat with guard hairs left in has been placed against one side of the loop of thread. The crooked end of a dubbing needle has been placed in the end of the loop.

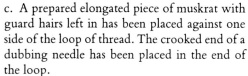

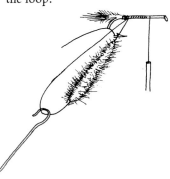

d. The loop is pulled taut with the dubbing needle.

e. The dubbing needle is twisted to the right as the fur and thread are spun into a ropelike form.

f. Fur rope has been grasped with a pair of hackle pliers and wound forward to form body of fly. As each turn is made around shank, pliers should further be twisted one turn to the right (clockwise) to maintain rope tension.

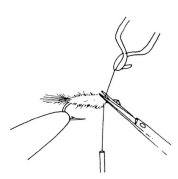

g. Excess end of fur rope being trimmed away.

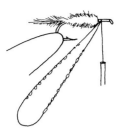

h. Another loop has been made and brushed with cement.

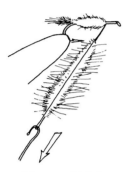

i. The second loop, which is used to form the collar, is lined on one side with fur that has the guard hairs fairly evenly aligned. In this case, the guard hairs are more important than the underfur.

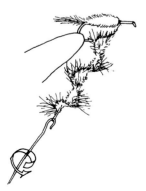

j. Second loop is being twisted into a rope.

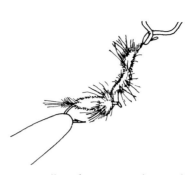

k. Fur rope collar is being wound around shank.

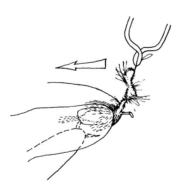

l. As collar is being wound forward around shank, left thumb and finger are used to stroke guard hair fibers rearward as each turn is being made so that both guard hairs and underfur are wound and fall neatly in place.

m. Collar has been formed and excess trimmed.

n. Ostrich herl is tied in and wound to form head of fly.

o. Completed Casual Dress.

CATE'S TURKEY

HOOK: Mustad 94840 (14–16)
THREAD: Black (Flymaster 6/0)
TAIL: Lemon wood duck flank fibers (gap width in length)
RIB: Fine gold wire wound full length of shank through body and peacock herl head
BODY: Four or five mottled turkey wing quill fibers tied in and wound around the shank as you would a piece of stranded yarn
HEAD: Three turns of peacock herl
HACKLE: Lemon wood duck flank, beard style, tied in front of peacock herl head

REMARKS: The peacock herl head is not formed directly behind the eye but sits back from it about a sixteenth of an inch to allow room for the wood duck beard and the tying off of thread.

This pattern is often fished in lakes, hence the light wire hook. In deeper or faster waters the Mustad 3906B hook may be used. Originated by Jerry Cate.

C.K. NYMPH

HOOK: Mustad 9672 (6–14)
THREAD: Black (Flymaster 6/0)
TAIL: Lemon wood duck flank fibers (gap width in length)
UNDERBODY: Fine lead wire spiraled around shank

PALMER RIB: Trimmed grizzly hackle palmered through body
BODY: Black wool

REMARKS: Hackle is trimmed to about half the width of the hook gap. Originated by Chuck Kraft.

CONDOR QUILL NYMPH

HOOK: Mustad 9671 (10–16)
THREAD: Black (Flymaster 6/0)
TAIL: Dark ginger hackle fibers (tied short, half gap width)
UNDERBODY: Two pieces of medium (.024) lead wire lashed to the sides of the shank, ends angle-cut to taper in to shank
BODY: Stripped condor quill dyed yellow (see model, Quill Gordon, pages 24–6)
WING CASE: Mottled brown turkey wing quill section (or equivalent) (pulled over)
LEGS: Dark ginger hen fibers (for wing case and legs, see model, Hendrickson Nymph)
THORAX: Peacock herl wound full

REMARKS: Since condor quill is almost nonexistent, the body of this pattern may be made of black and white turkey wing quill or other similar fibers (see Quill Gordon, pages 24–6). Originated by Leo Runkowski, this nymph imitation is also tied with a dyed insect green quill body.

COOPER BUG

HOOK: Mustad 3906B (12–16)
THREAD: Black (Flymaster 6/0)

TAIL: Natural deer body hair fibers (gray/brown)
SHELL: Continuation of excess tail fibers brought forward and lashed down behind the eye of the hook with excess clipped an eighth of an inch beyond the eye
BODY: Black chenille (size fine and extra fine depending on size of hook)

REMARKS: This "nymph" may be tied in various combinations of chenille and deer hair colors.

CREAM VARIANT NYMPH

HOOK: Mustad 9672 (10–12)
THREAD: Tan (Flymaster 6/0)
TAIL: Lemon wood duck flank fibers
RIB: Tan thread or tan single-strand floss
ABDOMEN: Amber dubbing fur
WING CASE: Light-shade Canada goose wing quill section
THORAX: Same as abdomen but fuller
LEGS: Golden ginger hen hackle, divided beard style

CRESS BUG

HOOK: Mustad 3906B (10–16)
THREAD: Olive (Flymaster 6/0)
BODY: Medium brown dubbing fur shaped to cress bug configuration (some of the guard hairs should be left in the fur)

DARK GREEN DRAKE NYMPH
(Troth)

HOOK: Mustad 3906B (8)
THREAD: Olive (Flymaster 6/0)
TAIL: Three dark moose body fibers
RIB: Heavy dark brown thread
ABDOMEN: Dark olive rabbit dubbing fur
WING CASE: Black duck wing quill section (folded over)
THORAX: Same as abdomen but fuller
LEGS: Partridge hackle dyed dark olive (or equivalent), beard style (to point of hook)

DARK HENDRICKSON NYMPH

HOOK: Mustad 9671 (10–16)
THREAD: Gray (Flymaster 6/0)
TAIL: Lemon wood duck flank fibers (1½ gap widths in length)
RIB: Fine gold or copper wire
ABDOMEN: Muskrat dubbing fur
WING CASE: Dark gray mallard wing quill section (folded over)
THORAX: Muskrat dubbing fur, fuller than abdomen
LEGS: Lemon wood duck flank fibers (or equivalent), beard style

DARK HENDRICKSON NYMPH (Troth)

HOOK: Mustad 3906B (10–12)
THREAD: Brown (Flymaster 6/0)

TAIL: Three moose body hair fibers (two gap widths in length)
RIB: Dark brown javelina (peccary fibers) wound in close spirals but leaving enough space for ostrich herl to come through to resemble gills
BODY: Dark brown ostrich herl
WING CASE: Natural black duck wing quill section
THORAX: Dark brown rabbit dubbing fur
LEGS: Dark brown partridge (or equivalent), beard style (to point of hook)

DIVING BEETLE

HOOK: Mustad 3906 (12)
THREAD: Black (Flymaster 6/0)
UNDERBODY: Fine lead wire
SHELL: Black nylon raffia
BODY: Rust-colored dubbing fur heavily applied
LEGS: One and a half turns of grouse hackle wound on prior to pulling shell forward
HEAD: Formed by folding raffia back on itself a short distance after having formed the back of the fly

REMARKS: Natural raffia may be substituted if nylon raffia (one brand name is Swiss Straw) cannot be obtained. This pattern, listed in the North Country Anglers catalog, is fished as a nymph though it is not normally recognized as such.

DUN VARIANT NYMPH (Flick)

HOOK: Mustad 9671 (10–12)
THREAD: Olive (Flymaster 6/0)
TAIL: Three peacock herl fibers (tied short, one-eighth inch past bend)
BODY: Claret seal fur and black wool dubbing blend
LEGS: Brown partridge (or equivalent) as wet fly collar (see model, Blue Dun, page 124)

ED BURKE NYMPH

HOOK: Mustad 3906B (12–16)
THREAD: Black (Flymaster 6/0)
TAIL: Black hackle fibers
RIB: Fine oval gold tinsel (over abdomen only)
BODY: Black dubbing fur
THORAX: Fuzzy black fur (or equivalent)
LEGS: Black hackle wound as a wet fly collar (see model, Blue Dun, page 124)

EMERGENT HARE'S EAR NYMPH (Troth)

HOOK: Mustad 3906B (10–16)
THREAD: Brown (Flymaster 6/0)
TAIL: Lemon wood duck flank fibers (two gap widths in length)
ABDOMEN: Hare's ear dubbing fur
THORAX: Hare's ear fur with guard hairs spun in a dubbing loop and wound full; hair fibers stroked rearward as turns are made

WING PAD: Gray marabou extending rearward from eye one-third the shank length

ESOPUS BROWN

HOOK: Mustad 9671 (12–14)
THREAD: Black (Flymaster 6/0)
TAIL: Three bronze peacock herl fibers (tied short, one-eighth inch past bend)
UNDERBODY: Two strips of fine lead wire, one on each side of shank
ABDOMEN: Dyed brown raffia, lacquered
WING CASE: Dark brown turkey tail section or black crow (folded over)
THORAX: Three strands of peacock herl wound around shank to eye
LEGS: Black hen hackle fibers (tied short), beard style

REMARKS: This pattern, originated by Woly Wolyniec, requires that the hook be bent into a slight S curve with a pair of pliers.

THE EVENING STAR
(see under The Sparrow)

FLEDERMOUSE (Rosborough)

HOOK: Mustad 9671 (8–14)
THREAD: Tan or brown (Flymaster 6/0)
TAIL: None
BODY: A blend of two parts muskrat belly, one part jackrabbit fur without guard hairs (hare's mask may be substituted), and two parts medium brown mink. (This makes for a heather dun mixture, according to Polly Rosborough.) The body is roughed up with tips of scissors or dubbing needle after completion.
HACKLE: A fur rope collar of Australian opossum. Remove some of the underfur so the fly does not get bulky. (See Casual Dress.)
WING CASE: Brown widgeon fibers over teal fibers (to center of shank) (dyed teal may be substituted for widgeon)
HEAD: Tying thread to eye twice normal length with two coats of clear head lacquer

THE GIMP
(Plate VIII)

HOOK: Mustad 3906 (10–16)
THREAD: Black (Flymaster 6/0)
TAIL: Natural medium to dark dun hen hackle fibers (1½ gap widths in length)
BODY: Gray wool
WING: Two "gimp" feathers from Lady Amherst or golden pheasant neck, one placed over the other
HACKLE: Natural dun hen hackle (same color as tail) wound as a wet fly collar (see model, Blue Dun, page 124)

REMARKS: This pattern, submitted by Walt Stockman, uses a feather for the wing which many fly tyers are unaware of. If you look under the white neck tippet feathers of a Lady Amherst pheasant, or under the orange tippet feathers of a golden pheasant, you will find a short, fuzzy, pale gray secondary feather about a half to three-quarters of an inch long and about an eighth of an inch in width. This is the so-called gimp feather. Tied in over the body, it gives a very natural impression of a buggy aquatic insect.

GIRDLE BUG
The same as Rubber Legs except that it uses dark-colored rubber hackle.

GOLD-RIBBED HARE'S EAR NYMPH

HOOK: Mustad 3906B (8–16)
THREAD: Dark brown (Flymaster 6/0)
TAIL: Brown hackle fibers (1½ gap widths in length)
RIB: Fine oval gold tinsel
ABDOMEN: Hare's mask and ear dubbing fur blend
WING CASE: Gray goose or gray duck wing quill section (folded over)
THORAX: Same as abdomen except fuller
LEGS: Guard hairs plucked out from under thorax with a dubbing needle

REMARKS: This is the American Express card in the nymph category of flies. You don't want to go astream without it.

GRAY DRAKE NYMPH (Troth)

HOOK: Mustad 9671 (10–12)
THREAD: Brown (Flymaster 6/0)
TAIL: Brown partridge fibers (1½ gap widths in length)
RIB: Gray ostrich herl

ABDOMEN: Hare's ear dubbing fur

WING CASE: Dark brown mottled turkey wing quill section (or equivalent) (folded over)

THORAX: Same as abdomen but fuller

LEGS: Brown partridge hackle, beard style (to hook point)

GRAY MARABOU NYMPH
(see Marabou Nymph)

GREEN DAMSEL NYMPH
(Rosborough)

HOOK: Mustad 38941 (6–8)

THREAD: Olive (Flymaster 6/0 or Monocord 3/0)

TAIL: Golden olive marabou (tied short, three-eighths to one-half inch past bend)

RIB: Green darning thread

ABDOMEN: A medium olive fuzzy type of yarn (mohair, Mohlon, etc.)

THORAX: Same as abdomen but much fuller

LEGS: Barred teal dyed medium olive, beard style (to hook point)

WING PAD: Medium olive marabou fluff (to center of body)

GREEN DRAKE NYMPH

HOOK: Mustad 9672 (8–12)

THREAD: Olive (Flymaster 6/0)

TAIL: Male ringneck pheasant tail fibers, light shade (three to five fibers 1½ gap widths in length)

RIB: Olive cotton thread or olive single-strand floss

BODY: Olive tan dubbing fur

WING CASE: Dark mottled turkey wing quill section (or equivalent) (folded over)

LEGS: Lemon wood duck flank fibers, beard style

GREEN MOUNTAIN DAMSEL

HOOK: Mustad 9672 (4–8)

THREAD: Olive (Monocord 3/0 or Flymaster 6/0)

TAIL: Dyed olive goose biots (tied forked) (gap width in length)

SHELL: Olive marabou over body (covers both abdomen and thorax)

RIB: Fine gold wire

ABDOMEN: Dark green seal fur (or equivalent)

THORAX: Same as abdomen but slightly fuller

WING PAD: Olive marabou extending rearward for one-third shank length

REMARKS: This pattern, originated by Randall Kaufmann, features a slim body. Only the thorax area becomes slightly fuller.

HARE'S EAR NYMPH
(Rosborough)

HOOK: Mustad 3906 (10–14)

THREAD: Black (Flymaster 6/0)

TAIL: None

BODY: A blend of two parts muskrat belly, one part jackrabbit back (substitute hare's mask fur if needed) without guard hairs, and two parts medium brown mink. Dubbing is wound around shank as a twisted fur rope (see Casual Dress).

GILLS: Gray squirrel back with guard hairs fashioned into rope and wound as a hackle collar. Stroke fibers rearward as each turn is made.

WING PAD: Speckled black and brown hen hackle feathers extending rearward one-third body length

HEAD: Black ostrich herl fibers

REMARKS: The original dressing for this pattern calls for the fur of a winter-killed pack rat to be used for the gills. I have been unable to find a listing of this animal in any of the current catalogs and thus have substituted the fur and guard hairs from the back of the gray squirrel.

HENDRICKSON NYMPH (Flick)

HOOK: Mustad 9671 (12–16)

THREAD: Olive (Flymaster 6/0)

TAIL: Lemon wood duck flank fibers (or equivalent) (1½ gap widths past bend)

RIB: Fine gold wire

ABDOMEN: A dubbing blend of red fox belly, beaver, and claret seal fur (mixed blend appears grayish brown)

WING CASE: Light shade of gray goose or duck quill section

LEGS: Brown partridge (or equivalent)

THORAX: Same as abdomen but fuller

REMARKS: This pattern by Art Flick is generally the one listed in most catalogs,

Tying Steps for Hendrickson Nymph

a. Tail and fine-wire rib have been tied to hook shank.

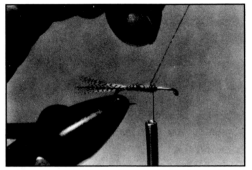

b. Body of dubbing fur has been formed and wire wound in open spiral to form segmentation. Excess wire is trimmed away.

c. Duck quill section and partridge feather have been tied in for wing case and legs.

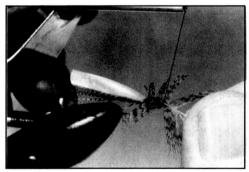

e. Partridge feather is being pulled forward beyond eye and secured with thread. Once secured, excess tip is cut away.

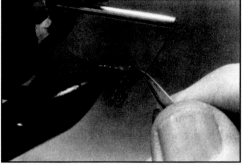

f. Duck quill section is pulled forward and also tied down with thread. Excess butt is trimmed away.

g. Completed Hendrickson Nymph. A thin coating of vinyl cement should be applied to top of wing case feather.

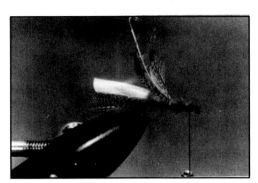

d. More fur has been dubbed on thread and wound for thorax. Some of fur has been wound against base of wing case and legs feather to produce more definition of bulge or hump. Thorax is always fuller than abdomen.

though Flick's name does not appear on many of them. Certain patterns become so familiar to us that they are accepted without regard to who originated them. But that's okay. The tribute is still there.

This pattern is the model for other flies using the particular construction methods of the wing case and legs. It is, perhaps, the most common method employed.

After the abdomen and a small portion of the thorax area have been formed, place the wing case section of light gray goose or duck quill on its back on top of the dubbing fur just slightly forward of the center of the hook shank and tie it down. The butt ends of the wing case section extend toward the eye. Then place a partridge hackle feather on top of the goose quill section, also on its back, with fibers curving slightly upward. The tip of the partridge hackle points toward the eye, and is tied down with thread. The tip of the partridge hackle feather has been separated from the lower fibers at the point where the feather is to be lashed to the shank. Any excess goose quill or partridge hackle protruding beyond the eye of the hook should be cut away at a point just before the eye. Wind the thread forward to the eye and back to its starting point to securely fasten both feathers to the shank.

The remainder of the thorax is now formed with additional dubbing. Force a bit of the dubbing against the two feathers lying on their backs, so that a slight hump is created when the wing case feather is later brought forward.

Bring the tying thread to a point just before the eye of the hook.

Grasp the partridge feather by the butt and pull it forward beyond the eye of the hook so that the fibers are now pointing outward and downward at the sides. The feather should be held slightly taut as the thread is brought around the stem just behind the eye of the hook.

Grasp the wing case goose quill feather and fold it forward also beyond the eye of the hook. Again hold it slightly taut as you bring the thread around the shank and the feather behind the eye of the hook. Bringing the wing case feather forward should force the partridge fibers downward a bit more to attain a natural semblance of legs. If the wing case feather does not force the partridge fibers downward just a bit, the goose quill section has probably been cut too thin, or if it forces the fibers downward too much, it has been cut too wide. The way the legs form will tell you just how wide the goose quill section should be cut the next time.

When selecting the partridge (or equivalent) hackle for the legs and checking for proper fiber length in relation to hook size, also look for feathers with a center stem that divides the fibers evenly. You will find that some feathers have fibers that are longer on one side than on the other. If you use these on your Hendrickson, you will have a completed nymph that has longer legs on either the left or the right side.

HENDRICKSON NYMPH (Troth)

HOOK: Mustad 3906B (10–12)
THREAD: Brown (Flymaster 6/0)

TAIL: Brown partridge fibers dyed olive (gap width past bend)

RIB: Dark brown thread

ABDOMEN: Dyed olive rabbit and natural brown mink fur, mixed

WING CASE: Natural black duck wing quill section (folded over)

THORAX: Same as abdomen but fuller

LEGS: Brown partridge fibers dyed olive, spread beard style

HENRY'S LAKE SPECIAL

HOOK: Mustad 9671 (6–10)

THREAD: Olive (Flymaster 6/0)

TAIL: Dyed brown goose biots (tied forked) (gap width in length)

PALMER RIB: Brown saddle hackle palmered through body and clipped to length of one-eighth inch

BODY: Peacock herl

REMARKS: This pattern is similar to the style of a Woolly Worm or Woolly Bugger. It is a favorite on Henry's Lake and Yellowstone Lake.

ISONYCHIA NYMPH

HOOK: Mustad 9671 (10–14)

THREAD: Brown (Flymaster 6/0)

TAIL: Three fibers from center tail of male ringneck pheasant

RIB: Tan cotton thread or tan single-strand floss

ABDOMEN: Claret seal fur (or equivalent) blended with brown dubbing fur (an equal amount of each)

WING CASE: Canada goose wing quill section

LEGS: Brown partridge hackle or equivalent (for wing case and legs, see model, Hendrickson Nymph)

THORAX: Same as abdomen but fuller

KEMP BUG

HOOK: Mustad 3906B (6–12)

THREAD: Black (Flymaster 6/0)

TAIL: Three or four strands of peacock herl (cut short and stubby, barely past bend)

BODY: Peacock herl

HACKLE: Furnace as a wet fly collar (see model, Blue Dun, page 124)

WING: Grizzly hackle tips tied flat and slightly splayed (delta style), angling backward for half shank length

REMARKS: Originated by Roy Donnelly and listed in Troth's Custom Flies catalog.

LARESE CASUAL
(Plate VIII)

HOOK: Mustad 9672 (10–12)

THREAD: Black (Flymaster 6/0)

TAIL: Guard hairs from red fox squirrel (twice gap width past bend)

RIB: Fine oval gold tinsel

ABDOMEN: Underfur from the orange-tan area near the base of the tail of a red fox squirrel, processed through a blender

THORAX: Blended fox squirrel with guard hairs left in. Wound on shank by means of spinning loop method. Fibers are stroked

rearward as each turn is made. (See Casual Dress.)

HACKLE: A mottled brown hen saddle feather wound as a wet fly collar (see model, Blue Dun, page 124)

REMARKS: This pattern, originated by Larry Larese, serves as an early-season, all-purpose nymph in the northern tier region of Pennsylvania, though it is rapidly spreading elsewhere. Selection and construction of materials are excellent for a lifelike breathing imitation.

LEADWING COACHMAN NYMPH

HOOK: Mustad 9671 (10–16)

THREAD: Black (Flymaster 6/0)

TAIL: Brown hackle fibers (1½ gap widths past bend)

BODY: Peacock herl

HACKLE: Dark brown as a wet fly collar and pulled down (see model, Blue Dun, page 124)

WING PAD: Mallard quill cut square, extending rearward one-third distance from eye

REMARKS: One of the smaller covert feathers from the shoulder of a duck wing is easily transformed into a wing pad feather with a pair of scissors.

LEPTOPHLEBIA NYMPH

HOOK: Mustad 9671 (12–18)
THREAD: Black (Flymaster 6/0)
TAIL: Three gray mini ostrich herl fibers (1½ gap widths past bend) (tied spread)
ABDOMEN: Stripped peacock quill (see model, Quill Gordon, pages 24–6)
WING CASE: Gray mallard wing quill section (or equivalent) (folded over)
THORAX: Muskrat dubbing fur
LEGS: Gray partridge hackle (or equivalent), beard style

LIGHT CAHILL NYMPH

HOOK: Mustad 9671 (10–16)
THREAD: Yellow (Flymaster 6/0)
TAIL: Lemon wood duck flank fibers (1½ gap widths past bend)
BODY: Creamy yellow dubbing fur
HACKLE: Dark cream as a wet fly collar and pulled down (see model, Blue Dun, page 124)
WING PAD: Mallard flank feather cut square, extending rearward one-third distance from eye

MAGGOT

HOOK: Mustad 3906B (12–16)
THREAD: Black (Flymaster 6/0)
SHELL: Dark brown duck quill section over entire body
BODY: Light cream latex
HACKLE: Dark brown as a wet fly collar (see model, Blue Dun, page 124)

REMARKS: It is suggested that an underbody of white floss be wound forward before the latex; otherwise the black thread may show through the body.

MARABOU NYMPH
(Plate VIII)

HOOK: Mustad 3906B (10–18)
THREAD: Black (Flymaster 6/0)
TAIL: Ten to twelve dark moose body hair fibers
RIB: Medium to fine gold wire, depending on hook size
BODY: Black marabou cut into small pieces, dubbed onto the tying thread, and wound to the eye; fuller at the thorax area
BACK AND WING CASE: Formed from the same section of moose fibers that formed the tail. Gold wire is wound four or five turns over the thread that secured the tail, then brought forward in an open spiral to the thorax area, where it is again wound around the fibers for two or three turns before it is tied down with thread and the excess cut away. Thread is then brought forward to the eye of the hook and the moose fibers brought forward again to be tied down behind the eye. Excesses are trimmed. Note: While it may take more moose fibers to form the back and wing case of this pattern than it does the tail, any excess fibers may simply be snipped out of the tail section.

LEGS: Formed by bending back and tying down excess butts (three on each side) and trimming to size

REMARKS: This pattern shows an unusual, yet simple method of forming a nymph. It not only gives a proper appearance but uses the correct material (marabou) to simulate the movement of a natural insect.

Marabou nymphs are also tied in marabou body shades of gray, amber, olive, and brown. Tying thread should match the body color. See pp. 174–5.

MARCH BROWN NYMPH (Flick)

HOOK: Mustad 9671 (10–14)
THREAD: Gray (Flymaster 6/0)
TAIL: Three fibers from center tail of male ringneck pheasant, equally spread (twice gap width past bend)
ABDOMEN: An equal blend of amber seal fur (or equivalent) and fawn-colored fox fur
WING CASE: A section of fibers from the side tail feathers of male ringneck pheasant
LEGS: Brown partridge (or equivalent) (for legs and wing case, see model, Hendrickson Nymph)
THORAX: Same as abdomen but fuller

MARCH BROWN NYMPH (Troth)

HOOK: Mustad 3906B (8–12)
THREAD: Brown (Flymaster 6/0)
TAIL: Three fibers from the center tail of

Tying Steps for Marabou Nymph

a. A clump of moose body hair has been tied to the hook shank just before the bend. The tips extend rearward and form the tail. A piece of medium gold wire has been tied to the shank in front of the tail. A black marabou feather has been cut into small pieces (about one-eighth to one-quarter inch) and adhered to a dubbing loop which has been twisted into a rope. (See rope technique procedure in model fly Casual Dress.)

b. Rope of twisted marabou has been wound forward for two-thirds of the hook-shank length.

c. Excess clump of moose body hair is pulled forward and tied down with tying thread.

e. Thorax area has also been formed by using the looped and twisted rope of marabou pieces. This area is fuller. Moose hair is held out of the way while some of the marabou rope is forced against its base to ensure a bulging wing case.

f. Excess moose hair is pulled forward once more and tied down with thread just behind the hook eye.

g. Three to four strands of moose hair fibers are pulled rearward and tied down with thread to serve as legs protruding from the sides of the abdomen. They are then trimmed to proper size.

d. Gold wire has been wound around area just forward of hook bend for three or four turns to thoroughly secure tail, after which it has been wound forward in an open spiral to a point directly in front of marabou abdomen, where it has been tied down with thread and the excess cut away.

h. Completed Marabou Nymph, a very scraggly but effective fly.

male ringneck pheasant, equally spread (twice gap width past bend)

RIB: Dark brown sewing thread

ABDOMEN: An equal blend of cream-colored fox fur and yellow seal fur (or equivalent)

WING CASE: Mottled brown turkey wing quill section (or equivalent)

THORAX: Same as abdomen but fuller

LEGS: Brown partridge (or equivalent) (for wing case and legs, see model, Hendrickson Nymph)

MARTINEZ BLACK NYMPH

HOOK: Mustad 9671 (10–14)

THREAD: Black (Flymaster 6/0)

TAIL: Natural guinea hen fibers (1½ gap widths past bend)

RIB: Fine oval gold tinsel

ABDOMEN: Black seal fur (or equivalent)

WING CASE: Green raffia (folded over)

THORAX: Black chenille

HACKLE: Gray partridge (or equivalent) as a wet fly collar (see model, Blue Dun, page 124)

MATT'S FUR NYMPH

HOOK: Mustad 9672 (6–12)

THREAD: Brown (Flymaster 6/0)

TAIL: Lemon wood duck flank fibers (1½ gap widths past bend)

RIB: Fine oval gold tinsel

ABDOMEN: An equal blend of natural otter fur and cream seal fur (or substitute)

WING CASE: Lemon wood duck flank fibers (folded over)

THORAX: Same as abdomen but fuller

LEGS: Formed by tying back leftover tip ends of wing case

REMARKS: The wing case is tied in such a way that the wood duck fibers point forward beyond the eye of the hook after being folded over. They should be measured so that when the fibers are forced rearward and tied down, the resulting legs are of a natural length. This pattern is featured in Randall Kaufmann's book *American Nymph Fly Tying Manual.* The pattern was originated by Matt Lavell.

MICHIGAN MAYFLY NYMPH

HOOK: Mustad 9671 (6–10)

THREAD: Black (Flymaster 6/0)

TAIL: Grizzly hackle fibers, spread slightly apart (1½ gap widths past bend)

RIB: Dark brown sewing thread

BODY: Brown Mohlon (or equivalent fuzzy type yarn) twisted and rotated one turn for each turn around the shank

LEGS: Grizzly hackle fibers

THORAX: Hare's ear dubbing fur

WING PAD: Brown ostrich trimmed to extend rearward from eye for one-third of the body

REMARKS: The grizzly hackle fiber legs should protrude from the sides of the thorax. This can be accomplished by winding the grizzly hackle through the thorax palmer style and then trimming all the fibers except those on the sides.

MINK NYMPH

HOOK: Mustad 3906B (10–14)
THREAD: Black (Flymaster 6/0)
BODY: Mink dubbing fur naturally tapered to head

REMARKS: This ultra-simple pattern is probably a takeoff on the Muskrat Nymph, except that it does not have a black ostrich herl head.

MONTANA NYMPH

HOOK: Mustad 9672 (6–12)
THREAD: Black (Flymaster 6/0)
TAIL: Black crow or black hackle fibers (gap width past bend)
ABDOMEN: Double-strand extra-fine black chenille
LEGS: Black hackle fibers, wound palmer style through thorax
THORAX: Size 1 or 2 (related to hook size) yellow chenille
WING CASE: Double-strand extra-fine black chenille brought over from abdomen

REMARKS: The double-strand black chenille forms both the abdomen and the wing case. After the abdomen has been formed, the black chenille is left hanging out of the way until the thorax and legs have been completed. Then it is pulled forward and tied down as the wing case.

MUSKRAT NYMPH

HOOK: Mustad 3906B, 9671 (10–16)
THREAD: Black (Flymaster 6/0)

BODY: Muskrat dubbing fur
HACKLE: Finely marked natural guinea hen fibers, beard style
HEAD: Black ostrich herl

REMARKS: A number of seasons ago I took a survey to find out which patterns were the top ten flies in various categories. I was a little surprised that the Muskrat Nymph was number one, surpassing even the old standby, the Gold-Ribbed Hare's Ear Nymph. Polly Rosborough deserves credit for the Muskrat Nymph and I doubt if even he knows how very popular this pattern is. It is carried by just about every catalog house and fly shop in the country.

When Rosborough ties this nymph, he likes to make a blend of muskrat belly, beaver belly, and jackrabbit fur (less guard hairs) and he forms the body using his famous rope method (see Casual Dress). Most tyers today simply tie it with muskrat dubbing fur and add a black ostrich herl head. The trout don't seem to mind.

NEEDLEFLY NYMPH

HOOK: Mustad 9672 (8–12)
THREAD: Black (Flymaster 6/0)
TAIL: Brown hackle fibers (1½ gap widths past bend)

BODY: Flat silver tinsel
HACKLE: Mottled gray/brown rump feather from male ringneck pheasant, tied spey fashion as a wet fly collar (see model, Blue Dun, page 124)
HEAD: Peacock herl

REMARKS: Originated by Dawn Holbrook.

OLIVE DUN NYMPH

HOOK: Mustad 9671 (14–18)
THREAD: Olive (Flymaster 6/0)
TAIL: Three fibers from center tail of male ringneck pheasant, spread (twice gap width past bend)
RIB: Brown sewing thread or brown single-strand floss
ABDOMEN: Olive gray dubbing fur
WING CASE: Mallard wing quill section (folded over)
THORAX: Same as abdomen but fuller
LEGS: Brown hackle, divided beard style

OLIVE MARABOU NYMPH
(see Marabou Nymph)

ORVIS ALL-PURPOSE NYMPH, DARK

HOOK: Mustad 38941 (8–16)
THREAD: Black (Flymaster 6/0)
TAIL: Three fibers from center tail of male ringneck pheasant, spread (1½ gap widths in length)
RIB: Fine gold wire
ABDOMEN: Dark brown dubbing fur

WING CASE: Dark brown white-tipped turkey tail section (folded over)

THORAX: Same as abdomen but fuller

LEGS: Black hen hackle, divided beard style

ORVIS ALL-PURPOSE NYMPH, LIGHT

HOOK: Mustad 38941 (8–16)

THREAD: Black (Flymaster 6/0)

TAIL: Lemon wood duck flank fibers (1½ gap widths past bend)

RIB: Brown sewing thread or brown single-strand floss

ABDOMEN: Cream buff red fox dubbing fur

WING CASE: Mottled mahogany section of fibers from center tail of male ringneck pheasant (folded over)

THORAX: Same as abdomen but fuller

LEGS: Dark cream hen hackle fibers, divided beard style

ORVIS ALL-PURPOSE NYMPH, MEDIUM

HOOK: Mustad 38941 (8–16)

THREAD: Black (Flymaster 6/0)

TAIL: Three fibers from center tail of male ringneck pheasant, spread (1½ gap widths past bend)

RIB: Fine gold wire

ABDOMEN: Grayish-brown red fox dubbing fur

WING CASE: Dark brown white-tipped turkey tail section (folded over)

THORAX: Same as abdomen but fuller

LEGS: Brown hen hackle fibers, divided beard style

OTTER NYMPH

HOOK: Mustad 9671 (10–14)

THREAD: Black (Flymaster 6/0)

TAIL: Mallard flank fibers (1½ gap widths past bend)

ABDOMEN: Tan otter dubbing fur

WING CASE: Section of mallard flank fibers (folded over)

THORAX: Same as abdomen but fuller

LEGS: Speckled light gray guinea hen fibers, divided beard style

PALE MORNING DUN NYMPH

HOOK: Mustad 9671 (12–18)

THREAD: Cream (Flymaster 6/0)

TAIL: Mallard flank fibers, sparse (1½ gap widths past bend)

ABDOMEN: Cream dubbing fur or poly dubbing

WING CASE: Light-shade duck wing quill section (folded over)

THORAX: Same as abdomen but fuller

LEGS: Speckled mallard breast feather fibers, divided beard style

REMARKS: There are more than a few versions of this pattern. This and the one following are two of the most popular.

PALE EVENING DUN NYMPH

HOOK: Mustad 3906B (14–18)

THREAD: Olive (Flymaster 6/0)

TAIL: Lemon wood duck flank fibers (1½ gap widths past bend)

RIB: Fine gold wire

ABDOMEN: Yellowish-gray dubbing fur

WING CASE: Light-shade mallard wing quill section (folded over)

THORAX: Same as abdomen but fuller

LEGS: Brown partridge hackle (or equivalent), divided beard style

PARTRIDGE AND BROWN NYMPH

HOOK: Mustad 3906B (12–14)

THREAD: Black (Flymaster 6/0)

TAIL: Lemon wood duck flank fibers (1½ gap widths past bend)

ABDOMEN: Stripped peacock tinted brown (see model, Quill Gordon, pages 24–6)

THORAX: Bronze peacock herl, full

LEGS: One turn of brown partridge hackle as wet fly collar (see model, Blue Dun, page 124)

REMARKS: Originated by Everett Caryl.

PEACOCK MIDGE NYMPH

HOOK: Mustad 9671 (18–22)

THREAD: Black (Flymaster 6/0)

TAIL: None

ABDOMEN AND THORAX: The quill from the bronze and green portion of the peacock eye wound around the shank so that the bronze portion forms the abdomen and the green portion the thorax

REMARKS: This all-purpose pattern serves as larvae for small caddis and diptera flies.

PELLIS MUSKRAT
(Plate VIII)

HOOK: Mustad 9671 (10–14)
THREAD: Black (Flymaster 6/0)
TAIL: Brown hackle fibers (1½ gap widths past bend)
PALMER RIB: Brown hackle palmered through body and clipped short (a stubby effect)
BODY: Muskrat dubbing fur
HACKLE: Brown as a wet fly collar (see model, Blue Dun, page 124)

REMARKS: Originated by Tom Pellis, this pattern is highly regarded in northern Pennsylvania.

PHEASANT TAIL

HOOK: Mustad 3906B (10–18)
THREAD: Black (Flymaster 6/0)
TAIL: Three fibers from center tail of male ringneck pheasant (gap width past bend)
BODY: Fibers from center tail of male ringneck pheasant twisted with gold wire and wound forward
WING CASE: Section of fibers from center tail of ringneck pheasant (folded over)

LEGS: Formed by cutting two or three fibers at the back end of the wing case and pulling them outward at a 90-degree angle

REMARKS: This is perhaps the most famous of the many patterns originated by Frank Sawyer, the legendary English riverkeeper and author of *Nymphs and the Trout.*

POTOMANTHUS NYMPH

HOOK: Mustad 9671 (10–12)
THREAD: Tan (Flymaster 6/0)
TAIL: Lemon wood duck flank fibers (1½ gap widths past bend)
RIB: Beige sewing thread or beige single-strand floss
ABDOMEN: Fawn amber dubbing fur
WING CASE: Mallard wing quill section (folded over)
THORAX: Same as abdomen but fuller
LEGS: Golden ginger hen hackle, divided beard style

PRINCE NYMPH
(also known as Black Forked Tail)

HOOK: Mustad 9671 (8–12)
THREAD: Black (Flymaster 6/0)
TAIL: Two black goose biots (tied forked) (gap width in length)
RIB: Fine oval silver tinsel
BODY: Black ostrich herl
HACKLE: Black hen hackle as a wet fly collar (see model, Blue Dun, page 124)
WING: Two white goose biots tied in the form of a V so that tips flare slightly upward and extend to bend of hook

REMARKS: Originated by Doug Prince. See also Brown Forked Tail.

RED FOX SQUIRREL HAIR NYMPH
(Plate VIII)

HOOK: Mustad 9671 (2–18)
THREAD: Dark brown (Flymaster 6/0)
TAIL: A few body hairs from back of red fox squirrel with some underfur left in (gap width past bend)
UNDERBODY: Lead wire around front half of shank
RIB: Oval gold tinsel (gold wire on sizes 16 and smaller)
ABDOMEN: Orange belly fur from red fox quirrel blended with 40% synthetic sparkle or Antron dubbing close in color to belly fur
THORAX: Back fur and guard hairs from red fox squirrel blended with 40% synthetic sparkle or Antron yarn in similar coloration

REMARKS: This pattern by Dave Whitlock is similar in appearance to the Gold-Ribbed Hare's Ear Nymph. It is used to represent many types of aquatic life, such as caddis pupa, mayfly nymphs, stonefly nymphs, and crustaceans. It is an all-purpose pattern for trout and landlocked salmon.

If red fox squirrel is unattainable, gray squirrel belly dyed orange may be substituted for the abdomen, and gray squirrel back fur and hair dyed orange may be substituted for the thorax.

REG'S HELLGRAMITE

HOOK: Mustad 79580 (8–10)
THREAD: Black (Flymaster 6/0)
TAIL: Black marabou, fairly thick (half again as long as shank)
PALMER RIB: Dark bronze blue dun hackle palmered through body
BODY: Dark chocolate brown dubbing fur

REMARKS: This pattern, originated by Reg Baird, may not look like much, but then, neither does the Woolly Bugger, to which it is similar. I'm sure that this pattern, like the Woolly Bugger or the Woolly Worm, is taken for many other things besides a hellgramite. Flies of this type having a multitude of breathing fibers are always highly effective.

RUBBER LEGS

HOOK: Mustad 9672 (2–10)
THREAD: Black (Flymaster 6/0 or Monocord 3/0)
TAIL: Two strands of white rubber hackle (tied forked) (1½ gap widths past bend)
BODY: Black chenille (related to hook size)
LEGS: White rubber hackle, spaced equally in thirds, extending from sides of body (six legs in all)
ANTENNAE: Two strands of white rubber hackle (same length as tail)

REMARKS: This pattern is tied both weighted and unweighted and also in body colors of olive, brown, yellow, and gray. This pattern is similar to the Girdle Bug, which generally uses dark gray rubber hackle. Excellent pattern for attracting fish of all kinds.

SCRAGGLY

HOOK: Mustad 3906B (12–18)
THREAD: Black (Flymaster 6/0)
TAIL: None
PALMER RIB: Grizzly hackle palmered through body and trimmed for a stubby or scraggly effect
BODY: Peacock herl
LEGS: Light brown hen hackle wound as a wet fly collar (see model, Blue Dun, page 124)

SLATE WING OLIVE

HOOK: Mustad 3906B (14–20)
THREAD: Olive (Flymaster 6/0)
TAIL: Three Canada goose quill fibers (tied spread) (1½ gap widths past bend)
RIB: Gray sewing thread or gray single-strand floss
ABDOMEN: Grayish-brown dubbing fur
WING CASE: Canada goose wing quill section (folded over)
THORAX: Same as abdomen but fuller
LEGS: Medium blue dun hen hackle fibers, divided beard style

SLATE WING OLIVE NYMPH
(Troth)

HOOK: Mustad 9671 (12)
THREAD: Olive (Flymaster 6/0)
TAIL: Brown partridge (or equivalent), fibers dyed dark olive (1½ gap widths past bend)
RIB: Dark brown thread
ABDOMEN: Dyed dark olive rabbit dubbing fur
WING CASE: Dyed black raffia (folded over)
THORAX: Same as abdomen but slightly fuller
LEGS: Brown partridge (or equivalent), dyed dark olive, tied spread as beard
HEAD: Dyed dark olive rabbit dubbing fur

THE SPARROW
(Plate VIII)

HOOK: Mustad 9671 (4–10)
THREAD: Gray (Flymaster 6/0)
TAIL: One or two short "marabou" ring-neck pheasant underrump feathers (gap width past bend) (the soft and fluffy feathers under the rump plumage, brown/gray in color)
BODY: A dubbing blend consisting of two-thirds gray squirrel body fur with guard hairs mixed in and one-third gray rabbit underfur
COLLAR HACKLE: A mottled gray and brown pheasant rump feather wound as a folded hackle (sparse, no more than two or three turns around the shank), the tips extending to the center of the tail.

HEAD HACKLE: One or two gray pheasant aftershaft feathers wound as a folded hackle forming a soft, fluffy head (see "aftershaft feather" in the glossary)

REMARKS: This pattern, which was originated by Jack Gartside, exemplifies the proper use of materials to achieve an impression of life. All of the materials used will pulse, breathe, and vibrate when fished and give the appearance of a natural insect. In fact, it is almost impossible not to catch trout or other fish with this fly. It also happens to be one of the simplest of patterns to tie at the vise.

Gartside also ties another version of this pattern, Evening Star, which is essentially a "Black Sparrow." It uses dyed black pheasant underrump feather for the tail, iridescent herl from a peacock eye for the body, and dyed black rump and aftershaft feathers for collar and head hackle.

Both the Sparrow and the Evening Star are fished as nymphs or wet flies and on occasion retrieved through the water as you would a streamer fly.

SPRING CREEK NYMPH

HOOK: Mustad 9671 (12–16)
THREAD: Tan (Flymaster 6/0)
TAIL: Brown partridge fibers (or equivalent) (1½ gap widths past bend)
BODY: Light olive tan dubbing fur

LEGS: Brown partridge hackle fibers, beard style
WING PAD: Brown ostrich herl extending rearward from eye for one-third length of shank

SQUIRREL

HOOK: Mustad 3906 (10–14)
THREAD: Black (Flymaster 6/0)
TAIL: Gray squirrel body fibers (gap width past bend)
BODY: Gray squirrel body fur with guard hairs mixed in (cut from skin and mixed in blender)
HACKLE: Two turns of squirrel body with guard hairs trapped between thread (as in Rosborough's Casual Dress) and stroked rearward when winding collar

REMARKS: This pattern should be tied weighted or fished with a weighted leader, since it will not readily sink because of all the fibers and underfur.

STONEFLY CREEPER

HOOK: Mustad 9672 (8–12)
THREAD: Primrose (pale yellow) (Flymaster 6/0)
TAIL: Two fibers from center tail of male ringneck pheasant tied forked (1½ gap widths past bend)
RIB: Stripped center stem quill from ginger neck or saddle hackle feather (see model, Red Quill, pages 24–6)
BODY: Yellow seal fur (or equivalent)

LEGS: Grouse hackle (or equivalent), beard style
WING: Lemon wood duck flank feather tied flat and extending over full length of body

REMARKS: Originated by Art Flick.

TELLICO NYMPH

HOOK: Mustad 3906B (10–14)
THREAD: Black (Flymaster 6/0)
TAIL: Guinea hen hackle fibers (1½ gap widths past bend)
SHELL: Section of fibers from one of the shorter (and lighter) male ringneck pheasant tails; covers entire body
RIB: Peacock herl
BODY: Yellow floss
LEGS: Brown hen hackle as a wet fly collar (see model, Blue Dun, page 124)

TIMBERLINE

HOOK: Mustad 3906B (12–16)
THREAD: Brown (Flymaster 6/0)
TAIL: Three moose body fibers (tied short, not quite gap width in length)
RIB: Copper wire
ABDOMEN: Hare's ear dubbing blend (do not include mask fur)
WING CASE: Underside section of cen-

ter tail of male ringneck pheasant (dark side showing on wing case) (folded over)

THORAX: Same as abdomen but fuller

LEGS: Ringneck fibers from excess wing case material folded back and tied slanting rearward (three on each side)

TRICORYTHODES NYMPH

HOOK: Mustad 94859 (20–22)

THREAD: Black (Flymaster 6/0)

TAIL: Dark dun hackle fibers (twice gap width past bend)

ABDOMEN: Dark brown dubbing fur

WING CASE: Dark-shade duck quill section (folded over)

THORAX: Same as abdomen but fuller

TRUEBLOOD'S OTTER NYMPH

HOOK: Mustad 3906 (8–14)

THREAD: Black (Flymaster 6/0)

TAIL: Brown partridge hackle fibers (or equivalent) (tied short, about one-half gap width in length)

BODY: Otter dubbing fur and natural cream seal fur (or equivalent) mixed (two parts otter, one part seal)

HACKLE: Brown partridge, beard style

TUPS INDISPENSABLE

HOOK: Mustad 9671 (12–16)

THREAD: Primrose (pale yellow) (Flymaster 6/0)

TAIL: Pale dun hackle tip (single unit of tip) (1½ gap widths past bend)

ABDOMEN: Light yellow floss

THORAX: Honey, red, and sulfur yellow fur mixed as blend

LEGS: Pale dun hen hackle as a wet fly collar (see model, Blue Dun, page 124)

TURKEY NYMPH

HOOK: Mustad 3906B (12–16)

THREAD: Black (Flymaster 6/0)

TAIL: Golden pheasant tippets (1½ gap widths past bend)

BODY: Medium blue dun muskrat dubbing fur

WING PAD: Mottled turkey wing quill section (or equivalent) (end V-notched) (to center of body)

LEGS: Dark ginger as a wet fly collar (see model, Blue Dun, page 124)

WATERBUG

HOOK: Mustad 9671 (8–12)

THREAD: Brown (Flymaster 6/0)

RIB: Fine gold wire

SHELL: Section of mallard flank fibers over entire body (gold wire rib goes around both shell and body)

BODY: Brown seal fur (or equivalent)

WESTERN GREEN DRAKE NYMPH
(Plate VIII)

HOOK: Mustad 9671 (10–12)

THREAD: Black (Flymaster 6/0)

TAIL: About six fibers from center tail of male ringneck pheasant, spread (gap width past bend)

RIB: Fine gold wire

ABDOMEN: Dark olive/brown dubbing fur

GILLS: A brown mini ostrich herl along each side of abdomen (rib of gold wire holds ostrich in place)

WING CASE: Very dark goose or duck quill section

LEGS: Brown partridge (or equivalent) (for wing case and legs, see model, Hendrickson Nymph)

THORAX: Same as abdomen but fuller and fluffed out a bit with dubbing needle

REMARKS: This pattern has a very seductive appearance and a goodly amount of moving, living fibers.

WHITE NYMPH

HOOK: Mustad 9672 (4–14)

THREAD: White (Flymaster 6/0)

TAIL: Two white goose biots (tied forked) (1½ gap widths past bend)

RIB: Cream Monocord

ABDOMEN: An equal blend of white rabbit and natural cream seal fur

WING CASE: White goose or duck wing quill section

Tying Steps for Hexegenia Wiggle Nymph

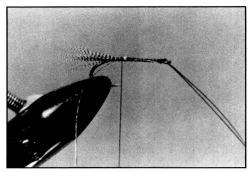

a. Rear hook of wiggle nymph which has tail tied in and a piece of gold wire tied in to be wound later. Hook eye, which has been straightened, has a piece of monofilament looped through it with both loose ends protruding downward through eye.

b. Body has been dubbed with fur and wire spiraled through it. Excess wire is trimmed away.

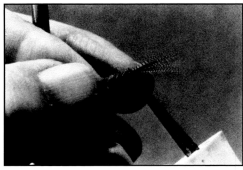

c. Point, barb, and bend of rear hook have been snipped off with a pair of wire cutters. Super Glue is being placed at junction of tail and remaining shank.

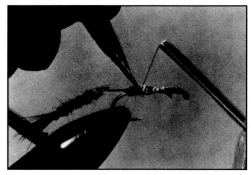

f. Rear quarter of fore hook has been wound with dubbing fur and the wing case feather (mottled turkey quill section) is being tied in just forward of the body.

g. Thorax area has been wound with dubbed fur and legs of wood duck flank fibers are being tied in beard style.

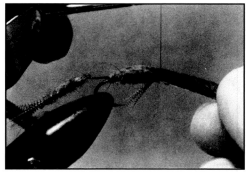

h. Turkey wing quill section is pulled forward over thorax and tied down with thread. Excess is then snipped away.

LEGS: White hen hackle (for wing case and legs, see model, Hendrickson Nymph)

THORAX: Same as abdomen but fuller

d. Fore hook has been placed in vise and mono-filament from rear hook is being tied to shank.

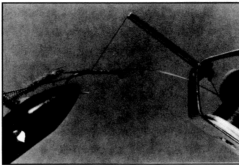

e. Both ends of monofilament have been lashed to shank up to eye of fore hook. One strand has been folded back and is being wound down with more thread. The other end of monofilament will be lashed to the other side of the shank. Then excess ends will be trimmed off.

i. Completed Hexegenia Wiggle Nymph.

REMARKS: This all-purpose white nymph pattern is tied to represent the stages of various nymphs during their molting process. In order to grow, the nymphs and larvae of all insects periodically shed their skins (or shells, or cases) and grow new ones to fit their expanded bodies. During the molting process they are very pale and almost colorless. There have been patterns on the market labeled Albino Nymph, but though the materials may serve the purpose, this terminology is wrong for the molting stage, since an albino is not a common natural occurrence.

Other materials which may be used to structure a white nymph pattern are cream latex or a white segmented body covered by a clear plastic shell.

Wiggle Nymphs

It is odd that this type of fly is not more popular than it is. Is it because these patterns seem to be more difficult to tie, or is it that the fly looks more like a lure than a fly?

The Wiggle Nymph, introduced by Doug Swisher and Carl Richards, is perhaps one of the more important contributions to fly fishing because it imitates a swimming motion so much like that of the natural itself. Unlike streamer flies, which are tied in tandem in order to trail a rear hook in case of short strikes, the Wiggle Nymph construction involves the snipping of the second hook high in the bend and leaving just a single point of the fore hook with which to strike the fish.

The Hexegenia Wiggle Nymph will serve as a model for the construction of this type of fly.

HEXEGENIA WIGGLE NYMPH

HOOK FOR REAR SECTION: Any standard ring-eye or a Mustad 3906 which has been formed into a ring-eye (2–6)

THREAD: Olive (Flymaster 6/0 or Monocord 3/0)

TAIL: Wood duck flank fibers or brown partridge fibers (1½ gap widths past end of rear hook)

RIB: Gold or copper wire

ABDOMEN (all of rear hook): Light tan dubbing fur (hare's ear and amber seal blended equally is a good combination)

HOOK FOR FORE SECTION: Mustad 3906 (2–6)

REMAINDER OF ABDOMEN: Same as on rear hook

WING CASE: Mottled brown turkey wing quill section (or equivalent) (folded over—pulled forward)

LEGS: Wood duck flank fibers or brown partridge fibers as beard-style hackle (or may also be formed in the manner of construction used in Hendrickson Nymph)

THORAX: Same as abdomen but fuller

1. Place a size 6 ring-eye hook in the vise (or insert a Mustad 3906), heat the eye, and bend it straight with a pair of flat-nosed pliers.

2. Tie in the tail and ribbing and dub the body. Wind the ribbing to the eye. Whip-finish and remove the rear portion of the fly from the vise. Cut the hook at the bend with a pair of wire cutters. Place a drop of Super Glue at the point where the body ends and a stub of wire remains.

3. Place a size 6 Mustad 3906 hook in the vise (this time do not straighten the eye). Cut a four-inch piece of ten-pound-test monofilament and loop it through the eye of the already formed rear hook. Place the two ends of the monofilament on top of the hook now in the vise and secure them with thread from the bend to the eye. Measure the length of the loop to make sure that the eye of the rear hook is no more than an eighth of an inch from the bend of the fore hook.

Double the loose ends of monofilament back along the sides of the hook shank and bind them down with thread. Clip the excess monofilament. Enough wrappings of thread should be taken around the mono and shank so that the rear hook will not slip. Super Glue easily solves the problem.

4. Form a short portion of dubbed body and tie in the wing case feather. Apply more dubbing to the thread and wind a fairly long thorax area. Remember, this imitation is tied over a two-hook area and the abdomen and thorax must remain in proportion to the two hook shanks.

5. Tie in the legs of wood duck fibers under the shank and just before the eye of the hook. Bring the wing case feather forward and tie it down. Snip the excess and whip-finish. Lacquer the wing case with Flexament or Plio Bond.

Other important Wiggle Nymph imitations follow.

MUSKRAT WIGGLE NYMPH

HOOK FOR REAR SECTION: Any standard ring-eye or Mustad 3906 which has been straightened into a ring-eye (12–16)

THREAD: Gray (Flymaster 6/0)

TAIL: Wood duck flank fibers (gap width past bend)

RIB: Copper or gold wire

ABDOMEN: Muskrat dubbing fur

HOOK FOR FORE SECTION: Mustad 3906 (12–16)

REST OF ABDOMEN: Muskrat dubbing fur

WING CASE: Mallard wing quill section

LEGS: Wood duck flank fibers, beard style

THORAX: Same as abdomen but fuller

SLATE BROWN WIGGLE NYMPH
(Plate VIII)

HOOK FOR REAR SECTION: Any standard ring-eye or Mustad 3906 which has been formed into a ring-eye (8–16)

THREAD: Olive (Flymaster 6/0)

TAIL: Wood duck flank fibers (gap width past bend)

RIB: Copper or gold wire

ABDOMEN: Dark reddish-brown dubbing fur (claret seal and dark brown rabbit mix well)

HOOK FOR FORE SECTION: Mustad 3906 (8–16)

REST OF ABDOMEN: Same as on rear hook

WING CASE: Dark gray duck wing quill section (folded over)

THORAX: Same as abdomen but fuller

LEGS: Wood duck flank fibers, beard style

STONEFLY WIGGLE NYMPH
(Plate VIII)

HOOK FOR REAR SECTION: Any standard ring-eye or Mustad 3906 which has been formed into a ring-eye (2–8)

THREAD: Black (Flymaster 6/0 or Monocord 3/0)

TAIL: Two dark gray goose biots (tied forked) (gap width past bend)

RIB: Fine oval silver tinsel

ABDOMEN: Dark brown dubbing fur (rabbit and seal mix provides extra movement)

HOOK FOR FORE SECTION: Mustad 3906 (2–8)

REST OF ABDOMEN: Same as rear hook

WING CASE: Mottled brown turkey wing quill section (or equivalent) (folded over)

LEGS: Brown hackle fibers (wound as in Montana Nymph)

THORAX: Amber tan fur (amber seal and hare's mask mixed)

YUK BUG

HOOK: Mustad 79580 (2–8)

THREAD: Black (Flymaster 6/0 or Monocord 3/0)

TAIL: Gray squirrel tail fibers (gap width past bend)

PALMER RIB: Badger hackle palmered through body

BODY: Black chenille (related to hook size)

LEGS: Three one-inch strands of white rubber hackle tied to top side of body, spaced in equal thirds on body (produces six half-inch legs)

REMARKS: This pattern is usually tied weighted.

ZUG BUG

HOOK: Mustad 3906B or 9671 (10–16)

THREAD: Black (Flymaster 6/0)

TAIL: Three peacock sword fibers (tied short, half gap width past bend)

RIB: Fine oval silver tinsel

BODY: Peacock herl

LEGS: Brown hackle tied as a wet fly collar (see model, Blue Dun, page 124)

WING PAD: Mallard flank feather, tip of which is cut square, extending rearward from eye one-third of body

REMARKS: This pattern used to be a favorite of Arnold Gingrich when fishing Esopus Creek in New York's Catskill Mountains.

Stonefly Nymphs

NATURAL STONEFLY nymphs come in a wide range of sizes and shapes and challenge the ingenuity of the creative fly tyer. Because of this variety of design there is very little standardization regarding this category. Thus, no proportion chart will be offered.

Hooks generally used are the Mustad models 9672, 79580, and 9575 from a size 2 for the larger *Pteronarcys* imitations down to a size 16 for the little black stonefly nymphs.

Materials for these imitations should be such that they allow the fly to sink rapidly while containing fibers or be of a consistency to provide lifelike movement. Most stonefly nymphs are tied weighted.

ASSAM DRAGON

HOOK: Mustad 9672 (4–10)

THREAD: Brown (Monocord 3/0)
TAIL: None
UNDERBODY: Lead wire
BODY: Natural brown seal fur on skin
HACKLE: Grizzly dyed brown (long and soft-fibered)

REMARKS: This pattern by Charles Brooks is actually an impression of several genera of dragonfly nymphs and is one of the featured flies in his book *Nymph Fishing for Larger Trout*. The fur strip for the body should measure one-quarter inch wide on a size 4 hook and one-sixteenth inch on a size 10. When the fur strip is being wound around the shank, the fibers should be stroked rearward as each turn is made. The hackle collar, which is wound in wet fly manner (see model, Blue Dun, page 124), is for two turns only around the shank.

BIRD'S STONEFLY NYMPH

HOOK: Mustad 9672 (4–10)
THREAD: Orange (Flymaster 6/0 or Monocord 3/0)
TAIL: Two dyed brown goose biots (tied forked) (gap width past bend)
BODY: Reddish-brown dubbing fur
WING CASE: Hen pheasant or brown turkey wing quill section (folded over)
LEGS: Brown hackle palmered through thorax
THORAX: Peacock herl

BLACK WILLOW STONEFLY NYMPH

HOOK: Mustad 9575 bent into a slight downward curve (6–10)
THREAD: Orange (Monocord 3/0)

Tying Steps for Black Willow Stonefly Nymph

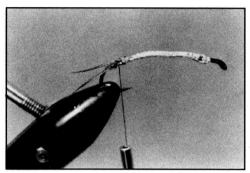

a. Hook has been slightly bent with pliers. Lead wire has been tied to each side of shank and two goose biots have been tied in for a forked tail.

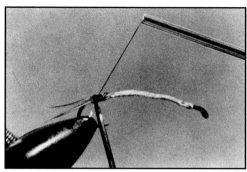

b. Tip end of Swannundaze oval rubbing material being tied in.

c. A dubbing rope has been formed with black seal and opossum mixture and is ready to be wound for abdomen. Tying thread has been brought to center of hook shank.

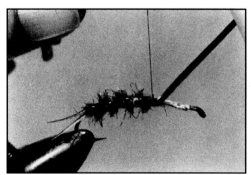

d. Swannundaze has been wound as a wide ribbing and is being tied down near center of hook shank.

e. Amber dubbing fur is being wound over the beginning of the thorax area.

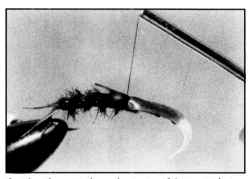

f. The first U-shaped piece of latex is being tied in to form part of the wing case. A bit more dubbing fur is then added to thorax area.

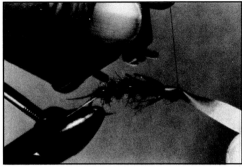

g. The second U-shaped piece of latex has been added slightly forward of the first and the excess has been folded back out of the way while the "church window" section of ringneck feather is being placed to be tied in for legs.

h. More fur being added for forward part of thorax area and two goose biots have been tied in to represent antennae.

i. Excess latex wing case section is now pulled forward and tied down about an eighth inch before eye of hook.

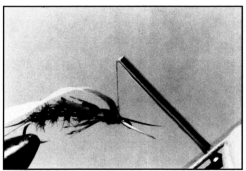

j. Excess latex has again been temporarily folded back and dubbing is once again added to complete thorax to eye of hook.

k. Latex has been brought forward to eye once more, where it is tied down and excess trimmed. Thread is wound around shank just behind eye to cover exposed stubs and form a neatly tapered head. Fly is complete.

TAIL: Orange goose biots (tied forked) (gap width past bend)

UNDERBODY: One strip of medium lead wire (.024) on each side

RIB: Black Swannundaze No. 15

ABDOMEN: An equal blend of dark brown Australian opossum and black seal fur

WING CASE: Dark amber latex trimmed to shape

THORAX: Dyed amber rabbit dubbing fur

LEGS: Ringneck pheasant "church window" fibers dyed amber

PRONOTUM: Excess latex from wing case pulled forward over remainder of thorax

ANTENNAE: Two orange goose biots (tied forked) (as long as tail fibers)

REMARKS: Originated by Craig Mathews. The wing case is made of two pieces of dyed amber latex the ends of which have been trimmed to a U shape. They are tied down at the center of the top of the thorax, with the lower piece of latex extending to the center of the body and the second, or overlapping, piece lying rearward over the first for half the distance. The excess latex is held in reserve until the legs and the rest of the thorax have been completed. It is then pulled forward and tied down behind the eye to form the pronotum.

BOX CANYON STONE

HOOK: Mustad 9672 (2–8)

THREAD: Black (Monocord 3/0)

TAIL: Black goose biots (tied forked) (gap width past bend)

BODY: Black wool

LEGS: Furnace hackle palmered through thorax

WING CASE: Mottled turkey wing quill (pulled over)

REMARKS: This pattern is nearly always tied weighted.

CATSKILL CURLER
(Plate VIII)

HOOK: Mustad 9672 (4–8)

THREAD: Brown (Monocord 3/0)

UNDERBODY: A strip of lead wire on each side of shank

TAIL: Two peccary fibers

ABDOMEN: Turkey tail fibers and brown thread twisted into rope

WING CASE: Dark brown turkey tail section coated with Flexament or Plio Bond

THORAX: Tan ostrich herl with tan thread twisted into rope

LEGS: Mottled light and dark brown hen ringneck pheasant tail fibers

HEAD: Formed from turkey section used for wing case

EYES: Painted on with black lacquer

REMARKS: This original pattern by Matthew Vinciguerra is a good example of what can happen to a pattern after its recipe has been passed from tyer to tyer. It has been misquoted, misinterpreted, and, in one instance, even mispronounced. Ted Niemeyer, one of the contributors to *Art Flick's Master*

Fly Tying Guide, lists the name of this pattern as the Catskill *Coiler,* since that was how it was, and still is, pronounced by a certain angler from Brooklyn who obtained the fly from Vinciguerra.

Though it is often tied incorrectly and its description in print is occasionally unrecognizable to its originator, it has stood the test of time. The structure of the double-folded wing case has been copied, varied, and innovated upon by tyers from East to West. Yet it needs no improvement. It is, in fact, a perfect model for other flies with a similar arrangement. I know the foregoing recipe is the correct one, for Vinciguerra instructed me in its procedure while taking the photographic sequences over my shoulder.

Procedure

Before beginning the actual tying of this pattern, prepare the turkey tail section to be used for the wing case. You will need a section (or several if you plan to tie more than one fly) of fibers measuring approximately a quarter inch wide and an inch and a half long. These are coated with Flexament or Plio Bond and placed on a piece of waxed paper. When they have dried, some of the wax will adhere to the quill section, leaving it supple and protected yet firm enough so that it does not split during the folding process.

The first item tied to the hook shank is the lead wire which extends from the bend to the eye. The end of each strip should be angle-cut so that it tapers naturally to the

Tying Steps for Catskill Curler

a. Lead wire has been secured from eye to bend.

b. Turkey quill section and piece of brown Monocord are tied in at bend.

c. Turkey quill section and Monocord are twisted into rope and wound forward for three or four turns. (For each turn around the shank, twist the hackle pliers one turn to the right.) At this time the turkey quill rope is allowed to hang downward with the weight of the hackle pliers while a peccary fiber is tied to each side of the body to form the separated tail.

g. Three strands of tan ostrich herl have been aligned with tan thread and twisted into a rope after being tied to shank. They are wound forward around shank for three turns. (With each turn around shank, twist hackle pliers to the right one turn.)

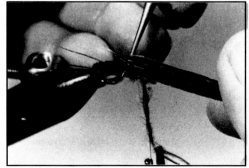

h. Wing case is being folded forward with the use of a dubbing needle. Fold is at the center of hook shank, and section is tied down one-third of the distance forward of the center. At this time another set of hen pheasant legs are added and ostrich herl is wound forward three more turns around shank.

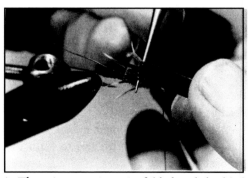

i. The wing case is again folded and doubled back and tied down at the second third of the distance between the center of shank and the eye.

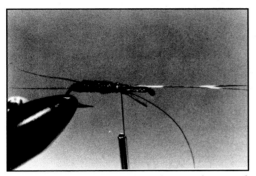

d. Peccary tail has been tied in and twisted rope of turkey quill and Monocord have been wound to a point slightly past center of shank. Excess quill and Monocord rope and excess peccary fibers are now trimmed away.

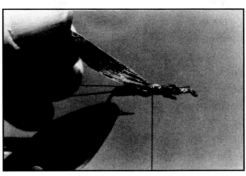

e. Previously prepared turkey quill section has been tied to center of shank on top of fore part of abdomen. Butt ends face eye of hook.

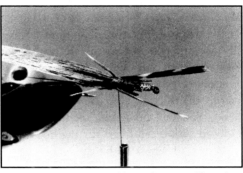

f. A narrow section of hen pheasant fibers has been tied to each side of the body.

j. Another set of legs has been added and ostrich herl has been wound to the eye. Wing case has been pulled forward and tied down directly behind eye, then folded rearward and tied down with thread just in front of last set of legs.

k. Excess wing case is being trimmed square between the folds to rear and front.

l. Completed Catskill Curler.

hook shank. The strips of lead which are fastened to the sides of the shank not only weight the fly but give it a flat appearance. Weighted Nymph Forms may be used in place of the strips of lead wire. Use head lacquer liberally and take enough thread windings to hold the strips of lead securely in place.

A short portion of the body is formed before the peccary tails are tied in at the bend. You will need long sections of dark mottled turkey tail fibers for the body. Cut a section of fibers about an eighth of an inch wide and also a piece of brown Monocord as long as the fibers. Tie both the thread and the tips of the fibers to the shank at the bend just behind the end of the strips of lead wire. Grasp the section of fibers and thread at their other end and twist them into a rope. Wind the rope of fibers and thread around the shank, progressing forward about three or four turns. As you make each turn around the shank, rotate the pliers one full turn. (If you don't rotate the pliers one turn for each turn around the shank, you will untwist the rope.)

Let the twisted rope of fibers hang downward with the weight of the pliers and tie one peccary fiber against each side of the partially formed body. By first partially forming the body the tail fibers are naturally separated.

Once the tail fibers have been tied in, continue with the twisted rope body of fibers and thread to the center of the hook shank. You may need to add another section of fibers and thread to accomplish this. When the abdomen has been completed, snip the excess material.

Place the prepared turkey tail section on the shank with the butt end facing the eye of the hook.

Tie in a short section of hen pheasant fibers on each side of the hook.

Take three tan strands of ostrich herl and align them with a piece of tan thread of the same length and tie them in by the tips. Again attach hackle pliers to the other end and twist them into a rope. Wind the twisted ostrich herl rope forward for three turns.

Fold the wing case using a dubbing needle and tie it down one-third of the distance from the center of the shank to the eye.

Add another pair of legs.

Add three more turns of twisted ostrich herl.

Fold the wing case forward once more as before.

Add the last pair of legs.

Add three more turns of ostrich herl rope.

Bend the wing case backward and tie it down with thread. Cut the wing case squarely about an eighth of an inch behind the eye of the hook to form the pronotum.

Place a touch of black lacquer on each side of the foremost part of the turkey quill section to form the eyes.

DELAWARE YELLOW STONEFLY

HOOK: Mustad 9672 (10)
THREAD: Black (Flymaster 6/0)
TAIL: Brown partridge hackle fibers (gap width past bend)
RIB: Black sewing thread
BODY: Yellow floss
LEGS: Brown partridge hackle fibers, beard style
WING: Bronze mallard flank fibers tied flat over body reaching to end of tail fibers

REMARKS: This pattern by Matthew Vinciguerra is tied in the manner of a wet fly, although Vinciguerra uses it as a stonefly imitation on the upper Delaware River.

EARLY BLACK STONEFLY NYMPH

HOOK: Mustad 9671 (10–16)
THREAD: Black (Flymaster 6/0)
TAIL: Two dark gray Canada goose biots (gap width past bend)
ABDOMEN: Iron dun dubbing fur (almost black)
WING CASE: Black goose wing quill section (double-folded; see model, Catskill Curler) (no pronotum)
THORAX: Same as abdomen but fuller
LEGS: Iron dun hen hackle fibers, divided beard style

EARLY BROWN STONEFLY NYMPH

HOOK: Mustad 9671 (10–14)
THREAD: Tan (Flymaster 6/0)
TAIL: Two turkey wing quill biots dyed tan (tied forked) (gap width past bend)
ABDOMEN: Medium brown dubbing fur
WING CASE: Dark brown mottled tur-

key wing quill section (double-folded; see model, Catskill Curler) (no pronotum)

THORAX: Same as abdomen but fuller

LEGS: Brown hen hackle fibers, divided beard style

FISHING POST STONEFLY, AMBER
(Plate VIII)

HOOK: Mustad 79580 (8)

THREAD: Brown (Flymaster 6/0 or Monocord 3/0)

TAIL: Brown goose biots (tied forked) (1½ gap widths past bend)

RIB: Copper wire

BODY: Fiery brown angora goat (or Fishing Post dubbing blend)

WING CASE: Dark brown mottled turkey tail section (triple-folded; see model, Catskill Curler)

LEGS: Ginger-colored Australian opossum (twisted-rope method)

ANTENNAE: Two dark brown mottled turkey tail fibers (cut back half as long as tail)

REMARKS: This exceptional pattern and the two following were originated by Tom Pellis. They are featured in the Fishing Post catalog.

The legs, which are the prominent feature, are constructed with the Polly Rosborough twisted fur rope method (see Casual Dress, page 163) and protrude almost a half inch from the sides of the fly, giving an impression of movement and life while being fished.

After sections of the rope of guard hairs and underfur have been wound around the shank, the top and bottom are trimmed or moved to the sides so that the hairs and fur protrude only from the sides. The legs are added after each folding of the wing case in the manner shown in the model fly Catskill Curler.

The Fishing Post has developed its own dubbing blend for these patterns, though the listed angora goat serves as well. These blends are available to the tyer through its catalog.

I'm really impressed with these patterns and would not hesitate to fish them anywhere, anytime.

FISHING POST STONEFLY, DARK

HOOK: Mustad 79580 (8)

THREAD: Brown (Flymaster 6/0 or Monocord 3/0)

TAIL: Brown goose biots (tied forked) (1½ gap widths past bend)

RIB: None (some segmentation occurs through using twisted-rope method for body)

BODY: Brown angora goat (or Fishing Post dubbing blend)

WING CASE: Dark brown mottled turkey section (triple-folded; see model, Catskill Curler)

LEGS: Brown Australian opossum (see model, Fishing Post Stonefly, Amber)

ANTENNAE: Two dark brown mottled turkey tail fibers (cut back half as long as tail)

FISHING POST STONEFLY, LIGHT

HOOK: Mustad 79580 (8)

THREAD: Cream or tan (Flymaster 6/0 or Monocord 3/0)

TAIL: Brown goose biots (tied forked) (1½ gap widths past bend)

RIB: Brown embroidery floss

BODY: Cream angora goat (or Fishing Post dubbing blend)

WING CASE: Mottled turkey quill section (triple-folded; see model, Catskill Curler)

LEGS: Cream Australian opossum (see model, Fishing Post Nymph, Amber)

ANTENNAE: Two light brown mottled turkey wing quill fibers (cut back half as long as tail)

GIANT BLACK NATURE NYMPH
(Plate VIII)

HOOK: Mustad 9575 (2–8)

THREAD: Black (Monocord 3/0)

TAIL: Goose or turkey biots dyed orange (gap width past bend)

RIB: Dark brown Swannundaze No. 21

ABDOMEN, top and sides: Dark brown seal fur (or equivalent)

ABDOMEN, belly: A strip of dyed orange angora fur yarn

WING CASE: Heavy chocolate brown latex cut to shape

THORAX: Dark brown seal fur (or equivalent)

LEGS: Dyed amber "church window" pheasant body feather fibers

PRONOTUM: Formed by excess end of latex wing case

HEAD: Black thread used to tie down end of pronotum

ANTENNAE: Goose or turkey biots dyed orange (as long as tail)

REMARKS: This pattern, which imitates one of our largest stoneflies, *Pteronarcys californica,* was originated by Craig Mathews. Except for the belly strip of orange angora yarn which is tied in under the shank at the bend and pulled forward and tied down at the thorax area, it is tied in the same manner as the Black Willow Stonefly Nymph. For details of construction see Black Willow Stonefly Nymph.

GIANT BLACK STONEFLY NYMPH

HOOK: Mustad 38941, slightly bent (2–6)

THREAD: Black (Monocord 3/0)

TAIL: Two dark gray (almost black) goose biots (tied forked) (gap width past bend)

ABDOMEN: Brown/black scraggly dubbing fur (seal or equivalent)

WING CASE: Dark brown mottled turkey wing quill section (double-folded; see model, Catskill Curler) (no pronotum)

THORAX: Same as abdomen but fuller

LEGS: Black hen hackle fibers, divided beard style

GIANT GOLDEN STONEFLY NYMPH

HOOK: Mustad 38941 slightly bent (4–8)

THREAD: Tan (Monocord 3/0)

TAIL: Two dyed amber goose biots (tied forked) (gap width past bend)

RIB: Medium brown dubbing fur spun on thread

ABDOMEN: Tan sandy fox dubbing fur

WING CASE: Mottled turkey wing quill section (double-folded; see model, Catskill Curler) (no pronotum)

THORAX: Same as abdomen but fuller

LEGS: Tan ringneck pheasant body feather fibers, divided beard style

REMARKS: This pattern and the Giant Black Stonefly Nymph are listed in the Orvis catalog.

GOLDEN STONE

HOOK: Mustad 79580 (6–10)

THREAD: Tan (Flymaster 6/0 or Monocord 3/0)

TAIL: Two ginger goose biots (tied forked) (gap width past bend)

RIB: Tan monofilament

ABDOMEN: Buff/gold seal fur (or equivalent)

WING CASE: Speckled turkey wing quill section dyed light orange. May be tied double-folded (see model, Catskill Curler) or as individual wing pad sections

THORAX: Same as abdomen but fuller

ANTENNAE: Two ginger goose biots (as long as tail)

LEGS: Grizzly hen hackle fibers dyed light orange, divided beard style

REMARKS: The Golden Stone, as with some other standard nymphs, may vary from shop to shop and from tyer to tyer.

GOLDEN STONE NYMPH (Rosborough)

HOOK: Mustad 9672 (4–6)

THREAD: Tan (Monocord 3/0)

TAIL: Teal flank fibers (gap width in length). Do not cut excess teal flank. Use long section of fibers.

RIB: Tan or gold sewing thread

ABDOMEN: Scraggly gold orlon or similar fuzzy yarn

SHELL: Excess teal section of fibers brought and pulled forward to beginning of thorax, where it is secured with thread and then further secured by winding the ribbing over it and the abdomen in an open segmented spiral

THORAX: Same as abdomen but fuller

WING PAD: A small dark teal neck feather tied in behind the head and extending rearward one-third of the shank (covers entire thorax area). The fibers of the sides of the teal neck feather are separated and stroked outward and downward to resemble legs.

HEAD: Formed by the thread (1½ times longer than standard)

GOLDEN STONEFLY NYMPH

HOOK: Mustad 9672 (6–10)

THREAD: Brown (Flymaster 6/0 or Monocord 3/0)

TAIL: Mahogany ringneck pheasant fibers (gap width past bend)

SHELL: Dark brown mottled turkey wing quill section over abdomen

RIB: Size A yellow nylon thread

ABDOMEN: Yellow floss

WING CASE: Dark brown mottled turkey wing quill section (pulled forward over thorax)

LEGS: Brown hackle palmered through thorax

THORAX: Peacock herl

REMARKS: This design is by Emil Grimm.

GRANDE STONEFLY NYMPH

HOOK: Mustad 9672 (4–12)

THREAD: Brown (Monocord 3/0 or Flymaster 6/0)

TAIL: Two brown hackle stems (tied forked) (gap width past bend) (trimmed with scissors to leave a stubby effect)

RIB: Oval gold tinsel

ABDOMEN: Beaver dubbing fur

WING CASE: Mottled brown turkey wing quill section (pulled forward over thorax)

LEGS: Brown hackle palmered through thorax

THORAX: Same as abdomen but fuller

ANTENNAE: Butt ends of turkey wing quill section trimmed to two ends extending beyond eye (as long as tail)

HARDBACK NYMPH
(Plate VIII)

HOOK: Mustad 9672 (6–12)

THREAD: Dark brown (Flymaster 6/0)

TAIL: Dark ginger hackle fibers

RIB: Size A black nylon thread

BODY: Pale green floss

HACKLE: Dark ginger as wet fly collar (see model, Blue Dun, page 124)

BACK: A coating of dark brown lacquer is applied to the back of the fly and allowed to dry to a hard glossy consistency (as many coats as necessary)

REMARKS: Originated by Emil Grimm, this pattern has long been a regional favorite in the East.

LITTLE BLACK STONEFLY NYMPH

HOOK: Mustad 9672 (10–18)

THREAD: Black (Flymaster 6/0)

TAIL: Dark brown goose biots (tied forked) (gap width past bend)

UNDERBODY: Fine lead wire

ABDOMEN: Dyed black mink or muskrat dubbing fur

THORAX: Same as abdomen but fuller

WING PAD: A dyed black goose wing quill section formed into shape of wing pad, extending rearward one-third of distance from eye

LEGS: Black hen hackle fibers, divided beard style

ANTENNAE: Dark brown goose biots (as long as tail)

LITTLE BROWN STONE

HOOK: Mustad 9672 (10–14)

THREAD: Brown (Flymaster 6/0)

TAIL: Brown partridge fibers (or equivalent) (gap width past bend)

RIB: Brown sewing thread (over abdomen area only)

BODY: Brown seal fur (or equivalent)

WING: A dark-cast grizzly hackle feather tied flat over body to bend

LEGS: Dark-cast grizzly hackle tied as a wet fly collar (see model, Blue Dun, page 124)

LITTLE YELLOW STONEFLY NYMPH

HOOK: Mustad 9671 (12–16)

THREAD: Yellow (Flymaster 6/0)

TAIL: Two amber goose biots (tied forked) (gap width past bend)

ABDOMEN: Amber dubbing fur

WING CASE: Cinnamon turkey tail section (double-folded; see model, Catskill Curler) (no pronotum)

THORAX: Same as abdomen but fuller

LEGS: Pale yellow hen hackle fibers, divided beard style

PERLA NYMPH

HOOK: Mustad 38941, slightly bent into curve (6–10)
THREAD: Tan (Flymaster 6/0 or Monocord 3/0)
TAIL: Two amber goose biots (tied forked) (gap width past bend)
ABDOMEN: Yellow/orange seal fur (or equivalent) (a blend of amber and yellow African goat is fine)
WING CASE: Mottled turkey wing quill section (double-folded; see model, Catskill Curler) (no pronotum)
THORAX: Same as abdomen but fuller
LEGS: Tan ringneck pheasant body feather, divided beard style

PTERONARCYS CALIFORNICA NYMPH

HOOK: Mustad 9575 (4–10)
THREAD: Black (Monocord 3/0)
TAIL: Two monofilament fibers dotted with marking pen (gap width past bend)
RIB: Four-pound-test monofilament
SHELL: Dark brown mottled turkey wing quill section
ABDOMEN: Black and brown seal fur mixed

WING CASE: Dark brown turkey section (pulled over) (see model, Hendrickson Nymph, page 170)
LEGS: Black hen neck hackle feather (pulled over)
THORAX: An equal blend of black, brown, and orange seal fur (or equivalent)

REMARKS: Originated by Dave McNeese. The shell or back of the nymph is tied down at the rear of the thorax and further secured with the mono ribbing which encircles both body and shell in an open spiral.

TED'S STONEFLY

HOOK: Mustad 9672 (6–12)
THREAD: Black (Flymaster 6/0)
TAIL: Two reddish-brown goose biots (tied forked) (gap width past bend)
ABDOMEN: Brown chenille (related to hook size)
WING CASE: Brown chenille
LEGS: Brown hackle palmered through thorax
THORAX: Orange chenille two sizes larger than abdomen

REMARKS: Except for the tail, this pattern is tied in the same manner as the Montana Nymph (page 176)

WHITLOCK BLACK NYMPH

HOOK: Mustad 79580 (4–10)
THREAD: Black (Flymaster 6/0 or Monocord 3/0)
TAIL: Two black peccary fibers (tied forked) (gap width past bend)
RIB: Fine oval silver tinsel
ABDOMEN: Black seal fur (or equivalent)
WING CASE: Seven to ten strands of peacock herl
LEGS: Black hackle palmered through thorax
THORAX: Same as abdomen but fuller
ANTENNAE: Two of the excess butts of the wing case left uncut, then trimmed to same length as tail
HEAD: Black

REMARKS: This pattern is one of a series of nymphs designed by Dave Whitlock. They are dressed in body colors of tan, gray, brown, and olive.

Part III

ATTRACTOR PATTERNS
AND BAITFISH IMITATIONS

Streamers and Bucktails

BECAUSE STREAMERS and buck-tails, for the most part, are dressed to imitate baitfish, the pattern recipes generally call for a long-shanked hook. The most popular of all the hooks used in this category is the Mustad 9575, not so much because of its length, since there are a few others having the 6XL designation, but because they are made with a looped eye which provides a platform of sorts upon which to lash the materials and form a neater and more secure head for the fly being tied. The looped-eye hook is also looked upon with favor by the angler since there are no abrupt, sharp edges which may cut a leader.

Some flies, such as muddlers and leeches, do not look like baitfish imitations at all but must be classified somehow. They are similar to bass bugs and their construction certainly indicates that they would be very effective if used as such. Still, these patterns are used primarily for trout and are listed under the heading of streamers and bucktails in most catalogs.

In many of the following patterns, the newer synthetic fibers may be substituted for the original, and in certain cases, a material which has more movement or life may replace an old-time favorite such as bucktail. In the event of any change from the original as it is known, a designation should be made to differentiate it from the original pattern. For example, if marabou is used to replace the white saddle hackle in the construction of the wing on the Black Ghost pattern, the improved pattern should be referred to as a Marabou Black Ghost, or Black Ghost, Marabou Wing.

Certain materials, however, do not require a change in or addition to the pattern name. The use of calf tail fibers, for instance, when bucktail is called for needs no notation. Calf tail fibers, because they are much finer and therefore much more suitable, especially in multiple wings, have been used without question in most of our streamer patterns. The use of some of the non-hollow deer belly hair fibers is also considered a free substitute when conditions suggest its use.

Though trout and other fish don't seem to care how neatly we dress our patterns, or how attractive they are, most anglers do care about the overall appearance. Commercial tyers especially will go to great lengths to make their imitations appealing to the eye so that the fly shop proprietor or manager has less trouble selling them, in turn, to the angler.

Strangely, in the dressing of streamer flies it is not so much the tying and arrangement of the materials on the hook that detracts from its appearance as it is how the head of the fly is finished off. Large, bulky heads or those with visible and uneven turns of thread seem to offset the natural flow of materials streaming rearward from that area. Small and neatly tapered heads, on the other hand, give a streamlined effect to the pattern. At times, especially when a triple or quadruple wing is called for in the recipe, the fly tyer wonders how he or she can produce a smaller, neater head. Multiple-wing constructions of such flies as the Black-Nosed Dace or the Gray Ghost always present a problem, especially for the amateur or novice fly tyer. The solution lies not only in the preparation and proper tapering of the materials as they are added to the hook but also in the use of the proper thread.

Though this category calls for larger hook sizes, generally in the 4 to 8 range, it is not necessary to go to a heavier thread. The Flymaster brand of thread, which is used for most of the standard dry flies and the smaller wets and nymphs, is perfectly adequate for streamer flies up to size 2 and even 1/0. You will require more turns of thread to secure the materials but you will be able to place the turns more carefully and evenly without adding bulk. Once the thread has been lacquered with a good head cement these flies with the finer thread will actually be more durable than those you might tie with a coarser, heavier thread.

Streamers and bucktails also look much better if the proper head lacquer is used to coat the head of the fly. Conventional head cement, while it will bond the thread wraps and prevent them from coming apart, does not always give a glossy, smooth appearance unless quite a number of coats are applied. There are a number of newer and better lacquers on the market today which do the job in one application. Among them are Wapsi Gloss Coat and Price Head Cement. Another, an old standby, is Cellire, a product from E. Veniard, Ltd., which creates a glossy head but usually requires a second coat.

In the selection of saddle hackle feathers for the winging of these patterns, you should keep in mind the overall fullness of the baitfish you are imitating. Saddle hackle feathers, which are narrow, may sometimes look great on a fly before they are fished; however, after they have been cast and are being retrieved through the water, the feathers slim down even more and make for a rather anemic representation of a baitfish. A wider and fuller feather will also slim down to some extent when being stripped back in a darting motion, but it will breathe and pulse a bit more than those that have too little fiber content to begin with.

When looking for saddle hackle feathers for streamer flies, you should keep your eyes open for those feathers that taper to a fair width at the point where they are to be tied to the shank before the head. A certain amount of web in the feather is desirable. Because most fly shops sell them in packs or bundles, you will be getting a variety of widths and curves, and you must match them properly before using them as wing parts. Saddle skins from India generally contain feathers that are much too narrow. Those from genetically raised birds are usually on the narrow side, though now and again you'll find a good one. What you want is the saddle skin from one of our larger domestic roosters that have not been raised for fly-tying purposes. They generally have the hackle you need, although they are fairly difficult to find in catalogs.

According to Bill Hunter, who lives in New Hampshire, where streamer flies are the rule rather than the exception, the neck hackles from a Chinese neck are ideally suited to this type of fly because of the amount of web in the larger feathers and the increased number of fibers per inch growing from the center stem. For jumbo streamers and tandem flies, Hunter uses two "schlappen" feathers on the inside and two saddle hackles on the outside of a four-feather wing. Schlappen feathers, found near the lower back of a rooster or hen, are fairly long, wide, and fully webbed. Not all suppliers carry schlappen feathers or, for that matter, Chinese necks, though one source should be Hunter's Angling Supplies. Your best bet is to have your dealer contact his wholesale feather supplier and order these feathers for you.

For streamer flies try to get all the good white hackles you can since they will dye readily to the many colors called for in the patterns that follow.

Comparison of Saddle Hackles
for Streamer Flies

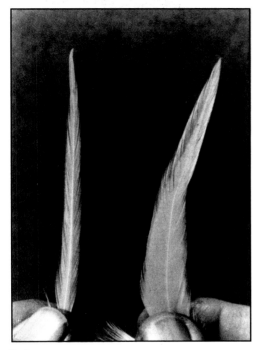

Left: too narrow
Right: ideal

The length of saddle hackle, bucktail, and other materials when used as a wing will also change in relation to the hook used. In other words, if you intend to tie a Black Ghost on an 8XL or 10XL hook, the length of the wing past the bend will be a bit shorter than called for in the recipe.

Many of the patterns call for a flat tinsel rib. In most instances I have not indicated whether this tinsel should be narrow, medium, or wide. This dimension also is related to hook size and shank length. Generally, you can use a narrow tinsel on size 8 and smaller hooks, a medium for sizes 2 to 6, and a wide flat tinsel on all hooks larger than size 2. The same holds true for the oval tinsel. Your eye is sometimes the best judge regarding these proportions.

Proportions

I'm a little hesitant to dictate the proportions of a fly that imitates baitfish and other aquatic creatures. In this category (as with nymphs) the fly tyer has much room for design and innovation. For example, the tail of the fly may be anywhere from just past the bend (some anglers feel that long tails mean short strikes) to more than a shank length beyond, or any distance in between. The same holds true for the wing. Nevertheless, if there were a proportion regarding this type of pattern I would describe it as follows. (Proportions are based on the Mustad 9575 hook.)

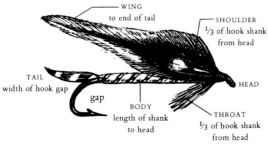

General Proportions for Streamers
TAIL: Width of hook gap
BODY: Length of hook shank
WING: Half a hook-shank length beyond bend
in flies without a tail; to the end of the tail on flies with a tail
THROAT: One-third of the hook shank rearward from the head
SHOULDER: One-third of the hook shank rearward from the head

ALASKA MARY ANN

HOOK: Mustad 9575 (2–10)
THREAD: Black (Flymaster 6/0)
TAIL: Dyed red hackle fibers (gap width past bend)
RIB: Fine flat silver tinsel
BODY: Beige floss
WING: White polar bear (or equivalent) (to end of tail)
CHEEKS: Jungle cock eyes (or equivalent) (second eye showing)
HEAD: Black

ALEXANDRA

HOOK: Mustad 9575 (4–10)
THREAD: Black (Flymaster 6/0)
TAIL: A narrow dyed red goose quill section (half shank length past bend) (see model, Alexandra, page 124)
RIB: Fine oval gold tinsel
BODY: Medium embossed silver tinsel
THROAT: Black saddle hackle wound as a wet fly collar and pulled down (tips extending to point of hook) (see model, Blue Dun, page 124)
WING: Ten to twelve strands of peacock herl (slightly past tip of tail)
HEAD: Black

REMARKS: This pattern, tied as a streamer fly, is basically a takeoff on the old standard wet fly Alexandra.

ALLIE'S FAVORITE

HOOK: Mustad 94720 (2–10)
THREAD: Black (Flymaster 6/0)
TAG: Flat silver tinsel
RIB: Medium flat silver tinsel
BODY: Red floss
THROAT: Sparse white bucktail reaching to bend of hook, then orange hackle followed by black hackle, both as beard extending rearward for one-third of shank
WING: Six strands of peacock herl, over which two orange saddle hackles flanked by two black saddle hackles (two gap widths past bend) (see model, Black Ghost)
CHEEKS: Jungle cock eyes (or equivalent) (tied long, third eye showing)
HEAD: Black

REMARKS: This pattern is often tied as a trolling streamer on an 8XL hook or in tandem.

AMERICAN BEAUTY

HOOK: Mustad 9575 (2–10)
THREAD: Black (Flymaster 6/0)
TAIL: None
BODY: Flat silver tinsel

WING: Sparse white bucktail, over which two red saddle hackles flanked by two silver doctor blue saddle hackles (half a shank length past bend) (see model, Black Ghost)
CHEEKS: Jungle cock eyes (or equivalent) (second eye showing)
HEAD: Black

ANDY'S SMELT

HOOK: Mustad 9575 (6–12)
THREAD: Black (Flymaster 6/0)
TAIL: A section of dyed red goose or duck quill fibers (see model, Alexandra) (quarter shank length past bend)
BODY: Flat silver tinsel
WING: White calf tail fibers topped by a single dyed blue mallard flank feather tied flat (both to end of tail)
HEAD: Black

AZTEC

HOOK: Mustad 7957BX (6–10)
THREAD: To match body color (Flymaster 6/0)
BODY: Olive, black, or brown acrylic knitting yarn
TAIL: Acrylic yarn (combed two shank lengths past bend)
WING: Acrylic yarn

REMARKS: The yarn which is to form the tail should be tied in first. A number of one-ply, 1½-inch pieces of yarn are used for the wing on the top of the shank and are tied

in with the body yarn along the shank in a construction similar to the Hi-Ti pattern listed in the saltwater section.

The yarn fibers, which are combed after the fly is completed, behave in an undulating manner when the fly is fished. This is a highly effective pattern, similar in appearance to a matuka fly.

Originator Dick Nelson expanded the Aztec series into many other patterns. Those who wish complete instructions for these flies should write to: Aztec Anglers, 14748 Golf Links Drive, Los Gatos, California 95030.

BABY SMELT

HOOK: Mustad 9575 (4–10)
THREAD: White (Flymaster 6/0)
TAIL: None
BODY: Flat silver tinsel
WING: Fluorescent pink bucktail flanked on each side by a pintail flank feather (both half a shank length past bend)
HEAD: Lacquered white

REMARKS: Originated by Bob Bouchea.

BALLOU SPECIAL

HOOK: Mustad 9575 (2–10)
THREAD: Black (Flymaster 6/0)

TAIL: Golden pheasant crest feather curving downward (gap width in length)

BODY: Flat silver tinsel

WING: Red bucktail, then white marabou, then ten to twelve strands of peacock herl (all half a shank length past bend)

CHEEKS: Jungle cock eyes (or equivalent) (second eye showing)

HEAD: Black

REMARKS: Be sure to use a rather fine bunch of red bucktail so that the head does not bulk too much.

BARNES SPECIAL

HOOK: Mustad 9575 (2–10)

THREAD: Red (Flymaster 6/0)

TAIL: Two jungle cock body feathers (tied short, just past bend) (or substitute two black saddle hackle tips)

RIB: Oval silver tinsel (medium on larger hooks, fine on sizes 8 and 10)

BODY: Flat silver tinsel

WING: Red bucktail, then white bucktail (both sparse), then two yellow saddle hackles flanked by two grizzly saddle hackles (all to end of tail)

THROAT: White hackle as a wet fly collar after wing has been secured (see model, Blue Dun, page 124)

HEAD: Red lacquer

REMARKS: This pattern is often tied on an 8XL hook or in tandem when used as a trolling streamer fly.

BARTON SPECIAL

HOOK: Mustad 9575 (4–8)

THREAD: White (Flymaster 6/0)

TAIL: A section of dyed red goose or duck quills (quarter shank length past bend) (see model, Alexandra)

BODY: Flat silver tinsel

THROAT: Red hackle fibers, beard style (extending rearward for one-third of the body)

WING: Yellow calf tail flanked by a mallard flank feather on each side (both extending to end of tail)

SHOULDERS: Dyed red mallard breast feather (one-quarter as long as wing)

HEAD: Painted silver with yellow eye and red pupil

BILL'S POLAR SHRIMP

HOOK: Mustad 36890 (1/0–2)

THREAD: Red (Flymaster 6/0 or Monocord 3/0)

TAIL: Fluorescent white Fishair (gap width past bend)

RIB: Medium oval silver tinsel

BODY: Fluorescent red wool

WING: Fluorescent white Fishair, over which a dozen strands of very fine silver Mylar tinsel (both to end of tail)

HEAD: Lacquered red

REMARKS: Originated by William Ryer.

BLACK AND WHITE STREAMER
(see Esopus Bucktail)

BLACK ANGUS
(Plate IX)

HOOK: Mustad 79580 (2–4)

THREAD: Black (flat waxed nylon size A)

TAIL: Four black neck or saddle hackle feathers (shank length past bend), flaring away from each other

UNDERBODY: Heavy lead wire (.036), double-wrapped from a quarter of an inch behind the eye to a point just rearward of the center of the shank

BODY: Black floss, neatly tapered to cover uneven grooves of underbody to a point just in front of lead wire

OVERBODY: Black marabou feathers wound around shank as a wet fly collar (see model, Blue Dun, page 124) (tied in after floss body has been formed)

HEAD: Black deer hair spun and trimmed to wedge shape (for technique, see also Irresistible, page 45), and Muddler Minnow)

REMARKS: You will need four or five long marabou feathers to form the overbody. While the limp marabou cannot be folded, it is stroked rearward after each turn is made in the manner of a wet fly collar. The idea is not to tie down the fibers but rather have them coming off the center stem and flowing rearward completely around the body for the entire length of the body.

The reason for the extra lead wire, just a

Tying Steps for Black Angus

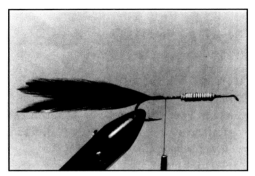

a. Four black hackles have been tied in for tail and forward half of hook shank has been weighted with heavy lead wire.

b. Shank and lead wire underbody have been wound with black floss.

c. Black marabou feather being tied in by tip.

e. Fourth marabou feather being tied in. Because of the lead wire underbody which increases shank diameter, you may need four or five plumes to completely surround shank with marabou.

f. Marabou body complete. This gives a feather-duster effect with marabou fibers protruding from all surfaces of the shank and flowing rearward.

g. Black deer hair has been spun around head area of hook shank.

d. Black marabou being wound around hook shank, one turn in front of the other as you would a folded hackle. (Marabou fibers must be stroked and pulled rearward as each turn is made to prevent them from being tied under with thread.)

h. Black deer hair has been trimmed to a wedge shape and some of the fibers allowed to flow back into the marabou so as to keep the fluffy fibers somewhat under control. Fly is complete.

bit forward of center on the shank, is that the fly should be fished on and off the bottom. The overload of marabou prevents that to some extent, hence the extra added weight.

This particular pattern came about when Angus Cameron asked me if I would be willing to construct a fly that was something like a Woolly Bugger, a muddler, and a leech for the large rainbows in Alaska. It had to be dark or black in color and stay on the bottom. I used marabou as the main ingredient simply because it has more movement than any other material and secured it like a wet fly to the shank since it was the one way I could get an abundance without losing the action or creating an imbalance in the way it rode the current. (This pattern will appear the same to the fish whether it rides right side up or upside down)

After he had returned from Alaska, Angus informed me that it was the top fish taker at the lodge that week. According to Ted Gerken of the Iliaska Lodge, the pattern has since become something of a standard. In a way, I'm not surprised, considering that it's like fishing a bugger, a muddler, and a leech all rolled up in one.

BLACK BEAUTY

HOOK: Mustad 9575 (2–10)
THREAD: Black (Flymaster 6/0)
TAIL: Red hackle fibers (gap width past bend)
RIB: Green tinsel (or equivalent)
BODY: Dark green floss
THROAT: Red hackle fibers, beard style (as long as tail)
WING: Four black saddle hackles (half shank length past bend) (see model, Black Ghost)
CHEEKS: Jungle cock eyes (or equivalent) (second eye showing)
HEAD: Black

BLACK GHOST

HOOK: Mustad 9575 (4–12)
THREAD: Black (Flymaster 6/0)
TAIL: Yellow hackle fibers (gap width in length)
RIB: Flat silver tinsel
BODY: Black floss
THROAT: Yellow hackle fibers, beard style (as long as tail)
WING: Four white saddle (or neck) hackles (half a shank length past bend)
CHEEKS (optional): Jungle cock eyes (or equivalent) (second eye showing)
HEAD: Black

REMARKS: The Black Ghost will serve as our model for other patterns of similar construction.

For most fly tyers, the setting of the hackle wing presents the greatest problem. When you consider that the hackle stems of saddle or neck feathers are formed in varying configurations from oval to triangular and when the tyer often has to use feathers from different necks or saddles, it is not surprising that these hackles, as they are being tied to the shank, tend to go their own way. Unless they are controlled, the results will often produce a wing that has one or two feathers askew, or another that refuses to behave.

A method that has served me well and results in the least amount of infighting is to prepare all four hackles first—that is, measure them for length and trim the appropriate fibers from the stem where they are to be tied in.

Procedure

1. Tie in tail, ribbing, and body floss. Wind and form the floss body and spiral the ribbing forward. Tie in the throat.

2. Place the two hackles which are to form the far side of the wing on the hook shank and take one turn of thread over the butts to temporarily hold them in place.

Take the two hackles which will form the near side of the wing and hold them against the hackles already in place and measure them for proper alignment.

3. Once they are aligned, grasp all four hackles just behind the trimmed butts and unwind the turn of thread that temporarily held the far side wing hackles. You should now have a unit of perfectly aligned hackle feathers between thumb and forefinger of your left hand.

4. Place all four hackles as a unit onto the hook shank once more and lash the trimmed butts to the shank, making sure that the thread covers them firmly from the eye to where the fibers begin. Do not release the pressure from your left thumb and forefinger until the hackle butts have been completely covered with thread. Use the entire platform of

the looped-eye hook for binding the hackles to the shank. A drop of head cement to the shank before tying in the hackle unit helps.

If the hackles are to be cocked—that is, tilted slightly upward at an angle away from the hook shank—bring your thread over the shank but under the wing (between the wing and the shank) directly behind the base of the wing and then continue on with the thread for two more turns over both wing and shank just forward of the previous turn.

You can now release the hackle feathers. They should remain in properly set position. If not, a little tugging and pulling is in order.

Alternate Method

Another method is used by Bill Hunter when teaching streamer tying in classes. It may just make the task of aligning hackle wings even easier than the first method. In any event, now you have a choice.

1. After measuring the saddle hackle feathers for wing length, strip the hackle fibers from the stem below the tie-in point. *Do not cut the excess stems* at this time.

2. The two hackle feathers forming the far side of the wing should be held to the hook shank with one turn of thread (this procedure is the same as in the first method) while the two hackles forming the near side of the wing are held against them to measure proper alignment. Then remove the single turn of thread and place the four feathers as a unit on top of the hook shank.

3. Place the wing unit on top of the hook shank but leave an eighth inch of space

between the point where the hackle fibers of the feather begin and where the thread is tying down the unit. Take six or seven turns of thread around the stripped quill stems of the four-feather unit. Turns of thread should be fairly snug.

4. Grasp the four-feather unit of wing between left thumb and forefinger. Make sure tips, top and bottom, are perfectly aligned. Grasp the four stripped hackle stems between your right thumb and forefinger and pull them forward in the direction beyond the eye of the hook until that part of the wing where the hackle fibers begin to emerge from the stems is pulled under the windings of thread. You are actually pulling the wing into the thread windings for a very short distance (about a sixteenth of an inch) and locking in the alignment.

5. Clip the excess quill stems and cover any stubs with windings of thread while also building a smooth taper for the head.

Both methods are shown in the succeeding photographic sequences.

The foregoing methods usually work most of the time. I believe what happens is this: When the hackles are tied in as a unit and a fair number of thread turns are taken around them over a space of approximately an eighth of an inch, the stems become slightly crunched and locked together in such a way that they cannot misbehave. Now and again, however, you may come across a hackle stem that no amount of restraint will discipline. In such a case, simply use another hackle.

The beard-style hackle on streamer flies is very easily accomplished if the hook is inverted and then the fibers tied in.

Winging Methods for Hackle Wing Streamer Flies (Black Ghost)

a. Tail, body, rib, and throat hackle have been tied in.

b. Four saddle hackles have been paired and are being measured for length as a wing.

c. Hackles have been tied to hook shank.

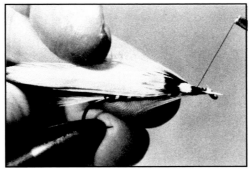

d. Thread has been wrapped to cover butts for distance of doubled wire in looped eye of hook. Hackle should be held firmly in place with left thumb and forefinger while this is being done.

e. Cheek of jungle cock eye being tied in.

f. Completed Black Ghost.

Alternate Winging Method

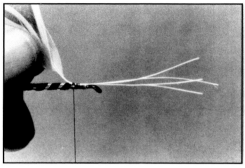

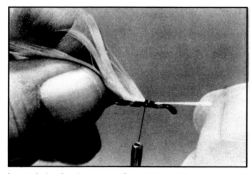

g. Four saddle hackles have been stripped of fibers, as opposed to being trimmed. Feathers have been aligned and four stems are being tied to hook shank.

h. While feathers are firmly held between left thumb and forefinger to maintain position and alignment, the stems are grasped between right thumb and forefinger and pulled forward until the first two or three feather fibers have been pulled under the thread wrappings.

i. The wing of four saddle hackles after being pulled under the thread wrappings.

BLACK GHOST, MARABOU

The same as Black Ghost except that the wing is made of white marabou.

BLACK MARABOU

HOOK: Mustad 9575 (4–12)
THREAD: Black (Flymaster 6/0)
TAIL: Red hackle fibers (gap width in length)
BODY: Flat silver tinsel or silver Mylar tubing
WING: A few strands of red calf tail, over which black marabou (both slightly past end of tail)
HEAD: Black

REMARKS: For the marabou wing, either a section of fibers from a long and fully fluted marabou plume or the single feather from a marabou short or "blood" feather may be used to form the entire wing. The blood feathers are generally from one and a half to three inches long and quite naturally tapered, so that a single feather will contain just the right amount of fibers for a proper wing.

BLACK MARABOU MUDDLER

HOOK: Mustad 79580, 38941 (4–10)
THREAD: Black (Monocord 3/0)
TAIL: Red hackle fibers (gap width in length)
BODY: Flat silver tinsel or silver Mylar tubing

WING: Black marabou topped with six strands of peacock herl (both to end of tail)

HEAD: Spun and clipped black deer hair (see model, Muddler Minnow)

REMARKS: This pattern is also tied weighted.

BLACK MUDDLER MINNOW
(see Muddler Minnow, Black)

BLACK-NOSED DACE

HOOK: Mustad 9575 (4–12)
THREAD: Red wool (tied short, half gap width in length)
RIB (optional): Oval silver tinsel
BODY: Flat silver tinsel
WING: White polar bear hair (or calf tail), over which black bear hair (or black skunk hair), over which natural brown bucktail from back of deer tail (all half a shank length past bend)
HEAD: Black

REMARKS: This Art Flick pattern was originally listed as having a flat silver tinsel body, though most tyers prefer to add the oval rib. It is also tied with embossed silver tinsel or Mylar tubing.

If the oval rib is used, it should be tied in at the bend by its cotton core and the thread brought forward to the head area. The flat silver tinsel is tied in at the head area and wound to the bend and back to the thread in connecting spirals. The rib is then brought forward to the thread in an open spiral and secured.

The multiple wing should have sparse clumps of polar bear, black bear, and brown bucktail primarily so that it will fish well beneath the surface of the water. The sparseness of the fibers also allows for the construction of a neatly tapered head. When trimming the excess butts near the head, they should be cut so that the white polar bear is clipped near the eye, the black bear slightly rearward of the first cut, and the brown bucktail still further rearward. This will ensure a naturally tapered head when the thread is wound over the butts and later lacquered.

BLUE RIBBON SCULPIN

HOOK: Mustad 3665A (1/0–6)
THREAD: Tan (Monocord size A)
UNDERBODY: Wide lead wire (.036 diameter), heavily applied
RIB: Gold wire
BODY: Cream seal fur (or equivalent)
PECTORAL FINS: Mottled gray/brown hen or prairie chicken body feathers (or hen mallard body feathers)

THROAT: Red wool
UNDERWING: Gray marabou fibers
WING: Grizzly dyed charcoal gray (quarter shank length past bend)
COLLAR: Natural deer hair (flared rearward half the length of body)
HEAD: Alternating bands of natural, black, and brown deer hair, spun and trimmed to sculpin head shape

REMARKS: This pattern by Craig Mathews was featured as one of his ten favorite flies in an article that appeared in the July 1983 issue of *Fly Fisherman.* It is tied in the same manner as the Whitlock Sculpin.

BLUE SMELT

HOOK: Mustad 9575 (4–12)
THREAD: Black (Flymaster 6/0)
TAIL: None
BODY: Flat silver tinsel
WING: White bucktail, over which blue bucktail topped with five or six strands of peacock herl (half a shank length past bend)
CHEEKS: Jungle cock eyes (or equivalent) (second eye showing)
HEAD: Black

BRADY'S SMELT
(Plate IX)

HOOK: Mustad 94720 (2–6)
THREAD: Black (Flymaster 6/0)
TAG: Oval silver tinsel
TAIL: Red hackle fibers (gap width past bend)

RIB: Medium oval silver tinsel
BODY: White floss
THROAT: Fine white deer leg hair fibers (near belly), under which four very fine strands of peacock herl (both extending to bend)
WING: Pintail flank feather tied flat, over which dyed light olive mallard flank feather (both extending rearward over body for three-quarters of shank length)
TOPPING: Six very fine strands of peacock herl (to end of tail)
HEAD: Black

REMARKS: This pattern should be hand-twitched while trolling. Originated by Dick Brady.

BRONZE GHOST

The same as Gray Ghost except that four bronze dun saddle hackles are used in wing.

BROWN GHOST

HOOK: Mustad 9575 (2–10)
THREAD: Black (Flymaster 6/0)
TAIL: None
RIB: Flat silver tinsel
BODY: Dark brown floss
THROAT: Sparse white bucktail covered with golden pheasant crest feather (both to point of hook)
WING: Golden pheasant crest feather (curving downward), over which four brown saddle hackles, topped with six strands of peacock herl (see models, Black Ghost and Gray Ghost)

SHOULDER: Dyed brown teal flank (one-third as long as wing)
CHEEKS: Jungle cock eyes (or equivalent) (second eye showing)
HEAD: Black

BUNNY FLY
(Plate IX)

HOOK: Mustad 9672 (2–6)
THREAD: Black (waxed Monocord 3/0)
TAIL: A strip of black rabbit on tanned skin (about one-eighth inch wide)
BODY: Remainder of black rabbit strip, wound around shank in connecting spirals to eye
HEAD: Black

REMARKS: This pattern was introduced to Henry's Fork Anglers by Mel Krieger. The rabbit fibers protrude from the hook shank on all sides, creating a pulsating, undulating motion much in the manner of marabou when it is being fished. This pattern is similar to leech flies and is also tied in brown, cream, olive, and gray.

CAPE COD WOOLLY WORM

HOOK: Mustad 38941, 9672, 9671 (8–14)
THREAD: Black (Flymaster 6/0)
TAIL: Black hen hackle fibers or black marabou (gap width in length)
PALMER RIB: Soft black hackle palmered through body
BODY: Black wool, fur, or chenille
HACKLE: Black hen as a wet fly collar (see model, Blue Dun, page 124)

REMARKS: This pattern was introduced to me by members of the United Fly Tyers when, after a fruitless day on Rhode Island's Wood River, and while other anglers were taking trout after trout, John Harder said to me, "Here, try this." I did and took four fish, one after the other. It is claimed that the less expertly tied this pattern is, the more fish it will take. It is an ugly, yet tantalizing, little morsel somewhat similar to the Woolly Bugger. It is tied in a variety of hook styles and sizes, but always in black.

CARDINELLE

HOOK: Mustad 9575 (2–12)
THREAD: Fluorescent fire orange (Flymaster 6/0)
TAIL: None
BODY: Fluorescent orange wool
WING: Fluorescent orange/pink calf tail, over which fluorescent pink marabou (half a shank length past bend)
HACKLE: Yellow tied as a wet fly collar (see model, Blue Dun, page 124)
HEAD: Fluorescent red

REMARKS: This original pattern by Paul Kukonen looks like nothing in nature. Yet it takes fish, though I have a suspicion they strike at the fly in sheer anger and irritation at the bright and gaudy colors.

CHAMPLAIN SPECIAL

HOOK: Mustad 9575 (2–10)
THREAD: Black (Flymaster 6/0)

TAIL: None
RIB: Medium flat gold tinsel
BODY: Yellow floss
THROAT: Red hackle fibers (to point of hook)
WING: White bucktail, then yellow bucktail (both sparse), then topped with five or six strands of peacock herl (all half a shank length past bend)
HEAD: Black

REMARKS: This pattern was rediscovered by Rodney Flagg in an old *Outdoor Life* magazine. It has proven to be one of his most successful streamers. It is also tied in tandem as a trolling streamer.

CHIEF NEEDAHBEH

HOOK: Mustad 9575 (2–10)
THREAD: Black (Flymaster 6/0)
TAG: Flat silver tinsel
TAIL: A section of red goose fibers (gap width past bend) (see model, Alexandra)
RIB: Fine flat silver tinsel
BODY: Red floss
WING: Two yellow saddle hackles flanked by two red saddle hackles (see model, Black Ghost)
HACKLE: Red hackle as a wet fly collar after wing has been constructed (see model, Blue Dun, page 124)
CHEEKS: Jungle cock eyes (or equivalent) (second eye showing)
HEAD: Black

COLONEL BATES

HOOK: Mustad 9575 (2–10)
THREAD: Black (Flymaster 6/0)
TAIL: Narrow section of red goose quill fibers (gap width in length) (see model, Alexandra)
BODY: Flat silver tinsel
THROAT: Dark brown hackle fibers, beard style (as long as tail)
WING: Two yellow saddle hackles (half a shank past bend) flanked by two white saddle hackles three-quarters the length of the yellow hackles (see model, Black Ghost)
SHOULDERS: Gray teal breast (half as long as white hackles)
CHEEKS: Jungle cock eyes (or equivalent) (second eye showing)
HEAD: Black with red band

REMARKS: This pattern was originated by Carrie Stevens and named after Joseph D. Bates, Jr., the noted fly-fishing author. The band of red thread is wound in after the cheeks have been secured and then the remainder of the head is wrapped with black thread. Clear head lacquer or varnish will cover both thread colors for a glossy finish.

COUNTERFEITER
(Plate IX)

HOOK: Mustad 9575, 94720, Partridge CS15 (Carrie Stevens hook) (2–10), or if in tandem, Mustad 3906 (4–6)
THREAD: Black (Flymaster 6/0)
TAIL: None

BODY: Flat silver tinsel
THROAT: Red impala (calf tail) covered by golden pheasant crest curving in to shank, beard style (one-third as long as wing)
WING: Sparse purple bucktail, over which four gray saddle hackles (one-half to one inch past bend)
SHOULDERS: Finely marked pintail flank (two-thirds as long as wing)
TOPPING: Silver pheasant crest feather (or peacock herl) (to end of wing)
CHEEKS: Jungle cock eyes (or equivalent) (third eye showing)
HEAD: Black

REMARKS: The sample fly I received was tied on a Partridge CS15 hook, which is a 10XL. However, the pattern can be tied on all the above-listed hooks, in which case minor adjustments should be made regarding the length of wing, throat, shoulders, and cheeks.

Robert Veverka originated this pattern for landlocked salmon. He is of those rare talents who can make a fly look so good you don't want to fish with it. He ties flies on a custom basis at fairly reasonable prices, considering the care and detail that go into the construction of each pattern.

His company, Counterfeiters in Flies, is listed in the Sources for Materials.

CUPSUPTIC

HOOK: Mustad 9575 (2–8)
THREAD: Black (Flymaster 6/0)

TAIL: Yellow hackle fibers (gap width in length)

BODY: Rear third: narrow band of peacock herl, then white floss, then narrow band of peacock herl; remainder: red floss with flat silver tinsel rib

THROAT: Yellow hackle fibers, beard style (as long as tail)

WING: Two red saddle hackles flanked by two furnace saddle hackles (half a shank length past bend) (see model, Black Ghost)

SHOULDERS: Gray saddle hackles (two-thirds as long as wing)

CHEEKS: Jungle cock eyes (or equivalent) (second eye showing)

HEAD: Black

REMARKS: In a multiple-wing construction such as this, it is sometimes easier if the right and left wing sections, shoulders, and cheeks are formed and cemented together as units before they are tied in.

DAHLBERG DIVER
(Plate IX)

HOOK: Mustad 3366 (2/0–10)

THREAD: Red (flat waxed nylon size A)

WEED GUARD: Monofilament of a lesser diameter than hook shank

TAIL: A few strands of gold Flashabou, over which a black marabou blood feather (both a shank length past bend) (the tail may be shouldered by two black sad-dle hackle feathers on each side flaring outward)

SKIRT (1): The tip ends of the first bunch of deer hair to be spun for the waist

WAIST: Black deer hair spun and trimmed (for hair-spinning technique, see Irresistible, page 45) to cover the rear half of the hook shank; trimmed to a rounded bullet shape on top and sides but flat on bottom

SKIRT (2): The tip ends of the first bunch of deer hair used to form the collar

COLLAR: Natural tan/gray deer hair flared and trimmed on top and sides of hook shank so that it forms a 180-degree collar twice as high as waist and head hair. The collar uses half the remaining distance between the waist and the hook eye on the shank.

HEAD: Black deer hair spun and trimmed to a rounded bullet shape on top and sides but flat on bottom

REMARKS: This pattern is unique and revolutionary. Larry Dahlberg, of Brainerd, Minnesota, who originated it, has created a fly that behaves like a spinning lure. By forming a trimmed deer hair collar which arcs higher than other body materials above the plane of the hook and trimming all the deer hair flush to the shank underneath, he has designed a fly that not only pops, gurgles, and pulses but dives and resurfaces.

Though originally tied for bass, this fly is now being tied in many colors and, in part, with other materials for trout, salmon, snook, and many other game fish. Its design has been incorporated into such patterns as sculpins, leeches, and minnows. When it is tied as a baitfish imitation, the waist of spun deer hair is sometimes replaced with braided Mylar or simply filled in with hackle or marabou. Other hooks, such as the Mustad 34007 when tying saltwater divers, may also be used. The trimmed hair collar and head and the stream-lined, flat trimmed body under the hook shank, however, remain unchanged, regard-less of other innovations.

The tying procedures are not difficult, but, like bass bugs, require a bit more time.

The monofilament weed guard is tied to the shank and down one-third of the bend area. When the fly has been completed, the free end of the monofilament is brought up through the hook eye and bound down with two turns of thread. The free end is pulled up until the lower curve of the monofila-ment rests just outside the bend and below the hook point. More turns of thread are then taken to secure the end directly behind the hook eye. The excess monofilament is then cut away.

When spinning the deer hair for the body, I like to remove the fly from the vise after the waist area has been spun and trim that sec-tion before adding the collar and head. I then replace the hook in the vise and spin on the collar and head hair. When spinning the collar, I hold the hair firmly by the tips and try not to allow the hair to rotate around the shank but to flare in place over the top and sides of the shank. When both collar and head have been spun, the fly is again removed from the vise and the trimming begins. Clipping deer hair is like sculpting. Some are better at it than others, but all of us improve with practice.

When the fly has been completed and the weed guard affixed, Flexament or vinyl cement should be applied to the thread windings and the front edge of the collar.

DARK SPRUCE

HOOK: Mustad 9575 (4–10)
THREAD: Black (Flymaster 6/0)
TAIL: Peacock sword fibers (gap width past bend)
BODY: Rear half, red floss; fore half, peacock herl
WING: Four furnace hackles (half shank length past bend) (see model, Black Ghost)
HACKLE: Furnace as a wet fly collar after wing is secured (see model, Blue Dun, page 124)
HEAD: Black

REMARKS: This pattern is sometimes tied on 3XL or 4XL hooks such as the Mustad 9672 or 79580.

DAVIS LEECH

HOOK: Mustad 9672 (8–10)
THREAD: Black (Flymaster 6/0)
RIB: Medium copper wire
BODY: Extra-fine black chenille (size 00)
WING: The butt end of a hackle feather having the softer, fluffier barbules cut to shank length and tied flat on top of shank

using Matuka technique (see Matuka Flies) of securing it with the copper ribbing
HEAD: Black

REMARKS: Listed in the Fly Shop catalog. Primarily a still water fly, this simple yet effective construction makes it an all-round pattern. It is also tied in olive.

DOLLY'S HAT
(Plate IX)

HOOK: Mustad 9575 (2–6)
THREAD: Black (Flymaster 6/0)
TAG: Oval silver tinsel
TAIL: None
RIB: Medium oval silver tinsel
BODY: Burnt orange floss
THROAT: Golden pheasant crest feather (curving upward into shank) covered by very fine white deer belly hair fibers (sparse) and then four extra-fine strands of peacock herl (all to bend of hook)
WING: Teal flank feather topped with six strands of extra-fine peacock herl (quarter inch past bend)
HEAD: Black

REMARKS: Originated by Dick Brady and used in the Moosehead Lake region of Maine for landlocked salmon.

DUSTY STREAMER

HOOK: Mustad 9575 (2–10)
THREAD: Black (Flymaster 6/0)
TAIL: None
RIB: Flat silver tinsel

BODY: Black floss
THROAT: Sparse white bucktail covering six strands of peacock herl (as long as wing)
WING: Four grizzly saddle hackles (slightly past bend)
CHEEKS: Jungle cock eyes (or equivalent) (second eye showing)
HEAD: Black

EDSON TIGER, DARK

HOOK: Mustad 9575 (4–10)
THREAD: Black (Flymaster 6/0)
TAG: Flat gold tinsel
TAIL: Yellow hackle fibers (gap width in length)
BODY: Yellow chenille (medium, size 1)
THROAT: Yellow hackle fibers, beard style (same length as tail)
WING: Brown bucktail dyed yellow (to end of tail)
CHEEKS: Jungle cock eyes (or equivalent) (only one eye showing)

EDSON TIGER, LIGHT

HOOK: Mustad 9575 (4–10)
THREAD: Black (Flymaster 6/0)
TAG: Flat gold tinsel
TAIL: Barred black and white wood duck flank fibers (gap width in length)
BODY: Peacock herl
WING: Yellow bucktail (or calf tail) (to end of tail), over which red hackle fibers (one-third the length of bucktail)

CHEEKS: Jungle cock eyes (or equivalent) (only one eye showing)
HEAD: Black

REMARKS: Both the Dark and the Light Edson Tiger were originated by William R. Edson.

ESOPUS BUCKTAIL
(also known as Black and White Streamer)

HOOK: Mustad 9575 (4–10)
THREAD: Black (Flymaster 6/0)
TAIL: Red calf tail fibers (tied short, half gap width in length)
BODY: Embossed silver tinsel
WING: White bucktail, over which black bucktail (both a gap width past bend) (calf tail fibers may be substituted)
CHEEKS: Jungle cock eyes (or equivalent) (only one eye showing)
HEAD: Black

FLAGG'S SMELT

HOOK: Mustad 9575 (2–6)
THREAD: White (Flymaster 6/0)
TAIL: Red calf tail fibers (gap width in length)
BODY: Silver Mylar tubing pressed flat against shank
THROAT: Sparse white bucktail (as long as body)
WING: Blue Fishair (sparse), then three strands of peacock herl (both to end of tail)

TOPPING: One slim mallard flank feather tied flat (half as long as wing)
CHEEKS (optional): Jungle cock eyes (or equivalent) (second eye showing)
HEAD: White

REMARKS: Originated by Rodney Flagg, this pattern is also tied as a trolling streamer on an 8XL hook or in tandem.

FLASHABOU STREAMER
(see Purple Flash)

FLOATING STREAMER

HOOK: Mustad 79580 (3/0–6)
THREAD: Clear sewing thread
TAIL: Portion of marabou wing (extending past end of quill body for about an inch)
BODY: Hollow goose quill plugged at open end with cork and Super Glue; red dots painted on quill body and then lacquered over with clear cement
WING: Long green marabou lashed to quill in crisscross fashion
HEAD: Painted yellow with black pupil

REMARKS: This excellent design by Charles Brooks imitates a crippled minnow not only in overall appearance but also in the pulsing movement of the marabou tail.

FRANK SMITH SPECIAL

HOOK: Mustad 9575 (6–12)
THREAD: Black (Flymaster 6/0)
TAIL: None

BODY: Flat silver tinsel
THROAT: White bucktail (or calf tail) (to bend)
WING: Natural brown calf tail over orange calf tail (both slightly past bend)
HEAD: Black

FROST'S BLUE SMELT

HOOK: Mustad 9575 or 94720 (4–12)
THREAD: White (Flymaster 6/0)
TAIL: None
TAG: Blue thread
BODY: Silver Mylar tubing secured at both ends with blue thread
WING: White bucktail, over which four strands of peacock herl, over which bright blue bucktail (all quarter inch past bend)
HEAD: Painted blue with white eyes and black pupil

REMARKS: This pattern, originated by Dick Frost, is primarily a lake trout and land-locked salmon fly. Angus Cameron, however, reports that it was recommended to him as an excellent choice for Icelandic Atlantic salmon. He says, "I used it three times and *each time killed a salmon with it*. My partner then killed two with it and two other fellow anglers killed two and one, respectively."

When it is used for landlocked salmon, this pattern is often tied in tandem or on an extra-long-shanked hook.

GOLDEN DARTER

HOOK: Mustad 9575 (4–10)
THREAD: Black (Flymaster 6/0)
TAIL: A section of fibers from a mottled brown turkey wing quill (see model, Alexandra, page 124)
RIB: Flat gold tinsel
BODY: Yellow floss
THROAT: Black hen hackle, beard style (as long as tail)
WING: Four golden badger saddle hackles (half a shank length past bend) (see model, Black Ghost)
CHEEKS: Jungle cock eyes (or equivalent) (one eye showing)
HEAD: Black

GOLDEN DARTER
(Orvis)

HOOK: Mustad 9575 (4–12)
THREAD: Black (Flymaster 6/0)
TAG: Red thread (used to secure Mylar at bend)
BODY: Gold Mylar tubing
THROAT: Guinea hen hackle fibers, beard style (gap width in length)
WING: Four furnace saddle hackles (half a shank length past bend) (see model, Black Ghost)
HEAD: Black

GOLDEN DEMON

HOOK: Mustad 9575 (4–10)
THREAD: Black (Flymaster 6/0)

TAIL: None
BODY: Flat gold tinsel
HACKLE: Hot orange as a wet fly collar and pulled down (see model, Blue Dun, page 124)
WING: Two bronze mallard flank feathers, one on top of the other (quarter inch past bend)
HEAD: Black

REMARKS: This pattern is sometimes tied with a body of yellow floss and a flat gold tinsel rib.

GOLDENHEAD

HOOK: Mustad 9575 (2–10)
THREAD: Black (Flymaster 6/0)
TAIL: None
RIB: Oval gold tinsel
BODY: Black floss
WING: Sparse white bucktail, over which two brown saddle hackles tied flat on top (both slightly past bend)
SHOULDER: Golden pheasant tippet feather (one-third as long as wing), tied flat on top
HEAD: Black

GOLDEN MINNOW
(Plate IX)

HOOK: Mustad 9575 (4–10)
THREAD: Red (Flymaster 6/0)
TAG: Red thread which secures Mylar tubing
BODY: Gold Mylar tubing

THROAT: Red hackle fibers, beard style (extending rearward for one-third of shank)
WING: White bucktail, then yellow bucktail, both sparse, flanked by dyed yellow mallard flank feathers (all slightly past bend)
HEAD: Gold lacquer with a painted red eye

REMARKS: This pattern, submitted by Rodney Flagg, is a spin-off of the Silver Minnow. It is very popular in Massachusetts.

GOLDEN MUDDLER MINNOW
(see Muddler Minnow, Golden)

GOVERNOR AIKEN

HOOK: Mustad 9575 (2–10)
THREAD: Black (Flymaster 6/0)
TAIL: Barred black and white wood duck flank fibers (gap width in length)
RIB: Medium oval silver tinsel (see model, Black-nosed Dace, page 209)
BODY: Flat silver tinsel
THROAT: White bucktail (to bend) covered with red calf tail (half the length of white bucktail) (both sparse)
WING: Lavender bucktail topped with six strands of peacock herl (half a shank length past bend)
CHEEKS: Jungle cock eyes (or equivalent) (second eye showing)
HEAD: Black

GRAVEL GERTIE

HOOK: Mustad 9575 (6–12)

THREAD: Black (Flymaster 6/0)

TAIL: Orange wool (tied short, eighth inch past bend)

BODY: Medium black and white chenille wound simultaneously to form alternate barring

THROAT: Pink wool, as beard (as long as tail)

WING: White calf tail (to end of tail) topped with a few fibers of red fox squirrel tail (half the length of white calf tail)

HEAD: Black

REMARKS: This pattern is listed in the Hook and Feathers catalog.

GRAY GHOST
(Plate IX)

HOOK: Mustad 9575 (2–12)

THREAD: Black (Flymaster 6/0)

TAIL: None

RIB: Medium flat silver tinsel

BODY: Orange floss

THROAT: Golden pheasant crest next to underside of shank (curving in to shank) covered with sparse white bucktail (both to bend)

WING: Golden pheasant crest feather (curv-

ing downward), over which four light to medium blue dun saddle hackles, over which a topping of six strands of peacock herl (all half a shank length past bend) (see model, Black Ghost)

SHOULDER: Silver pheasant body feather (one-third the length of body)

CHEEKS: Jungle cock eyes (or equivalent) (second eye showing)

HEAD: Black

REMARKS: This famous pattern was originated by Carrie Stevens. In the original recipe, the topping of peacock herl was located below the shank and dressed as part of the throat. Many anglers prefer the herl as a topping since the fly rides on a more even keel when being trolled or retrieved. The color of the Gray Ghost saddle hackles is often in dispute, and fly tyers have used all shades of blue dun from light to dark and some of the off-shades in bronze. Some will claim to have seen one of the original flies tied by Stevens, but it is probable that the color of those original feathers may have faded. (Color fading occurs in both natural and dyed materials over a period of time, depending on light or climatic conditions.) Since the fly is used mostly as a smelt imitation, it is best to adjust the wing color to the natural species and environmental variations thereof. (Depending on water habitat, seasonal changes, and individual traits, all species, whether animals, insects, or fish, take on individual hues.) However, no matter what shade is used for the wing, the fly does not seem to lose its effectiveness.

It is a good idea to construct the wing,

shoulders, and cheeks as left and right units and then tie them to the shank, which is the method used by Stevens.

GRAY GHOST, MARABOU WING

The same as Gray Ghost except that the wing is constructed of dyed blue dun marabou.

GRAY TIGER

HOOK: Mustad 9575 (6–12)

THREAD: Black (Flymaster 6/0)

TAIL: Quill section from silver pheasant body or wing feather (white with black stripes) (see model, Alexandra) (gap width in length)

BODY: Fine white chenille (size 0)

THROAT: Red hackle fibers, beard style (as long as tail)

WING: Gray squirrel tail fibers topped with a single mallard flank feather (both to end of tail)

HEAD: Black

GREEN GHOST

HOOK: Mustad 9575 (4–10)

THREAD: Black (Flymaster 6/0)

TAIL: None

TAG: Flat silver tinsel

RIB: Fine flat silver tinsel

BODY: Orange floss

THROAT: Five strands of very fine peacock herl next to underside of hook shank covered with white bucktail (both to bend)

WING: Four green saddle hackles topped with a golden pheasant crest feather (half a shank length past bend) (see model, Black Ghost)

SHOULDERS: Silver pheasant body feather (half the length of body)

CHEEKS: Jungle cock eyes (or equivalent) (second eye showing)

HEAD: Black

GREEN MUDDLER
(see Muddler Minnow, Green)

GREEN WONDER

HOOK: Mustad 9575 (2–10)
THREAD: Black (Flymaster 6/0)
TAIL: None
BODY: Flat silver tinsel
WING: Sparse white bucktail, then four dyed green grizzly saddle hackles topped with six strands of peacock herl (all a quarter shank length past bend) (see model, Black Ghost)
HEAD: Black

GREYHOUND

HOOK: Mustad 94720 or Partridge CS15 (Carrie Stevens' hook) (2–8)
THREAD: Black (Flymaster 6/0)
TAG: Flat silver tinsel
TAIL: Red hackle fibers (gap width past bend)
RIB: Medium flat silver tinsel

THROAT: White bucktail along underside of shank (to bend), then red hackle fibers as beard (one-third the length of bucktail)

WING: Five strands of peacock herl, over which four light gray saddle hackles (both to end of tail) (see model, Black Ghost)

SHOULDERS: Jungle cock body feathers (or equivalent) (one-third as long as body)

CHEEKS: Jungle cock eyes (or equivalent) (second eye showing)

HEAD: Black

REMARKS: This Carrie Stevens pattern is also tied as a tandem streamer.

GRIZZLY KING STREAMER

HOOK: Mustad 9575 (4–12)
THREAD: Black (Flymaster 6/0)
TAIL: Red hackle fibers (gap width in length)
RIB: Flat silver tinsel
BODY: Green floss
THROAT: Grizzly hackle fibers, beard style (as long as tail)
WING: Four grizzly saddle hackles (half a shank length past bend) (see model, Black Ghost)
SHOULDERS: Barred teal body feather (one-half the length of body)
HEAD: Black

HARRIS SPECIAL

HOOK: Mustad 9575 (2–10)
THREAD: Black (Flymaster 6/0)

TAIL: Golden pheasant tippet fibers (gap width in length)
BODY: Flat gold tinsel
THROAT: Red bucktail (two-thirds the length of wing)
WING: White bucktail, over which a natural lemon wood duck flank feather tied flat on top (both to end of tail)
HEAD: Black

HORNBERG
(Plate IX)

HOOK: Mustad 38941, 9671 (6–10)
THREAD: Black (Flymaster 6/0)
TAIL: None
BODY: Flat silver tinsel
WING: Dyed yellow calf tail fibers tied to tilt at a slightly upward angle and flanked by two mallard flank feathers (half a shank length past bend)
CHEEKS: Jungle cock eyes (or equivalent) (second eye showing)
HACKLE: Grizzly and brown mixed tied as a dry fly collar
HEAD: Black

REMARKS: Though this pattern is listed in the streamer and bucktail section of most catalogs, it may also be used as a dry fly imitating some of the adult caddis and stonefly naturals common in most streams. The Hornberg is an all-purpose favorite, especially highly regarded in the New England states, where a number of variations have evolved.

In the following seven patterns, only the

variations from the original are listed. The rest of the pattern remains the same.

HORNBERG, BLACK

BODY: Flat silver tinsel
WING: Mallard flank dyed black
HACKLE: Brown and black mixed

HORNBERG, BLUE

THREAD: Blue
BODY: Light blue floss
WING: Mallard dyed light blue
HACKLE: Grizzly

HORNBERG, BRONZE

BODY: Flat gold tinsel
UNDERWING: Hot orange hackle tips
WING: Bronze mallard flank (small feathers)
HACKLE: Golden badger

HORNBERG, CINNAMON

THREAD: Orange
BODY: Flat gold tinsel
WING: Mallard dyed imitation wood duck
HACKLE: Brown

HORNBERG, DARK

THREAD: Brown
BODY: A dubbing mixture of tan fur, olive fur, and muskrat fur in three equal parts
WING: Bronze mallard flank feather
HACKLE: Brown and blue dun mixed

HORNBERG, GREEN

THREAD: Olive
BODY: Medium olive dubbing fur
WING: Mallard flank dyed olive green
HACKLE: Dyed olive

HORNBERG, YELLOW

THREAD: Yellow
BODY: Flat gold tinsel
WING: Mallard dyed yellow
HACKLE: Dyed olive

There is yet another variation of this pattern, introduced by Dick Stewart, which features a downwing type wing tied flat over the body.

HORNBERG, DOWNWING
(Plate IX)

HOOK: Mustad 9671, 38941 (6–16)
THREAD: Black (Flymaster 6/0)
BODY: Flat silver tinsel
UNDERWING: Yellow hackle fibers (to bend)
WING: Two mallard flank feathers folded and applied tent-shaped over body (gap width past bend)
HACKLE: Brown and grizzly mixed and tied as a dry fly collar

REMARKS: The wing is made by taking two narrow mallard flank feathers and tying them on top of the hook shank. When the thread catches the feather, it pulls the fibers

downward from the center stem, thus folding, or tenting, them downward on each side of the shank. This wing more closely imitates the adult caddis and stonefly naturals. Two more variations of the downwing type follow. The hook remains the same in each.

HORNBERG, DOWNWING ORANGE

THREAD: Orange
BODY: Flat silver tinsel
UNDERWING: Orange hackle fibers (to bend)
WING: Two mallard flank feathers folded and applied tent-shaped over body just past bend
HACKLE: Grizzly

HORNBERG, DOWNWING RED

THREAD: Red
BODY: Flat silver tinsel
UNDERWING: Red hackle fibers (to bend)
WING: Two mallard flank feathers folded and applied tent-shaped over body just past bend
HACKLE: Grizzly

HOUSATONIC SPECIAL

HOOK: Mustad 9575 (4–10)
THREAD: Black (Flymaster 6/0)

TAIL: White calf tail fibers (gap width past bend)
BODY: Oxford gray wool tapered into thorax
WING: Natural brown bucktail fibers from tail of white-tailed deer
HEAD: Black

REMARKS: This innovation comes from Walt Stockman.

ILIASKA BLACK MUDDLER

HOOK: Mustad 79580 (4–6)
THREAD: Black (Monocord 3/0)
TAIL: Crow or raven wing quill section (or dyed black goose quill section) (see model, Alexandra) (gap width past bend)
RIB: Medium oval gold tinsel
UNDERBODY: Wrapped with medium lead wire (.024)
BODY: Gold-colored wool
WING: Crow or raven wing quills (to center of tail, tips curving downward) (or dyed black goose or turkey wing quill sections)
HEAD: Dyed black deer hair spun and trimmed to muddler head (see model, Muddler Minnow). The first flaring of hair fibers also serves to form a short collar over portions of wing and body. Flared collar fibers extend to end of wing.

REMARKS: Ted Gerken of the Iliaska Lodge in Illiamna, Alaska, regards this pattern as a super fall and spring rainbow fly.

JANE CRAIG

HOOK: Mustad 9575 (2–10)
THREAD: Black (Flymaster 6/0)
TAIL: None
BODY: Flat silver tinsel
THROAT: White hackle fibers, beard style (gap width in length)
WING: Six white saddle hackles topped by eight strands of peacock herl (all half a shank length past bend) (see model, Black Ghost)
CHEEKS: Jungle cock eyes (or equivalent) (second eye showing)
HEAD: Black

JANSSEN'S MARABOU LEECH

HOOK: Mustad 9672 (4–8)
THREAD: Black (Monocord 3/0)
TAIL: Black marabou (shank length past bend)
BODY: Black fuzzy yarn
WING: Black marabou (to end of tail)
HEAD: Black

REMARKS: Developed by Hal Janssen. Also tied in body and wing colors of brown and olive.

JANSSEN MINNOW
(Plate IX)

HOOK: Mustad 9672, 9674 (4–8)
THREAD: White (Monocord 3/0)
TAIL: Yellow marabou fluff (gap width in length)
BODY: Mylar piping over pre-shaped form, then painted appropriate color scheme, then epoxied
EYES: Painted yellow with black pupil

REMARKS: This is actually a series of minnow imitations designed by Hal Janssen and formed in the manner of Andre Puyans's Threadfin Shad (which see). When I first saw a sample of this pattern, I wondered what the price per fly would be. Actually, at about three dollars each, these flies are a bargain, for they involve the individual painting of various color lines and spots to imitate the coloration of brook, brown, or rainbow trout and threadfin shad. A challenge for the artistic fly tyer.

JOE'S SMELT
(Plate IX)

HOOK: Mustad 9575, 94720 (2–10)
THREAD: Black (Flymaster 6/0)
TAIL: Red calf tail fibers (tied short, half gap width in length)
TAG: Red thread to secure Mylar
BODY: Silver Mylar tubing
THROAT: Mylar painted red for one-quarter body length
WING: Narrow pintail flank feather tied flat on top (to end of tail)

HEAD: Painted black with yellow eye and black pupil

REMARKS: This pattern, designed by Joe Sterling, is a highly regarded landlocked salmon and trout fly in the Northeast.

As often happens with popular patterns, this one has undergone variations. One of the newer versions calls for an underbody wrapped with Mylar tinsel enclosed in a body of pearlescent tubing. Pearlescent tubing is slightly transparent and the glitter of the silver Mylar underneath bleeds through the outer shell, creating a very lifelike effect. The underbody may also be changed by using Mylar in other colors, such as purple, green, gold, and so forth.

This pattern is quite often tied in tandem.

KING SMELT

HOOK: Mustad 94720 (2–10)
THREAD: Black (Flymaster 6/0)
TAIL: None
BODY: Flat silver tinsel
WING: Sparse bunches of the following from bottom to top: white bucktail, purple bucktail, blue bucktail, green bucktail, black bucktail (all gap width past bend)
HEAD: Black with white eye and red pupil

LADY GHOST

HOOK: Mustad 9575 (2–10)
THREAD: Black (Flymaster 6/0)
TAIL: None
RIB: Oval silver tinsel

BODY: Flat silver tinsel
THROAT: Six very fine strands of peacock herl along underside of shank, under which a few fibers of white bucktail (both as long as wing), under which a golden pheasant crest feather curving upward
WING: Golden pheasant crest feather (curving downward), over which four badger saddle hackles (both half a shank length past bend) (see model, Black Ghost)
SHOULDERS: Reeves's pheasant body feathers (gold with black edge) (one-third as long as wing) (substitute: ringneck pheasant "church window" body feathers)
CHEEKS: Jungle cock eyes (or equivalent) (second eye showing)
HEAD: Black

LEAD EYE RABBIT LEECH
(Plate IX)

HOOK: Mustad 3906B (2–6)
THREAD: Black (Monocord 3/0)
EYES: Pre-formed lead eyes (see materials section for description and source) lacquered yellow and painted with a black pupil
TAIL: A strip of tanned rabbit (two shank lengths past bend)
BODY: Tanned rabbit strip, wound around shank from bend to a point in front of eyes

REMARKS: The strip used for the tail is no more than a quarter inch wide and tapers to a point. To form the body, a thin strip (no more than a sixteenth of an inch wide) is

wound around the shank as you would a hackle and tied off in front of the eyes. This pattern is tied in natural and dyed rabbit colors. It is the first I know of to feature the newly manufactured lead eyes.

LIGHT SPRUCE

HOOK: Mustad 9575 (2–10)
THREAD: Black (Flymaster 6/0)
TAIL: Three or four peacock sword fibers (gap width past bend)
BODY: Rear half, red floss; fore half, peacock herl
WING: Four badger saddle hackles (half a shank length past bend) (see model, Black Ghost)
THROAT: Badger hackle tied as a wet fly collar after wing has been secured (see model, Blue Dun, page 124)
HEAD: Black

LITTLE BROOK TROUT

HOOK: Mustad 9575 (4–12)
THREAD: Black (Flymaster 6/0)
TAIL: Green calf tail fibers over a strand of red floss (gap width in length)
RIB: Fine flat silver tinsel
BODY: Cream spun fur or cream dubbing fur
THROAT: Hot orange calf tail fibers, beard style (as long as tail)
WING: Sparse bunches of the following from bottom to top: white calf tail, orange calf tail, badger fur guard hair fibers (all slightly past tail)

CHEEKS (optional): Jungle cock eyes (or equivalent) (second eye showing)

HEAD: Black

REMARKS: Be sure to use the stagger-cut method for a neatly tapered head.

LITTLE BROWN TROUT

HOOK: Mustad 9575 (4–12)

THREAD: Black (Flymaster 6/0)

TAIL: Tan ringneck pheasant body feather fibers (gap width past bend)

RIB: Oval gold tinsel

BODY: White wool

WING: Sparse bunches of the following from bottom to top: yellow calf tail, reddish-orange calf tail, dyed brown squirrel tail (all slightly past end of tail)

CHEEKS: Jungle cock eyes (or equivalent) (second eye showing)

LITTLE RAINBOW TROUT

HOOK: Mustad 9575 (4–12)

THREAD: Black (Flymaster 6/0)

TAIL: Green calf tail fibers (gap width past bend)

RIB: Fine flat silver tinsel

BODY: Very pale pink dubbing fur

WING: Sparse bunches of the following from bottom to top: white calf tail, pink calf tail, green calf tail, badger fur guard hair fibers (all slightly past end of tail)

CHEEKS: Jungle cock eyes (or equivalent) (second eye showing)

HEAD: Black

THE LLAMA
(Plate IX)

HOOK: Mustad 9575, 79580, 38941 (6–12)

THREAD: Black (Flymaster 6/0)

TAIL: Grizzly hackle fibers (gap width past bend)

RIB: Flat gold tinsel (medium for sizes 6–8, fine for sizes 10–12)

BODY: Red floss

WING: Woodchuck guard hair fibers with color bands showing from head to tail of black, tan, black, and white tip (all to end of tail)

HACKLE: Grizzly wound as a wet fly collar after wing has been secured (see model, Blue Dun, page 124)

HEAD: Painted black with white eye and black pupil

REMARKS: Originated by Miles Tourtilloutt. The woodchuck wing is the primary ingredient in this pattern. You'll notice that I have listed three different models of hooks ranging from a 6XL down to a 3XL. This will allow the tyer to match the hook to the barring and length of woodchuck guard hairs so that the bands of black, tan, black, and white tip may be produced without difficulty. (The length and barring on woodchucks may differ from animal to animal.) This pattern is one of the very few in which the wing itself is the decisive factor in the hook used. In short, you match the hook to the guard hairs.

When tying in the wing, leave some of the underfur in with the guard hairs, as this will allow the fly to pulse and breathe better when being fished. Should you have this pattern with you on the stream, hold it in the running water and observe it. You'll see it pulse and vibrate on its own, without any movement on your part.

Llamas have also been tied using other color combinations. Here are two more.

LLAMA, BLACK

HOOK: Mustad 9575, 79580, 38941 (6–12)

THREAD: Black (Flymaster 6/0)

TAIL: Grizzly hackle fibers (gap width in length)

RIB: Flat gold tinsel (medium for sizes 6–8, fine for sizes 10–12)

BODY: Black floss

WING: Woodchuck guard hair fibers (to end of tail)

HACKLE: Grizzly as a wet fly collar (see model, Blue Dun, page 124)

HEAD: Black with white eye and black pupil

LLAMA, WHITE

HOOK: Mustad 9575, 79580, 38941 (6–12)

THREAD: Black (Flymaster 6/0)

TAIL: Grizzly hackle fibers (gap width in length)

RIB: Flat silver tinsel (medium for sizes 6–8, fine for sizes 10–12)

BODY: White floss

HACKLE: Grizzly as a wet fly collar (see model, Blue Dun, page 124)

HEAD: Black with white eye and black pupil

REMARKS: Llama patterns have also been used for fishing the Atlantic salmon in New Brunswick and Labrador. In these instances, the bodies are sometimes made of fluorescent red floss.

MAGOG SMELT

HOOK: Mustad 9575 (2-10)
THREAD: Black (Flymaster 6/0)
TAIL: Teal flank fibers (gap width past bend)
BODY: Flat silver tinsel
THROAT: Red hackle fibers, beard style (as long as tail)
WING: Sparse strands of the following from bottom to top: white calf tail, yellow calf tail, lavender calf tail, topped with peacock herl (all half a shank length past bend)
SHOULDERS: Barred teal flank feather (one-third as long as wing)
HEAD: Black

MANSFIELD

HOOK: Mustad 9575 (4-12)
THREAD: Black (Flymaster 6/0)
TAIL: None
BODY: Flat silver tinsel
THROAT: Red bucktail (as long as body)
WING: A few strands of white bucktail, over which four bright orange saddle hackles (both half a shank length past bend) (see model, Black Ghost)

CHEEKS: Jungle cock eyes (or equivalent) (second eye showing)
HEAD: Black

MARABOU MUDDLER MINNOW
(see Black Marabou Muddler and White Marabou Muddler)

Matuka Flies

Matuka patterns are a style of tying a streamer fly which originated in New Zealand and were introduced to our modern-day anglers by Doug Swisher and Carl Richards in their book *Fly Fishing Strategy.* Whereas in conventional streamer patterns the wing is tied in behind the head and allowed to flow freely past the bend, matuka flies have the wing lashed to the hook shank by means of the ribbing material, usually gold or silver oval tinsel. The ribbing itself is carefully wound around the stem but between the hackle fibers protruding from the wing so that the fibers themselves are still free to move and pulse. Dressed in this manner, the fibers from the lashed downwing represent the fins of a baitfish. The extension of the wing beyond the bend is free to move, but because of the technique involved this freely moving part of the wing does not easily get caught in the hook gap as sometimes happens with the hackle wings on standard patterns.

The construction of a matuka type wing is relatively simple and proficiency comes with a little practice.

1. Tie in a ribbing of medium oval tinsel at the bend.

2. Form a body of wool, floss, chenille, or dubbing fur. A soft body is preferable to a hard body since the ribbing bites into a soft material more readily and the turns of ribbing around the body and wing are more easily controlled.

3. Tie in the wing at the head area of the hook. (A wing may consist of two or four hackles depending on how full you want it to be.) Secure the butt ends well since you will be pulling and tugging on the saddle hackles just beyond the bend of the hook.

After the wing has been measured for length, some tyers prefer to remove those fibers from the side of the wing which comes in contact with the body. This removal of hackle from the underside of the wing eliminates the problem of trapped fibers.

4. Pull the saddle hackle wing rearward with your left thumb and forefinger so that it is slightly taut. Stroke the fibers of the wing forward (toward the hook eye) and try to separate them just a bit where the first turn of ribbing is to be made near the bend. Bring the ribbing around the hook shank and through the saddle hackle fibers. The first turn is usually the most difficult. Continue with the ribbing in an open spiral toward the head, bringing it around the body and the hackle fibers as you progress forward.

5. When you have reached the head area, tie the ribbing down with enough thread

Tying Steps for Matuka Fly

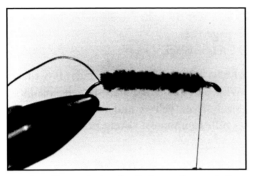

a. Chenille and tinsel rib have been tied to hook.

b. Fibers have been removed from one side of four saddle hackle feathers and the aligned set is being measured along top of hook shank.

c. Hackles have been secured behind eye of hook and excess butts trimmed. First turn of tinsel rib is being taken around hackle and chenille near bend.

d. Tinsel rib is being spiraled around body and between fibers of saddle hackle to thread, where it is later tied off and the excess trimmed.

e. An additional saddle hackle feather is being tied in to form a collar on the fly.

f. Completed matuka fly.

turns so that it does not slip. Secure it well.

You will notice that no matter how many times you attempt this tying of a matuka wing there are always a few hackle fibers that have been pressed down with the thread. Use the point of your dubbing needle to free these fibers.

Ron Macuga solved his problem of matted-down fibers by threading the ribbing through a wide-eyed sewing needle. He uses the point of the needle to divide the fibers neatly and evenly and, as if he were actually sewing, allows the ribbing to follow through the hackle fibers. Once through the fibers with the ribbing, he tightens it against the body as he spirals it forward for the next turn.

Most pattern recipes call for rooster neck or saddle hackle feathers for the wings of matuka flies. However, Doug Swisher prefers to use hen hackle if it can be found in the proper length. Hen hackle fibers, whether from the neck, saddle, or body, if they have the proper length, color, and proportion, are more desirable in that the webby fibers pulse and vibrate more actively when fished.

Matuka patterns may be tied in endless color variations. There are really no set patterns. The following are just a few of the different color combinations listed in the mail-order catalogs.

BLACK MATUKA

HOOK: Mustad 9575 (2–10)
THREAD: Black (Flymaster 6/0)
TAIL: None
RIB: Medium oval silver tinsel
BODY: Black chenille, wool, or dubbing fur
WING: Four black rooster or hen neck or saddle hackles (half a shank length beyond bend)
COLLAR (optional): Black as a wet fly collar (see model, Blue Dun, page 124)
HEAD: Black

FURNACE MATUKA

HOOK: Mustad 9575 (2–10)
THREAD: Black (Flymaster 6/0)
TAIL: None
RIB: Medium oval gold tinsel
BODY: Brown chenille, wool, or dubbing fur
WING: Four furnace rooster or hen neck or saddle hackles (half a shank length past bend)
COLLAR (optional): Furnace as a wet fly collar (see model, Blue Dun, page 124)
HEAD: Black

REMARKS: Sometimes badger saddle hackles are used with a lighter brown or tan body

OLIVE MATUKA

HOOK: Mustad 9575 (2–10)
THREAD: Black (Flymaster 6/0)
TAIL: None
RIB: Medium oval gold tinsel
BODY: Olive chenille, wool, or dubbing fur
WING: Four dyed olive grizzly rooster or hen neck or saddle hackles (half a shank length past bend)
COLLAR (optional): Grizzly dyed olive as a wet fly collar (see model, Blue Dun, page 124)
HEAD: Black

REMARKS: This is a particular favorite of Swisher's. The wing may also be made of grizzly dyed yellow and the body of cream chenille to imitate a young perch.

MAYNARD MARVEL (No. 1)
(Plate IX)

HOOK: Mustad 94720 (2–8)
THREAD: Black (Flymaster 6/0)
TAIL: Red wool yarn (barely past bend)
BODY: Embossed silver tinsel
THROAT: Red calf tail fibers, beard style (for half the length of body)
WING: Twelve golden pheasant crest feathers (gap width past bend)
SHOULDERS: Black hackle feather (to center of body)
HEAD: Black with yellow eye and red pupil

REMARKS: There seems to be some confusion as to which is the correct Maynard Marvel. The above was sent to me by Bill Hunter. It is very similar to what Dick Stewart, co-author of *Trolling Flies for Trout and Salmon*, has now listed as the Golden Marvel, but he makes a distinction between the two. Both Hunter and Stewart are extremely knowledgeable fly tyers and I'm not going to even attempt to find out who is correct in this. In this case, it's up to the tyer and angler to decide which to tie and which to fish.

According to Hunter, the original fly, as designed by Ora Smith of Keene, New Hampshire (and sometimes called the Keene Fly), was tied with twenty-four golden pheasant crest feathers and layered as a wing in alternating lengths of one short, one long, one short, and so on. Says Hunter, "This fly still catches an awful lot of fish in spite of the fact that it is a pain to tie and expensive to boot."

Another version of the Maynard Marvel follows.

MAYNARD MARVEL (No. 2)

HOOK: Mustad 9575 (4–12)
THREAD: Black (Flymaster 6/0)
TAIL: Red hackle fibers (gap width past bend)
BODY: Embossed silver tinsel
THROAT: Red hackle fibers, beard style (same length as tail)
WING: Golden pheasant crest (curving downward), over which a sparse bunch of light blue bucktail, over which a mallard flank feather tied flat on top (all half a shank length past bend)
HEAD: Black

MICKEY FINN

HOOK: Mustad 9575 (2–12)
THREAD: Black (Flymaster 6/0)

TAIL: None
RIB: Oval silver tinsel (see model, Black-Nosed Dace)
BODY: Flat silver tinsel
WING: Yellow, then red, then yellow calf tail (or bucktail) (all half a shank length past bend)
HEAD: Black

REMARKS: Be sure to stagger-cut the butts of the wing fibers for a neatly tapered head. The original of this famous fly, once called simply Red and Yellow Bucktail, was popularized by John Alden Knight. The top layer of yellow bucktail equals the thickness of the combined red and yellow bucktail beneath it.

MILLER'S RIVER SPECIAL

HOOK: Mustad 9575 (2–10)
THREAD: Black (Flymaster 6/0)
TAIL: Golden pheasant tippets (gap width past bend)
RIB: Oval gold tinsel
BODY: Flat gold tinsel (for rib and body, see model, Black-Nosed Dace)
WING: Yellow bucktail, over which black bucktail (both half a shank length beyond bend)
SHOULDERS: Red side feathers from golden pheasant (half the length of wing) (substitute: dyed red hackle feather)

CHEEKS: Jungle cock eyes (or equivalent) (only one eye showing)
HEAD: Black

MOBEY DICK

HOOK: Mustad 9575, 79580 (6–12)
THREAD: Black (Flymaster 6/0)
TAIL: Golden pheasant tippet fibers (gap width past bend)
PALMER RIB: Brown saddle hackle palmered through body
BODY: Peacock herl
WING: Mallard fibers dyed light bronze dun (to end of tail) (tied over the back as in a Hendrickson wet fly)
HEAD: Black

REMARKS: Originated by David Goulet, who states that he has no idea what this pattern imitates but it is nevertheless a constant fish taker.

MOHAIR LEECH, BLACK

HOOK: Mustad 9672 (4–8)
THREAD: Black (waxed Monocord 3/0)
TAIL, BODY, AND WING: A long black-fibered fuzzy yarn is left as a tail and also wound as a body. The body fibers are then combed out to the rear to give the leech effect. Tail is a full shank-length long.

REMARKS: This pattern, listed in Henry's Fork Angler News, was created by Doug Siebert. It is also tied in olive, brown, and purple.

MOOSE RIVER STREAMER

HOOK: Mustad 9575 (2–8)
THREAD: Black (Flymaster 6/0)
TAIL: None
BODY: Flat silver tinsel
WING: White bucktail, over which four badger saddle hackles topped by six strands of peacock herl (all half a shank length past bend) (see model, Black Ghost)
SHOULDERS: Golden pheasant tippet feathers (one-third as long as wing)
HEAD: Black

MUDDLER MINNOW

HOOK: Mustad 38941, 79580 (2–14)
THREAD: Gray (Monocord 3/0 or, on very large sizes, flat waxed nylon size A)
TAIL: A short section of mottled turkey wing quill (not quite gap width in length), fibers arching upward or downward to taste.
BODY: Flat gold tinsel
UNDERWING: Gray squirrel tail fibers, fairly sparse (to end of tail)
WING: Two mottled turkey wing quill sections tied slightly tented off top side of body and angling upward with tips to bend (tips may angle upward or downward to tyer's preference)
HEAD: Spun and trimmed deer hair. Some of the fibers from the first flaring and

spinning of deer hair are left angling rearward as sort of a hackle collar surrounding all but the bottom of the body.

REMARKS: This most popular of all listed bucktail and streamer type patterns looks the least like a baitfish imitation. Yet it does service as a dry (hopper), a wet (tadpole), and a groveler (sculpin), and almost whatever you care to make it do or whatever the fish takes it for. It has even been tied on jig heads by spin fishermen. It has been copied, incorporated, and improved upon in countless other patterns. It is tied with big heads, small heads, flat-shaped, pear-shaped, square-shaped, and however-you-want-to-trim-it heads. Wing tips and tail tip are tied curving up or down depending on the tyer's style and preference. All of them work. Credit for this phenomenal pattern goes to Don Gapen.

Construction of the Muddler Minnow is not difficult, but because it is such an important fly, a review is in order.

1. Tie in the tail section of turkey quill fibers (about seven or eight fibers on a size 6 hook). Wind the thread over the butt ends of the turkey quill to a point a quarter shank length before the eye. (Winding over the butt ends as opposed to cutting them away at the bend makes for a smoother body.)

2. Tie in the gold tinsel and wind it to the bend in connecting spirals and then back again, over itself, to the thread. Secure it with the tying thread.

3. Tie in a small bunch of squirrel tail fibers the tips of which extend to the center of the tail.

4. Cut a left and a right section of mottled turkey wing quill fibers (or any suitable substitute) and tie them to the shank as you would a wet fly wing (see model, Black Gnat, pages 9–11). I like my tips to curve upward, more in the manner of a hopper wing.

5. Wind the thread to the eye and back to the wing, filling in uneven areas.

6. The best deer body hair for the Muddler Minnow is that from a mule deer. It spins better than the white-tailed and the barring at the tips is much narrower and presents a neater appearance. Cut a clump of deer hair (slightly more than the diameter of a wooden matchstick) and hold it against the near side of the hook shank where the tying thread was left so that the tips point rearward about three-quarters of the wing length. Bring the thread around the shank and deer hair and pull the thread toward you. The hair will flare on your side of the hook shank. Because thread and some excess butt material are covering the shank at this point, the deer hair will not spin around the entire shank. It should, however, fill in the area of the shank facing you.

Place an equal amount of deer hair on the far side of the shank, bring the thread around it two times, and once more pull it toward you. The hair will flare on the far side.

If a larger head is desired, add more deer hair in front of the hair just flared.

7. Remove the fly from the vise and trim the head to a square or wedge shape. The area under the hook shank just behind the eye should be trimmed relatively flat. My own preference is a more or less triangular

Tying Steps for Muddler Minnow

a. Tip of turkey quill section has been tied in for tail. Note that excess has been brought forward two-thirds of shank and covered with thread before being trimmed to assure a smooth body.

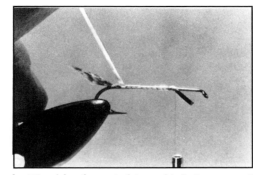

b. Tinsel has been tied in and is being wound rearward. It is then reversed and wound back to starting point in connecting spirals.

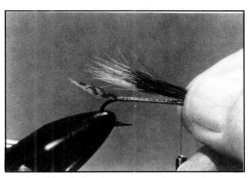

c. Tinsel body has been secured and a clump of squirrel tail fibers are being measured along shank prior to being tied in.

d. Turkey wing quill sections have been paired and tied to hook shank. Excess butts are then trimmed.

e. A medium-sized clump of deer hair has been placed on each side of the hook directly in front of tied-down turkey butts.

f. Deer hair is being spun around forward end of hook shank. (For spinning technique, see Irresistible, page 45)

g. Deer hair is being trimmed to Muddler Minnow head shape.

h. Completed Muddler Minnow.

i. Another completed Muddler Minnow on which the turkey wing quills have been tied in with the wing tips curving downward.

wedge shape somewhat like a sculpin. I just feel I can fish it better. However, any of the shapes work well.

Some fly tyers like to lacquer their turkey wing quill sections so they do not split. However, the split wings seem to work very well when fished. Perhaps it's because they have more movement.

Muddler Minnows are often tied weighted when they are to be fished deep.

Other Muddler Minnow variations follow.

MUDDLER MINNOW, BLACK

HOOK: Mustad 9672, 38941 (2–14)
THREAD: Black (Monocord 3/0)
TAIL: Bronze turkey quill section
BODY: Flat gold tinsel
UNDERWING: Black squirrel tail fibers
WING: Bronze turkey wing quill sections
HEAD AND COLLAR: Dyed black deer
  hair spun and trimmed

MUDDLER MINNOW, GOLDEN (Graves)

The same as the standard Muddler Minnow except that the turkey wing quills and tail section are dyed a golden color. Designed by Ralph Graves of Roscoe, New York.

MUDDLER MINNOW, GREEN

HOOK: Mustad 38941, 9672 (4–14)
THREAD: Olive (Monocord 3/0)
TAIL: Mottled turkey quill section

BODY: Fluorescent green nylon tow or wool

UNDERWING: Calf tail dyed grass green

WING: Mottled turkey wing quill sections

HEAD AND COLLAR: Top part, brown deer hair dyed olive; bottom part, natural brown/gray deer hair

REMARKS: The head of this fly must be flared and pieced in.

MUDDLER MINNOW, ORANGE

HOOK: Mustad 9672, 38941 (2–14)

THREAD: Gray (Monocord 3/0)

TAIL: Mottled turkey quill section

BODY: Fluorescent orange nylon tow or wool

UNDERWING: Orange calf tail

WING: Mottled turkey wing quill sections

HEAD AND COLLAR: Top part, brown deer hair dyed orange; bottom part, natural brown/gray deer hair

REMARKS: The head of this fly must be flared and pieced in.

MUDDLER MINNOW, WHITE

HOOK: Mustad 38941, 79580, 9672 (2–14)

THREAD: White (Monocord 3/0)

TAIL: Light mottled turkey quill section

BUTT: Red wool

RIB: Fine silver tinsel

BODY: White wool

UNDERWING: White calf tail fibers, over

which teal flank fibers, both sparse (to center of tail)

WING: Light-shade mottled turkey wing quill sections

COLLAR: Natural brown deer hair flared rearward to butt surrounding body

HEAD: White deer hair spun and trimmed to shape

REMARKS: There are a few variations of this pattern. The above is the original as designed by Dan Bailey, who used a cross between the Muddler Minnow and the Bumble Puppy. It was nicknamed the Mizzoulian Spook by Vince Hamilin, author of the Alley Oop comic strip.

MUDDLER MINNOW, YELLOW

HOOK: Mustad 38941, 9672 (2–14)

THREAD: Gray (Monocord 3/0)

TAIL: Mottled turkey wing quill section

BODY: Flat gold tinsel

UNDERWING: Red fox squirrel tail fibers

WING: Dyed yellow mottled turkey wing quill sections

HEAD AND COLLAR: Natural gray/brown deer hair spun and trimmed

NEEDLE SMELT

HOOK: Mustad 9575 (2–10)

THREAD: Black (Flymaster 6/0)

TAIL: None

BODY: Embossed silver tinsel

WING: Deep yellow bucktail, over which

four gray saddle hackles (half a shank length past bend) (see model, Black Ghost)

CHEEKS: Jungle cock eyes (or equivalent) (second eye showing)

HEAD: Painted black with white eye and black pupil

NINE THREE

HOOK: Mustad 9575 (2–10)

THREAD: Black (Flymaster 6/0)

TAIL: None

BODY: Flat silver tinsel

WING: White bucktail (or calf tail), over which two green saddle hackles flanked by two black saddle hackles (all half a shank length past bend) (see model, Black Ghost)

CHEEKS: Jungle cock eyes (or equivalent) (second eye showing)

HEAD: Black

REMARKS: This pattern is also tied in tandem for landlocked salmon.

NOTHING

HOOK: Mustad 9575 (10)

THREAD: Black (Flymaster 6/0)

TAIL: White calf tail fibers (gap width past bend)

BODY: White wool

WING: White calf tail (barely past end of tail)

HEAD: Black

REMARKS: Ted Gerken states that this all-white fly imitates the fry of trout and salmon and is exceptionally effective for spring rainbow and char fishing in Alaska.

ORANGE MUDDLER MINNOW
(see Muddler Minnow, Orange)

PEARL FLASH

HOOK: Mustad 9575 (2–10)
THREAD: White (Flymaster 6/0)
BUTT OR TAG: Red thread to secure end of Mylar tubing
BODY: Silver Mylar tubing
THROAT: White bucktail (or calf tail) fibers (as long as wing)
WING: Pearlescent Flashabou wing material (gap width past bend)
HEAD: Painted white with yellow eye and black pupil

REMARKS: Featured by Flagg's Flies, Barre, Massachusetts.

PINK LADY STREAMER

HOOK: Mustad 9575 (2–10)
THREAD: Red (Flymaster 6/0)

TAIL: None
RIB: Flat gold tinsel
BODY: Pink wool
THROAT: Yellow hackle fibers, beard style (gap width in length)
WING: White bucktail (or calf tail), over which two orange saddle hackles flanked by two grizzly saddle hackles (all half a shank length past bend) (see model, Black Ghost)
SHOULDERS: Mallard flank feathers (one-third as long as wing)
CHEEKS: Jungle cock eyes (or equivalent) (second eye showing)
HEAD: Red

REMARKS: When selecting mallard flank feathers for the shoulders on streamer flies, always choose the shorter feathers since they taper in width more quickly. The larger flank feathers are too long and by the time you stroke the excess rearward to form the shorter shoulder section, there is very little left.

PINTAIL SMELT
(Plate IX)

HOOK: Mustad 9575, 79580 (6–8)
THREAD: White (Flymaster 6/0)
TAIL: None
BODY: Embossed silver tinsel
UNDERWING: Pale pink bucktail, sparse (to bend)

WING: One pintail flank feather on each side covering the shank (Hornberg style) (tips extending quarter shank length past bend)
HEAD: Painted yellow with black pupil

REMARKS: David Goulet, its originator, states that this local (Massachusetts) favorite is a well-guarded secret which should be made public. I suspect there are those anglers who disagree with Goulet.

PLATTE RIVER STREAMER

HOOK: Mustad 79580 (2–8)
THREAD: Black (Flymaster 6/0)
TAIL: None
RIB: Oval gold tinsel
BODY: Brown chenille (size 2 for hook sizes 2–4, size 1 for hook sizes 6–8)
WING: Two brown saddle hackles flanked by two yellow saddle hackles cocking slightly upward (half a shank length past bend) (see model, Black Ghost)
HACKLE: Brown and yellow mixed and wound as a dry fly collar
HEAD: Black

PURPLE FLASH

HOOK: Mustad 9575 (4–10)
THREAD: White (Flymaster 6/0)
BUTT: Red thread used to secure Mylar tubing
BODY: Silver Mylar tubing
THROAT: White bucktail (or calf tail) (as long as wing)

WING: Purple Flashabou wing material (gap width past bend)

HEAD: Painted white with yellow eyes and black pupil

REMARKS: This pattern, submitted by Rodney Flagg, is also tied with other wing colors in Flashabou, which then changes the pattern name accordingly: Black Flash, Pearl Flash, Copper Flash, and so on.

QUEEN BEE

HOOK: Mustad 9575 (2–8)
THREAD: Black (Flymaster 6/0)
TAIL: None
BODY: Flat silver tinsel
THROAT: Red hackle fibers, beard style (gap width in length)
WING: Yellow bucktail, over which white bucktail, both sparse, over which four brown saddle hackles (all half a shank length past bend) (see model, Black Ghost)
CHEEKS: Jungle cock eyes (or equivalent) (second eye showing)
HEAD: Black

QUICKSILVER

HOOK: Mustad 9575 (2–6)
THREAD: Black (Flymaster 6/0)
TAIL: None
RIB: Flat silver tinsel
BODY: White floss
THROAT: White bucktail (sparse) next to underside of shank (as long as wing), cov-

ered by a beard of red hackle fibers (one-quarter the length of the bucktail)
WING: Four natural black saddle hackles with an olive cast topped by six strands of extra-fine peacock herl (one-third shank length past bend)
SHOULDERS: Ringneck pheasant "church window" body feathers (one-third the length of body)
HEAD: Black

REMARKS: Originated by William Quick, who states that this fly is deadly about the second week in June on Moosehead Lake, Maine, when he is fishing for landlocked salmon.

RAINY DAY SPECIAL

HOOK: Mustad 9575, 94720 (2–6)
THREAD: Green or olive (Flymaster 6/0)
TAIL: None
TAG: Oval silver tinsel
RIB: Oval silver tinsel
BODY: Fluorescent green floss
THROAT: Green hackle fibers (half the shank length)
WING: Dyed fluorescent green white-tailed deer belly hair (very fine), over which six extra-fine strands of peacock herl (all half a shank length past bend)
HEAD: Painted green

REMARKS: "When the water is high, murky, and roily, and especially in the rain, this fly is a killer," says Dick Brady. The pattern is used for landlocked salmon in Maine.

RANGELEY CENTENNIAL

HOOK: Mustad 94720 (2–10)
THREAD: Black
TAIL: None
RIB: Oval silver tinsel
BODY: Red floss
THROAT: White bucktail next to shank under which is yellow bucktail, both sparse (both as long as body)
WING: Two yellow saddle hackles flanked by two white saddle hackles (both a gap width past bend). Both are then covered by two red saddle hackles two-thirds as long as the former. (see model, Black Ghost)
CHEEKS: Jungle cock eyes (or equivalent) (second eye showing)
HEAD: Black

RED/GRAY GHOST

The same as Gray Ghost except that it uses red bucktail in place of golden pheasant crest for both throat and wing.

RED AND WHITE BUCKTAIL

HOOK: Mustad 9575 (2–10)
THREAD: Black (Flymaster 6/0)
TAIL: None
RIB: Oval silver tinsel (see model, Black-nosed Dace, page 209)
BODY: Flat silver tinsel
WING: White bucktail, over which red bucktail, both sparse, topped by five or six strands of peacock herl (all half a shank length past bend)
HEAD: Black

RED AND WHITE STREAMER

HOOK: Mustad 36890 (3/0)
THREAD: Black (Monocord 3/0)
TAIL: White bucktail (gap width past bend)
RIB: Medium flat silver tinsel
UNDERBODY: Medium lead wire (.024)
BODY: White wool
WING: White bucktail over red bucktail (half a shank length past bend)
TOPPING (optional): White marabou

REMARKS: This extra-large pattern is used for king (chinook) and silver (coho) salmon in Alaska and has taken fish up to forty pounds, according to Ted Gerken.

RIPOGENUS SMELT

HOOK: Mustad 9575 (2–10)
THREAD: Black (Flymaster 6/0)
TAIL: None
TAG: Flat silver tinsel
RIB: Flat silver tinsel
BODY: Fluorescent orange floss
THROAT: Four strands of peacock herl next to underside of shank, under which a few strands of white bucktail (both as long as wing), both covered with a small golden pheasant crest feather (one-third as long)
WING: Two grizzly saddle hackles flanked by two light blue saddle hackles (both a gap width past bend) (see model, Black Ghost)

CHEEKS: Barred teal flank feathers (one-third as long as body)
HEAD: Black

REMARKS: Originated by Edward Reif.

ROYAL COACHMAN BUCKTAIL

HOOK: Mustad 9575 (4–12)
THREAD: Black (Flymaster 6/0)
TAIL: Golden pheasant tippet fibers (gap width past bend)
BODY: Peacock herl divided by a wide band of red floss
THROAT: Brown hackle fibers, beard style (as long as tail)
WING: White bucktail (or calf tail) (half a shank length past bend)
HEAD: Black

RYER'S COHO

HOOK: Mustad 9575 (1/0–4)
THREAD: Red (Monocord 3/0)
TAIL: Orange bucktail (gap width past bend)
RIB: Medium flat silver tinsel
UNDERBODY: Medium lead wire (.024)
BODY: White wool
WING: Orange bucktail over white bucktail (both to end of tail)
HEAD: Red

RYER'S SOCKEYE
(Plate IX)

HOOK: Mustad 79580 (2)
THREAD: Red (Flymaster 6/0 or Monocord 3/0)
TAIL: Red over yellow bucktail (gap width past bend)
RIB: Medium flat silver tinsel
UNDERBODY: Medium lead wire (.024)
BODY: Medium orange chenille (size 1)
WING: Red over yellow bucktail (both to end of tail)
HEAD: Red

REMARKS: Both Ryer's Coho and Ryer's Sockeye were originated by William Ryer, who has used them effectively fishing Alaska.

SHENK SCULPIN

HOOK: Mustad 9672 (2–6)
THREAD: Black (Monocord 3/0)
TAIL: Black marabou (half a shank length past bend)
BODY: Black rabbit fur, full and tapered
PECTORAL FINS: Dark mottled turkey reinforced with vinyl cement
WING: Black marabou (to end of tail)
HEAD: Spun and trimmed black deer hair (see model, Irresistible, page 45) (trimmed to flat wedge shape, like a sculpin's head)

REMARKS: Designed by Ed Shenk. When you trim the head to sculpin shape, some of the deer hair fibers may be allowed to flare rearward and blend in with the marabou wing so that there is a flow from front to rear.

SILVER DARTER

HOOK: Mustad 9575 (4–10)
THREAD: Black (Flymaster 6/0)
TAIL: Teal flank fibers (gap width past bend)
RIB: Fine flat silver tinsel
BODY: White floss
THROAT: Peacock sword fibers, as beard (same length as tail)
WING: Four badger saddle hackles (half a shank length past bend) (see model, Black Ghost)
CHEEKS: Jungle cock eyes (or equivalent) (only one eye showing)
HEAD: Black

REMARKS: This pattern is sometimes tied with Mylar tubing for the body, in which case the tail is omitted.

SILVER DEMON

HOOK: Mustad 9672 (8–12)
THREAD: Black (Flymaster 6/0)
TAIL: Bright orange calf tail fibers (gap width in length)
BODY: Flat silver tinsel
THROAT: Bright orange calf tail fibers, beard style (as long as tail)

UNDERWING: Bright blue calf tail fibers (to end of tail)
WING: One mallard flank feather tied flat on top (to end of tail)
HEAD: Black

SILVER MINNOW

HOOK: Mustad 9575 (2–10)
THREAD: White (Flymaster 6/0)
TAIL: Grizzly hackle fibers (gap width past bend)
UNDERBODY: White floss to build shape and taper, or if weighted, white floss to smooth lead wire and pre-shape
BODY: Flat embossed silver tinsel
THROAT: Red hackle fibers, fairly long (reaching to hook point)
WING: White bucktail, over which blue bucktail topped by a single mallard flank feather tenting over bucktail (all half a shank length past bend)
HEAD: Painted silver with black eye and yellow pupil

SILVER SHINER

HOOK: Mustad 9575 (2–10)
THREAD: Black (Flymaster 6/0)
TAIL: White calf tail fibers (gap width past bend)
RIB: Flat silver tinsel
BODY: White floss

WING: Olive marabou over white marabou (half a shank length past bend)
HEAD: Black

SLIM RICHARD
(Plate IX)

HOOK: Mustad 9575, 94720 (2–6)
THREAD: Black (Flymaster 6/0)
TAIL: Red hackle fibers (gap width past bend)
BODY: Flat silver tinsel
WING: Very fine white belly hair from white-tailed deer (hindquarters area), over which a single natural dark blue dun saddle hackle (fairly thin) tied flat over body, over which four extra-fine peacock herl fibers (all to end of tail)
HEAD: Black

REMARKS: Originated by Dick Brady for fishing landlocked salmon in Maine.

SOCKEYE JOHN

HOOK: Mustad 79580 (2)
THREAD: Black (Monocord 3/0)
TAIL: None
BODY: Flat silver tinsel
WING: Black bear hair (half a shank length past bend)
HEAD: Black

REMARKS: This sockeye salmon pattern comes from the Iliaska Lodge in Illiamna, Alaska.

SOFT HACKLE STREAMER

HOOK: Mustad 3406 (for fresh water), 34007 (for salt water) (1/0–6)

THREAD: To match wing color (Flymaster 6/0)

BODY: None

UNDERWING: Two strands of Flashabou material (as long as wing)

WING: Marabou blood feather wound as a wet fly hackle (shank length past bend)

COLLAR: Mallard flank, pheasant rump, guinea hen body feather, or other appropriate feather wound as a wet fly hackle (extending rearward half the length of the wing)

HEAD: Lacquered with clear cement to allow color of thread to show through

REMARKS: This innovation by Jack Gartside may, at first glance, appear to be nothing more than a marabou streamer of sorts. What's different about it, however, is that the marabou blood feather is tied in by the tip and wound around the shank behind the eye as you would a hackle feather on a wet fly. The marabou completely surrounds the entire hook shank and acts as both wing and body. (This is similar to the design I used in the pattern Black Angus, where the marabou was wound as a folded hackle along the entire length of the hook shank.)

The hackle collar is also wound in the same manner so that it too surrounds the wing and hook shank.

Gartside leaves it to the tyer to choose his wing and collar colors. The sample I received for trout and other freshwater fish was dressed with two strands of gold Flashabou, a yellow marabou wing, and a collar of mallard flank. Yellow thread was used. Another sample used olive marabou with a dyed olive mallard flank collar. Saltwater versions, using the Mustad 34007 hook, employ white, blue and white, red and white mixtures of marabou (two blood feathers can be wound as one for special effects) with guinea fowl or mallard flank as the collar. Variations are, of course, as endless as the imagination and there is no point in listing such. The idea is a sound one in that this type of construction prevents any separation of wing from body (since both are the same) when the fly is fished and actually adds to a pulsing, breathing lifelike impression.

SPECTRUM SMELT

HOOK: Mustad 94720 (4–6)

THREAD: White (Flymaster 6/0)

TAIL: None

BODY: Silver Mylar tubing

BUTT: White thread to secure tubing

THROAT: Sparse white bucktail (to bend)

WING: A few strands each of light blue, pink, and light yellow bucktail mixed together, over which a similar sparse mixture of green, purple, and orange bucktail, over which a topping of four strands of peacock herl (all extending barely past bend)

HEAD: Painted silver with black on top

REMARKS: Originated by Dick Stewart of North Country Angler.

SPITFIRE

HOOK: Mustad 9672 (4–10)

THREAD: Black (Flymaster 6/0)

TAIL: A section of dyed red goose quill fibers (1½ gap widths past bend) (see model, Alexandra, page 124)

PALMER RIB: Brown hackle palmered through body

BODY: Medium black chenille (size 1)

WING: None

HACKLE: Guinea hen body feather wound as a wet fly collar (tips to point of hook) (see model, Blue Dun, page 124)

HEAD: Black

REMARKS: This Don Gapen pattern is now almost fifty years old. It is listed as a trout streamer pattern but would also easily pass as a wet fly.

SPRUCE MATUKA

The same as the Light Spruce or Dark Spruce streamer fly except that the wing is tied to the shank using the matuka method (see page 222).

SPUDDLER

HOOK: Mustad 79580, 9672 (2–12)

THREAD: Gray (Monocord 3/0)

TAIL: Brown bear hair or brown calf tail (gap width past bend)

BODY: Cream wool or cream poly yarn

WING: Red fox squirrel tail, over which four grizzly dyed brown saddle hackles tied flat on top (extending half a shank length past bend) (sometimes cree saddle hackles are used)

GILLS: A short band of red wool which covers the wrappings and butts of wing

HEAD: Brown antelope spun and trimmed to a sculpin's head (wedge-shaped and flat on bottom) (see model, Irresistible, page 45)

REMARKS: This pattern was developed in Dan Bailey's Fly Shop with the help of Red Monical and Don Williams. It evolved out of the Muddler Minnow and the Spruce Fly, two of the more effective patterns fished in the West. The Spuddler is now listed in just about every catalog.

SQUIRREL TAIL

HOOK: Mustad 9575 (4–10)

THREAD: Black (Flymaster 6/0)

TAIL: None

RIB: Oval silver tinsel

BODY: Flat silver tinsel (for rib and body, see model, Black-Nosed Dace)

WING: A few strands of white calf tail, over which gray squirrel tail fibers (half a shank length past bend)

HEAD: Black with yellow eye and black pupil

SUNDOWNER

HOOK: Mustad 94720 (2–4)

THREAD: Black (Flymaster 6/0)

TAG: Medium flat silver tinsel, used to secure Flashabou

BODY: Pearlescent Flashabou wound around shank as you would tinsel (about eight strands are used as one)

THROAT: Very fine white belly hair from white-tailed deer (hindquarters area) next to shank, under which are three or four very fine strands of peacock herl covered by a golden pheasant crest feather (all to bend)

WING: Four dark olive/gray saddle hackles, over which six very fine strands of peacock herl (all a gap width past bend)

SHOULDERS: "Church window" body feathers from male ringneck pheasant (one-fourth the length of wing)

HEAD: Black

REMARKS: "I use this fly just before dark," states Dick Brady. The pattern is a trolling streamer for landlocked salmon in Maine.

SUPERVISOR

HOOK: Mustad 9575 (4–12)

THREAD: Black (Flymaster 6/0)

TAIL: A piece of red wool (tied short, barely past bend)

BODY: Flat silver tinsel

THROAT: White hackle fibers, beard style (gap width in length)

WING: White bucktail, over which four light bright blue saddle hackles topped by six strands of peacock herl (all half a shank length past bend) (see model, Black Ghost)

SHOULDERS: Bright light green saddle hackles (one on each side) covering one-third of blue saddle hackles

CHEEKS: Jungle cock eyes (or equivalent) (third eye showing)

HEAD: Black

REMARKS: This famous smelt imitation was originated by Joseph F. Stickney of Saco, Maine.

SWIFT RIVER

HOOK: Mustad 3665A (6–10)

THREAD: Black

TAIL: Golden pheasant tippet fibers (gap width past bend)

RIB: Flat silver tinsel

BODY: Bright green wool

THROAT: Red hackle fibers, beard style (as long as tail)

WING: Brown bucktail over white bucktail (both half a shank length past bend)

TED'S YESTERDAY
(Plate IX)

HOOK: Mustad 36890, 9575 (3/0–6)

THREAD: Black (Flymaster 6/0 or Monocord 3/0)

TAIL: Red hackle fibers (gap width past bend)

RIB: Flat silver tinsel

BODY: White wool

THROAT: Red calf tail fibers, beard style (as long as tail)

WING: White calf tail fibers (to bend), over which two badger saddle hackles (almost twice as long as calf tail)

HEAD: Black

REMARKS: This is a great name for a fly. Originated by Ted Gerken of Illiamna, Alaska.

THREADFIN SHAD
(Plate IX)

HOOK: Mustad 9674 or similar ring-eye (2–10)

THREAD: Gray (Flymaster 6/0 or Monocord 3/0)

TAIL: Gray marabou (slightly longer than gap width)

UNDERBODY: Pre-formed with metallic tape or Styrofoam, depending on whether the fly is a sinker or floater. The lead shields from dental X-ray slides are ideal. Go see your dentist. (For underbody construction, see model, Zonker.)

BODY: Mylar tubing

FIN: Marabou clipped short, tied in at bend and brought forward over body as a shell and tied down behind head; cement applied on top of Mylar body to keep fin in place along back

HEAD: Gray with white eye and red pupil (or if weighted, gray with white eye and black pupil)

REMARKS: This pattern was originated by Andre Puyans and is one of the few baitfish imitations that look the part while still retaining the impression of life. The flash of the Mylar and the action of the marabou fibers in both fin and tail make this fly an extremely effective pattern. It has been used for all kinds of fish in addition to trout.

Puyans is a truly innovative fly tyer who is responsible for many fly patterns (see also the A.P. series of nymphs). Tyers such as Puyans, Troth, Rosborough, and certain others are responsible not only for the patterns they have originated but also for the many offshoots of these patterns that other tyers design on the basis of the originals. In short, they are the ones that start the trends.

Thunder Creek Patterns

Not long ago most of the mail-order catalogs displayed a variety of fly patterns known as the Thunder Creek series. I suspect the reason for the decline of the flies today is that the companies just cannot get enough professional fly tyers to meet the demand. That these patterns consistently take fish has been proven time and time again. They are not tied as quickly as, say, a standard Black-Nosed Dace or, for that matter, a Marabou Muddler, and not all fly tyers take the time and trouble to fashion these patterns properly—that is, in a neat and precise manner as outlined by Keith Fulsher in his book *Tying and Fishing the Thunder Creek Series*. The bucktail fibers which form the wing, usually in a two-tone or three-tone effect, must be carefully separated and precisely fastened to the shank. Then there is the varnishing of the head to a hardness that will permit the painting of an optic eye, which in itself involves three coats of lacquer and the drying time in between. (Fulsher now uses a half-hour epoxy which does the job with one coat.) Yet these flies are truly among the most accurate and beautiful imitations of a baitfish using the old standard bucktail fibers.

I will detail the tying of one of the patterns and then list a few more of the popular ones. For those of you who wish to take this interest further, I suggest you try to obtain a copy of Fulsher's book, now available only through out-of-print book dealers.

THUNDER CREEK BLACK-NOSED DACE
(Plate IX)

HOOK: Partridge Thunder Creek or equivalent ring-eye (2–10)

THREAD: White (Flymaster 6/0 or Monocord 3/0), later lacquered red

BODY: Embossed silver tinsel

WING: Lateral stripe, black bucktail; top, brown bucktail; bottom, white bucktail

HEAD: Pulled-back deer hair; clear varnish with creamy yellow eye (mix white and yellow lacquer) and black pupil

REMARKS: The following construction procedures apply.

1. Spiral thread from eye to bend forming a thread base. Tie tinsel in at bend. Bring thread forward to a point one-quarter shank length before eye. Wind tinsel to thread and tie down.

2. Tie in a sparse bunch of black bucktail fibers with the tips extending past the bend a distance equal to the gap width. Secure the fibers to the shank by winding the thread over them to a point directly behind the eye and then back to a point a quarter of the hook shank behind the eye. This is the base area upon which the head will later be formed. Clip excess butts.

3. Tie in a small bunch of brown bucktail fibers (make sure the tips are first evenly aligned), this time with the tips protruding beyond the eye of the hook. These fibers will later be forced rearward, so before you take too many turns to secure them, bring the fibers rearward and measure them to see that the tips will later align with the black bucktail tips. These tips are secured to the shank for the same distance as the black bucktail, from the eye to a quarter shank length behind the eye. When you secure the butt ends to the shank, try to flatten them so that they cover the hook shank from side to side yet do not slip below the horizontal plane of the hook. Take extra turns of thread directly against the eye so that when the fibers are forced rearward the curve of the fibers from the reversal is just behind the eye. Clip excess butts.

4. Turn the hook upside down in your vise and tie in an equal amount of white bucktail fibers, measuring them to make sure that when they are reversed rearward the tips will be slightly shorter than the others. The same procedure used in securing the brown bucktail fibers also applies with the white ones. Clip excess butts.

5. Apply head lacquer to all the windings and add more turns of thread to even out any grooves or dips in the tie-down area. Bring the thread back to a position one-quarter of the hook shank behind the eye, or the base of what will be the head.

6. Invert the hook so that it is once again in an upright position. Grasp the brown and white bucktail fibers and force them rearward so that the tips align with the tips of the black bucktail. You will be pulling the brown over the top of the shank and along the sides and the white along the bottom of the shank and along the sides. As you pull them taut, make sure that there is a distinct division between the brown and the white bucktail and also that a thin line of black bucktail shows through. This takes a little practice to get it just right. If you don't succeed on the first try, let them go and start over.

When the fibers are properly aligned, hold them tautly by the tip ends and bring your thread over and around all the bucktail fibers at the base of the head for six or seven turns. The turns of thread should be next to each other, forming a neat band which, when lacquered red on the bottom half, simulates the red gills of baitfish. Whip-finish in the same area and snip. (Since you are using white thread, you will have to lacquer it red after the whip finish to form the gills.) This is a recent change by the originator, Keith Fulsher.

7. Apply three coats of clear head varnish, allowing each one to dry thoroughly before applying the next, or apply one coat of half-hour epoxy, allowing the excess to run into the bucktail fibers.

When the varnish has dried, paint a yellow eye on each side of the head. Allow the eyes to dry. Then paint the center of each yellow eye with black lacquer. A dowel or nail head does the job fairly well for the eyes on the head. You will need different sizes for each and, of course, different sizes for the differently sized hooks.

In the case of this pattern, the Black-Nosed Dace, a black line should also be painted on the head to show the continuation of the lateral line of the black bucktail.

For photographic purposes only, black thread was used in the following sequences.

THUNDER CREEK GOLDEN SHINER

HOOK: Partridge Thunder Creek or equivalent ring-eye (4/0–6)
THREAD: White (Flymaster 6/0 or Monocord 3/0), painted red for gills after fly is completed
BODY: Yellow tinsel
WING: Lateral stripe, dyed yellow bucktail; top, brown fibers from dyed green bucktail; bottom, white bucktail
HEAD: Clear varnish with cream eye and black pupil

Tying Steps for Thunder Creek Series (Black-Nosed Dace)

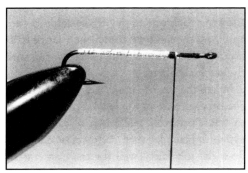

a. Embossed silver tinsel has been tied in and wound to form body.

b. Black bucktail fibers have been tied in and excess trimmed.

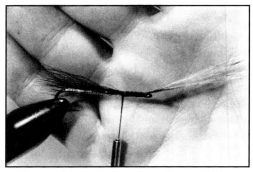

c. Brown bucktail fibers have been tied in so that tips extend beyond eye of hook. These fibers should first be measured for length to make sure that when they are later pulled rearward the tips will align with those of the black bucktail.

d. Hook has been reversed and white bucktail fibers have been tied in with tips forward. Length of white tips is just slightly shorter than brown bucktail tips.

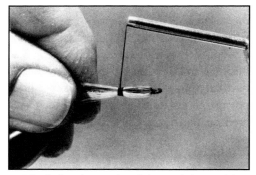

e. Hook has been placed in upright position once more. Brown bucktail has been pulled along top of shank to rear and white bucktail along bottom. They are being held tautly as thread is wound around them behind head area.

f. Completed Thunder Creek Black-Nosed Dace, lacquered and with eyes painted in.

THE BOOK OF FLY PATTERNS 239

THUNDER CREEK RAINBOW TROUT
(Plate IX)

HOOK: Partridge Thunder Creek or equivalent ring-eye (2–10)
THREAD: White (Flymaster 6/0 or Monocord 3/0), painted red for gills after fly is completed
BODY: Embossed silver tinsel
WING: Lateral stripe, true pink bucktail; top, brown portion of dyed green bucktail; bottom, white bucktail
HEAD: Clear varnish with cream eye and black pupil

THUNDER CREEK REDFIN SHINER
(Plate IX)

HOOK: Partridge Thunder Creek or equivalent ring-eye (4/0–10)
THREAD: White (Flymaster 6/0 or Monocord 3/0), painted red for gills after fly is completed
RIB: Embossed silver tinsel
BODY: Deep pink or fluorescent red floss
WING: Top, natural brown bucktail; bottom, white bucktail (no lateral stripe)
HEAD: Clear varnish with cream eye and black pupil

REMARKS: A later design created by Fulsher, which he considers to be a better redfin imitation, has a body of embossed silver tinsel and the bottom portion of the wing is white bucktail over red bucktail.

The red is very sparse and extends only to the bend of the hook and is tied to the shank in a conventional manner.

THUNDER CREEK SILVER SHINER

HOOK: Partridge Thunder Creek or equivalent ring-eye (1/0–10)
THREAD: White (Flymaster 6/0 or Monocord 3/0), painted red for gills after fly is completed
BODY: Embossed silver tinsel
WING: Top, brown bucktail; bottom, white bucktail (no lateral stripe)
HEAD: Clear varnish with cream eye and black pupil

THUNDER CREEK SMELT

HOOK: Partridge Thunder Creek or equivalent ring-eye (1/0–6)
THREAD: White (Flymaster 6/0 or Monocord 3/0), painted red for gills after fly is completed
BODY: Embossed silver tinsel
WING: Lateral stripe, orchid bucktail; top, brown bucktail; bottom, white bucktail
HEAD: Clear varnish with cream eye and black pupil

TRI-COLOR

HOOK: Mustad 94720, 9575 (2–10)
THREAD: Black (Flymaster 6/0)

TAIL: None
RIB: Oval silver tinsel
BODY: Flat silver tinsel (for rib and body, see model, Black-Nosed Dace)
THROAT: White bucktail (as long as wing)
WING: Orange bucktail, over which green bucktail, both slightly past bend on 8XL hook (longer on 6XL hook)
CHEEKS: Jungle cock eyes (or equivalent) (third eye showing)
HEAD: Black

TROUT FIN BUCKTAIL

HOOK: Mustad 9575 (4–10)
THREAD: Black (Flymaster 6/0)
TAIL: A section of dyed red goose quill fibers (see model, Alexandra, page 124) (gap width past bend)
RIB: Oval silver tinsel
BODY: Flat silver tinsel (for rib and body, see model, Black-Nosed Dace)
WING: Sparse white bucktail, over which sparse black bucktail, over which a bunch of orange bucktail equal in thickness to both white and black bucktail (all half a shank length past bend)
HEAD: Black

A.S. TRUDE STREAMER

HOOK: Mustad 79580 (4–10)
THREAD: Black (Flymaster 6/0)
TAIL: None
RIB: Oval silver tinsel
BODY: Red wool

WING: Red fox squirrel tail (quarter shank length past bend)
HACKLE: Brown as a wet fly collar (see model, Blue Dun, page 124)
HEAD: Black

WARDEN'S WORRY

HOOK: Mustad 9575 (2–10)
THREAD: Black (Flymaster 6/0)
TAG: Flat gold tinsel
TAIL: Dyed red duck quill section (see model, Alexandra, page 124) (slightly more than gap width in length)
RIB: Fine oval gold tinsel
BODY: Hare's mask dubbing fur dyed yellow/orange
THROAT: Yellow hackle as a wet fly collar and pulled down (see model, Blue Dun, page 124)
WING: Light brown bucktail or calf tail (half a shank length past bend)
HEAD: Black

WHITE MARABOU

HOOK: Mustad 9575 (4–12)
THREAD: Red (Flymaster 6/0)
TAIL: Dyed red hackle fibers (gap width past bend)
BODY: Flat silver tinsel (or silver Mylar tubing)
WING: White marabou topped with six strands of peacock herl (all half a shank length past bend)
HEAD: Red

WHITE MARABOU MUDDLER

HOOK: Mustad 79580, 38941 (4–10)
THREAD: Gray (Monocord 3/0)
TAIL: Dyed red hackle fibers (gap width past bend)
BODY: Flat silver tinsel
WING: White marabou topped with six strands of peacock herl (half a shank length past bend)
COLLAR: Hair fibers from first flaring of deer hair (almost to bend and surrounding body)
HEAD: Spun and trimmed natural gray deer hair to Muddler Minnow head shape (see Irresistible, page 45, and Muddler Minnow, page 227)

REMARKS: This pattern is often tied weighted for fishing deep.

WHITE MUDDLER MINNOW
(see Muddler Minnow, White)

WHITE RABBIT LEECH

HOOK: Mustad 79580 (6)
THREAD: White (Monocord 3/0)

RIB: White thread used to lash wing to shank matuka style (see Matuka Flies for construction techniques)
WING AND TAIL: White rabbit on fur strip (eighth inch wide) (a full shank length past bend)

REMARKS: A leech innovation by Ted Gerken.

WHITEFISH STREAMER

HOOK: Mustad 36620 or equivalent ring-eye (2–8)
THREAD: White (Monocord 3/0)
TAIL: None
UNDERBODY: Yarn or lead wire (depending on whether fished shallow or deep)
BODY: Embossed silver tinsel
THROAT: White marabou, sparse (to bend)
WING: Blue marabou, over which green marabou, over which five strands of peacock herl (all slightly past bend)
HEAD: White wool on bottom, blue mixed with brown wool on top, tied as a flared and trimmed Woolhead Sculpin (which see)
EYES: Doll eyes, white with black center

REMARKS: Originated by Craig Mathews, this type of fly is also effective for bass, pike, and assorted saltwater species.

WHITLOCK MATUKA SCULPIN

HOOK: Mustad 36890 (3/0–10)
THREAD: Gray (flat waxed nylon size A)
TAIL: Extension of wing (shank length past bend)
RIB: Medium oval gold tinsel
UNDERBODY: Medium to heavy lead wire (.024–.036)
BODY: Tan yarn
WING: Four dyed brown grizzly saddle hackles, matuka style (see Matuka Flies)
PECTORAL FINS: Prairie chicken body feathers, one on each side (or substitute hen mallard body feathers)
GILLS: A short band of red wool
HEAD: Spun and trimmed deer hair in color bands of brown, black, and tan. Part of the first flaring of deer hair is allowed to flow rearward as a collar over half the body. Head is trimmed to wedge shape (see model, Irresistible, page 45)

REMARKS: Originated by Dave Whitlock. The coloration of this pattern may be changed to match the coloration of different species of sculpins. It is always weighted when used as such an imitation, since the fly should be fished near the bottom. However, this pattern also makes an excellent bass bug and may be tied unweighted if such is the angler's preference.

WINNEPESAUKEE SMELT

HOOK: Mustad 94720 (2–6)
THREAD: Black (Flymaster 6/0 or Monocord 3/0)
TAIL: None
BODY: Flat silver tinsel
WING: Sparse white bucktail, over which four strands of peacock herl, over which a few fibers of lavender bucktail, over which white marabou (all extending slightly past bend)
TOPPING: Two natural blue silver pheasant crest feathers (as long as wing) (substitute: blue/black ostrich herl)
HEAD: Black with yellow eye and black pupil

WOOD SPECIAL

HOOK: Mustad 9575 (2–10)
THREAD: Black (Flymaster 6/0)
TAIL: Golden pheasant tippets (gap width past bend)
RIB: Flat silver tinsel
BODY: Fluorescent orange chenille
THROAT: Brown hackle fibers, beard style (as long as tail)
WING: Lemon wood duck flank feather tied flat on top (to end of tail)
CHEEKS: Jungle cock eyes (or equivalent) (second eye showing)
COLLAR: Grizzly as a wet fly collar after

wing and cheeks have been formed (see model, Blue Dun, page 124)

REMARKS: Originated by Joe Sterling.

Woolhead Sculpins

BLACK WOOLHEAD SCULPIN

HOOK: Mustad 79580 (4)
THREAD: Black (Monocord 3/0)
TAIL: Extension of wing (shank length past bend)
UNDERBODY: Heavy lead wire (.036)
RIB: Medium oval gold tinsel to secure wing matuka style (see Matuka Flies)
BODY: Black wool
WING: An eighth-inch-wide strip of dyed black rabbit on tanned skin tied in matuka style (for construction, see Matuka Flies)
PECTORAL FINS: One black hen neck feather on each side
HEAD: Black wool fashioned into sculpin-shaped head

REMARKS: This pattern was submitted by Ted Gerken of the Iliaska Lodge in Illiamna, Alaska, who uses it for the fall run of giant rainbow trout in that region. James Bonnet writes that the head of this pattern should be made from a type of matted wool such as is used to make fly patches on fishing vests. Bonnet states that it is best to build up the head of the fly with other materials before applying the wool (chenille, floss, etc.). This type of wool does flare and it is trimmed to shape in the manner of spun deer hair.

I have not found a listing for this type of wool in any of the catalogs, but Blue Ribbon Flies in West Yellowstone, Montana, carries it for fly tyers. Conventional wool, such as that sold by the skein for knitting, can also be used to form the head of this pattern. This wool does not flare as readily but, if tied on top of a base of chenille, does crimp upward nicely. You will have to piece in short sections of the wool to fill the head area and then trim it.

The appearance of this type of fly and the reports of its success certainly seem to warrant the effort to tie it.

BLUE RIBBON WOOLHEAD SCULPIN
(Plate IX)

HOOK: Mustad 9674 or equivalent ring-eye (2–6)
THREAD: Gray (Monocord 3/0)
RIB: Medium copper wire
BODY: White wool
PECTORAL FINS: Grizzly hen hackle feathers protruding from behind head on sides of shank

WING: Two webby grizzly hackles dyed dark blue, tied flat on top (half a shank length past bend)
HEAD: Flared and trimmed patch wool (or see method for yarn wool under Black Woolhead Sculpin) in three distinct colors, progressing from wing to eye, of blue, dark brown, and tan

REMARKS: Originated by Craig Mathews (of Blue Ribbon Flies), who states that though the woolhead type of sculpin is relatively new to most anglers, he and his tyers have been dressing them in this manner for years, and best of all, have been taking more than their share of trout with this type of pattern.

OLIVE WOOLHEAD SCULPIN

HOOK: Mustad 9674 or equivalent ring-eye (2–6)
THREAD: Olive or gray (Monocord 3/0)
TAIL: Extension of wing (shank length past bend)
RIB: Medium copper wire
BODY: Dark olive wool
WING: Tan rabbit dyed light olive as a fur strip, one-eighth inch wide, secured to shank matuka style (for construction, see Matuka Flies)
PECTORAL FINS: Mottled partridge or grouse (or equivalent) body feathers dyed orange, protruding from behind head on both sides of shank
HEAD: Wool dyed olive with black band of wool across center (see model, Black

Woolhead Sculpin), to shape of sculpin's head

REMARKS: Design by Craig Mathews.

PHEASANT WOOLHEAD SCULPIN

HOOK: Mustad 9674 or equivalent ring-eye (2–6)
THREAD: Gray (Monocord 3/0)
RIB: Medium copper wire
BODY: White wool
WING: Two mottled tan feathers from the lower body of male ringneck pheasant tied flat on top of shank (half a shank length past bend)
PECTORAL FINS: "Church window" body feathers from ringneck pheasant, protruding from behind head on sides of shank
HEAD: Flared and trimmed patch wool in two colors: rear two-thirds, olive; fore third, black (see model, Black Woolhead Sculpin), trimmed to shape of sculpin's head

REMARKS: Design by Craig Mathews.

WOOLLY BUGGER
(Plate IX)

HOOK: Mustad 79580 (4–16)
THREAD: Black (Flymaster 6/0)
TAIL: Black marabou blood feathers (almost as long as shank)
PALMER RIB: Black saddle hackle palmered through body

BODY: Dark olive chenille (related to hook size)

REMARKS: Though tied today in a variety of colors and hook models, this is the original pattern as designed by Russell Blessing.

The Woolly Bugger may never win any beauty contests, yet this unappealing ugly has found favor with anglers from the Carolinas to Alaska and from the Catskills to the Rockies. It is unimpressive in appearance, imitates nothing in particular, yet seems to stimulate and excite trout and other fish for reasons they alone know. It has, in fact, usurped the timeworn cliché formerly reserved for the Adams, namely: "When in doubt, use a Woolly Bugger."

Though originated by Blessing, the Woolly Bugger would not have been more than a local favorite had it not been for Barry Beck, who was so enamored of this pattern that he not only fished it but promoted it, wrote about it, and sold it through his store. Beck is never without this pattern and fishes it all over the world.

Another well-traveled angler, Angus Cameron, regards the Woolly Bugger as the "daredevil" of flies and has fished it for rainbow trout and arctic char in Alaska and for Atlantic salmon in Iceland with phenomenal success. He writes: "The Icelandic gillie I had took the fly out of the first salmon I took on the Woolly Bugger and was visibly repelled by the sheer ugliness and unlikeliness of the fly. 'If I had not seen it with my own eyes I wouldn't have believed it' is the way the gillie put it."

Angus likes to add a few strands of Flashabou material to the marabou tail. One of his favorite color combinations is to use black and bright yellow in both the tail and the body with strands of Flashabou added.

From what I can gather, the Woolly Bugger may very well be one of the most important patterns added to our fly box in the last generation.

Following are some other popular variations of the Woolly Bugger.

WOOLLY BUGGER, BLACK

TAIL: Black
PALMER RIB: Black
BODY: Black

WOOLLY BUGGER, BROWN AND TAN

TAIL: Brown marabou
PALMER RIB: Brown saddle hackle
BODY: Tan chenille

WOOLLY BUGGER, GRIZZLY AND WHITE

TAIL: White marabou
PALMER RIB: Grizzly saddle hackle
BODY: White chenille

Woolly Buggers are often tied weighted for fishing deep.

YELLOW BREECHES STREAMER

HOOK: Mustad 9575 (4–12)
THREAD: Black (Flymaster 6/0)
TAIL: None
RIB: Fine oval silver tinsel
BODY: Flat silver tinsel (for rib and body, see model, Black-Nosed Dace)
THROAT: Red hackle fibers (half as long as body)
WING: Yellow marabou, then brown marabou, topped with six strands of peacock herl (all half a shank length past bend)
CHEEKS: Jungle cock eyes (or equivalent) (second eye showing)
HEAD: Black

YELLOW MARABOU

HOOK: Mustad 9575 (4–12)
THREAD: Black (Flymaster 6/0)
TAIL: Dyed red hackle fibers (gap width in length)
BODY: Flat silver tinsel or silver Mylar tubing
WING: Yellow marabou topped with six strands of peacock herl (both half a shank length past bend)
HEAD: Black

YELLOW MUDDLER MINNOW
(see Muddler Minnow, Yellow)

YELLOW PERCH

HOOK: Mustad 9575 (2–10)
THREAD: Black (Flymaster 6/0)
TAIL: Golden pheasant tippet fibers (gap width past bend)
RIB: Flat gold tinsel
BODY: Cream floss
THROAT: Orange hackle fibers, beard style (as long as tail)
WING: Two dyed yellow grizzly saddle hackles flanked by two yellow saddle hackles (both half a shank length past bend) (see model, Black Ghost)
CHEEKS: Jungle cock eyes (or equivalent) (second eye showing)
HEAD: Black

YORKS KENNEBEGO

HOOK: Mustad 9575 (4–12)
THREAD: Black (Flymaster 6/0)
TAIL: Golden pheasant crest (curving upward, mirroring bend)
BUTT: Red floss
RIB: Oval silver tinsel
BODY: Flat silver tinsel (for rib and body, see model, Black-Nosed Dace)
THROAT: Red hackle fibers, beard style (gap width in length)
WING: Four golden badger saddle hackles (half a shank length past bend) (see model, Black Ghost)
TOPPING: Red hackle fibers (about three-quarters of an inch long)
CHEEKS: Jungle cock eyes (or equivalent) (second eye showing)
HEAD: Black

ZOMBIE

HOOK: Mustad 94720 (2–10)
THREAD: Black (Flymaster 6/0)
TAIL: None
BODY: Flat silver tinsel
THROAT: White bucktail, sparse (as long as wing)
WING: Pink bucktail, over which light blue bucktail, both sparse, over which four black saddle hackles (all slightly past bend) (see model, Black Ghost)
SHOULDERS: Black-edged white body feather from Lady Amherst pheasant neck (one-third as long as wing)
CHEEKS: Jungle cock eyes (or equivalent) (second eye showing)
HEAD: Black

REMARKS: Often tied in tandem as a trolling streamer

ZONKER

HOOK: Mustad 9674 or equivalent long-shanked ring-eye (2–6)
THREAD: Black and red (Flymaster 6/0 or Monocord 3/0)
UNDERBODY: Trimbrite metallic tape (or equivalent)
BODY: Silver Mylar tubing
BUTT OR TAG: Red thread used to secure Mylar tubing near bend and to lash the end of the wing strip to body
HACKLE: Grizzly as wet fly collar and pulled down (see model, Blue Dun, page 124)
WING: A tanned strip of natural brown/gray rabbit
HEAD: Black

REMARKS: Originated by Dan Byford.

1. The underbody is formed by placing a section of metallic tape down both sides of the hook shank from a point on the shank just over the hook barb to a fifth of the shank length before the eye. The width of the section is half the size of the hook gap. Next measure a point on the hook shank one-third of the distance back from the eye. Make an angle cut from this point on the metallic tape to both ends of the folded-down section. This will form a natural shape tapering to the belly area and upward again toward the head. Super Glue should be used to hold the metallic section to the shank. If you are tying a number of Zonkers of a particular size, simply remove the folded metallic sheet and use it as a model to make a number of them with the same proportions.

2. Cut a piece of Mylar tubing. (The size of the tubing will depend on your hook size. The tubing is usually sold in diameters of 1/16th, 1/8th, and 3/16th of an inch but commonly only listed as small, medium, and large. For sizes 2 and 4, you will need the large size; for hook sizes 6 and 8, the medium will do.)

Slip the Mylar over the hook and underbody and secure it near the bend with red thread. Do not cut the excess Mylar but allow the open end of the tubing to extend beyond the tying thread into the curve of the bend for an eighth inch or so. Sort of a flared Mylar tail, you might say. Also, do not cut the red thread at this time.

3. Attach your black tying thread to the shank behind the eye.

You will need a piece of tanned natural brown/gray rabbit fur cut into a strip approximately 1/8th to 3/16th of an inch wide and almost twice as long as the shank. Tie the wide end of the strip to the shank at the head area.

4. Take the grizzly hackle which is to form the collar and tie it in by the tip. Using the folded-hackle method described in the model fly Blue Dun (page 124), wind it as a wet fly collar. Build a neatly tapered head while covering exposed bits of material and whip-finish the thread and cut it off.

5. Coat the top of the Mylar tubing with one of the better glues and hold the fur strip tautly rearward as you tie it down near the bend with the red thread left hanging there. Whip-finish. Apply head lacquer to the wrappings at the head and the bend.

Note: The underbody of this pattern can also be made using strips from an aluminum beer or soda can (prior to the Zonker there were quite a number of flies dressed in such a manner using aluminum or tin for the underbody and Mylar for the scaly shape), or if the fly is intended to be fished deep, thin flat sheets of lead are used.

Tying Steps for the Zonker

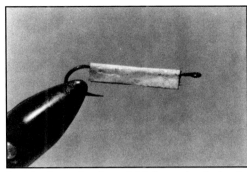

a. Piece of metal strip (weighted or otherwise) which will form underbody.

b. Metal strip has been folded over hook shank.

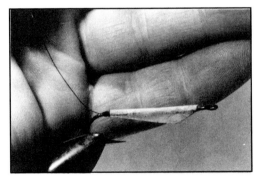

c. Metal strip has been trimmed to shape. A piece of red thread has been attached to the bend. Use a fairly strong thread, such as a size A Monocord.

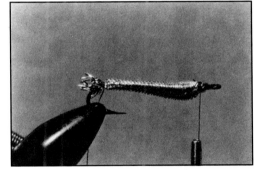

d. Mylar tubing has been forced over the hook eye and the metal underbody. It is tied down at the head with the thread from the tying bobbin and at the bend with the red thread. Half-hitch the red thread after the Mylar has been secured. Do not cut the excess red thread. Note that the exposed stranded ends of Mylar are allowed to extend rearward just past the bend.

e. A section of natural brown/gray rabbit fur on skin being measured for length.

f. Strip of rabbit fur has been tied in about a quarter inch behind the hook eye.

g. Grizzly hackle collar being tied in.

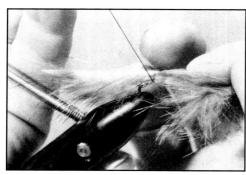

h. Guard hairs and fur have been separated and red thread is securing rabbit strip at bend.

i. Completed Zonker.

Tandem or Trolling Streamers

Most of the patterns listed so far in this section can be tied in tandem and in quite a number of instances they are. There are two reasons for making a tandem streamer. First, the tandem streamer can be used to imitate some of the larger baitfish, such as smelt or alewife, and second, it satisfies those anglers who are fearful of a short strike. Tandem streamers are tied with the materials distributed over two hooks instead of one. Using hooks in tandem as opposed to a single extra-long-shanked hook also gives the fish less leverage to work with.

Though they may be cast in the conventional manner if the proper rod, line, and leader are used, these heavier dual-hook affairs are generally trolled from a canoe or a small boat. Because of the large size of the imitation, the choice of materials in certain recipes is more selective. For example, the hackle feathers that form the wings of many of these patterns will sometimes be of the larger neck feathers of a domestic rooster rather than feathers from the saddle. Saddle hackles are usually too slim for these larger flies and when drawn through the water behind a canoe the hackles sleek down too severely,

whereas the wider-barbuled neck hackle retains more of its shape. There are some very successful anglers, however, such as Dick Brady, who prefer the super-sleek, streamlined effect.

If the size of the fly is larger, the proportions must change accordingly. Though the hooks used in a tandem rig are not very large, the overall effect is that of a fly tied on a long-shanked 3/0 to 5/0 hook.

The tying of tandem flies only appears to be difficult—you just have to do them one hook at a time. For those of you who wish to delve deeper into this art, I recommend *Trolling Flies for Trout and Salmon,* by Dick Stewart and Bob Leeman. This book covers nearly every pattern that has ever been tied in tandem, quite a number of which are displayed in full color.

My version of how the two hooks in a tandem fly are connected and dressed may not be the method most commonly used, but I don't think your fly will come apart when it is taken by a fish. The Black Ghost is here listed out of alphabetical order because it once more serves as a model for the other patterns in this section.

BLACK GHOST

HOOK SIZE: Mustad 3906B (2–6)
THREAD: Black (Flymaster 6/0 or Monocord 3/0)
TAIL: Yellow hackle fibers (gap width past bend on rear hook)
RIB: Medium flat silver tinsel
BODY: Black floss

THROAT: Yellow hackle fibers (as long as tail fibers)
WING: Four white saddle or neck hackles (to end of tail)
CHEEKS (optional): Jungle cock eyes (or equivalent) (second eye showing)
HEAD: Black

NOTE: The hooks used on this and other patterns is the Mustad model 3906B or equivalent.

1. Cut a five-inch section of twenty-pound-test stainless-steel trolling wire and fold it in two. (My own preference in this wire is the stranded type.) Insert the folded end through the eye of the hook far enough so that the hook can be looped through the wire. Pull the wire snug to the eye and clamp the hook in your vise. The two free ends of the wire should now protrude beyond the eye for two and a half inches.

2. Spiral some black thread onto the shank of the hook. Apply head cement to the steel wire where it is looped around the hook behind the eye. Wind the thread over the wire behind the eye, securing it well, and then bring the thread to the bend of the hook.

3. Tie in the yellow hackle fibers for the tail, then the rib of flat silver tinsel, and then the black floss for the body. Wind the floss and rib forward to form the body of the rear hook. Whip-finish your thread and remove the rear portion of the Black Ghost from the vise.

4. Place your second Mustad 3906B size 4 in the vise and spiral your thread onto the shank from behind the eye to the bend.

5. Push the free ends of the two wires

coming from the eye of the rear hook down through the eye of the hook in the vise. Hold the rear hook in a tandem position behind the one in the vise so that approximately three-quarters to one inch separates the eye of the rear hook from the bend of the fore hook. Wind your thread over the wire which is now lying along the top of the shank of the fore hook. Secure it well.

Bend the free ends of wire protruding downward from the eye of the fore hook backward along the bottom of the shank and secure them to the shank with more windings of thread. They should reach rearward along the underside of the shank to a point just above the hook point. Snip any excess beyond this area. Apply head cement to the thread windings along the shank and wind the thread forward to the eye and then back to the bend two or three times for added security. Then leave the thread hanging at the bend area.

Again tie in your tinsel rib and black floss and form the body of the fore hook. Be sure to leave adequate space before the eye for the wing, throat, and head.

6. Tie in your beard-style yellow hackle fibers for the throat.

7. Select four fairly wide white neck or saddle hackles which, when tied in, will reach to the end of the tail on the rear hook (see Black Ghost standard, page 207), for construction details).

8. Tie in the jungle cock eyes for the cheeks.

9. Build a neatly tapered head and whip-finish. Lacquer the head with black lacquer.

Assembling a Tandem Pattern (Black Ghost)

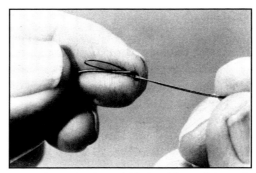

a. Steel wire has been folded and looped through eye of rear hook.

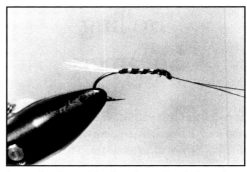

b. Tail, rib, and body of rear hook have been formed.

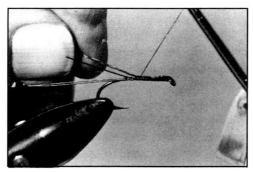

e. Both strands of wire have been pulled through eye and are being fastened to shank. Excess is then trimmed.

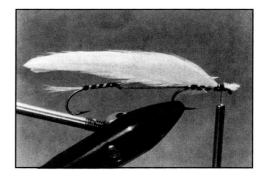

f. Four long saddle hackles have been tied in (see method under Black Ghost, page 207) and throat hackle tied in.

Again, any streamer pattern can be made into a tandem fly. Simply look upon the two hooks and the connecting wire as one long hook and judge the proportions. One of the major changes that occur on a tandem rig is that the wing rarely extends very far beyond the bend. Usually it goes just past it or, at the most, to the end of the tail if there is a tail.

The rear hook in a tandem setup is sometimes tied inverted—that is, it rides upside down while the fore hook rides right side up. This is a preference of some anglers. For that matter, some prefer a double hook as the rear section. Again, a matter of preference. Actually, I've found that if the fish wants the imitation badly enough, a single short-shanked hook with six inches of material trailing behind it won't keep the fish from becoming hooked. There are those other times, however, perhaps when the fish has earlier had its fill, when it may wish to play around a bit. Then the rear hook serves the angler very well.

A listing of some of the flies usually tied in tandem follows. It does not include those already listed in the preceding section on standard streamers and bucktails. The hooks used for all the following patterns will be the Mustad model 3906B unless otherwise specified.

AA SPECIAL

HOOK SIZE: Mustad 3906B (2–6)
THREAD: Red (Flymaster 6/0 or Monocord 3/0)
RIB: Flat silver tinsel
BODY: Red floss

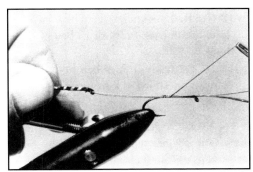

c. Two strands of wire coming from rear hook being tied to fore hook.

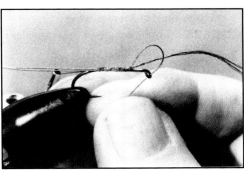

d. Wire has been secured with thread and is now being bent and forced through eye to be folded rearward.

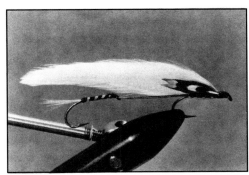

g. Jungle cock eyes have been added for cheeks to complete Black Ghost tandem.

WING: White, yellow, red, then blue bucktail, in that order, all sparse, flanked by three strands of peacock herl on each side (all to end of bend)

TOPPING: Two dark grizzly hackles dyed to a brownish cast (gap width past bend)

HEAD: Red

ASTRONAUT

HOOK SIZE: Mustad 3906B (2–4)

THREAD: Black (Flymaster 6/0 or Monocord 3/0)

BODY: Embossed silver tinsel

THROAT: Four strands of peacock herl next to shank, under which a few strands of fine white goat hair (or deer belly hair) (both as long as wing)

WING: Two brown saddle hackles flanked by two grizzly saddle hackles (see model, Black Ghost, page 207) (to end of bend of rear hook)

CHEEKS: Jungle cock eyes (or equivalent) (second eye showing)

HEAD: Black

EAST GRAND LAKE SPECIAL

HOOK SIZE: Mustad 3906B (2–6)

THREAD: Black (Flymaster 6/0 or Monocord 3/0)

BODY: Flat silver tinsel

WING: Sparse white bucktail, then red bucktail, over which four dark grizzly neck or saddle hackles (all to bend)

SHOULDERS: Silver pheasant body feathers (one-third as long as wing)

CHEEKS: Jungle cock eyes (or equivalent) (second eye showing)

HEAD: Black

FLASHABOU TANDEM
(Plate IX)

HOOK SIZE: Mustad 3906B (2–4)

THREAD: White (Flymaster 6/0 or Monocord 3/0)

BODY: Flat silver tinsel

MID-BODY: Five red beads on wire between hooks (allow space)

THROAT: White bucktail (to bend of rear hook)

WING: Flashabou material in any of the following colors: pearlescent, purple, copper, silver, black

HEAD: White with yellow eye and black pupil

REMARKS: Rodney Flagg states that this pattern has been his best seller for the past two seasons. One favorite, called the Pearl and Black Smelt, features a wing of black Flashabou over silver Flashabou material.

FOOTER SPECIAL
(Plate IX)

HOOK: Mustad 9672 (2–6)

THREAD: Black (Flymaster 6/0 or Monocord 3/0)

BODY: Flat gold tinsel

THROAT: Dark blue bucktail next to underside of shank covered with five strands of peacock herl (all to bend of rear hook)

WING: Red bucktail, over which two yellow saddle hackles (both to bend of rear hook)

SHOULDERS: Guinea hen body feather (almost one-third as long as wing)

HEAD: Black

REMARKS: Originated by David Footer of Lewiston, Maine, who is regarded by many as perhaps the finest taxidermist in the United States and Canada specializing in brook trout and salmon.

GOLDEN EAGLE

HOOK SIZE: Mustad 3906B (2–4)

THREAD: Red (Flymaster 6/0 or Monocord 3/0)

BODY: Gold Mylar tubing

BUTT OR TAG: Red thread securing Mylar at bend

THROAT: Lavender bucktail next to underside of shank, under which white bucktail, both sparse (both as long as wing)

WING: Six strands of peacock herl, over which two ginger grizzly saddle hackles (both slightly past bend of rear hook)

SHOULDERS: Black-tipped bronze breast feather from male ringneck pheasant (one-fourth as long as wing)

CHEEKS: Jungle cock eyes (or equivalent) (second eye showing)

HEAD: Red

REMARKS: The Mylar tubing body may be individually formed on both rear and fore hooks or it may be made to serve as one continuous body by covering the rear hook, the wire, and the fore hook.

GOVERNOR BARROWS

HOOK SIZE: Mustad 3906B (2–4)
THREAD: Black (Flymaster 6/0 or Monocord 3/0)
BODY: Embossed silver tinsel
THROAT: White bucktail next to underside of shank, under which is blue bucktail, under which is red bucktail, all sparse (all as long as wing)
WING: Five strands of peacock herl, over which four yellow neck or saddle hackles (all slightly past bend of rear hook) (See model, Black Ghost, page 207)
SHOULDERS: Lemon wood duck flank feathers (one-third as long as wing)
CHEEKS: Jungle cock eyes (or equivalent) (second eye showing)
HEAD: Black

GRAY GHOST
Variations on a Theme

In addition to the standard Gray Ghost, which is a popular tandem rig in its own right (for pattern recipe, see Gray Ghost, page 216), there are a number of offshoots designed in tandem as trolling flies.

FLUORESCENT-BODIED GRAY GHOST

HOOK SIZE: Mustad 3906B (2–4)
THREAD: Black (Flymaster 6/0 or Monocord 3/0)
RIB: None
BODY: Fluorescent red wool
THROAT: White bucktail covered by golden pheasant crest (to bend of rear hook)
WING: Golden pheasant crest, over which a few strands of silver Flashabou wing material, over which five strands of peacock herl, over which four light gray saddle hackles (see model, Black Ghost, page 207) (all slightly past bend)
SHOULDERS: Silver pheasant body feathers (one-fourth length of wing)
CHEEKS: None
HEAD: Black

REMARKS: Rodney Flagg states that this is also an excellent pattern for big rainbow trout in lakes. This pattern is often tied on the IOXL Carrie Stevens streamer hook, Partridge model CS15.

FLUORESCENT PINK (GRAY) GHOST

HOOK SIZE: Mustad 3906B (2–4)
THREAD: Black (Flymaster 6/0 or Monocord 3/0)
RIB: Flat silver tinsel
BODY: Orange floss
THROAT: White bucktail covered by

golden pheasant crest (to bend of rear hook)
WING: Golden pheasant crest, over which six strands of peacock herl, over which four fluorescent pink saddle hackles (see model, Black Ghost, page 207) (all slightly past bend of rear hook)
SHOULDERS: Silver pheasant body feathers (one-fourth the length of wing)
CHEEKS: None
HEAD: Black

WASHED-OUT GRAY GHOST

HOOK SIZE: Mustad 3906B (2–4)
THREAD: Black (Flymaster 6/0 or Monocord 3/0)
RIB: Flat silver tinsel
BODY: Orange floss
THROAT: White bucktail covered by golden pheasant crest feather (to bend of rear hook)
WING: Golden pheasant crest feather, over which six strands of peacock herl, over which four ginger saddle hackles (see model, Black Ghost, page 207) (all slightly past bend of rear hook)
SHOULDERS: Silver pheasant body feathers (one-fourth as long as wing)
CHEEKS: Jungle cock eyes (or equivalent) (second eye showing)
HEAD: Black

REMARKS: According to Joe Sterling, this pattern is a great favorite in East Grand Lake in Maine.

KENNEBEGO SMELT

HOOK SIZE: Mustad 3906B (2–4)
THREAD: Black (Flymaster 6/0 or Monocord 3/0)
RIB: Oval silver tinsel
BODY: Flat silver tinsel
THROAT: Sparse white bucktail (to bend
of rear hook), under which yellow hackle
as beard (one-fourth the length of bucktail)
WING: Red bucktail, then blue bucktail
(both sparse), over which four natural black
saddle or neck hackles (see model, Black
Ghost, page 207), over which five strands
of peacock herl (all slightly past bend of
rear hook)
CHEEKS: Jungle cock eyes (or equivalent)
(second eye showing)
HEAD: Black

REMARKS: Sometimes tied on a 10XL
Carrie Stevens hook, Partridge model CS15.

KEVIN'S WARRIOR
(Plate IX)

HOOK SIZE: Mustad 3906B (2–4)
THREAD: Black (Flymaster 6/0 or Monocord 3/0)
RIB: Medium oval silver tinsel
BODY: Flat silver tinsel
THROAT: Very fine white deer hair from
legs/belly area of a white-tailed deer, covering four strands of pearlescent Flashabou
material (both as long as wing)
WING: Four very dark natural dun saddle
hackles (fairly slim) (see model, Black

Ghost, page 207), over which six very fine
strands of peacock herl (all slightly past
bend)
HEAD: Black

REMARKS: This pattern is one of Dick
Brady's favorites when trolling for landlocked
salmon in Maine. Brady recommends that
the fly be twitched with very sharp jerks
during the trolling process.
  Kevin's Warrior is normally tied on a 10XL
Partridge CS15 hook. When it is tied as a
tandem streamer, a golden pheasant crest
feather is added to the throat between the
Flashabou material and the white deer hair
fibers and a cheek of jungle cock eyes with
the second eye showing is incorporated.

LIBBY'S CAL

HOOK SIZE: Mustad 3906B (2–6)
THREAD: Fluorescent red (Flymaster 6/0)
RIB: Flat silver tinsel
BODY: Fluorescent red floss
WING: Sparse white bucktail, over which
two yellow saddle or neck hackles flanked
by two grizzly hackles (see model, Black
Ghost, page 207) (all slightly past bend)
TOPPING: Three strands of peacock herl

SHOULDERS: Silver pheasant body feathers (one-fourth as long as wing)
HEAD: Fluorescent red

LIGGET SPECIAL

HOOK SIZE: Mustad 3906B (2–6)
THREAD: Black (Flymaster 6/0 or Mono-
cord 3/0)
RIB: Oval silver tinsel
BODY: Flat silver tinsel
WING: White, red, and yellow bucktail, in
that order (all to end of rear hook if in
tandem; slightly past bend if a single long
shank)
CHEEKS: Jungle cock eyes (or equivalent)
(second eye showing)
HEAD: Black

REMARKS: Often tied on a 10XL Partridge
CS15 hook.

MEREDITH SPECIAL

HOOK SIZE: Mustad 3906B (2–4)
THREAD: White (Flymaster 6/0 or Monocord 3/0)
THROAT: White imitation bucktail (Fishair or equivalent) (to bend)
WING: Four medium blue dun saddle
hackles (see model, Black Ghost, page 207)
(slightly past bend)
SHOULDERS: Mallard flank feathers (one-
third as long as wing)
HEAD: Painted silver with yellow eye and
black pupil

MISS JULIE

HOOK SIZE: Mustad 3906B (2–4)
THREAD: Black (Flymaster 6/0 or Mono-
cord 3/0)
RIB: Flat silver tinsel
BODY: Light orange floss
WING: White, orange, white, black buck-
tail, all sparse, in that order (slightly past
bend of rear hook)
CHEEKS: Jungle cock eyes (or equivalent)
(only one eye showing)
HEAD: Black

MISS SHARON

HOOK SIZE: Mustad 3906B (2–6)
THREAD: Black (Flymaster 6/0 or Mono-
cord 3/0)
RIB: Flat silver tinsel
BODY: Red floss
WING: Red, white, orange, black bucktail,
all sparse, in that order (to bend of rear
hook)
HEAD: Black

MONTREAL

HOOK SIZE: Mustad 3906B (2–4)
THREAD: Black (Flymaster 6/0 or Mono-
cord 3/0)
RIB: Flat gold tinsel
BODY: Claret floss
WING: Red bucktail, over which four claret
saddle or neck hackles (see model, Black
Ghost, page 207) (all barely past bend)
TOPPING: Five strands of peacock herl
HEAD: Black

MORNING GLORY

HOOK SIZE: Mustad 3906B (2–4)
THREAD: Red (Flymaster 6/0 or Monocord 3/0)
TAG: Flat silver tinsel (rear hook only if in
tandem)
RIB: Flat silver tinsel
BODY: Red floss
THROAT: White bucktail (to bend), under
which dark blue silver pheasant crest
feather (one-third the length of bucktail)
(substitute: dark blue calf tail or dyed dark
blue golden pheasant crest feather)
WING: Silver pheasant crest feather (or
substitute), over which four yellow saddle
hackles (see model, Black Ghost, page 207)
(all slightly past bend)
SHOULDERS: Red body feathers from
golden pheasant (one-third as long as wing)
CHEEKS: Jungle cock eyes (or equivalent)
(third eye showing)
HEAD: Red with black band in center

REMARKS: Often tied on a 10XL Carrie
Stevens hook, Partridge model CS15.

PARMACHENE BELLE

HOOK SIZE: Mustad 3906B (2–4)
THREAD: Black (Flymaster 6/0 or Mono-
cord 3/0)
RIB: Flat gold tinsel
BODY: Yellow floss
WING: White bucktail, over which yellow
bucktail, both sparse (barely past bend)
SHOULDERS: White over red saddle
hackles (two-thirds the length of wing)
HEAD: Black

PARSON TOM

HOOK SIZE: Mustad 3906B (2–4)
THREAD: Black (Flymaster 6/0 or Mono-
cord 3/0)
RIB: Oval silver tinsel
BODY: Flat silver tinsel
THROAT: White bucktail (as long as wing)
WING: Five strands of peacock herl, over
which four light blue saddle or neck
hackles flanked by two grizzly hackles (all
slightly past bend of rear hook) (see model,
Black Ghost, page 207)
SHOULDERS: Silver pheasant body feath-
ers (one-third as long as wing)
CHEEKS: Jungle cock eyes (or equivalent)
(second eye showing)
HEAD: Black

SENATOR MUSKIE

HOOK SIZE: Mustad 3906B (2–4)

THREAD: Red (Flymaster 6/0 or Monocord 3/0)

RIB: Oval silver tinsel

WING: White, orange, green bucktail, all
sparse, in that order, over which two grizzly saddle or neck hackles (all slightly past
bend)

TOPPING: Five strands of peacock herl

HEAD: Red

Salmon Flies

SALMON FLIES fall into two categories: those that are to be fished and those that are to be framed and admired. This distinction is more commonly known as being either a fully dressed, built wing salmon fly or a hair wing type. We will be primarily concerned with the hair wing type, since they are the ones most fished and most often cataloged by mail-order companies and stocked by fly shops. And, for the most part, the patterns that follow are those which are familiar to anglers in the United States and Canada. The tying of the fully dressed classic salmon flies, such as the Jock Scott, Green Highlander, and Durham Ranger, is such a specialized category that it needs to be pursued in its own right.

Salmon flies are almost always dressed on hooks that have been specifically designed and manufactured for the express purpose of salmon fly tying and fishing. They are always black and have an upturned looped eye. I suspect these are merely traditional features, and if we dressed our patterns on other hooks, it would not matter in the least to the salmon. A few notable exceptions to tying on the traditional hooks have to do with the dressing of such flies as the Bombers and Buck Bugs and now and then a nymph.

Salmon flies are rarely ever tied with lead wire underbodies, for the simple reason that in most salmon rivers the weighting of the fly is illegal. There are more ways than one to skin a cat, however, and salmon tyer/anglers, being a resourceful lot, indulge in various maneuvers when they intend their patterns to be fished deeper. They use heavier-gauge hooks, larger hooks, double hooks. They load the hook with a double wrap of extra-heavy tinsel, tie the patterns sparsely, or use a sink tip line with a short leader, or a combination of any and all of these methods.

Double hooks are probably the answer for most anglers when the water is high. They are also the answer for some who feel that the double hook holds the fish more securely. However, others believe the two points work against each other and allow the salmon its freedom. This is a classic and ongoing controversy. As far as hooks go, most patterns are tied on the Partridge salmon brand or the Mustad model 36890. Both have a slightly longer shank than the average wet fly trout hook, with the Mustad having a slight edge in shank length in a given size. When the water is low, a longer, lighter hook, aptly called a low water salmon hook, is employed. The wise angler carries his patterns dressed on both types in addition to doubles to be prepared for any situation.

When patterns are tied on double salmon hooks, the overall proportions in a given recipe remain the same. This is not true, however, when a pattern is dressed as a low water fly.

Low water flies not only employ a much lighter hook but they are dressed sparsely or some materials are omitted. You might say that they shed much of their outer garments the way we do when the weather becomes warm. It just happens that low water conditions prevail in many salmon rivers during the summer months, especially in August and September.

Whereas the forming of the tag, tip, and tail of the fly begins at the bend on a standard salmon pattern, these components in a low water fly are moved forward, beginning anywhere along the shank from a point two-thirds rearward from the eye to the exact center of the shank. This is a specialized type of fly tying which may vary from area to area and from tyer to tyer. For those of you who are interested in pursuing the tying of these flies further, I recommend Poul Jorgensen's book *Salmon Flies.*

In the pages that follow you will also see that tinsel, both flat and oval, is used on just about every pattern listed. Unless specified otherwise, the following rule should apply when selecting tinsel sizes for related hook sizes.

Hook Size	Tinsel Size
6–10	Fine
2–4	Medium
I/0 and larger	Wide

The designations fine, medium, and wide, though they do not give you the width in inches in a flat tinsel or the gauge of thickness in the oval, do come very close to what you will need for the scale indicated above. Some manufacturers may be a hair wider or finer than others, but the deviation is so small it is not even worth considering. E. Veniard, Ltd., of Thornton Heath, England, offers flat and embossed tinsels in no fewer than eleven sizes and ovals in six.

As for tinsel quality, if you can obtain some of the coated tinsels made in France, you will be ahead of the game. Though they are more expensive, those tinsels that have gone through a process which coats them with a protective chemical will not tarnish and thus will last much longer and retain their appearance. A shiny bright tinsel will also create more flash and attraction when it is being fished.

A glossy head adds to the attractiveness of a salmon fly and lacquers should be chosen with this in mind. Keith Fulsher and Charles Krom, who tied the salmon flies for Plate X, use a half-hour epoxy to achieve a high gloss on their patterns.

General Proportions for a Hair Wing Salmon Fly
TAIL: * To end of bend
TAG: Over hook barb
TIP: Between hook barb and point

*Many salmon fly patterns feature a tail of a golden pheasant crest feather. The upward curve of this feather is usually always symmetrically opposite to the curve of the bend.

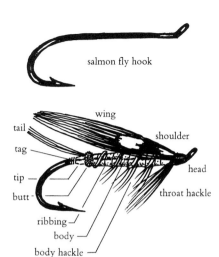

BUTT: Over point of hook
BODY: Length of shank to beginning of looped eye
WING: To end of bend or even with tip of tail
THROAT: Half to three-quarters to point of hook
PALMER RIB: Width of hook gap
SHOULDER: One-third to one-half length of wing (may vary)
CHEEKS: May vary
HEAD: Lacquered and small and neat

Unlike some categories of flies, salmon flies have fairly consistent proportions. Unless stated otherwise, the following listing of patterns will follow the proportions outlined above.

Many tyers feel that the tying of salmon flies, even of the hair wing variety, is just too difficult. This is quite untrue. The difficulty lies only in their imagination when they read a lengthy pattern description and are discouraged before they begin. The secret to tying a salmon fly is to take it one step at a time, progressing from the tail to the head.

I have selected the Dusty Miller as our model to illustrate these steps.

AKROYD

HOOK: Mustad 36890, Partridge salmon (2–10)
THREAD: Black (Flymaster 6/0)
RIB: Oval silver tinsel
BODY: Rear half, orange seal fur (or equivalent); fore half, black floss with yellow hackle palmered through floss
THROAT: Barred teal flank fibers, sparse, beard style
WING: White bucktail, over which red fox squirrel tail fibers (both sparse and slightly past bend)
HEAD: Black

REMARKS: There are variations of this pattern, including a golden pheasant crest tail and a tag of silver tinsel. It is also, at times, dressed with jungle cock cheeks. The transition from a fully dressed fly to a hair wing is never entirely smooth and sometimes there are variations from region to region and tyer to tyer.

BLACK BEAR, GREEN BUTT

HOOK: Mustad 36890, Partridge Salmon (4–10)
THREAD: Black (Flymaster 6/0)
TAG: Oval gold tinsel
TAIL: Black hackle fibers

BUTT: Fluorescent green wool
RIB: Oval gold tinsel
BODY: Black wool
WING: Black bear hair fibers, sparse (slightly past bend)
HACKLE: Black hen hackle, beard style
HEAD: Black

REMARKS: The body of this pattern is sometimes tied with black floss or peacock herl, and here and there it may feature a tail of golden pheasant crest. The original of this series, the Black Bear, is rarely listed in catalogs today. The use of peacock herl, which gives the body extra action, is a recent change from the floss or wool body.

BLACK BEAR, ORANGE BUTT
(Plate X)

The same as Black Bear, Green Butt, except has a fluorescent orange butt.

You can tie butts in this pattern of as many colors as are manufactured. However, the Green Butt and the Orange Butt are the most popular.

BLACK COSSEBOOM
(see Cosseboom, Black)

BLACK DOSE

HOOK: Mustad 36890, Partridge salmon (4–10)
THREAD: Black (Flymaster 6/0)
TAG: Oval silver tinsel
TIP: Pale yellow floss

TAIL: Golden pheasant crest covered half its length by red hackle fibers
RIB: Oval silver tinsel
PALMER RIB: Black hackle palmered through body
BODY: Black floss
WING: Four peacock sword fibers, over which a small bunch of black bear fibers (both to end of tail)
THROAT: Black hen hackle wound as a wet fly collar (see model, Blue Dun, page 124)
CHEEKS: Jungle cock eyes (or equivalent) (second eye showing)
HEAD: Black

BLACK FITCH TAIL
(Plate X)

HOOK: Mustad 36890, Partridge salmon (4–10)
THREAD: Black (Flymaster 6/0)
TAG: Flat silver tinsel
TIP: Fluorescent orange or green floss
TAIL: Golden pheasant crest feather
RIB: Flat silver tinsel
BODY: Black floss
THROAT: Black hen hackle fibers, beard style
WING: Black fitch tail
HEAD: Black

BLACK PARADISE

HOOK: Mustad 36890, Partridge salmon (4–10)

THREAD: Black (Flymaster 6/0)

TAG: Oval gold tinsel

TIP: Fluorescent orange floss

TAIL: Red hackle fibers, sparse (barely past bend)

RIB: Oval gold tinsel over butt and body

BUTT: Medium blue floss

BODY: Coarse underfur from a black bear

THROAT: Grizzly hackle covered with guinea hen hackle, both sparse, beard style

WING: Black bear hair fibers, sparse (to end of tail)

SHOULDER: A small iridescent feather from a bird of paradise

HEAD: Black

REMARKS: Originated by Charles De Feo. A good substitute for the shoulder feather is the small bluish-green neck feathers of the peacock.

BLACK RAT

HOOK: Mustad 36890, Partridge salmon (4–10)

THREAD: Red (Flymaster 6/0)

TAG: Oval silver tinsel

TAIL: Golden pheasant crest

RIB: Oval silver tinsel

BODY: Black seal fur (or equivalent)

WING: Gray fox guard hair fibers

HACKLE: Grizzly wound as a wet fly collar (see model, Blue Dun, page 124)

CHEEKS: Jungle cock eyes (or equivalent) (only one eye showing)

HEAD: Red

BLUE CHARM

HOOK: Mustad 36890, Partridge salmon (4–10)

THREAD: Black (Flymaster 6/0)

TAG: Oval silver tinsel followed by yellow floss

TAIL: Golden pheasant crest

RIB: Oval silver tinsel

BODY: Black floss

THROAT: Medium bright blue hackle fibers, beard style

WING: Gray squirrel tail fibers (to end of tail)

HEAD: Black

REMARKS: Some tyers feel that the use of woodchuck guard hairs for the wing comes closer to the original feather wing of bronze mallard and barred teal.

BLUE DOCTOR

HOOK: Mustad 36890, Partridge salmon (4–10)

THREAD: Red (Flymaster 6/0)

TAG: Oval silver tinsel

TIP: Golden yellow floss

TAIL: Golden pheasant crest feather

BUTT: Red floss

RIB: Oval silver tinsel

BODY: Light blue floss

THROAT: Light blue hackle as a wet fly

collar and pulled down (see model, Blue Dun, page 124)

WING: Gray squirrel tail fibers

HEAD: Red

BLUE RAT
(Plate X)

HOOK: Mustad 36890, Partridge salmon (2–10)

THREAD: Red (Flymaster 6/0)

TAG: Oval gold tinsel

TAIL: Three or four peacock sword fibers, short (to end of bend)

RIB: Fine oval gold tinsel

BODY: Rear two-thirds, kingfisher blue floss; fore third, peacock herl (a strand of the floss left to extend rearward to center of tail, as in Rusty Rat)

WING: Gray fox guard hairs

CHEEKS: Jungle cock eyes (or equivalent) (second eye showing), covered half their length by hen hackle body feathers dyed kingfisher blue

THROAT: Grizzly hen hackle as a wet fly collar (tied in after wing and cheeks have been secured) (see model, Blue Dun, page 124)

HEAD: Red

REMARKS: Originated by Poul Jorgensen.

BLUE SAPPHIRE
(Plate X)

HOOK: Mustad 36890, Partridge salmon (2–10)

THREAD: Black (Flymaster 6/0)
TAG: Oval gold tinsel
TIP: Yellow floss
TAIL: Golden pheasant crest topped half
  its length with bright blue hackle fibers
RIB: Fine oval gold tinsel
BODY: Black floss
PALMER RIB: One black and one royal
  blue hackle palmered through body
  (wound as one by folding one inside the
  other and winding forward in an open
  spiral as you would a wet fly hackle)
THROAT: Royal blue hackle fibers, beard
  style
WING: Red fox squirrel tail fibers over
  medium bright blue calf tail fibers
HEAD: Black

BROWN FAIRY
(Plate X)

HOOK: Mustad 36890, Partridge salmon
  (2–10)
THREAD: Black (Flymaster 6/0)
TAG: Oval gold tinsel
RIB: Oval gold tinsel
BODY: Medium brown floss
PALMER RIB: Brown hackle palmered
  through fore half of body, terminating in
  a throat collar
WING: Red fox squirrel tail fibers
CHEEKS: Jungle cock eyes (or equivalent)
  (second eye showing)
HEAD: Black

BUCK BUG
(see in Salmon Dry Flies, page 117)

BUTTERFLY
(see Ingall's Butterfly)

COLBURN SPECIAL
(Plate X)

HOOK: Mustad 36890, Partridge salmon
  (2–10)
THREAD: Black (Flymaster 6/0)
TAG: Oval silver tinsel
TAIL: Black calf tail over green calf tail
BODY: Fluorescent green floss fully shaped
  with a black ostrich herl wound in the
  center
WING: Black calf tail over green calf tail
  (to end of tail)
THROAT: Yellow hackle wound as a wet
  fly collar (see model, Blue Dun, page 124)
HEAD: Black

CONRAD

HOOK: Mustad 36890, Partridge salmon
  (2–10)
THREAD: Black (Flymaster 6/0)
TAG: Oval silver tinsel
TIP: Fluorescent green floss
TAIL: Black hackle fibers (barely past bend)
RIB: Oval silver tinsel
BODY: Black floss or wool
THROAT: Black hackle fibers, beard style

WING: Black bear hair (to end of tail)
HEAD: Black

COPPER KILLER

HOOK: Mustad 36890, Partridge salmon
  (4–10)
THREAD: Red (Flymaster 6/0)
TAG: Copper wire or tinsel
TIP: Fluorescent green floss
TAIL: Red fox squirrel tail fibers (slightly
  past bend)
BUTT: Red floss
RIB: Oval copper tinsel
BODY: Flat copper tinsel
THROAT: Bright orange hackle, beard
  style
WING: Red fox squirrel tail fibers (to end
  of tail)
HEAD: Red

COSSEBOOM

HOOK: Mustad 36890, Partridge salmon
  (4–10)
THREAD: Red (Flymaster 6/0)
TAG: Embossed silver tinsel
TAIL: Medium olive floss, a short strand
  (barely past bend)
RIB: Embossed silver tinsel
BODY: Medium olive floss
WING: Gray squirrel tail fibers (to end of
  tail)
THROAT: Lemon yellow hackle as a wet
  fly collar (see model, Blue Dun, page 124)
CHEEKS (optional): Jungle cock eyes (or
  equivalent) (one eye showing)
HEAD: Red

COSSEBOOM, BLACK
(Plate X)

HOOK: Mustad 36890, Partridge salmon (2–10)
THREAD: Red (Flymaster 6/0)
TAG: Embossed silver tinsel
TAIL: Black floss, a short strand (barely past bend)
RIB: Embossed silver tinsel
BODY: Black floss
WING: Gray squirrel tail fibers (to end of tail)
THROAT: Black hackle as a wet fly collar (see model, Blue Dun, page 124)
HEAD: Red

REMARKS: The Cosseboom series of flies was originated by John Cosseboom, and the fly is sometimes listed as the Cosseboom Special.

CROSSFIELD
(Plate X)

HOOK: Mustad 36890, Partridge salmon (4–10)
THREAD: Black (Flymaster 6/0)
TAG: Oval silver tinsel
TAIL: Golden pheasant crest feather
BODY: Embossed silver tinsel
THROAT: Bright blue hackle fibers, beard style
WING: Gray squirrel tail fibers
HEAD: Black

CULLMAN'S CHOICE

HOOK: Mustad 36890, Partridge salmon (2–10)
THREAD: Black (Flymaster 6/0)
TAIL: Brown hackle fibers, short (to end of bend)
RIB: Oval gold tinsel
BODY: Bright apple green floss
THROAT: White hen hackle, beard style
WING: Black bear hair, over which a silver pheasant crest feather
HEAD: Black

REMARKS: Originated by Lee Wulff.

DE FEO'S BLACK DIAMOND
(Plate X)

HOOK: Mustad 36890, Partridge salmon (4–10)
THREAD: Black (Flymaster 6/0)
TAG: Flat silver tinsel
TIP: Fluorescent orange floss
TAIL: Golden pheasant crest
BUTT: Black wool
RIB: Oval silver tinsel
BODY: Flat silver tinsel
THROAT: Brown hackle fibers, beard style
WING: Black squirrel tail over a strand of fluorescent red floss
TOPPING: Golden pheasant crest feather
CHEEKS: Two very small jungle cock eyes (or equivalent) (only one eye showing)
HEAD: Black

REMARKS: Originated by Charles De Feo, who spent much time on the salmon rivers

he loved. De Feo was respected for his knowledge of the use of fly-tying materials, which resulted in many innovative designs of salmon flies. Other fly tyers always sought him out and were never turned away. Harold Campbell, who at one time may have owned the largest collection of salmon fly materials in the world, used to bring De Feo various exotic feathers and furs without charge just to obtain a few De Feo originals. It is unfortunate indeed that De Feo never published his designs or innovations.

Most of the De Feo originals are not cataloged by the mail-order houses. Some of his patterns, however, appear in *Atlantic Salmon Flies and Fishing* by Joseph D. Bates, Jr., and nearly all his prominent hair wing patterns are listed in *Hair Wing Atlantic Salmon Flies,* by Keith Fulsher and Charles Krom.

DUNKELD

HOOK: Mustad 36890, Partridge salmon (2–10)
THREAD: Black (Flymaster 6/0)
TAG: Fine oval gold tinsel
TAIL: Golden pheasant crest feather topped by red hackle fibers half as long
BUTT: Black ostrich herl
BODY: Embossed gold tinsel
HACKLE: Hot orange as a wet fly collar (see model, Blue Dun, page 124)
WING: A small mixed bunch of red, yellow, and blue bucktail topped by red fox squirrel tail fibers

CHEEKS: Jungle cock eyes (or equivalent)
(second eye showing)
HEAD: Black

DUSTY MILLER

HOOK: Mustad 36890, Partridge salmon
(2–10)
THREAD: Black (Flymaster 6/0)
TAG: Oval silver tinsel
TIP: Yellow floss
TAIL: A golden pheasant crest, over which
red hackle fibers half as long
BUTT: Black ostrich herl
RIB: Fine oval silver tinsel
BODY: Rear two-thirds, embossed silver
tinsel; fore third, orange floss
THROAT: Natural guinea hen fibers, beard
style
WING: A sparse mixed bunch of orange,
red, and yellow polar bear or calf tail,
over which a small bunch of natural brown
bucktail or red fox squirrel tail fibers
TOPPING: A golden pheasant crest feather
CHEEKS: Jungle cock eyes (or equivalent)
(second eye showing)
HEAD: Black

REMARKS: This pattern is among those
derived from the classics which may show
variations in the hair wing version due simply to the tyer's translation from the original.
It uses more than the usual amount of materials found in a hair wing pattern and thus
serves well as a model for similar techniques
used in other salmon flies.

1. Spiral thread onto the shank beginning
at a point behind the eye and winding rearward in open spirals to a position on the
shank just above the barb.

2. For the tag you will need a short section (three to four inches) of oval silver tinsel.
Since I'm demonstrating this on a size 6
hook, I'm using a tinsel size designated fine.
Strip a bit of tinsel from one end, exposing
the cotton core. Tie the cotton core to the
shank by winding the thread over it and
forward for five or six turns. Wind the tinsel
to the thread and tie it down. Snip the excess.

3. Cut a short section of single-strand yellow floss and tie it to the shank just forward
of the tinsel by winding the thread forward
and over it for several turns, securing it. Wind
the floss *rearward* to cover some of the turns
of the oval tinsel but leaving a short section
exposed as the tag. Wind the floss forward
once more and tie it down with the thread.
Clip the excess.

4. Tie in a golden pheasant crest feather so
that the tip curves upward and mirrors the
bend. Pluck a few red hackle fibers from a
dyed bright red feather and tie them in on
top of the crest feather so the tips extend
rearward and cover the crest feather for half
its length. Both the crest feather and the
hackle fibers should be lashed to the shank at
a point just above the hook point. Clip the
excess butts.

5. Tie in a natural black ostrich herl fiber
and secure it to the shank by winding the
thread over it for three turns to the rear and
then three turns forward. Wind the herl to
the thread in connecting spirals for three or

four turns. Tie it down with the thread and
clip the excess.

I have often wondered what purpose the
butt of ostrich herl serves. It is used on many
patterns. The only conjecture I can come up
with is that sometime in the obscure past a
salmon fly tyer, having formed some intri-
cate assembly of tag, tip, and tail, was in a
dilemma over what to do with the body
bulk formed at the rear end of the shank.
What better way to hide the tying off of four
separate materials than a few turns of ostrich
herl, especially black. Looks pretty good. In
fact, it looks traditional.

6. Cut another section of fine oval silver
tinsel, de-core one end, and tie it in under the
shank in front of the ostrich herl butt. Place
it rearward, out of the way for now.

7. Cut a section of embossed silver tinsel
(this is usually available only in a medium
size). Bring your thread to the center of the
hook shank. Tie the tip of the tinsel in under
the shank of the hook. Wind the tinsel rearward to the butt and then, in connecting
spirals, forward to a point slightly past the
center of the shank. Tie it down and clip the
excess.

8. Bring your thread slightly forward of
where the tinsel was tied down. Tie in a
section of orange floss. Bring the thread forward to the head of the hook where the
looped eye comes together with the shank.
Wind the floss rearward to a point one-third
of the shank length behind the head and then
forward again, forming a smooth, even forward body. Secure the floss with the thread
and snip the excess.

9. Grasp the oval tinsel rib left idling in the rear and wind it in an open spiral around both the embossed tinsel and then the orange floss to the thread. Tie it down and clip the excess. There should be five rings of oval tinsel formed around the body of the fly.

10. Cut a section of fibers (approximately a quarter inch wide) from a guinea hen feather and tie them in as the throat. The tips should extend halfway to the point of the hook.

11. Cut a few fibers each of orange, red, and yellow polar bear and mix the shades between your fingers. Align the tips. Tie them in as the wing so that the tips reach to the end of the tail. Cut a section of natural brown bucktail or red fox squirrel tail fibers, fairly sparse, and tie them in on top of the polar bear or bucktail. Trim all excess butts with an angle cut to ensure a neatly tapered eye.

12. Tie in the topping of a golden pheasant crest curving downward to meet the tips of the wing fibers. Trim excess butt.

13. Select two medium-sized jungle cock eyes and tie them in for the cheeks. If you lacquer the inside of each feather with head cement, the positioning becomes much easier. The second eye of each feather should be showing on each side.

14. Cover any exposed butts with thread while simultaneously making the head area smooth, even, and gently tapered. Do not build up a bulky thread head. Whip-finish the thread.

15. Apply black head lacquer or epoxy to form a glossy head. Use more than one coat if needed to achieve the desired result.

Tying Steps for Dusty Miller

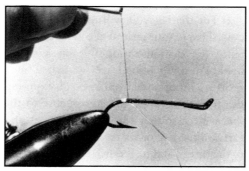

a. Oval tinsel tag being tied in.

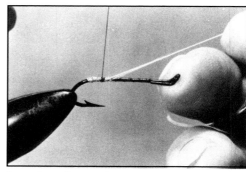

b. Yellow floss tip being tied in.

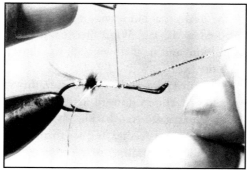

f. Embossed silver tinsel has been tied in and wound around shank to form rear portion of body.

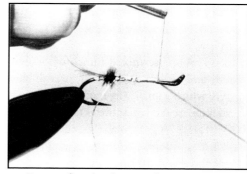

g. Orange floss has been tied in and wound to form fore portion of body.

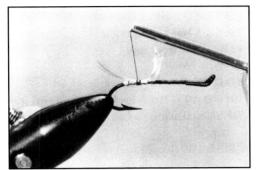

c. Golden pheasant crest tail being tied in.

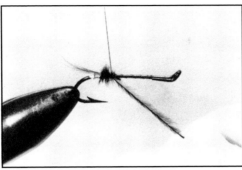

d. Ostrich herl butt being tied in.

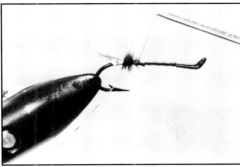

e. Oval silver tinsel being tied in for ribbing.

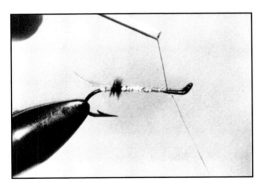

h. Oval tinsel rib has been wound forward in open spiral to form ribbing.

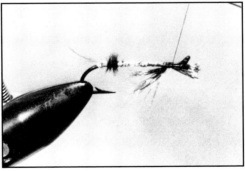

i. Guinea hen fibers have been tied in to form throat hackle.

j. Mixed section of orange, red, and yellow polar bear fibers being measured to end of tail prior to being tied in.

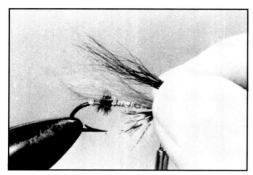

k. Brown bucktail fibers being measured along top of polar bear fibers prior to being tied in.

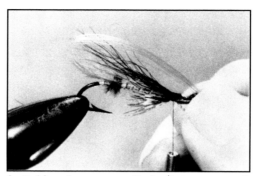

l. Golden pheasant crest feather being measured and curving downward to tip of tail prior to being tied in.

m. Jungle cock eyes being tied in for cheeks.

n. Completed Dusty Miller with lacquer applied to head.

ENGLEHARDT SPECIAL

HOOK: Mustad 36890, Partridge salmon (2–10)
THREAD: Black (Flymaster 6/0)
TAG: Oval gold tinsel
RIB: Oval gold tinsel
TAIL: None
BODY: Bronze peacock herl
THROAT: Black hackle fibers, beard style
WING: Black bear hair fibers (slightly past bend)
CHEEKS: Jungle cock eyes (or equivalent) (only one eye showing)
HEAD: Black

FEATHERDUSTER

HOOK: Mustad 36890, Partridge salmon (2–10)
THREAD: Black (Flymaster 6/0)
TAIL (optional): Golden pheasant tippet fibers
BODY: Wound with a double-folded orange and grizzly saddle hackle
HACKLE: Guinea hen dyed orange and wound as a wet fly collar

REMARKS: The Featherduster series employs the technique of the folded hackle (see model, Blue Dun, page 124), but in this case two feathers are folded either together or separately and then wound as one over the entire length of the hook shank. If they are folded one at a time, they are placed one inside the other before being tied to the shank. In this pattern the orange saddle hackle would be placed inside the grizzly, tied to the shank by the tips, then wound forward. As each turn is being made around the shank, the fibers are stroked rearward.

Featherdusters are sometimes tied with an underbody of flat silver or gold tinsel, or with a layer of one of the fluorescent flosses, such as green, orange, or red. This is usually not necessary, however, since the folded hackle, wound in close connecting spirals, completely hides the underbody.

Featherdusters may be tied in any combination desired, although the three described here are the most popular.

FEATHERDUSTER, BLACK

HOOK: Mustad 36890, Partridge salmon (2–10)
THREAD: Black (Flymaster 6/0)
TAIL: Black hackle fibers
BODY: Dyed orange grizzly saddle hackle within black saddle hackle, both folded and wound in connecting spirals the full length of the hook shank
HACKLE: Guinea hen dyed orange as a wet fly collar (see model, Blue Dun, page 124)
HEAD: Black

FEATHERDUSTER, BLACK AND YELLOW

HOOK: Mustad 36890, Partridge salmon (2–10)
THREAD: Black (Flymaster 6/0)
TAIL: Yellow and black hackle fibers mixed
BODY: Black and yellow saddle hackles wound as one in connecting spirals the length of the shank, the yellow inside the black as a folded hackle
HACKLE: Guinea hen dyed yellow as a wet fly hackle
HEAD: Black

GARRY
(also known as Yellow Dog)
(Plate X)

HOOK: Mustad 36890, Partridge salmon (2/0–6)
THREAD: Black (Flymaster 6/0)
TAG: Oval silver tinsel
TIP: Yellow floss
TAIL: Dyed red goose quill section (three or four fibers) over golden pheasant crest feather
RIB: Oval silver tinsel
BODY: Black floss
THROAT: Dyed blue guinea hen hackle, beard style
WING: Yellow calf tail over red calf tail, both sparse
HEAD: Black

REMARKS: This British hair wing pattern is often tied in very large sizes up to 7/0.

Now and then jungle cock eyes are tied in as shoulders or cheeks.

GOLD RAT

HOOK: Mustad 36890, Partridge salmon (2–10)
THREAD: Red (Flymaster 6/0)
TAG: Flat silver tinsel
TAIL: Golden pheasant crest dyed red
RIB: Oval silver tinsel
BODY: Flat gold tinsel
WING: Gray fox guard hairs
THROAT: Grizzly hackle as a wet fly collar (see model, Blue Dun, page 124)
HEAD: Red

GREEN BUTT
(see Black Bear, Green Butt)

GREEN HIGHLANDER
(Plate X)

HOOK: Mustad 36890, Partridge salmon (4–10)
THREAD: Black (Flymaster 6/0)
TAG: Flat silver tinsel
TIP: Pale yellow floss
TAIL: Golden pheasant crest feather, over which teal flank fibers half as long as crest
BUTT: Black ostrich herl
RIB: Oval silver tinsel
BODY: Rear third, light gold floss; fore two-thirds, bright green floss

PALMER RIB: Bright green hackle palmered over green floss only

WING: A few golden pheasant tippet fibers, over which a sparse bunch of green and yellow calf tail fibers mixed together

THROAT: Canary yellow hackle as a wet fly collar (see model, Blue Dun, page 124)

CHEEKS: Jungle cock eyes (or equivalent) (second eye showing)

HEAD: Black

HAGGIS

HOOK: Mustad 36890, Partridge salmon (2–10)

THREAD: Black

TAG: Oval silver tinsel

RIB: Oval silver tinsel

BODY: Black floss

WING: Black bear

TOPPING: Black bucktail (sparse), used only if extra flotation is desired (shank length past bend)

THROAT: From a dyed yellow hackle feather a few strands of the fluffy hackle near the base mixed with a few soft fibers found just above

HEAD: Black

REMARKS: Originated by Lee Wulff.

HAIRY MARY

HOOK: Mustad 36890, Partridge salmon (4–10)

THREAD: Black (Flymaster 6/0)

TAG: Oval gold tinsel

TAIL: Golden pheasant crest feather

RIB: Oval gold tinsel

BODY: Black floss

THROAT: Bright blue hackle fibers, beard style

WING: Brown fitch tail fibers

HEAD: Black

HATHAWAY SPECIAL

HOOK: Mustad 36890, Partridge salmon (2–10)

THREAD: Black (Flymaster 6/0)

TAIL: None

RIB: Peacock herl and brown hackle

BODY: Yellow wool

WING: Red fox squirrel tail fibers (slightly past bend)

HEAD: Black

REMARKS: This pattern, submitted by Rodney Flagg, deviates from the normal overall salmon fly structure. It has no tail, tag, or tip, and the rib of peacock herl and hackle produces a slightly unusual effect.

When forming the rib, the peacock herl should be wound forward in an open spiral first and then the hackle is wound to follow in its track. The rib hackle fibers are slightly longer than the hook-gap width. The tips of the wing extend past the bend for approximately half a gap width.

HOT ORANGE

HOOK: Mustad 36890, Partridge salmon (4–10)

THREAD: Black (Flymaster 6/0)

TAG: Flat gold tinsel

TIP: Yellow floss

TAIL: Golden pheasant crest feather

RIB: Flat gold tinsel

BODY: Black floss

THROAT: Hot orange as a wet fly collar and pulled down (see model, Blue Dun, page 124)

WING: Dyed black squirrel tail fibers

HEAD: Black

INGALL'S BUTTERFLY

HOOK: Mustad 36890, 90240, Partridge salmon (6–10)

THREAD: Black (Flymaster 6/0)

TAIL: Dyed red hackle fibers (almost a gap width past bend)

BODY: Peacock herl

WING: White goat hair divided and slanting rearward (to bend)

HACKLE: Brown as a dry fly collar

HEAD: Black

REMARKS: The original version of this pattern calls for the hackle collar to be wound

both in front and in back of the wings. This gets too involved because of the rearward slant of the wing. Most tyers today simply wind the hackle collar in front of the wing.

The wing can be formed by tying the fibers in as a conventional streamer or bucktail wing and then dividing the fibers with thread and raising them off the hook shank, or they may be formed by tying them to the shank as a divided split hair wing (as in the Hair Wing Royal Coachman) and forcing them to slant rearward by using the reverse-figure-eight technique of securing a dry fly wing. In the latter case, the fibers will quiver and pulse as they are being fished, since the fibers, after having been pushed down by the force of the current, always try to resume their natural set position. Do the salmon realize all the trouble we go to?

JEANNIE

HOOK: Mustad 36890, Partridge salmon (2–10)
THREAD: Black (Flymaster 6/0)
TAG: Oval silver tinsel
TAIL: Golden pheasant crest feather
RIB: Oval silver tinsel
BODY: Rear third, lemon yellow floss; fore two-thirds, black floss
THROAT: Black hackle fibers, beard style
WING: Red fox squirrel tail fibers
CHEEKS: Jungle cock eyes (or equivalent) (second eye showing)
HEAD: Black

JOCK SCOTT

HOOK: Mustad 36890, Partridge salmon (2–10)
THREAD: Black (Flymaster 6/0)
TAG: Flat silver tinsel
TIP: Yellow floss
TAIL: Golden pheasant crest topped for half its length with orange hackle fibers
BUTT: Black ostrich herl
RIB: Flat silver tinsel
BODY: Rear half, yellow floss; fore half, black seal fur (or equivalent)
WING: The mixed fibers of yellow, red, and blue calf tail, all sparse, over which a small bunch of natural brown calf tail or bucktail
THROAT: Black hen hackle as a wet fly collar and pulled down (see model, Blue Dun, page 124)
HEAD: Black

LADY JOAN

HOOK: Mustad 36890, Partridge salmon (2–10)
THREAD: Black
TAIL: None
TAG: Oval gold tinsel
BODY: Burnt orange floss
RIB: Oval gold tinsel
THROAT: From a dyed yellow hackle feather a few strands of the fluffy hackle near the base mixed with a few soft fibers found just above

WING: Black bear hair, over which gray squirrel tail fibers
HEAD: Black
REMARKS: Originated by Lee Wulff.

LAXA BLUE
(Plate X)

HOOK: Mustad 36890, Partridge salmon (2–10)
THREAD: Black (Flymaster 6/0)
TAG: Flat silver tinsel
TIP: Fluorescent orange floss (or fluorescent green floss)
RIB: Flat silver tinsel
BODY: Black floss
THROAT: Bright blue hackle fibers, beard style
WING: Bright blue calf tail fibers
CHEEKS: Jungle cock eyes (or equivalent) (second eye showing)
HEAD: Black

LOGIE

HOOK: Mustad 36890, Partridge salmon (2–10)
THREAD: Black (Flymaster 6/0)
TAG: Oval silver tinsel
TAIL: Golden pheasant crest feather
RIB: Oval silver tinsel
BODY: Rear half, yellow floss; fore half, claret floss
THROAT: Light blue hackle fibers, beard style

WING: Red fox squirrel tail fibers over dyed yellow monga ringtail fibers
HEAD: Black

MUDDLER MINNOW, SALMON
(see Salmon Muddler Minnow)

NIGHT HAWK

HOOK: Mustad 36890, Partridge salmon (2–10)
THREAD: Red (Flymaster 6/0)
TAG: Fine oval silver tinsel
TIP: Yellow floss
TAIL: A golden pheasant crest feather, over which a few blue hackle fibers not quite as long as crest
BUTT: Fluorescent red floss
RIB: Oval silver tinsel
BODY: Flat silver tinsel
THROAT: Black hackle fibers, beard style
WING: Black bear or dyed black squirrel tail fibers
WING: Golden pheasant crest feather curving downward to meet tail crest
HEAD: Red

NIPISIGUIT GREY

HOOK: Mustad 36890, Partridge salmon (2–10)
THREAD: Black (Flymaster 6/0)
TAG: Oval gold tinsel
TIP: Yellow floss
TAIL: Golden pheasant crest feather

BUTT: Peacock herl
RIB: Oval gold tinsel
BODY: Muskrat dubbing fur
THROAT: Grizzly hackle, beard style
WING: Black bear hair
HEAD: Black

ONSET

HOOK: Mustad 36890, Partridge salmon (2–10)
THREAD: Black (Flymaster 6/0)
TAG: Flat silver tinsel
TIP: Yellow floss
TAIL: Golden pheasant crest feather
RIB: Flat silver tinsel
BODY: Rear third, yellow floss; fore two-thirds, orange floss
THROAT: Medium blue dun hackle, beard style
WING: Gray squirrel tail fibers
HEAD: Black

ORANGE BLOSSOM
(Plate X)

HOOK: Mustad 36890, Partridge salmon (2/0–8)
THREAD: Black (Flymaster 6/0)
TAG: Oval silver tinsel
TIP: Yellow floss
TAIL: Golden pheasant crest feather
BUTT: Black ostrich herl
RIB: Oval silver tinsel
BODY: Rear half, embossed silver tinsel; fore half, yellow seal fur palmered with dyed yellow hackle

WING: Brown and white calf tail fibers mixed
CHEEKS: Jungle cock eyes (or equivalent) (only one eye showing)
THROAT: Orange hackle as a wet fly collar (tips almost to point of hook) (see model, Blue Dun, page 124)
HEAD: Black

ORANGE CHARM

HOOK: Mustad 36890, Partridge salmon (2/0–8)
THREAD: Black (Flymaster 6/0)
TAG: Flat silver tinsel
TIP: Fluorescent orange floss
TAIL: Golden pheasant crest feather
RIB: Medium flat silver tinsel
BODY: Black floss
THROAT: Orange hackle fibers, beard style
WING: Red fox squirrel tail fibers
HEAD: Black

ORIOLE
(Plate X)

HOOK: Mustad 36890, Partridge salmon (4–10)
THREAD: Black (Flymaster 6/0)
TAG: Fine gold oval tinsel
TAIL: Red body feathers from golden pheasant (or red hackle fibers)
RIB: Fine oval gold tinsel
BODY: Black wool
THROAT: Brown hackle wound as a wet

fly collar and pulled down (see model, Blue Dun, page 124)

WING: Dyed yellow squirrel tail or woodchuck guard hair fibers

HEAD: Black

PACK RAT
(Plate X)

HOOK: Mustad 36890, Partridge salmon (2–10)

THREAD: Black (Flymaster 6/0)

TAG: Flat gold tinsel

TAIL: Fiery brown guard hair fibers from under rear leg area of a woodchuck (slightly past bend)

RIB: Oval gold tinsel

BODY: Rear third, hare's ear dubbing fur

PALMER RIB: Grizzly hackle palmered through fore two-thirds of body

BODY: Fore two-thirds, peacock herl

WING: Woodchuck guard hair fibers from back of animal

THROAT: Black hen hackle as a wet fly collar (see model, Blue Dun, page 124)

HEAD: Black

PALE TORRISH
(sometimes listed as Yellow Torrish)

HOOK: Mustad 36890, Partridge salmon (2–10)

THREAD: Black (Flymaster 6/0)

TAG: Flat silver tinsel

TIP: Yellow floss

TAIL: A golden pheasant crest feather

topped with blended strands of fluorescent red and orange floss

BUTT: Black ostrich herl

BODY: Flat silver tinsel divided by a yellow hackle tied like a throat, beard style, directly in front of which a butt of black ostrich herl

THROAT: Yellow hackle, beard style

WING: Dyed yellow gray squirrel tail fibers topped with a golden pheasant crest feather

CHEEKS: Jungle cock eyes (or equivalent) (second eye showing)

HEAD: Black

RAY'S RED

HOOK: Mustad 36890, Partridge salmon (2–10)

THREAD: Fluorescent red (Flymaster 6/0)

TIP: Fluorescent red wool

TAIL: Hot orange floss, short

RIB: Embossed silver tinsel

BODY: Hot orange floss

WING: Gray squirrel tail fibers dyed hot orange

HEAD: Fluorescent red

RED ABBEY

HOOK: Mustad 36890, Partridge salmon (2–10)

THREAD: Black (Flymaster 6/0)

TAG: Oval silver tinsel

TAIL: Dyed red goose quill section

RIB: Flat silver tinsel

BODY: Red floss

WING: Red pine squirrel tail fibers

THROAT: Brown hackle as a wet fly collar (see model, Blue Dun, page 124)

HEAD: Black

RED BUTT MIRAMICHI
(Plate X)

HOOK: Mustad 36890, Partridge salmon (2–10)

THREAD: Black (Flymaster 6/0)

TAIL: None

BUTT: Fluorescent red floss

RIB: Oval gold tinsel

BODY: Black floss

THROAT: Black hackle fibers, beard style

WING: Natural tan bucktail or calf tail (slightly past bend)

HEAD: Black

ROGER'S FANCY

HOOK: Mustad 36890, Partridge salmon (4–10)

THREAD: Black (Flymaster 6/0)

TAG: Oval silver tinsel

TIP: Fluorescent green floss

TAIL: Three or four peacock sword fibers

RIB: Oval silver tinsel

BODY: Bright green seal fur (or equivalent)

THROAT: Yellow hackle fibers, under which green hackle fibers, beard style

WING: Gray fox guard hair fibers (or badger guard hair fibers)

HEAD: Black

ROSS SPECIAL

HOOK: Mustad 36890, Partridge salmon (2–10)

THREAD: Black (Flymaster 6/0)

TAG: Oval silver tinsel

TAIL: Golden pheasant crest feather

RIB: Oval silver tinsel

BODY: Red wool

THROAT: Yellow hackle fibers, beard style

WING: Red fox squirrel tail fibers

CHEEKS: Jungle cock eyes (or equivalent) (only one eye showing)

HEAD: Black

RUELLAND SPECIAL

HOOK: Mustad 36890, Partridge salmon (2–10)

THREAD: Black (Flymaster 6/0)

TAG: Oval silver tinsel

TIP: Fluorescent green floss

TAIL: Green calf tail fibers

BUTT: Peacock herl

RIB: Extra-fine black chenille (size 00)

BODY: Flat green tinsel

WING: Black bear hair fibers

THROAT: Two grizzly hackle tips tied

beard style, with the remainder of one of the feathers wound as a wet fly collar

HEAD: Black

RUSTY RAT
(Plate X)

HOOK: Mustad 36890, Partridge salmon (4–10)

THREAD: Red (Flymaster 6/0)

TAG: Oval gold tinsel

TAIL: Three peacock sword fibers

RIB: Oval gold tinsel

BODY: Rear half, orange floss (a free strand of orange floss is folded back to form a veil to center of tail); fore half, peacock herl

WING: Gray fox guard hairs, sparse

THROAT: Grizzly hackle as a wet fly collar (see model, Blue Dun, page 124)

CHEEKS (optional): Jungle cock eyes (or equivalent) (only one eye showing)

HEAD: Red

REMARKS: Woodchuck guard hair fibers make an excellent substitute for gray fox hair for the wing.

SALMON HORNBERG

HOOK: Mustad 36890, Partridge salmon (4–8)

THREAD: Black (Flymaster 6/0)

TAIL: None

BODY: Flat silver tinsel

WING: Two yellow neck or saddle hackle feathers (or a sparse bunch of yellow calf

tail) flanked by two mallard flank feathers (slightly past bend)

CHEEKS: Jungle cock eyes (or equivalent) (second eye showing)

HACKLE: Brown and grizzly mixed and wound as a dry fly collar

HEAD: Black

REMARKS: This is almost identical to the Hornberg listed in the streamer flies section. Though it is much better known as a trout pattern, it is also quite effective as a salmon fly.

SALMON MUDDLER MINNOW

HOOK: Mustad 36890, Partridge salmon (2–10)

THREAD: Gray (Monocord 3/0)

TAIL: Mottled turkey wing quill section (curving upward, mirroring bend)

BODY: Flat gold tinsel

WING: Gray squirrel tail fibers, over which and slightly straddling hook shank two mottled turkey wing quill sections (one on each side), both to meet and align with tip of tail

HEAD: Spun and trimmed natural brown/gray deer hair, a portion of which is allowed to flow rearward as a collar over the body

REMARKS: For construction details, see Muddler Minnow (page 227). If you use one of the salmon fly hooks listed in this recipe, you will be spinning the deer hair on a double-wire shank, so the hair will have to be flared at several locations around the shank so that all areas are fully covered before the trimming begins.

SHEEPSCOT SPECIAL (No. 2)
(Plate X)

HOOK: Mustad 36890, Partridge salmon (2–10)
THREAD: Black (Flymaster 6/0)
TAG: Oval gold tinsel
TAIL: Orange floss, short
RIB: Oval gold tinsel
BODY: Orange floss
WING: Red fox squirrel tail fibers
THROAT: Furnace hackle as a wet fly collar and pulled down (see model, Blue Dun, page 124)
HEAD: Black

SILVER BLUE
(Plate X)

HOOK: Mustad 36890, Partridge salmon (4–10)
THREAD: Black (Flymaster 6/0)
TAG: Oval silver tinsel
TAIL: Golden pheasant crest feather
RIB: Oval silver tinsel
BODY: Flat silver tinsel
THROAT: Pale blue hackle fibers, beard style

WING: Gray squirrel tail fibers
HEAD: Black

SILVER DOCTOR

HOOK: Mustad 36890, Partridge salmon (2–10)
THREAD: Red (Flymaster 6/0)
TAG: Oval silver tinsel
TAIL: Golden pheasant crest feather topped by red hackle fibers half as long
BUTT: Red wool
BODY: Flat silver tinsel
RIB: Oval silver tinsel
THROAT: Natural guinea fowl hackle, beard style
WING: A small mixed bunch of red, yellow, and blue bucktail topped with red fox squirrel tail fibers
SHOULDER: Two turns of light blue hackle wound as a wet fly collar (see model, Blue Dun, page 124)
CHEEKS: Jungle cock eyes (or equivalent) (second eye showing)
HEAD: Red

SILVER DOWNEASTER

HOOK: Mustad 36890, Partridge salmon (2–10)
THREAD: Black (Flymaster 6/0)
TAG: Fine oval gold tinsel
TAIL: Golden pheasant crest feather
BUTT: Black ostrich herl
RIB: Fine oval silver tinsel
BODY: Flat silver tinsel
THROAT: Orange hen hackle as a wet fly

collar and pulled down (see model, Blue Dun, page 124)
WING: Black bear hair or black squirrel tail
HEAD: Black

SILVER GRAY

HOOK: Mustad 36890, Partridge salmon (4–10)
THREAD: Black (Flymaster 6/0)
TAG: Flat silver tinsel
TIP: Yellow floss
TAIL: Golden pheasant crest feather
BUTT: Black ostrich herl
RIB: Oval silver tinsel
BODY: Flat silver tinsel
THROAT: Badger hackle, short (gap width in length), beard style
WING: Gray squirrel tail mixed with orange and yellow calf tail fibers
CHEEKS (optional): Jungle cock eyes (or equivalent) (second eye showing)
HEAD: Black

SILVER MONKEY

HOOK: Mustad 36890, Partridge salmon (2–10)
THREAD: Black (Flymaster 6/0)
TAG: Oval silver tinsel
TAIL: Golden pheasant crest feather

BUTT: Black ostrich herl
RIB: Oval silver tinsel
BODY: Flat silver tinsel
THROAT: Grizzly hackle, beard style
WING: Strands of fluorescent yellow and green floss, over which mottled gray silver monkey hair fibers
CHEEKS: Jungle cock eyes (or equivalent) (only one eye showing)
HEAD: Black

REMARKS: Originated by Charles De Feo. Substitutes for silver monkey include gray fox guard hairs and mottled woodchuck tail guard hairs.

SILVER RAT
(Plate X)

HOOK: Mustad 36890, Partridge salmon (2–10)
THREAD: Red (Flymaster 6/0)
TAG: Oval gold tinsel
TAIL: Golden pheasant crest feather
RIB: Oval gold tinsel
BODY: Flat silver tinsel
WING: Gray fox guard hairs
THROAT: Grizzly hackle wound as a wet fly collar (see model, Blue Dun, page 124)
CHEEKS: Jungle cock eyes (or equivalent) (only one eye showing)
HEAD: Red

REMARKS: This pattern, along with other light-shaded flies, is a favorite among anglers on bright sunny days.

STOAT TAIL

HOOK: Mustad 36890, Partridge salmon (2–10)
THREAD: Black (Flymaster 6/0)
TAG: Oval silver tinsel
TAIL: Golden pheasant crest feather
RIB: Oval silver tinsel
BODY: Black floss
THROAT: Black hackle fibers, beard style
WING: Black stoat tail (ermine, fitch, or mink)
HEAD: Black

SWEEP

HOOK: Mustad 36890, Partridge salmon (2–10)
THREAD: Black (Flymaster 6/0)
TAG: Oval gold tinsel
TAIL: Golden pheasant crest feather
BUTT: Black ostrich herl
RIB: Oval gold tinsel
BODY: Black floss
THROAT: Black hackle fibers, beard style
WING: Black bear hair
CHEEKS: Blue kingfisher body feathers (substitute: dyed bright blue hen hackle tips)
HEAD: Black

THUNDER AND LIGHTNING

HOOK: Mustad 36890, Partridge salmon (4–10)

THREAD: Black (Flymaster 6/0)
TAG: Oval silver tinsel
TIP: Yellow floss
TAIL: Golden pheasant crest feather
BUTT: Black ostrich herl
RIB: Oval gold tinsel
BODY: Black floss
PALMER RIB: Hot orange hackle palmered through fore third of body only
THROAT: Dyed blue guinea hen hackle as a wet fly collar and pulled down (see model, Blue Dun, page 124)
WING: Orange polar bear (or calf tail), over which natural brown bucktail, over which dyed yellow calf tail, all sparse bunches
CHEEKS: Jungle cock eyes (or equivalent) (second eye showing)
HEAD: Black

UNDERTAKER

HOOK: Mustad 36890, Partridge salmon (2–10)
THREAD: Black (Flymaster 6/0)
TAG: Flat gold tinsel
TIP: Fluorescent green floss followed by fluorescent orange floss
RIB: Oval gold tinsel
BODY: Peacock herl
THROAT: Black hackle fibers, beard style
WING: Black bear hair
CHEEKS: Jungle cock eyes (or equivalent) (only one eye showing)
HEAD: Black

Steelhead Flies

STEELHEAD FLIES are not very different from streamer patterns or salmon flies and may have evolved from one or the other in the past. This does not imply that there are no original steelhead patterns; there are, in fact, thousands. The brief listing here includes only those most often cataloged by fly shops because they have proven effective.

The patterns described here are, for the most part, those which are popular in the Northwest. The Great Lakes patterns, even though intended for the same fish which has its origins in the rivers from northern California up into British Columbia, differ slightly and have their own innovations.

Hooks for steelhead flies vary, though the most frequently used seem to be the black up-eye salmon hooks of the English or Norwegian variety. The Eagle Claw 1197B is also cataloged and used by a number of fly shops and tyers. The black salmon hook lends a more classic appearance and this may be one reason for its popularity. The weight of the hook is determined by whether the fly is to be fished deep or shallow.

The tail fibers on steelhead flies do not vary quite as much as in streamer and bucktail flies. Tails are usually as long as the hook gap is wide and in some cases just a bit shorter.

The hackle on these patterns is generally of a wet fly collar style tied in after the wing has been secured. In cases where it is tied in before the wing, it is either pulled down to act as a full beard or, and preferably, the fibers on top of the shank are pulled out or trimmed.

Thread used is either the Flymaster brand in size 6/0 or the Monocord variety. Here again, the finer Flymaster permits a neater head, especially in a multiple wing. Hook size also indicates which will perform better.

ADMIRAL
(Plate XI)

HOOK: Partridge salmon (4–8)
THREAD: Black (Flymaster 6/0)
TAIL: Red hackle fibers (gap width in length)
RIB: Flat gold tinsel
BODY: Bright red wool or fluorescent red wool
HACKLE: Red hackle as a wet fly collar and pulled down (see model, Blue Dun, page 124)
WING: White bucktail (to end of tail)
HEAD: Black

REMARKS: This version (the Admiral has several) was submitted by Ed Haas of Forks of Salmon, California.

BABINE SPECIAL

HOOK: Eagle Claw 1197N, Mustad 36890 (2–6)
THREAD: Red (Flymaster 6/0 or Monocord 3/0)
BODY: Fluorescent hot pink chenille wound in two separate humps to represent salmon eggs; a red hackle wound dry fly style at the center division between the two chenille humps
HACKLE: White as a dry fly collar

REMARKS: This pattern may very well have been the forerunner for the two-egg sperm fly used so successfully not only in the rivers of the Northwest but in the streams feeding the Great Lakes from New York to Michigan. There are quite a few variations of this pattern.

BADGER YELLOW
(Plate XI)

HOOK: Eagle Claw 1197B or Partridge salmon (6)

THREAD: Black (Flymaster 6/0)
TAIL: Red hackle fibers (gap width past bend)
BODY: Fluorescent yellow chenille (size 2)
HACKLE: Badger hackle palmered through body from center of shank to head
HEAD: Black

BLACK BEAUTY
(Plate XI)

HOOK: Low water salmon (4–6)
THREAD: Black (Flymaster 6/0)
TAIL: Black hackle fibers (gap width past bend)
BODY: Fluorescent red floss
HACKLE: Black as a wet fly collar (see model, Blue Dun, page 124)
HEAD: Black

BLACK DEMON
(Plate XI)

HOOK: Low water salmon (4–6)
THREAD: Black (Flymaster 6/0)
TAIL: Barred black and white wood duck fibers (gap width past bend)
BODY: Flat gold tinsel
HACKLE: Orange as a wet fly collar (tips to point of hook) (see model, Blue Dun, page 124)
WING: Black bear hair
HEAD: Black

BLACK GORDON
(Plate XI)

HOOK: Low water salmon (2–6)
THREAD: Black (Flymaster 6/0)
RIB: Fine flat gold tinsel
BODY: Rear third, red wool; fore two-thirds, black wool
HACKLE: Black as a wet fly collar and pulled down (see model, Blue Dun, page 124)
WING: Natural black squirrel tail or black bear fibers.

REMARKS: This pattern, tied for me by Edward L. Haas, features an alternative material for the wing, as do many of the patterns Haas ties. Whether you use squirrel tail fibers or the coarser material of black bear depends on the type of water you are fishing. In still or quiet waters, the softer natural black squirrel tail fibers pulse and undulate more than the stiffer and heavier black bear hairs, and conversely, in fast water, the black bear, because of its consistency, will vibrate and pulse whereas the softer squirrel tail fibers will sleek down and not perform as well.

BLACK PRINCE
(Plate XI)

HOOK: Low water salmon (2–6)
THREAD: Black (Flymaster 6/0)
TAIL: Red hackle fibers (gap width past bend)
RIB: Fine flat silver tinsel

BODY: Rear half, yellow wool; fore half, black wool

HACKLE: Black as a wet fly collar (see model, Blue Dun, page 124)

WING: Black squirrel tail (tips to center of tail)

HEAD: Black

BLACK SPOOK
(Plate XI)

HOOK: Low water salmon (4–8)

THREAD: Black (Flymaster 6/0)

TAIL: Black hackle fibers (gap width past bend)

RIB: Medium flat gold tinsel

BODY: Red floss

HACKLE: Black as a wet fly collar (see model, Blue Dun, page 124)

WING: White bucktail (to center of tail)

HEAD: Black

BOBBIE DUNN

HOOK: Eagle Claw 1197B, Mustad 36890 (2–6)

THREAD: Black (Flymaster 6/0 or Monocord 3/0)

TAIL: Red bucktail fibers (gap width past bend)

BODY: Copper wire in connecting spirals

WING: White bucktail, over which a sparse bunch of red bucktail (both to center of tail)

HEAD: Black

BOSQUITO
(Plate XI)

HOOK: Eagle Claw 1197B (2–6)

THREAD: White (Flymaster 6/0 or Monocord 3/0)

TAIL: Red hackle fibers (gap width past bend) (sometimes two red hackle tips flaring outward)

RIB: Fine flat gold tinsel

BODY: Yellow wool (sometimes yellow chenille)

HACKLE: Black as a wet fly collar (see model, Blue Dun, page 124)

WING: White polar bear or white calf tail fibers (to center of tail)

HEAD: White

BOSS

HOOK: Eagle Claw 1197B, Mustad 36890 (2–6)

THREAD: Fluorescent fire orange (Monocord 3/0)

TAIL: Black monga ringtail fibers (or dyed black squirrel tail or black bear hair) (gap width past bend)

RIB: Medium flat silver tinsel

BODY: Black chenille

HACKLE: Fluorescent hot orange as a wet fly collar (see model, Blue Dun, page 124)

EYES: Silver bead chain links (eighth-inch diameter)

REMARKS: The tying of bead chain links to represent eyes is not difficult. However, unless the thread wrappings securing the chain links to the hook shank are properly wound, the eyes may swivel or be easily pulled off center. On a hook such as the Eagle Claw 1197B or some of the equivalent Mustad hooks, there is no flat platform upon which to rest the round stem connecting the two beads. Therefore, in addition to crisscrossing the thread around the bead chain links and the hook shank, the thread must also be wound on a horizontal plane under the bead chain links so that a platform can be constructed. I have found that if you place a drop of Crazy Glue (or any of the equivalent Super Glues) on the link stem and the hook shank, before the winding of thread to secure the links, the bead eyes will stay in place. Even then, it takes a goodly number of thread wraps, almost filling up the space to the top of the bead eyes, to make them thoroughly secure.

If you are winding these bead eyes on a salmon hook with a looped eye, you will not have this problem, because the end of the shank forming the loop aligns itself to the shank, forming a platform and preventing the swiveling of the bead chain link eyes.

BOULTON SPECIAL

HOOK: Eagle Claw 1197B, Mustad 36890 (2–6)

THREAD: Black (Flymaster 6/0)

TAIL: A red golden pheasant breast feather (gap width past bend)

BODY: Embossed silver tinsel

WING: Two badger saddle hackles flanked by two white saddle hackles flaring away (outward) from each other (see model, Black Ghost, page 207) (to end of tail)

HACKLE: A red golden pheasant breast feather, beard style (as long as tail)

HEAD: Black

BRAD'S BRAT

HOOK: Eagle Claw 1197B, Mustad 36890 (2–8)

THREAD: Black (Flymaster 6/0)

TIP: Fine flat gold tinsel

TAIL: White over orange bucktail, both sparse (gap width past bend)

BODY: Rear half, orange wool; fore half, red wool

HACKLE: Brown as a wet fly collar and pulled down (see model, Blue Dun, page 124)

WING: White bucktail, over which sparse orange bucktail (to center of tail)

HEAD: Black

REMARKS: This pattern, originated by Enos Bradner, is sometimes tied with cheeks of jungle cock eyes (or equivalent).

BRINDLE BUG
(Plate XI)

HOOK: Eagle Claw 1197B, Partridge salmon (2–6)

THREAD: Black (Flymaster 6/0 or Monocord 3/0)

TAIL: Two brown hackle tips flaring away from each other and tilted slightly upward (45-degree angle) (gap width past bend)

RIB (optional): Fine oval silver tinsel

BODY: Black and yellow variegated chenille (size 1)

HACKLE: Brown as a wet fly collar (see model, Blue Dun, page 124)

HEAD: Black

REMARKS: The tail is often tied using a single hackle tip.

BURLAP
(Plate XI)

HOOK: Eagle Claw 1197B, low water salmon (2–8)

THREAD: Gray, brown, or black (Flymaster 6/0)

TAIL: Natural gray deer hair fibers (gap width past bend)

BODY: Burlap sack material

HACKLE: Grizzly as a wet fly collar (see model, Blue Dun, page 124) (tips to point of hook)

REMARKS: Attributed to Arnold Arana and Ted Towendolly, this pattern is often

tied weighted. An early springtime version consists of a body of burlap and yellow wool with a black hackle.

CHAPPIE

HOOK: Eagle Claw 1197B, Mustad 36890 (2–8)

THREAD: Black (Flymaster 6/0)

TAIL: Two narrow grizzly hackle tips flaring outward from each other (gap width past bend)

RIB: Fine flat gold tinsel

BODY: Orange wool

HACKLE: Grizzly as a wet fly collar and pulled down (see model, Blue Dun, page 124)

WING: Two grizzly saddle hackles flaring away from each other (outward) (to center of tail)

HEAD: Black

CLARET SPEY

HOOK: Partridge salmon (4–8)

THREAD: Claret (Flymaster 6/0)

TAIL: None

BODY: Rear half, blue floss with fine flat

silver tinsel rib; fore half, blue seal fur
with oval silver tinsel rib

HACKLE: Gray heron wound as a wet fly
collar spey fashion (extending a full shank
length past bend) (see model, Blue Dun,
page 124) (substitute: gray ringneck pheasant rump feathers)

WING (optional): Four claret hackle tips
(to bend)

CHEEKS (optional): Jungle cock eyes (or
equivalent) (second eye showing)

HEAD: Claret

REMARKS: Originated by Robert Veverka.

COMET

HOOK: Eagle Claw 1197B, Mustad 36890
(2–8)

THREAD: Yellow (Monocord 3/0)

TAIL: Orange calf tail (as long as shank)

BODY: Oval silver tinsel

HACKLE: Yellow and orange wound together as a wet fly collar (see model, Blue
Dun, page 124)

EYES: Silver bead chain links (see model,
Boss)

REMARKS: There are a variety of comet
type patterns, and I suppose one could even
call these a subcategory of steelhead flies.

CONWAY SPECIAL

HOOK: Partridge salmon (4–8)

THREAD: Black (Flymaster 6/0)

TIP: Fine flat gold tinsel

TAIL: Red and white hackle fibers mixed
(gap width past bend)

RIB: Fine flat gold tinsel

PALMER RIB: Yellow hackle palmered
though body in an open spiral

BODY: Yellow wool

HACKLE: Red and yellow wound together
as a wet fly collar and pulled down (see
model, Blue Dun, page 124)

WING: A white goose quill section with a
thin strip of red goose quill section married to white on top and bottom (see
model, Parmachene Belle, page 134) (wing
tips to end of tail)

REMARKS: Originated by Dan Conway.

COPPER DEMON

HOOK: Eagle Claw 1197B, Mustad 36890
(2–6)

THREAD: Black (Flymaster 6/0)

TAIL: Orange marabou, short (one-third
gap width past bend)

UNDERBODY: Orange floss for taper

BODY: Oval copper tinsel

HACKLE: Hot orange as a wet fly collar
and pulled down (see model, Blue Dun,
page 124)

WING: Dyed hot orange calf tail (to end of
tail)

HEAD: Black

CUMMINGS' SPECIAL

HOOK: Eagle Claw 1197B, Mustad 36890
(2–8)

THREAD: Black (Flymaster 6/0)

TAIL: None

RIB: Fine oval gold tinsel

BODY: Rear third, yellow wool; fore two-
thirds, claret wool

HACKLE: Dyed claret as a wet fly collar
and pulled down (see model, Blue Dun,
page 124)

WING: Natural dark brown bucktail (gap
width past bend)

CHEEKS: Jungle cock eyes (or equivalent)
(second eye showing)

HEAD: Black

DR. SPRATELY

HOOK: Partridge salmon (2–10)

THREAD: Black (Flymaster 6/0)

TAIL: Grizzly hackle fibers (gap width past
bend)

RIB: Medium flat silver tinsel

BODY: Black floss

HACKLE: Grizzly, beard style (same length
as tail)

WING: Ringneck pheasant tail fibers (to
end of tail)

HEAD: Black

FALL FAVORITE
(Plate XI)

HOOK: Low water salmon (4–8)

THREAD: Red (Flymaster 6/0)

TAIL: None
BODY: Embossed silver tinsel
HACKLE: Bright red as a wet fly collar (see model, Blue Dun, page 124) (tips to point of hook)
WING: Hot orange polar bear (or equivalent) (to bend)
HEAD: Red

REMARKS: Polar bear fur is now illegal in the United States. Most fly tyers substitute calf tail, though white monga ringtail is good, and, if you can get some, the guard hairs from the American opossum are very silky and approximate the lustrousness of polar bear.

FLAME

HOOK: Eagle Claw 1197B, Mustad 36890 (4–8)
THREAD: Fluorescent fire orange (Monocord 3/0)
EYES: No. 6 silver bead chain links (eighth-inch diameter) (see model, Boss)
TAIL: Black bear hair fibers (gap width past bend) (substitute: skunk hair fibers)
RIB: Oval silver tinsel
BODY: Fluorescent red wool
HACKLE: Fluorescent orange as a wet fly collar (see model, Blue Dun, page 124)
HEAD: Fire orange

GOLDEN DEMON

HOOK: Eagle Claw 1197B, Mustad 36890 (2–6)

THREAD: Black (Flymaster 6/0)
TAIL: Golden pheasant crest feather curving upward to mirror bend
BODY: Oval gold tinsel in connecting spirals
HACKLE: Hot orange as a wet fly collar and pulled down (see model, Blue Dun, page 124)
WING: Red fox squirrel tail fibers (to end of tail)
HEAD: Black

ILIASKA IMP
(see under Salmon Egg Fly)

INDIAN FLY
(Plate XI)

HOOK: Low water salmon (2–8)
THREAD: Black (Flymaster 6/0)
TAIL: White hackle fibers (gap width past bend)
RIB: Fine flat silver tinsel
BODY: Rear half, yellow wool; fore half, red wool
HACKLE: Brown as a wet fly collar (as long-fibered as tail) (see model, Blue Dun, page 124)
WING: Natural black squirrel tail or black bear fibers (to end of tail) (see Black Gordon for reasons for choice)
HEAD: Black

JOE O'DONNELL

HOOK: Eagle Claw 1197B, Mustad 36890 (2–8)
THREAD: Red (Flymaster 6/0)
TAIL: Red and yellow hackle fibers mixed (gap width past bend)
BODY: Medium cream chenille (size 2)
WING: Two badger saddle hackles flaring outward (to end of tail)
HACKLE: Red and yellow wound together as a wet fly collar (see model, Blue Dun, page 124)
HEAD: Red

KALAMA SPECIAL
(Plate XI)

HOOK: Eagle Claw 1197B, Partridge salmon (2–8)
THREAD: Black (Flymaster 6/0)
TAIL: Red hackle fibers (gap width past bend)
PALMER RIB: Golden badger saddle hackle palmered through body with two extra turns taken at base of head
BODY: Yellow wool
WING: White bucktail (to center of tail)
HEAD: Black

KILLER
(Plate XI)

HOOK: Low water salmon (2–8)
THREAD: Black (Flymaster 6/0)
TAIL: Red hackle fibers (gap width past bend)

RIB: Medium flat silver tinsel

BODY: Bright red wool

HACKLE: Bright red as a wet fly collar (see model, Blue Dun, page 124)

WING: Natural black squirrel tail or black bear hair (see Black Gordon for reasons for choice)

HEAD: Black

McGINTY

HOOK: Eagle Claw 1197B, Mustad 36890 (2–8)

THREAD: Black (Flymaster 6/0)

TAIL: Red hackle fibers and bronze mallard flank fibers mixed (gap width past bend)

BODY: Medium black and yellow chenille wound as one

HACKLE: Brown as a wet fly collar and pulled down (see model, Blue Dun, page 124)

WING: Gray squirrel tail fibers (to center of tail)

HEAD: Black

McLEOD'S UGLY
(Plate XI)

HOOK: Eagle Claw 1197B, Partridge salmon (2–8)

THREAD: Black (Flymaster 6/0)

TAIL: Base fluff from red hackle feather (gap width past bend)

PALMER RIB: Grizzly hackle palmered through body with two extra turns taken

as collar (palmer rib fibers as long as gap width)

BODY: Medium black chenille (size 1)

WING: Natural black squirrel tail (or equivalent) (to end of tail)

HEAD: Black (some anglers prefer a red head)

NIGHT OWL

HOOK: Eagle Claw 1197B, Partridge salmon (2–6)

THREAD: White (Flymaster 6/0)

TAIL: Yellow hackle fibers (gap width past bend)

BUTT: Red chenille or wool

BODY: Oval silver tinsel

HACKLE: Orange as a wet fly collar (see model, Blue Dun, page 124)

WING: White calf tail (to center of tail)

HEAD: White

ORANGE DEMON

HOOK: Eagle Claw 1197B, Mustad 7957BX (2–8)

THREAD: Orange (Flymaster 6/0 or Monocord 3/0)

TAIL: Hot orange hackle fibers (gap width past bend)

BODY: Fluorescent yellow wool

HACKLE: Hot orange as a wet fly collar (see model, Blue Dun, page 124)

WING: Black bear hair (to center of tail)

HEAD: Orange

REMARKS: Originated by Lloyd Silvius. Sometimes the body is tied with fluorescent green wool.

ORANGE SHRIMP

HOOK: Eagle Claw 1197B (2–8)

THREAD: Orange (Flymaster 6/0 or Monocord 3/0)

TIP: Flat gold tinsel

TAIL: Red hackle fibers (gap width past bend)

RIB: Flat gold tinsel

BODY: Fluorescent orange wool

HACKLE: Orange as a wet fly collar and pulled down (see model, Blue Dun, page 124)

WING: White polar bear hair (or calf tail), over which a few strands of hot orange calf tail (all to end of tail)

CHEEKS (optional): Jungle cock eyes (or equivalent) (second eye showing)

HEAD: Orange

ORLEANS BARBER
(Plate XI)

HOOK: Eagle Claw 1197B, Partridge salmon (2–6)

THREAD: Black (Flymaster 6/0 or Monocord 3/0)

TAIL: Barred black and white wood duck fibers (gap width past bend)

BODY: Red chenille (size 1 or 2)

HACKLE: Grizzly as a wet fly collar (see model, Blue Dun, page 124)

WING: None

HEAD: Black

ORPHAN
(Plate XI)

HOOK: Low water salmon (2–8)

THREAD: Black

TAIL: Mallard flank fibers (gap width past bend)

RIB: Fine flat gold tinsel

BODY: Dark olive chenille (size 1)

HACKLE: Grizzly as a wet fly collar and pulled down (see model, Blue Dun, page 124)

WING: Gray squirrel tail fibers (to center of tail)

HEAD: Black

PAINTED LADY

HOOK: Partridge salmon (2–6)

THREAD: Black (Flymaster 6/0)

TAIL: A section of dyed orange goose fibers (gap width past bend)

LATERAL STRIPE: Fluorescent pink floss

BODY: Flat silver tinsel painted fluorescent yellow on top

WING: Yellow bucktail, over which orange bucktail (both to center of tail)

HEAD: Black with white eye and black pupil

REMARKS: After the tail is tied in, four strands of fluorescent floss are tied in on each side of the shank at the bend. The tinsel body is tied in and wound forward. The top of the tinsel body is painted fluorescent yellow. Then the floss is brought forward along the upper half of each side of the shank and tied down where the tinsel body ends, forming a lateral stripe. Then wings and head are added to complete the fly.

PETE'S SPECIAL

HOOK: Eagle Claw 1197B, Mustad 36890 (2–6)

THREAD: Black (Flymaster 6/0)

TAIL: Red hackle fibers (gap width in length)

BODY: Rear third, fluorescent green chenille; fore two-thirds, fluorescent red chenille (size 1 or 2)

HACKLE: Orange as a wet fly collar (see model, Blue Dun, page 124)

WING: White bucktail or calf tail (to end of tail)

HEAD: Black

REMARKS: Originated by Peter McVey.

POLAR SHRIMP
(Plate XI)

HOOK: Eagle Claw 1197B, Partridge salmon (2–8)

THREAD: White (Flymaster 6/0 or Monocord 3/0)

TAIL: Red hackle fibers (gap width past bend)

RIB: Fine silver wire

BODY: Orange wool (sometimes chenille)

HACKLE: Orange as a wet fly collar (see model, Blue Dun, page 124)

WING: White polar bear (or calf tail) (to end of tail)

HEAD: Red (sometimes white)

PURPLE PERIL
(Plate XI)

HOOK: Eagle Claw 1197B, Partridge salmon (2–8)

THREAD: Black (Flymaster 6/0 or Monocord 3/0)

TAG (optional): Flat silver tinsel

TAIL: Purple hackle fibers (or lavender) (gap width past bend)

RIB: Flat silver tinsel

BODY: Purple wool

HACKLE: Purple as a wet fly collar and pulled down (see model, Blue Dun, page 124)

WING: Natural black squirrel tail (to center of tail)

HEAD: Black

RAJAH

HOOK: Eagle Claw 1197B, Mustad 36890 (2–8)

THREAD: Black

TAIL: Fluorescent pink calf tail (gap width past bend)

BODY: Rear two-thirds, embossed silver tinsel; fore third, fluorescent pink chenille ribbed with embossed silver tinsel

WING: White polar bear hair (or equivalent) (to end of tail)

HACKLE: Fluorescent pink hackle as a wet fly collar, very long (tied in after wing has been secured) (see model, Blue Dun, page 124)

HEAD: Black

RED OPTIC

HOOK: Eagle Claw 1197B, Mustad 7970, Mustad 7957BX (2–4)

THREAD: Black (Monocord 3/0)

TAIL: None

BODY: Oval silver tinsel in connecting spirals

WING: Red bucktail fibers (shank length past bend)

HEAD: Formed by splitting a brass bead and securing it to the shank or building a thread head, either of which is painted black with a yellow eye and a black pupil

REMARKS: Optics are a style of pattern originated by Jim Pray. They are usually tied on a short-shanked hook such as the Mustad 7970, but occasionally on others.

RIO GRANDE KING

HOOK: Low water salmon (2–8)

THREAD: Black (Flymaster 6/0)

TIP: Fine flat gold tinsel

TAIL: Yellow hackle fibers (gap width past bend)

BODY: Black chenille (size 1)

HACKLE: Brown as a wet fly collar and pulled down (see model, Blue Dun, page 124)

WING: White bucktail (to center of tail)

HEAD: Black

ROGUE RIVER SPECIAL

HOOK: Eagle Claw 1197B, Mustad 36890 (2–8)

THREAD: White (Flymaster 6/0 or Monocord 3/0)

TAIL: Two orange hackle tips flaring away from each other (gap width past bend)

RIB: Fine oval gold tinsel

BODY: Rear third, yellow wool; fore two-thirds, red wool

WING: White bucktail divided as in a dry fly wing but slanting rearward over body (to tips of tail)

CHEEKS: Jungle cock eyes (or equivalent) (second eye showing)

HEAD: White

REMARKS: Sometimes the head is made black.

SALMON EGG FLY

HOOK: Mustad 3906, 3906B (6)

THREAD: White or red (Flymaster 6/0 or Monocord 3/0)

BODY: Glo-Bug yarn flared and trimmed to salmon egg shape (see model, Black Woolhead Sculpin, page 241)

REMARKS: These flies are made in a variety of colors from white through peach, orange, deep orange, and deep pink. They are referred to as Salmon Egg Fly, Single-Egg Fly, Glo-Bug Egg Fly, and in some cases acquire personalized name tags. One such is the Iliaska Imp, designed by Ted Gerken, which features a pink center in an all-white Glo-Bug yarn egg. The Iliaska Imp was named by Angus Cameron to prevent Gerken from giving it some other illicit or nondescript status. It is reputed to be one of the deadliest single-egg patterns for rainbows and to serve well as a steelhead and Pacific salmon fly pattern.

SCARLET WOMAN

HOOK: Mustad 36890, Partridge salmon (2–6)
THREAD: Red (Flymaster 6/0)
TAIL: None
BODY: Oval silver tinsel in connecting spirals
WING: Two large jungle cock eyes glued back to back and extending slightly past bend
SHOULDERS: Two red goose quill sections half the width of jungle cock, extending rearward not quite as far as jungle cock
HACKLE: Hot orange as throat, beard style
HEAD: Red

REMARKS: Originated by Martin Tolley.

SILVER ANT
(Plate XI)

HOOK: Eagle Claw 1197B, low water salmon (4–8)
THREAD: Black (Flymaster 6/0)
TAIL: Yellow hackle fibers (gap width past bend)
BODY: Embossed silver tinsel
HACKLE: Red as a wet fly collar (see model, Blue Dun, page 124)
WING: Natural black squirrel tail or black bear (to center) (See Black Gordon for reason for choice)
HEAD: Black

SILVER HILTON
(Plate XI)

HOOK: Eagle Claw 1197B, low water salmon (4–8)
THREAD: Black (Flymaster 6/0)
TAIL: Mallard flank fibers (gap width past bend)
RIB: Fine flat silver tinsel
BODY: Black chenille (size 1)
WING: Two grizzly hackle feathers flaring away from each other (to end of tail)
HACKLE: Grizzly wound as a wet fly collar in front of wing (see model, Blue Dun, page 124)
HEAD: Black

SKAGIT CUTTHROAT

HOOK: Eagle Claw 1197B, Partridge salmon (2–6)
THREAD: Black (Flymaster 6/0)
TAIL: Fluorescent red and orange hackle fibers mixed (gap width past bend)
BUTT: Fluorescent orange chenille (size 1 or 2)
BODY: Silver Mylar tubing

WING: White polar bear (or equivalent) (to end of tail)
SHOULDERS: Red goose wing quill sections (six or seven fibers) (one-third as long as wing)
HEAD: Black

SKUNK
(Plate XI)

HOOK: Eagle Claw 1197B, low water salmon (2–8)
THREAD: Black (Flymaster 6/0)
TAIL: Red hackle fibers (gap width past bend)
BUTT (optional): Fluorescent green chenille
RIB: Fine flat silver tinsel (sometimes oval)
BODY: Black chenille (size 1)
HACKLE: Black as a wet fly collar (see model, Blue Dun, page 124)
WING: White polar bear (or equivalent) (to center of tail)
HEAD: Black

REMARKS: When the optional butt of fluorescent green chenille is used, the pattern is sometimes referred to as the Skunk, Green Butt.

SKYKOMISH SUNRISE
(Plate XI)

HOOK: Eagle Claw 1197B, Partridge salmon, low water salmon (2–8)
THREAD: Sometimes black, sometimes red, sometimes white (Flymaster 6/0)

TAIL: Red and yellow hackle fibers mixed (gap width past bend)

RIB: Fine flat silver tinsel

BODY: Medium red chenille (size 1 or 2)

HACKLE: Red and yellow wound together as a wet fly collar and pulled down (see model, Blue Dun, page 124)

WING: Polar bear (or equivalent) (to end of tail)

HEAD: White, red, or black

SPRING WIGGLER

HOOK: Mustad 79580 (2–12)

THREAD: Black (Flymaster 6/0)

PALMER RIB: Grizzly hackle palmered through body

BODY: Burnt orange seal fur or burnt orange chenille (size 1)

TAIL, SHELL, AND HEAD: Fox squirrel tail fibers, fairly full, tied down at the bend so that the tips extend beyond the bend almost a full shank length. The squirrel tail fibers are then fastened to the shank just before the eye of the hook, forming a shell. The excess butts are trimmed beyond the eye of the hook so that a stub of head protrudes just past the hook eye.

REMARKS: Originated by Ron Spring, this pattern has become a favorite fly for the anglers fishing the Great Lakes tributaries.

STILLAQUAMISH SUNRISE

HOOK: Eagle Claw 1197B, Mustad 36890 (2–8)

THREAD: Fluorescent fire orange (Flymaster 6/0)

TAIL: Yellow and red hackle fibers mixed (gap width past bend)

RIB: Medium flat silver tinsel

BODY: Yellow chenille (size 1 or 2)

HACKLE: Orange as a wet fly collar and pulled down (see model, Blue Dun, page 124)

WING: White polar bear (or equivalent) (to end of tail)

HEAD: Red

THOR

HOOK: Eagle Claw 1197B, Mustad 36890 (2–8)

THREAD: Black (Flymaster 6/0)

TAIL: Hot orange hackle fibers (gap width past bend)

BODY: Red or dark red chenille (size 1)

HACKLE: Coachman brown as a wet fly collar and pulled down (see model, Blue Dun, page 124)

WING: White polar bear (or equivalent) (to end of tail)

HEAD: Black

TWO-EGG SPERM FLY

HOOK: Mustad 7957BX, 3906 (2–6)

THREAD: White (Flymaster 6/0)

REAR EGG: Fluorescent orange chenille (size 2 or 3)

HACKLE: White at center between the two chenille egg balls

FRONT EGG: Same as rear egg

REMARKS: This very simple pattern was designed to imitate the salmon eggs which steelhead feed upon. In some cases a wing of white marabou is added to simulate the flow of sperm over the eggs. These patterns are occasionally tied weighted.

UMPQUA SPECIAL
(Plate XI)

HOOK: Eagle Claw 1197B, Partridge salmon (2–8)

THREAD: Red (Flymaster 6/0)

TAIL: White bucktail (gap width past bend) (or soft white hackle)

RIB: Fine flat silver tinsel

BODY: Rear third, yellow wool; fore two-thirds, red wool

WING: White bucktail (to end of tail), over which red bucktail (two-thirds as long as white)

HEAD: Black

VAN LUVEN
(Plate XI)

HOOK: Partridge salmon (4–8)

THREAD: Black (Flymaster 6/0)

TAIL: Red hackle fibers (gap width past bend)

RIB: Fine flat silver tinsel

BODY: Red floss
HACKLE: Brown as a wet fly collar (see model, Blue Dun, page 124)
WING: White bucktail (to end of tail)
HEAD: Black

Steelhead Dry Fly Patterns

It's rare to find a section devoted solely to dry fly patterns for steelhead fishing. I have not found such a separate category in any of the current catalogs, including those from the western mail-order houses or the Great Lakes region. The dry fly is, of course, fished for steelhead as it is for the Atlantic salmon, but unless the proper conditions or situations prevail, most anglers do not find it as effective as the wet fly.

Western rivers, more often than not, are deep and wide, and this is another reason why the wet fly is preferred. Trey Combs, in *Steelhead Fly Fishing and Flies,* tells us that Harry Lemire, a well-known steelheader and gifted fly tyer, accomplished a most unusual feat by taking a steelhead of over twenty pounds on a dry fly. (The pattern was a

Black Irresistible designed by Lemire featuring a hackle collar trimmed close to the shank on the bottom. Except for the trimmed hackle, this pattern is the same as the Irresistible but dressed completely in black.) What makes this such an accomplishment is that the larger fish generally do not rise to the dry fly as readily as the smaller ones.

With few exceptions, the dry flies that are used for steelhead are those that were designed for trout. These include the Wulff-type patterns, the spun-hair Bombers and Irresistible, the larger hair wing caddis dry flies, and occasionally even such classic patterns as the March Brown or Bivisible.

BULKLEY MOUSE

HOOK: Partridge Wilson Dry Fly (4–10)
THREAD: Black (Flymaster 6/0 or Monocord 3/0)
TAIL: Tan deer or elk hair, tips extending to a point on shank directly above hook barb
BODY: Forward, or butt, section of tail lashed to shank with crisscross windings of thread
WING: Tan deer or elk hair flaring upward at a 45-degree angle (tips to end of tail)
HEAD: Flared and clipped deer or elk hair.

REMARKS: This particular fly was designed for steelhead and given to me by Collin Schadrech, who states that the Bulkley Mouse has proven to be effective on the Bulkley River in British Columbia and in most situations outfished all of the more popular wet flies. This fly is, in fact, the only pattern listed in a brochure printed by River West Tours in Telkwa, British Columbia, where Schadrech is a licensed guide. He further states that this pattern is taken "with reckless abandon."

The Bulkley Mouse, which has a wing similar to that of an Elk Hair Caddis, is tied somewhat like a low water salmon fly in that the tail, body, and wing are formed on the forward two-thirds of the hook. This pattern is also listed under general steelhead patterns in the Fly Shop catalog as the Disco Mouse and is tied using black deer or elk hair. The Fly Shop catalog states that it is also effective on the Babine and Kispiox drainages.

Saltwater Flies

THERE ARE very few saltwater patterns that have become recognized standards. Offhand, the only two I can think of are the various Lefty Deceivers and the Joe Brooks Blonde series, both of which are more of a fly design than a pattern since the wing, tail, and body may be changed. The saltwater category of flies is still a wide-open area, with many opportunities for pioneering. Each season sees innovations and improvements on what has been, and because of the introduction of a wealth of new materials such as Flashabou, pearlescent type tinsels, body glass, and V-rib material, newer patterns are constantly being devised. Angler/tyers are forever experimenting, and what may be in vogue one season may not even be catalogued the next.

Those saltwater anglers with a background in freshwater fishing and fly tying generally have an advantage in fly design and presentation. Familiarity with various materials, how they appear when wet, how imitative they become, and how they behave when fished is a prerequisite to success. Many freshwater patterns, especially those imitating baitfish, are as effective in salt water as they are in rivers, lakes, or streams. Angus Cameron and Jim Grace, while fishing for jack crevalle off Florida's west coast, noticed that the fish were taking something on the surface. Grace, a noted guide, asked if Angus happened to have any bass hair bugs with him. "I did," says Cameron, "and the jacks took them voraciously." On another occasion, when fishing for snook, a Gray Ghost streamer took the first fish.

The following patterns have proven successful in salt water. Most are listed by the catalog houses, but some are used quietly but effectively by local anglers who share them only with friends. The Snook Fly by Jim Hopkins is such a pattern and, as far as I know, has never appeared in print. Yet this fly is used repeatedly by clients who seek out his services in Florida.

Every saltwater fly tyer seems to have his own idea of how long a wing or tail should be, and it hardly matters as long as the pattern is behaving in a natural manner. Hooks used are generally stainless steel and preferred threads are those of fine diameter but with more tensile strength.

ARGENTINE BLONDE

HOOK: Mustad 34007 (1/0–2/0)
THREAD: Black (Monocord 3/0 or Flymaster 6/0)
TAIL: White bucktail fibers

BODY: Flat gold tinsel

WING: Medium blue bucktail

HEAD: Black

REMARKS: The Blonde series of flies was originated by Joe Brooks. Tail and wing are always made of bucktail of varying colors, depending upon the pattern. The tail is almost always two hook shanks long and the wing reaches almost to the end of the tail. The bucktail fibers in both wing and tail amount to roughly the diameter of a wooden matchstick.

The Blonde series of flies is used for various game fish, including striped bass, bluefish, jack crevalle, and others.

BALLYHOO

HOOK: Mustad 34007 (1/0–2/0)

THREAD: White (Nylon 2/0 or Monocord 3/0)

TAIL: A dozen white saddles four inches long flanked by two strips of silver Mylar on each side

BODY: White tying thread painted green on top

REMARKS: Originated by Lefty Kreh for various saltwater game fish.

BEND BACK
(Plate XII)

HOOK: Mustad 34007 (2–6)

THREAD: Black (Monocord 3/0)

TAG: Red wool

BODY: Fluorescent green chenille

WING: Grizzly hackle dyed green or squirrel tail dyed green (or equivalent) (tied inverted)

HEAD: Black

REMARKS: The Bend Back pattern is tied in other body colors and varying wing formations. It is used for snook, bonefish, and other species.

BLACK BEAUTY
BONEFISH FLY

HOOK: Mustad 34007 (4–8)

THREAD: Black (Flymaster 6/0 or Monocord 3/0)

BODY: Black wool or similar yarn

WING: Six strands of fine flat silver Mylar tied on underside of shank, over which black poly yarn (gap width past bend)

HEAD: Black

BLUE CRAB
(Plate XII)

HOOK: Mustad 34007 (1/0–2)

THREAD: White (flat waxed nylon size A)

BOTTOM: Three or four mallard flank feathers dyed yellow

TOP: Two or three ringneck rump feathers, over which three or four ringneck mottled "church window" feathers half as long

REMARKS: This pattern, originated by Lew Jewett, is usually tied weighted. Both topside and belly feathers are tied in a fanlike fashion extending slightly past the hook bend, giving the overall appearance of a flat triangle. When fished, the hook should ride inverted with yellow side skimming along the bottom. Sometimes a monofilament weed guard is added to prevent snagging. It is used for permit and bonefish.

BONBRIGHT TARPON FLY

HOOK: Mustad 34007 (5/0)

THREAD: Red or white (Monocord 3/0 or nylon 2/0)

TAIL: Two white flanked by two red hackle tips (gap width past bend)

BODY: Flat silver tinsel

WING: Four white saddle hackles (shank length past bend) (see model, Black Ghost, page 207)

CHEEKS: A section of red goose quill a quarter inch wide extending to end of body, over which jungle cock eyes covering two-thirds of goose quill

HACKLE: Wound as a dry fly collar (hackle size equals gap width)

REMARKS: Originated by Howard Bonbright.

BONEFISH LEECH

HOOK: Mustad 34007 (4–8)
THREAD: Yellow (Monocord 3/0)
TAIL: White marabou, over which yellow marabou (both a shank length past bend)
BODY: Yellow yarn (acrylic or wool) wound, flared, and trimmed to shape

REMARKS: Use the butt ends of the marabou to build up the hook shank. Wind a yarn body in the normal manner. Cut a number of half-inch sections of yarn and tie them to the body from bend to eye so that they flare upward. When the shank has been covered with flared pieces of yarn, run a fine-tooth comb through the fibers to make them expand and fluff. Then trim with scissors. Procedure is similar to that used for the Woolhead Sculpin (page 241)

BONEFISH SPECIAL
(see Chico's Bonefish Special)

BROWN SNAPPING SHRIMP

HOOK: Mustad 34007 (2–6)
THREAD: Black (Monocord 3/0)
BODY: Rear third, rust ultra-translucent dubbing; fore two-thirds, beige ultra-translucent dubbing
WING: Brown Fishair (1½ shank lengths past bend) (tied inverted)
HEAD: Black

REMARKS: Originated by Chico Fernandez for bonefish.

CHICO'S BONEFISH SPECIAL
(Plate XII)

HOOK: Mustad 34007 (4)
THREAD: Black (Monocord 3/0)
TAIL: Orange marabou (slightly past bend)
BODY: Flat gold tinsel overwrapped with gold monofilament
WING: White bucktail, over which two grizzly saddle hackles (both a shank length past bend) (tied on underside of shank; hook is first inverted in vise)
HEAD: Black

REMARKS: Originated by Chico Fernandez.

CHICO'S SHALLOW WATER TARPON FLY
(Plate XII)

HOOK: Mustad 34007 (3/0–5/0)
THREAD: Orange (Monocord 3/0)
WING/TAIL: One orange saddle hackle flanked by two grizzly saddle hackles on each side (six hackles in all) flaring outward from each other (tied in at bend and extending two shank lengths past bend)
COLLAR: Grizzly and orange mixed (tied in at bend)
BODY: Remainder of shank covered with thread and coated with orange lacquer

REMARKS: Originated by Chico Fernandez.

CHINESE CLAW

HOOK: Mustad 34007 (3/0–5/0)
THREAD: Black (Monocord 3/0)
TAIL/WING: Two yellow saddle hackles flanked by four grizzly saddle hackles (three on each side) flaring outward (all two shank lengths past bend)
COLLAR: Black and grizzly saddle hackles mixed (fiber length slightly more than gap width) (tied in just forward of bend)
BODY: Remainder of shank covered with black thread and lacquered.

REMARKS: Used for tarpon.

COCKROACH
(Plate XII)

HOOK: Mustad 34007 (2/0–4/0)
THREAD: Red (Monocord 3/0 or nylon 2/0)
TAIL/WING: Six grizzly saddles tied in near bend and extending two to two and a half inches beyond bend (shiny sides facing outward)
WING: Gray squirrel tail fibers tied in near head so that they completely surround shank and extend a quarter inch past bend and blend in with the grizzly saddle hackles
HEAD: Red

REMARKS: This Lefty Kreh original, a version of the Lefty's Deceiver for tarpon, is also tied with a wing of red fox squirrel tail fibers and a black head.

CRAZY CHARLIE, CREAM
(Plate XII)

HOOK: Mustad 34007 (4)
THREAD: White or cream (Monocord 3/0)
EYES: Silver bead chain links (eighth-inch diameter) (see model, Boss, page 275)
BODY: Pearlescent Mylar tinsel, over which is wound clear V-rib material, both extending halfway down into bend
WING: Cream/tan calf tail fibers tied on underside of shank and extending slightly past bend
HEAD: White or cream

REMARKS: This very popular bonefish pattern featured by the Orvis Company is an adaptation of the Nasty Charlie pattern originated by Bob Nauheim.

The bead chain eyes, which ride on the bottom of this inverted fly, must be securely fastened so that they do not twist off in either direction. For technique of securing to shank, see the pattern, Boss (page 275).

The Crazy Charlie pattern is also tied in pink, using pink calf tail for the wing, and in brown. The brown version uses an underbody of flat gold Mylar tinsel under the V rib, eyes of gold bead chain links, and wing of natural brown calf tail fibers.

DIAMOND HEAD
(Plate XII)

HOOK: Mustad 34007 (4–6)
THREAD: Yellow (Monocord 3/0)
EYES: Silver bead chain links (eighth-inch diameter) (see model, Boss, page 275)

TAIL: Ten to twelve pearlescent Flashabou fibers (tied short, barely past bend)
BODY: Pearlescent mylar tinsel over-wrapped with V-rib material
WING: A dozen strands of pearlescent Flashabou fibers flanked by two white hackle tips on each side (all a gap width past bend)
HEAD: Yellow chenille (size 1) wound behind, between, and in front of the bead chain eyes

REMARKS: This bonefish pattern, somewhat similar to the styles of Nasty Charlie, Crazy Charlie, and Mini Puff, is also tied with a head of red chenille.

FINGER MULLET
(Plate XII)

HOOK: Mustad 34007 (1/0–4/0)
THREAD: White (Monocord)
EYES: Silver bead chain links painted black (quarter-inch diameter) (see model, Boss, page 275)
TAIL: Two grizzly saddle hackles aligned with shiny side out (1½ shank lengths past bend)
REAR COLLAR: A bunch of brown antelope hair spun and flared around shank at bend and flowing rearward to blend in with the beginning of the tail feathers
BODY: White deer hair spun and trimmed to a shape flat on the sides and about as high as the gap width (see model, Irresistible, page 45)

REMARKS: This pattern is used for various saltwater game fish.

FRANKIE BELLE BONEFISH FLY

HOOK: Mustad 34007 (1–4)
THREAD: White (Flymaster 6/0 or Monocord 3/0)
BODY: White chenille (size 1 or 2)
WING: Natural brown bucktail tied on underside of shank (gap width past bend)
SHOULDERS: One grizzly hackle on each side of bucktail and as long
HEAD: White

FRANKIE BELLE POLY BONEFISH FLY

HOOK: Mustad 34007 (4–8)
THREAD: Red (Flymaster 6/0 or Monocord 3/0)
BODY: Fluorescent green chenille (size 1)
WING: White poly yarn tied on underside of shank (gap width past bend)
SHOULDERS: One grizzly hackle on each side of poly yarn and as long
HEAD: Red

REMARKS: You will find that most bonefish flies are tied in the inverted position, which helps keep these flies weedless and prevents them from snagging the bottom in the shallow waters where they are fished. This method also hides the hook point, barb, and lower bend to some extent.

GIBBS STRIPER FLY

HOOK: Mustad 34007 (1/0)
THREAD: Black (Flymaster 6/0 or Monocord 3/0)
BODY: Flat silver tinsel
WING: White bucktail (1½ shank lengths
past bend)
THROAT: Dyed red hackle fibers (halfway
to point of hook)
SHOULDERS: A section of dyed blue
goose quill fibers approximately an eighth
of an inch wide (gap width past bend)
CHEEKS: Jungle cock breast feather (or
substitute) extending rearward half a shank
length
HEAD: Black with yellow eye and red pupil

REMARKS: Originated by Harold Gibbs.
The jungle cock breast feather, which is black
with a white stripe, may be imitated with a
hen body feather of similar marking.

GLASS MINNOW
(Plate XII)

HOOK: Mustad 34007 (2/0-2)
THREAD: Black (Monocord 3/0)
BODY: Flat silver Mylar overwrapped with
V-rib material
WING: Green bucktail over white bucktail
(both a shank length past bend)
SHOULDERS: Two or three strips of
fine silver Mylar as a lateral stripe (three-
quarters as long as wing)
HEAD: Black with yellow eye and black
pupil

REMARKS: Used for various saltwater
game fish such as stripers, bluefish, and snook.

GOLDEN CLAW
TARPON FLY

HOOK: Mustad 34007 (3/0-5/0)
THREAD: Red (Monocord 3/0 or nylon
2/0)
TAIL/WING: Two grizzly saddle hackles
covered by four hot orange saddle hackles
(three feathers on each side) extending
approximately two to two and a half inches
past bend (all six hackles tied in at bend)
COLLAR: Grizzly and hot orange mixed
and wound as a dry fly collar covering
the rear quarter of shank
BODY: Shank is covered with bright red
thread to the eye and lacquered with clear
cement

REMARKS: Most tarpon flies have their
hackles tied in at the bend so that they do not
foul under the hook gap.

GOLDEN MANTIS SHRIMP

HOOK: Mustad 34007 (2-8)
THREAD: Red (Monocord 3/0)
BODY: Fluorescent green chenille (size 1
or 2)

WING: Golden yellow Fishair flanked by
two grizzly saddle hackles (both a shank
length past bend) (tied inverted)
HEAD: Red

REMARKS: Used primarily for bonefish.

GRASS SHRIMP (SATER)

HOOK: Mustad 34007 (1-4)
THREAD: Gray (Monocord 3/0)
TAIL: Olive saddle hackle tip tied down
into bend to imitate natural
SHELL: A strip of polyethylene material
RIB: Six-pound-test monofilament over shell
and body in an open spiral
PALMER RIB: Olive gray saddle hackle
palmered through body with two extra
turns of hackle near the eye; hackle on top
of shank is clipped close to body
BODY: Dark olive wool, over which is
wound gray seal fur (or equivalent)
EYES: Burnt stubs of twenty-pound-test
monofilament

REMARKS: This very effective striper and
weakfish pattern, originated by Robert Sater,
may seem to present a difficulty factor in the
tying because of its many components. It is,
however, relatively simple if the sequences
are followed in order. Briefly, here are the
steps.

1. Wind the tying thread onto the shank
from the eye to the bend. Tie in a single olive
hackle tip, forcing it downward into the bend.
Clip excess.

2. Tie in the six-pound-test monofilament
rib as far into the bend as the hackle tip.

3. Tie in the polyethylene strip. The strip can be made from a plastic poly bag. It should be about two inches long and taper from an eighth inch at one end to a quarter inch at the other. The narrow end is tied in directly in front of the monofilament rib.

4. Tie in the palmer rib of olive gray saddle hackle feather directly in front of the point where you tied down the poly strip. The hackle should be tied in at the tip as a folded hackle. (For technique of folding a hackle, see Blue Dun, page 124.)

5. Tie in a piece of dark olive yarn and wind it to the eye and back again to the thread. This will build the underbody of your fly.

6. Make a dubbing loop with your thread (double it and tie it over itself). (See also Casual Dress, pages 163–5, for technique of making a fur rope.) Coat the two sides of the thread loop with head cement and place elongated sections of gray seal fur (or equivalent) on the inside of the thread loop. Insert a crocheting needle or the crook of a dubbing needle into the loop and twist it until it forms into a rope. Move your tying thread to the eye of the hook. Grasp the fur rope with your hackle pliers and wind it forward, forming a fuzzy seal fur body. (You may have to repeat this step if the fur rope you have made is not long enough. I usually do it in two stages.) With a pair of scissors, trim any excess or wayward fibers that seem out of place.

7. Wind the palmer rib forward to the thread. Make sure the fibers slant rearward as you wind forward in an open spiral. Take an extra turn or two around the shank just before the eye. This area should have a little heavier concentration of hackle. Secure the hackle with the tying thread and snip the excess. Trim all the fibers from the top of the hook shank.

8. Pull the poly strip forward along the top of the hook shank and tie it down behind the eye. Clip the excess.

9. Wind the monofilament rib in an open spiral to the eye and tie it down with the thread. Clip the excess. The last spiral before the eye should be wider than the others to represent the back of the natural shrimp.

10. Cut a one-inch section of twenty-pound-test monofilament and hold it between the jaws of your hackle pliers. Put a flame to each end, burning back the monofilament and forming a pair of burnt stubs to resemble the eyes of the shrimp. Tie the eyes to the shank directly in back of the hook eye with crisscross windings of thread. Whip-finish.
Note: The poly strip, monofilament rib, and eye materials used in the photographic sequence were coated with a marking pen so they would photograph more clearly. Black tying thread was also used. The tyer, however, should use the colors listed in the recipe.

Tying Steps for Sater Grass Shrimp

a. Olive saddle hackle tip being tied down into bend of hook. Excess is trimmed off.

e. Olive yarn has been wound to eye and back to bend for underbody. Gray seal fur has been inserted into loop of thread prior to forming twisted rope.

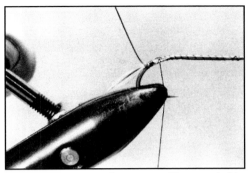

b. Piece of six-pound-test monofilament tied in at bend.

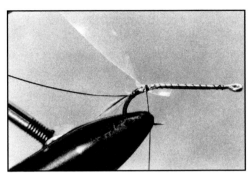

c. Strip of polyethylene bag tied in at bend.

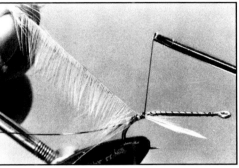

d. Olive gray saddle hackle feather being tied in by tip. Excess tip is trimmed off.

f. Tying thread has been brought to point before eye of hook. Gray seal fur is being twisted into rope.

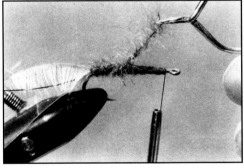

g. Gray seal fur rope being wound forward to form scraggly body.

h. Saddle hackle being wound in open spiral through body.

i. Hackle fibers on top being trimmed away.

j. Polyethylene strip being pulled forward and tied down behind hook eye.

k. Monofilament being wound forward in open spiral to form segmentation and being tied down behind hook eye. Burnt mono eyes have also been tied in.

l. Burning a section of twenty-pound-test monofilament to form eyes.

m. Completed Sater Grass Shrimp.

GREEN BONEFISH FLY

HOOK: Mustad 34007 (4–8)
THREAD: Black (Flymaster 6/0)
BODY: Flat silver tinsel
WING: Six strands of fine flat silver Mylar tied on the underside of shank covered by bright green strands of poly yarn (both a gap width past bend)
HEAD: Black

HI-TI

HOOK: Mustad 34007 (1/0–5/0)
THREAD: Red (Monocord 3/0)
TAIL: White bucktail, sparse (1½ shank lengths past bend)
WING: Four sparse sections of white bucktail tied an equal distance apart along the top of the shank and reaching to the end of the tail. A fifth clump of bucktail of blue, red, green, or yellow is tied in just before the eye and reaches back to align with the tips of the tail.

REMARKS: The wing sections must be tied in one clump at a time and the thread windings should be neat and connected to give the appearance of a red body under the wing.

HONEY BLONDE
(Plate XII)

HOOK: Mustad 34007 (1/0–2/0)
THREAD: Red (Flymaster 6/0 or Monocord 3/0)
TAIL: Yellow bucktail (twice shank length)
BODY: Flat gold tinsel
WING: Yellow bucktail (almost to end of tail)
HEAD: Red

REMARKS: Used for stripers, bluefish, and various other game fish.

HOPKINS TARPON FLY
(Plate XII)

HOOK: Mustad 34007 (3/0–5/0)
THREAD: Red
TAIL/WING: Six yellow saddle hackles (three on each side) flaring outward from each other, two hook shanks in length, flanked on each side by half a dozen lime green Flashabou fibers two-thirds as long
BODY: Red hackle palmered dry fly style in connecting spirals to head
HEAD: Red

REMARKS: Originated by Jim Hopkins.

HORROR
(Plate XII)

HOOK: Mustad 34007 (2–8)
THREAD: Red (Flymaster 6/0 or Monocord 3/0)
BODY: Rear two-thirds, yellow chenille (size 1 or 2); fore third, yellow chenille

WING: Natural brown bucktail tied on underside of shank between two-part chenille body (tips of bucktail extend half a shank length past bend)
HEAD: Red

REMARKS: Sometimes fluorescent orange chenille is used for the body. This pattern, originated by Pete Perinchief, is regarded as the first effective reverse wing style of bonefish flies.

LEFTY'S DECEIVER
(Plate XII)

HOOK: Mustad 34007 (2–3/0)
THREAD: Red (Flymaster 6/0 or Monocord 3/0)
TAIL/WING: Eight to ten white saddle hackles tied in at bend and extending approximately two and a half inches past bend. These are shouldered by six to eight strands of fine flat silver Mylar tinsel half as long as the saddle hackles.
BODY: Flat silver tinsel
WING: White bucktail tied so that it surrounds the shank and dense enough to form a fish shape when wet. Tips of fibers extend rearward as far as the Mylar tinsel.
TOPPING: Six to eight strands of peacock herl
HEAD: Red

REMARKS: This most popular of all saltwater flies is credited to Lefty Kreh. Kreh wanted a full-bodied fly, yet one that would sink rapidly after being cast—hence this particular design and construction. The Deceiver is used for various saltwater game fish and some of our larger freshwater species.

LEFTY'S DECEIVER, BLACK

HOOK: Mustad 34007 (2–3/0)
THREAD: Black (Flymaster 6/0 or Monocord 3/0)
TAIL/WING: Six to eight black saddle hackles tied in at bend and extending approximately two and a half inches beyond bend. These are shouldered by six to eight strands of fine flat silver Mylar tinsel half as long as the saddle hackles.
BODY: Flat silver tinsel
WING: Black bucktail tied so that it surrounds the shank and dense enough to form a fish shape when wet. Tips of fibers extend rearward as far as the Mylar tinsel.
TOPPING: Eight to ten strands of peacock herl
HEAD: Black

Lefty's Deceiver Series

As with popular flies in other categories, the Deceiver has been copied, improvised upon, and become a model for numerous other dressings. Some of the more popular colors cataloged by fly shops are the following.

BLUE AND WHITE DECEIVER

TAIL: White saddle hackles shouldered by silver Mylar
BODY: Flat silver tinsel
WING: White bucktail
TOPPING: Blue bucktail, over which peacock herl
HEAD: Black (sometimes with an optic eye)

GREEN AND WHITE DECEIVER

TAIL: White saddle hackles shouldered by silver Mylar
BODY: Flat silver tinsel
WING: White bucktail
TOPPING: Green bucktail, over which peacock herl
HEAD: Black

GREEN AND YELLOW DECEIVER

TAIL: Yellow saddle hackles shouldered by silver Mylar
BODY: Flat silver tinsel
WING: Yellow bucktail

TOPPING: Green bucktail, over which peacock herl
HEAD: Black

RED AND WHITE DECEIVER

TAIL: White saddle hackles shouldered by silver Mylar
BODY: Flat silver tinsel
WING: White bucktail
TOPPING: Red bucktail, over which peacock herl
HEAD: Black

RED AND YELLOW DECEIVER

TAIL: Yellow saddle hackles shouldered by silver Mylar
BODY: Flat silver tinsel
WING: Yellow bucktail
TOPPING: Red bucktail, over which peacock herl
HEAD: Black

WHITE DECEIVER

The same as Lefty's Deceiver but no topping.

YELLOW DECEIVER

TAIL: Yellow saddle hackles shouldered by silver Mylar
BODY: Flat silver tinsel
WING: Yellow bucktail
HEAD: Red (sometimes with an optic eye)

REMARKS: Many Deceivers are now constructed with an optic eye of black head, white eye, and black pupil, or red head, white eye, and black pupil.

LOVING BASS FLY

HOOK: Mustad 34007 (10)
THREAD: Black (Flymaster 6/0 or Monocord 3/0)
BODY: None
WING: White bucktail (shank length past bend)
HACKLE: Dyed red and wound as a dry fly collar (hackle size equals gap width)
HEAD: Black

REMARKS: Originated by Tom Loving for striped bass.

McNALLY SMELT

HOOK: Mustad 34007 (1/0–3/0)
THREAD: White (Monocord 3/0)
BODY: Flat silver Mylar tinsel
WING: White bucktail, fairly heavily applied (extending rearward two shank lengths past bend)

TOPPING: Fifteen to twenty strands of peacock herl
HEAD: White

REMARKS: Originated by Tom McNally for various species.

MINI PUFF
(Plate XII)

HOOK: Mustad 34007 (4–6)
THREAD: Beige (Monocord 3/0)
EYES: Silver bead chain links (eighth-inch diameter) (see model, Boss, page 275)
WING: Red fox squirrel tail fibers, over which two slim saddle hackles dyed orange (both a gap width past bend) (tied inverted)
HEAD: Beige chenille wound one turn behind bead chain eyes and one turn in front (like a little puff ball)

REMARKS: The hook shank remains bare. This quick-sinking pattern is a favorite for bonefish in the Bahamas.

NASTY CHARLIE
(Plate XII)

HOOK: Mustad 34007 (4)
THREAD: White (Monocord 3/0)
EYES: Silver bead chain links (eighth-inch diameter)
TAIL: Eight to ten strands of pearlescent Flashabou material (barely past bend)
BODY: Silver Mylar tinsel covered with fifteen-pound-test clear monofilament
WING: Four white saddle hackles (gap width past bend) (tied inverted)

REMARKS: Originated by Bob Nauheim for bonefish, this pattern has been copied and given other names.

NEEDLEFISH
(Plate XII)

HOOK: Mustad 34007 (3/0)
THREAD: Green (Monocord size A) (white can be used if later lacquered green)
TAIL: Two light blue saddle hackles, aligned with shiny side facing outward and extending one and a half shank lengths past bend, flanked by a sparse bunch of white bucktail on each side two-thirds as long as the saddle hackle
REAR COLLAR: Green marabou wound around shank at the bend like a skirt surrounding the tail for a third of its length
EYES: Large bead chain links painted yellow, quarter inch diameter tied an eighth of an inch forward of the skirt of marabou (see model, Boss, page 275)
BODY: Green Monocord fairly heavy between skirt collar and the eyes and tapering to a narrower diameter from the bead chain eyes to the eye of the hook. Thread is then coated with green lacquer.

REMARKS: Used for tarpon and other large game fish.

PALMER DILLER

HOOK: Mustad 34007 (1/0)
THREAD: Black (Monocord 3/0)
BODY: Flat silver tinsel

WING: Blue bucktail, over which red bucktail, over which white bucktail (all 1½ shank lengths past bend)

HEAD: Black

REMARKS: This striped bass pattern was originated by Harvey Flint.

PERMIT FLY
(Plate XII)

HOOK: Mustad 34007 (1/0–4)

THREAD: Tan (Monocord 3/0)

TAIL: Badger guard hair fibers flanked by two furnace saddle hackles (both a shank length past bend)

HACKLE: Furnace as a dry fly collar at bend

BODY: Tan chenille (size 1 or 2)

EYES: Glass eyes in an amber or orange shade

REMARKS: Also tied with dark brown calf tail fibers flanked by two dyed brown grizzly saddle hackles to form the tail, with a body of dark brown chenille.

PIGTAILS

HOOK: Mustad 34007 (1/0)

THREAD: Black (Flymaster 6/0 or Monocord 3/0)

BODY: Flat silver tinsel

THROAT: Red hackle fibers (almost to point of hook)

WING: Green bucktail, over which yellow bucktail, over which white bucktail (all a shank length past bend)

TOPPING: Six to eight strands of peacock herl (as long as wing)

HEAD: Black

REMARKS: Originated by Edward A. Materne. Primarily a striped bass pattern.

PINK SHRIMP

HOOK: Mustad 34007 (2–8)

THREAD: Gray (Flymaster 6/0 or Monocord 3/0)

TAIL: Pink bucktail (gap width past bend and slightly downward)

BODY: Flat silver tinsel

HOOD: Pink bucktail

HACKLE: Pink palmered through body and clipped on top (hackle size equals gap width)

REMARKS: The tail and hood are made from one clump of deer hair. After the tail has been formed, the excess bucktail is simply folded back and secured with a few turns of thread. After the body and hackle legs have been formed, the deer hair is brought forward over the body to form the hood. Originally designed for bonefish.

PLATINUM BLONDE

HOOK: Mustad 34007 (1/0–2/0)

THREAD: Red (Flymaster 6/0 or Monocord 3/0)

TAIL: White bucktail (twice shank length)

BODY: Flat silver tinsel

WING: White bucktail (almost as long as tail)

HEAD: Red

PURPLE ISLE TARPON FLY

HOOK: Mustad 34007 (3/0–5/0)

THREAD: White (Monocord 3/0)

TAIL/WING: A dozen strands of purple Flashabou, a shank length past bend, shouldered by three dyed royal blue grizzly saddles on each side, flaring outward and extending rearward two shank lengths past bend

BODY: Rear quarter of shank collared with purple fluff feathers from a rooster neck; second quarter of shank wound with purple neck hackle dry fly style; fore half of shank wound with thread lacquered with purple nail polish (or equivalent)

REMARKS: Originated by Mary Beth DeWierke. Dick Williams, a guide in Islamorada, Florida, states, "It is one of the best tarpon flies I have ever used."

RED AND YELLOW TARPON FLY
(see Stu Apte Tarpon Fly)

SAILFISH
(Plate XII)

HOOK: Mustad 34007 (4/0)

THREAD: White (flat waxed nylon size A or Monocord size A)

TAIL: White hair fibers, fairly full (six inches past bend)

BODY: Thread wrappings covering butts of tail fibers to wing area

WING: White hair fibers, four inches long, over which light green hair fibers, over which medium blue hair fibers topped with a dozen strands of green and silver Flashabou. Total thickness of wing is equal to tail (each about two matchsticks in diameter)

HEAD: White and lacquered with clear Cellire or varnish

REMARKS: The wing and tail can be made of deer tail, polar bear, goat, sheep, or a synthetic imitation, as long as it has the length. Used for billfish and other large species of saltwater game fish.

SALTY BEADY EYE
(Plate XII)

HOOK: Mustad 34007 (3/0–8)

THREAD: Color to suit, though usually white (flat waxed nylon size A or Kevlar)

TAIL: Four to six saddle hackles flaring outward (away from each other) (two shank lengths beyond bend)

EYES: Quarter-inch split brass bead

BODY: Medium silver Mylar tubing

SKIRT: Formed by de-coring ends of Mylar tubing

REMARKS: Originated by Matthew Vinciguerra for weakfish, striped bass, and other saltwater species. See p. 298 for tying steps.

After the tail of saddle hackles has been tied in at the bend, a twelve-inch piece of thread is tied in and left idling at the bend. The hook shank is then covered with tying thread to the eye and the thread is brought back to rest at a point one-quarter of an inch before the eye. Thread color is usually white, though red or other shades may be used if a particular color is desired for the lateral stripe.

The brass bead is split halfway (or may be purchased already split) and forced onto the shank behind the eye. The open end of the split on the bead should face up. Thread is then wound in front and in back of the bead and also through the split to secure it to the shank. Enough turns of thread should be taken so that the bead does not move or rotate.

A four-inch section of de-cored Mylar tubing is forced through the front of the eye of the hook. It's best to first create a small opening between the woven strands of Mylar with a dubbing needle. Half the Mylar tubing is pulled rearward along the top half of the shank and the other half along the bottom. Both are tied down with the thread that was previously tied in at the bend. After the Mylar is secured to the shank, the thread is whip-finished and the excess Mylar cut a half inch beyond the bend. The half inch of leftover Mylar is then unwoven with the point of a dubbing needle to form the flared skirt around the beginning of the tail fibers.

The beads are painted black or other colors for the optic effect and both body and eyes are coated with five-minute epoxy to protect the fly.

These flies may also be made with the Mylar formed rearward along the sides of the hook shank. In addition to the Salty Beady Eye, Vinciguerra also ties this pattern in other sizes and colors for use in fresh water.

SALTY DIVER, DARK
(Plate XII)

HOOK: Mustad 34007 (1/0)

THREAD: Red (Monocord size A)

BODY: Red thread wrapped around shank halfway down bend to center of shank

WING: Orange marabou, over which brown marabou tied in at center of shank and extending a shank length past bend, flanked by a grizzly hackle on each side flaring outward and topped by eight to ten strands of copper Flashabou

HACKLE: Grizzly dyed orange wound as a dry fly collar four to six turns from center of shank toward eye

TOPPING: Brown deer hair flared on top of shank, then black deer hair flared on top of brown deer hair. Tip ends of brown and black deer hair extend rearward as a top skirt to the bend. Butt ends of deer hair are trimmed even with orange deer hair head on the bottom but allowed to fan above orange deer hair head for a quarter of an inch.

HEAD: Orange deer hair spun and trimmed to a wedge shape (see Muddler Minnow, page 227)

REMARKS: This pattern is usually tied with a twenty-pound-test monofilament weed guard. Used for bonefish and other species.

Tying Steps for Salty Beady Eye

a. Saddle hackles have been tied in at bend and a twelve-inch piece of white thread has been tied in just in front of the saddle hackles.

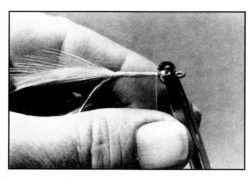

b. A split brass bead is being crimped onto shank behind hook eye.

c. Dubbing needle is used to form opening between braided strands of Mylar.

d. Mylar tubing has been forced over eye of hook.

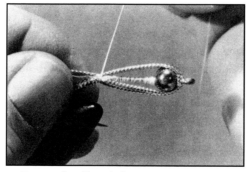

e. Two ends of braided Mylar being secured to shank at bend.

f. Excess mylar has been trimmed and the remainder, between tie-down point and end of hook, is being de-braided with dubbing needle to complete the fly.

SANDS BONEFISH FLY

HOOK: Mustad 34007 (1/0–4)
THREAD: Black (Flymaster 6/0 or Monocord 3/0)
BODY: None
WING: White bucktail (a shank length past
bend) flanked by two yellow saddle hackles
covered by two grizzly saddle hackles (both
as long as bucktail)
HEAD: Black

REMARKS: Originated by Hagen Sands.

SEA DUCER
(Plate XII)

HOOK: Mustad 34007 (1/0–4)
THREAD: Red (Monocord size A)
TAIL: Six white saddle hackles flaring away
from each other (three on each side) extending two shank lengths past bend,
flanked by three fine strands of silver Mylar
on each side
BODY: White saddle hackle palmered along
shank in connecting spirals to a point a
quarter shank distance before the eye
COLLAR: Red saddle hackle as a wet fly
collar (length of palmered body fibers and
collar slightly more than gap width)
HEAD: Red

REMARKS: This very old pattern, named
and popularized by Chico Fernandez, is used
for snook, tarpon, dolphin, and other species.
It is also tied in other tail and body colors of
yellow, yellow and grizzly mixed, and white,
blue, and grizzly mixed.

SILVERSIDES
(Plate XII)

HOOK: Mustad 34007 (2–4)
THREAD: White (Monocord 3/0)
TAIL: Olive marabou (gap width past bend)
BODY: Formed in the manner of Janssen's
Minnow (page 219) and Threadfin Shad
(page 236); painted a pale olive gold on
top half and silver Mylar allowed to show
through on bottom half; has a black lat-
eral stripe
EYES: Painted white with black pupil

REMARKS: As in the pattern Janssen's
Minnow, this is a hard, realistic imitation.
The results are usually as good as the tyer's
artistic talents with a paintbrush. It is used
for various species such as striped bass, bluefish, and snook.

SKIPPING BUG
(Plate XII)

HOOK: Long-shanked, kinked (2/0–3/0)
THREAD: White (Monocord 3/0)
BODY: Shaped and painted cork, Styro-
foam, or equivalent

REMARKS: Originated by Bill Gallasch.
When stripers, bluefish, and certain other
game fish are feeding on the surface, this
particular type of fly (perhaps "lure" is a
better word) is deadly. You don't want to be
without it.

Skipping bugs are handcrafted affairs. Generally cork is used, though some of the newer
Styrofoam materials are much tougher. You
will need a long-shanked, kinked hook. I
used to use the Mustad 9082A, but I don't
believe this model is made anymore. Saltwater fly rodders prefer hooks that are stainless,
tinned, nickel-plated, or have a similar finish,
but even a bronzed hook will do. If you're
fishing for bluefish or a similar toothy species,
you'll do well to use the cheapest material,
both in hook and in body form, since the
popper type fly may not last more than a fish
or two anyway.

Popular colors of skipping bugs are white;
red and white; blue and white; red and yellow;
and black and white. The darker color usually forms the fore third, or head, of the bug.

Making a skipping bug does not come
under the art of fly tying. Even if you are a
poor craftsman, the fish don't seem to care.

A clump of bucktail, about the same length
as the body, is lashed to the hook shank at
the bend. A piece of cork is cut and shaped
so that it has a natural, oblong taper and a
slightly angled cut at the face, or fore end.
(Sometimes these bodies can be purchased
pre-shaped and pre-cut, but I have not found
them listed in the larger sizes.)

A slot is cut on the underside of the cork,
which is then slipped onto the kinked part of
the hook shank. Winding a base of thread on
the shank and covering it with glue allows
the cork to hold its position more securely.
Cement is also added to the crevice of the
slot after the cork cylinder has been affixed.
Any remaining gaps or apertures are filled in
with wood putty or the like.

The cork body gets a final sanding for
smoothness and it is then painted the desired

color. Some tyers prefer to paint eyes on their bugs and use two sizes of dowels to form a white eye and a black pupil, or a yellow eye and a black pupil.

SNOOK FLY
(Plate XII)

HOOK: Mustad 34007 (2/0)

THREAD: White and (for head) hot orange (Danville flat waxed nylon size A)

TAIL: None

BODY: None

WING: A clump of white bucktail or goat hair (the thickness of a wooden matchstick) extending past the bend for one and a half inches, flanked and covered by two or three wide white streamer hackles on each side as long as the bucktail. The bucktail fibers are tied to the shank in such a manner that they completely surround it and the hackle feathers are secured flat against the sides, hiding and covering the shank.

SHOULDERS: Half a dozen lime green or pearlescent Flashabou fibers on each side, as a lateral stripe, extending rearward three-quarters of wing length

NOTE: At this point, construction is temporarily halted so that the weed guard may be affixed (see below).

TOPPING: Six strands of peacock herl (as long as wing)

HEAD: Painted hot orange with white eye and black pupil

REMARKS: This original pattern was designed by Jim Hopkins, a transplanted Beaver-

kill angler who now resides in Naples, Florida, where he is considered by many to be *the* guide and expert when it comes to snook fishing.

This pattern offers little difficulty, but a weed guard is necessary when fishing for snook lying behind mangrove roots. The weed guard is made from a piece of stainless-steel leader material (.017 gauge).

Cut a two-inch section and with a pair of duck-billed pliers bend one end of the wire into a U. Bend the wire once more, forming a right angle to the U.

Slip the end of the U-shaped wire through the eye of the hook from the bottom up so that the short end lies on top of the shank just before the eye.

Secure it with a couple of turns of thread and let it hang straight downward for now.

Tie in the six strands of peacock herl for the topping.

Build a head in the normal manner using a hot orange thread. Whip-finish. Apply a liberal coat of head cement.

Paint or dowel on the optic eyes. They can be white with a black pupil or yellow with a black pupil. Allow to dry completely.

Lacquer the entire head with a good five-minute epoxy. Hopkins uses one called Formula No. 4, which will not fade or discolor in salt water.

When the epoxy has dried, bend the hook guard backward to within a quarter inch of the hook point and make a final small bend with the pliers. Clip excess beyond that.

Tying Steps for Snook Fly

a. White goat hair or bucktail has been tied to shank.

e. Weed guard being secured to shank with thread.

b. Three white saddle hackles have been tied in to flank white hair fibers on each side, and half a dozen lime green Flashabou fibers have been added as shoulders.

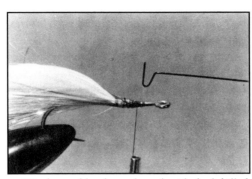

c. Weed guard has been shaped with duck-billed pliers.

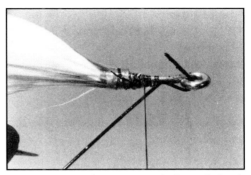

d. Weed guard being inserted through hook eye from under shank.

f. Peacock herl topping being tied in.

g. Completed Snook Fly with built-up head of thread which has been lacquered and painted with eyes. Note also that end of weed guard has been bent to parallel hook shank.

STRAWBERRY BLONDE

HOOK: Mustad 34007 (1/0–2/0)

THREAD: Black (Flymaster 6/0 or Monocord 3/0)

TAIL: Orange bucktail (twice shank length past bend)

BODY: Flat gold tinsel

WING: Red bucktail (almost as long as tail)

HEAD: Black

REMARKS: Used for striped bass, bluefish, and other species.

STU APTE TARPON FLY

HOOK: Mustad 34007 (3/0–5/0)

THREAD: Red (2/0 nylon or 3/0 Monocord)

TAIL/WING: Two bright orange saddle hackles covered by two yellow saddle hackles off each side of shank at bend, flaring outward from each other (dull side facing out) and extending beyond bend approximately two and a half inches

HACKLE: Orange and yellow saddle hackles wound as a dry fly collar and covering the rear third of the shank (hackle size equals gap width)

REMARKS: The hook shank of this pattern is wrapped with red thread forward of the collar, almost to the eye. A short space on the shank (an eighth to a quarter inch) is left bare. The thread is then painted with fluorescent orange or red lacquer.

This pattern is sometimes tied using red and yellow saddle hackles. Also, some angler/tyers prefer to have four yellow hackles covering the red or the orange.

TARPON FLY (No. 2)
(Plate XII)

HOOK: Mustad 34007 (1/0–2/0)

THREAD: Red

TAIL: Red calf tail fibers (1½ shank lengths past bend)

BODY: Flat gold tinsel overwrapped with twenty-pound-test Stren golden fluorescent monofilament line (substitute: yellow body glass for overwrap)

WING: Orange calf tail fibers (almost to tips of red tail fibers)

HEAD: Red

REMARKS: This design by Jim Hopkins is similar to the Strawberry Blonde, except that the wing and tail colors are reversed and the body of gold tinsel is overwrapped with a clear material, giving it a translucent effect.

The pattern is used for tarpon under fifty pounds and for these it is a favorite in southwestern Florida.

WHISTLER, RED AND WHITE

HOOK: Mustad 34007 (3/0)

THREAD: Red (Monocord 3/0)

EYES: Silver bead chain links (see model, Boss, page 275) (quarter-inch diameter)

TAIL: White bucktail tied full (about two matchsticks in diameter) flanked by a sparse bunch of red bucktail on each side to form a lateral stripe (all two shank lengths past bend)

BODY: Rear third, red chenille (size 3); middle third, white saddle hackle palmered to bead chain eyes

REMARKS: This pattern is also tied with yellow bucktail for the tail flanked by two grizzly saddle hackles. Another, listed as Harold's Whistler, is tied with a black bucktail flanked by grizzly saddles dyed brown, a rear third body of black chenille, and a palmered middle third body of grizzly saddle hackle dyed brown. The Whistler originated with Dan Blanton.

Part IV

COLOR PLATES
AND APPENDIXES

Adams   Black Gnat   Blue Dun   Brown Bivisible   Delaware Adams   Female Beaverkill

Ginger Quill   Henryville Special   Katterman   Mosquito   Royal Coachman   Fan Wing Royal Coachman

(all above flies tied by Walt Dette)

Blue Winged Olive (Flick)   Conover   Cream Variant   Dark Cahill   Dun Variant   Gray Fox

Gray Fox Variant   Light Cahill   Light Hendrickson   March Brown   Quill Gordon   Little Sulfur Dun (tied by Mary Dette Clark)

(all of the above tied by Winnie Dette except Little Sulfur Dun)

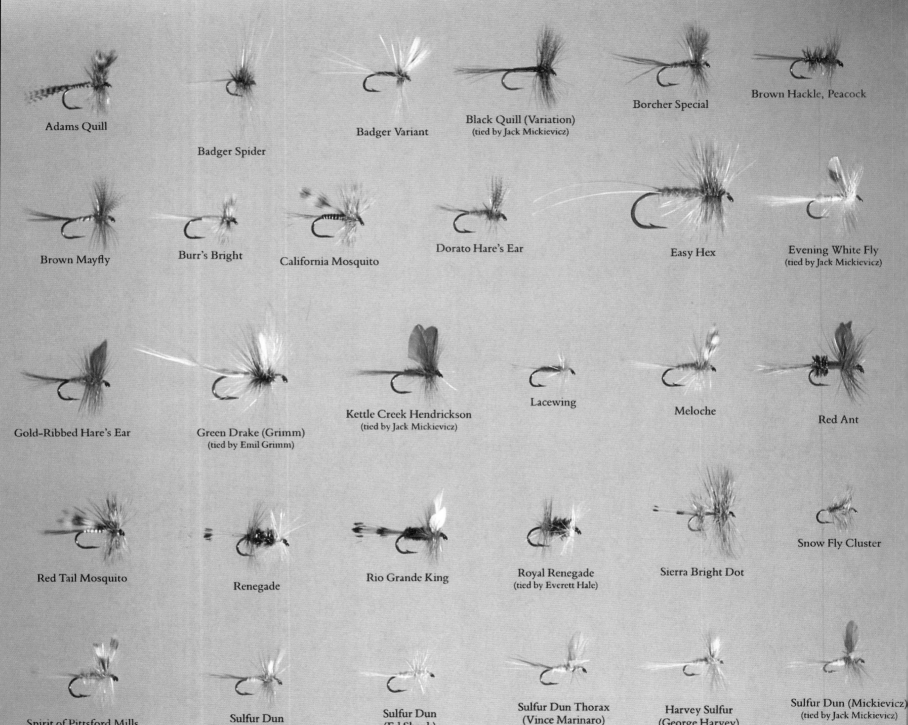

PLATE II STANDARD DRY FLIES

Adams Quill

Badger Spider

Badger Variant

Black Quill (Variation)
(tied by Jack Mickievicz)

Borcher Special

Brown Hackle, Peacock

Brown Mayfly

Burr's Bright

California Mosquito

Dorato Hare's Ear

Easy Hex

Evening White Fly
(tied by Jack Mickievicz)

Gold-Ribbed Hare's Ear

Green Drake (Grimm)
(tied by Emil Grimm)

Kettle Creek Hendrickson
(tied by Jack Mickievicz)

Lacewing

Meloche

Red Ant

Red Tail Mosquito

Renegade

Rio Grande King

Royal Renegade
(tied by Everett Hale)

Sierra Bright Dot

Snow Fly Cluster

Spirit of Pittsford Mills

Sulfur Dun
(Charles Fox)

Sulfur Dun
(Ed Shenk)

Sulfur Dun Thorax
(Vince Marinaro)

Harvey Sulfur
(George Harvey)

Sulfur Dun (Mickievicz)
(tied by Jack Mickievicz)

Adams Irresistible
(tied by Doug Pope)

Adams Wulff
(tied by Peter Burton)

Ausable Wulff
(tied by Herb Dickerson)

Brown Drake

Coachman Trude

Coffin Fly
(tied by Mary Dette Clark)

Goofus Bug
(tied by Doug Pope)

Gray Wulff
(tied by Walt Dette)

Green Drake
(Western)

Grizzly Wulff
(tied by Herb Dickerson)

H & L Variant

The Usual
(tied by Herb Dickerson)

Humpy
(tied by Kathy Buchner)

Eastern Humpy

Ken's No-Hackle Hex
(tied by Jay Neve)

Michigan Caddis

Mr. Rapidan

Polar Hex
(tied by Jay Neve)

Royal Wulff
(tied by Walt Dette)

Soda Butte Special
(tied by Peter Burton)

Hendrickson Sparkle Dun
(tied by Craig Mathews)

Troth Hair Spider
(tied by Al Troth)

Haystack
(tied by Herb Dickerson)

Kolzer Yellow

White Wulff
(tied by Walt Dette)

PLATE IV

CADDIS DRY FLIES

Au Sable King
(Tied by Frank Cupp)

Chuck Caddis

Dark Caddis
(Rosborough)

Delta Wing Caddis, Gray

Elk Hair Caddis
(tied by Al Troth)

Goddard Caddis
(tied by Ralph Kanz)

Gus's Grannom

Hare's Ear Fluttering Caddis
(tied by Jack Mickievicz)

Hemingway Caddis

Hermaphrodite, Olive
(tied by David Goulet)

October Caddis

Peacock Caddis

Pheasant Caddis

Saco Caddis

Solomon's
Hair Wing, Gray

Spent Partridge Caddis
(tied by Dick Jabens)

Stalker Caddis, Night
(tied by Peter Burton)

Wisconsin Fa
(tied by Robert Sch

TERRESTRIALS

Beetle

Elk Hair Flying Ant
(tied by Jack Gartside)

Gartside Pheasant Hopper
(tied by Jack Gartside)

Green Leaf Hopper

Henry's Fork Hopper

Inchworm

Jassid

Jay/Dave's Hopper
(tied by Kathy Buchner)

John's Elk Hair Hopper

Letort Cricket

McMurray Ant

Michigan Hopper

Muddler Hopper

Rod's Black Ant
(tied by Rod Yerger)

Woodchuck Hopper

PLATE V

MIDGES AND SPINNERS

Brown Drake
Spinner

Adams Midge

Tricorythodes
Dun

Tricorythodes
Male Spinner

Tricorythodes
Female Spinner

Hexegenia Spinner

PARACHUTE FLIES

Adams Parachute

Brown Drake Paradrake
(tied by Rob Van Kirk)

Clumper Midge
(tied by Si Upson)

Elk Wing Parachute Caddis
(tied by Tom Rosenbauer)

Loop Wing
Paradun, Olive

Rio Grande
King Parachute

THORAX AND NO-HACKLE FLIES

Adams Thorax

Brown Drake Thorax

Quill Gordon Thorax

Slate/Olive No-Hackle
(tied by Rene Harrop)

Gray/Yellow No-Hackle
(tied by Rene Harrop)

ADULT STONEFLIES

Bi-Fly Yellow

Fluttering Golden Stonefly

Henry's Fork Salmon Fly
(tied by Rob Van Kirk)

MacSalmon
(tied by Al Troth)

Reg's Little Stonefly
(tied by Reg Baird)

Jughead

K's Butt Salmon Fly
(tied by Dave McCarthy)

Sofa Pillow

Swann's Stonefly

Stimulator

PLATE VI   UNDERWATER VIEW OF VARIOUS TYPES OF DRY FLIES

Standard Adams · Adams Silhouette · Adams Thorax · Adams Parachute · Hairwing Royal Coachman

Hendrickson (Flick) · Cut Wing Blue Winged Olive · Compara Dun Light Cahill · No Hackle (Gray/Yellow) · Cream Variant

The purpose of the above photographs is to show what the trout sees when a particular type of dry fly floats into its "window." While the view of flies from below may seem somewhat distorted to us, trout have no problems discerning one from another. Even with the distortion, it is obvious that those patterns in which the bodies are closer to the surface of the water have a more prominent wing silhouette. The most realistic in appearance of these is the No-Hackle. This, however, does not necessarily prove that trout prefer those with the more perfect outline. The hackled flies, such as the Standard Adams, the Hendrickson, and the Cream Variant, create an illusion of movement which, under certain stream conditions, will trigger a response when others don't. Generally, it is conceded that the fully-hackled type fly will fish better in fast or riffly water while the low-bodied or hackle-less type creates a better posture or impression in slower or poollike water. Though they are shown here as the trout sees them, I leave it to the individual fly tyer to decide which to tie and to use when fishing.

All the patterns shown on this plate were photographed by Dr. Frederic Oswalt. (see page 114)

 Black Gnat

 Blue Dun

 Coachman

 Cowdung

 Dark Cahill

 Dark Hendrickson

 Female Beaverkill

 Ginger Quill

 Gold-Ribbed Hare's Ear

 Leadwing Coachman

 Light Cahill

 Light Hendrickson

 March Brown

 Pale Evening Dun

 Quill Gordon

 Royal Coachman

 Blue Winged Olive

(all of the above tied by Mary Dette Clark)

LARVAE, PUPAE AND SHRIMP

 Cream Peeking Caddis

 Cro Caddis

 Emergent Pupa, Ginger

 Gill Ribbed Larva
(tied by Pete Zito)

 Jorgensen Fur Caddis Pupa, Gray

 Latex Larva, Cream
(tied by Pete Zito)

 Olive Scud

 Solomon's Caddis Pupa, Gray
(tied by Pete Zito)

 Sow Bug

 Speckled Sedge

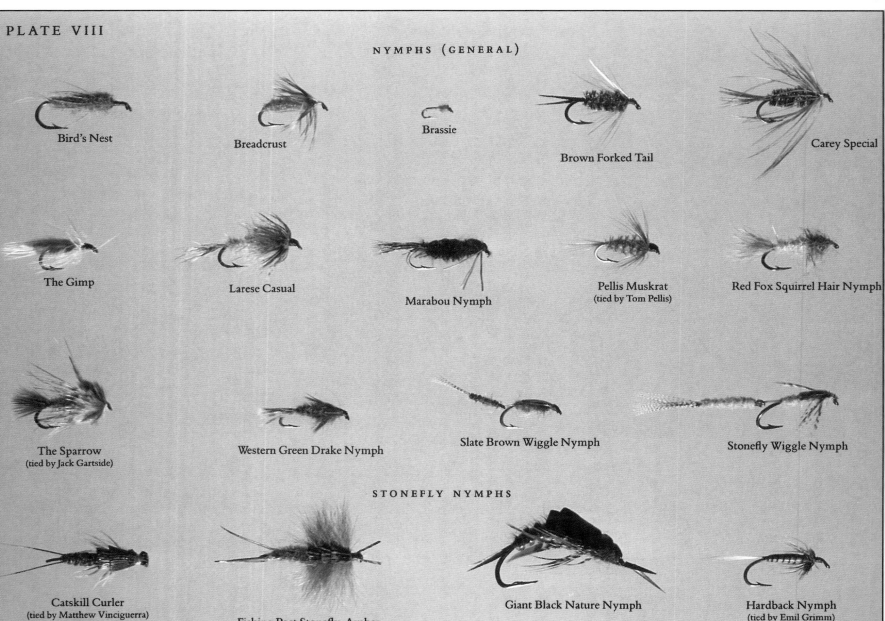

PLATE VIII

NYMPHS (GENERAL)

Bird's Nest

Breadcrust

Brassie

Brown Forked Tail

Carey Special

The Gimp

Larese Casual

Marabou Nymph

Pellis Muskrat
(tied by Tom Pellis)

Red Fox Squirrel Hair Nymph

The Sparrow
(tied by Jack Gartside)

Western Green Drake Nymph

Slate Brown Wiggle Nymph

Stonefly Wiggle Nymph

STONEFLY NYMPHS

Catskill Curler
(tied by Matthew Vinciguerra)

Fishing Post Stonefly, Amber

Giant Black Nature Nymph

Hardback Nymph
(tied by Emil Grimm)

EMERGERS

Green Drake Emerger

Mosquito Emerger

Partridge and Orange
Emerger

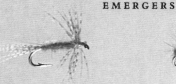

Philo Caddis Emerger
(tied by Jack Gartside)

Philo Mayfly Emerger
(tied by Jack Gartside)

Timberline Emerger

Brady's Smelt
(tied by Dick Brady)

Counterfeiter

Dolly's Hat
(tied by Dick Brady)

The Llama

Janssen Minnow

Golden Minnow
(tied by Rodney Flagg)

Gray Ghost

Hornberg

Slim Richard

Joe's Smelt

Lead Eye Rabbit Leech

Maynard Marvel
(No. 1)

Pintail Smelt
(tied by David Goulet)

Ted's Yesterday

Ryer's Sockeye

Threadfin Shad

Hornberg,
Downwing

Thunder Creek
Black-Nosed Dace
(tied by Keith Fulsher)

Thunder Creek
Rainbow Trout
(tied by Keith Fulsher)

Thunder Creek
Redfin Shiner
(tied by Keith Fulsher)

Blue Ribbon Woolhead Sculpin

Woolly Bugger

Black Angus

Bunny Fly

Dahlberg Diver

Flashabou Tandem
(tied by Rodney Flagg)

Footer Special
(tied by David Footer)

Kevin's Warrior
(tied by Dick Brady)

PLATE X

SALMON FLIES

Black Bear, Orange Butt

Black Fitch Tail

Blue Rat

Blue Sapphire

Brown Fairy

Colburn Special

Black Cosseboom

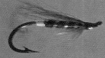
Crossfield

(all of the above tied by Keith Fulsher)

Green Highlander

Pack Rat

De Feo's Black Diamond

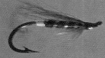
Laxa Blue

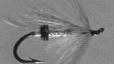
Orange Blossom

Oriole

Garry

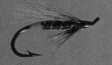
Red Butt Miramichi

Rusty Rat

Sheepscot Special (No. 2)

Silver Blue

Silver Rat

(all of the above tied by Charles Krom)

SALMON DRY FLIES

Ausable Wulff
(tied by Herb Dickerson)

Buck Bug

Woodchuck Wulff

Bomber

MacIntosh

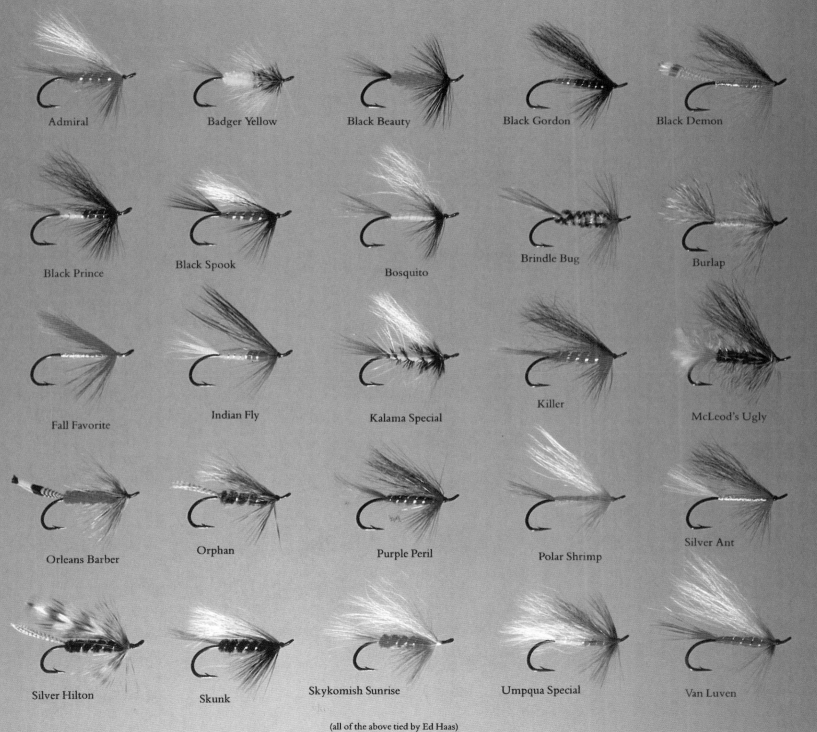

Admiral

Badger Yellow

Black Beauty

Black Gordon

Black Demon

Black Prince

Black Spook

Bosquito

Brindle Bug

Burlap

Fall Favorite

Indian Fly

Kalama Special

Killer

McLeod's Ugly

Orleans Barber

Orphan

Purple Peril

Polar Shrimp

Silver Ant

Silver Hilton

Skunk

Skykomish Sunrise

Umpqua Special

Van Luven

(all of the above tied by Ed Haas)

PLATE XII SALT WATER FLIES

Bend Back

Blue Crab

Chico's Bonefish Special

Mini Puff

Nasty Charlie

Horror

Diamond Head

Crazy Charlie, Cream

Glass Minnow

Cockroach

Finger Mullet

Honey Blonde

Hopkin's Tarpon Fly
(tied by Jim Hopkins)

Lefty's Deceiver

Chico's Shallow Water Tarpon Fly

Permit Fly

Needlefish

Salty Beady Eye
(tied by Matthew Vinciguerra)

Salty Diver, Dark

Tarpon Fly (No. 2)
(tied by Jim Hopkins)

Snook Fly
(tied by Jim Hopkins)

Skipping Bug

Sea Ducer

Silversides

Sailfish

Hooks

THERE IS, believe it or not, more than one hook manufacturer, yet O. Mustad and Son of Gjøvik, Norway, seems to have some 95 percent of the business of selling hooks to fly tyers. It is not only because Mustad makes a good hook, but primarily because this brand has been used for so many years and referred to in so many volumes of fly-tying literature that the name Mustad has become a household word among fly tyers. When pattern recipes are copied for a new book or article or for inclusion in catalogs, the Mustad name is brought forward. Most fly tyers have grown accustomed to one model or another for a particular dry fly or nymph, and very few will experiment with other hooks if the pattern calls for a Mustad. Mustad, in short, must be quite happy going round and round in a seemingly unending cycle.

Mustad manufactures a greater variety of fly-tying hooks than other companies, and special-izes in hooks for almost all categories of flies, producing short, long, fine, extra-fine, stout, and what have you variations for the simulation of a multitude of insects in both fast and slow water. The company will even make special hooks to order if a minimum quantity is ordered by the dealer or fly tyer.

Still, while Mustad hooks do the job, there are some hooks from other manufacturers which are just as good, and in some cases, better for a particular pattern. I have used Mustad hooks for over thirty years, yet I would be remiss if I did not at least report the hooks of some of the other companies to show you what they have to offer. In my opinion, there are a few models worth your consideration.

Some fly tyers prefer the English hook made by Partridge. The Partridge hook is handmade. In fact, it is individually handled, one hook at a time, in no fewer than five separate operations, which include pointing, forging, bowing (making the eye of the hook), setting (positioning the eye of the hook in an up or down angle), and counting and inspection. (Partridge does not use a weighing device; thus when hooks are counted into packages they are inspected at the same time. Flawed hooks are simply discarded.) Three other operations are semi-automated, but even here a worker stands by to check for accuracy and quality. Needless to say, the Partridge hook is more expensive than most, but the manufacturer claims that the extra cost is offset by a higher percentage of perfectly formed hooks. Indeed, I cannot remember ever having found a faulty hook in one of their packages.

Partridge dry fly hooks are made of very fine wire, endearing them to not a few fly tyers. With these hooks, a bit of common sense is called for. When fishing in slow-moving waters such as the English meadow streams, a fine wire hook, sparsely dressed, may be perfect. On the other hand, when fishing some of our faster, swifter rivers harboring good-sized fish, a bit more steel is required. The Captain Hamilton, a really fine dry fly hook made by Partridge, also features a short point and much smaller barb for quick penetration. Many prefer this hook over its equivalent, the standard Mustad 94840. Depending on the conditions, I will use either the Captain Hamilton or the Mustad 94840 for much of my dry fly fishing.

Partridge, finally, seems to be making some well-deserved friends in this country and is being featured in more and more catalogs.

Surprisingly, the VMC hook, which is manufactured in France and distributed by VMC in St. Paul, Minnesota, is carried by very few suppliers. VMC is the new kid on the block and, I suppose, simply has not gotten to know the neighborhood yet. I hope this will change, since the hooks are well made and have impressed me. The steel seems to be of exceptional quality and the hook points outstandingly sharp. While VMC does not carry the variety of styles required by most fly tyers, there are a few models well worth investigating. The company advertises that its hooks are being made with new machinery using modern technology. One dealer who does list them in its catalog is the Fly Shop in Redding, California.

TIEMCO, or TMC as it is known when referring to a model number, is also another relatively new hook on the market. The choice of styles is limited: three dry fly hooks, two nymph hooks, and one streamer model. The hooks are made in Japan, and as with quite a number of things coming from that country today, the quality is good. It is my understanding that TIEMCO uses a new technology involving chemicals to point and barb the hooks. They appear to be finely pointed with a small barb similar to the Partridge and the steel seems very strong for its fine diameter. Some of these hooks are carried by the Orvis Company under its own name.

The thing to remember about all hooks is that they are the last link between you and the fish. If the hook point is not sharp, you may not hook the fish in the first place. If the temper of the steel is faulty, the hook may straighten out or break. The design must be correct for the imitation being tied. Hook eyes should close properly since small gaps or openings invite leader abrasion. These are the things to check before putting a hook in your vise.

In most mail-order catalogs you will see reference made to certain terms describing specific hooks. They are here interpreted.

HOOK BENDS
Only three types of hook bends need concern the fly tyer today, namely, the model perfect round, the sproat, and the limerick.

HOOK EYES
In order to save space, catalog designers may abbreviate the terms denoting hook-eye shape.

Turned-down Tapered Eye (TDTE): The eye has been turned down in the same direction as the hook point. "Tapered" means that the end of the wire forming the eye has a diminishing diameter and is tapered in to the shank. Now and then you will find reference to a "ball eye," in which the end of the wire has not been tapered.

Turned-up Eye (TUE): The eye has been angled upward in the opposite direction of the hook point.

Ringed Eye: The eye is on a horizontal plane with the hook shank.

Looped Eye: May be up or down. The wire is brought back alongside the shank and the doubled end is left open. This type of eye will not fray leaders.

HOOK FINISH
Nearly all hooks, with the exception of those made of stainless steel, have a protective coat of some sort. The most common is the bronzed finish, used mostly on trout flies. Japanned black is another type of coating, found nearly always on salmon hooks. Other coatings are of tin, nickel, cadmium, and gold plate.

HOOK SIZE, SHANK LENGTH, AND WIRE VARIATIONS
Hooks are measured in even sizes from size 2 (large) to 28 (small). Larger hooks are designated by a zero placed after their numbers, such as 1/0 (smallest) to 9/0 (largest).

You will find some hooks designated as 1X long (1XL) or 3X long (3XL) or, for that matter, as 2X short (2XS). This means that they are longer or shorter in shank length when compared to other models in the same size. There is no standard formula for determining shank lengths, since these may vary from manufacturer to manufacturer. However, a formula which may be employed is this: A 1X long hook in a size 12 has the same shank length as a standard size 10. For example, if you were to take a Mustad 3906 size 10 and place it against the shank of a Mustad 3906B size 12, the shank lengths would be equal, though the gap and bend size would be different.

HOOK WEIGHTS

Hook wires are designated as standard, light, or heavy, and this is even more widely interpreted by manufacturers. What Partridge calls standard may be light for Mustad, whereas a VMC or TIEMCO standard may fall somewhere in between. Generally speaking, when a hook is made of 3X fine (3XF) wire it is much finer when compared to a hook by the *same* manufacturer. Stout or heavy-wire hooks are usually designated as such.

In the overall weight of the hook, the shank length also has some bearing. You will decide for yourself which hook is best for a given purpose after examining all the hooks of various manufacturers. The suggestions in the pattern listings in this book are those of the originator, or those, in my opinion, which will best serve the recipe or the fishing situation.

FORGED

All hooks are cold-forged after they have been bent into the round, sproat, or limerick bends forming their special shape. Because the process of bending may cause stress in the structure of the metal wire, the hooks are placed between two steel surfaces which are brought together against the hook, thus forging strength and uniformity back into the hook in the areas of the bend, barb, and point.

STRAIGHT

Usually after the word "forged" you will find the word "straight." This means that the hook point and barb at the bottom of the bend have not been offset and that the bend has been perfectly formed so that the hook point is directly under the shank.

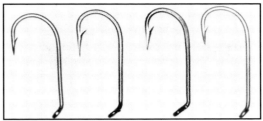

Partridge L3A   Mustad 94840   VMC 9280   TIEMCO 100

A Magnified Look at Hook Point, Barb, and Bend Design by Manufacturer (all size 12 dry fly hooks)

HOLLOW POINT

This term is confusing, for the point of a hook cannot be hollow. The term simply means that the sides of the hook point are very slightly concave rather than rounded.

DRY FLY HOOKS

MUSTAD 94840

Hollow point, forged, straight, turned-down tapered eye, bronzed, extra-fine wire. Sizes 2–28. This is the most used hook in fly tying today. It has become the standard for most dry flies. Features a model perfect bend.

PARTRIDGE L3A

Labeled the Captain Hamilton dry fly hook, this is a lightweight (probably 2XF), bronzed hook with the most perfect model perfect bend; it is gaining more interest among anglers in the United States. Barb is very short, as is the point of the hook, more so than on hooks of other manufacturers. This assures both quick penetration and easy removal. The downward angle of the down eye is slight, somewhere between the

Mustad 94840 down eye and a ringed eye. Hook gap is slightly wider than that of the Mustad. Sizes 8–22.

VMC 9280

This hook is similar to the Mustad 94840 but has a slightly shorter point, which makes for easier penetration. The bend is a modified model perfect. Features a specially forged and bronzed shank with a turned-down eye that tapers snugly back to the shank with no apparent open area that has to be closed by thread. Wire is listed as extra light, but this is really a standard light wire (about the same as the Mustad 94840). This is a superlative hook for standard dry flies and adult caddis. Sizes 6–20.

VMC 9281

The same as the VMC 9280 except that it has an up eye.

PARTRIDGE L4A

The same as the Partridge L3A except that it is made of extra-fine wire. This is a delicate hook capable of carrying sparse materials and still floating the fly. I suspect that in sizes 16 and smaller extra care must be taken with the fish or the hook may straighten.

PARTRIDGE L3B

The same as the L3A except has a turned-up eye.

TMC 100

This TIEMCO dry fly hook features fine wire, is forged, and has a modified model perfect bend with a wide gap. Barb and hook points are short, similar to the Partridge style. This is a nice hook.

MUSTAD 94833

Hollow point, forged, straight, turned-down tapered eye, bronzed, 3XF wire. Sizes 2–20. This hook should only be used when materials will not support a standard light-wire hook, especially in sizes 16 and smaller. (If a light-wire hook is required, use a Partridge.)

MUSTAD 94842

The same as the Mustad 94840 except has an up eye.

MUSTAD 94845

The same as the Mustad 94840 except that it is barbless. This hook is becoming more and more popular because of catch and release programs promoted by Trout Unlimited and the Federation of Fly Fishermen. Sizes 10–22.

MUSTAD 94836

The same as the Mustad 94840 except that it is IX short. This is a compact yet strong hook for many mayflies and adult caddis imitations.

WET FLY HOOKS

MUSTAD 3906

Hollow point, sproat bend, turned-down tapered eye, bronzed. Sizes 2–20. This may just be the most popular hook used on wet flies. It is made of heavy wire on a standard-length shank.

MUSTAD 3906B

The same as the Mustad 3906 except that it is IX long. It is sometimes used for nymphs as well as wet flies.

VMC 8526

Similar to the Mustad 3906 but seems to be made of stouter steel. Bronzed, turned-down tapered eye which closes very snugly, sproat bend with an extra-sharp point. An exceptionally good wet fly hook. Sizes 8–16.

VMC 8527

The same as the VMC 8526 except that it is IX long. Similar to the Mustad 3906B. Sizes 8–16.

PARTRIDGE L2A

A medium-weight wet fly hook with a down eye and model perfect bend. Has a wider gap than the Mustad. A hook to try. Sizes 2–20.

PARTRIDGE G3A

A heavy-wire bronzed sproat bend hook to get the fly down deeper. It is flat-forged and has a gentle angle to its down eye. Similar to the Mustad 3906 except for its extra weight.

PARTRIDGE K12ST

A recent introduction for use as a larva hook. It is japanned black with a ring eye and a slightly curved shank. It is approximately a 3XL and should have good hooking capabilities compared to similarly styled hooks.

PARTRIDGE K4A

Designed for shrimp, scuds, and larvae, this hook has a rounded shank with a down eye. It is made of heavy wire and an extra-wide gap since good clearance is usually lost in this type of design. Sizes 10–16.

PARTRIDGE K2B

Also known as the Yorkshire Sedge, this hook features a slightly curved shank with an up eye.

Especially designed for caddis larvae imitations. Sizes 10–14.

MUSTAD 37160

This is a 6X long-shanked hook which has been bent into a curve for caddis larvae and scud patterns. When using this hook always select a hook a size smaller than the size of fly because of the long shank. In other words, if you are tying a size 14 caddis larva, use a size 16 hook. Gap clearance on this hook is poor. The Partridge K2B is a better choice.

MUSTAD 7957B

Hollow point, forged, straight, turned-down tapered eye, bronzed. This is a slightly heavier hook than the Mustad 94840. It is used in smaller sizes (16–18) for dry flies and in larger sizes for bass bugs.

MUSTAD 7957BX

The same as the Mustad 7957B except that it is made of much heavier wire.

MUSTAD 7948A

Very similar to the Mustad 7957B except that it is a hair shorter. Also used as a dry fly hook in the smaller sizes when extra strength of wire is required.

NYMPH HOOKS

VMC 9279

A really fine nymph hook similar to the Mustad 9671 but with perhaps a bit heavier steel. It has a 2X long shank and a model perfect bend. It is bronzed, forged, and has a down-tapered eye. A good choice for most mayfly and some of the smaller stonefly nymphs. Sizes 2–18.

MUSTAD 9671
Model perfect bend, heavy wire, bronzed, turned-down tapered eye, hollow point. One of the most used hooks for mayfly nymphs.

MUSTAD 9672
The same as the Mustad 9671 except that it has a 3X long shank. Used on both mayfly and stonefly nymphs as well as on hoppers and muddlers. A very versatile hook. Sizes 2–16.

PARTRIDGE H1A
Bronzed, down eye, 2X long with a wider gap than Mustad or VMC. Barb is fine and hook point short for quick penetration and easy release. Perhaps a shade lighter in weight than the Mustad 9671. Sizes 2–16.

MUSTAD 79580
Turned-down tapered eye, bronzed, model perfect bend. A 4X long-shanked hook used on sculpins, muddlers, and some hoppers. Now and then it is used for streamer patterns. A good all-around hook. Sizes 2–16.

PARTRIDGE H3ST
This specially designed hook for flat-bodied nymphs features a split shank that angles outward and comes back together near the bend. Originated by Keith Draper for the Partridge Company.

STREAMER AND BUCKTAIL HOOKS

MUSTAD 9575
The favorite streamer hook of most fly tyers. This is a 6X long, hollow point, bronzed hook with a limerick bend. Its special feature is the looped eye which prevents fraying of leaders and also presents a flat surface upon which to tie the materials for the wing. Sizes 2–14.

MUSTAD 3665A
The same as the Mustad 9575 except that it has a tapered down eye.

MUSTAD 79580
See under Nymph Hooks.

VMC 9283
A 4XL hook with a model perfect bend. Similar to the Mustad 79580. Bronzed, down eye, forged. Good for muddlers, hoppers, and the larger stoneflies. Sizes 2–18.

MUSTAD 38941
Hollow point, sproat bend, turned-down tapered eye, 3X long shank. Used primarily for hoppers and muddlers. Sizes 2–14.

MUSTAD 9674
Hollow point, forged, straight, bronzed with a 4X long shank. A ringed-eye hook. Sizes 2–14.

MUSTAD 94720
Hollow point, forged, straight, turned-down tapered eye. Features an 8X long shank. Used most often for landlocked salmon and lake trout flies. Sizes 2–12.

MUSTAD 36620
Hollow point, forged, straight, bronzed. Has a 6X long shank and a ringed eye. Used for tying the Thunder Creek series of streamer flies. Sizes 2–12.

PARTRIDGE CS15
Labeled as a 10XL long-shanked streamer hook, this model was specially designed to duplicate the hook used by Carrie Stevens when she dressed her famous patterns, such as the Gray Ghost. It is listed in the Hunter's Angling catalog.

PARTRIDGE CS5
A relatively new hook by Partridge in its Connoisseurs series (advertised as the Keith Fulsher Thunder Creek hook). Made of extra-heavy, round, high-carbon Sheffield steel wire, it features a small, tightly closed ringed eye for tying Thunder Creek style flies and others requiring this configuration. Shank is 6X long with a round bend and generous gap. Point is short but sharp and the barb is small. Finish is a blue-black.

PARTRIDGE CS2
Featured as a steelhead and salmon hook. It is japanned black with a looped-down eye and made of extra-heavy wire. A fine-looking hook. Sizes 4–10.

MUSTAD 7970
Hollow point, bronzed, turned-down ball eye. This hook is featured as 5X strong, indicating a rather heavy wire. Used primarily for steelhead flies. Sizes 2–10.

EAGLE CLAW 1197B
Heavy wire, long-shanked, down eye, bronzed. A favorite hook for western steelhead and coho salmon. Sizes 2–10.

EAGLE CLAW 1197N
The same as Eagle Claw 1197B except that it has a nickel finish.

SALMON HOOKS

PARTRIDGE SINGLE SALMON HOOK (M)
Japanned black, looped-up eye, standard shank.
A favorite worldwide. Sizes 2/0–10.

PARTRIDGE LOW WATER SINGLE (N)
The same as the code M except that it has
lighter wire. Sizes 2/0–10.

WILSON DRY FLY SALMON HOOK
Also made by Partridge, this has been the standard hook for salmon dry flies. It is japanned
black, has a looped-up eye and a sproat bend.
Sizes 2–12.

**PARTRIDGE WILSON DOUBLE
LOW WATER SALMON HOOK**
Features a fairly small looped-up eye, a desir-
able trait. Japanned black. Sizes 5/0–12.

MUSTAD 36890
Japanned black with a turned-up looped eye.
One of the more popular salmon fly hooks in
the United States. Sizes 3/0–10.

MUSTAD 3582C
A japanned-black double salmon hook with a
turned-up oval eye. Also a favorite in the United
States. Sizes 5/0–10.

MUSTAD 90240
Japanned black, turned-up looped eye, fine wire.
This hook, which has a shorter shank than the
Wilson salmon dry fly hook, is preferred by
some tyers since its proportions are closer to
conventional dry fly standards. Sizes 2–10.

SALTWATER HOOKS

MUSTAD 34007
Stainless steel, superior point, sproat bend,
forged, and features a ringed eye. Perhaps the
most popular of all saltwater fly hooks. Sizes
5/0–8.

MUSTAD 3407
The same as the Mustad 34007 except that it is
tinned. Some anglers do not like to use a stainless-
steel hook such as the Mustad 34007 because it
will not disintegrate if left in the fish, hence this
alternative. Same size range.

MUSTAD 3408B
The same as the Mustad 3407 except that it has
down eye.

BASS BUG AND
PANFISH HOOKS

MUSTAD 33900
Ringed eye, bronzed, with a sproat bend. This
hook features a kinked or hump shank which
prevents it from twisting when inserting into
the slot of a cork popper. Sizes 3/0–12.

MUSTAD 33903
The same as the Mustad 33900 except that it has
an extra-long shank, which is preferred by many
tyers of popping bugs.

MUSTAD 37187
Sometimes called the "Stinger," this hook features a ringed eye and a wide gap. It is made of
light wire for tying bass hair bugs and other
flies. Sizes 1/0–6.

Fly-Tying Materials

THE PRIMARY purpose of this section is to give you a better understanding of the materials that are related to the patterns in this book and to let you know where the rarer ones may be obtained. (Where a material is easily obtainable, I have listed no sources.) In addition, it also contains some of the newer materials, especially those of a synthetic nature, which may one day replace some of the old standards, or result in the formation of new designs and futuristic patterns. Some of these materials are already in use though they have not shown up in pattern recipes as such. That there are many, many other materials which can be used for fly tying goes without saying, and that more will be discovered and developed is a certainty as long as flies are tied.

As with most things, a little common sense in the use of materials will serve the fly tyer well and in the long run save time and money. Familiarity with the various furs and feathers will enable you to substitute when necessary, to improvise when you are in a creative mood, and overall to have a broader scope in the tying of all the categories of flies.

It is not my intention to delve into all the uses of fly-tying materials. That is a subject unto itself. For those who wish to pursue it further, I have listed several publications in the bibliography that deal with this area in much greater detail.

AFRICAN GOAT: One of the more popular fur blends serving as a substitute for the restricted English seal's fur is the African Goat. It was first developed as a dubbing fur by Jack Mickievicz of Jack's Tackle and introduced to the fly-tying public by the Orvis Company. It is easier to work with than seal fur while still retaining the bristliness and glitter of the natural seal.

Quite a bit of work is involved in preparing this particular blend. The natural fibers of the African Goat are some five to six inches long and must first be cut into quarter-inch lengths. It is then fed into a mangling machine to further reduce the fibers to an intermingled mass. Thereafter it is placed in a blender with other colors to form the particular shade desired. It is sometimes listed as Angora Goat by the fly shops which retail it. Some companies which carry it are the Orvis Company, Kaufmann's Streamborn Flies, and Hunter's Angling Supplies.

ANGORA SPUN FUR (see Spun Fur)

ANTELOPE: The hair of this western animal is used primarily for spinning hair-bodied flies. The head of the Spuddler pattern is a good example. Color ranges from a light reddish brown from the back of the animal to white on the underside. The fibers near the skin are more of a pale gray. Antelope hair is much coarser and heavier than that of either the white-tailed deer or the mule deer and will not pack as tightly. It is also a bit fragile and may break under the pressure of tying thread. Nor does it take as well to dyeing. For these reasons, it is not much used.

ANTRON: Antron was originally manufactured by Du Pont for the clothing and garment industry for the purpose of producing a very fine frosted effect in fabrics. When it was no longer fashionable it was taken out of production. The frosted, sparkling type of fiber was, however, of interest to fly tyers in general and in particular to Gary LaFontaine, who used it to form the bodies of the emerging pupa imitations he described in his book *Caddisflies.*

For a time it seemed that this product would no longer be available to fly tyers. But Jack Mickievicz found a solution. He persuaded Du Pont to make one bale of clear Antron, which is the very least their machines would turn out and which weighs almost 800 pounds. Mickievicz is now the only supplier of Antron in the country, but considering how much he did obtain, that should last quite a while.

Antron dubs fairly easily and has the sparkle. For those dealers who wish to obtain it for their shops, I suggest you contact Jack's Tackle, a wholesale distributor. Dealers who list it in their catalogs are North Country Angler, Kaufmann's Streamborn Flies, and Dale Clemens Custom Tackle. Any of the commercially sold yarns which are listed as "sparkle" or "frosted" may be substituted.

BADGER: A creamy tan fur sometimes used for dubbing material. However, it is primarily the guard hairs which most fly tyers are interested in. These are of a cream color with black and white barring at the tips.

BEAD CHAIN: This is the type you will find on a key chain. It is manufactured in a gold and silver color and used to form the optic eyes on certain steelhead and saltwater patterns. Two who carry this item are the Orvis Company and Kaufmann's Streamborn Flies.

BEADS: Though used quite often in terminal tackle rigs in saltwater fishing and in certain specialized situations in freshwater fishing, the various colored beads are mostly used as attractors on some of the larger tandem streamers. They are carried by some bait and tackle shops and most hobby shops. One fly shop that keeps a stock on hand is Flagg's Flies.

BEAVER: The velvety-soft underfur of this water animal is highly water-resistant and thus very desirable for forming the bodies on dry flies. Color range is from silver gray near the base to brown gray near the tips. Because of its silky nature it is often mixed with muskrat fur for easier spinning onto thread for the bodies of such flies as the Adams, Blue Dun, and other blue dun body patterns. Readily available from most sources.

BIOTS: A term given to the short fibers growing from the narrow side of a primary flight feather of such birds as geese and turkeys. Biots are used as tails and antennae on various nymph patterns. In addition to natural shades, the short side fibers of white goose and barred black and white turkey primaries can be dyed for special effects. Incidentally, if you plan to dye some of these fibers yourself, you should first peel the narrow-fibered edge from the quill feather, bend it in a circle, and staple the two ends together. This will keep the fibers open so that the dye can penetrate the inside areas. Natural and dyed biots are carried by the Orvis Company, Kaufmann's Streamborn Flies, and Fly Fisher's Paradise, among others.

BLACK BEAR: Black bear guard hairs are not always all-black. Prime condition consists of a lustrous sheen with tips tapering to a point. Used mostly in streamer and salmon flies. Readily available.

BODY GILL MATERIAL: This is a relatively new item, introduced by Traun River Products. It is sold in sheet form and appears to be made of some type of foam-rubber material, one side of which is covered with minuscule fibers. I wrapped one for the body of a nymph and the tiny fibers do seem to represent insectlike gills.

The label on the package states that it can also be used for the bodies of dry flies, so I placed a piece of it in a glass of water. I squeezed it, submerged it, and held it under until it was thoroughly waterlogged, and it still surfaced. I think fly tyers will find this an interesting material to work with.

BODY GLASS: This material is an oval plastic similar to Swannundaze but perhaps a bit softer. It is used for the bodies of stonefly nymphs and caddis larvae. From Traun River Products, it comes in a great range of colors, including clear.

BRONZE MALLARD: The feathers come from the shoulder area of a drake mallard. They are barred in a rich deep brown color. This highly prized feather, which is used in salmon and streamer flies, is fairly expensive since there are only two to three pairs of prime feathers on each bird. Two supply houses that carry them are Donegal and Hunter's Angling Supplies. Depending upon availability, they are an in-and-out item with many fly shops. The wise fly tyer asks his duck-hunting friends to save these and other feathers for him.

BRONZE TURKEY: Both the body feathers and certain wing quills of the wild turkey and the domestic brown turkey have some bronze coloration to them. When the feathers achieve this shade there is also a small amount of iridescence to them, especially in the body feathers. As with speckled or mottled brown turkey wing quills, the bronze turkey quill is expensive when it is available. The best source for these feathers is the turkey hunter, who will throw them away unless you ask him to save them for you. Now and again this item may be found in a supply shop.

BUCKTAIL: Generally refers to the tail of a white-tailed deer although the hair fibers from the western black-tailed deer, though a bit shorter, are also excellent. Tails are brown to brown/black on top and white on the bottom. They are easily dyed to any color desired and are readily available in all fly shops.

BUGGY NYMPH MATERIAL: A pre-blended translucent synthetic fur in twenty colors for making nymph bodies. It can also be used as a substitute for seal fur. Sold by the Fly Shop.

BURLAP: The same material which burlap bags are made of. It is used in the famous pattern of the same name but can also be wound as the body for other categories of flies, especially nymphs. This scraggly material is generally

not packaged and listed by fly shops, though I did find it cataloged by the Fly Shop, who went to the trouble of dyeing it in half a dozen different colors.

CADDIS WING MATERIAL: This is a hand-painted reproduction of a caddis wing which is imprinted upon a suitable fabric of very fine mesh. There are over fifty clearly outlined impressions to a sheet, ranging in size from 8 to 20. For use as caddis wings, they are first cut from the sheet and trimmed and then folded down a center line and finally fastened to the hook shank. They present a very realistic appearance. From Traun River Products.

CALF SKIN: Fibers from the skin of a calf are much straighter than those on the tail and are preferred for the wings on hair-winged dry flies. They are generally not long enough for bucktail and streamer wings. Color range is similar to that of the tail. For reasons I don't understand, not all fly shops carry this item. Two outfits that do catalog it are Murray's Fly Shop and the Orvis Company.

CALF TAIL: Sometimes referred to or listed as kip tail or impala. Hair fibers from the tail of a calf are finer than bucktail and do not flare when being fastened to a hook shank. They are used in both dry fly and streamer type patterns. Depending on the purpose for which they are to be used, a certain amount of care should be taken in their selection since some calf tails may have fibers that are simply too crinkly for the fly intended. They are available in natural white, black, and brown and easily dyed into any color.

CAMEL HAIR DUBBING: Something old, yet something new. I never envisioned camels having an underfur which could be used as a dubbing. They do, and a good one at that. When I first received samples of this fur I spun a few bodies. It dubs quite easily, tapers extremely well without loose ends yet seems to retain a "buggy" roughness which is desirable, especially in wet flies and nymphs. As a floater it is about on a par with rabbit fur and better than any of the synthetics, and is thus an excellent candidate for dry flies. It absorbs floatants and fly dopes well. It is blended and packaged by the Wapsi Fly Company, a wholesale distributor. The only two shops I know of that carry it are Hunter's Angling Supplies and the Orvis Company, though I suspect it will soon be widely distributed. It is now available in a dozen of the more popular fly-tying colors.

CANADA GOOSE: Of primary interest to the fly tyer are the medium to dark gray wing quills, which form wet fly wings, wing cases, and legs and antennae on nymphs. The body feathers are rarely used.

CARIBOU: Hair is pale gray on the back of this animal to white on the underside. It is perhaps the finest of all deer type fibers and is ideal for the spun and trimmed deer hair bodies of the smaller flies (it is used for very little else). Harry Darbee, the famed Catskill fly tyer, preferred this material for his Rat-Faced McDougals. Readily available at most fly shops.

CARPET THREAD: A common item found in most department stores and local supermarkets. Because of its heavy gauge it is often used as a ribbing to form the segmentation on nymphs.

CENTER STEM QUILL: This is the center stem of a rooster or saddle hackle feather after the fibers have been removed. It is not usually sold in this prepared condition by fly shops. The fly tyer must do his or her own stripping and preparation. (For method, see Red Quill, page 26.)

CHENILLE: This manufactured item is usually made of rayon and is available in every fly shop in a wide variety of colors, including many fluorescent shades. Size designations and relationships follow.

Manufacturer's Designation	Equivalent Listing	Approximate Diameter	Approximate Related Hook Size
00	extra fine	3/32"	12 and smaller
0	fine	1/8"	8–10
1	medium	5/32"	4–6
2	large	3/16"	1/0–2
3	extra large	1/4"	2/0 and larger

Chenille has been used on the bodies of flies in almost all categories, including the dry fly, for which it is, of course, not suited because of its absorbency.

Cotton chenille, which has a much softer texture, is used as Honey Bug material to create a fly by that name which imitates certain caddis larvae. It is very popular in Pennsylvania; two dealers that carry it are Jack's Tackle and Beckie's.

Tinsel chenille is woven from fine tinsel or Mylar and is used primarily in attractor type flies.

Speckled or variegated chenille is made by weaving any two colors to form a two-toned effect, such as black and green or black and yellow. It may also be manufactured with tinsel, such as the black chenille with a silver oval rib to form the body of a Black Woolly Worm.

Except for cotton chenille, just about all the chenille sold by dealers today comes from the Danville Chenille Company in South Danville, New Hampshire. They sell directly and only to distributors.

CHINESE BOAR: The very fine, yet very durable fibers from this animal make for ideal tails and antennae on both dry flies and nymphs. The natural shades range from cream to tan to black, but they are easily dyed into other colors. Available through some dealers, two of which are the Fly Shop and Murray's Fly Shop.

CHIPMUNK: The fur and guard hairs of this animal are of a texture not dissimilar to a hare's mask or a squirrel. Color ranges from light brown to black throughout the skin and it is usually sheared with both guard hairs and underfur to form a coarse blend for a scraggly type body.

The tail fibers of the chipmunk are almost identical in barring to that of a woodchuck and are excellent for the tailing and the winging of small caddis flies. Chipmunk tail fibers, however, do not have the water-resistant quality of woodchuck fibers.

The hide and the tail of chipmunks are not usually sold in fly shops. You have to go out and get your own, either through hunting or as a road kill. In some states it is considered a varmint or a pest animal.

CINNAMON TURKEY: I still have in my possession some natural cinnamon turkey tails and I am reluctant to tie with them since I don't know where to obtain more. I suspect that this color in its natural form was derived through some special breeding. Most fly tyers today, when a pattern recipe calls for such a feather, must resort to dyeing white turkey tails into the desired cinnamon shade.

COASTAL DEER HAIR: When patterns call for coastal deer hair, they are referring to the hair fibers of the western black-tailed deer. These fibers are much shorter and finer than those of the white-tailed deer or the mule deer and have a narrower barring of color bands at the tip, and are thus an excellent choice for caddis fly wings and certain hair wings. It is available in some fly shops, especially those in the western states.

CONDOR: Condor quill, stripped condor quill, condor secondaries, and all such are no longer available commercially to the fly tyer. The Andes condor is protected in South America and importation into the United States is forbidden. In fact, the purchase or sale of these feathers is a felony. That the stripped wing quill fibers of these birds make the best bodies for such flies as the Quill Gordon, Ginger Quill, and others is unquestioned. They not only have the proper segmentation but are very tough. In their unstripped condition they have been used to make the bodies of dry flies.

The only way to obtain condor feathers today is to make friends with a zookeeper or someone who has a license to work with these birds. Then, when the bird molts and drops its feathers, or dies of old age, you may become a grateful recipient.

Substitutes for condor include goose primary quills in the unstripped stage and the light-shaded portion of a wild turkey wing quill, which can be used for the body of a Quill Gordon. Or you can resort to the stripped peacock quill. (See Quill Gordon, pages 24–6)

COPPER WIRE: (see under Tinsels)

COTTON THREAD: Sewing thread is found in most department stores, supermarkets, and yarn shops. This thread, like carpet thread, is fairly heavy and flattens out nicely for use in forming segmentation on wet flies and nymphs.

CROW: The feathers from this bird are not generally available through fly shops since the bird is protected under federal migratory bird regulations. It is, however, hunted in season in most states, and that is your source. These wary birds are rarely found as a road kill. Feathers are all-black and have numerous uses. Substitutes for crow are rooster or hen wing quill and body feathers.

CRYSTAL HAIR: A very fine synthetic fiber in a wide array of colors which is used to blend in with bucktail, calf tail, marabou, and other winging material for bucktails, streamers, and saltwater flies. What makes this fiber unusual is that each single strand is twisted during the manufacturing process and this gives it a glistening effect of alternating colors. The yellow sample I received, for example, appears to be yellow with lime green bands, yet when you run it through your fingers or hold it tautly, taking out the twist, it appears to be of one color, a kind of pearlescent yellow. This is truly an exciting new material to work with. It is available to dealers through Fly Fishing Specialties.

DAZZLE-AIRE: This is a synthetic yarn used in the knitting of sweaters and is found in most department stores, knitting supply shops, and the like. It comes in a variety of colors highlighted with glints of silver, sparkle, or dazzle. It is used for the bodies of caddis pupae and some other flies.

A word of caution: Products such as this may go the way of Antron (which see) due to changes in fashion. It is only mentioned here so that when you see a pattern listing this or a similar brand, you will know what type of yarn you will need if you have to make a substitution, such as Antron or any yarn sold as frosted or sparkle.

DEER HAIR: When a pattern recipe calls for clipped, spun, or flared deer hair it is generally referring to the back or underside hair fibers of the white-tailed deer. These hair fibers are hollow and when the pressure of the thread is brought against them they flare, or pop up, and when the thread is wound around the shank at the same moment the fibers also partially revolve around the shank, or spin, as it were.

The hair fibers on the back and sides of the white-tailed deer are generally of a pale gray color from the base upward, changing to brown near the tips and terminating in a tan tip. The underside fibers are white, and are dyed into various shades and used mostly for bass bugs. The hairs around the legs, under the haunches, and in the tail (see also Bucktail) do not spin readily and should not be used for spun hair bodies. White-tailed deer hair is available in all fly shops.

Mule deer is perhaps even better for spinning deer hair bodies, and the color is a more pronounced gray, but few eastern fly tyers are aware of this because the shops in this region, more often than not, stock only the white-tailed deer body hair. It is only now and then listed in catalogs. Some who do stock it, however, are Jacklin's Fly Shop, Hunter's Angling Supplies, and Little Dixie Flies.

The hair of these animals may also be obtained from deer hunters, and certainly the local taxidermist should have more scraps and trimmings than he knows what to do with.

DEER MASK: The hair fibers on the face of a white-tailed deer, and other species for that matter, are shorter and finer than body hair and have a narrower band of tip. These fibers are used for caddis flies and hair wings, and they are the primary ingredient in the fly patterns known as Compara Duns. Because of the time and trouble it takes to skin the mask from the head of the animal, this particular piece of hide is more expensive than an equivalent patch of body hair. Here again, if you have a friend who is a hunter, you can ask him to save you the head so that you can skin it out yourself. Of course, if this happens to be a buck deer of trophy proportions you can forget it.

This item is only now and again available in supply shops. Some who do carry it are the Beaverkill Angler, Buchner Fly Designs, Valley Angler, and Hunter's Angling Supplies.

DOLL EYES (see Glass Eyes)

DUCK, DUCK WING QUILLS: The feathers of all waterfowl are used in fly tying. They are especially desirable in dry flies because the wing quills and body feathers are highly water-resistant, due to the natural oils in the plumage.

The wing quills of ducks form the wings of many of our standard dry and wet fly patterns and also the wing cases on nymphs. Wild ducks such as mallard, widgeon, and pintail generally have wing quill feathers ranging from light to dark gray. White duck wing quills, which are dyed into numerous bright colors, are obtained from the domestic duck.

Duck wing quill feathers are sold in all fly shops either by the matched pair or matched set of wings. The latter is the better value since you don't have to pay for the pairing and packaging and usually there is the additional bonus of some small shoulder feathers to tie with.

See Mallard and Wood Duck for the use of flank and breast feathers.

ELK, ELK HAIR, ELK RUMP: The colors of this animal range from cream, tan, light brown, reddish brown to dark brown. The hair fibers are used in numerous patterns, most notably in the Elk Hair Caddis. The hair from the leg, which is shorter and stiffer, is ideal for such downwing type patterns as caddis flies and stoneflies. The hair is not commonly used for spinning deer hair bodies since it does not flare as readily as the hair of either the white-tailed or the mule deer.

EMBOSSED TINSEL (see under Tinsels)

ENGLISH HARE'S MASK AND EARS (see Hare's Mask)

EVERGLOW, EVERGLO: This is a braided synthetic fiber similar to Mylar tubing except that the luminescent materials glow in the dark. Sizes are slightly larger than standard Mylar braiding but can be used comfortably with most streamers and saltwater patterns. It is made in a range of fluorescent colors.

As with Mylar, you must first de-core this type of tubing. However, don't discard the fibrous and glistening synthetic yarn which forms the core, since it makes an interesting

wing in its own right. Carried by the Fly Shop and the Orvis Company, among others.

FANTAFOAM: A soft synthetic foam which has been cut into very thin sheets and is available in a wide range of colors. It is used for the bodies of emergers and dry flies. It is slightly lighter than water. Available to dealers through Fly Fishing Specialties.

FELT PENS: Waterproof marking pens are used by fly tyers for certain two-tone effects on nymphs and, in some cases, for quick color adjustments at streamside. The full color range is more available in hobby shops, whereas the materials houses carry mostly what are considered fly-tying colors.

FISHAIR: This synthetic nylon type fiber with a lustrous sheen is manufactured primarily as a substitute for polar bear hair and as a stronger equivalent for bucktail when durability is required. It is a favorite among saltwater anglers in pursuit of such toothy game fish as bluefish and barracuda. It is available from most supply houses in a full color range, including the fluorescents. It is packaged in size lengths of 2½, 4, and 6 inches.

FISHING POST NYMPH BLEND: A rug yarn type synthetic blend of high luster designed by the Fishing Post. Ideal for nymphs and as a substitute for seal fur in salmon flies.

FITCH, FITCH TAIL: The underfur of the fitch, in part, consists of a soft creamy yellow fur which is the ideal color for the Light Cahill, both dry and wet fly, and some of the Sulfur

Dun patterns. Other sections of the fur range from cream to gray/cream.

The guard hairs from the tail of the fitch are used mostly in salmon flies. They are generally dark brown to almost black.

FLASHABOU: Introduced by Larry Dahlberg. A form of Mylar cut into very fine, almost hairlike strands approximately ten inches long. It is used in the construction of wings on bucktails, streamers, and saltwater flies and, in some cases, salmon flies. It comes in a fairly wide range of colors, such as silver, gold, bronze, green, blue, and the especially favored pearlescent. It is similar to marabou in that it is very light, soft, and supple. It will pulse and move easily when fished. Most tyers prefer to mix this material with other fibers such as bucktail or calf tail as a compound wing to add glitter and flash.

Flashabou has become so popular so fast simply because it does many of the things we want a material to do—that is, attract, vibrate, and lure game fish to our offering. I suspect it will be the cause of many "improved" versions of existing patterns. It has, in fact, already been added to quite a number of standard flies. Here again, if Flashabou is incorporated into the wing of an existing known pattern, it should be acknowledged. For example, if you were to add Flashabou to the Black Ghost, the pattern should be called Black Ghost, Flashabou, or Flashabou Black Ghost.

Without question, Flashabou is here to stay. It is carried by most fly shops and is also available under other trade names, such as Marabou Tinsel, distributed by Jack's Tackle, and Sparkleboy, distributed by D. H. Thompson, the famous toolmaker.

FLOSS: Nearly all of the floss sold today by the fly shops throughout the United States comes from the Danville Chenille Company in South Danville, New Hampshire. The floss is made of rayon and is manufactured in a wide range of colors, including the fluorescent shades. Danville also manufactures an acetate floss which can be molded with acetate solution to form flat bodies on nymphs.

Flosses are available in single-, double-, and four-stranded yarns, so that for ease of handling they may be adjusted to the largest and smallest of hooks.

The only silk floss I know of that is still being manufactured is the Pearsall brand sold by E. Veniard of Thornton Heath, England, and it is still used by fly tyers who specialize in the tying of salmon flies. Silk floss is a bit more difficult to work with than rayon.

FLY-RITE: This synthetic dubbing blend of polypropylene fibers was first introduced by Doug Swisher and Carl Richards and is now distributed nationwide in forty colors representing the most popular insect hatches from coast to coast.

Fly-Rite is easy to dub onto thread and forms a neat and precise body. However, because of its spongelike absorbency of water, it is not recommended for the bodies of dry flies. Available at most fly shops.

FOX FUR, GRAY FOX: The guard hairs of the gray fox are of prime interest to fly tyers, especially to those who dress salmon flies. The black, white, and black-tipped fibers are used in many patterns but especially noted for their use in the wings of the Rat series of flies, such as the Rusty Rat, Silver Rat, and Black Rat, among others. A package of skin with gray fox guard hairs is usually more expensive than an equal package of red fox since the best and most prominently barred fibers come from the middle back of the animal and a furrier is unlike to have very much scrap fur from this area. Thus, when distributors buy bulk furs, this popular section is usually in short supply. When a distributor has to resort to buying whole skins, even damaged ones, he has to pay more for them, hence the inflated price tag.

The underfur of the gray fox, though it does not have the color range of the red, is also usable. Incidentally, gray foxes are just as careless as red foxes, and you will find a certain amount of the pink-cast urine-burned dubbing near their rear underside.

FOX FUR, RED FOX: A favored fur for dubbing, the red fox has a varied range of colors from the desirable pink-cast urine-burned fur from the belly, the sandy beige fur which becomes part of the mixture in the March Brown, the fawn/tan shades, the creamy color that is listed for the Light Cahill, down through the pale and medium gray shades of the sides and back. The dubbing fur from the tail of the red fox is slightly coarser and if this material is placed in a hot orange dye bath it results in the often used "dirty orange" color.

Guard hairs from the red fox have, on rare occasions, been used for winging streamer or bucktail flies.

FURRY FOAM: A foam-rubber material covered on both sides with very short and fuzzy synthetic fibers. It is used for the quick formation of bodies on nymphs and wet flies. It is somewhat elastic, which allows for a certain degree of control regarding body diameters.

Color range is quite comprehensive in relation to aquatic insects.

GIMP FEATHER: Any of the short, fuzzy secondary feathers found under the orange or white tippet feathers of the golden or Lady Amherst pheasant neck capes. They are barely half an inch long and range from light to medium gray. They are used as wing cases for nymphs. (See The Gimp, page 168.) They are rarely listed separately, but you can obtain them in any fly shop that carries the neck capes of the golden or Lady Amherst pheasant. One enterprising fly shop that does go to the trouble of packaging these tiny feathers is Joe's Tackle.

GLASS EYES: Unless you're tying bass bugs, certain large streamers, or saltwater flies, you may never use this group of materials. Glass eyes, or doll eyes, are manufactured for use in the making of stuffed animals and toys and they come in various shapes, sizes, and colors. Some, listed as Audible Eyes by the Fly Shop, contain loose pupil-like pellets or disks which move freely about, adding extra life to the pattern when it is fished. Some come with wire attached for wrapping around the shank, while others are glued in. A number of dealers carry them. You might try the Orvis Company, Kaufmann's Streamborn Flies, or Traun River Products.

GLO-BUG YARN: A soft synthetic fiber similar to nylon tow which is primarily used for making salmon egg flies for steelhead and salmon fishing. It is available in a wide range of colors in most fly shops. Tyers and dealers interested in this and other Glo-Bug products should contact the Bug Shop (which only deals in this yarn), 3342 Dodson Lane, Anderson, California 96007. They deal in both wholesale and retail. Also advertised is a Glo-Bug Tying Instruction Sheet.

GOAT HAIR: These soft white fibers are used in salmon and streamer flies. The texture is finer than that of deer or calf tail. Goat hair is rarely found in supply shops, but a few that do carry it are Turner's Fly Shop, Buchner Fly Designs, and Joe's Tackle.

GOLDEN PHEASANT: Two of the most frequently used materials, especially in the tying of salmon flies, come from the head and the neck of this bird. The tippet feathers of orange with black bands are a familiar sight on the Royal Coachman pattern, while the shining and lustrous golden pheasant crest feather forms the tail and topping of many salmon flies.

The feathers from the body are used less frequently, although the red plumage from the sides substitutes for the restricted Indian crow and the golden yellow back feathers serve in place of toucan.

Not too long ago the entire skin, including neck and crest, was obtainable at a reasonably low price. Today, these feathers command a respectable price. Golden pheasant is available through most fly shops, though most of the dealers carry only the neck and crest. Some who do carry the entire skins are Angling Specialties and Donegal.

GOLD WIRE (see under Tinsels)

GRAY FOX (see Fox Fur, Gray Fox)

GROUNDHOG (see Woodchuck)

GROUSE: When a pattern lists grouse in its recipe, you may have good reason for confusion. Does it refer to the ruffed grouse, a game bird whose natural range covers much of the United States and Canada, or the blue grouse, which inhabits the West, or the English or Scottish bird? When an Englishman says "grouse" he is referring only to the red grouse, a beloved game bird whose scientific name is *Lagopus lagopus* (which is the same species as our willow ptarmigan).

Some of the confusion arises from the fact that many patterns have evolved from fly dressings which originated in the British Isles and the name "grouse" crossed the Atlantic without further identification. American tyers, designing their own patterns for native waters, did not hesitate to use what was available here—in effect, the ruffed grouse. In New England, the ruffed grouse is occasionally called "partridge," which further complicates things. Fortunately there is a similarity in plumage coloration among the various grouses and partridges, and when a pattern calls for gray or brown grouse, a small barred feather from any of the grouses or partridges may be used. The birds offered by fly shops are the ruffed grouse and less frequently the blue grouse. Red grouse imported from England is illegal here, but ruffed grouse or Hungarian partridge may be substituted for it.

GUINEA HEN, GUINEA FOWL: These commercially raised birds have body feathers that are black with white spots—polka-dotted, you might say. Fly tyers favor the neck with its smaller hackles and smaller white spots, or flecks. All of the body feathers are used in wet flies, nymphs, streamers, and salmon flies to form legs, beards, throats, shoulders, and folded hackle collars. The feathers are also dyed in various shades for differing effects.

HACKLE: Unless otherwise specified, the word "hackle" refers to the feathers from the neck or saddle area of a male chicken, or rooster. When the fibers of a hen chicken are required, as in the case of wet flies, the description will read "hen hackle," and if other types of feathers are used, the pattern recipe may designate "partridge hackle" or "guinea fowl hackle" or whatever the case may be. Even strands of rubber and hair fibers may, at times, be referred to as hackle.

Hackle for a dry fly requires that the fibers or barbs (see glossary) on the hackle feather be stiff and resilient, since they must radiate firmly from the hook shank in order to support the fly as it floats on the surface of the water. Hackles for wet flies should be softer so that they can pulse and move beneath the surface. The requisite for streamer patterns is length and fullness in order to maintain a proper silhouette.

For those who are interested in the properties, qualities, and an in-depth study of hackles and their various uses, I recommend *The Metz Book of Hackle* listed in the bibliography.

Natural Hackle Colors

The following listing of colors as they occur in roosters are those most commonly used in fly tying. White, cream, and certain variant types of necks may be used for dyeing into colors not reproduced naturally or for certain shades which may be in short supply.

White: Self-explanatory; occasionally you will find a hint of cream on the feathers on a white neck.

Cream: Off-white, pale beige, and not really quite dark enough for the pattern Light Cahill, though it is often used in this recipe.

Cream Ginger: A dark cream, occasionally with a glint of yellow throughout. A favorite for the Cahills and Sulfur patterns.

Golden Ginger: A golden buff color. Somewhere between a dark cream and a dark ginger.

Dark Ginger: Sometimes called "red game," this is a light brown shade with reddish highlights.

Brown: Darker than dark ginger and in a medium range of brown but still retaining a lifelike or fiery luster. Note: There is such a range of shadings between dark ginger and brown that an overlap occurs when they are graded to color. Since nearly everyone sees color differently, a dark ginger neck may be called a brown by one fly tyer and a brown labeled a dark ginger by another.

Coachman Brown: A rich dark mahogany brown.

Blue Dun: Ranges from very pale gray to almost black. Preferred necks are those which have feathers that are dusted or speckled with lighter contrasting flecks since they more closely imitate the natural markings of an aquatic insect.

Black: Preferably with a glossy or lustrous finish on the outside of the feather.

Iron Blue Dun: Appears black but is actually a very dark gray.

Badger: A cream to golden feather which has a black section running down the middle. The black portion is actually the webby part of the feather.

Furnace: A dark ginger to brown feather with a black center.

Cock Y Bondhu: A furnace type hackle which, in addition to the black center stripe, is edged in black at the ends of the fibers.

Grizzly: A black hackle with white barring. Depending on the predominance of white or black, these hackles are listed in patterns as dark-cast grizzly or light-cast grizzly. When combined with a brown hackle they produce a rusty dun effect.

Ginger Grizzly: A cream neck with dark ginger barring. Sometimes referred to as "ginger variant."

Red Grizzly: A brown neck with cream or cream ginger barring. Sometimes called "red variant."

Cree: A feather containing black, cream, and brown barring. Dark-cast cree hackles are referred to as "instant Adams" since they will tie this pattern by themselves and do not require one brown and one grizzly for the collar.

Variants: Any neck with a variation of color in its hackles.

Sandy Dun: A color derived through special breeding by the Metz Hatchery. Shade is a pale tannish gray suitable for many light-colored flies such as the Pale Morning Dun.

Sandy Brown: Specially bred by the Metz Hatchery, this neck features a dark ginger hackle with a pale dun center stripe.

Splash: A purebred neck used by the Metz Hatchery to cross with other strains to produce blue dun colors. Hackles on this neck are either blue gray or white and occasionally an individual hackle contains both colors.

Bronze Dun: True bronze dun, which has a measure of brown shading in with the gray, is rarely available in a natural neck. This effect is more readily obtained by dyeing.

HACKLE SIZE: All hackles have barbules, or fibers, which grow on each side of the center quill. The length of these fibers determines what size they will be on a related hook. The sizing of hackle fiber length for a dry fly is relatively simple. With a standard hook such as a Mustad 94840 or its equivalent, the length of the fiber should measure three-quarters of the shank length. Another rule tyers follow is that the fiber length should be equal to one and a half times the gap width. Manufacturers of fly-tying tools have simplified this even further by making various sorts of hackle gauges upon which the fibers of a given hackle can be measured for related hook sizes.

HAIRLINE: A dubbing blend made from rabbit underfur. Available from Angler's Junction and Frontier Anglers.

HAIRTRON: A commercially manufactured blend of the synthetic Antron and natural rabbit underfur. Available in a wide range of colors through Kaufmann's Streamborn.

HARE'S MASK, HARE'S EARS: (English Hare's Mask) This is the entire face area of the hare which is skinned out. Sometimes the ears are offered for sale separately. The mask fur contains tan, gray, and reddish-brown fur and has both the soft underfur and an outer covering of coarse guard hairs. The ears have almost no underfur and are covered with short, scraggly fibers, or guard hairs. Most fly tyers cut the fur from both the mask and the ears and blend it so that it is of one consistency containing both the softer underfur and the short, coarser fibers. When it is blended in this manner it is still relatively easy to spin onto thread as a dubbed body while retaining its scraggly appearance, thus making for an effective and lifelike imitation. Though it is used on many nymphs and wet flies, it is most famous in its application on its namesake, the Gold-Ribbed Hare's Ear.

Hare's mask fur is also dyed into many other colors, such as olive, brown, and black, and is available both as an entire dyed mask and in the form of a dyed blend.

HORSE HAIR: This item was, at one time, commonly used as a ribbing material for wet flies. Though rarely cataloged today, it is listed by Murray's Fly Shop and the Ojai Fisherman. Most commonly used colors are brown and black.

IMPALA: I suppose at one time the tail fibers of this animal were used for fly tying. Now, when this material is listed, the general meaning is calf tail.

IRISE DUBBING MATERIAL: This is a somewhat coarse, lustrous, synthetic dubbing material with fine fragments of a Spectraflash or Flashabou type material blended in. It can be used as a sparkle dubbing for caddis pupae or simply to highlight the bodies of nymphs. It is available in a variety of colors through Traun River Products.

JACKRABBIT: Similar to the fur from a hare's mask, this item is rarely listed by the catalog houses. It is used by Polly Rosborough in a few of his fuzzy nymphs. For western fly tyers it is available through hunting and road kills.

JAVELINA (see Peccary)

JUNGLE COCK, JUNGLE FOWL: This restricted item still appears on streamer and salmon flies. I suppose that most of our tyers have been fortunate enough to find supplies which were imported prior to the ban of 1969 or they are spending the bucks for the genetically raised jungle fowl skins.

Though the jungle cock body feather, a black oblong with a narrow white to creamy yellow stripe, is used on a few patterns, it is the "eyed" feather that is most sought after. In fact, if it were not for this eyed feather, I doubt whether the jungle cock would be used for any purpose in fly tying.

The jungle cock eye or nail feather ranges from a half to one and a half inches in length. It is black with an ovoid white to creamy yellow spot near the tip of the feather which is of an enameled consistency or, if you will, like nail polish. To the rear of this first ovoid white spot there is another, more elongated white enameled section, sometimes called the "second eye," and behind that yet another, even narrower white section which qualifies more as a stripe than a spot. When fastened to the shank as eyes, cheeks, or shoulders on streamer or salmon flies, they may be tied in exposing one, two, or even three eyes, depending upon the pattern requirements.

The enameled or eyed section of the jungle cock eye feather is fairly brittle and will easily split. Many of these feathers, in fact, when they are first obtained already have splits in them, especially the larger ones. These splits may be repaired by wetting thumb and forefinger with head cement and pulling the feather between them. It is allowed to dry and then another coat of head cement is applied for yet a bit more durability.

Most fly shops do not carry jungle cock, since it is quite difficult to obtain capes that can be stocked legally. They do, however, carry a variety of imitations, the best of which are those manufactured by the Ti-Rite Company in St. Paul, Minnesota, which through a photographic process transfers the image of the real thing onto a piece of opaque frosted plastic

equal in thickness to that of a natural jungle cock eye.

Two suppliers who carry the real thing legally are Thomas and Thomas and Letort Limited.

KAPOK: Kapok is a seed plant fiber which, because of its buoyant properties, was once used for the making of life jackets. Its natural color is cream but it has been dyed into other shades and is sold under the brand name of K–Dubbing.

KIP TAIL: A kip is the hide of a young animal, such as a cow. Thus, calf tails may be referred to as kip tails by farmers or slaughterhouses and the term has been picked up by those buying and selling them for the fly-tying market (see also Calf Tail).

LACQUERS AND CEMENTS: Head lacquers have two uses: to act as a glue or tacky substance to prevent thread from unraveling, and to give a lustrous finish to heads and to form optic eyes. There are a number of lacquers, head cements, and varnishes on the market today. It's up to you to decide what your need is in relation to the types of flies you tie. The following are but a few of those offered in the various catalogs.

Head Cement: This is the most common labeling. Head cements are made from various chemicals, the most common of which is a celluloid cement.

Cellire: Sold by E. Veniard, Ltd., this product is imported by some dealers in this country. (Hunter's Angling Supplies carries it.) It is available in clear, white, black, red, and yellow and produces a highly glossy finish. It is used mostly by salmon fly tyers.

Price Head Cement: Used as a gloss coat, this quick-drying cement comes with a brush for quick application, though the brush is too large for use on small flies.

Pro-Kote: Manufactured and distributed by Peter Phelps of the Bedford Sportsman in Bedford Hills, New York, this is a highly penetrating type of cement. Phelps makes it in a number of viscosities, from an almost watery liquid to a heavier fluid (a small drop will hold at the point of a dubbing needle).

Wapsi Fly Head Cement: This fairly recent introduction by the Wapsi Fly Company features a cotton cellulose cement that stays clear and doesn't deteriorate. It penetrates into the thread windings and material fibers. If a glossy head is called for, a second coat should be applied.

Wapsi Gloss Coat: This product is formulated for a quick buildup so that a glossy coat can be achieved in one application.

Fritz Von Schlegel Head Cement: I suspect quite a few fly tyers will want to try this specially formulated head cement which is almost of the consistency of water. The bottle has a patented flow-control valve, so that when you turn the bottle upside down, a fine brush embedded in a cartridge pops down with enough liquid cement on it to lacquer the head of the fly. Following the cartridge downward is a steel ball which seals off the rest of the fluid so that none is inadvertently spilled. It's a gimmick that seems to work quite well.

Plio Bond: A rubber-based glue that is slightly supple and pliable after drying. Used to lacquer wing cases and hopper type wings because of the soft, yet durable result.

Vinyl Cement: Like Plio Bond, this cement dries to a soft durability and is used on Muddler Minnow and hopper wings and the feathers that form wing cases on nymphs. It has an advantage over rubber cements in that it does not dull the color of the material upon which it is used. Some shops that carry it are Jack's Tackle and the Fishnet.

Flexament: An Orvis Company product that has the virtues of vinyl cement and Plio Bond, drying to a strong and flexible consistency.

Acrylic Paints: Some dealers, such as the Fly Shop, are listing acrylic type paints in metallic and pearlescent shades. These are quick-drying and can be used to paint hard pre-shaped bodies on such patterns as Janssen's Minnow or to produce unusual effects on streamer heads. They are also readily available in a great variety of shades in art stores.

Nail Polish: A visit to the local pharmacy will also add to your collection of lacquer for heads and cements in general. Nail polish works very well.

LADY AMHERST PHEASANT: The neck and crest feathers of this pheasant are used occasionally, mostly on salmon flies. Lady Amherst tippets, the neck feathers, are white with a black band on their rounded tips, the crest is of a brilliant metallic red. The white tippets are often dyed and used as shoulder substitutes for other feathers. (See also Gimp Feather.)

The green and white body plumage is rarely used, though the tail, white with black barring on its long fibers, is sought after by salmon fly tyers. Because of its limited use and the high price of the tail feathers, not every fly shop carries it. Some that do are Donegal, Angler's Ruff, and Hunter's Angling Supplies.

LATEX: A very thin sheet of rubberized material which is cut into strips to form the bodies of caddis larvae and the wing cases on stonefly nymphs. Manufactured in a cream color but can be dyed. Traun River Products has introduced a form of latex which is marbled brown over a clear sheet of stretchable material. It does not, however, stretch quite as much as the original. The only trouble with latex is that it will melt in a hot fly box.

LEAD EYES: A recent design by Tom Schmuecker features the molding of lead into "eyes" which can be tied to the hook shank without the usual problems of twisting or separating encountered in the use of split shot. These molded eyes look like miniature dumbbells with the ends sheared off. They are manufactured in plain lead which can be lacquered any color and in nickel-plate for those who favor the silver bead chain look. They are available in six sizes ranging from 1/100th to 1/10th of an ounce and are available to dealers through the Wapsi Fly Company.

LEAD WIRE: The material most commonly used for the weighting of nymphs and some streamer flies is the fine round lead wire sold for use by electricians. This is available in what are called amp sizes. Translated into diameters, the following designations result:

1 amp	= fine	= .016	= hook sizes 10–12
2 amp	= medium	= .024	= hook sizes 6–8
3 amp	= wide	= .036	= hook sizes 2–4

The wire is usually wound around the shank in coils or cut into strips for lashing to the sides of the shank, depending on the configuration desired. The side shank strip method is usually employed when imitating flat-bodied nymphs.

LEMON WOOD DUCK FLANK: The natural shade of the flank feather of the male wood duck, which is a barred lemon brown. (See also Wood Duck.)

LIGAS ULTRA TRANSLUCENT DUBBING: A coarse, high-sheen synthetic substitute for seal fur similar to Sealex, Unseal, and others. Blended in a full color range.

MACRAMÉ YARN: A fibered stringy yarn which has found its way to the fly tyer's bench. Not listed in catalogs. A visit to the local nursery, florist, or arts and crafts shop may secure some.

MAGIC SPINNER WING MATERIAL: A synthetic fabric of a very fine denier from which you can peel a desired amount of fibers to use in the formation of a spinner wing. It surpasses poly yarn in presenting a natural appearance. It is available in iridescent white, olive, gray, and brown, and can be colored any shade with a marking pen. Available through Traun River Products and sold under the name Magic Wing by the Orvis Company.

MAHOGANY RINGNECK TAIL (see Ringneck Pheasant and Ringneck tail)

MALLARD, MALLARD FLANK, MALLARD WING QUILLS: It is to the fly tyer's good fortune that this particular species of waterfowl is fairly abundant since quite a few of its feathers are used in countless fly patterns. It is readily available from the catalogs and fly shops and can also be found on shooting preserves and game farms.

The drake mallard is the most sought after. Its barred pearl gray flank feathers serve for such flies as the Gray Fox and can also be dyed to a lemon brown shade to imitate the natural wood duck flank feather, which is scarce. The barred flank feathers are also dyed into shades of yellow, insect green, and bronze dun for other imitations.

On the inside of the drake wing shoulders are found the natural bronze barred feathers so often called for in salmon, streamer, and wet flies. On the average drake, there are usually four good feathers of this color. Only the older birds have more, usually six.

The pale gray barred breast feathers are not nearly as frequently used. Yet if they are well marked and placed back to back and tied as a tufted wing, they are ideal for the dry fly.

The wing quills, which are slate gray in color, are the most used of all duck quills for such standards as the Blue Dun, Blue Quill, and Ginger Quill.

Hen mallards are used primarily for their wing quills, though the mottled tan/brown and white body feathers serve well as a substitute for prairie chicken when imitating the pectoral fins of sculpin type flies.

The black duck, darker than the mallard, is used mostly for its wing quills.

MANDARIN DUCK (see under Wood Duck)

MARABOU: Once a by-product of the marabou stork, these feathers today come from the white turkey. Marabou is usually available in varying lengths from two-inch shorts to full plumes some eight to nine inches long.

I prefer the shorter "blood" feathers in about the two- to three-inch range simply because only one feather is required to make a wing and I can skip the procedure of aligning the fibers. The longer feathers must first have their side fibers aligned before they are trimmed from the stem and many times you simply can't gather enough of them between thumb and forefinger to form a full-bodied wing, resulting in yet another alignment and trimming and a matching of the first unit with the second. Too much work.

Marabou is easily dyed into all colors and is readily available in every fly shop, or should be.

MASTERBLEND: Manufactured and distributed by Jack Mickievicz of Jack's Tackle, this blend comprises a mix of natural furs. It was first designed for the Leonard Rod Company, but since that company's disappearance from the fly-tying scene it is now available to all dealers.

I should add a word or two here about Jack Mickievicz, whose name appears quite frequently under various patterns. Mickievicz is perhaps the most innovative developer of materials in the country today. He has been responsible, directly or indirectly, for a great majority of the natural fur and synthetic blends on the market, whether they bear his name or not. He is the only one I know of who invested in a machine, of no small size and expenditure, which, with its thousands of tiny teeth on numerous steel rollers, literally chews, digests, and reduces any fiber to the purest form of dubbing. This machine has been nicknamed "the Mangler" (though Jack has another name for it ever since it took off a portion of his index finger).

In addition to his own blends, he has been manufacturing and packaging furs and synthetic blends for Orvis, Wapsi, Dale Clemens, and a host of others.

His knowledge of animal furs, feathers, and all types of synthetics is a result of dogged research, experiment, and development. He knows more about colors and combinations than any other tyer I have met.

MICROWEB: A realistic thin, webby material used for the making of wings on mayflies, caddis flies, and stoneflies. Sold in black, gray, olive, and white. One dealer who carries it is Murray's Fly Shop.

MICROFIBITS (see Spinner Tail Material)

MINK, MINK FUR, MINK TAIL: The underfur of the mink, which is available in natural brown, beige, blue dun, and white, is soft, water-resistant, and fairly easy to dub. Its only drawback is the short guard hairs which make the dubbing a bit prickly unless the fur is carefully cut from the skin and the short fibers meticulously pulled out. Most dealers, however, simply shear off as much of the upper guard hairs as possible and next shear the fur close to the skin. It is then dyed and blended into various desirable shades to imitate the abdomen and thorax area of various aquatic insects.

Mink tail guard hairs in natural black, brown, blue dun, beige, and bleached ginger are used for the winging of caddis flies and other patterns. The fibers are about an inch in length and are firm and glossy. When they are tied as a downwing, a drop of head cement should be placed on the thread windings around the hook shank before the fibers are lashed and secured to the shank; otherwise they may easily be pulled out.

MOHAIR: A coarse and fuzzy knitting yarn, available in many colors, found in most department stores or knitting supply shops. The scraggly fibers make for a buggy and lifelike imitation. It is possible to cut mohair into short sections, an eighth to a quarter of an inch long, and blend them to achieve a particularly desired color.

MOHLON: To my knowledge, this synthetic material is no longer available as a knitting yarn through the usual outlets, though some fly shops may have a certain amount of stock left over. Murray's Fly Shop has a supply in black, brown, olive, gray, and tan. Mohlon was introduced by Polly Rosborough in his *Tying and Fishing the Fuzzy Nymphs.* Mohair is a good substitute.

MOLE: This fur is not widely listed today, yet it is one of the softest and smoothest to tie with and is used to form the bodies of dries, wets, and nymphs. One outfit that does catalog it is Hook and Hackle.

MONGA RINGTAIL: The tail of the ringtail cat, or cacomistle, found in the southwestern United States and Mexico, features alternating bands of fairly long, soft and silken black and white fibers. They make excellent material for wings on streamer and bucktail type flies. They are often dyed in red, green, yellow, and other colors. Surprisingly, very few fly shops stock them, but you will find them listed in the catalogs of the Fly Shop and Hunter's Angling Supplies.

MONOFILAMENT: All forms of monofilament have been used for the bodies, tails, antennae, and even eyes of nymph type patterns. Ernest Schwiebert in *Nymphs* was one of the first to mention its use in regard to the construction of the abdomen of these insects.

Today, a form of flat oval monofilament (such as that manufactured by the Cortland Line Company under the trade name Cobra) is the type most commonly used for bodies. This product is not packaged for fly tying as such. You simply purchase a spool of it at the lines and reels counter and take it home and cut it to size.

To use monofilament line to form the eyes on shrimp patterns or nymphs, cut it to a one-inch length and put a flame to both ends. As the mono burns back, it forms a tiny black ball at each end. When you reach the desired proportion, blow out the flame.

MOOSE HAIR, MOOSE MANE: The moose offers strong, firm, and durable hair fibers in black, dark brown, and light gray. They range in length from one to two inches on most of the body and are used for tailing and winging many of our western dry flies and for the forked tails on nymphs and other patterns. Moose hair, though it does spin, is rarely used for spun and trimmed hair bodies.

Moose mane fibers, which are found on the upper back, are much longer, usually from four to six inches in length, and come in both white (a very pale gray) and black shades. By winding one dark and one light fiber around the shank simultaneously you will form a segmented body such as is used in the pattern Mosquito.

MOTTLED TURKEY WING QUILL (see under Turkey)

MULE DEER (see under Deer Hair)

MUSKRAT: This is perhaps the most favored of all furs among fly tyers. The underfur ranges from a silver blue-gray on the underside of the animal to a perfect medium blue dun gray on its back, with a tinge of bronzy brown at the outer tips of the underfur. It is very highly water-resistant and dubs extremely well, qualities that make it the most commonly used fur for such patterns as the Adams, Blue Dun, and a multitude of others. The guard hairs are rarely used.

MYLAR: A synthetic non-tarnishing form of tinsel which was first introduced on the market in laminated sheet form, gold on one side and silver on the other. It was sold by supply houses in an eight-by-ten format or cut into halves and quarters. Most of the Mylar tinsel available today comes on spools in the usual tinsel sizes. (See also Tinsels.)

MYLAR TUBING (or Piping) This is a braided form of Mylar consisting of very fine strands of either gold or silver which are interwoven around a cotton core. It is used mostly for forming bodies on streamer flies. Most Mylar tubings and other forms of braiding come in the following sizes:

Small   = 1/8″ diameter = hook sizes 8 and smaller
Medium = 3/16″ diameter = hook sizes 2–6
Large   = 1/4″ diameter = hook sizes 2/0 and larger

The relationship to hook size is only approximate since the smaller diameters can be squeezed onto some fairly large hooks and, conversely, a large-sized braid can be used on a smaller hook for certain effects. Sizing also depends on whether some kind of material is first wound around the hook shank to form a shaped underbody. Underbodies can be made from floss, foam strips, most yarns, or, in some cases, plastic or metal that has been pre-shaped and glued to the shank, as in the case of the Zonker and the Threadfin Shad.

Mylar is also braided without a core and here the diameter is roughly equal to that of wide oval tinsel. When it is wound as a body, however, it lies flat and reflects more light, somewhat like embossed tinsel, because of the broken surface.

Another form of tubing which is becoming very popular is the pearlescent type which is braided in the same manner as Mylar but is made of a strong polyester material. It is carried in the same size range as Mylar.

NATUREBLEND: A specialized blend of natural furs designed to imitate the body color of the natural insect. Manufactured and distributed through Jack's Tackle.

NUTRIA: The fur which comes from the nutria, or coypu, a South American water animal in the rodent family. Its underfur is a natural shade of brown and it dubs fairly well. It is not cataloged very often, but one supplier who lists it is Jacklin's Fly Shop.

NYLON TOW: A soft fibrous nylon yarn in a fairly thick diameter (a quarter inch) in various fluorescent shades. It can be used as a streamer wing or tied down so that it flares and can be trimmed to shape as you would deer body hair. It is often used to form a salmon egg imitation.

NYMPH FORM, NYMPH WEIGHT: These items are manufactured for the purpose of easily forming a flat-bodied nymph. They were first introduced by Robert Boyle of Cold Spring, New York, and then manufactured by Peter Phelps of the Bedford Sportsman in Bedford Hills, New York. They have since been copied by other manufacturers. They are available both in heavy plastic and in lead, the choice depending on how deep the nymph is to be fished.

OPOSSUM, AMERICAN: The American opossum, with its soft pale cream and almost translucent fur, is rarely ever used or sold in fly shops. Yet the fur, which is a bit glassy and on the stringy side, certainly must have a number of uses in fly tying. One odd example I received from a member of the Philadelphia Fly Tyers was a streamer pattern dressed with secondary guard hairs of this animal which had been dyed three different colors. My first impression was that the tyer had used extremely fine polar bear. If the underfur is cut into small sections of a quarter inch or so and then blended by itself or with other furs, it will also make a good substitute for seal fur.

This animal is often found as a road kill and that may have to be your source, though I did find one listing of it in the Jacklin's Fly Shop catalog.

OPOSSUM, AUSTRALIAN: This is one of the easiest of all furs to dub onto thread. The natural color of this animal ranges from a soft gray on the back to cream on the underside. Areas around the legs show shades of reddish brown and fawn tan. Quite often this fur is bleached into lighter shades of ginger and some off-tones of rusty orange and soft fiery brown, which fit well into many patterns.

The tail of the Australian opossum, unlike the ratlike tail of our native opossum, has black silken fibers which are excellent for the winging of streamer flies.

This fur is readily available at most fly shops and from furriers.

OPTIC EYES (see Glass Eyes)

ORLON: A synthetic knitting yarn that comes in a variety of colors and may be obtained by the skein in department stores and knitting supply shops.

OSTRICH PLUMES: Ostrich plumes can be a very expensive item since they are primarily harvested for the feather district in New York City to be sold to millinery, theater, costuming, and related industries. Large, fully shaped, and neatly formed plumes will, at the wholesale level, bring somewhere between three and five dollars. Yet they are available to fly tyers from supply houses at very reasonable prices because we get the leftovers or those that do not otherwise make the grade.

The plumes range in size from five to six inches to almost three feet in length. Natural colors include black, gray, beige/brown, and white, and the feathers can be dyed into a variety of other shades by commercial dyers. If you try to dye these yourself you may be disappointed, since conventional dyeing causes the fibers to mat. I have not yet discovered the process feather merchants use to achieve their results.

The smaller and shorter-flued ostrich plumes are called mini ostrich by catalog houses. These are used mostly as feelers or gills on nymphs and larvae. The larger plumes are used on nymphs and wet flies for wing cases, ribbing, and thoraxes. In salmon fly tying they are used as butts and in streamer flies as soft pulsing and undulating wings.

OTTER: An aquatic animal with soft brown to tan cream underfur which is used for both dry flies and subsurface patterns.

PARTRIDGE: "Partridge," or "partridge hackle," when used in a pattern recipe, nearly always refers to the brown back or gray breast feathers of the gray partridge (*Perdix perdix*), more commonly known as the Hungarian partridge. These feathers are relatively small (about the size of white wood duck breast feathers or less) and have a soft, subtle, almost speckled barring. They are used as tails, beards, legs, and hackle collars on wet flies and nymphs.

Substitutes often used in place of this feather include the chukar partridge and grouse, as well as the back or saddle hackle feathers of hen chickens having similar markings.

The word "partridge" should not be confused with the loose interpretation sometimes given to the ruffed grouse, which in some regions of New England is also called partridge or "pah-tridge."

Some sources for partridge are Fly Fisher's Paradise, Donegal, Egger's, and Turner's Fly Shop.

PEACOCK, PEACOCK EYE, PEACOCK HERL, PEACOCK SWORD: Peacock is to a fly shop what bread is to a grocery store. If ever there was a fiber grown specifically for the tying of flies, the herled fiber from a peacock eyed tail would be it.

Peacock eyed tails, swords, and other feathers are collected in India (where the birds are sacred) after the bird has molted and dropped its feathers.

In addition to the heavily flued or herled fibers below the eye of a peacock tail, the fibers in the eye itself are stripped of their barbules and become the stripped quill bodies for Quill Gordons, Ginger Quills, and other patterns.

Peacock sword feathers, with their shorter and more staggered flued fibers, are used mostly by the salmon fly tyer for tails and throats.

Though they are seldom seen in fly shops, the wing quills, both the mottled and the cinnamon, are highly sought after and some fly tyers consider them superior to the old-fashioned mottled turkey wing quill and the cinnamon turkey tail.

The body feathers of the peacock are of an iridescent blue and gold and would make excellent cheeks and shoulders, but these also are rarely cataloged.

Peacock eyed tails, swords, and strung peacock herl (used mostly for streamer flies since the flues are too short) are sold in every fly shop. One outfit that specializes in the mottled wing quills is Donegal.

PEARLESCENT DIAMOND BRAID: Made in the same manner as Mylar tubing (which see) except that a pearlescent material is woven around a cotton core.

PECCARY: Sometimes referred to as javelina, this wild pig, the only one native to the southwestern United States and Mexico, has a hide covered with bristly fibers that are barred black and white and terminate in a black tip. Though fairly stiff, the fibers have a certain amount of flex to them and are ideally used to form the tails and antennae on stonefly nymphs.

PHEASANT (see Golden Pheasant, Lady Amherst Pheasant, Ringneck Pheasant, Silver Pheasant)

PINTAIL DUCK: The feathers most sought after on this duck are the narrow flank feathers of the drake. They are approximately four to five inches long and just over half an inch wide. The pearl blue-gray barring is much finer than that of mallard flank, though mallard may be substituted if pintail is unavailable. The feathers are used primarily on streamer flies when dressing smelt imitations.

Very few suppliers list this item since it is fairly scarce, but you will find it cataloged by Joe's Tackle and the Classic and Custom Fly Shop.

The wing quills of this large duck offer excellent winging material for both wet and dry flies.

POLAR BEAR: The hair of the federally protected polar bear is still much sought after in the tying of salmon, streamer, and steelhead flies. The silky-smooth, yet firm hair fibers are of a lustrous white to cream shade and are often dyed into other bright colors. Incidentally, when dyeing this fiber you should be careful not to let the tapered ends touch the hot sides of the dyeing container since this will singe and blunt them. Polar bear hair ranges in length from an inch to almost five inches, with an average size of two inches.

Substitutes for polar bear include calf tail, goat hair, yak, American opossum, and a variety of synthetic equivalents such as Fishair and other nylon products. The synthetics are usually available in a variety of colors.

Polar bear hair may still be obtained from some taxidermists in the form of cuttings and trimmings, and some fly shops may still have

an existing supply, though I suspect the price has far surpassed the normal inflationary process.

POLAR BEAR, IMITATION: I have not seen this synthetic material listed of late and it may well have been replaced by Fishair (which see). It is made of soft, silken, synthetic fibers and is intended to replace the protected polar bear.

POLLY WIGGLE: An elongated form of poly yarn which is used for streamer flies. Has a pulsing, undulating action when being retrieved through the water.

POLYCELON: A thin, foam-rubber-like material in a variety of shades which can be used for dry fly bodies, wing cases on emergers, terrestrial bodies, and other patterns where high floating qualities are desired.

POLYETHYLENE STRIP: Polyethylene bags are often cut into strips to form the shell on such flies as shrimp and scuds (see the pattern, Grass Shrimp, pages 289–92). You don't buy them. You buy the materials usually packaged inside them and regard them as a fringe benefit.

POLYPROPYLENE YARN: A smooth-fibered yarn manufactured by Phentex in a variety of colors. It has a specific gravity which is lighter than water. Used primarily as spinner wings on dry flies and occasionally as streamer winging material.

POLY II SHEET MATERIAL: Manufactured by Fly-Rite, this product is used mostly at streamside by fly tyers trying to match a specific hatch. It consists of an unwoven nylon cloth such as that used in dress patterns. The soft, fuzzy fibers can be scraped off with thumb and finger-

nail and dubbed onto thread. It is not very frequently cataloged, though Dan Bailey's Fly Shop lists it.

PORCUPINE: Both the quills, which may be white or white with black tips, and the much softer bristles of this animal are used. The hollow quill will at times be lashed to the shank to form the body of a fly such as the Green Drake Spinner featured by Vincent Marinaro in *A Modern Dry Fly Code,* while the bristles form tails and antennae on nymphs. Some fly shops that carry it are Rusin's Fly and Tackle and Donegal.

PRAIRIE CHICKEN: The widely barred brown/tan and white body feathers are used as gills in the Whitlock Matuka Sculpin and similar patterns. This bird is rarely available through fly shops, though Blue Ribbon Flies has been known to have a supply. I believe there is a limited hunting season on them in certain western states and the fly tyers in these areas may either shoot their own or beg the feathers from hunters. Substitutes for this bird are hen mallard, Hungarian partridge, and ruffed grouse.

PRISMATIC BODY MATERIAL: Used primarily on streamer flies and hair bugs, this synthetic product has an adhesive surface on one side for easy placement and attachment and is available in iridescent shades of orange, gray, violet, gold, silver, and yellow. It is available through Traun River Products.

RABBIT: The soft long-fibered underfur of both the domestic rabbit and the cottontail is a great boon to fly tyers. The fur blends easily not only with itself but with furs of many other animals. It is often used as a binding and adhesive fiber in conjunction with some of the coarser furs such as seal. The cottontail is a natural blue-gray in color while the hair of the domestic white rabbit is easily dyed into any required shade. Moreover, it is the least expensive of all furs and the supply is almost unlimited.

Rabbit fur is often used with the guard hairs intact to form the collars of such patterns as the Jorgensen Fur Caddis Pupa. It is readily available at all fly shops both as packaged pieces on the skin or as a blend in various fly-tying shades.

RAFFIA: Imported from Madagascar, raffia is the leafstalk of a palm which is used primarily for weaving baskets. Its natural color is tan but it can be dyed into other shades. It is used for the bodies of dry flies, wet flies, and nymphs.

RAVEN: A fairly large black bird similar to the crow (which see). Not listed in catalogs or usually found in supply houses since it is protected under federal migratory bird laws. If hunting seasons apply, it may be obtained during the legal season or possibly as a road kill. The substitute for raven is the crow or the natural or dyed black feathers of the common chicken.

RED FOX SQUIRREL TAIL (see Squirrel)

REDI RABBIT: A product developed by Jack Mickievicz which uses the underfur of rabbit exclusively. The resulting blends are imitative of the bodies of our most important aquatic insects. Available to dealers and fly tyers through Jack's Tackle.

REEVES PHEASANT: The plumage from this bird is rarely used and seldom cataloged. Body feathers are brownish orange with black barring around the outer edge.

RINGNECK PHEASANT, RINGNECK TAIL: This bird, a native of Asia, is raised domestically in both England and the United States and survives and breeds quite well in the wild as well as in many of our farmland areas. Thus the varied and beautiful plumage is in ample supply.

The male bird is the most prized, from its metallic green head down to its long-fibered blue-gray rump feathers, which are used as spey hackle in salmon and steelhead patterns. The body plumage includes various mottled and faintly barred "church window" feathers, so-called because they resemble arched stained-glass windows. Other body feathers are of a rich bronze golden tan, some of which terminate in a black tip. There are also shorter side feathers which could be used as legs or throat hackles on nymphs, wet flies, and salmon flies. The tips of these fibers are mostly blue-gray but others are tan or green and tan. Occasionally you will come across a bird with utterly different plumage which is the result of cross-breeding by shooting preserves. One preserve I know of even raised this bird in pure white.

The hen ringneck pheasant is of a mottled light tan shade, and though not as plentiful in fly-tying shops (most states restrict the shooting of hens, and preserves only keep enough for breeding), its feathers are also in demand for legs, throat hackle, and the like. The wing quills of the hen and the cock bird are also used, though infrequently.

The tail of the male ringneck is famous for its fibers, which form the tail of many mayfly

patterns. Color is a barred mahogany. Readily available.

RUBBER HACKLE: This item is usually sold in inch-wide flat rubber strips which have been pre-scored so that very fine strands can be peeled off. Basic colors are white, medium blue-gray, and dark gray. A recent catalog introduction labeled Living Rubber Legs features a wider range of colors, used mostly by tyers of bass bugs and poppers. In conventional fly tying these rubber strands are used as feelers and antennae on some of our western flies, such as the Yuk Bug and the Bitch Creek.

Rubber hackle behaves in a tantalizing manner when it is twitched while being fished. Certain traditionalists might hesitate to use such a fly, but as long as the fly can be cast in the normal manner with a fly rod, the pattern qualifies. Bass spin fishermen have no such compunctions. They have long known of the virtues of rubber hackle and taken advantage of it.

SCHLAPPEN: A name used in the feather industry for the long, soft feathers found near the lower back of a rooster or hen chicken. They are fairly long, wide, and fully webbed and are often used by tyers of streamer flies to obtain a full-bodied wing effect.

SEALEX: A lustrous synthetic fur blend developed by Poul Jorgensen as a substitute for the non-importable natural coarse seal's fur originally obtained from England. It is available in most of the bright colors used by salmon fly tyers and also blended into shades for may fly and caddis imitations. Available to dealers through Umpqua Feather Merchants, Inc. (See also Unseal.)

SEAL FUR: There are two kinds of seal fur. One is the coarse, glassy, fibrous fur of the Greenland or hair seal and the other the soft, velvety underfur of the Pacific fur seal.

Seal fur is still available, though few fly shops, if any, carry it. I believe that a limited amount of these animals are allowed to be harvested and thus wind up with the furriers, from whom a few scraps or damaged skins may be acquired.

The fur of the Greenland or hair seal, which is sheared and blended and dyed in England for such supply houses as E. Veniard, Ltd., is the one that has gained popularity, not only for its use in many salmon fly patterns but also for the coarse scraggly bodies of many of our nymphs. Its natural color is cream. Unfortunately, this item is restricted for import and substitutes are, more or less, the order of the day. Some of these include African Goat, Unseal, Fishing Post Nymph Blend, Ligas Ultra Translucent Dubbing, and any others having a coarse and glistening fiber.

Unless specified otherwise, anytime a pattern calls for a body made of seal fur it is referring to the coarse, hard-to-dub, glassy hair seal variety. One dealer who still lists the genuine article is Wallace W. Doak and Sons.

SILVER PHEASANT: Still readily available to distributors in this country under a special import quota system through the federal Fish and Wildlife Service, silver pheasant is primarily used for its body feathers, which are white with black stripes. The feathers are used as shoulders on streamer and salmon flies. The Gray Ghost pattern is one example.

The silver pheasant also has a fairly long dark blue crest, which is used as topping on some streamer patterns.

SILVER WIRE (see under Tinsels)

SKUNK: Though this animal is often available as a road kill, I don't advise collecting it unless you have a strong stomach. It is extremely difficult to eliminate the penetrating odor once it has been released.

Fortunately, the glistening black and white tail, which makes excellent wing material for streamer flies, is available through some supply houses and through the furrier. The body hair is rarely used. Two shops that list the tail in their catalogs are Bud Lilly's Trout Shop and Evening Rise Fly Tyers.

SNOWSHOE RABBIT FEET: The fur on the hind feet of a snowshoe rabbit is not unlike seal fur in coarseness. I suspect it was Francis Betters of the Adirondack Sport Shop in Wilmington, New York, who made this fur popular by using it on his famous The Usual pattern. Betters has the advantage of living in the north country where this hare is prevalent. It is also available from the Beaverkill Angler.

SPECKLED TURKEY (see Turkey)

SPECTRAFLASH: Similar to polypropylene bag material except that it is produced in a pearlescent shade. Like the poly bags, it is cut to size to form the hood or shell back on shrimp and scuds. Available to dealers through Traun River Products. Spectraflash II is laminated to a fine, white synthetic fabric for more durability.

SPECTRAFLASH-HAIR: A product introduced by Traun River Products along the same lines as Flashabou. They offer a full color range, including some shades that differ from Flashabou. Like Flashabou, this is simply a great new material for fly tyers which will find its way into many types of patterns.

SPECTRAFLASH TUBING: A type of pearlescent Mylar tubing in shades of pearl, rose, red, yellow, light green, dark green, gray, orange, and brown. Streamer fly tyers should love this one, since it opens new vistas for imitating the variously colored baitfish in both fresh and salt water.

SPECTRUM: A very fine synthetic dubbing made from polyester. It is easy to dub and is blended into a variety of aquatic insect body colors. Some dealers that carry it are Henry's Fork Anglers, Hunter's Angling Supplies, and the Fly Shop.

SPINNER TAIL MATERIAL (also sold under the trade name Microfibits): A super-fine, yet fairly tough synthetic fiber produced in a number of insect colors, including white, cream, blue dun, olive, grizzly, and cree. I suspect that John Betts, of *Synthetic Flies* fame, is directly responsible for the development of this material. It is ideal for tails on mayflies and feelers and legs on nymphs. Introduced by Traun River Products and available to dealers and fly tyers through their distributorship.

SPUN FUR: Made from the fibers of the Angora rabbit, this natural yarn was once listed in most catalogs. A few still carry it, one of which is Murray's Fly Shop. Of late I have not noticed it in department stores and it is possible that Angora sweaters are now knitted with synthetic fibers. It used to be available in a wide variety of colors, and its soft trailing fibers made it ideal for leeches and other subsurface patterns.

SQUIRREL, SQUIRREL TAIL: The tail fibers of the gray squirrel, for some three-quarters of their length from the skin out, are a barred tan and black, terminating in a wide black band and a white tip. The tail fibers are used in countless fly patterns, including streamers, salmon flies, and some surface downwing patterns.

The body hair and fur of the gray squirrel can be sheared and blended to produce a coarse blue-gray mottled effect for bodies of both nymphs and dry flies.

The tail of the red fox squirrel on its back or top side is barred a reddish tan (almost ginger) and black for three-quarters of its length from the skin out and terminates in a wide black band with a reddish-brown tip. The underside tail fibers are of a solid ginger orange shade but also end with the wide black band and reddish-brown tip. Incidentally, you will find off-shades in both the red fox and the gray squirrel coloration from time to time. Length of tail fibers of both species may be anywhere from one and a half to two and a half inches, depending on age and the individual animal.

The body hair of the red fox squirrel is a mottled tan, black, and white on the back and a beautiful natural orange on the underside. Both are cut and blended into a fur for bodies of wet flies and nymphs.

Both gray and red fox squirrel tails are available at most supply houses. The body fur is carried by only a few shops, two of which are the Classic and Custom Fly Shop and Jack's Tackle.

The black squirrel, at least in this country, is a melanistic phase of the gray squirrel. Natural black squirrel tails are rarely listed in catalogs because the supply is too limited. These fibers, however, are among the most prized by the tyers of salmon and steelhead flies.

The tail fibers and body fur of the much smaller eastern pine squirrel have a lovely rusty brown coloration. The body fur is often sheared and blended to form a substitute material for the Gold-Ribbed Hare's Ear patterns. This animal, hunted as a pest in some states, is also occasionally found as a road kill. It is prevalent in the northern regions of New York, Vermont, New Hampshire, and Pennsylvania.

One dealer who lists both the pine squirrel and a species of natural black squirrel tail is Wallace W. Doak and Sons.

STARLING: The starling's body feathers are black with a creamy yellow/white spot and they are often used as a substitute for jungle cock eyes. They are also used in soft-hackled fly patterns such as the Starling and Herl. Full skins of the bird (which is hunted as a pest in many states) are now and again available in some fly shops. They are listed by Little Dixie Flies.

STOAT TAIL: When a pattern recipe calls for stoat tail fibers, it is referring to the hair of the brown phase of an ermine tail. However, because of the strong similarity, not only ermine but fitch, mink, or weasel may be substituted. Stoat is rarely listed in American catalogs, but others of the weasel family are.

STRIPPED GOOSE (see Biots)

STRIPPED HACKLE STEM QUILL (see Center Stem Quill)

STRIPPED PEACOCK QUILL: Refers to the de-flued fibers from a peacock eyed tail. (See also Peacock, and for method, see Quill Gordon, pages 24–6.)

SWANNUNDAZE: This soft vinyl/type of plastic material, which is flat on one side and oval on the other, is used to form the bodies of stone-fly nymphs and caddis larve. It is manufactured in a variety of colors, including clear and some translucent shades. Swannundaze was first used by Frank Johnson of Lyndhurst, New Jersey, on a stonefly nymph imitation while fishing the upper Delaware River. He introduced it to a number of dealers, and it has since become one of the major innovations in the last decade. It is now available in nearly every fly shop throughout the world.

Incidentally, quite a number of new patterns have evolved that are directly attributable to Swannundaze.

SWISS STRAW: You might call this a synthetic equivalent of raffia. It is used for wing cases on nymphs and shell backs on shrimp and scuds. Comes in a variety of colors. One dealer that lists it is the Fly Shop.

TEAL, TEAL FLANK: Though all the feathers of the green-winged teal may be used, the drake of this species of duck is known primarily for its heavily pronounced barred flank feathers, which are a pale gray with black bands. They are mostly used in salmon and streamer flies, though they are also ideal for the formation of a prominent upright wing on a dry fly. Some tyers prefer them for the wings of the Adams instead of the standard grizzly hackle tips.

Teal breast has a fainter barring but is also used, at times, for cheeks, shoulders, and throats. The wing quills of both the drake and the hen, though smaller than mallard or pintail, are used for the divided wings on some of the smaller mayfly imitations.

Teal is not very readily available in fly shops since imports are restricted and native supplies are not numerous. Some that do carry it are the Fishing Post, Dan Bailey's Fly Shop, and the Orvis Company.

THREAD: Except when used as the head of a streamer, salmon, or steelhead pattern or as a ribbing on a wet fly or nymph, thread should always be unobtrusive. It should be fine enough so that it does not bulk up the fly in any way and its color should be such that it blends in with the overall shade of the imitation. In most of the categories of patterns in this book I've recommended the 6/0 size of the Flymaster brand of thread. This particular brand lies fairly flat, is waxed so that it easily winds around the hook shank and will spin all but the coarsest of dubbings without additional waxing, and comes in a full color range to suit almost all recipes. Now and then, however, you will come across situations where another type of thread is warranted and the following listing should meet these requirements.

Monocord: This type of thread comes in sizes 3/0 and A and in both waxed and unwaxed versions. It lies very flat and many tyers prefer it for the tying of some of our larger stonefly imitations, streamers, and saltwater patterns. I will occasionally use this thread for the spinning of deer hair bodies on such flies as the Irresistible since it is stronger and more pressure can be applied. This thread has one drawback in that it is fairly elastic and stretches more than the average nylons. It comes in a very full range of colors.

Silk Thread: This type of thread has no stretch at all and for that reason alone it is preferred by some tyers, even though it is not as strong or as durable as nylon or other

synthetics. In black and white it is available in all sizes, including an extremely fine 8/0. In other colors it is usually not available in diameters smaller than 2/0.

Midge Thread: This extremely fine thread, sometimes referred to as Spiderweb thread, measures an approximate 14/0 on the scale and is used by quite a few tyers for the tying of midge type flies in sizes 20 and smaller. It is available only in white but can be tinted any color with a marking pen. Its only disadvantage is that it gathers static electricity and flares all over the place when you are working with it.

Flat Waxed Nylon Thread: This was first introduced by Andre Puyans of Creative Sports. It is very strong yet lies flat and is ideal for spinning deer hair heads on the larger muddlers, sculpins, and bass flies. It comes in a variety of colors.

Kevlar Thread: A recent introduction of exceptional tensile strength for its diameter (about equal to a size A Monocord) which is gaining favor with bass bug tyers and those who use large quantities of deer hair. It is just now seeing its way into various fly shops. The Fly Shop carries it under the name of Super Thread in yellow, brown, olive, and pink, and I believe this range will be expanded shortly. A similar thread in an orange shade is carried by Traun River Products under the name Galaxy Wonder Thread. Incidentally, if you are tempted to test this thread by trying to break it with your hands, be careful. It's somewhat like monofilament (but much stronger) and may cut into your fingers before it breaks.

TINSELS: Although tinsel is manufactured worldwide, French tinsel is the kind most often sought by fly tyers because it is coated with a

protective layer of varnish which keeps it from tarnishing.

Metallic tinsels are usually made in gold and silver in sizes ranging from 1/32nd to 1/16th of an inch, generally listed simply as fine, medium, and wide. E. Veniard, Ltd., carries an exceptional size range (eleven sizes of flat tinsel and six sizes of oval tinsel), using much smaller increments between the finest and the widest.

Embossed tinsels, which are run through a special dye to break up the flat surface, are also available in gold and silver, though most dealers only carry them in the medium size.

Tinsels are also made in a copper color, though this shade is often a synthetic product today.

An oval tinsel is one in which a fine strand of gold or silver tinsel is wound around a cotton core. If the manufacturing process on an oval tinsel is of poor quality, the tinsel may unravel from the cotton core while the fly is being tied. I've found that if you coat this type of tinsel with head lacquer first and let it dry fully, this problem will be solved.

Though not a tinsel as such, most manufacturers also produce single strands of fine gold and silver wire, which are used mostly on smaller flies. These add just the faintest amount of glitter to the pattern and also serve as a binding on fur bodies and other materials. They are used, in some patterns, as a counter-wrap over stripped peacock quill bodies to reinforce them against abrasion.

Tinsels made of Mylar and other synthetics are easier to handle, do not kink, and are non-tarnishing. Mylar in tinsel form is available in many colors, including pearlescent, which makes for a realistic body that displays subtle color changes when the fly is retrieved underwater. Mylar tinsels also lend themselves

THE BOOK OF FLY PATTERNS 331

to mixing with other materials in streamer type wings since they are supple enough to flow, flex, and weave almost as naturally as some hair fibers. Lefty Kreh introduced this type of arrangement when he designed Lefty's Deceiver, and the material Flashabou (which see) incorporates this technique in the fullest sense.

Tinsels of all types are available at nearly every fly shop. Some that specialize in the offbeat shades are Traun River Products, the Orvis Company, and the Fly Shop.

TURKEY (wild and domestic): The speckled or mottled oak turkey wing quills, which are used so often for so many purposes by fly tyers, were once a common item, in the days when the brown or bronze turkey was raised for consumption. Today, just about all of the domestically raised turkeys are white, not because they taste better, but because they look better to the consumer. When a brown turkey is defeathered small bluish-purple marks are left on the skin; in the white bird these are indiscernible.

Mottled turkey wing quills and other feathers may still be obtained from the wily wild bird, which is being hunted in more and more states every season. Here again, as with other game birds and animals, making the acquaintance of those in the hunting fraternity may increase your supply of these feathers. One enterprising fly tyer, Thomas Horan of Shamokin, Pennsylvania, is raising the brown turkey for its feathers, but because it is a business and feed prices being what they are, a pair of mottled brown turkey wing quills may set you back some four to five dollars. The mottled turkey wing quill may be anywhere from eight inches to over a foot long. The markings are from a light white speckled brown to a dark oak leaf mottled brown, which make them favorites for wing cases on stonefly nymphs and wings of hoppers and muddlers.

The tail feathers of the brown turkey are a very deep brown with yet deeper brown barring. The tips of these feathers are white.

The body feathers, which are brown or bronze and are sometimes called "flats," are also used. These feathers are somewhat triangular in shape and taper down at the sides with the tip, or top, squared off, almost as if it were cut to make it look even.

Turkey flats from the white turkey can be dyed to various shades for use as wings on dry flies and emergers. They have also been used for some of the Swisher/Richards no-hackle patterns. Because the white turkey is so abundant, the feathers from this bird are among the least expensive.

The wing quills from the white turkey can easily be dyed to all shades except mottled. You can, however, make your own mottled feathers by first dyeing a number of white wing quills to a light shade of brown or tan and then, with a marking pen or paintbrush, design your own muddler or hopper wings.

Substitutes for turkey include any of the other larger mottled wing quills, such as those of the peacock (though these may be just as scarce). Some dealers, such as the Fly Shop, offer bleached turkey wing quills. These are the black and white pointer feathers which have been bleached down to a shade of brown and white. Also used are what are called "foto feathers," which are produced from white turkey wing quills by a silk-screen process. Just about every fly shop offers turkey in one form or another.

UNSEAL: Derived from a product called "Aunt Lydia's rug yarn," this lustrous synthetic was first discovered by Poul Jorgensen and blended by him under the trade name of Sealex (which see) as a substitute for the non-importable seal fur. For a number of years Sealex was not available and Jack Mickievicz, evolving still other colors, produced the same product under the trade name of Unseal. It is available to all dealers through the Jack's Tackle distributorship. This type of imitation seal fur dubbing is, in all probability, being made by others under various brand names.

V-RIB MATERIAL: A clear plastic oval material similar to Swannundaze but much finer and softer and with much more stretchability. It is used to form segmented bodies on nymph and larval imitations, and is featured on certain bonefish patterns such as the Crazy Charlie. Two dealers that carry it are the Orvis Company and the Fly Shop.

WHISKERS: The whiskers of most animals make excellent material for tails and antennae because they are finely tapered yet firm in texture. They are usually available through a furrier outlet as scrap fur still attached to the masks of foxes, fitch, opossum, and other popular coat-making skins.

WIDGEON, BALDPATE WIDGEON: A fairly large duck with slate gray wing quills which are excellent for dry flies and wet flies. The drake features a barred pinkish-brown flank feather somewhat similar to that of wood duck flank, though the markings are softer and subtler.

It is not often listed in catalogs, but I did find it cataloged by the Ojai Fisherman. It may be obtained from hunters during legal gunning seasons. Though it is fairly widely distributed throughout the United States, it is more common in western regions.

WIRE (see under Tinsels)

WOODCHUCK (Groundhog): The hide from this animal may be the most underrated and underused of all furs and fibers, though it does seem to be gaining more popularity in recent years.

The guard hairs of the woodchuck, which range from black to tan to black with white tips, are perhaps the most versatile of all hair fibers in their many uses. They are supple enough when tied full length as a wing for streamer and salmon flies yet firm but easily manageable as upright wings on mayfly imitations and downwings on caddis flies. The fine barring, which is evenly and definitively pronounced, provides a color mixture much like a grizzly hackle, a breakup effect, if you will, which gives an impression of bugginess and life. Woodchuck fibers, though not hollow, are extremely high floaters and much more durable than deer hair fibers. In addition to the barred fibers on the back of the animal, you will find cream, tan, and fiery brown guard hairs along the underside and in the area where the legs emerge from the body.

The underfur, which is very coarse, can be cut and blended and used as a scraggly body fur on nymphs and other patterns.

Even though this animal is abundant and, in fact, considered a pest by many farmers, it is not readily available. John Harder of the Orvis Company personally uses a pattern called the Chuck Caddis, which features a wing made of woodchuck guard hairs, and considers it one of his most effective patterns. However, he does not list it in the Orvis catalog because he is unable to obtain enough woodchuck hides for his tyers and customers. Woodchuck is often hunted and also found as a road kill, especially in early spring when the fur is in prime shape. Two dealers who do list it in their catalogs are Wallace W. Doak and Sons and Buchner Fly Designs. Some distributors who carry it when they can get it are the Wapsi Fly Company and Raymond C. Rumpf and Son.

WOODCOCK, ENGLISH: You will occasionally see reference made to the feathers of this bird, for both body and wing plumage, which are of a barred dark brown. It is, however, restricted for import and I have been unable to find a listing of it anywhere. Suitable substitutes include grouse, English partridge (also restricted but available here and there), or any bird with small feathers of similar coloration.

The American woodcock is also used now and again for its feathers, but this bird does not have the barring contained in the English version.

WOOD DUCK: One of the most beautiful of all waterfowl, the American drake wood duck is a delight to painters, photographers, and wood carvers and the grand prize to fly tyers. Beginning at the head, one finds a long metallic green crest which blends into shades of blue and purple at the sides. The neck and throat are purple flecked with white. The flank feathers, sometimes called "fly tyer's gold," are of a lemon brown, barred with very fine dark brown bands throughout while others, closer to the shoulder, terminate in a white and black barring of much wider dimensions. The breast feathers are pure white and fairly short with just about the perfect flare for the making of fan wings.

The lemon brown flank feather is, of course, the most valued, since it is used for every type of fly imaginable, from dry flies to wet flies as winging material, to legs and tails on nymphs and wet flies, and to throats, tails, wings, and shoulders on streamer and salmon flies.

A few decades ago the mandarin duck was listed in many catalogs as a substitute for the American wood duck since the flank feathers are almost identical. They are, in fact, so much alike that the American wood duck has been listed as a substitute for the mandarin duck in many listings. Mandarin duck is, however, now a restricted item and has not been available in years, though you may come across some old stock hidden in the back of a fly shop here and there.

Not all fly shops list natural wood duck for sale, since it is fairly scarce. Unlike the mallard, it is not raised domestically for shooting preserves. The only available source for some dealers is the limited supply brought in by hunters, though even this procedure is illegal in some states and further limits the supply. Your best bet here is to make the acquaintance of some duck hunters and beg some of these prized feathers from them. Sadly, most of the plumage of this duck is discarded after the bird has been plucked and prepared for the table. Two shops that list this item are Hook and Feathers and the Ojai Fisherman.

WOOD DUCK, IMITATION: Made by dyeing mallard or teal flank to the shade of natural lemon brown wood duck flank. One favored old-time recipe for obtaining the shade was to dye mallard flank in tea. Another, even better method, according to Jack Mickievicz, is to immerse it in a bath of boiled onion skins. Available in all fly shops.

WOOL: Available in carded form from most supply houses, and sold by the skein in department stores and knitting supply shops. The color range is almost limitless. Certain suppliers, such as Jacklin's Fly Shop, carry raw wool in heavy bulk skeins which are used on some of the larger stonefly nymphs. Still others, such as Traun River Products, carry a fluffy type of wool, used in the knitting of sweaters, having a soft and silken texture. Wool is subject to the varied fashion whims of clothing manufacturers, and somehow fly tyers eventually discover and make use of every type.

ZEBRA MANE: The long black and white fibers found on the mane of the zebra make excellent ribbing. Generally not listed by fly shops but available through furriers specializing in the making of rugs and ornamental interior designs.

Sources for Materials and Related Information

THE PURPOSE of this section is to give the fly tyer every possible lead as to where he can obtain the materials he needs or any related information for the tying of his flies. I undertake the following listing with a certain amount of trepidation, since there are bound to be some companies or individuals I've overlooked, though quite unintentionally. Obviously, I cannot mention every fly shop in the country and have thus limited the listing to those who do business by mail order. This in no way implies that the tyer should neglect his local fly shop if there is one within driving distance of his home. Actually, the tyer should approach the local dealer first, since a personal visit allows the tyer to select qualities and colors for himself as opposed to relying on the judgment of another, however expert and well intentioned, many miles away. For the benefit of the local fly shop, sports store, and tackle shop, I have included the names of various reliable distributors so that they can obtain supplies at a fair wholesale price and thus compete with others in the industry.

I have tried to list every mail-order house I could find in the advertising sections of the various publications in our field, in addition to others I know, with or without catalogs, that will ship orders by mail. If I have missed someone, by all means let me know so that I can rectify the matter in a later printing. I'm sure that by the time this book comes off the press there will be other, newer dealers on the scene and some of those listed herein will have folded their tents.

Below I have provided a somewhat detailed description of what each of the companies carry and have noted whether they sell retail, wholesale, or both. If a specific or unusual item is needed, I suggest you first look for it in the section dealing with fly-tying materials, which in many cases will refer you to the company or companies that carry it. Incidentally, in that section some dealers are mentioned more than others, for the simple reason that the latest catalogs I have received from them are more up-to-date than others. Also, some dealers will specialize in the new or unusual or list something that others do not as yet carry. Food for thought for all you dealers.

One final word: If I can be of help in any manner regarding materials, or if there are suggestions you wish to make that will be of benefit to other fly tyers, by all means drop me a line in care of the publisher.

ANGLER'S JUNCTION
5606 Alameda, N.E.
Albuquerque, New Mexico 87113
(505) 821-0500

Carries fly-tying tools, hooks, a fly-tying kit, and a good range of flies. Catalog includes fly-fishing and assorted accessory items. Books on various subjects available. Owner is John Wirth, Jr.

ANGLER'S PRO SHOP
224 Old Bethlehem Pike
Souderton, Pennsylvania 18964
(215) 721-4909
Both retail and wholesale. No catalog at this time, but responds to mail-order requests. Carries a complete line of fly-fishing materials in addition to one of the most comprehensive listings of fly-fishing and fly-tying books available. Owner is Herb Van Dyke.

ANGLER'S PRODUCTS
2071½ 30th Street
Boulder, Colorado 80302
(303) 443-6425
Wholesale to dealers and commercial tyers only. Carries a full line of fly-tying materials, hooks, and tools. Wally Allen, owner.

ANGLER'S RUFF
16 Glen Head Road
Glen Head, New York 11545
(516) 676-0087
Val and Lauren Antonucci, who own and run the Ruff, have a compact and classy catalog which may be obtained for $1. They carry a full line of materials, books, and flies and specialize in salmon fly tying and flies.

ANGLING SPECIALTIES
P.O. Box 6
Lethbridge, Alberta
Canada T1J 3Y3
(403) 328-5252

Featured are tools, materials, hooks, accessories, and books. Fairly comprehensive catalog. Does not carry flies in catalog as of this writing.

DAN BAILEY'S FLY SHOP
209 West Park Street
Livingston, Montana 59047
(406) 222-1673
This is, of course, one of the oldest establishments. Now operated by Dan's son John Bailey. A lovely catalog with clear, full-color photographs of some 300 fly patterns. Specializes in western patterns but not to the exclusion of favorites in other regions. Also carries a full line of fly-fishing equipment, materials, books, hooks, and tools.

BAIRD'S "SNOW COUNTRY"
Box 22
Clementsvale, Nova Scotia
Canada B0S 1G0
Catalog features flies for the region, materials, and an assortment of hackle. Reg Baird, the owner, carries some things in his shop you won't find elsewhere.

L. L. BEAN, INC.
2091 Main Street
Freeport, Maine 04033
(207) 865-3111
This grand old company, which is famous for its quality line of outdoor clothing, has only recently thrown its hat into the fly-tying ring. It now publishes a catalog devoted solely to fly fishing which includes a section featuring the latest in tools and materials. Also runs a fly-fishing school.

BEAVERKILL ANGLER
Broad Street
Roscoe, New York 12776
(607) 498-5194
No catalog, but does quite a bit of mail-order business. Budge and Dot Loekle, the owners, carry a full line of materials, flies, and equipment and are a distributor for McMurray Ant bodies and parts. Detailed maps of the Beaverkill, Willowemoc, and all branches of the Delaware River are kept in stock.

BECKIE'S
1336 Orange Street
Berwick, Pennsylvania 18603
(717) 752-2011
A small but thoroughly thought-out catalog. Carries flies, materials, hooks, books, and general fly-fishing equipment, and usually introduces innovative ideas, such as the Turkey Flat Emergers. Owners Barry and Cathy Beck also run schools for fly tying.

BLUE RIBBON FLIES
P.O. Box 1037
West Yellowstone, Montana 59758
(406) 646-9365
Retail and wholesale. Retail catalog also includes news and maps of the area and local fishing information. Craig Mathews, owner, also conducts fishing trips and guide services. Specializing in western flies but carries all others. A good supply of materials, hooks, and books.

BOB'S HACKLE FARM AND FLY SHOP
872 Anthony Highway
Chambersburg, Pennsylvania 17201
(717) 352-7470
Bob and Linda Wetzel have assembled a compact little catalog dealing primarily with fly tying materials and tools. Their specialty item

is necks of rooster raised on their farm, in grizzly and other colors.

BUCHNER FLY DESIGNS
P.O. Box 1022
Jackson, Wyoming 83001
(307) 733-4944
   Formerly High Country Flies. A very neat little catalog which has all the important items Jay and Kathy Buchner carry, a full selection of meticulously tied flies, and a comprehensive listing of materials.

PETER BURTON
R.D. 1, Pleasant View Terrace
Middlebury, Vermont 05753
(802) 388-6876
   Does not have a catalog, but answers all mail-order inquiries. Specializes in flies for the area, some materials, and some accessories.

CABELLA'S
812 13th Avenue
Sidney, Nebraska 69160
(800) 237-8888
   One of the largest all-around fishing and hunting catalogs with good service and quality products: flies, materials, hooks, books, and fly-fishing equipment.

CHUCK'S TACKLE
283 Buckhead Avenue, N.E.
Atlanta, Georgia 30305
(404) 233-5065
   Gary and Bob Merriman's knowledge and experience show in the selection of their products for both fresh- and saltwater. No catalog as yet, but they will respond to any mail-order inquiries.

CLASSIC AND CUSTOM FLY SHOP
477 Pleasant Street
Holyoke, Massachusetts 01040
   David Goulet, owner, is also the fly tyer on the premises. Catalog features a full range of fly styles, hooks, books, materials, and assorted fly-fishing tackle.

DALE CLEMENS CUSTOM TACKLE, INC.
444 Schantz Spring Road
Allentown, Pennsylvania 18104
   Deals in both retail and wholesale, specializing in fly-tying materials. For those who are interested in rod building, Clemens carries a complete line of rod parts, blanks, and assorted tools and accessories.

CLOUSER'S FLY SHOP
101 Ulrich Street
Middletown, Pennsylvania 17057
(717) 944-6541
   This catalog, a simple homemade affair, doesn't look like much at first glance. But a closer look will tell you that owner Bob Clouser is extremely knowledgeable in the area of flies and materials for small mouth bass. In fact, he specializes in this area and offers guided trips on the Susquehanna and other rivers for those so inclined. The materials section of the catalog is very complete.

COLD SPRING ANGLERS
13 N. Letort Dr.
Carlisle, Pennsylvania 17013
(717) 245-2646
   In addition to general fly fishing equipment this catalog carries a fairly complete line of hooks, vises, and feathers and furs. Operated by Herb and Kathy Weigl.

COUNTERFEITER IN FLIES
R.D. 1, Box 315
Underhill, Vermont 05489
(802) 899-2049
   Robert Veverka, the owner, ties flies on a custom basis at fairly reasonable prices considering the care and detail that go into the construction of each pattern. Specializes in salmon, landlocked salmon, steelhead, streamers and bucktails, and some of the old English-style wet flies. He will mail a color brochure upon request which lists the exquisite patterns he ties.

CREATIVE SPORTS
2335 Boulevard Circle
Walnut Creek, California 94595
(415) 938-2255
   Owned and operated by Andre Puyans, an extremely resourceful innovator of fly patterns. Mail-order and retail shop, though catalog may not be available. Worthwhile calling for special flies, materials, and tackle.

WALLACE W. DOAK AND SONS, LTD.
P.O. Box 95
Doaktown, New Brunswick
Canada E0C 1G0
   A tastefully assembled catalog with color plates of salmon flies in the centerfold. Jerry and Bonnie Doak carry a wide assortment of salmon and trout fly patterns. There is a good range of materials, hooks, and tools with an accent on quality tackle.

DONEGAL
677 Route 208
Monroe, New York 10950
(914) 782-4600
   Operated by Paul I. Filippone. Catalog and retail shop feature quality tackle with accent on

salmon flies and materials. Good range of hooks, books, and accessories. Stocks unusual and hard-to-find items. Holds fly-tying lessons during the winter season.

EAGLE RIVER TRADING COMPANY
P.O. Box 1810
Wakefield, Massachusetts 01880
(617) 245-0755

This outfit is a distributor for Partridge hooks in the United States. Brochure lists these hooks and specialized tools. Also carries specialized books with accent on salmon fishing. Bill Grady, who runs the operation, plans to expand into a full line of materials and fishing equipment.

EDDIE'S FLIES AND TACKLE
303 Broadway
Bangor, Maine 04401

Eddie Reif ties many of the fly patterns in his catalog and is a knowledgeable Maine fishing guide. Carries a full line of materials and related fly-fishing equipment. Book list is comprehensive.

EGGER'S
P.O. Box 1344
Cumming, Georgia 30130

Deals primarily in materials, hooks, and tools. Geared to the fly tyer. Run by Hart and Marj Egger.

ESOPUS FLY FISHER
Box 206, Main Street
Phoenicia, New York 12464
(914) 688-5305

Emil and Kay Grimm have no catalog, but they fill mail-order requests. Fully equipped retail shop has a wide selection of materials, flies, tools, hooks, and books. Fly-tying classes also available.

EVENING RISE FLY TYERS
R.D. 2, Box 269
Plank Road
Navron, Pennsylvania 17555
(717) 442-4372

Operated by Nicholas J. Delle Donne, Jr., this mail-order company features a catalog with a good listing of tools, materials, hooks, books, and flies. There is a $1 charge for the first catalog.

THE FISHING POST
114 North Main Street
Greensburg, Pennsylvania 15601
(412) 832-8383

The owners are very knowledgeable in the fly-tying field. Their full line of materials and some exceptionally interesting ideas reflect their progressive imagination. Catalog is also well rounded in other areas.

THE FISHNET
Route 9
Cold Spring, New York 10516
(914) 265-3319

Al Purdy, the owner and manager, is an experienced angler and fly tyer and the shop reflects his expertise in the selection of quality materials. His mail brochure listing includes tools, materials, hooks, books, and related fishing items.

FLAGG'S FLIES
Box 574, Old Stage Road
Barre, Massachusetts 01005

The company mails a small but concise catalog which specializes in streamer and trolling flies. Also listed are tools, hooks, and materials. Rodney Flagg, the owner, raises a few of his own chickens, some of which are caped out with the entire skin intact.

THE FLY FISHER
315 Columbine Street
Denver, Colorado 80206
(303) 322-5014

This truly full-line shop, run by Ken Walters, has no catalog as yet, but has been replying to mail-order requests for years. Walters can also clue you in to some of the better fishing in the area since he seems to be field-testing new flies and equipment quite often.

FLY FISHER'S PARADISE
Box 448, Pike Street
Lemont, Pennsylvania 16851
(814) 234-4189

Run by Steve Sywensky and Dan Shields. Catalog deals primarily with flies and materials. The company conducts free seminars during the pre-season months which deal with the various styles of fly tying, knot tying, and stream techniques.

FLY FISHING SPECIALTIES
315 Lincoln Street
Roseville, California 95678
(916) 786-3470

Wholesale to dealers only. Terry Hellekson, who runs this outfit, always introduces something new to the trade, such as the Crystal Hair and Fantafoam materials. Catalog lists a complete line of fly-tying materials, hooks, books, and other items.

THE FLY SHOP
4140 Churn Creek Road
Redding, California 96002
(916) 222-3555

A very complete and progressive catalog with new materials always being introduced. Owners Mike Michalak and Brad Jackson offer free expertise regardless of the region to be fished. The company also features fishing trips to remote areas from Alaska to Christmas Island.

FREELAND OUTFITTERS
10060 Big Lake Road
Clarkston, Michigan 48016
(313) 625-4238

Wholesale to dealers only. Mike Freeland, the owner, has put together an easy-to-read catalog specializing primarily in tools, hooks, and fly-tying materials. Accent is on current and contemporary items, with a full range of the new synthetics plus a good assortment of blended furs.

FRONTIER ANGLERS
P.O. Box 11
Dillon, Montana 59725
(800) 228-5263

Catalog contains a good range of materials, hooks, tools, and books. An all-around selection of flies and fishing equipment. Company also features a guide service for southwestern Montana.

TED GODFREY
3509 Pleasant Plains Drive
Reisterstown, Maryland 21136
(301) 239-8468

Ted Godfrey specializes in salmon fishing. Flies are custom-tied. Features the sheep series eel flies, ball-headed riffling patterns, and flies for Iceland. One page of salmon flies in full color.

HENRY'S FORK ANGLERS
P.O. Box 487
St. Anthony, Idaho 83445
(208) 624-3995 (Winter)
(208) 558-7525 (Summer)

Catalog is in black and white but carries a superb display of the most popular western flies in addition to fly-fishing equipment. Also materials, tools, hooks, and many other sundries. Mike Lawson, the owner, is a professional fly tyer and licensed river guide.

E. HILLE
815 Railway Street
Williamsport, Pennsylvania 17701

This catalog carries some of the best dyes found anywhere. Operated by Bill O'Connor, this long-established company carries a full line of fly-tying materials and tools.

HOOK AND FEATHERS
Route 4, P.O. Box 400
Rangeley, Maine 04970
(207) 864-3309

Formerly the Rangeley Region Sports Shop. Catalog cost is $1. Carries a full line of fly-tying materials, hooks, tools, and flies. Related fishing equipment.

THE HOOK AND HACKLE COMPANY
P.O. Box 1003
Plattsburgh, New York 12901
(518) 561-5893

A fairly full catalog of many pages, with accent on materials, hooks, tools, books, and flies in addition to fly-fishing equipment.

HUNTER'S ANGLING SUPPLIES
Central Square
New Boston, New Hampshire 03070
(603) 487-3388

Bill Hunter has a reputation of refusing to sell anything but the best. If he won't tie with a material himself, he won't ship it. Catalog, which costs $3, is well rounded and highlights salmon flies and materials; the flies are reproduced in

color. Also books trips to various fishing camps throughout the world.

JACK'S TACKLE
1262 Valley Forge Road
Phoenixville, Pennsylvania 19460
(215) 933-9160

Although the catalog appears infrequently, owner Jack Mickievicz handles mail orders for the full range of materials, especially dubbing blends, and carries the usual array of hooks, books, tools, and flies. Wholesale and retail.

BOB JACKLIN'S FLY SHOP
P.O. Box 310
West Yellowstone, Montana 59758
(406) 646-7336

Catalog features western-style flies to go along with the float trips offered by the company. Bob Jacklin has a good range of tools, hooks, and materials as well as a comprehensive stock of fly-fishing equipment.

JOE'S TACKLE
Route 1, Box 156
Danforth, Maine 04424
(207) 448-2909

Joe Sterling lists quite a few expensive antique or used bamboo rods in his catalog. However, he is also strong in flies, especially streamer types, and carries a full line of tools, hooks, books, and materials.

KAUFMANN'S STREAMBORN FLIES
P.O. Box 23032
Portland, Oregon 97223
Retail Shop:
12963 S.W. Pacific Highway (99W)
Tigard, Oregon 97223

Superb catalog. Full-color fly section always has something new in a fully rounded selection. Photos are clear enough to tie from. Materials, tools, hooks, fly-fishing equipment, and books are more than adequate. This outfit is run by Randall and Lance Kaufmann, who check things out firsthand and feature trips to various streams around the world.

KETTLE CREEK TACKLE SHOP
HCR 62, Box 140
Renovo, Pa. 17764
(717) 923-1416

Owned and operated by Phil Baldacchino, the shop carries a full line of fly tying and fishing equipment. Specialty items include formulated dubbing blends for matching specific hatches.

LETORT LIMITED
P.O. Box 417
Boiling Springs, Pennsylvania 17007
(717) 258-3010

Formerly the Yellow Breeches Fly Shop. Complete catalog covers flies, materials, hooks, books, tools, tapes, and fly-fishing equipment. There is a $2 charge for the catalog, which has tips and articles by various noted authorities.

BUD LILLY'S TROUT SHOP
West Yellowstone, Montana 59758
(406) 646-7801

Very neat and complete catalog. Full range of flies, tools, hooks, books, and materials. Features guided trips and free general information service. Retail shop is open seven days a week.

LITTLE DIXIE FLIES
3801 Eminence Avenue
Berkeley, Missouri 63134

Operated by Robert Schneider, who puts out a small but complete catalog dealing primarily in flies, materials, and books. A young company which is growing and extends itself to the tyer.

MAXWELL MacPHERSON
10 Hillside Avenue
Bristol, New Hampshire 03222
(603) 744-3313

The twenty-two-page full-color catalog printed on a heavy glossy stock features a selection of salmon flies. Offers a custom tying service for just about any salmon fly pattern, whether old or new. There is a $1 charge for the catalog but the photographs are well worth it.

DAVE McNEESE
330 Liberty Street
Salem, Oregon 97301

Carries a complete line of flies and materials. McNeese is an exceptional fly tyer and particular about his materials. Catalog is not always available, but he will mail-order without one.

MARRIOTT'S FLY FISHING STORE
2634 W. Orangethorpe
Fullerton, California 92633
(714) 525-1827

In addition to a very complete catalog featuring the latest in fishing equipment and fly tying supplies, owner Robert M. (Bob) Marriott offers extensive courses in fly tying and fly fishing, some of which are conducted by leading experts in the field such as Poul Jorgensen and Lefty Kreh. For those in the area, Marriott operates two other stores, one located in Laguna Niguel, California ((714) 582-3699) and one in Burbank, California ((818) 843-7888)

MERRICK TACKLE
2655 Merrick Road
Bellmore, New York 11710
(516) 781-6777

This catalog is large and comprehensive, covering a lot of ground in general fishing tackle and the like, and reflects an extensive list of materials, flies, and equipment. Specializes in hard-to-find equipment and carries more angling books than most.

MIDWEST TROUTFITTERS
P.O. Box 666
Adrian, Michigan 49221
(517) 263-0561

Carries a full line of fly-tying materials and flies. Catalog also features books and related fly-fishing equipment.

MURRAY'S FLY SHOP
P.O. Box 156
Edinburg, Virginia 22824
(703) 984-4142

Quality catalog which carries a number of unusual fly-tying materials and a few fly patterns not carried anywhere else. Harry Murray has always been particular in his selection of stock. He is also knowledgeable regarding the area's fishing prospects.

NATIONAL FEATHERCRAFT
9010 St. Charles Rock Road
St. Louis, Missouri 63117
(314) 427-1707

More of an information sheet than a catalog. However, Ed Story, the owner, always has some exceptionally high-quality materials in stock in addition to some unusual offerings.

NORTH COUNTRY ANGLER
Route 16, Box 156
North Conway, New Hampshire 03860
(603) 356-6000
  This outfit has one of the largest selections of flies found anywhere. Dick Stewart specializes in offbeat patterns, streamers, and landlocked salmon flies as well as the conventional patterns. Also listed are materials and related fly-fishing items.

OJAI FISHERMAN
218 North Encinal Avenue
Ojai, California 93023
(805) 653-7642
  Catalog lists a full range of flies, some of which are rarely listed anywhere else, in addition to a full line of materials, hooks, tools, and fly-fishing equipment. Also carries Veniard dyes. Book listing is very comprehensive.

THE ORVIS COMPANY
Manchester, Vermont 05254
(802) 362-1300
  This enjoyable catalog is printed in full color from front to back and includes everything you'll ever need for fly fishing. For the fly tyer Orvis now prints a special catalog which includes materials, hooks, tools, and various sundries with an accent on quality and current designs.

PENNSYLVANIA OUTDOOR WAREHOUSE
1508 Memorial Avenue
Williamsport, Pennsylvania 17701
(800) 441-7685
  Large catalog for which there is a charge of $2. Lists flies, tools, hooks, and a wide range of fishing accessories.

PETER PHELPS
c/o The Bedford Sportsman
Depot Plaza
Bedford Hills, New York 10507
(914) 666-8092
  Though primarily a retail shop dealing in materials, hooks, tools, and books, Phelps is the manufacturer and distributor of the Xuron vise, Pro-Kote head cement, and Nymph Form, among others. Phelps will sell on a mail-order basis if called regarding a particular item. There is no catalog as such, though brochures for specific items are available.

REED TACKLE
P.O. Box 390
Caldwell, New Jersey 07006
  A catalog of many tackle-craft items with a full range of fly-tying materials, hooks, tools, and some books. Has been in business for almost half a century. Quality and service are reliable.

THE RIVER'S EDGE
2012 North 7th Avenue
Bozeman, Montana 59715
(406) 586-5373
  Run by Greg Lilly (formerly of Bud Lilly's Trout Shop) and Dave Corcoran, this relatively new outfit prints a catalog featuring a full range of fly-fishing and fly-tying equipment.

ROCKY MOUNTAIN DUBBING COMPANY
P.O. Box 1478
Lander, Wyoming 82520
(307) 856-4094
  Strictly wholesale to dealers. Steve Kennerk, who owns the company, sells a variety of bulk and pre-packaged furs and hairs, some of which are offbeat. Rabbit strips for Zonkers and leeches are one of his specialties.

ROGUE RIVER ANGLERS
3156 Rogue River Highway
Gold Hill, Oregon 97525
  A wholesale distributor for various fly-tying materials and tools. Keeps up with current trends.

RAYMOND C. RUMPF AND SON
P.O. Box 319
Sellersville, Pennsylvania 18960
(215) 257-0141
  A very complete distributor catalog for dealers only. Specializes in furs, feathers, hooks, threads, and related fly-tying equipment. Also a full selection of books.

RUSIN'S FLY AND TACKLE
396 Cliff Street
Fairview, New Jersey 07022
  Catalog deals only in flies, tools, and materials. Rusin is a professional fly tyer and tries to offer quality products.

SCELBA AND SON, INC.
P.O. Box 25
Springfield, New Jersey 07081
(201) 623-4133
  A basic catalog dealing in tools, materials, hooks, and a selection of fly-tying books.

SIMON PETER
R.D. 7, Box 312
Route 206 South
Newton, New Jersey 07860
(201) 786-6919
  Fairly large catalog dealing mostly with general fishing tackle, but does have a section for fly-tying tools and materials.

SKIP'S TACKLE
P.O. Box 8549
Erie, Pennsylvania 16505
(814) 833-8425
Strictly wholesale to dealers only. Catalog features tools, hooks, and materials. Also lists a book section containing over 200 titles.

STEWART CUSTOM TACKLE
17310 N.E. Halsey
Portland, Oregon 97230
(503) 254-2359
Catalog features a complete line of fly-tying materials and related fly-fishing items. Retail shop is even more fully stocked.

STREAM DESIGNS
80 Porterfield Road
Rexdale, Ontario
Canada M9W 3J8
(416) 742-8631
A brochure rather than a catalog, but well designed, featuring quality materials, flies, hooks, and tackle. Operated by Bill Hayes.

STREAMLIFE INNOVATIONS
P.O. Box 266
Hailey, Idaho 83333
(208) 788-3649
Fred Arbona's catalog features the offbeat flies, such as special cut wing mayflies, ostrich-bodied nymphs, and extended body patterns, in addition to some conventional type flies. Also lists fly-tying materials.

DOUG SWISHER
West Fork Route
Darby, Montana 59829
(406) 363-6659

The unique styles, flies, and materials introduced and used by Swisher are the primary ingredients in this catalog. Also featured are the fly-fishing schools and clinics he runs.

THE TACKLE SHOP
P.O. Box 369
Richardson, Texas 75080
(214) 231-5982
Large catalog which features molds, rod and lure components, and general fishing accessories. Does not carry flies at this time, but does list many materials, hooks, and tools.

JERRY TAYLOR
Route 1, Box 462
Newberry, Florida 32669
Deals primarily in unusual fly-tying materials in natural feathers and furs. Worth investigation by fly tyers everywhere.

THOMAS AND THOMAS
22 Third Street, Box 32
Turners Falls, Massachusetts 01376
(413) 863-9727
A portion of this comprehensive, 100-page catalog is in color. Features the sale of legally raised jungle cock skins in addition to a full range of materials. Comprehensive book section. Also books trips to Alaska, Canada, and Norway.

TRAUN RIVER PRODUCTS
c/o Rudi Heger
Hauptstrasse 6
8227 Siegsdorf
West Germany
This company is translating its catalog into English so that American fly tyers and dealers can take advantage of its unusual output. Rudi Heger and Roman Moser develop new designs

and concepts on a regular basis, some of which may be found in the fly-tying materials section of this book. Traun River Products sells both retail and wholesale.

TURNER'S FLY SHOP
R.R. 1
Aspen, Nova Scotia
Canada B0H 1E0
(902) 833-2303
Catalog features the MacIntosh series of salmon dry flies in addition to many other patterns. Also carries materials, hooks, tools, and fly-fishing equipment.

UMPQUA FEATHER MERCHANTS
P.O. Box 700
Glide, Oregon 97443
(503) 496-3512
Wholesale to the trade only. Specializes in imported flies and has made available to dealers a number of selected items including VMC hooks, Sealex dubbing, Antron sparkle blends, Traun River innovations, Krystal Flash and others. Carries a full line of standard materials such as feathers and furs, fly tying tools and books.

UNIVERSAL VISE CORP.
P.O. Box 626, 16 Union Avenue
Westfield, Massachusetts 01086
(413) 568-0964
Full-color catalog and price list to dealers only. Deals strictly in the wholesale of materials, hooks, tools, and books. Has a long-established reputation.

THE VALLEY ANGLER
56 Padanaram Road
Danbury, Connecticut 06810
(203) 792-8324

No catalog, but phone or mail orders are accepted. Lou Kish and Scott Bennett carry a complete line of materials and flies in addition to a quality array of fly-fishing equipment, and put on occasional special events for tyers.

E. VENIARD, LTD.
138 Northwood Road
Thornton Heath, England CR4 8YG
   Wholesale to the trade only. Specializes in domestic and exotic fly-tying materials, hooks, tools, books, dyes, and quite a number of items not found in the usual catalogs. Well worth having.

WAPSI FLY COMPANY
Highway 201 North
Route 5, Box 57E
Mountain Home, Arkansas 72653
(501) 425-9500
   Wholesale to dealers only. Tom Schmuecker, who runs things, sees to it that the quality of all products remains at a high standard. This is a materials company dealing in both bulk and packaged items in a wide selection, both natural and synthetic.

WORLD WIDE OUTFITTERS, INC.
425 Teconi Circle
Santa Rosa, California 95401
(707) 545-4657
   Strictly a wholesale distributor dealing in flies, materials, tools, and books. Dave Inks, who runs the place, will get your store just about anything you want. Also sends out a dealer newsletter.

JOAN AND LEE WULFF
Box CC
Livingston Manor, New York 12758
(914) 439-4060
   The brochures and catalog are highly specialized and deal primarily in the flies, hooks, and tackle associated with these two world-renowned experts on fly fishing, who also run a superb fly-fishing school on the Beaverkill River.

ROD YERGER
Box 294
Lawrence, Pennsylvania 15055
   Catalog contains custom flies, some of which are of unusual design. Something new to be learned here.

ORGANIZATIONS

There are always newer sources to be found, different styles of tying to be learned. The following organizations and periodicals should be useful as sources of information about things that interest the fly tyer.

FEDERATION OF FLY FISHERS
P.O. Box 1088
West Yellowstone, Montana 59758
   This national organization prints a quality magazine, *The Flyfisher,* four times a year, geared to both the angler and the fly tyer. Now and again there is interesting and informative reference to fly patterns, their construction, and their histories. The Federation also conducts conclaves throughout the United States in addition to a national get-together, usually held in West Yellowstone, which in itself is worth the

time and money. You'll derive much from this organization.

TROUT UNLIMITED
501 Church Street
Vienna, Virginia 22180
   Trout Unlimited has chapters within driving distance of most areas. Its primary goals are the restoration of polluted waters and the protection of trout streams. Nearly all chapters offer classes in fly tying and fishing, usually with a nominal fee that may be applied toward membership. Its quarterly magazine, *Trout,* is sent to all members.

UNITED FLY TYERS, INC.
P.O. Box 220
Maynard, Massachusetts 01754
   This organization, created over twenty-five years ago, is solely for fly tyers. It publishes a magazine, *Roundtable,* four times a year, which is filled from cover to cover with ideas, tying instructions, new patterns, and other related information. I have personally saved every issue I've ever received. Some of the earlier issues, which in the early sixties were printed on a mimeograph machine (the magazine is now on a fairly heavy glossy stock and quite attractive), have become collector's items. Well worth joining.

PERIODICALS

FLY FISHERMAN MAGAZINE
2245 Kohn Road
Harrisburg, Pennsylvania 17105
   A bimonthly with a special section in each issue devoted to fly tying.

FLY FISHERMAN'S BUYER'S GUIDE

Obtained through *Fly Fisherman Magazine.* Published yearly. Without a doubt, every fly tyer, dealer, and distributor should make sure he gets a copy of this guide each time it comes out. It lists all the manufacturers, distributors, and most of the dealers of flies, materials, tools, hooks, and the like, with emphasis on current trends.

FLY TYER
Box 1231
North Conway, New Hampshire 03860

A quarterly magazine dealing solely with fly patterns and methods of construction. Most fly tyers save every issue for reference, and the dealers who rack it are usually sold out before the next one arrives.

ROD & REEL
P.O. Box 370
Camden, Maine 04843

Published five times a year, with most features and departments dealing with fly fishing. Does, however, have some fly tying in the form of patterns or instructions in nearly every issue.

OUT-OF-PRINT BOOKS

The following bookdealers specialize in angling books that are no longer available from the publisher. Supply and demand dictate prices here. Most of them send out an updated listing every few months or so since titles are constantly changing.

ADAMS ANGLING BOOKS & PARAPHERNALIA
1170 Keeler Avenue
Berkeley, California 94708
(415) 849-1324

KENNETH ANDERSON
38 Silver Street
Auburn, Massachusetts 01501
(617) 832-3524

THE ANGLER'S ART
P.O. Box 148
Plainfield, Pennsylvania 17081
(717) 243-9721

Carries new, used, and out-of-print titles relating to all aspects of fly fishing. Over 500 titles in stock. There is a $2 charge for their catalog. Catalog is free if request is accompanied by an order.

ANGLER'S & SHOOTER'S BOOKSHELF
Goshen, Connecticut 06756
(203) 491-2500

JUDITH BOWMAN
Pound Ridge Road
Bedford, New York 10506
(914) 234-7543

ALEC JACKSON
Box 386
Kenmore, Washington 98028
(206) 488-9806

PISCES & CAPRICORN BOOKS
514 Linden Avenue
Albion, Michigan 49224

Glossary

FLY-TYING TERMS can sometimes be confusing, since a fair number of them are used to mean different things. The following explanations should prove helpful in clearing up some of those which seem a bit ambiguous. Specific fly-tying materials are described on pages 311–33.

ABDOMEN: In the tying of mayfly and stonefly nymphs, this refers to the rear portion of the body, comprising approximately two-thirds of the overall body length. The abdomen is never the entire body of an artificial fly. (See Body.)

AFTERSHAFT, AFTERSHAFT FEATHER: A much smaller, softer, fluffier, and almost down-like feather which grows with a separate stem of its own from the base of a primary feather. For example, an aftershaft feather may be found growing below the lowest fibers on a hackle feather just above where it emerges from the skin.

ANTENNAE: Sometimes referred to as feelers, this component of nymph and scud imitations is formed with a wide variety of materials, including strands of rubber hackle. The most popular antenna or feeler material is perhaps the short side of goose or turkey wing quills, called biots. Many anglers feel that this addition is more of a hindrance, in that it gets in the way while tying a leader to the fly. While fish will take the fly whether it has feelers or not, if the material used in the antennae is soft enough to weave or pulse, it will add to the overall liveliness of the pattern when it is fished.

BARB: The projection on a hook cut into the wire near the point which prevents, to a degree, a fish from coming off after it has been hooked. Most hooks are manufactured with barbs, but some are not, such as the Mustad model 94845, which is made barbless so that trout may be released without undue harm.

"Barb" is also the correct name for the fiber growing from the center stem of a rooster hackle feather or, for that matter, a hackle feather on any bird. In fly tying we refer to barbs as fibers or hackle fibers.

BARBULES: Small hooklike projections from the sides of hackle fibers (barbs) which adhere to adjacent barbules and cause the barbs to cling to one another. A good example of this hooking or clinging quality may be seen in hen hackle or the adhering fibers of duck quills. The "webbiness" of certain parts of a hackle is caused by these minuscule barbules adhering to one another, thus giving a closed or joined effect. Fortunately, there are very few barbules on the upper half of a rooster neck hackle and it is this lack of barbules that makes the dry fly hackle feather barbule-free or, as we know it, web-free.

BEARD: The material, usually hackle fibers, that is tied on the underside of the hook shank on a streamer, wet fly, or salmon fly. When a pattern calls for a hackle to be constructed "beard style," it means that the fibers are tied in as a unit as opposed to being wound as a hackle collar. The word "beard" is interchangeable with "throat" or "throat hackle," both signifying the tying of a material under the hook shank. Beards are usually one-third of the hook shank in length and extend from behind the eye toward the point of the hook.

BLEND: A fly tyer's term for the material used for a part of the fly, usually the body, that is made of a mixture of more than one material or of different colors of one or more kinds of material. Blends may be of synthetic or natural materials and in some cases a mixture of both. (However, any individual fur, such as muskrat, may also be considered a blend if the fibers have been mixed in a blender or coffee grinder or simply intermingled by hand or in a jar of water.) Blending mixes two or more furs or synthetic materials of different colors to form a uniform consistency of dubbing. Rough furs are also blended with soft silky furs to obtain a dubbing blend that spins easily onto the thread while still retaining a coarse-fibered effect.

The easiest method of blending furs or synthetics is by means of an inexpensive coffee grinder having very little capacity. The larger blenders or food processors generally whip the material to the top of the cylinder and thus lose some of the intermingling effect.

BODY: That portion wound around the shank of the hook from the bend to a point before the eye where the wing is tied in. In nymph patterns, especially stonefly nymphs, the body is often divided into two parts: the abdomen and the thorax. Though both abdomen and thorax together form the body, they are listed separately since, in most cases, they are constructed differently or with different materials. The thorax portion of almost all bodies is larger in diameter than the abdomen.

BULLET-SHAPED: Refers to bodies or heads which are constructed of spun and trimmed deer hair. The body of a fly such as the Irresistible may be considered bullet-shaped, with the pointed or narrow end tapering in to the bend and the widest part abutting the wings. On muddler type patterns the narrow end is nearer the eye with the wider area expanding rearward.

BUTT: The ends of materials which are to be trimmed, or cut away and discarded. A butt is also the lower or bottom portion (fuller and with fuzzier fiber content) of a hackle feather or a clump of deer hair. It always refers to the part which grows in or is closest to the hide of an animal or bird. The butt of a hackle feather is at the opposite end from the finely tapered tip.

In salmon fly terminology, a butt is nearly always a black ostrich herl fiber which has been wound around the shank near the bend at a spot precisely over the point of the hook. This type of butt is tied in after tip, tag, and tail have been affixed.

In another meaning—again nearly always related to salmon flies—"butt" refers to a very short type of tail, usually of floss, as in the

Black Bear, Green Butt, or a band of floss as in the Buck Bug.

CHEEKS: Fairly short pieces of material, very commonly of jungle cock eyes or an equivalent, tied in on the sides of a pattern just behind the head and extending rearward for a quarter or a third of the length of the hook shank. Cheeks are mostly found in recipes for streamer and salmon flies, occasionally for steelhead flies, wet flies, and saltwater patterns.

CIGAR SHAPE: The shape of the body of a fly, usually in the streamer category, which is constructed of wool or floss. The taper is narrow near the bend, swells near the center of the shank, and may or may not taper in as it reaches the wing area.

CLIPPED DEER HAIR: A type of body or head or any other part of a fly which is formed by spinning and trimming deer or other suitable hair fibers. (For the process, see Irresistible, page 45.)

CLUMP: A section or bunch of fibers, whether of hair or feathers. The size of a clump should always be specified, such as "a matchstick-sized clump" or "a clump of ten to twelve fibers."

COLLAR: A hackle feather that is wound around the hook shank behind the eye to form a band on a dry fly or wet fly. The dry fly collar stands erect, with the fibers at a 90-degree angle to the hook shank. A wet fly collar extends rearward, generally at a 45-degree angle (or less), to the hook shank. On a fur collar, the fibers of a specific animal are trapped between two strands of thread and wound around the shank as you would a hackle feather.

COUNTER-WIND, COUNTER-WRAP: To work thread and materials around the shank counterclockwise—that is, in the opposite direction from conventional tying sequences. This method is usually used in connection with wire tinsels, which are counter-wound to secure the more fragile bodies, such as stripped peacock herl.

COVERT FEATHERS: Small feathers found on the shoulders of wings and the upper portion of the tail feathers of most birds, covering the bases of the larger feathers. The covert feathers on a duck, for example, overlap the base quills of the secondary and flight feathers.

CUT WING: Any feather which has been shaped by a wing-burning tool, wing cutter, or other device to form the shaped wing on a dry fly.

DEER-BODIED: Refers to a fly whose body is constructed of deer hair.

DELTA WING: A wing, used primarily on caddis dry flies, that is tied to the shank so that it slants rearward at approximately a 45-degree angle to the shank.

DIVIDED BEARD: A style of tying beard or throat hackle (see Beard) in which the fibers are divided so that equal amounts protrude downward and rearward from each side of the hook shank behind the eye. The easiest way to form a beard hackle of this type is to snip the center stem of a hackle feather, forming a V of hackle from both sides of the stem, and place the fibers onto the shank from above so that they sit astride.

DOWNWING: Refers to any fly pattern, usually an imitation of an adult caddis or stonefly, on which the wing is tied on top of and parallel to the hook shank.

DUB: To spin a piece of fur or synthetic material onto a piece of waxed thread which is then wound around the hook shank to form the body of a fly. The secret of forming a precise and neatly tapered body is to use only small pinches of fur or other material. Using large quantities not only presents a problem in the spinning process itself but usually results in a bulky and uneven body. Underfur or synthetic equivalents should always be spun onto the thread in one direction only. Back-and-forth motions of thumb and forefinger are counterproductive.

DUBBING: Any material that can be spun or twisted onto thread, regardless of its makeup. The most common forms of dubbing are natural underfurs of animals and synthetic fibers which have been reduced to blendable consistency and feel and behave like the natural. But when a fly tyer refers to a material as "dubbing fur," he or she always means the underfur of an animal.

DUBBING NOODLE: A form of dubbing material which has been teased and stretched into an elongated mass that can be tied to the hook shank as you would a piece of wool and, with the aid of the tying thread, can be wound forward to form the body. Dubbing noodles are also placed between two strands of thread which are then spun in one direction a number of times, thus locking in the noodle permanently within the thread before winding it

around the shank to form the body. (See also Fur Rope.)

EGG SAC: Any material which can be used to represent female mayflies or caddis flies in ovipositing condition. Common materials used are chenille, floss, and the dyed butt end of a feathered quill. Egg sacs are tied in before the tail is secured to the shank.

EXTENDED BODY: A body—usually of an imitation mayfly dun—that reaches well past the bend and curves slightly upward in the manner of the natural insect. The most common material used is deer body hair which has been wound and counter-wound with thread in a crisscross fashion to compact it in its extended state beyond the bend.

FAN WING: A dry fly wing made from duck breast feathers having a natural or pronounced flare. These feathers are placed back to back to each other and mirror each other after they have been secured to the shank. The Fan Wing Royal Coachman exemplifies this type of wing. The white breast feathers of the male wood duck are among the most favored by tyers for this type of construction.

FEELERS (see Antennae)

FIBER: A unit of hackle or hair from a feather or a piece of fur. For example, a feather from a rooster neck is said to have either stiff fibers or soft fibers depending on its overall quality. The true name of these hackle fibers is "barbs," though few fly tyers call them that. The hair from the tail of a squirrel or a calf tail, the coarse hair of a deer, and the guard hairs of a mink may all be referred to as fibers or hair fibers.

FLARE: To cause a fiber, such as deer or elk hair, to spring up or out at an angle, as in the flared wing of the Elk Hair Caddis.

FLAT WING: A wing usually made of duck, turkey, or goose quill sections which are tied flat over the body of the fly, and used mostly in adult caddis and stonefly imitations.

FLIGHT FEATHERS: The leading long feathers on a bird's wing. Fly tyers use these primary wing quills from such birds as ducks, geese, and turkeys mainly in the construction of wings and wing cases on dry flies, wet flies, and nymphs.

FLUES: The barbules or individual fibers of such fine-textured feathers as ostrich and peacock herl. On a peacock herl, for example, the flues are the small, fuzzy barbules protruding from a single herled fiber. When these are longer than average length the fiber is considered a wide-flued herl.

FLYMPH: A coined word describing a fly pattern that serves as both a wet fly and a nymph. Introduced by Vern Hidy in *The Art of Tying the Wet Fly and Flymph.*

FOLDED HACKLE: Any hackle which is stroked and manipulated by the fingers so that all the fibers protrude in one general direction. (For technique, see Blue Dun, page 124.)

FORKED TAIL: A construction in which two sections of a material, usually hackle fibers, come off the shank at the bend at a 45-degree angle. Goose biots are also commonly used for this type of tail.

FRONT HACKLE: The hackle closest to the eye of the hook, such as the white hackle in a bivisible pattern.

FUR ROPE: Similar to a fur noodle (which see). Promoted by Polly Rosborough in his book *Tying and Fishing the Fuzzy Nymph,* the technique involves trapping a coarse type of fur between two strands of thread and spinning the thread (twisting it) to form a segmented type of fur rope which is wound forward to form the body. (For process, see Casual Dress, pages 163–5.)

GILLS: The minuscule respiratory organs of a nymph or larva, located on the sides of the body and usually imitated by such fine flues as peacock or ostrich herl.

With streamer flies or sculpin type imitations, "gills" refers to the area where the organs of these baitfish would be located. Usually imitated with a red material, such as hair, hackle, or wool.

GUARD HAIRS: The outer fibers of an animal's pelage which are firmer and more resilient than the fur fibers underneath. A mink has guard hairs that may be half an inch or more in length in addition to a soft velvety underfur. A deer's pelt seems to be made entirely of guard hairs, but on closer inspection, we find a softer, almost woolly fiber near the skin.

HACKLE: When denoting a part of a fly pattern, this term refers to a rooster neck or saddle feather which is wound around the shank behind the hook eye to form the collar on a dry fly, or the fibers of a rooster or hen feather tied under the shank behind the hook eye to represent legs on a wet fly.

HACKLE COLLAR (see Collar)

HAIR WING: A type of wing used mostly on dry flies that may be made with calf tail, deer hair, bucktail, woodchuck hair, and other animal fibers, as well as with synthetic substitutes for hair.

HERL: The slender quill of any feather, such as ostrich or peacock, having very fine barbs, or fibers, along its length. Both ostrich and peacock herl are used to simulate the gills of many nymphs, pupae, and crustaceans.

HOOD: A covering of material from the tail to the wing by another material. Sometimes called a shell or shell back. A shrimp type pattern, for example, may have a body of olive seal fur and a hood of goose quill section.

LEGS: Imitation appendages constructed from various materials, whether of hackle, deer hair, turkey fibers, or scraggly dubbing fur, to simulate the legs of nymphs, scuds, and terrestrials.

MARRIED FEATHERS: The assimilation of differently colored quill sections of a bird or the joining together of the quill sections of birds of different species to form a single unit. If you take a goose primary quill, you can easily separate one section of fibers from the rest. You can also join this section of fibers (barbs) with another by stroking the two units with thumb and forefinger and gently nudging them against each other. Most such fibers have very tiny hooks (barbules) which intermesh so that they hold their form as a wing when in flight. Married wings are made by stroking and nudging differently colored fibers against each other. A good example is the wet fly pattern Parmachene Belle.

OPTIC EYE: The eye of an imitation baitfish, which may be formed by lacquering the head of the fly with black lacquer and then hand-painting in an iris and a pupil. Optic eyes are also made of pre-fashioned materials such as bead chain links, doll eyes, and glass eyes.

OUTRIGGER: A style of tying tail fibers, or wing or hackle collar fibers, so that they are forked (like an outrigger) to better support the fly on the surface of the water.

PALMER: The technique of tying a feather rib through the body of a fly by winding a hackle in an open or closed spiral, usually over some other body material, from the bend to a position behind the wings or head of the pattern. A palmered fly is one which has been wound with hackle in an open spiral the entire length of the hook shank.

In a palmer rib the hackle is wound as you would a ribbing of tinsel in an open spiral over the body of the fly.

PARACHUTE: A style of forming a horizontal hackle collar by winding hackle around the base of another material, usually a clump of calf tail or deer hair.

PECTORAL FINS: That part of a baitfish imitation (such as spuddlers or sculpins) constructed with small mottled breast feathers which have an inherent natural curve and flare outward after they are tied in to represent the pectoral fins.

PRONOTUM: In fly tying, the smaller pad between the two wing pads of the thorax and the head of a stonefly imitation. In entomology, the dorsal sclerite of the prothorax of an insect.

PULLED OVER, PULLED FORWARD: Generally applies to a material which is used as a wing case or shell and which has been tied to the hook shank during an early process and achieves proper formation at a later time. For example, a turkey wing quill section of fibers may be tied in at the center of the shank (at a point where the abdomen merges into the thorax of a nymph imitation) and left idling while the thorax and the legs are being formed. Then when the forward section of thorax and legs have been completed, the wing case is "pulled over" or "pulled forward" over the thorax and tied down behind the head. Some tyers may simply say "over" when referring to this procedure.

In the case of a shell, as in a scud or shrimp imitation, the process is the same except that the material is "pulled over" from the bend to the eye.

QUILL: In general usage, a quill is the central shaft, usually hollow, of a feather from which the fibers (barbs) emanate, and usually refers to the larger feathers of the wing or tail. Fly tyers use this type of quill only on specialized flies, such as the Vince Marinaro Pontoon Hopper or the peeled sheath of large quills as used in the Niemeyer stoneflies.

"Quill" may also refer to an entire section of fibers, such as goose, duck, or turkey quills when they are used to form the wings of wet

flies, dry flies, and hoppers or the wing cases of nymphs.

Certain flies, such as the Ginger Quill, Quill Gordon, and others, derive their name from the use of what we incorrectly call a peacock quill. In the peacock eyed tail, these are the stems emanating from the central quill which are stripped of their fibers. The stripped stem of hackle feathers, as used in the Red Quill pattern, is considered a true quill.

And then there are porcupine quills, those white- or white and black-tipped, smooth, hollow affairs that behave much like barbed hooks once they penetrate your skin. These are now and then used in fly tying.

RIB, RIBBING: A tinsel that is wound around the body in an open spiral to the wing area. On salmon flies or streamer patterns the use of tinsel as a ribbing material serves to add flash and thus attract the attention of the fish. A rib may also be formed with quill or other materials and in such instances it may be used to lend a suggestion of segmentation in imitation of an aquatic insect. (See Palmer and Segmentation.)

SEGMENTATION: The forming of divisions along the body of such flies as nymphs and wet flies. To imitate the natural banding of nymphs, scuds, and other aquatic insects, fly tyers may use a two-toned material, such as a light tan peacock quill with a darker leading edge, to form the body or abdomen. In other patterns materials of two different colors, such as a light and a dark moose mane fiber, are wound simultaneously to produce a banded or segmented effect. Segmentation may also be effected by the use of a ribbing material wound in an open spiral through the body of the pattern being tied, such as winding a black thread over a body of green floss.

SHELL (see Hood)

SHOULDER: In salmon and streamer fly nomenclature, a construction made of any feathered material (and occasionally hair fibers) which is tied in on the side of the shank near the head and extends rearward usually for a third or half of the body length of the fly. The pattern Gray Ghost features a shoulder made from the body feathers of the silver pheasant.

An exception to the general rule of tying shoulder feathers in at the head area occurs in some saltwater patterns where the wing material is tied in at the bend of the hook. Here a shoulder feather is tied in to flank the wing or tail feathers.

SLATE DUCK WING QUILLS: Refers to the natural slate gray color of wing quills (usually of a mallard). There is much confusion about this color; when it is called for, simply use any natural gray duck quills that are not too light.

SPENT WING: The wing of a dry fly which is tied to the shank so that it extends outward on a horizontal plane and at right angles to the hook shank. The style is used to imitate the spinner stage of mayflies after they have oviposited and lie exhausted, or spent, on the surface of the stream.

SPEY HACKLE: Used primarily in salmon and steelhead patterns to form "spey flies." Spey hackle consists mostly of rump feathers from various pheasants, though the old English flies used the tail feathers of roosters. Heron, a prohibited feather, was also used in the construction of spey type patterns. Spey hackle is tied in behind the eye of the hook and wound as a doubled or folded hackle surrounding the shank behind the eye and extending past the hook bend.

SPINNER: A type of dry fly pattern constructed to imitate the spinner, or spent, stage of an adult mayfly (see Spent Wing).

SPINNING: The hair fibers from such animals as the white-tailed deer, mule deer, and antelope are hollow and will flare when thread pressure is brought against them on the hook shank. When two loose loops of thread are brought over a clump of this type of fibers and wound around the shank in a continuing motion, the hair fibers, in addition to flaring, also rotate around the shank. This rotating and flaring of deer hair around the hook shank is called spinning (see Irresistible, page 45) and its end result is called spun (or clipped) deer hair.

STAGGER CUT: The trimming of excess material in progressive stages to form a natural taper for the body or head of the fly. For example, the excess butts extending rearward from the lashed-down wing on a dry fly are trimmed away by cutting one-third of the excess directly behind the wing, a second third at the center of the hook shank and the final third just before the bend, thus providing a gradually inclined underbody over which a body of fur or other material is formed.

STRIP, STRIPPING: Usually applies to peacock eyed quills, condor quills, and other large feathers, or the center stem of hackle feathers. Stripping the flues or barbules from a quill may involve the use of Clorox to dissolve them. Other methods include hand stripping or dipping in paraffin and then stripping between thumb and forefinger. (See Quill Gordon and Red Quill, pages 24–6 and 26–7.)

Sometimes a larger quill, such as from a goose flight feather, is stripped of its sheath and this outer layer is used to form a quill strip to be used on the bodies of stonefly nymphs. This process involves soaking the quill in water for an hour or so in order to soften it, after which a single-edge razor blade is used to slice into and through the outer layer only so that the sheath of quill can be peeled from the quill stem.

TAG: In salmon fly terminology, the tag is the first material to be tied to the shank and forms the rearmost material at the bend.

TAIL: That part of the fly which extends beyond the bend to imitate the tail of a natural insect. In the case of dry flies, the tail also supports the fly on the surface of the water.

TAILING: Any material which can be used for the construction of a tail in the various categories of fly patterns.

TANDEM FLIES: Usually refers to certain types of streamer flies which are to be fished for landlocked salmon and lake trout. Because the imitations have to be fairly long in order to imitate certain baitfish, such as smelt, and because anglers believe that a fish will sometimes strike short, two hooks on these flies are fastened together by means of steel wire or monofilament—that is, connected in tandem. (For assembly technique, see page 248.)

TENTING: The forming of a material to obtain

a tentlike shape. Materials such as turkey or duck quill sections are tied in so that the upper edges of the sections meet and touch while the rest of the quill sections angle downward at a 45-degree angle. Used mostly in the construction of wings of caddis dry flies and hoppers.

THORAX: The forward portion of the body of an aquatic insect or its imitation. In fly patterns this area is packed more fully with materials than the abdomen. (See Body.)

THROAT: Has the same meaning as "beard," but "throat" is the term used in salmon fly terminology and in relation to streamer and steelhead flies. It usually consists of hackle, though hair fibers are also used, which is tied in under the hook shank at the head area and extends rearward for a quarter to a third of the shank length. On certain streamer flies, however, especially the trolling or tandem variety, a throat may extend to the bend or even be as long as the wing. (See Beard.)

TIP: On salmon flies, this is the second material, usually floss, to be tied in after the tag. On wet flies, it refers to a piece of tinsel, and sometimes other material, which is tied in before the tail.

TOPPING: In salmon fly tying, topping is quite often a golden pheasant crest feather which curves over all the other materials that make up the wing. However, the term is also applied to other materials, especially if a different material is added to an already complex wing. For example, a wing made of three shades of bucktail flanked by two or four pairs of saddle hackles may have a topping of half a dozen strands of peacock herl or a dark blue silver pheasant crest.

TROLLING FLIES: Usually refers to flies which are tied in tandem, although some patterns are tied on single hooks of extra-long shank length. (See Tandem Flies.)

TUFTED WING: A term coined by Walt Dette to describe a process in which a pair of smaller wood duck or other breast feathers are pressed between thumb and forefinger to achieve a more durable clump effect while still retaining a semblance of flare and separation. Used mostly on smaller flies to establish a respectable silhouette.

UPRIGHT CLUMP: A single unit of fibers, such as calf tail, deer hair, poly yarn, or other, which has been constructed as a wing, usually in parachute type flies, to stand vertically erect at a 90-degree angle from the shank.

VARIANT: A type of dry fly in which the hackle collar is usually tied two or three sizes larger than normal, such as in the Gray Fox Variant or Cream Variant. These patterns, in most cases, do not have wings.

In its second meaning, variant refers to colors or markings of certain shades of hackle, such as ginger variant or red variant. It is also taken further to mean those hackles, with the exception of grizzly, which have some kind of barring in them. Examples of these are chinchillas and crees.

VEIL: A material, other than the wing, which is used to cover part of the body, such as the floss veiling in the salmon fly pattern Rusty Rat. Basically a salmon fly term.

WHIP FINISH: A type of knot used to tie off the thread after a fly has been completed so that the windings do not unravel. Similar to the type used by rod builders when wrapping guides on a blank. It is, in effect, a multiple half hitch knot. There are devices called whip finishers, the best of which is the type invented by Frank Matarelli, which perform this function for the fly tyer.

WING: On dry flies and wet flies, the wing imitates the wing of a natural insect. However, when material is affixed to the same area on the hook shank on streamer, steelhead, and salmon flies, it is also called a wing even though baitfish, which these flies generally represent, do not have wings.

To "wing" a fly is to construct a wing of one type or another. "Wing material" refers to anything that can be used to form a wing.

The wings on dry flies are nearly always in an upright position, except when the fly is tied spent or, in the case of adult caddis and stoneflies, when the wing is tied flat or tented over the body in a downwing position. On streamer flies and the like, the wing usually lies on top of the hook shank and parallel with it.

WING BULGE: A puffing or bulging of the wing case just prior to emergence, when the natural insect has arrived at the water's surface and its wings are ready to unfold. To imitate this condition, fly tyers tie a ball of dubbing, either natural or synthetic, on top of the thorax area.

WING CASE: In a natural insect this refers to an undeveloped wing or one which has not as yet begun to unfold. In the nymphal stage this case lies fairly flat over the back of the insect at the thorax area. When the nymph reaches the emerger stage, the case is more fully pronounced, somewhat like a miniature puff ball, ready to crack open and fluff its wings.

The wing case on an artificial fly may be made with turkey or duck wing quill sections which are tucked in fore and aft over the thorax area. We may also use pre-shaped individual feathers having mottled coloring which have been cut to shape or burned out with a tool and carefully placed over the forward part of the imitation to simulate the natural.

WING PAD: A formation, usually of a breast feather, which is tied in behind the eye of the hook and cut off squarely about a third of the shank rearward. A wing pad is always a single feather tied flat over the top of the shank covering the thorax area. It is not tucked in between the thorax and abdomen like a standard wing case.

WING SLATS: Short sections of duck wing quills tied to the shank along the forward side of the body to imitate the undeveloped wings emerging from the sides of the body of the caddis pupa.

Bibliography

THE FOLLOWING books have been selected as worthwhile reading and reference material that will enable the fly tyer to broaden his knowledge of fly patterns and the manner in which they are constructed. I have consulted many of these titles in my research for this book to assure overall accuracy of detail. You will find, in some instances, that the authors are not always in agreement regarding some of the pattern recipes and some of the methods used in their construction. Yet there is something to be learned from each of them.

All of the following books are a permanent part of my angling library simply because I tie flies professionally. Some, too specialized in content, are rarely perused. Still, I must have them because I may just be invited to go fishing for bonefish off Christmas Island or trolling for landlocked salmon in Maine, and I will have to tie a few patterns for this kind of fishing. In short, they are there if I ever need them. If you're like me and you enjoy tying flies and it is your intention one day to fish all the streams and oceans of the world, start collecting.

ATHERTON, JOHN
The Fly and the Fish. Rockville Centre, N.Y.: Freshet Press, 1971.

Originally published by the Macmillan Company in 1951. Of particular interest to the fly tyer is Chapter VII, entitled "Flies and Impressionism." Atherton, an avid angler and innovative fly tyer, was also a wildlife artist and this led him to some original thoughts regarding the appearance of a fly to a trout. His book contains full descriptions of the many and varied patterns he used, some of which are still found in current catalogs.

BATES, JOSEPH D., JR.
Atlantic Salmon Flies and Fishing. Harrisburg, Pa.: Stackpole, 1970.

This has long been the bible for both anglers and tyers using the North American hair wing patterns. Although the book is out of print, it may still be found (at higher prices) at the various used-book dealers. Contains the pattern descriptions, origins, and, in most cases, brief histories of some of the best-known salmon flies used today. A must for anyone tying salmon flies or fishing for salmon.

Streamers and Bucktails: The Big Fish Flies. New York: Alfred A. Knopf, 1979.

A revised and updated version of the original *Streamer Fly Tying and Fishing,* published by Stackpole in 1950 and again in 1966. Bates seems to have a bent for plain hard work. There is a monumental amount of research involved here, producing a harvest of valuable information for fly tyers everywhere. A very important book.

BAY, KENNETH E.
The American Fly Tyer's Handbook. New York: Winchester Press, 1979.

A fully photographed step-by-step sequence of fifteen different flies by as many contributors: Walter Burr, Ted Godfrey, Edward Graham, Hal Janssen, Charles Krom, Gary LaFontaine, Chauncy Lively, John McKim, John Merwin, Sid Neff, Ted Niemeyer, Eric Peper, John Schollenberger, Dick Surette, and Ralph Wahl. Contains some unique approaches to important patterns and methods.

BAY, KENNETH E., AND HERMAN KESSLER
Salt Water Flies. Philadelphia: Lippincott, 1972.

Over fifty pattern descriptions of the most popular saltwater flies, including pattern recipes for flies for such game fish as tarpon, bonefish, bluefish, stripers, and weakfish. Photographic tying sequences for nine major flies. An important book for the saltwater angler/tyer. Out of print but still available through some fly shops.

BERGMAN, RAY
Trout. New York: Alfred A. Knopf, 1938.

Still in print after almost fifty years, which proves it more than time-tested. Some of the numerous fly patterns are no longer listed in current catalogs, but it is amazing how many are still being used. This is a book to be read again and again.

BETTS, JOHN
Synthetic Flies. John Betts, 1980.

Hand-printed by John's own hand and published by himself, this unique book deals with the construction of flies using primarily synthetic fibers, such as paintbrush bristles, plastic bags, and various fabrics. This type of fly tying is not everyone's cup of tea, but the unusual and vastly different patterns do work extremely well. I don't know where you can get a copy of this book except from John himself. At present he resides in Denver, Colorado. He can also be located through the *Roundtable,* the United Fly Tyers' magazine, which occasionally runs one of his articles.

BLADES, WILLIAM F.
Fishing Flies and Fly Tying. Harrisburg, Pa.: Stackpole, 1951, 1962, 1979.

Both a fly-tying and a pattern book containing much useful information in all categories of flies.

BORGER, GARY
Naturals. Harrisburg, Pa.: Stackpole, 1980.

Deals primarily with the habits of the natural insects we imitate, but has valuable pattern recipes derived from this study.

Nymphing. Harrisburg, Pa.: Stackpole, 1980.

A basic book about nymphs and nymph fishing. Borger is a digger who burrows deeply into all that intrigues him. Many of the patterns are the result of study at the vise and research on the stream.

BOYLE, ROBERT H.,
AND DAVE WHITLOCK
The Fly Tyer's Almanac. New York: Crown, 1975; Nick Lyons Books, 1982.

The Second Fly Tyer's Almanac. Philadelphia: Lippincott, 1978.

Both books have a wealth of information for the fly tyer, including specialized patterns and unique tying instructions for offbeat imitations. *The Second Fly Tyer's Almanac* is out of print, but a few copies are still available in some of the fly shops. It will probably become an expensive collector's item.

BROOKS, CHARLES
Nymph Fishing for Larger Trout. New York: Crown, 1976.

Brooks is the kind of angler/tyer who won't write about a technique or procedure unless he has assured himself that it does indeed work well. Here the accent is on nymphs, especially the larger stoneflies, and his ideas are reflected in original patterns, many of which are cataloged by fly shops throughout the West. An important book.

The Trout and the Stream. New York: Crown, 1974.

Contains important fly patterns and instructions relating to the imitation of natural insects on western waters. Again, a very important book.

CAUCCI, AL, AND BOB NASTASI
Hatches. New York: Comparahatch, 1975.

Primarily a book on entomology for the angler and in that regard one of the best. For the fly tyer, it contains information regarding fly patterns of the Compara Dun type and some instructions.

COMBS, TREY
Steelhead Fly Fishing and Flies. Portland, Ore.: Salmon-Trout-Steelhead, 1976.

This book belongs on the shelf of all those interested in steelhead patterns. Includes eight full-color plates in addition to numerous important pattern descriptions that provide, in most cases, the history and origins of the recipes. This is also a fine angling book regarding this species.

DENNIS, JACK
Western Trout Fly Tying Manual. Jackson Hole, Wyo.: Snake River Books, 1974.

Contains many pattern descriptions important to fly tyers everywhere. It is also filled with photographic illustrations showing technique and method in various categories. My only criticism concerns the procedure used in the dressing of the dry fly, in which the wing is tied in after the tail and body have been formed. Since the wing sets the overall proportions on a dry fly and is usually the most difficult part, it should be the first material tied to the shank of the hook. However, the knowledgeable fly tyer will take this into consideration and use the proper process. This minor comment notwithstanding, the book is well worth having.

Western Trout Fly Tying Manual, Vol. II. Jackson Hole, Wyo.: Snake River Books, 1980.

In this even larger volume, Dennis covers the special flies of the West, such as the Elk Hair Caddis, Bailey's Damsel, the Gartside Pheasant Hopper, the Matuka Sculpin, and a host of others. Be sure to obtain a copy of this one.

DUBOIS, DONALD
The Fisherman's Handbook of Trout Flies. New York: A. S. Barnes, 1960.

When this book first appeared, it did not fare too well. Now that it is out of print, it is sought by tyers and collectors regardless of the higher price. There must have been many, many hours of research and work involved in assembling and coding the 5,939 flies presented here. A good reference work.

FLICK, ART
Art Flick's New Streamside Guide. New York: Crown, 1969; Nick Lyons Books, 1982.

The standard for mayfly dressings in the Northeast. It contains the recipes for the major hatches on such rivers as the Beaverkill, Delaware, Esopus, and Schoharie in New York and similar streams as far west as Michigan. The Hendrickson, Quill Gordon, March Brown, and Green Drake are a few of the patterns closely associated with this important little book.

Art Flick's Master Fly Tying Guide. New York: Crown, 1972.

Tying instructions for different categories of flies are provided by qualified experts in each area: Swisher and Richards on no-hackle flies, Niemeyer on wet flies and nymphs, Flick on dries, Whitlock on western patterns, Schwiebert on salmon flies, Lefty Kreh on saltwater flies, Ed Koch on terrestrials and midges, and Helen Shaw on streamer, bucktail, and bass patterns.

FLING, PAUL N.,
AND DONALD L. PUTERBAUGH
Expert Fly Tying. New York: Sterling Publishing Co., 1982.

Contains a number of unusual techniques that should interest any fly tyer. One such is a simple and more efficient method for constructing an extended body.

FULSHER, KEITH
Tying and Fishing the Thunder Creek Series. Rockville Centre, N.Y.: Freshet Press, 1973.

Specializes in the tying of patterns relating to the Thunder Creek series of flies, which features a reverse wing. This fine book is now out of print, but may be obtained through a secondhand-book dealer.

FULSHER, KEITH, AND CHARLES KROM
Hair Wing Atlantic Salmon Flies. North Conway, N.H.: Fly Tyer, Inc., 1981.

A modern compilation of the most important North American hair wing salmon fly patterns, including tying instructions. Four full-color plates. For the salmon fly tyer, a must.

HELLEKSON, TERRY
Popular Fly Patterns. Salt Lake City: Peregrine-Smith, 1979.

One of the best fly pattern books ever published. Over 800 useful flies with eight color plates. Hellekson has done his research well, checking into origins, presenting a few tying tips where needed, and even making this type of book a bit more interesting with an occasional anecdote. An unusually fine reference work.

JENNINGS, PRESTON
A Book of Trout Flies. New York: Crown, 1970.

First published as a Derrydale edition in 1935, this book is still referred to by many of today's tyers and anglers. Discusses not only the patterns but the hackle and materials that go into them. A good book to have.

JORGENSEN, POUL
Dressing Flies for Fresh and Salt Water. Rockville Centre, N.Y.: Freshet Press, 1973.

One of the first truly fine books to appear on the market in the early 1970s. Covers all areas of fly tying. Photography and color plates are excellent. This book, unfortunately, is out of print. Prices for copies at used-book dealers are high, but the book is well worth the expense.

Jorgensen is at this time preparing a much-expanded version for the Johnson Publishing Company in Boulder, Colorado, which is intended to replace the out-of-print original. It is to be entitled *How to Tie Flies for Fresh and Salt Water Gamefish* and will include a chapter concerning realistic and artistic fishing flies.

Modern Fly Dressings for the Practical Angler. New York: Winchester Press, 1976.

A book of fly patterns and tying tips. Another volume to have on hand for reference.

Salmon Flies. Harrisburg, Pa.: Stackpole, 1978.

Covers all aspects of salmon fly tying and includes the procedures for the difficult General Practitioner. If you tie salmon flies, you should have a copy.

Modern Trout Flies. N.Y.: Doubleday, 1979; Nick Lyons Books, 1982.

Originally available as *The Jorgensen Trout Fly Charts,* this book specializes in trout flies only, covering dries, wets, streamers, and nymphs. Contains pattern descriptions and a separate section with brief fly-tying tips relating to the patterns. What makes this book special is the superb color photography by Lee Bolton.

KAUFMANN, RANDALL
American Nymph Fly Tying Manual. Portland, Ore.: Frank Amato Publications, 1975.

A fine book devoted entirely to nymphs. The approximately 200 important patterns are covered individually in pattern requirements and tying instructions. There are eight full-color plates of flies. A very important book.

LaFONTAINE, GARY
Caddisflies. New York: Nick Lyons Books, 1981.

More of a book concerning angler entomology, which LaFontaine covers in depth and detail. In this regard alone the book is worth the price. It does have patterns that reflect the exhaustive research and includes the popular emergent caddis pupa and the use of Antron fibers.

LEISENRING, JAMES, AND VERN HIDY
The Art of Tying the Wet Fly and Flymph. New York: Crown, 1971.

Some time-honored and still effective trout patterns are presented here. The original book by Leisenring was published in 1941. The addition of the flymph by Hidy thirty years later brought another wrinkle to the wet fly.

LEISER, ERIC
Fly Tying Materials. New York: Crown, 1973; Nick Lyons Books, 1982.

A book for fly tyers. Contains chapters on tools, hooks, and materials and how to use them. Includes methods for dyeing, photodyeing, protection of materials, and skinning and cleaning road-killed animals and birds.

The Complete Book of Fly Tying. New York: Alfred A. Knopf, 1977.

Fly-tying instructions for the beginner and the advanced. Detailed, step-by-step, fully illustrated procedures for tying all categories of flies for freshwater and saltwater species.

The Metz Book of Hackle. New York: Nick Lyons Books, 1986.

An in-depth look at the feathers of the common chicken, especially the rooster neck. Determining quality, special uses, money-saving tips, protection of hackle and dyeing are some of the subjects covered. A very important book for fly tyers.

LEISER, ERIC, AND ROBERT H. BOYLE
Stoneflies for the Angler. New York: Alfred A. Knopf, 1982.

Specialized patterns and tying instructions for the larger stoneflies. Includes Boyle's K's Butt Salmon Fly and the White Nymph. Also a listing of patterns from regional anglers from coast to coast.

LEONARD, J. EDSON
Flies. New York: A. S. Barnes, 1950.

Contains pattern recipes for 2,200 flies plus instructions for various types of tying. This standard reference guide for fly tyers should definitely be in your library.

LIVELY, CHAUNCY
Chauncy Lively's Fly Box. Harrisburg, Pa.: Stackpole, 1980.

Lively is a unique fly tyer who is always using a new approach to many types of patterns. This book contains a collection of his innovations for dries, nymphs, midges, and terrestrials. Much to be learned here.

MARINARO, VINCENT
A Modern Dry Fly Code. New York: Crown, 1970.

When this book first appeared in 1950, it did not sell well. Yet shortly before its reprinting in 1970, a used copy was selling for almost two hundred dollars. Marinaro was before his time, but anglers and tyers finally caught up with him. He has set a number of standards in both angling and fly tying. This remains a fine reference work.

McKIM, JOHN F.
Fly Tying: Adventures in Fur, Feathers and Fun. Missoula, Mont.: Mountain Press, 1982.

An unusual but very interesting approach to fly patterns and their dressings. There are new things to be learned here in the numerous patterns displayed.

NEMES, SYLVESTER
The Soft-Hackled Fly. Old Greenwich, Conn.: The Chatham Press, 1975.

Discusses the wet fly as it was many, many years ago and describes the use of soft-feathered materials such as partridge, woodcock, grouse, and starling in the making of a pattern that moves and pulses as it is being fished beneath the surface of the water. This type of pattern is still among the most effective any angler can use. The information contained herein is of value to fly tyers everywhere.

The Orvis Index of Fly Patterns. Manchester, Vt.: Orvis Company, 1978.

Compiled and edited by John Harder, who runs the flies and materials department at the Orvis Company, this index includes all the flies carried by the company and periodically adds supplements to incorporate the newer flies as they appear on the market. There is a full-color photograph of every fly, and the almost cardboard-like glossy pages are held in a ring binder so that they can easily be turned and held open. There are some tying tips, especially in the more difficult patterns. An excellent reference work for fly patterns.

ROSBOROUGH, E. H. "POLLY"
Tying and Fishing the Fuzzy Nymphs. Harrisburg, Pa.: Stackpole, 1978.

This is a small book in terms of size, yet it has more important fish-taking patterns and unique methods of fly construction than most larger publications. Many of Rosborough's methods and processes have, in fact, been used as basic

procedures in other fly-tying books. This one absolutely belongs on your bookshelf.

SCHWIEBERT, ERNEST
Matching the Hatch. New York: Macmillan, 1955.

Nymphs. New York: Winchester Press, 1973.

Two books that need no introduction. Schwiebert delves into angling entomology and interprets his findings in patterns of his own origin.

SHAW, HELEN
Fly Tying. New York: Ronald Press, 1963; Wylie, 1981.

One of the best books for the beginning fly tyer. Does not contain patterns and does not attempt to tie any. Yet each element, such as wing, body, tail, hackle, or type of materials handled is treated individually by means of full-page photography.

SMEDLEY, HAROLD HINSDALE
Fly Patterns and Their Origins. Muskegon, Mich.: Westshore Publications, 1943.

This small hard-cover book sold for $2.50 when it was first published. You'll pay much more for it if you find a copy today. In addition to pattern descriptions, it gives the history and origins of many of the flies still popular today. Some of the patterns included are the Adams, Hendrickson, and Bivisible.

STEWART, RICHARD
Universal Fly Tying Guide. Brattleboro, Vt.: Stephen Greene Press, 1979.

For the price, this soft-cover book printed on a solid stock of glossy paper can't be beat as a basic fly pattern reference for some of our favorite and most popular flies. It contains approxi-

mately 150 fly recipes in all categories, all of which are shown in full color. Another section, also in full color, depicts the various common materials used in fly tying. Also included is a brief treatise on how to tie the various dries, wets, nymphs, and streamer flies.

The Hook Book. Intervale, NH: Northland Press, Inc. A soft cover book devoted to an in depth study of hook styles. Lists all the major manufacturers of fly tying hooks and is thoroughly illustrated. A good reference work for those who wish to know more about the hooks on which they dress their flies.

STEWART, RICHARD, AND BOB LEEMAN
Trolling Flies for Trout and Salmon. Brattleboro, Vt.: Stephen Greene Press, 1982.

A specialized soft-cover book dealing with the patterns used for landlocked salmon and lake trout. A must for those who fish for these species and in this type of water. Thirty-two color plates highlight the more important flies in the more than 200 recipes listed. Stewart and Leeman give credit to the originators wherever possible and in certain cases include brief histories of the flies. A good book.

SOLOMON, LARRY, AND ERIC LEISER
The Caddis and the Angler. Harrisburg, Pa.: Stackpole, 1978.

A basic book for those interested in the tying of caddis flies. Contains tying instructions for both adult and subsurface forms of this insect. Includes fly patterns from regional experts throughout the country.

SURETTE, DICK
Trout and Salmon Fly Index. Harrisburg, Pa.: Stackpole, 1978.

Some 200 fly patterns in various categories are depicted page by page in color (one fly pattern to a page). Along with the original recipe, Surette also gives the history and origin of each fly. This soft-cover book is bound in a plastic ring binding, making it easy to work from. Very neatly done and a good reference work.

SURETTE, DICK, Editor
Fly Tyer Pattern Bible. North Conway, N.H.: Saco River Publishing Corp., 1985.

A collection of 672 patterns which have previously appeared in issues of *Fly Tyer* magazine. Also contains a number of tying tips and assorted information. Flies are portrayed in color. An excellent reference book for your library.

SWISHER, DOUG, AND CARL RICHARDS
Selective Trout. New York: Crown, 1971.

Contains the fly patterns that were originated by the authors to simulate a hackleless dry fly, as well as much vital information for fly tyers everywhere. The in-depth research involved makes for a fine reference work.

Tying the Swisher/Richards Flies. Harrisburg, Pa.: Stackpole, 1979.

Includes the tying instructions from the authors' two previous books, *Selective Trout* and *Fly Fishing Strategy* and other assorted flies. Some good hints and tips here.

TALLEUR, RICHARD
Mastering the Art of Fly Tying. Harrisburg, Pa.: Stackpole, 1979.

Contains tying instructions for some two dozen patterns and an in-depth study of tools, hooks, and hackle.

VENIARD, JOHN
Fly Dresser's Guide. London: A. C. Black, 1952.

This English book has much information regarding the construction methods for fly patterns. Also includes a good number of recipes.

WILLIAMS, A. COURTNEY
A Dictionary of Trout Flies. London: A. C. Black, 1949.

This book has been reprinted a number of times. Most of the fly patterns are English, but

for those who wish to trace origins and derive a bit of historical knowledge, this book is for you. Some of the patterns are, of course, the forerunners of some of our popular flies. Contains a wealth of side information.

WILSON, BOB, AND RICHARD PARKS
Tying and Fishing the West's Best Dry Flies. Portland, Ore.: Frank Amato Publications, 1978.

Contains pattern descriptions of almost a hundred of the more popular flies used in the West along with tying instructions. Mayflies, caddis flies, stoneflies, and terrestrials are the major areas covered. Also includes a directory of western fly shops and the most popular patterns sold by them.

WULFF, LEE
Lee Wulff on Flies. Harrisburg, Pa.: Stackpole, 1980.

Contains over a dozen patterns originated by Wulff along with interesting reasons why particular patterns are tied in a specific manner. Well worth delving into.

Index

A NOTE ABOUT THE AUTHOR

Eric Leiser is a master fly tyer, teacher, and expert on the materials of the craft. He is the author of *Fly Tying Materials, The Caddis and the Angler* (with Larry Solomon), *Stoneflies for the Angler* (with Robert H. Boyle), and *The Complete Book of Fly Tying*. He is on the board of the United Fly Tyers and is an active member of Theodore Gordon Fly Fishers, the Federation of Fly Fishermen, and Trout Unlimited. Born in Brooklyn, he now lives in Wappingers Falls, New York.

A NOTE ABOUT THE TYPE

This book has been set in a digitized version of the well-known Monotype face, Bembo. The roman is a copy of a letter cut for the celebrated Venetian printer Aldus Manutius by Francesco Griffo, and first used in Cardinal Bembo's *De Aetna* of 1495. The companion italic is an adaption of the chancery script type designed by the Roman calligrapher and printer Lodovico degli Arrighi, called Vincentino, and used by him during the 1520's.

Composed by Superior Type, Champaign, Illinois.

Designed by
Peter A. Andersen